[Everyone's an Author]

Everyone's an Author

ANDREA LUNSFORD
STANFORD UNIVERSITY

MICHAL BRODY
SAN FRANCISCO STATE UNIVERSITY

LISA EDE
OREGON STATE UNIVERSITY

BEVERLY J. MOSS
THE OHIO STATE UNIVERSITY

CAROLE CLARK PAPPER
HOFSTRA UNIVERSITY

KEITH WALTERS
PORTLAND STATE UNIVERSITY

W. W. NORTON AND COMPANY
New York • London

W. W. Norton & Company has been independent since its founding in 1923, when William Warder Norton and Mary D. Herter Norton first published lectures delivered at the People's Institute, the adult education division of New York City's Cooper Union. The firm soon expanded its program beyond the Institute, publishing books by celebrated academics from America and abroad. By mid-century, the two major pillars of Norton's publishing program—trade books and college texts—were firmly established. In the 1950s, the Norton family transferred control of the company to its employees, and today—with a staff of four hundred and a comparable number of trade, college, and professional titles published each year—W. W. Norton & Company stands as the largest and oldest publishing house owned wholly by its employees.

First Edition

Editor: Marilyn Moller
Editorial assistants: Erica Wneks, Tenyia Lee
Managing editor: Marian Johnson
Developmental editor: John Elliott
Project editor: Rebecca Homiski
Marketing manager: Lib Triplett
Emedia editor: Cliff Landesman
Photo editor: Trish Marx
Production manager: Jane Searle
Design director: Rubina Yeh
Designer: Jo Anne Metsch
Composition and layout: Carole Desnoes
Manufacturing: RR Donnelley Crawfordsville

Library of Congress Cataloging-in-Publication Data

Lunsford, Andrea A., 1942–
    Everyone's an author with readings / Andrea Lunsford . . . [et al.].
       p. cm.
    Includes bibliographical references and index.
    ISBN 978-0-393-91201-2 (pbk.)
    1. English language--Rhetoric. 2. Report writing. 3. Authorship. 4. College readers.
I. Title.
    PE1408.L874 2012
    808'.042--dc23   2012017465

W. W. Norton & Company, Inc., 500 Fifth Avenue, New York, NY 10110
www.wwnorton.com

W. W. Norton & Company, Ltd., Castle House, 75/76 Wells Street, London W1T 3QT

3 4 5 6 7 8 9 0

For our students, authors all.

Preface

**HEN WE BEGAN TEACHING** (we won't even say how many years our combined teaching careers have spanned), our students wrote traditional academic essays by hand—or sometimes typed them on type-writers.

But that was then. Those were the days when writing was some-thing students were assigned, rather than something they did every sin-gle day and night. When "text" was a noun, not a verb. When tweets were sounds birds made. When blogs didn't exist. Today the writing scene has changed radically. Now students write, text, tweet, and post to every-thing from *Facebook* to *Blackboard* to *YouTube* at home, in the library, on the bus, while crossing the street. Writing is ubiquitous—they barely even notice it.

What students are learning to write has changed as well. Instead of "essays," students today engage a range of genres: position papers, anal-yses of all kinds, reports, narratives—and more. In addition, they work across media, embedding images and even sound and video in what they write. They do research: not just for assigned "research papers" but for pretty much everything they write. And they write and research not just to report or analyze but to join conversations. With the click of a mouse they can respond to a *Washington Post* blog, publishing their views along-side those of the *Post* writer. They can create posters for the We Are the 99% *Facebook* page, post a review of a novel on Amazon, contribute to a wiki, submit a poem or story to their college literary magazine, assemble a digital portfolio to use in applying to graduate school. The work of these students speaks clearly to a sea change in literacy and to a major premise of this book: if you have access to a computer, you can publish what you write. Today, everyone can be an author.

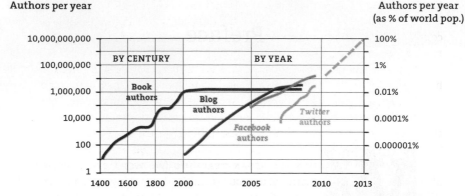

Authors per year

Authors per year
(as % of world pop.)

Number of authors who published in each year for various media since 1400 by century (left) and by year (right). *Source*: Denis G. Pelli and Charles Bigelow, "A Writing Revolution," *Seedmagazine.com*, 20 Oct. 2009, Web, 3 Jan. 2012.

We began to get a hint of this shift nearly a decade ago. In a 2009 analysis in *Seed* magazine, researchers Denis Pelli and Charles Bigelow argue that while "nearly universal literacy is a defining characteristic of today's modern civilization, nearly universal authorship will shape tomorrow's."[1] They go on to offer a graph of the history of "authorship" from 1400 projected through 2013, noting that while we've seen steep rises in authorship before (especially around 1500 and 1800), the current rise is more precipitous by far.

This most recent spike in authorship calls into question Roland Barthes' 1967 pronouncement of "the death of the author." But in some ways, Barthes was right: while universal authorship is now a possibility, what constitutes "authorship" has changed so profoundly that many of the old characteristics of "the author" are indeed dead. In brief, where "authors" were once a small, elite group (made up mostly of men), today's authors are more likely to include ordinary people who are now able to get their voices out there for others to hear. Moreover, these authors are more likely to be working together in teams large or small to produce messages of every imaginable kind.

Tracking another shift, rhetorician Deborah Brandt suggests that now that a majority of Americans make their living in the so-called informa-

1. Denis G. Pelli and Charles Bigelow, "A Writing Revolution," *Seedmagazine.com*, 20 Oct. 2009, Web, 3 Jan. 2012.

tion economy, where writing is part of what they do during their workday, it could be said that "writing is . . . eclipsing reading as the literate skill of consequence."[2] Pelli and Bigelow put this shift more starkly, saying, "As readers, we consume. As authors, we create."

Today's authors are certainly creators, in the broadest sense: protestors have used *Twitter* to organize and demonstrate against regimes across the Middle East, with results that are still cascading around us. Fans create websites for those who follow certain bands, TV shows, sports teams, games. As this book goes to press, U.S. presidential candidates are using *Facebook* and *Twitter* to broadcast their messages, raise money, and mobilize voters.

Consumers have also gained new power thanks to social media. Think of the role that customer reviews posted on sites like *Craigslist* or Amazon now play. Or consider the case of David Carroll, a musician whose guitar was broken on a United Airlines flight. When United rebuffed his requests for remuneration, Carroll wrote and posted the song "United Breaks Guitars" on *YouTube*. In two days, the song reeled in half a million hits, which was all it took for United to change its mind—and even to ask Carroll for permission to use his song in customer service training sessions!

Clearly, we are experiencing a major transition in what it means to be a writer. Such a massive shift brings challenges as well as opportunities. Many worry, for example, about the dangers the internet poses to our privacy. As the authors of this text, we also understand that being a *productive* author means accepting certain responsibilities: working fairly and generously with others; taking seriously the challenges of writing with authority; standing behind the texts we create; being scrupulous about where we get information and how we use it; and using available technologies in wise and productive ways.

This book aims to guide student writers as they take on the responsibilities, challenges, and joys of authorship. As teachers who have been active participants in the "literacy revolution" brought on by changes in technologies and modes of communication, we've been learning with our students how best to engage such changes. As scholars, we have read widely in what many refer to as the "new literacies"; as researchers, we have studied the changing scene of writing with excitement. Our goal in writing this new textbook has been to take some of the best ideas animating the field of rhetoric and writing and make them accessible to and usable by students and teachers. *Everyone's an Author* attempts to meet those goals in several ways.

---

2. Deborah Brandt, "Writing at Work," Hunter College, New York, 12 Nov. 2011, Lecture.

Highlights

- *On genres and media.* We cover the genres students need to write, with examples from across media, including readings that incorporate images, audio, video, and more. Chapter 12 offers help "Choosing Genres" when the choice is theirs.

- *On social media.* We've tried to bridge the gap between the writing students do on social media sites and the writing they do in college. We reject the notion that *Google* is making us stupid; in fact, we find that student writers are adept at crafting messages that will reach their intended audiences *because* of their constant use of social media. Chapter 27 on "Moving from Social Media to Academic Writing" shows how the rhetorical strategies they use instinctively on *Facebook* and other social media sites could be used in academic writing.

- *On the need for rhetoric.* We make students aware of the importance of rhetoric—with chapters on "Thinking Rhetorically," "Rhetorical Situations," "Writing and Rhetoric as a Field of Study," and "Writing and Rhetoric in the Workplace" and prompts throughout the book to help students think about their own rhetorical situations.

- *On academic writing.* We've tried to demystify academic writing—and to show students how to enter academic conversations. Chapter 28 on "Meeting the Demands of Academic Writing" explains conventions students need to follow, from stating claims explicitly to using appropriate disciplinary formats.

- *On collaboration.* Chapter 4 offers advice on working successfully with others and on the ways in which writers today might be authors one moment, members of an audience the next—and what these shifting roles mean for students as writers and readers.

- *On research.* We provide the guidance students need for dealing with massive amounts of information. The challenge today's students face is not gathering data, but making sense of it and using it effectively in support of their own arguments—and we hope that Chapter 21 will help them in "Synthesizing Ideas." It's no surprise that recent studies show that in the face of so much information, students cite getting started as the biggest hurdle in doing research, so we've written Chapter 15 to help them do so.

- *On style.* We pay attention to style, with guidelines that will help students think carefully and creatively about the stylistic choices open to them—from the words they choose to the way they write a sentence to how they design what they write.

- *50+ readings—and more posted weekly on Tumblr.* Each of the Genre chapters includes 2 or 3 readings, and there's an anthology of 36 readings in the back of the book. The anthology is organized alphabetically by author and includes menus on the inside back cover that categorize readings by both genres and themes. The book is designed as 2 books in one, rhetoric in front and anthology in back. Links in the margins help navigate between the parts—and allow instructors to center a syllabus on either rhetoric or reader. In addition, Michal Brody will be posting articles, cartoons, videos, speeches, photos, and more on everyonesanauthor.tumblr.com regularly for students to read, analyze, reflect on—and respond to. All readings include thought-provoking questions and writing prompts.

- *Menus, directories, documentation templates, and a glossary/index* make the book easy to understand—and to use.

Everyone's an Author is available in two versions, with and without an anthology of readings. The version with readings has been edited by Michal Brody and includes thirty-five wonderful readings, many of them appearing in a composition textbook for the first time. Readings are arranged alphabetically by author, with menus indexing the readings by genre and theme. And the book is formatted as two books in one, rhetoric in front and readings in the back. You can therefore center your course on either the rhetoric or the readings, since links in the margins will help you draw from the other part as you wish to.

What's Online

As an ebook. Both versions of *Everyone's an Author* are available as ebooks, and include all the readings and images found in the print book. Available at less than half the price of the print books, the ebooks are completely searchable and allow readers to highlight and attach sticky notes.

Everyonesanauthor.tumblr.com. Please visit our *Tumblr* site, where you'll find essays, articles, cartoons, videos, photos, speeches, interviews, and more—and where your students (and you) can post comments, questions, and more in those same media. They can also post their own writing or other texts they want to share, and to tag posts to participate in conversations about particular topics. Michal Brody is hosting the site and will be posting new items weekly, along with questions to prompt response—and all the authors will be participating. We look forward to meeting you there!

FRED. We're pleased to introduce Fred, our new online commenting system. Created by CritiqueIt and customized for college writers, Fred allows you to respond to drafts in writing, and also with audio or video—and lets students do so as well.

wwnorton.com/instructors is where you'll find the companion Norton coursepack. Go here for model essays, grammar quizzes, documentation guidelines for MLA, APA, *Chicago*, and CSE styles—and much more.

Instructors' Notes. At wwnorton.com/instructors, you'll find a site full of advice for teaching this book and for teaching writing more generally: how to create a syllabus, respond to writing, help students whose primary language isn't English, and more. You'll also find short videos of each of the authors, speaking on topics that we are often asked about—Beverly Moss on how to take advantage of the writing center, Carole Clark Papper on how to incorporate multimodal writing into your courses, Lisa Ede on how to help students collaborate productively, Keith Walters on advice for teachers whose classes include both L1 and L2 students, and Andrea Lunsford on why we believe that everyone today is an author.

Acknowledgments

We are profoundly grateful to the many people who have helped bring *Everyone's an Author* into existence. Indeed, this text provides a perfect example of what an eighteenth-century German encyclopedia meant when it defined *book* as "the work of many hands." Certainly *Everyone's an Author* is the work of many hands, and among those hands none have been more instrumental than those of Marilyn Moller: the breadth of her vision is matched by her meticulous attention to detail, keen sense of style and design, and ability to get more work done than anyone we have ever known. Throughout the process of composing this text, she has set the bar high for us, and we've tried hard to reach it. Special thanks as well to Rebecca Homiski, whose wizardry with images has added so substantially to our text—and whose attention to its visual presentation has made it a book that's both beautiful and easy to use. And a big thank you to John Elliott for his careful and graceful line editing of the words that make up the text.

We are similarly grateful to many others who contributed their talents to this book, especially Carole Desnoes and Jane Searle, for all they did to produce this book in record time (no small undertaking). Thanks as well to Megan Jackson and Trish Marx for their work clearing the many text and image permissions; to Ana Cooke and Kristin Bowen for their help with the research chapters; and to Betsye Mullaney and Marian Johnson for making time to read many chapters, pencils in hand. Last but certainly not least, we thank Erica Wnek for undertaking countless tasks large and small with energy and unprecedented efficiency.

The design of this book is something we are particularly proud of, and for that we offer very special thanks to five amazing designers. Stephen Doyle created the spectacular cover that embodies a key message of our book: that we live in a world made of words and images. Carin Berger created the whimsical illuminated alphabet, also made of text, that opens every chapter. JoAnne Metsch did the lovely interior design. And Debra Morton-Hoyt and Rubina Yeh oversaw the whole thing as well as adding their own elegant touches on every page. Best thanks to all of them.

Everyone's an Author is more than just a print book, and we thank the emedia team of Peter Kay, Peter Lesser, and especially Cliff Landesman, for creating the superb ebook, *Tumblr* site, and instructors' site. And we also send a big shout out to Michal Brody for her imaginative work in creating and editing the *Tumblr* site.

Special thanks to the fabled Norton Travelers, who will be working with us to introduce teachers across the country to what *Everyone's an Author* can offer them. And a big thank you to Lib Triplett, Ashley Cain, and Doug Day for helping us keep our eye on our audience, teachers and students at colleges where rhetorics of this kind are assigned. Finally, we are grateful to Roby Harrington, Julia Reidhead, and Steve Dunn, who have given their unwavering support to this project for nearly a decade now. We are fortunate indeed to have had the talent and hard work of this distinguished Norton team.

An astute and extremely helpful group of reviewers has helped us more than we can say: we have depended on their good pedagogical sense and advice in revising every chapter of this book. So special thanks to: Edward Baldwin, College of Southern Nevada; Michelle Ballif, University of Georgia; Larry Beason, University of South Alabama, Mobile; Kevin Boyle, College of

Southern Nevada; Elizabeth Brockman, Central Michigan University; Stephen Brown, University of Nevada, Las Vegas; Vicki Byard, Northeastern Illinois University; Beth Daniell, Kennesaw State University; Douglas Day, Texas State University; Nancy DeJoy, Michigan State University; Debra Dew, University of Colorado, Colorado Springs; Ronda Dively, Southern Illinois University, Carbondale; Douglas Downs, Montana State University; Suellynn Duffey, University of Missouri, St. Louis; Anne Dvorak, Longview Community College; Patricia Ericsson, Washington State University; Frank Farmer, University of Kansas; Casie Fedukovich, North Carolina State University; Lauren Fitzgerald, Yeshiva University; Diana Grumbles, Southern Methodist University; Ann Guess, Alvin Community College; Michael Harker, Georgia State University; Charlotte Hogg, Texas Christian University; Melissa Ianetta, University of Delaware; Jordynn Jack, University of North Carolina, Chapel Hill; Sara Jameson, Oregon State University; David A. Jolliffe, University of Arkansas; Ann Jurecic, Rutgers University; Connie Kendall, University of Cincinnati; William Lalicker, West Chester University; Phillip Marzluf, Kansas State University; Richard Matzen, Woodbury University; Moriah McCracken, The University of Texas, Pan American; Mary Pat McQueeney, Johnson County Community College; Clyde Moneyhun, Boise State University; Whitney Myers, Texas Wesleyan University; Carroll Ferguson Nardone, Sam Houston State University; Rolf Norgaard, University of Colorado, Boulder; Katherine Durham Oldmixon, Huston-Tillotson University; Matthew Oliver, Old Dominion University; Gary Olson, Idaho State University; Jason Palmeri, Miami University–Ohio; Paula Patch, Elon University; Scott Payne, University of Central Arkansas; Mary Jo Reiff, University of Kansas; Albert Rouzie, Ohio University; Alison Russell, Xavier University; Kathleen J. Ryan, University of Montana; Emily Robins Sharpe, Penn State University; Eddie Singleton, The Ohio State University; Allison Smith, Middle Tennessee State University; Deborah Coxwell Teague, Florida State University; Rex Veeder, St. Cloud State University; Matthew Wiles, University of Louisville; Mary Wright, Christopher Newport University.

Collectively, we have taught for over 150 years: that's a lot of classes, a lot of students—and we are grateful for every single one of them. We owe some of the best moments of our lives to them—and in our most challenging moments, they have inspired us to carry on. In *Everyone's an Author,* we are particularly grateful to the student writers whose work adds so much to this text: Ade Adegboyega, Rutgers University; Amanda Baker, The Ohio State University; Christine Bowman, Oregon State University; Sam Forman, Grinnell College; Julia Landauer, Stanford University; Melanie Luken, The

Ohio State University; David Pasini, The Ohio State University; Walter Przybylowski, Rutgers University; Melissa Rubin, Hofstra University; Katherine Spriggs, Stanford University; Shuqiao Song, Stanford University; Saurabh Vaish, Hofstra University; Kameron Wiles, Ball State University.

Each of us also has special debts of gratitude. Andrea Lunsford thanks her students and colleagues at the Bread Loaf Graduate School of English and in the Program in Writing and Rhetoric at Stanford, along with her sisters Ellen Ashdown and Liz Middleton, friends and life supporters Shirley Brice Heath, Betty Bailey, Cheryl Glenn, and Jackie Royster; editor and friend Carolyn Lengel; and especially—and forever—her grandnieces Audrey and Lila Ashdown, who are already budding authors.

Michal Brody would like to thank her two wonderful families in California and Yucatan who so graciously support (and endure) her crazy and restless transnational life. Her conversations—both the actual and the imagined—with each and all of those loved ones provide the constant impetus to reach for both the texture and depth of experience and the clarity with which to express it. She also thanks her students in both countries, who remind her every day that we are all teachers, all learners.

Lisa Ede thanks her husband, Greg Pfarr, for his support, for his commitment to his own art, and for their year-round vegetable garden. Thanks as well to her siblings, who have stuck together through thick and thin: Leni Ede Smith, Andrew Ede, Sara Ede Rowkamp, Jeffrey Ede, Michele Ede Smith, Laurie Ede Drake, Robert Ede, and Julie Ede Campbell. She also thanks her colleagues in the Oregon State School of Writing, Literature, and Film for their encouragement and support. Special thanks go to the school's director, Anita Helle, and to their amazing administrative staff: Ann Leen, Aurora Terhune, and Felicia Phillips.

Beverly Moss thanks her parents, Harry and Sarah Moss, for their love, encouragement, and confidence in her when her own wavered. In addition, she thanks her Ohio State and Bread Loaf students who inspire her and teach her so much about teaching. She also wants to express gratitude to her colleagues in Rhetoric, Composition, and Literacy at Ohio State for their incredible support. Finally, she thanks two of her own former English teachers, Dorothy Bratton and Jackie Royster, for the way they modeled excellence inside and outside the classroom.

Carole Clark Papper would like to thank her husband, Bob, and wonderful children—Dana, Matt, Zack, and Kate—without whose loving support little would happen and nothing would matter. In addition, she is grateful to the Hofstra University Writing Center faculty and tutors whose dedication and commitment to students always inspire.

Keith Walters thanks his partner of thirty years, Jonathan Tamez, for sharing a love of life, language, travel, flowers, and beauty. He is also grateful to his students in Tunisia, South Carolina, Texas, and Oregon, who have challenged him to find ways of talking about what good writing is and how to do it.

Finally, we thank those who have taught us—who first helped us learn to hold a pencil and print our names, who inspired a love of language and of reading and writing, who encouraged us to take chances in writing our lives as best we could, who prodded and pushed when we needed it, and who most of all set brilliant examples for us to follow. One person who taught all of us—about rhetoric, about writing, and about life—was Edward P. J. Corbett. We remember him with love and with gratitude.

—Andrea Lunsford, Michal Brody, Lisa Ede,
Beverly Moss, Carole Clark Papper, Keith Walters

CONTENTS

8 Writing a Narrative / "Here's What Happened" *101*

Across Fields / Media / Cultures and Communities / Genres

CHARACTERISTIC FEATURES

A ROADMAP

READINGS

9 Writing Analytically / "Let's Take a Closer Look" *137*

Across Fields / Media / Cultures and Communities / Genres

CHARACTERISTIC FEATURES

Is Everyone an Author?

**E'VE CHOSEN A PROVOCATIVE TITLE** for this book, so it's fair to ask if we've gotten it right, if everyone is an author. Let's take just a few examples that can help to make the point:

- A student creates a *Facebook* page, which immediately finds a large audience of other interested students.

- A visitor to the United States sends an email message to a few friends and family members in Slovakia—and they begin forwarding it. The message circles the globe in a day.

- A professor assigns students in her class to work together to write a number of entries for *Wikipedia*, and they are surprised to find how quickly their entries are revised by others.

- An airline executive writes a letter of apology for unconscionable delays in service and publishes the letter in newspapers, where millions will read it.

- A small group of high school students who are keen on cooking post their recipe for Crazy Candy Cookies on their *Cook's Corner* blog and are overwhelmed with the number of responses to their invention.

- Five women nominated for the Academy Award for Best Actress prepare acceptance speeches: One of them will deliver the speech live before a national audience.

- You get your next assignment in your college writing class and set out to do the research necessary to complete it. When you're finished, you turn in your twelve-page argument to your instructor and classmates for their responses—and you also post it on your webpage under "What I'm Writing Now."

All of these examples represent important messages written by people who probably do not consider themselves authors. Yet they illustrate what we mean when we say that today "everyone's an author." Once upon a time, the ability to compose a message that reached wide and varied audiences was restricted to a small group; now, however, this opportunity is available to anyone with access to the internet.

The word *author* has a long history, but it is most associated with the rise of print and the ability of a writer to claim what he or she has written as property. The first copyright act, in the early eighteenth century, ruled that authors held the primary rights to their work. And while anyone could potentially be a writer, an author was someone whose work had been published. That rough definition worked pretty well until recently, when traditional copyright laws began to show the strain of their 300-year history, most notably with the simple and easy file sharing that the internet makes possible.

In fact, the web has blurred the distinction between writers and authors, offering anyone with access to a computer the opportunity to publish what they write. Whether or not you own a computer, if you have access to one (at school, at a library), you can publish what you write and thus make what you say available to readers around the world.

Think for a minute about the impact of blogs, which first appeared in 1997. As this book goes to press, there are more than 156 million public blogs, a trend that shows no sign of slowing down. Add to blogs the rise of *Facebook, Twitter, YouTube, Google+,* and other social networking sites for ever more evidence to support our claim: Today, everyone's an author. Moreover, twenty-first-century authors just don't fit the image of the Romantic writer, alone in a garret, struggling to bring forth something unique. Rather, today's authors are part of a huge, often global, conversation; they build on what others have thought and written, they create mash-ups and remixes, and they practice teamwork at almost every turn. They are authoring for the digital age.

Redefining Writing

If the definition of *author* has changed in recent years, so has our understanding of the definition, nature, and scope of *writing*.

Writing, for example, now includes much more than words, as images and graphics take on the job of conveying an important part of the meaning. In addition, writing can now include sound, video streaming, and other media. Perhaps more important, writing now often contains many voices, as information from the web is incorporated into the texts we write with increasing ease. Finally, as we noted above, writing today is almost always part of a larger conversation. Rather than rising mysteriously from the depths of a writer's original thoughts, a stereotype made popular during the Romantic period, writing almost always responds to some other written piece or to other ideas. If "no man [or woman] is an island, apart from the main," then the same holds true for writing.

Writing now is also often highly collaborative. You work with a team to produce an illustrated report, the basis of which is used by members of the team to make a key presentation to management; you and a colleague carry out an experiment, argue over and write up the results together, and present your findings to a class; a business class project calls on you and others in your group to divide up the work along lines of expertise and then to pool your efforts in meeting the assignment. In all of these cases, writing is also performative—it performs an action or, in the words of many students we have talked with, it "makes something happen in the world."

Perhaps most notable, this expanded sense of writing challenges us to think very carefully about what our writing is for and whom it can and might reach. Email provides a good case in point. In the aftermath of the September 11 attacks, Tamim Ansary, a writer who was born in Afghanistan, found himself stunned by the number of people calling for bombing Afghanistan "back to the Stone Age." He sent an email to a few friends expressing his horror at the events, his condemnation of Osama bin Laden and the Taliban, and his hope that those in the United States would not act on the basis of gross stereotyping. The few dozen friends to whom Ansary wrote hit their forward buttons. Within days, the letter had circled the globe more than once, and Ansary's words were published by the Africa News Service, the *Philippine Daily Inquirer,* the *Evening Standard* in London, the *San Francisco Chronicle,* and many other papers in the United States, as well as on many websites.

Authors or writers whose messages can be instantly transported around the world need to consider those who will receive those messages. As the example of Tamim Ansary shows, no longer can writers assume that they write only to a specified audience or that they can easily control the dissemination of their messages. We now live not only in a city, a state, and a country but in a global community as well—and we write, intentionally or not, to speakers of many languages, to members of many cultures, to believers of many creeds.

Everyone's a Researcher

Since all writing responds to the ideas and words of others, it usually draws on some kind of research. Think for a moment of how often you carry out research. We're guessing that a little reflection will turn up lots of examples: You may find yourself digging up information on the pricing of new cars, searching *Craigslist* or the want ads for a good job, comparing two new MP3 players, looking up statistics on a favorite sports figure, or searching for a recipe for tabbouleh. All of these everyday activities involve research. In addition, many of your most important life decisions involve research— what colleges to apply to, what jobs to pursue, where to live, and more. Once you begin to think about research in this broad way—as a form of inquiry related to important decisions—you'll probably find that research is something you do almost every day. Moreover, you'll see the ways in which the research you do adds to your credibility—giving you the authority that goes along with being an author.

But research today is very different from research of only a few decades ago. Take the example of the concordance, an alphabetized listing of topics and words in a work that gathers up every instance of that topic or word in the work. Before the computer age, concordances were done by hand: the first full concordance to the works of Shakespeare took decades of eye-straining, painstaking research, counting, and sorting. Some scholars spent years, even whole careers, developing concordances that then served as major resources for other scholars. As soon as Shakespeare's plays and poems were in digital form—voilà!—a concordance could be produced automatically and accessed by writers with the click of a mouse.

To take a more recent example, first-year college students just twenty years ago had no access to the internet. Just think of how easy it is now to check temperatures around the world, track a news story, or keep up to the minute on stock prices. These are items that you can *Google*, but you may also have many expensive subscription databases available to you through your school's library. It's not too much of an exaggeration to say that the world is literally at your fingertips.

What has *not* changed is the need to carry out research with great care, to read all sources with a critical eye, and to evaluate sources before depending on them for an important decision or using them in your own work. What also has not changed is the sheer thrill research can bring: While much research work can seem plodding and even repetitious, the excitement of discovering materials you didn't know existed, of analyzing information in a new way, or of tracing a question through one particular historical period brings its own reward. Moreover, your research adds to what philosopher Kenneth Burke calls "the conversation of humankind," as you build on what others have done and begin to make significant contributions of your own to the world's accumulated knowledge.

Everyone's a Student

More than 2,000 years ago, the Roman writer Quintilian set out a plan for education, beginning with birth and ending only with old age and death. Surprisingly enough, Quintilian's recommendation for a lifelong education has never been more relevant than it is in the twenty-first century, as knowledge is increasing and changing so fast that most people must continue to be active learners long after they graduate from college. This explosion of knowledge also puts great demands on communication. As a result, one of your biggest challenges will be learning how to learn and how to communicate what you have learned across wider distances, to larger and increasingly diverse sets of audiences, and using an expanding range of media and genres.

When did you first decide to attend college, and what paths did you take to achieve that goal? Chances are greater today than at any time in our past that you may have taken time off to work before beginning college, or that you returned to college for new training when your job changed, or that you are attending college while working part-time or even full-time. These characteristics of college students are not new, but they are increasingly important, indicating that the path to college is not as straightforward as it was once thought to be. In addition, college is now clearly a part of a process of lifetime learning: you are likely to hold a number of positions—and each new position will call for new learning.

Citizens today need more years of education and more advanced skills than ever before: Even entry-level jobs now call for a college diploma. But what you'll need isn't just a college education. Instead, you'll need an education that puts you in a position to take responsibility for your own learning and to take a direct, hands-on approach to that learning. Most of us learn best by *doing* what we're trying to learn rather than just being told about it. What does this change mean in practice? First, it means you will be doing much more writing, speaking, and researching than ever before. You may, for instance, conduct research on an economic trend and then use that research to create a theory capable of accounting for the trend; you may join a research group in an electrical engineering class that designs, tests, and implements a new system; you may be a member of a writing class that works to build a website for the local fire department, writes brochures for a nonprofit agency, or makes presentations before municipal boards. In each case, you will be doing what you are studying, whether it is economics, engineering, or writing.

Without a doubt, the challenges and opportunities for students today are immense. The chapters that follow try to keep these challenges and opportunities in the foreground, offering you concrete ways to think about yourself as a writer—and yes, as an author; to think carefully about the rhetorical situations you face and about the many and varied audiences for your work; and to expand your writing repertoire to include new genres, new media, and new ways of producing and communicating knowledge.

Everyone's an Author

PART I

The Need for Rhetoric and Writing

CLOSE YOUR EYES and imagine a world without any form of language—no spoken or written words, no drawings, no mathematical formulas, no music—no way, that is, to communicate or express yourself. It's pretty hard to imagine such a world, and with good reason. For better or worse, we seem to be hardwired to communicate, to long to express ourselves to others. That's why philosopher Kenneth Burke says that people are, at their essence, "symbol-using animals" who have a basic need to communicate.

We can look across history and find early attempts to create systems of communication. Think, for instance, of

 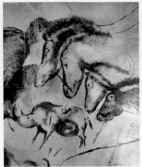 

Horses in prehistoric art: Uffington White Horse, Oxfordshire, England (approx. 3,000 years old); Chauvet Cave, near Vallon-Pont-d'Arc, France (approx. 31,000 years old); rock paintings, Bhimbetka, India (approx. 30,000 years old).

the chalk horses of England, huge figures carved into trenches that were then filled with white chalk some 3,500 years ago. What do they say? Do they mark the territory in some way? Are they celebratory? Whatever their original intent, they echo the need to communicate to us from millennia away.

Cave paintings, many of them hauntingly beautiful, have been discovered across Europe, some thought to be 30,000 years old. Such communicative art—all early forms of writing—has been discovered in many other places, from Africa to Australia to South America to Asia.

While these carvings and paintings have been interpreted in many different ways, they all attest to the human desire to leave messages. And we don't need to look far to find other very early attempts to communicate— from makeshift drums and whistles to early pictographic languages to the symbols associated with the earliest astronomers.

As languages and other symbolic forms of communication like our own alphabet evolved, so did a need for ways to interpret and organize these forms and to use them in new and inventive ways. And out of these needs grew rhetoric—the great art, theory, and practice of communication. In discussing rhetoric, Aristotle says we need to understand this art for two main reasons: first, in order to express our own ideas and thoughts, and second, to protect ourselves from those who would try to manipulate or harm us. Language, then, can be used for good or ill, to provide information that may help someone—or that may be deliberately misleading.

We believe the need for understanding rhetoric may be greater today than at any time in our history. At first glance, it may look as if communication has never been easier. We can send messages in a nanosecond, reaching people in all parts of the world with ease. We can broadcast our thoughts, hopes, and dreams—and invectives—on email, blogs, *Faccbook* status up dates, tweets, text messages, and a plethora of other means.

So far, perhaps, so good. But consider the story of the Tower of Babel, told in different ways in both the Qur'an and the Bible. When the people sought to build a tower that would reach to the heavens, God responded to their hubris by creating so many languages that communication became impossible—and the tower had to be abandoned. As with the languages in Babel, the means of communication are proliferating today, bringing with them the potential for miscommunication. From the old game of passing a message around a circle by whispering it to the person next to you—only to see it emerge at the end of the exercise bearing little if any resemblance to its original—to the challenge of trying to communicate across vast differences in languages and cultures, we face challenges that our parents and grandparents never did.

In a time when new (and sometimes confusing) forms of communication are available to us, many are looking for ways to aid in the process of

Pieter Brueghel the Elder, *Tower of Babel*, 1563.

YAHOO! BABEL FISH [Search]

日本語

修辞のための必要性

Search the web with this text

Translate again   (Enter up to 150 words)

the need for rhetoric

English to Japanese   Translate

Babel Fish's translation of "the need for rhetoric" from English to Japanese.

communication. *Google Translate* and *Yahoo! Babel Fish,* for example, are attempts to offer instant translation of texts from one language to another.

Such new technologies and tools can certainly help us as we move into twenty-first-century global villages. But they are not likely to reduce the need for an art and a theory that can inform them—and that can evaluate their usefulness, calculate their pros and cons, and improve on them. Rhetoric responds to this need. Along with writing, which we define broadly to include speaking and drawing and performing as well as the literal inscription of words, rhetoric offers you solid ground on which to build your education as well as your communicative ability and style. The chapters that follow will introduce you more fully to rhetoric and writing—and engage you in acquiring and using their powers.

ONE

Thinking Rhetorically

The only real alternative to war is rhetoric.

—WAYNE BOOTH

ROFESSOR WAYNE BOOTH made this statement at a national conference of scholars and teachers of writing held only months after 9/11, and it quickly drew a range of responses: Just what did Booth mean by this stark statement? How could rhetoric—the art and practice of persuasion—act as a counter to war?

Throughout his long career, Booth explored these questions, identifying rhetoric as an ethical art that begins with deep and intense listening and that searches for mutual understanding and common ground as an alternative to violence and war. Put another way, two of the most potent tools we have for persuasion are language and violence: When words fail us, violence often wins the day. Booth, a noted critic and scholar, sees the careful, ethical use of language as our best approach to keeping violence and war at bay. Years later, Booth's words echoed again, during the start of the Arab Spring of 2011 as a vast gathering of Egyptian citizens protested in Cairo's Tahrir Square, using rhetorical means of persuasion—including posters, tweets, *Facebook* status updates, songs, and more—to eventually persuade President Hosni Mubarak to step down.

So how can you go about developing your own careful, ethical use of language? Our short answer: by learning to think and act rhetorically, that is, by developing habits of mind that begin with listening and

Protestors in Cairo's Tahrir Square use banners, flags, raised fists, and their own voices to communicate their positions.

searching for understanding before you decide what you yourself think and try to persuade others to listen to and act on what you say.

Learning to think rhetorically will serve you well as you negotiate your way through the complexities of life in today's world. In many situations in your everyday life, you'll need to communicate successfully with others in order to get things done, and done in a responsible and ethical way. On the job, for example, you may need to bring coworkers to consensus on how best to raise productivity when there is little, if any, money for raises. Or in your college community, you may find yourself negotiating difficult waters. When a group of students became aware of how little the temporary workers on their campus were paid, for example, they met with the workers, listening hard and gathering information. They then mounted a campaign using flyers, newsletters, photographs, speeches, and sit-ins—in other words, using the available means of persuasion—to win attention and convince the administration to raise the workers' pay. These students were thinking and acting rhetorically, and doing so responsibly and ethically.

Note that these students, like the protesters in Tahrir Square, worked closely together, both with the workers and with each other. In other words, none of us can manage such actions all by ourselves; we need to engage in

Students use posters and face-to-face conversation to protest the low wages paid to campus workers at Harvard.

conversation with others. Perhaps that's what philosopher Kenneth Burke had in mind when he created his famous "parlor" metaphor for life:

> Imagine that you enter a parlor. You come late. When you arrive, others have long preceded you, and they are engaged in a heated discussion, a discussion too heated for them to pause and tell you exactly what it is about. . . .You listen for a while, until you decide that you have caught the tenor of the argument; then you put in your oar.
>
> —KENNETH BURKE, *The Philosophy of Literary Form*

In this parable, each of us is much like the person arriving late to a room full of animated conversation; we don't understand what is going on. Yet instead of butting in or trying to take over, we listen closely until we catch on to what people are saying. Then we join in, using language and rhetorical strategies to engage with others as we add our own voices to the conversation.

This book aims to teach you to *think and act rhetorically*—to listen carefully and then to "put in your oar," join conversations about important issues, and develop strong critical and ethical habits of mind that will help you engage with others in responsible ways. In this chapter, you'll learn more about several specific practices that will help you develop the habit of thinking rhetorically.

First, Listen

We have two ears and one mouth so we may listen more and talk less.

—EPICTETUS

Thinking rhetorically begins with listening, with being willing to hear the words of others in an open and understanding way. It means paying attention to what others say *as a way* of getting started on your own contributions to the conversation. Think of the times you are grateful to others for listening closely to you: when you are talking through a conflict with a family member or even when you are trying to explain to a salesperson just what it is you are looking for. On those occasions, you want the person you are addressing to really listen.

Hear What Others Are Saying—and Think about Why

When you enter any conversation, whether academic, professional, or personal, take the time needed to understand what is being said rather than rushing to a conclusion or a judgment. Listen carefully to what others are saying and consider what motivates them to do so: Where are they coming from?

Developing such habits of mind will be useful to you almost every day, whether you are participating in a class discussion, negotiating with friends over what film is most worth seeing, or studying a local ballot issue to decide how you'll vote. In each case, thinking rhetorically means being flexible and fair, able to hear and consider varying—and sometimes conflicting—points of view.

In ancient Rome, Cicero argued that considering alternative points of view and counterarguments was key to making a successful argument, and it is just as important today. Even when you disagree with a point of view— perhaps especially when you disagree with it—allow yourself to see the issue from the viewpoint of its advocates before you reject their positions. You may be convinced that hydrogen fuel will be the solution to global warming—but check your enthusiasm for it until you have thought hard about others' perspectives and carefully considered alternative solutions.

Thinking hard about others' views also includes considering the larger context and how it shapes what they are saying. This aspect of rhetorical thinking goes beyond the kind of close reading you probably learned to do in high school literature classes, where you looked very closely at a particular text and interpreted it on its own terms, without looking at secondary sources or outside influences. When you think rhetorically, you take a step further and put that close analysis into a larger context—historical, political, or cultural, for example.

In analyzing the issue of gay marriage, for instance, you would not merely consider your own thinking or do a close reading of texts that address the issue. In addition, you would look at the whole debate in context by considering its historical development over time, thinking about the broader political agendas of both those who advocate for and oppose gay marriage, asking what economic ramifications adopting—or rejecting—gay marriage might have, examining the role of religion in the debate, and so on. In short, you would try to see the issue from as many different perspectives and in as broad a context as possible before you formulate your own stance. When you write, you draw on these sources—what others have said about the issue—to support your own position and consider counterarguments to it.

See how carefully Brent Staples considers the positions and reasoning that he is opposing, p. 935.

What Do You Think—and Why?

Examining all points of view, all angles, on any issue will engage you in some tough thinking about your own stance—literally, where you are coming from on an issue—and why you think as you do. Such self-scrutiny can eventually clarify your stance or perhaps even change your mind; in either case, you stand to gain. Just as you need to think hard about the motivations of others, it's important to examine your own motivations in detail, asking yourself what influences in your life lead you to think as you do or to take certain positions. Then you can reconsider your motivations and reflect on their relationship to those of others, including your audience—those you wish to engage in conversation or debate.

In your college assignments, you probably have multiple motivations and purposes, one of which is to convince your instructor that you are a serious and hardworking student. But think about additional purposes as well: What could you learn from doing the assignment? How can doing it help you attain goals you have?

Beyond the classroom, examining your own stance and motivation is equally important. Suppose you are urging fellow members of a campus group to raise money for AIDS research. On one level, you are dedicated to helping science find a means of eradicating this disease. But when you think a bit harder, you might find that you have additional motivations: to oppose those who would rather raise money for a social event, to be able to list this fund-raising for science on your résumé, perhaps to change the organization's direction. As this example shows, examining what you think and why helps you to challenge your own position—and to make sure that your approach to the topic is appropriate and effective.

Do Your Homework

Rhetorical thinking calls on you to do some homework, to find out everything you can about what's been said about your topic, to **ANALYZE** what you find—and then to **SYNTHESIZE** that information to inform your own ideas. To put it another way, you want your own thinking to be deeply informed, to reflect more than just your own opinion.

To take an everyday example, you should do some pretty serious thinking when deciding on a major purchase, such as a new car. You'll want to begin by considering the purchase in the larger context of your life. What motivates you to buy a car? Do you need one for work? Do you want it in part as a status symbol? Are you concerned about the environment and want to switch to an electric vehicle? Who besides you might be affected by this decision? A thoughtful analysis of the context and your specific motivations and purposes can guide you in drawing up a preliminary list of cars to consider.

Then you'll need to do some research, checking out reports on safety records, efficiency, cost, and so on. Sometimes it can be hard to evaluate such sources: How much should you trust the mileage statistics provided by the carmaker, for example? For this reason you should consult multiple sources and check them against one another.

You will also want to consider your findings in light of your priorities. Cost, for instance, may not be as high on your priority list as energy efficiency. Such careful thinking will help you come to a sound decision, and then to explain it to others. If your parents, for instance, are helping you buy the car, you'll want to consider what their responses to your decision will be, anticipating questions they may ask and how to respond.

Doing your homework also means taking an analytic approach, focus-

TAKE A LOOK at the 2011 Super Bowl Chrysler ad at <u>wwnorton.com/write/everyone</u> <u>links</u>. You'll see many scenes from Detroit, and here are some of the words in the ad: "What does this city know about luxury? What does a town that's been to hell and back know about the finer things in life? I'll tell you, more than most!" What kind of rhetorical thinking did the ad writers do? Who was their target audience, and how did they go about appealing to them? This was an award-winning ad—but how successful do you think it was as an ad? In other words, did it sell a lot of cars? If you were going to write an ad for a car you like, what words would you use, and why?

ing on *how* various rhetorical strategies and appeals work to persuade you. You may have been bowled over by a powerful advertisement for a new car—one you saw on Super Bowl Sunday that has been in your mind ever since. So what made that advertisement so memorable? To answer that question, you'll need to study the ad closely, determining just what qualities—a clever script? memorable music? celebrity actors? a provocative message?—worked to create the effect the ad had on you. This is the kind of analysis and research you will do when you engage in rhetorical thinking.

Give Credit

As part of engaging with what others have thought and said, you'll want to give credit where credit is due. Acknowledging the work of others will help build your own **ETHOS**, or character, showing that you have not only done your homework but that you want to credit those who have influenced you. The great physicist and astronomer Isaac Newton demonstrated the art of giving credit when he wrote to his rival Robert Hooke in 1676, saying:

> What Descartes did was a good step. You have added much in several ways, and especially in taking the colours of thin plates into philosophical consideration. If I have seen a little further it is by standing on the shoulders of giants.   —ISAAC NEWTON, letter to Robert Hooke

In this letter, Newton acknowledges the work of Descartes as well as of Hooke before saying, with a fair amount of modesty, that his own advancements were made possible by their work. In doing so, he is thinking—and acting—rhetorically.

You can give credit informally, as Newton did in this letter, or you can do so formally with a full citation. Which method you choose will depend on your purpose and context. Academic writing, for instance, usually calls for formal citations, but if you are writing for a personal blog, you might embed a link that connects to another's work—or just give an informal shout-out to a friend who contributed to your thinking. In each case, you'll want to be specific about what ideas or words you've drawn from others, as Newton does in referring to Hooke's consideration of the colors of thin plates. Such care in crediting your sources contributes to your credibility—and is an important part of ethical, careful rhetorical thinking.

Be Imaginative

Remember that intuition and imagination can often lead to great insights. While you want to think analytically and carefully, don't be afraid to take chances. A little imagination can lead you to new ideas—about a topic you're studying and about how to approach the topic in a way that will interest others. Such insights and intuitions can often pay off big-time. One student athlete we know was interested in how the mass media covered the Olympics, and he began doing research on the coverage in *Sports Illustrated* from different periods. So far, so good: He was gathering information and would be able to write an essay showing that the magazine had been a major promoter of the Olympics.

   While looking through old issues of *Sports Illustrated*, however, he kept feeling that something he was seeing in the early issues was different from current issues of the magazine . . . something that felt important to him

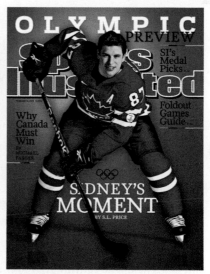

Two *Sports Illustrated* covers depicting hockey players in the Winter Olympics. The cover on the left, from 1980, showcases the U.S. team's "miracle on ice" victory win over the heavily favored USSR team. The one on the right, from 2010, pictures Canada's superstar Sidney "Sid the Kid" Crosby, who scored the game-winning shot in the gold medal game against the United States.

though he couldn't quite articulate it. This hunch led him to make an imaginative leap, to articulate for himself what that difference was. Excited that he was on to something, he returned to his chronological examination of the magazine. On closer inspection, he found that over the decades of its Olympics coverage, that magazine had slowly but surely moved from focusing on teams to depicting *only* individual stars. This discovery led him to make an argument he would never have made had he not paid attention to his imagination, to his creative hunch—that the evolution of sports from a focus on the team to a focus on individual stars is perfectly captured in the pages of *Sports Illustrated*. It also helped him write a much more interesting—and more persuasive—essay, one that captured the attention not only of his instructor and classmates but of a local sports newsmagazine, which reprinted his essay along with a picture of its author. Like this student, you can benefit by using your imagination and listening to your inner hunches. They can pay off for you as they did for him.

Put in Your Oar

So rhetorical thinking offers a way of coming to any situation with a tool kit of strategies that will help you understand that situation and "put in your oar" to act effectively within it. When you think rhetorically, you ask yourself certain questions:

- How do you want to come across to your audience?
- How can you appear knowledgeable, fair, and well informed?
- What can you do to represent yourself in a positive way?
- What can you do to show respect both for your audience and for those whose work and thinking you engage with?
- How can you demonstrate that you have your audience's best interests at heart?

This kind of rhetorical thinking will help ensure that your words will be listened to and taken seriously.

We can find examples of such a rhetorical approach in all fields of study and in all walks of life. Take, for instance, the landmark essay by James Watson and Francis Crick on the discovery of DNA, published in *Na-*

ture in 1953. This essay shows Watson and Crick to be thinking rhetorically throughout, acutely aware of their audience (major scientists throughout the world) as well as of competitors who were simultaneously working on the same issue.

Here is Wayne Booth's analysis of Watson and Crick's use of rhetoric:

> In [Watson and Crick's] report, what do we find? Actually scores of *rhetorical* choices that they made to strengthen the appeal of their scientific claim. (Biographies and autobiographies have by now revealed that they did a lot of conscientious revising, not of the data but of the mode of presentation; and their lives were filled, before and after the triumph, with a great deal of rhetoric-charged conflict.) We could easily compose a dozen different versions of their report, all proclaiming the same scientific results. But most alternatives would prove less engaging to the intended audience. They open, for example, with
>
>> "*We wish to suggest* a structure" that has "*novel* features which are of *considerable* biological *interest*." *(My italics, of course)*
>
> Why didn't they say, instead: "We shall here demonstrate a *startling, totally new structure* that will *shatter* everyone's conception of the biological world"? Well, obviously their rhetorical choice presents an ethos much more attractive to most cautious readers than does my exaggerated alternative. A bit later they say
>
>> "We have made the *usual chemical assumptions,* namely . . ."
>
> Why didn't they say, "*As we all know*"? Both expressions acknowledge reliance on warrants, commonplaces within a given rhetorical domain. But their version sounds more thoughtful and authoritative, especially with the word "chemical." Referring to Pauling and Corey, they say
>
>> "They *kindly* have made their manuscript available."
>
> Okay, guys, drop the rhetoric and just cut that word "kindly." What has that got to do with your scientific case? Well, it obviously strengthens the authors' ethos: we are nice guys dealing trustfully with other nice guys, in a rhetorical community.
>
> And on they go, with "*In our opinion*" (rather than "We proclaim" or "We insist" or "We have miraculously discovered": again ethos—we're

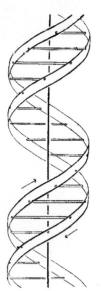

The original sketch showing the structure of DNA that appeared in Watson and Crick's article.

not dogmatic); and Fraser's *"suggested"* structure is *"rather ill-defined"* (rather than "his structure is stupid" or "obviously faulty"—we *are* nice guys, right?)

And on to scores of other such choices.

—WAYNE BOOTH, *The Rhetoric of Rhetoric*

Booth shows in each instance how Watson and Crick's exquisite understanding of their rhetorical situation—especially of their audience and of the stakes involved in making their claim—had a great deal to do with how that claim was received. (They won the Nobel Prize!)

As the example of Watson and Crick illustrates, rhetorical thinking involves certain habits of mind that can and should lead to something—often to an action, to making something happen. And when it comes to taking action, those who think rhetorically are in a very strong position. They have listened attentively and thought carefully and methodically; viewed their topic from many alternate perspectives; done their homework; and engaged with the words and thoughts of others. This kind of rhetorical thinking will help you to get in on conversations—and will increase the likelihood that your ideas will be heard and will inspire actions that take root and prosper.

Indeed, the ability to think rhetorically is of great importance in today's global world, as Professors Gerald Graff and Cathy Birkenstein explain:

> The ability to enter complex, many-sided conversations has taken on a special urgency in today's diverse, post-9/11 world, where the future for all of us may depend on our ability to put ourselves in the shoes of those who think very differently from us. Listening carefully to others, including those who disagree with us, and then engaging with them thoughtfully and respectfully . . . can help us see beyond our own pet beliefs, which may not be shared by everyone. The mere act of acknowledging that someone might disagree with us may not seem like a way to change the world; but it does have the potential to jog us out of our comfort zones, to get us thinking critically about our own beliefs, and perhaps even to change our minds.
>
> —GERALD GRAFF AND CATHY BIRKENSTEIN, *"They Say / I Say"*

In the long run, if enough of us learn to think rhetorically, we just might achieve Booth's goal—to use words (and images) in thoughtful and constructive ways as an alternative to violence and war.

READ *Margaret Mead's words closely, and then think of at least one historical example in which a "small group of thoughtful citizens" has changed the world for the better. Then think about your own life and the ways in which you have worked with others to bring about some kind of change. In what ways were you called upon to think and act rhetorically to do so?*

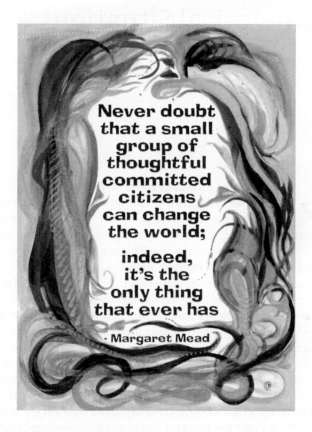

Never doubt
that a small
group of
thoughtful
committed
citizens
can change
the world;

indeed,
it's the
only thing
that ever has

- Margaret Mead

TWO

Rhetorical Situations

S PART OF A COLLEGE APPLICATION, a high school student writes a personal statement about what she plans to study, and why. A baseball fan posts a piece on a New York Yankees blog analyzing data to show why a beloved pitcher probably won't be elected to the Hall of Fame. Eighty-seven readers respond, some praising his analysis, others questioning his conclusions and offering their own analyses. The officers of a small company address the annual shareholders' meeting to report on how the firm is doing, using *PowerPoint* slides to call attention to their most important points. They take questions afterward, and two people raise their hands. Our baseball fan sees on *Twitter* that the Yankees have signed a star pitcher he thinks they don't really need—and fires off a tweet saying so. The student in our first example takes a deep breath and logs on to the website of the college she wants to attend to see if she's been accepted. Good news: She's in. Come September she's at the library, working on an essay for her first-year composition course—and texting her friends as she works.

In each of these scenarios, an author is writing (or speaking from written notes) in a different set of specific circumstances—addressing certain audiences for a particular purpose, using certain technologies, and so on. So it is whenever we write. Whether we're texting a friend, outlining an oral presentation, or writing an essay, we do so within a spe-

Three different rhetorical situations: a lone writer texting (*top left*); a student giving an oral presentation in class (*top right*); and members of a community group collaborating on a group project (*bottom left*).

cific rhetorical situation. We have a purpose, an audience, a stance, a genre, a medium, a design—all of which exist in some larger context. This chapter covers each of these elements and provides prompts to help you think about some of the choices you have as you negotiate your own rhetorical situations.

Every rhetorical situation presents its own unique constraints and opportunities, and as authors, we need to think strategically about our own situation. Adding to a class wiki presents a different challenge from writing an in-class essay exam, putting together a résumé and cover letter for a job, or working with fellow members of a campus choir to draft a grant proposal to the student government requesting funding so the choir can go on tour the following year. A group of neighbors developing a proposal to present at a community meeting will need to attend to both the written text they will submit and the oral arguments they will make. They may also need to create slides or other visuals to support their proposal.

The workplace creates still other kinds of rhetorical situations with their own distinctive features. Reporters, for instance, must always consider their deadlines as well as their ethical obligations—to the public, to the persons or institutions they write about, and to the story they are reporting. A reporter working for six months to investigate corporate wrongdoing faces different challenges from one who covers local sports day to day. The medium—print, video, radio, podcast, blog, or some combination of these or other media—also influences how reporters write their stories.

Think about Your Own Rhetorical Situation

Lynne Truss writes in a large-circulation newspaper about her own personal habits with the medium of texting. See how she navigated that complicated rhetorical situation on p. 939.

It is important to start thinking about your rhetorical situation early in your writing process. As a student, you'll often be given assignments with very specific guidelines—to follow the conventions of a particular genre, in a certain medium, by a specific date. Nevertheless, even the most fully developed assignment cannot address every aspect of any particular rhetorical situation.

Effective writers—whether students, journalists, teachers, or your mom—know how to analyze their rhetorical situation. They may conduct this analysis unconsciously and instinctively, drawing upon the rhetorical common sense they have developed as writers, readers, speakers, and listeners. Particularly when you are writing in a new genre or discipline, though—a situation that you'll surely face as a college student—it can be helpful to analyze your rhetorical situation more systematically.

THINK ABOUT YOUR GENRE

- *Have you been assigned a specific genre?* If not, do any words in the assignment imply a certain genre? *Evaluate* may signal a review, for example, and *explain why* could indicate a causal analysis.

- *If you get to choose your genre,* consider your purpose. If you want to convince readers to recycle their trash, you would likely write an argument. If, however, you want to explain how to go about recycling, your purpose would call for a process analysis.

- *Does your genre require a certain organization?* A process analysis, for instance, is often organized chronologically, whereas an annotated bibliography is almost always organized alphabetically.

- *How does your genre affect your* TONE *?* A lab report, for example, generally calls for a different tone than a film review.

- *Are certain design features expected in your genre?* You would likely need to include images in a review of an art show, for instance, or be required to use a certain font size for a research paper.

THINK ABOUT YOUR AUDIENCE

- *Who is your intended audience?* An instructor? A supervisor? Classmates? Members of a particular organization? Visitors to a website? Who else might see or hear what you say?

- *How are members of your audience like and unlike you?* Consider demographics such as age, gender, religion, income, education, occupation, or political attitudes.

- *What's your relationship with your audience?* An instructor or supervisor, for example, holds considerable authority over you. Other audiences may be friends, coworkers, or (especially online) complete strangers. What expectations about the text might they have because of your relationship? You'd need to be careful not to sound too informal to a committee considering you for a scholarship, or too bossy to a group of friends.

- *If you have a choice of medium,* which one(s) would best reach your intended audience?

- *What do you want your audience to think or do* as a result of what you say? Take your ideas seriously? Respond to you? Take some kind of action? How will you signal to them what you want?

- *Can you assume your audience will be interested* in what you say, or will you need to get them interested? Are they likely to resist any of your ideas?

- *How much does your audience know about your topic?* How much background information do they need? Will they expect—or be put off by—the use of technical jargon? Will you need to define any terms?

- *Will your audience expect a particular genre?* If you're writing about Mozart for a music class, you might analyze something he wrote; if, however, you're posting comments on *Amazon* about a new CD, you'd be more likely to write some kind of review.

THINK ABOUT YOUR PURPOSE

- *How would you describe your own motivation for writing?* To fulfill a course assignment? To meet a personal or professional commitment? To express your ideas to someone? For fun?

- *What is your primary goal?* To inform your audience about something? To persuade them to think a certain way? To call them to action? To entertain them? Something else? Do you have other goals as well?

- *How do your goals influence your choice of genre, medium, and design?* For example, if you want to persuade neighbors to recycle, you may choose to make colorful posters for display in public places. If you want to inform a corporation about what recycling programs accomplish, you may want to write a report using charts and examples.

THINK ABOUT YOUR STANCE

- *What's your attitude toward your topic?* Objective? Strongly supportive? Mildly skeptical? Amused? Angry?

- *What's your relationship with your audience?* Do you know them? Are they teachers? friends? strangers? How do you want to be seen by them—as a serious student? an effective leader? an informed citizen?

- *How can you best convey your stance in your writing?* What TONE do you want it to have?

- *How will your stance and tone be received by your audience?* Will they be surprised by it?

THINK ABOUT THE LARGER CONTEXT

- *What else has been said about your topic,* and how does that affect what you will say? What would be the most effective way for you to add your voice to the conversation?

- *Do you have any constraints?* When is this writing due? Given your current to-do list and the nature and significance of this project, how much time and energy can you put into it?

- *How much independence do you have as a writer* in this situation? To what extent do you need to meet the expectations of others, such as an instructor or supervisor? If this writing is an assignment, how can you approach it in a way that makes it matter to you?

THINK ABOUT YOUR MEDIUM AND DESIGN

- *If you get to choose your medium,* which one will work best for your audience and purpose? Print? Spoken? Digital? Some combination?

- *How will the medium determine what you can and cannot do?* For example, if you're writing on *Facebook,* how might the medium influence your TONE ? If you're submitting an essay online, you could include video, but if you were writing the same essay in print, you'd only be able to include a still shot from the video.

- *Does your medium favor certain conventions?* Paragraphs work well in print, but *PowerPoint* presentations usually rely on bulleted phrases instead. If you are writing online, you can include links to sources and background information.

- *What's the look most appropriate to your rhetorical situation?* Serious? Warm and inviting? Whimsical? What design elements will help you project that look?

- *Should you include visuals?* Is there anything in your text that would benefit from them? Will your audience expect them? What kind would be appropriate—photographs? video? maps? Is there any statistical material that would be easier to understand as a table, chart, or graph?

- *If you're writing a spoken or digital text,* should you include audio or video?

MAKE A LIST of all the writing that you remember doing in the last week. Be sure to include everything from texting and tweeting to more formal academic or work-related writing. Choose three examples that strike you as quite different from one another and write an analysis of the rhetorical situation you faced for each one, drawing upon the guidelines in this chapter.

THREE

Writing Processes

**HINK OF SOMETHING YOU LIKE TO DO**: ride a bike, play a certain video game, grow your favorite vegetables. If you think about it, you'll see that each of these activities involves a process and that when you first started learning it took some effort to make the process go well. Eventually, however, the process became familiar, and now you just do a lot of it automatically.

Writing is much the same. It, too, is a process: a series of activities that take some effort to do well. At some level, everyone who writes knows this—from a child illustrating a story who erases part of a picture thinking, "That tree just doesn't look right," to college students working over an extended period of time on a research paper.

But as with any process, you can negotiate your *writing process* in ways that will make it work for you. The goal of this chapter is to help you make the most of the many writing demands you'll encounter at school, at work, and elsewhere. No single writing process works for every author, so now is a good time to develop a repertoire of writing strategies that will enable you to become an efficient, productive, effective writer.

Develop writing habits that work for you. Think about how you habitually approach a writing task and then examine those habits to make sure they are working well. You may write best early in the day—or at night. You may need solitude and quiet—or you may need music or white noise around you. A neat work area may be helpful to you—or not. So think carefully about what habits seem to produce your best work. But be careful: If you think you do your best work while multitasking, think again. Research increasingly challenges that assumption!

WRITING PROCESSES / A Roadmap

Understand your assignment. Read every assignment you get very carefully, and make sure you understand what it asks you to do. Does it specify a topic? a theme? a genre? Look for words like "argue," "evaluate," and "analyze"—these are words that specify a GENRE and thus point you toward approaching your topic in a certain way. An assignment that asks you to analyze, for example, lets you know that you should break down your topic into parts that can then be examined closely. If your assignment doesn't name a genre, think about which genre will best suit your rhetorical situation.

Come up with a topic. If you haven't been assigned a specific topic, figure out what you want to write about. Think of things you are particularly interested in and want to know more about—or something that puzzles you or poses a problem you'd like to solve or that gets you fired up. Don't worry if the topic you come up with isn't very specific: as you do research on it, you will be able to narrow and refine it. Coming up with a broad topic is just the beginning, a way of getting started.

Keep your RHETORICAL SITUATION in mind. Whether you're writing an argument or a narrative, working alone or with a group, you will have a purpose, an audience, a stance, a medium, a design, and a context—all things that you should be thinking about as you make your way through your own writing process.

Schedule your time. Remember that you must fit any writing project into your busy schedule, so you need to think about how to use your time most wisely. However you keep yourself on track, remember that taking a series of small steps is easier than a huge jump. So schedule goals for yourself: doing so will build your confidence and reinforce good writing habits.

Generate ideas. Most of us find that it helps to explore our ideas in writing. Here are some activities for generating ideas:

- *Brainstorming.* Take a few minutes to focus on your topic or thesis (or a broad idea you want to develop into a specific topic or thesis) and make a list—using words or phrases—of everything that occurs to you about this subject. Be sure not to censor yourself and to let your ideas flow as freely as possible. Then review what you have written, looking for promising ideas and relationships that you can further develop.

- *Clustering.* Take a sheet of paper and write a word or phrase that best summarizes or evokes your topic. Draw a circle around this word. Now fill in the page by adding related words and ideas, circling them and connecting them to the original word. Then look at all the circles to see what patterns you can find or where your ideas seem to be leading.

- *Freewriting.* Write as freely as possible without stopping. To freewrite, simply write about whatever comes into your head in relation to a particular idea or topic for five to ten minutes. You may be surprised at the complexity and power of the ideas that you have developed through this process.

- *Looping.* Looping is an extended and directed kind of freewriting. Begin by establishing a subject and then freewrite for five to ten minutes. Look at what you've written. Identify the most important or interesting or promising idea and write a sentence summarizing it. Use this sentence to start another "loop" of freewriting. Repeat this process as many times as necessary.

- *Drawing or sketching.* Many writers create images that help guide their thinking. You may be able to spur your thought by drawing a picture of your topic. If you are writing about recycling on your campus, what does that topic look like? Drawing it may lead to a creative breakthrough. Could you create a series of sketches that would capture the movement or structure of an essay you're writing?

- *Questioning.* Think of your topic as a news story, and explore it using questions based on the following categories: Who? What? Where? When? Why? How? Who or what's involved? Where and when did something happen? Why and how did a situation change?

Come up with a tentative THESIS, a statement that identifies your topic and the point you want to make about that topic.

1. *What point do you want to make about your topic?* Try writing it out as a promise to your audience: *In this essay, I will present reasons for becoming a vegetarian.*

2. *Ask some questions about what you've written.* Will it engage your intended audience? Can you actually do what you say you will do—that is, do you have the time and resources necessary to do so?

3. *Try plotting out a thesis in two parts,* the first announcing your topic, the second making some claim about the topic: *Adopting a vegetarian diet will improve health, help local farms, and reduce the carbon footprint.*

4. *Do you need to qualify your thesis?* You don't want to overstate your case—or to make a claim that you'll have trouble supporting. Adding words such as *could, might, likely,* or *potentially* can help qualify what you say: *Adopting a vegetarian diet will <u>likely</u> improve health, <u>might</u> help local farms, and <u>could potentially</u> reduce the carbon footprint.*

Keep in mind that at this point in your process, this is a tentative thesis, one that could change as you write and revise.

Plan and write out a draft. While all writers plan, draft, and revise, they may do so in radically different ways. You may prefer to do most of your planning in your head, and then start drafting. Perhaps you do your best work by writing down explicit plans, sketches, or outlines before you begin to draft. Or you may like simply to start writing and see where it takes you. As always, pay attention to what works best for you.

Look at your draft with a critical eye, get response, and revise. Each of the genre chapters in this book includes guidelines for reading a draft carefully and revising: **ARGUMENTS** (p. 87), **NARRATIVES** (p. 126), **ANALYSES** (p. 168), **REPORTS** (p. 210), and **REVIEWS** (p. 254).

• *Read over your draft* closely with your purpose, your thesis, and your audience in mind. After every paragraph, ask yourself how it supports your thesis and whether it will be clear to your audience. Refer to Chapter 13 for guidance in analyzing your argument. And now might be a good time to **OUTLINE** your text in order to check for organization.

- *Get response from others*—from your instructor, your classmates, your friends. Tell them about any questions or concerns you have about the draft, and ask for their advice. But remember: you don't have to take all the advice you get, just what you consider helpful. You're the author!

- *Revise.* If you're writing in one of the genres in this book, refer to the guidelines listed above.

Edit and proofread. Now's the time to pay close attention to the details of your writing, to check your paragraphs, your sentences, your words, and your punctuation. For help editing your writing for style, see Chapter 26. For help with the conventions of academic writing see Chapter 28. For help editing your sentences, see Chapter 30. And don't forget to check for common mistakes: Chapter 31. Finally, take the time to proofread. Read with an eye for typos and inconsistencies. Make sure all your sentences are complete. Run a spell checker, but be aware that it is no substitute for careful proofreading.

Approach Your Writing Pragmatically

Gerald Graff's essay on p. 787 might help you appreciate that you already have a lot of everyday skills that you can apply to your own writing process.

Even if you have a writing process that works well for you, that doesn't mean you complete all writing tasks the same way—or that you should. It's just common sense that you spend more time and take more care with your writing process for a fifteen-page research paper that counts 40 percent of your final grade than you would for a much briefer essay that counts 10 percent of that grade. Take a tip from social scientist Herbert Simon, who coined the word "satisfice," blending *satisfy* and *suffice*. Writers who satisfice approach a writing task pragmatically, considering how important it is, any time constraints, what else they have to do, the nature of the task itself, and how well prepared they feel to complete it. That is, they make *realistic* decisions about their writing processes. So be realistic: What do you *need* to do to complete an assignment effectively—and what *can* you do?

TAKE TIME TO REFLECT on what you've written. What worked well? What was a struggle? What do you plan to do differently next time? Identify one passage in your writing that you like a lot, and then think about what you like about it. What goals do you have for yourself as a writer?

FOUR

The Need for Collaboration

Here Comes Everybody!

*ERE COMES EVERYBODY* is the title of NYU professor Clay Shirky's book about "what happens when people are given the tools to do things together, without needing traditional organizational structures" to do them. Put another way, Shirky's book is about how technology has led to connectivity and how connectivity has led to easy and innovative collaborations. Here's what we mean:

- A group of students creates a *Wikipedia* entry devoted to Latino/a comics. Within hours, dozens of others from around the world have joined in, helping to expand and refine the entry.

- Romance writer Eloisa James maintains a website that invites readers to ask questions about characters, request rewrites of chapters, and even suggest alternative chapters.

- Assigned to write an essay about twenty-first-century grassroots social movements, a student starts by researching what has been written on this topic (reading news magazines and online news sites), choosing a specific topic—the Occupy Wall Street movement—and then figuring out what he wants to say. As he writes the essay, he weaves the views of others (carefully cited) into his own, thus adding his voice to the conversation about that topic.

"On back porch, opening jars of fireflies, releasing them into nite air. Beautiful things should be allowed to go free."
—@BettyDraper

- Fans of the hit TV show *Mad Men* take over the characters, and soon hundreds of "Betty Drapers" are tweeting the innermost thoughts of the lonely housewife—big news to the writers of the show and no doubt to Betty herself, if she had actually existed!

Even the student mentioned above, sitting alone at his computer with all of his research, depends on others. In short, writers seldom—if ever—write alone. Collaboration is inevitable and essential. This chapter will help you think about the role that collaboration plays in your life and especially how it affects the work you do as a writer and reader.

THINK ABOUT READING AND WRITING that you do regularly online— email, blog postings, wikis—everything. In what ways are you an author, and in what ways are you a member of an audience? To what extent does each activity involve collaboration with others, and how would it be different if there were no collaboration at all?

What Collaboration Means for Authors—and Audiences

The examples above show some of the ways that authors collaborate— and how they sometimes even trade places with their audiences. Those tweeting Betty Drapers are members of an audience who decide to take on authorship; author Eloisa James becomes an audience for her readers' suggestions and ideas; the student reading and writing about grassroots social movements is an audience to those authors whose work he reads and then an author when he responds to their views in his own essay. Welcome to the digital age, where authors and audiences shift roles and collaborate constantly—and indeed, where there's hardly any way to avoid doing so.

Once upon a time, newspapers reported information and events; today, they include blogs that serve as forums for discussing, challenging, even changing that information. Readers who were once passive consumers of the news can now be active participants in writing about that news.

To take one other familiar example, players of the first video games were an audience for a story that was written by the game's designers. That's not the case in many of today's role-playing games, however, where the players/audience get to customize their characters and write their own story—very often in collaboration with other players. Consider, for example, the aptly named MMORPGs (massively multiplayer online role-playing games) such as *World of Warcraft,* in which a large number of people play as a group, or the more serious video game *World without Oil*, in which almost 2,000 individuals from twelve countries collaborated over the course of a month to imagine how to deal with a global oil crisis. Not only do such games offer opportunities for collaboration, but it's also actually impossible for any one player to play on his or her own.

Collaborations take place for all kinds of purposes. David L. Hoyt describes one of these on p. 823.

Collaboration is an everyday matter. We collaborate for fun, as when a flash mob suddenly appears and starts dancing to "Thriller" or singing the Hallelujah Chorus and then just as suddenly disappears. And we collaborate for more serious purposes, as when many people contribute over time to develop a *Wikipedia* entry or when people promoting a particular cause use social media to stay connected and to plan future actions (think Occupy Wall Street). For these and other purposes, collaboration is a necessity. As media professor Henry Jenkins puts it, ours is "a world where no one knows everything, but everyone knows something." Putting those somethings together is what happens when we collaborate.

THINK BEYOND WORDS

TAKE A LOOK at some favorite flash mobs at wwnorton.com/write/everyonelinks. *Some promote a cause, others sell a product, still others celebrate something or someone. The one picture above, from Berlin, is a tribute to Michael Jackson. We think you'll agree that in addition to fulfilling various purposes, they can be great fun. What ideas do you have for an effective flash mob? In what ways would the flash mob accomplish your goal better than a piece of writing might do?*

What Does Collaboration Mean for You as a Student?

As a student, you'll have many occasions to collaborate, as when you meet in class with a group of students to discuss a question posed by your teacher or to respond to each other's writing. Other occasions call for full-fledged collaboration, as when you work with a team to research and write a report, carry out and evaluate an experiment, or construct a website.

As a writer, you'll be in constant collaboration with others, from teachers and classmates who read and respond to your drafts to the audiences you're addressing—and don't forget those whose work you read and cite. Academic writing in particular calls on you to engage with the ideas of others—to listen to and think about what they say, to respond to views you don't agree with, and to weave the ideas of others (those you agree with and those you don't) into your own arguments. Very often you may even present your own views as a direct response to what others say—in fact, when you think of it, the main reason we make arguments at all is because someone has said or done something that we want to respond to. And one reason we make academic arguments is to add our voices to conversations about topics that we're studying, things that matter to us.

And consider your nonacademic writing, particularly that which you do online. Whether you're texting friends, posting or following others on *Facebook* or *Twitter* or *Tumblr*, viewing or contributing to *Wikipedia* or *YouTube* or *Flickr*, it all assumes and makes possible a back-and-forth—a collaboration. You might be an author or an audience or both. These are all ways that we regularly communicate—and collaborate—with others.

GO TO Wikipedia *and work with several classmates to choose an entry that interests you and then revise or add to it. Or, if you don't find what you're looking for, create a new entry yourselves. Revisit in a few days to see what others may have added to (or removed from) your entry.*

Collaboration at Work

Collaboration almost certainly plays a role in your work life. Indeed, teamwork is central to most businesses and industries. Engineers work in teams to design power plants; editors and designers work together to publish books and magazines; businesses from Best Buy to *Google* rely on teams to develop and market new products. Given the role that information technologies now play in our lives, whatever work you do—whether it is that of en-

At the Los Angeles headquarters of *I.D.* magazine, CEO Kelly Bush leads a videoconference with members of her New York staff.

gineer, health-care worker, bookstore owner, chemist, or teacher—you will find yourself continually communicating with others. The effectiveness of these communications will depend to a large extent on your ability to collaborate effectively.

Today's global culture can raise particular challenges for communication. Increasing numbers of workers are telecommuting—spending time at their desktops rather than at a desk in an office with other workers. Even when they are working from a centralized office, workers often need to communicate with colleagues elsewhere in the world and in other time zones. Digital humanities professor Cathy Davidson describes how one company holds global conference calls:

> Everyone chats using Sametime, IBM's internal synchronous chat tool, and has a text window open during the conversation. Anyone can be typing in a comment or a question (backchatting) while any other two people are speaking. Participants are both listening to the main conversation between whichever two people happen to be talking while also reading the comments, questions, and answers that any of the other participants might be texting. The conversation continues in response to both the talk and the text.
>
> —CATHY DAVIDSON, *Now You See It: How the Brain Science of Attention Will Transform the Way We Live, Work, and Learn*

A dizzying scenario to be sure—and an excellent reminder of both the challenges and the opportunities that the future holds for all who wish to make our voices heard in today's global culture. As a student in college, you are well positioned to prepare yourself for this future—which is in fact not the future at all but our present moment. Rather than taking your online writing for granted as "just fun," learn from it. Take advantage as well of the opportunities that your school provides to learn with and from people with diverse cultural backgrounds. Such collaborative interactions are intrinsically satisfying, and they can also help prepare you to communicate effectively in the twenty-first century.

Some Tips for Collaborating Effectively

As a college student, you will often be asked to work collaboratively with others. Sometimes that collaboration will be fleeting and low risk—for example, to work with a group to respond to questions about a reading and then to share the group's ideas with the class. Other collaborations are more extended and high risk, as when you have a major group project that will count for a significant percentage of everyone's final grade.

Extended collaborative assignments can be a challenge. Members of the group may have differing goals—for instance, if two members will accept nothing less than an A and others are just hoping for a C. Other problems can result as well, such as with domineering members of the team or those who don't participate at all. And the logistics of collaborating on a major project can be a challenge. Here are some tips that can help ensure efficient, congenial, and productive team relationships when you are working on an extended collaborative project.

- *Find ways of recognizing everyone.* For example, each group member could talk about a strength that he or she can contribute to the project.

- *Listen carefully*—and respectfully—to every group member.

- *Establish some ground rules.* Whether online or face-to-face, the way your group runs its meetings can make or break your collaborative effort. Spend part of your first meeting exploring your assignment and figuring out how often the group will meet, the responsibilities of each member, and so on.

- *Make an effort to develop trust and group identity.* To get started, everyone could share some pertinent information, such as their favorite spots for writing or their typical writing processes. Remember, too, that socializing can play an important role in the development of group identity. Sharing a pizza together while brainstorming can pay off down the road. However, remember to stay focused on the project.

- *Get organized.* Use an agenda to organize your meetings, and be sure that someone takes notes. Don't count on anyone's memory, and don't leave all the note-taking to one person! You may want to take turns developing the agenda, reminding everyone of upcoming meetings via email or text message, maintaining written records, and so on.

- *Develop nonthreatening ways to deal with problems.* Rather than telling someone that their ideas are unclear, for instance, you might say, "I'm having trouble making the connection between your suggestion and my understanding of what we're discussing." Just a simple shift from *your* to *my* can defuse difficult situations. And remember that tact, thoughtfulness, and a sense of humor can go a long way toward resolving any interpersonal issues.

- *Build in regular reality checks* to nip any potential problems in the bud— for example, to reserve some time to discuss how the group is working and how it could be better. Try not to criticize anyone; instead focus on what's working and what could be improved.

- *Encourage the free play of ideas,* one of the most important benefits of working collaboratively. Think carefully about when your group should strive for consensus and when you should not. You want to avoid interpersonal conflicts that slow you down.

- *Expect the unexpected.* Someone's computer may crash, interlibrary loan materials may arrive later than expected. Someone else may be sick on the day when she was supposed to write a key section of your text. Try to build in extra time for the unexpected.

- *Be flexible about how you meet.* If getting together in person poses problems, use online chat or *Google Docs* to meet and work. Your school might provide a course management system that includes discussion forums, wikis, and file-sharing folders—all of which will prove helpful for collaborative work.

Remember that when you engage in group work, you need to attend to both the task and the group. And keep in mind that each member of the group should be valued and that the process should be satisfying to all.

FIVE

Writing and Rhetoric as a Field of Study

**HETORICIAN SUSAN MILLER** neatly sums up why we study rhetoric: "If you want to know how power works, you must understand how language works—and that's what the study of rhetoric is all about." As Miller's statement underscores, mastery of the tools of rhetoric—writing, reading, speaking, and listening—is more crucial today than ever before, so much so that employers rank the ability to communicate well at the top of their list of the qualities they look for in those they hire. A survey of 120 American corporations, for instance, concludes that in today's workplace writing is a "threshold skill" for hiring and promotion.

So it's no surprise that colleges and universities are responding by establishing departments, programs, and courses that allow students to choose writing and rhetoric as a field of study. Check out the website for the University of Texas's Department of Rhetoric and Writing, for example, and you'll find this statement: "Analytical, communicative, and persuasive skills are in demand in almost every profession. . . . The Rhetoric and Writing major . . . produces sophisticated communicators." Michigan State's Department of Rhetoric, Writing, and American Cultures defines its goal as "to prepare students to be culturally and technologically engaged thinkers, writers, researchers, teachers, and citizens."

Educational leaders also speak to the need for careful study of writing and rhetoric. In an interview, Stanford University president John Hennessy (who was a professor of engineering before he became presi-

The website of the Department of Rhetoric and Writing at the University of Texas focuses on rhetoricians. From left: Demosthenes, a Roman woman of Pompeii, Aristotle, and Frederick Douglass.

dent) reflected on his own experience to make the point: "[In college] we had a notion that engineers had to know how to use slide rules or calculators or computers, but not how to write. And that is the biggest falsehood you could possibly perpetrate on young people. I think writing and rhetoric . . . are the two most valuable skills across any discipline in any field."

You have strong reasons, then, to consider writing and rhetoric as a field of study, whether you choose it as a major or a minor or simply to take advantage of opportunities to take classes in writing and rhetoric.

What Will You Learn by Studying Writing and Rhetoric?

What will it mean—what will you learn—if you choose writing and rhetoric as a field of study? As the quotations above suggest, this field focuses on effective, ethical communication, whether written, visual, or spoken—that is, it concentrates on how words and images can change our minds, earn our agreement, and shape our identities and lives. Members of this field recognize that in complex societies such as ours, those who can produce powerful written, spoken, visual, or digital messages have some distinct advantages.

That's the "big picture" of writing and rhetoric as a field of study. But this field will also introduce you to powerful practitioners of rhetoric, from the ancient Sumerian priestess Enheduanna (whose impassioned writing argued for the supremacy of the goddess Inanna over male gods), to the an-

The website of the Department of Rhetoric & Writing Studies at San Diego State University focuses on the media of communication.

cient Roman orator Cicero (whose words in support of the Roman Republic were so dangerous that they cost him his life), to twentieth-century rhetorical theorists such as Kenneth Burke (who argues that "wherever there is persuasion, there is rhetoric"), to contemporary leaders like Barack Obama and Aung San Suu Kyi.

Most important, as a student of rhetoric and writing, you will learn to think about how a text gets its message across, rather than just focusing on what the message is. In other words, as a student of rhetoric and writing, you will learn to think rhetorically. And in doing so, you'll read, analyze, and respond to important works of rhetoric throughout history, from Plato's attack on rhetoric as deception and trickery in his *Phaedrus* to Sei Shonogan's mischievous and memorable *Pillow Book*, which offers advice and observations about life in eleventh-century Japan, to the powerful speeches of Maria Stewart, Chief Sitting Bull, Sojourner Truth, Mohandas Gandhi, John F. Kennedy, and Martin Luther King Jr.

> I have something to say to the world, and I have taken English 12 in order to say it well.
> —W. E. B. DU BOIS

You may engage in a variety of research projects. For example, you may study how values and beliefs shape debates over public policy, or you may consider the knowledge, skills, and tools involved in workplace literacy practices. You might study how rhetorical strategies like metaphor and narrative shape communication in the public sphere—or how emerging technologies shape social practices and communication.

Like all fields, this one has a number of subfields:

- Digital rhetoric
- Visual rhetoric

- Literacy studies
- Technical, professional, and business communication
- Editing and publishing
- The history of rhetoric and of writing
- The teaching of writing and rhetoric
- Writing program administration
- Teaching English as a second or foreign language
- Community literacy

As a student of rhetoric and writing, you will likely find courses on many of these topics. In addition, you may take courses on such topics as gender and writing, the rhetoric of film, American Indian rhetorics, African American rhetorics, Asian American rhetorics, the rhetoric of graphic narratives (comics!), or the rhetoric of science—to name just a few.

Thinking rhetorically helped Emily Martin to understand how our ideas about the meeting of egg and sperm are formed by much more than science alone. See what she figured out on p. 845.

What Jobs Will Writing and Rhetoric Prepare You For?

A major or minor in rhetoric and writing will prepare you well for any number of pursuits. It offers excellent preparation for law, for example, and it can lead toward any career that calls for effective communication: public relations, advertising, nonprofit work, political and community organizing, publishing, international relations, media, and entertainment. (And don't forget the numerous advantages of studying a second language. Doing so helps you gain insight both into the rhetoric of other cultures and of your own.)

The study of writing and rhetoric can be a springboard for a number of good jobs. Many of our students, for example, have gone on to become teachers of language arts, history, or social studies; some have gone overseas to teach English as a foreign language. We know another student who, after majoring in writing and rhetoric, became a speechwriter and researcher for a U.S. senator. Still another landed a job as an editorial assistant with a publishing firm in New York City. One former student is now a junior associate in an advertising firm in Chicago, and another is working as an assistant writer for BET. Not long ago, one of us was on an airplane when a fellow passenger noticed the business card on her luggage and said,

Don't tell me words don't matter. "I have a dream"—just words? "We hold these truths to be self-evident, that all men are created equal"— just words?

—BARACK OBAMA

When there is more than one language, more than one culture, and more than one rhetorical tradition, the basic question of communication never goes away in terms of who has the floor, who understands what's being said, and who gets listened to.

—LU MING MAO

"You must be a rhetorician; we just hired a rhetorician this week." The fellow passenger was the CEO of an insurance company, and his firm, he said, had hired a student with an extensive background in writing and rhetoric as a group leader in the public relations department. As these examples show, studying writing and rhetoric is a field of study that can lead to many opportunities!

If your school does not offer a major or minor in rhetoric and writing, check out the possibility of developing an independent major or minor. Chances are, you'll find courses in a variety of departments that could help you achieve expertise in writing and rhetoric; communications, new media, anthropology, linguistics, English, design, and international relations are just some of the departments that might have courses you could take. But whatever your major, you'll be wise to take courses that focus on rhetoric, writing, or speaking. These are skills that have always been important to those who succeed, but in today's world they have become in many ways the new basics.

FIND OUT whether there is a writing and rhetoric program or department at your school. If not, look for courses on writing and speaking and rhetoric in various other departments, or look in your course catalog to locate courses that are marked with a W to indicate that they are writing intensive. See if there is a writing center on your campus—and if you find one, check out its services. Finally, think about what role writing, speaking, and rhetoric are likely to play in your future.

SIX

Writing and Rhetoric in the Workplace

LASH FORWARD FIVE OR TEN YEARS. You've graduated from college, maybe from graduate or professional school as well; you're on the job. And whatever that job is, one thing is certain: Your ability to communicate— through writing, speaking, and other means—will be crucial to your success. If you're an engineer, you'll be writing **PROPOSALS**, specifications, and directions and maybe giving presentations to prospective clients. If you're a teacher, you'll be writing lesson plans and student **EVALUATIONS**. If you're a health-care practitioner, you'll be writing medical **NARRATIVES** and patient charts and speaking with patients and their families. If you're an accountant, you'll be **ANALYZING** data. If you're a sales representative, you'll be writing **REPORTS** and marketing copy as well as presenting pitches to customers. So strong is the demand for good communicators that virtually every survey of employers reports that the ability to write and speak well is the skill they value most.

Becoming a strong writer, speaker, and presenter isn't rocket science or a gift from the gods: It's a product of careful choices, hard work, and lots of practice. This chapter offers advice on some of the writing and speaking you'll need to do for work, first to get a job and then once you're on the job.

Strong writing and speaking skills are essential in the workplace—from finding (and landing) a job to performing the tasks that job will require.

Consider Your Rhetorical Situation

Whether you have a job or are searching for one, you'll be communicating with many different audiences for many different purposes—and so you should get in the habit of thinking systematically about your rhetorical situation. Here are some questions that can guide you:

- *What's your* PURPOSE*?* Are you seeking information? an interview? a specific job? Are you asking someone to do something for you? Are you discussing a possible job, plan, or project? Are you presenting a proposal? negotiating a salary?

- *Who's your* AUDIENCE*?* Someone you know or have been referred to? A human resources director? A colleague? A person you would report to? Someone you know nothing about? If it's someone you don't know, what do you know about him or her—and what can you find out by looking on a company website?

- *What's your* STANCE*?* How do you want to present yourself—as eager? curious? confident? knowledgeable? professional? friendly? earnest? If you're looking for a job, what experience do you bring—and how can you demonstrate what you could contribute?

- *What's the* CONTEXT*?* Are you responding to an ad? writing a cover letter to go with an application or a proposal or some other document? presenting to a large group? If you're applying for a job, how many steps are involved? What can you find out about the organization by doing some research online?

- *What* GENRES *should you use?* Are you writing a letter? composing a résumé? reporting information? arguing a position or for some kind of action? reviewing someone's work (or being reviewed)?

- *What* MEDIA *will you use?* If you're sending a letter or résumé, should you use email or U.S. mail? If you're participating in a discussion or interview, will it be face-to-face? on the phone? over *Skype*? in a webinar? If you're giving a presentation, should you include slides or handouts?

Be Professional

The words you choose, the way you construct sentences, the way you design a letter or résumé, even your email address create an impression for prospective employers—which you want to be good. And it's even more important once you're on the job, for then you'll be representing both yourself and the organization you work for. Careless errors that might result in a few points off a grade at school can have greater consequences in the working world, from not getting an interview to not winning a contract to actually losing a job. Whether you're writing letters or résumés, presenting samples of your work, or participating in an interview, every word is crucial for making your goals clear and for establishing your credibility with employers, colleagues, or clients. This advice is underscored by business schools everywhere:

> Business people who never expected to be doing much writing find that the Internet forces everyone to exchange written messages. . . . Poor writing reflects badly on us, and it limits the influence we can have on others. Excellent writing correlates with the ability to think well, analyze, make decisions and persuade.
>
> —UNIVERSITY OF CONNECTICUT SCHOOL OF BUSINESS

Job Letters

In email or print, letters are important documents for conducting a job search. You will almost certainly write some inquiry letters, looking for information or asking about possible positions. On other occasions, you will send application letters about specific jobs you're interested in. And you will also have occasions to send thank-you letters. For all the job-related letters you'll write, here are some tried-and-true tips:

- Be direct and brief. Say what you want, and why. Assume that your readers will be scanning for just the information they need; make it easy for them to find it.

- Focus more on how you can help the company or organization than on why working there would be good for you. Be careful not to start too many sentences with *I*.

- State your interest and qualifications in a way that makes your readers want to speak with you—or hire you.

- Design letters carefully, making sure they look neat and professional. Use a single typeface—Times New Roman or Arial are always appropriate. Remember that the look of your letters says a lot about who you are.

- Use capitalization and punctuation the way you would in an academic essay. Don't include emoticons or cute little icons.

- Address readers by name and title (Dear Ms. Willett) or by first name and last if you're not sure about the correct title (Dear Mary Helen Willett). If an advertisement lists only an office, use that in your salutation (Dear Office of Human Resources). If you can't find a person or an office to use, check the company's website—or make a call to the company headquarters to find out more about whom you should address.

- Proofread, proofread, proofread! Make sure that nothing is misspelled.

Inquiry letters. Sometimes you may want to send a letter looking for information about a position, an industry, an organization, or something else. If you admire someone's work, or are interested in a particular company, do some research. You can probably find company email addresses, or maybe they're on *Twitter*. Write to ask if they would speak with you.

Inquiry letters should be brief but at the same time say what you're looking for, and why. Introduce yourself, and explain your interest in the organization or the person's work. Be enthusiastic but direct about what you're asking for—information about an organization? an opportunity to meet with someone? Remember to include your contact information. If you're looking for a job, you might attach your résumé, or enclose it if you are sending the letter by mail.

Shuqiao Song read a book on designing presentations that she liked very much and that helped improve her own presentation skills. When she noticed in the book that the author had a business near her college, Song sent the following email:

From: Shuqiao Song <ssong@gmail.com>

Date: Sunday, May 31, 2009 8:28 PM

To: Nancy Duarte <nduarte@presentations.com>

Subject: interested in communications design

Dear Ms. Duarte:

I'm a sophomore at Stanford University, where I recently took a rhetoric course on graphic novels in which we studied your book *slide:ology* for examples of successful presentations. I loved your book and was inspired to incorporate your suggestions and model my own presentation and slides on the advice in your book.

The words and images in the graphic novel that I analyzed in my presentation interact in unusual and fascinating ways, and my research on this topic led me to some insights about the way that speech, written text, and images could interact in my presentation. I've attached a video file of the presentation, which I hope you'll find interesting. My performance is far from perfect, but reading your book really changed the way I thought about presenting and helped me analyze the elements of good (and bad) presentations.

Your book also made me aware of the field of communications design, and I'm interested to learn more about it. Would you be willing to meet with me and to tell me about your work and how I can learn more about the field?

Thank you so much for considering this request. I hope to have the opportunity to speak with you.

Sincerely yours,
Shuqiao Song
650-799-8484

Application letters. When you're writing to apply for a job—or a grant, or something else—you'll usually need to write an application letter. This kind of letter is ordinarily sent along with a résumé, so it should be relatively short and to the point, saying what you are applying for and why you are interested in it. If you're applying for a specific position, say how you heard about it. Most important of all, try to show readers why they should consider your application—and here you need to think in terms of why hiring you would be good for them, not for you. Finally, identify anything you are including with your letter: your résumé, a writing sample, and so on.

Ade Adegboyega saw an advertisement for a summer internship at a ticket sales and service company. He was majoring in exercise science and sport management and had some experience in ticket sales and related services, so he was quick to apply. See the letter he sent on the next page.

Sample Application Letter

89 Laurel Ave.
Irvington, NJ 07111
June 14, 2011

Sender's address.

Frank Miller, Sales Manager
The ASR Group
3120 Industrial Blvd.
Suite A200
Atlanta, GA 30318

Recipient's name and address.

Dear Mr. Miller:

I am writing in response to your Teamworkonline.com posting for a summer intern in ticket sales and services. I believe that I have skills and experience that would enable me to contribute to your organization, and I am interested in this position.

Direct, to-the-point opening that mentions how he heard about position.

I am a sophomore at Rutgers University, majoring in exercise science and sport management, graduating in May 2013. The enclosed résumé provides details of my skills, education, and work experience. One item that may be of particular interest to you is my work in the ticket sales department at the Prudential Center. This experience taught me how to analyze sales patterns and meet sales quotas and promotional objectives. I've also worked as an office assistant and would also be able to contribute to the production of reports. All my jobs have helped me learn to communicate effectively with both colleagues and vendors.

Refers to enclosed résumé and relevant experience and skills.

I would welcome the opportunity to put my experience and abilities to work for the ASR Group sport management department and to discuss the position further with you. I can be reached at 862-773-4074 or ade.adegbo@scarletmail.rutgers.edu. Thank you for considering my application.

Contact information.

Sincerely,

Ade Adegboyega

Ade Adegboyega

Thank-you letters. Send a thank-you letter to anyone you speak with or who helps you when you're looking for a job. Whether you talk to someone in person, on the phone, or over email, you should thank him or her in writing. Doing so is a sign of respect and demonstrates your seriousness and your ability to follow through. When you're writing to someone who's interviewed you, try to reference something discussed in the interview, to raise a new question that might extend the conversation, and to provide additional thoughts about why the position would be an excellent match for your abilities and interests. And be sure to send a thank-you promptly, within a day or two of your interview. It's usually best to send it via email, especially if the employer will be making a decision soon. When Scott Williams was looking for a job, he was careful to write thank-you emails after every interview, like this one:

From: Scott Williams <sjwilliams@optonline.net>

Date: Friday, March 30, 2012 4:35 PM

To: Yuri Davison <davisony@graceco.com>

Subject: Thank You

Dear Mr. Davison,

Thank you for meeting with me yesterday and for taking so much time to explain the work your firm does. As an economics major, my studies were mostly theoretical so I was especially interested to hear about the day-to-day work at a private equity firm.

It's exciting to know that Grace & Company might be looking for a junior analyst in the near future, and I'm pleased to attach a sample of my writing, as you requested. It's an analytical paper I wrote about the music of Franz Liszt.

Thank you again for your time and consideration. I hope you'll keep me in mind if you do decide you need a junior analyst. In the meantime, would it be a good idea for me to take a class to prepare for the Series 7 exam? There's no telling what the future holds, but I know that I want to work in finance, and that is something I could get working on now.

Sincerely,
Scott Williams
203-875-9634

Note that Williams wrote this letter the day after his interview and that he references some specific things discussed and poses a question that gives reason for the conversation to continue. Now take a look at another letter, which demonstrates what *not* to do:

From: Libby White <lib.white@me.com>

Date: Sunday, October 25, 2009 4:13 PM

To: Alexander Elliott <aelliott@sales.maxco.com>

Subject: Thanks!

Mr. Elliott,

Thank you so much for giving me the opportunity to speak with you about your Sales Representative position. I am extremely excited about the possibility of working for you. Having now received the answers to my many questions about the sales position, I am even more thrilled to have the opportunity to interview for the position.

I greatly appreciate your taking the time to answer my questions so patiently and thoroughly. I hope we speak again in the future.

Thanks again,
Libby White
646-432-2533

While the interview was held on October 19, this email wasn't sent until October 25, suggesting to the employer that the writer was not very efficient or perhaps not genuinely interested in the job—or both. The writer focuses her message more on herself than on the position and the company, and both the subject line (thanks!) and the ending salutation (thanks again) are too informal. You probably won't be surprised to find that this applicant did not get the job.

Résumés

Your résumé provides an overview of your education and work experience—and thus is usually your most important chance to create a strong and favorable impression. While busy employers may not take time to read all the materials you send them, they will certainly take a close look at your résumé. For that reason, you'll need to write and design it carefully. As a piece of writing that represents you, you want it to look good and to be easy to read. Keep it to one page—just enough to showcase your experience and your ability to present yourself thoughtfully. The sample résumés on pp. 51 and 52 list experience in chronological order, but you might consider using reverse-chronological order if your recent experiences show a progression toward the kind of job you'd like to attain.

Format. Be prepared to submit your document in a variety of ways: MS Word, rich text format (RTF) or plain text, PDF, HTML, or keyword-optimized. Because browsers or company systems can translate files in different ways, having a clean, simple setup will prevent your résumé from being relegated to the "toss pile" because it has defaulted to something that's difficult to read. If you're submitting your résumé online, check how it looks in the major browsers—*Firefox, Chrome, Safari,* and *Internet Explorer* as this book goes to press. Try to determine which formats your audience requires.

Design. Use headings to organize your information and highlight key information with bullets. If you're able to save your résumé as a PDF, you can use some of the design features available in word-processing programs. But because you'll likely have to adapt to various file formats, make your design as simple as possible: fonts and indents won't always carry over.

You may also need to create a plain-text *scannable résumé,* designed to be read by a computer. Scannable résumés use a single font, with no italics, boldface, or indents, and they need to use keywords such as *sales* or *analysis* to match terms in job descriptions the computer is likely to be reading for. Scannable résumés use nouns instead of verbs to describe responsibilities and experiences. If a company you're applying to wants résumés in a particular format, be sure to deliver it that way.

If you have a specific job objective, you might list that objective at the top, just under your name and contact information. Be sure to mention any courses or experience that are relevant to that objective. If you're applying to be a teaching assistant at an elementary school, for example, you'll want to list any substitute teaching or babysitting experience and your CPR certification. And you might want to put experience that is most relevant to your goals first, as Ade Adegboyega did on this résumé he sent in for an internship at a ticket sales and service company.

Sample Print Résumé

Ade Adegboyega •——————————— *Name in boldface.*
89 Laurel Ave.
Irvington, NJ 07111
862-773-4074
ade.adegbo@scarletmail.rutgers.edu

OBJECTIVE
To obtain an internship related to the field of sport management.

EDUCATION
Rutgers University, New Brunswick, NJ (2009–present)
- School of Arts and Science
- Major: Exercise Science and Sport Management •——————— *Headings and bullets used*
- Minor: Economics   *to highlight information.*
- Bachelor of Science expected May 2013

EXPERIENCE
Prudential Center, Newark, NJ (Oct. 2007–Sept. 2009) •——— *Experience directly*
Ticket Sales Associate   *relevant to the job listed*
- Responded to inbound sales calls, responded to inquiries, and   *first; other experience in*
  provided information and/or follow-up materials as requested   *chronological order.*
- Maintained knowledge of ticket plan programs and ticket holder
  preferences

Answer, Rutgers University Center for Applied Psychology,
Piscataway, NJ (Sept. 2009–present)
Office Assistant at national organization for sex education
- Oversee database management for quality assurance
- Assist staff with administrative duties as requested
- Compile statistical information for program coordinators
- Distribute incoming mail and prepare outgoing mail

Rutgers Recreation, New Brunswick, NJ (Jan. 2010–present)
Intramural Referee
- Look for violations of rules during play
- Impose penalties on players as necessary
- Explain the rules governing a specific sport

COMPUTER SKILLS
Microsoft Word, Excel, PowerPoint, Access, programming

ACTIVITIES
Intramural soccer
Rutgers Brazilian Jiu Jitsu Club •——————————————— *Length kept to one page.*

Sample Scannable Résumé

Ade Adegboyega

Key words for computer searches.

Key words: ticket sales; oversight; sport; referee; economics; compilation of statistics; administrative duties

Address
89 Laurel Ave.
Irvington, NJ 07111
Phone: 862-773-4074
Email: ade.adegbo@scarletmail.rutgers.edu

Education

All information in a single font, flush left, with no bold, italics, or underlining.

B.S. in Exercise Science and Sport Management, minor in Economics, Rutgers, New Brunswick, NJ, expected May 2013

Experience
Ticket Sales Associate, Oct. 2007–Sept. 2009
Prudential Center, Newark, NJ

Nouns rather than verbs used to list responsibilities and experiences.

Response to inbound sales calls and inquiries; provision of information and/or follow-up materials as requested
Knowledge of ticket plan programs and ticket holder preferences

Office Assistant, Sept. 2009–present
Answer, Rutgers University Center for Applied Psychology, Piscataway, NJ
Oversight of database management for quality assurance; assistance of staff with administrative duties as requested; compilation of statistics for program coordinators as requested; distribution of incoming mail and preparation of outgoing mail

Intramural Referee, Jan. 2010–present
Rutgers Recreation, New Brunswick, NJ
Determination of rule violations during play; imposition of penalties on players; explanation of rules governing a specific sport

Computer Skills
Microsoft Word, Excel, PowerPoint, Access, programming

Activities
Intramural soccer
Rutgers Brazilian Jiu Jitsu Club

References

Often prospective employers will ask for references—professors or past supervisors who can speak about your work and your work ethic. Your first step is to develop relationships with teachers and others who might serve as references. Start early in your college career; visit your teachers during office hours, discuss your goals with them—and keep in touch. When you feel comfortable enough, ask if they would be willing to be a reference for you.

When it comes time to ask for a specific reference, be sure to provide them with helpful information: a description of the position, your résumé and cover letter, and samples of your work. Give ample notice—never less than a week or two to write a letter. If the letter will be mailed, be sure to provide stamped, addressed envelopes. Remember to thank your references at every step—when they agree to be a reference, after they recommend you, and when you get the position!

Writing Samples

You may be asked to submit a writing sample or even a portfolio of your work. For some positions, you may want to choose work that demonstrates certain kinds of writing, but often you'll just need to show something that demonstrates your writing ability. Include a brief cover note with your sample explaining what it is, why you are proud of it, and why you've chosen to submit it. Label the sample with your name and contact information, and take care with its presentation: Place it in a folder if you're delivering it in person or as a neatly designed document if you're sending it via email.

When Elizabeth Sanders interviewed for a position as a student events coordinator for a campus research institute that specified "experience organizing and publicizing campus events" as a qualification, she was asked to bring a portfolio of her work along. She chose work that showcased writing that would matter for that job—two brochures she wrote, designed, and produced; an interview she'd conducted with a visiting speaker; and a press release—and then wrote a cover statement listing what was in her portfolio and describing how each item addressed the job she was applying for.

Scott Williams was asked to submit a writing sample after his interview at a private equity firm. Having just graduated from college, he chose an analytical paper he'd written as a junior and attached it to his thank-you email.

Both Sanders and Williams were careful to choose examples that demonstrated their best work and to present it in a professional manner. In this case, their hard work paid off: Both got the jobs they were seeking. But even if they hadn't, they would have gained important experience to use when starting the next job search.

Job Interviews

When it comes time to interview, you'll need to prepare. Review the job description and plan how you will talk about your experiences as they relate to each required skill. Research the department and organization that you'd be working for. Make a list of questions you can imagine being asked and come up with answers to each. Prepare your own list of questions that you'd like to ask. Ask a friend to do a mock interview with you for practice.

The day of the interview, be on time, dress appropriately, and bring extra copies of your résumé, cover letter, references, and any other materials that were requested. Of course you'll be nervous, but be sure to *listen*—and to think before responding. And remember to smile! Here are a few questions that interviewers might ask that you can use to practice and build your own list of potential questions:

- Why are you interested in this industry or field?
- What do you know and like about our organization?
- What is your greatest strength? weakness?
- Can you explain a time that you successfully collaborated on a project?

Today, many employers use *Skype* or other videoconferencing technologies to conduct interviews. If you're asked to do an interview of this kind, you should practice speaking over *Skype* with a friend. Remember to look and speak directly into the camera in order to come as close as possible to establishing eye contact with your interviewers. And be sure to speak carefully, enunciating each word in case the connection is less than ideal.

Writing on the Job

The fact is that almost any job you take will call for writing—and for speaking and presenting as well. Regardless of what job you do, you will surely

Remember to focus on the camera, rather than the screen, during a videoconference.

be writing email. You will also likely be composing **EVALUATIONS** as well as letters of recommendations for others and carrying out **ANALYSES** of all kinds. Many jobs will call on you to write a whole range of **REPORTS** and to give presentations using *PowerPoint, Prezi,* or other presentation software.

As rhetorician Deborah Brandt points out, most of those working in the United States today spend part of their day writing:

> A large majority of Americans . . . now make their living in the so-called information economy, people who produce, distribute, process, manipulate or vend mostly written work during a significant percentage of the workday. At the turn of the 20th century, information workers represented 10 percent of all employees. By 1959, they had grown to more than 30 percent; by 1970, they were at 50 percent and now are 75 percent of the employed population. . . . As the nature of work in the United States has changed—toward making and managing information and knowledge—intense pressure has come to bear on the productive side of literacy, the writing side, made all the more intense . . . with the wide distribution of communication technologies that enable writing, that put keyboards and audiences readily at hand.
>
> —DEBORAH BRANDT, "Writing at Work"

So writing is going to be key to your future success. And the greatest success will come to those who know how to present themselves most effectively and who develop a strong work ethic, seeking mentorship and constructive criticism, and literally writing and speaking their way to success. Remember that getting—and keeping—a job depend on some basic rhetorical principles that will never go out of style:

- Become a strong and proactive team player who **COLLABORATES** well with others.
- Know your **AUDIENCE**, and make the effort to meet them more than halfway, with respect and a willingness to listen and learn from them.
- Clarify your goals and **PURPOSES**, and stick to them—but also know when and how to compromise.
- Consider the **RHETORICAL SITUATION** of any task you take on, and make sure that what you are doing is appropriate in that context.
- Know your own strengths and weaknesses, and strive to build on the former and minimize the latter.
- Learn from your mistakes.

Some years ago, when we surveyed members of professional associations asking them about the writing they did as part of their job, we received a letter from an engineer, who said the following: "It has come to my attention that those who are skilled in communication—and especially in writing and speaking—are the ones who get ahead in my firm. Would you be willing to correspond with me about how I might improve these skills?" Our guess is that there are thousands of new employees who would echo this sentiment, and this chapter is an attempt to respond to those requests.

PART II

Genres of Writing

WHEN YOU WERE A LITTLE KID, did you have certain kinds of clothes you liked to wear? Six-year-old Audrey describes her wardrobe this way: "I have school clothes—they're okay, I guess. And I have dress-up clothes, like for when I go to the *Nutcracker* or a fancy party. But my favorites are my make-believe clothes: Snow White, Alice in Wonderland, and especially Princess Tiana. She's my favorite!" What Audrey displays here is a fairly sophisticated sense of genres, ways that we categorize things. You see genres everywhere—in literature (think poetry, fiction, drama), in movies (westerns, film noir, action adventure), and in music (punk rock, country, classical).

These genres are never static or fixed. Rather, they are flexible and expand and change over time.

And when we talk about writing, we often talk about kinds—genres—of writing: narratives, lab reports, reviews, résumés, personal statements, letters, essays, and so on. Like all genres, those associated with writing have evolved over time as writers find new ways to communicate.

In the ancient world, for example, personal communication involved carving symbols into clay tablets or, a bit later, having a scribe record your message on papyrus. For communicating with speed, couriers memorized letters and raced to deliver them orally to the receiver. Once paper arrived on the scene and letters were less costly and easier to produce, they evolved into multiple subgenres: the business letter, the personal letter, the condolence letter, and so on. Today, letters have further evolved into electronic forms—emails, *Facebook* postings, tweets. It's hard to predict how these genres of personal communication will evolve in the future, but when they do, we know they will stretch to accommodate new ways and new media, as genres always do. In short, genres reflect current expectations while also shaping—and sometimes even changing—them.

In college, instructors will ask you to use particular genres, most likely including the ones we feature in this book: position papers, narratives, analyses, reports, and reviews. You may need to write a critical analysis of a short story or an analysis of a painting. In such a case, knowing the characteristic features of an analysis will be particularly helpful. And you may want or need to combine genres. You might find yourself, for example, introducing your analysis with a short narrative or concluding the analysis with an argument about the value of the work you are analyzing.

Of course, you may not always be asked to write in a particular genre: Your instructor may give you a topic, or ask you to select one, and then have you write about that topic in whatever way you choose. In this case, you will need to think carefully about what genre will be most appropriate for addressing that topic. You can begin by thinking about your rhetorical situation—your purpose, your audience, and your best means of reaching them. This rhetorical situation will help you determine the genre you need. You wouldn't apply for a business job by leaving a voicemail message saying, "Please give me this job; I'm sure I can do it," but by sending a letter of application that follows the form widely recognized and accepted in the business world.

Even though new social expectations and new media will continue to stretch traditional genres and to produce new ones as well, the underlying

Communication throughout the ages, from clay tablets to couriers delivering messages to tweets and texts.

reason for using genres remains: We have a deep need to communicate with one another, and genres help us meet that need efficiently, appropriately, and often even elegantly. You will see such genre-driven communication taking place everywhere on the web, from reviews written by Amazon customers, to comments posted to newspaper blogs, to the personal ads posted to many matchmaking services. Want to learn how to use any of these genres? Just log on and study a number of them, noting what the best ones have in common. Then plunge in and write one yourself.

The chapters that follow introduce five genres you will often be assigned in college. Each genre chapter identifies and explains the genre's characteristic features; discusses how, when, where, and why you might employ the genre most appropriately; provides a roadmap to guide you in writing that genre; and presents three examples. Chapter 12 will help you choose genres when the choice is yours. We hope that you'll use these chapters to explore some of the most frequently assigned college genres—and to adapt those genres to your own purposes and goals.

SEVEN

"This Is Where I Stand"
Arguing a Position

S O WHAT'S YOUR POSITION ON THAT?" This familiar phrase pops up almost everywhere, from talk radio to blogs, from political press conferences to classroom seminars. In fact, much of the work you do as an author responds, in some way, to this question.

After all, taking a position is something you do many times daily: You visit your advisor's office to explain in person your reasons for dropping a course; you send an email to a friend listing all the reasons she should see a certain film; you post a comment on a *YouTube* video; in an economics class discussion, you offer your own position on consumer spending patterns in response to someone else's; you survey the most recent research on abstinence-only sex education and then write a letter to the editor of your local newspaper advocating (or denouncing) such an approach. In all these cases, you're doing what philosopher Kenneth Burke calls "putting in your oar," taking and supporting positions of your own in conversation with others around you.

Look around, and you'll see other positions being articulated all over the place. Here's one we saw recently on a t-shirt:

Work to eat.

Eat to live.

Live to bike.

Bike to work.

The central argument here is clear: Bike to work. One of the reasons it's so effective is the clever way that the last sentence isn't quite parallel to the others. (In the first three, *to* can be replaced by *in order to*; in the last case, it can't.) Another reason it works well is the form of the argument, which is a series of short commands, each beginning with the same word that the previous sentence ends with. This pattern is even clearer when presented visually in its original format:

This chapter offers guidelines for writing an academic essay that takes a position. As you'll see, taking a position in an academic context often differs in crucial ways from doing so in other contexts. At the same time, many of the principles discussed will serve you well when stating a position generally.

THINK ABOUT the genre. Stop for a moment and begin jotting down every time you've had to take a position on something—anything at all—in the last few days. The list will surely soon grow long if you're like most of us. Then take an informal survey, noting down every time in one day someone around you takes a position. This informal research should convince you that the rhetorical genre of taking a position is central to many of your daily activities.

Across Academic Fields

Position papers are written in many fields, and a quick web search reveals that a number of disciplines offer specific guidelines for composing them. In *philosophy*, a position paper is a brief persuasive essay designed to express a precise opinion about some issue or some philosopher's viewpoint. In *computer science*, position papers consider a number of perspectives on an issue before finally offering the writer's own position. In *political science*, position papers often critique a major argument or text, first summarizing and analyzing its main points and then interpreting them in the context of other texts. Many college courses ask students to take a position in response to a course reading, specifying that they state it clearly, support it with evidence and logical reasons, and cite all sources consulted. So one challenge you'll face when you're asked to write a position paper in various disciplines will be to determine exactly what is expected of you.

Across Media

Different media present different resources and challenges when it comes to taking positions. Setting up a *website* about animal abuse gives you the possibility of creating links to evidence or additional information, whereas writing a traditional *essay* on that topic for a print magazine requires that

**THINK
BEYOND
WORDS**

TAKE A LOOK at the website of Mutt Love Rescue, a dog adoption organization in Washington, D.C., where you can see photos of available dogs, find out about fostering a dog, and more. Click on "Saving a Life" to see their appeal for donations, along with photos of some of the "lucky pups." How compelling do you find their argument? How does the use of words and images contribute to their appeal—is one more important? How would you revise this site to make it more effective—add video? audio? statistics? testimonials? more written information (or less)? Go to the Mutt Love Rescue link at wwnorton.com/write/everyonelinks to access the site.

you provide all the relevant evidence and reasons on the page. It is very easy to incorporate color images or video clips of many kinds in the webpage, but the magazine's budget may not allow for color at all. If you give a *lecture* about animal abuse to a student group, you'll mostly be talking, though you may use PowerPoint slides to help your listeners follow the structure of your comments, to remind them of your main points, and to show graphs or photos that will appeal to their sense of reason or their emotions. Finally, if your marketing class is designing a fundraising *TV commercial* for a non-profit organization that works to stop animal abuse, you'll likely be able to use images and even music to drive home your point, but you might have only thirty seconds to get the message across.

Remember that persuasion is always about connecting with an audience, meeting them where they are, and helping them see why your position is one they should take seriously or even adopt. To achieve that goal, you have to help your audience understand why you're excited or sad or optimistic or however else you feel about your topic. Spend some time examining the ways that the particular medium you're using can support or undermine a message. If that medium doesn't help you make your point convincingly or effectively, then you might ask whether you've taken advantage of what it offers or whether you need to consider another.

Across Cultures and Communities

Taking a position in cultures or communities other than your own poses special challenges. Advertising—a clear case of taking a position—is full of humorous tales of cross-cultural failure. When Pepsi first sought to break into the *Chinese* market, for example, its slogan, "Pepsi Brings You Back to Life," got mangled in translation, coming out as "Pepsi Brings Your Ancestors Back from the Grave."

Such errors in translation aren't limited to advertising. In March 2009, during her first meeting with *Russian* foreign minister Sergei Lavrov, President Barack Obama's U.S. secretary of state, Hillary Clinton, wanted to mark a clear break with the way the United States and Russia had related (or failed to relate) during the George W. Bush presidency. As a symbol of the new position the United States would be taking toward Russia, she offered Lavrov a gift, a large red button of the sort you would push in an emergency, labeled in English and Russian. In English, it said *reset*. As soon as Lavrov pointed out that the Russian inscription on the button didn't translate as "reset" but as "overcharged," a word with particularly negative connotations in Russian, Secretary Clinton herself was red-faced. Although everyone laughed at the incident and Clinton made sure that Lavrov soon received a button with the Russian equivalent of *reset*, her efforts to take a position effectively were undercut by the translation gaffe despite her best intentions. These examples remind us that taking a position in a culture you don't know intimately is risky.

Far more problematic than questions of translation are questions of stance. When taking a position in *American academic contexts*, you're almost always expected to state your position explicitly while acknowledging your awareness of other possible positions. In contrast, in some cultures and communities, you would generally avoid stating your opinion directly; rather, you would hint at it. In yet others, you would be expected to state your mind forthrightly, paying little attention to what others think about the issue or to how your words might make them feel.

Equally important, how people are expected to frame positions they take varies greatly—but systematically—within a culture, depending on their place in the social hierarchy as employee or supervisor, student or teacher, ruler or governed. To complicate matters, the expectations with respect to outsiders are almost always different from those for the locals. Most Americans (or Canadians or Mexicans or Cubans) might be quick to criticize their own government among friends, but they don't necessarily grant outsiders the same privilege. A word to the wise: Humility is in order, especially when taking a position in communities or cultures of which you're not a member. Don't assume that what works at home will work elsewhere. A safe first step is to listen and observe carefully when in a new context, paying special attention to how people communicate any positions they are taking.

Across Genres

Arguing a position, as we've pointed out, is something that you do, in small ways or large, almost every day—and even across a range of genres. You might, for instance, find yourself writing a letter to the editor of your local newspaper lamenting the closure of the local library—and setting forth your position that it must be kept open at all costs. Similarly, an annual **REPORT** would likely set out the company's position on collective bargaining with employees. After taking in a highly anticipated film, you might tweet a 144-character **REVIEW**, arguing that it wasn't as good as you'd expected.

LOOK TO SEE where and how positions are expressed around you, considering posters, editorials, songs, Facebook postings, blog entries, and so on. Then choose one that most interests you—or that is most irritating to you—and spend some time thinking about how it presents its position. How does it appeal to you—or why does it fail to appeal? What kinds of words, images, or sounds does it use as support for its position? If you were going to revise it for a different audience, what would you do? If you were going to create it in another medium, how would it be different?

CHARACTERISTIC FEATURES

Given the many different forms of writing that take a position, no one-size-fits-all approach to composing them is possible. We can, however, identify the following characteristic features common to writing where the author is taking a position:

- An explicit position
- A response to what others have said or done
- Appropriate background information
- A clear indication of why the topic matters
- Good reasons and evidence
- Attention to more than one point of view
- An authoritative tone
- An appeal to readers' values

An Explicit Position

Stating a position explicitly is easier said than done, since the complexity of most important issues can make it hard to articulate a position in a crystal-clear way. But it's very important to do so insofar as possible; nothing will lose an audience faster than hemming and hawing or drowning your position in a sea of qualifications. At the same time, in most academic contexts (as well as many others), a position stated baldly with no qualifications or nuances may alienate many readers.

In a syndicated column from March 2009, just as the severity of the financial downturn was finally sinking in, *New York Times* columnist Thomas Friedman, writing for an American audience, explained:

Let's today step out of the normal boundaries of analysis of our economic crisis and ask a radical question: What if the crisis of 2008 represents something much more fundamental than a deep recession? What If It's telling us that the whole growth model we created over the last 50 years is simply unsustainable economically and ecologically and that 2008 was when we hit the wall—when Mother Nature and the market both said: "No more."

We have created a system for growth that depended on our building more and more stores to sell more and more stuff made in more and more factories in China, powered by more and more coal that would cause more and more climate change but earn China more and more dollars to buy more and more U.S. T-bills so Americans would have more and more money to build more and more stores and sell more and more stuff that would employ more and more Chinese. . . .

We can't do this anymore.

—THOMAS FRIEDMAN, "The Inflection Is Near?"

Friedman's position is clear and explicit: Americans' assumptions about their country's economic relationship with China and the behavior growing out of these assumptions must change. Although such a strong position may alienate some readers, all readers have a clear understanding of where Friedman stands.

A Response to What Others Have Said or Done

Crucially, position papers respond to other positions. That is, they are motivated by something that has been said or done by others—and are part of an ongoing conversation. In the example above, Thomas Friedman explicitly questions a popular position—namely that despite the current economic downturn, Americans and people around the world will eventually be able to continue the patterns of consumption they have created over the past few decades. His response is a rejection of this position, signaled with his emphatic "we can't do this anymore." Readers of the *Times* website had a chance to respond to Friedman and thus to make their own contributions to the conversation.

In some cases, the position being responded to is used as part of the argument. The all-star "Yes, We Can" video that was widely viewed on *YouTube* during the 2008 election uses this latter strategy. Based on a speech by then-candidate Barack Obama, the video's soundtrack acknowledges the "chorus

Responding to an argument offers a good opportunity to establish your position. See how a large corporation responds to a barrage of criticism on p. 875.

of cynics" but turns this acknowledgment into part of the argument itself, as you can see in the italicized lines below.

> It was a creed written into the founding documents that declared the destiny of a nation. Yes, we can.
>
> It was whispered by slaves and abolitionists as they blazed a trail toward freedom. Yes, we can.
>
> It was sung by immigrants as they struck out from distant shores and pioneers who pushed westward against an unforgiving wilderness. Yes, we can.
>
> It was the call of workers who organized; women who reached for the ballots; a President who chose the moon as our new frontier; and a King who took us to the mountaintop and pointed the way to the Promised Land.
>
> Yes, we can to justice and equality. Yes, we can to opportunity and prosperity. Yes, we can heal this nation. Yes, we can repair this world. Yes, we can.
>
> We know the battle ahead will be long, but always remember that no matter what obstacles stand in our way, nothing can stand in the way of the power of millions of voices calling for change.
>
> *We have been told we cannot do this by a chorus of cynics. They will only grow louder and more dissonant.*
>
> *We've been asked to pause for a reality check. We've been warned against offering the people of this nation false hope.*
>
> But in the unlikely story that is America, there has never been anything false about hope.
>
> Now the hopes of the little girl who goes to a crumbling school in Dillon are the same as the dreams of the boy who learns on the streets of LA.
>
> We will remember that there is something happening in America; that we are not as divided as our politics suggests; that we are one people, we are one nation, and together, we will begin the next great chapter in the American story with three words that will ring from coast to coast, from sea to shining sea: Yes, we can.
>
> —WILL.I.AM, "Yes, We Can"

In fact, the position being taken here extended far beyond what Obama himself said. The video's argument was an explicit response to those who claimed "No, we can't" achieve "justice and equality," "heal this nation," and so on. However, another argument it was making was that U.S. voters could and would elect an African American as their president for the first time, a position that is implicit rather than explicit.

*WATCH THE VIDEO of "Yes, We Can." Consider how the medium—video, with the
addition of music, voice-overs, written words (like "hope" and "yes, we can"), and
images of singers and of Obama delivering the speech—contributes to the power of the
argument. Go to the link at* wwnorton.com/write/everyonelinks *to access the full video.*

In online writing, authors often simply provide a brief reference with a
link to help orient readers to another position within an ongoing conversation. In academic position papers, authors are expected not only to respond
to other positions but also to acknowledge those positions explicitly—a situation that is often not the case when you take a position in other contexts
and in some cultures. Later in this chapter, you will meet Katherine Spriggs,
who staked out a position on "buying local" in an essay written for one of
her college courses. In this brief excerpt from her essay, she responds directly to those who say buying local will have negative environmental effects:

> It has also been argued that buying locally will be detrimental to the envi-
> ronment because small farms are not as efficient in their use of resources
> as large farms. This is a common misconception and actually depends on
> how economists measure efficiency. Small farms are less efficient than
> large farms in the total output of one crop per acre, but they are more
> efficient in total output of all crops per acre (McCauley).
>
> —KATHERINE SPRIGGS, "On Buying Local"

In a short space, this author identifies an argument that others have made
about the position she is taking and then responds explicitly to it.

⁓⊚ THINK ABOUT YOUR WRITING as part of a larger, ongoing conversation. Examine something that you have recently written—an email message, a love letter, an essay for a class—about an issue or topic that matters to you and that expresses a position. Check to see whether it makes clear your motivation for writing and the position(s) to which you were responding. If these aren't clear, try revising your text to make them explicitly clear.

Appropriate Background Information

The amount of background information needed—historical background, definitions, contextual information—will vary widely depending on the scope of your topic, your audience, and your medium. If you are preparing a position paper on the effects of global warming for an environmental group, any background information provided will represent extensive, often detailed, and sometimes highly technical knowledge. If, on the other hand, you are preparing a poster to display on campus that summarizes your position on an increase in tuition, you can probably assume your audience will need little background information—for which you will have only limited space anyway.

The "Yes, We Can" video, as an advertisement in a political campaign, provided no background information other than what was contained in segments of the Obama speech on which it is based. Rather, it assumed that viewers would know a great deal about the context of the election and Obama's candidacy. In online writing, links can often do much of the work of filling readers in on background information; they are especially convenient because readers have the option of clicking on them or not, depending on how much information they need or want.

In academic contexts, writers are generally expected to provide a great deal of background information. When the president of Rensselaer Polytechnic Institute, Shirley Ann Jackson, addressed the Society of Women Engineers in 2003, she argued that government, education, private industry, and nonprofit organizations must form a coalition to attract women and minority group members into science and engineering careers because of the need the United States has and will have in coming years for experts in these fields. But to make that argument, she first needed to provide background information about the scope and urgency of the need itself:

A recent study by the U.S. General Accounting Office reveals that fully 15 percent of NASA's current scientific and engineering staff is already eligible to retire. During the next five years, that number will increase to 25 percent. NASA Administrator Sean O'Keefe testified before the Congress earlier this year that his agency's scientists and engineers, aged 60 and older, outnumber those aged 30 and younger by a factor of nearly three to one.

The same story is playing out at the U.S. Environmental Protection Agency (EPA), an important participant in this conference. A recent internal workforce assessment project, looking out to the year 2020, made some startling discoveries about the relatively short term.

Nearly 80 percent of the agency's Senior Executive Service employees —virtually its entire leadership cadre—will be eligible to retire by 2005. When we broaden the cohort to include senior scientists at the GS-14 and GS-15 levels, we find that 60 percent will be eligible to retire by 2005.

—SHIRLEY ANN JACKSON, "Engineering Education in the 21st Century"

These facts and statistics provide background information designed to convince her listeners that in order to meet this crisis, the country must recruit large numbers of students into the sciences and engineering; given the size of the need, it's logical to try to recruit more women and members of ethnic minority groups, who have historically been underrepresented in these fields.

Background information is not always statistical and impersonal, even in academic contexts. In an essay written for *Academe,* a publication of the

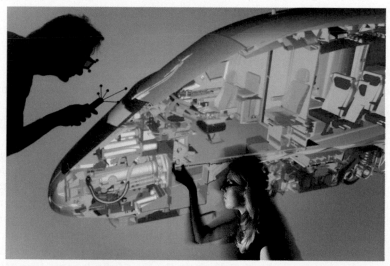

A female German engineer designs the high-speed train Velaro Rus using virtual reality projections.

American Association of University Professors, Randall Hicks, a professor of chemistry at Wheaton College, argues that it is harder for working-class students to become professors than it is for children of college-educated parents. The background information he provides is startlingly personal:

> "I'll break his goddamned hands," my father said. I wonder if he remembers saying it. Nearly twenty-five years later, his words still linger in my mind. My father had spent the entire day in the auto body shop only to come home and head to the garage for more work on the side. I may have finished my homework, and, tired of roughhousing with my brother, gone out to help him scrape the paint off his current project, some classic car that he was restoring. "It's okay for a hobby, but if somebody tells me that he's thinking of doing it for a living, I'll break his goddamned hands." Although we had no firm plans and little financial means to do so, he was telling me that he expected me to get an education.
>
> —RANDALL HICKS

Isn't nitrogen fascinating? No? Check out how Michael Pollan makes chemistry information interesting on p. 897.

Note how this story provides readers with important background information for Hicks' argument. Immediately, we learn relevant information about him and the environment that shaped him; thus, we understand part of his passionate commitment to this topic: He learned, indirectly, from his father to put a high value on education, since doing so in his father's view would allow Hicks to get a job that would be better than something that is just "okay for a hobby."

A Clear Indication of Why the Topic Matters

No matter what the topic, one of an author's tasks is to demonstrate that the issue is real and significant—and thus to motivate readers to read on or listeners to keep listening. Rarely can you assume your audience sees why your argument matters.

As a student, you'll sometimes be assigned to write a position paper on a particular topic; in those cases, you'll have to find ways to make the topic interesting for you, as writer, although you can assume the topic matters to the person who assigned it. On other occasions you may take it upon yourself to set out your position on something you care deeply about; then you will need to help your audience understand why they should care.

In a column in the *Washington Post*, Marie Cocco is strongly critical of the media coverage of Sarah Palin from the time Palin became John McCain's running mate in 2008 until her resignation as governor of Alaska in

Sarah Palin speaking at rallies in North Carolina (*left*) and Pennsylvania (*right*). Note how the photographers' perspectives affect the way we see her.

July 2009. Writing later that month, Cocco recounts incident after incident in which the media treated Palin in ways that, for Cocco, can only be labeled sexist. Twice during the essay, she mentions the treatment that Hillary Clinton received as a candidate, and twice she mentions the suffragists who fought for women's right to vote during the early twentieth century:

> When did such a savage strain of sexism become acceptable public discourse? Why does the same combination of bemused condescension and uninhibited vitriol that the media of a century ago showed toward the suffragists persist today?
>
> Palin most likely will fade away as a meaningful figure to all but her admirers on the far right. It is more relevant to ask not what she will do next but how the political media will treat the next Sarah Palin or Hillary Clinton—who, you may recall, was subjected to a *Washington Post* analysis of a bare hint of cleavage beneath a business suit. It appeared months before the first Democratic primary vote was cast.
>
> More than 100 years of sexist media treatment of women political leaders is, for me, quite enough. Whether it is for anyone else remains to be seen. —MARIE COCCO, "Trashing as Old as Suffrage"

In this passage, Cocco moves far beyond the single case of Sarah Palin to see larger societal forces at work that trouble her profoundly; in other words, the real problem is how the media covers female political leaders generally.

The creators of the "Yes, We Can" video certainly believed the election of 2008 mattered, as demonstrated in the values they appealed to and the range of people they included in the video. (If you watch carefully, you will see that one of the people participating was signing American Sign Language as she sang, explicit evidence that the Deaf, too, are part of the "we" who can.) Similarly, Thomas Friedman certainly thinks America's response to the economic downturn that began in 2008 is important. When he writes that the 2008 crisis might be "something much more fundamental than a deep recession," and "the whole growth model . . . is simply unsustainable," his tone conveys a sense of urgency. In all these cases, the writers share the conviction that what they're writing about matters not just to them but to us all, and they work hard to make that conviction evident.

 ⌇⦿ *EXAMINE SOMETHING YOU'VE WRITTEN* that takes a strong position. *Catalog the specific ways you make clear to your readers that the topic matters to you—and should to them.*

Good Reasons and Evidence

See how Barbara Ehrenreich went about getting firsthand information in order to write about low-wage workers in Florida, p. 761.

Positions are only as good as the reasons and evidence that support them, so part of every author's task in arguing a position is to provide the strongest possible reasons for the position and evidence for those reasons. Evidence may take many forms, but among the most often used, especially in academic contexts, are facts; firsthand material gathered from observations, interviews, or surveys; data from experiments; examples; expert testimony (often in the form of what scholars have written); precedents; statistics; and personal experience. In online writing, evidence is often provided through carefully chosen links.

In a 2006 essay from the *New York Times* op-ed page, Jennifer Delahunty, dean of admissions at Kenyon College, seeks to explain to her own daughter why she was rejected by one of the colleges she had applied to. Delahunty's explanation—the position her essay takes—is that the rejection was due at least in part to the fact that young women, even accomplished ones, face particular challenges in getting into prestigious colleges:

> She had not . . . been named a National Merit Finalist, dug a well for a village in Africa or climbed to the top of Mount Rainier. She is a smart, well-meaning, hard-working teenage girl, but in this day and age of swollen applicant pools that are decidedly female, that wasn't enough. . . .
> Had she been a male applicant, there would have been little, if any,

hesitation to admit. The reality is that because young men are rarer, they're more valued applicants. Today, two-thirds of colleges and universities report that they get more female than male applicants, and more than 56 percent of undergraduates nationwide are women. Demographers predict that by 2009, only 42 percent of all baccalaureate degrees awarded in the United States will be given to men.

　　　　　　　　　—JENNIFER DELAHUNTY, "To All the Girls I've Rejected"

Delahunty offers two related reasons that her daughter had not been admitted. First, for all her daughter's accomplishments, they were not as impressive as those of other applicants. Here she provides specific evidence (her daughter was not a National Merit finalist, nor had she "dug a well for a village in Africa or climbed to the top of Mount Rainier") that makes the reason memorable and convincing.

The second reason focuses on the fact that male applicants in general have an easier time of it than female applicants to many schools. This time her evidence is of a different sort; she uses three sets of statistics to show that young men are rarer and therefore more valued applicants. Note that Delahunty expects readers to share her knowledge that something seen as valuable takes on additional value when it is rare.

The scientific community typically takes the long view in terms of gathering evidence in support of the positions it takes. Certainly that was true in the case of smoking, when decades of research paved the way for a statement on the relationship between smoking and cancer. The 1964 Surgeon General's report on the health consequences of smoking notes:

> The U.S. Public Health Service first became officially engaged in an appraisal of the available data on smoking and health in June, 1956, when, under the instigation of the Surgeon General, a scientific Study Group on the subject was established jointly by the National Cancer Institute, the National Heart Institute, the American Cancer Society, and the American Heart Association. After appraising sixteen independent studies carried on in five countries over a period of eighteen years, this group concluded that there is a causal relationship between excessive smoking of cigarettes and lung cancer.
>
> 　　　　　—*Smoking and Health: Report of the Advisory Committee*
> 　　　　　　　*of the Surgeon General of the Public Health Service*

In this case, the Surgeon General's study group analyzed evidence gathered over eighteen years before reaching its conclusion.

Attention to More than One Point of View

Considering multiple, often opposing, points of view is a hallmark of any strong position paper, particularly in an academic context. By showing that you understand and have carefully evaluated other viewpoints, you show respect for the issue and for your audience while showing that you have done your homework on your topic.

In a journal article on climate change caused by humans, Naomi Oreskes takes a position based on a careful analysis of 928 scientific articles published in well-known and respected journals. Some people, she says, "suggest that there might be substantive disagreement in the scientific community about the reality of anthropogenic climate change. This is not the case." Yet in spite of the very strong consensus Oreskes bases her claim on, she still acknowledges other possible viewpoints:

> Admittedly, [some] authors evaluating impacts, developing methods, or studying paleoclimatic change might believe that current climate change is natural. . . . The scientific consensus might, of course, be wrong. If the history of science teaches anything, it is humility, and no one can be faulted for failing to act on what is not known.
>
> —NAOMI ORESKES, "Beyond the Ivory Tower: The Scientific Consensus on Climate Change"

Thus does Oreskes acknowledge that the consensus she found in the articles she examined might be challenged by other articles she did not consider and that any consensus, no matter how strong, might ultimately prove to be wrong.

Sometimes you'll want to both acknowledge and reply to other viewpoints, especially if you can answer any objections persuasively. Here is Jennifer Delahunty, noting—and ruling out—the possibility that college admissions officers do not give careful consideration to all applicants.

> Rest assured that admissions officers are not cavalier in making their decisions. Last week, the 10 officers at my college sat around a table, 12 hours every day, deliberating the applications of hundreds of talented young men and women. While gulping down coffee and poring over statistics, we heard about a young woman from Kentucky we were not yet ready to admit outright. She was the leader/president/editor/captain/lead actress in every activity in her school. She had taken six advanced placement courses and had been selected for a prestigious state leadership program.

In her free time, this whirlwind of achievement had accumulated more than 300 hours of community service in four different organizations.

Few of us sitting around the table were as talented and as directed at age 17 as this young woman. Unfortunately, her test scores and grade point average placed her in the middle of our pool. We had to have a debate before we decided to swallow the middling scores and write "admit" next to her name.

—JENNIFER DELAHUNTY, "To All the Girls I've Rejected"

Delahunty provides evidence from a specific case, demonstrating persuasively that the admissions officers at her college take their job seriously.

Even bumper stickers can subtly acknowledge more than one position, as does this one from late 2008:

I Support Our Troops
I Question Our Policies

This bumper sticker states two positions that initially might seem contradictory, arguing that supporting the country's troops and questioning our government's foreign policies are not mutually exclusive.

An Authoritative Tone

Particularly in academic contexts, authors make a point of taking an authoritative tone. Even if your goal is to encourage readers to examine a number of alternatives without suggesting which one is best, you should try to do so in a way that shows you know which alternatives are worth examining and why. Likewise, even if you are taking a strong position, you should seek to appear reasonable and rational. The 1964 Surgeon General's report on the consequences of smoking does not vacillate: Smoking causes cancer. At the same time, in taking this position, it briefly outlines the history of the issue and the evidence on which the claim is logically based, avoiding emotional language and carefully specifying which forms of smoking ("excessive" cigarettes) and cancer (lung) the claim involves.

Jennifer Delahunty establishes her authority in other ways. Her description of ten admissions officers putting in twelve-hour days going through hundreds of applications and "poring over statistics" backs up her forthright assertion, "Rest assured that admissions officers are not cavalier in making their decisions." Later in the essay, acknowledging her own struggles to weigh issues of fairness to highly qualified young women against the need to maintain gender balance in incoming classes, Delahunty not only demonstrates that she knows what she is writing about but also invites readers to think about the complexity of the situation without offering them any easy answers. In short, she is simultaneously reasonable and authoritative, a challenge you'll frequently face in American academic culture.

An Appeal to Readers' Values

Implicitly or explicitly, authors need to appeal to readers' values, especially when taking a strong position. The creators of the "Yes, We Can" video clearly appealed to a number of cultural values that Americans hold dear, such as justice and equality (with references to the country's founding documents, slaves and abolitionists, workers and women who fought to organize and to vote, the civil rights movement) and opportunity, prosperity, and adventure (immigrants, pioneers, the space program). Similarly, we find appeals to values in the Obama speech's talk of hope and in the use of "from sea to shining sea" from "America the Beautiful," a song known to virtually all Americans. The refrain "yes, we can" is itself a highly charged appeal to the audience's sense of democratic ideals.

Similarly, the authors of the Surgeon General's report linking smoking and cancer made assumptions about the values of likely readers: They would want conclusions based on scientific evidence, itself the result of numerous experimental studies. In contrast, both Randall Hicks and Jennifer Delahunty assume that their readers will trust values based on lived experience. Hicks offers a searing childhood memory that suggests the benefits of listening to and heeding a father's words, while Delahunty embodies the self-assurance of a confident professional and a mother's love.

Online contexts are particularly interesting for considering appeals to values since you can rarely be sure who your actual readers are and you certainly can't control who will see a text you create. Yet appealing to values is no less important in online situations and may, in fact, take on a greater role in arguing positions effectively. In this case, writers often seek to create their ideal audience through the words and images they choose. (In the "Yes, We Can" video, every viewer—or at least every American viewer—becomes potentially a part of the "we.") Online environments remind us that as writers, we are always imagining who our audience is and appealing to what we imagine our audience's values to be.

ARGUING A POSITION / An Annotated Example

RUSSEL HONORÉ wrote this essay for *This I Believe*, a not-for-profit organization that sponsors "a public dialogue about belief, one essay at a time." The essay was later broadcast on *NPR's Weekend Edition* on March 1, 2009. Honoré is
a retired lieutenant general in the U.S. Army who has contributed to response
efforts to Hurricanes Katrina and Rita in 2005 and other natural disasters.

Work Is a Blessing
RUSSEL HONORÉ

I GREW UP IN Lakeland, Louisiana, one of 12 children. We all lived
on my parents' subsistence farm. We grew cotton, sugar cane,
corn, hogs, chickens and had a large garden, but it didn't bring in
much cash. So when I was 12, I got a part-time job on a dairy farm
down the road, helping to milk cows. We milked 65 cows at five in
the morning and again at two in the afternoon, seven days a week.

> *Background information.*

In the kitchen one Saturday before daylight, I remember complaining to my father and grandfather about having to go milk
those cows. My father said, "Ya know, boy, to work is a blessing."

> *A position taken in response to another position.*

I looked at those two men who'd worked harder than I ever
had—my father eking out a living on that farm and my grandfather
farming and working as a carpenter during the Depression. I had
a feeling I had been told something really important, but it took
many years before it sunk in.

> *Admitting his own slowness to understand what his father meant contributes to his authoritative tone.*

Going to college was a rare privilege for a kid from Lakeland,
Louisiana. My father told me if I picked something to study that
I liked doing, I'd always look forward to my work. But he also

added, "Even having a job you hate is better than not having a job at all." I wanted to be a farmer, but I joined the ROTC program to help pay for college. And what started out as an obligation to the Army became a way of life that I stayed committed to for 37 years, three months and three days.

Citing his father, Honoré shows his attention to more than one point of view about work.

In the late 1980s, during a visit to Bangladesh, I saw a woman with a baby on her back, breaking bricks with a hammer. I asked a Bangladesh military escort why they weren't using a machine, which would have been a lot easier. He told me a machine would put that lady out of work. Breaking those bricks meant she'd earn enough money to feed herself and her baby that day. And as bad as that woman's job was, it was enough to keep a small family alive. It reminded me of my father's words: To work is a blessing.

Reasons and evidence for how the author came to see work as a blessing.

Serving in the United States Army overseas, I saw a lot of people like that woman in Bangladesh. And I have come to believe that people without jobs are not free. They are victims of crime, the ideology of terrorism, poor health, depression and social unrest. These victims become the illegal immigrants, the slaves of human trafficking, the drug dealers, the street gang members. I've seen it over and over again on the U.S. border, in Somalia, the Congo, Afghanistan and in New Orleans. People who have jobs can have a home, send their kids to school, develop a sense of pride, contribute to the good of the community, and even help others. When we can work, we're free. We're blessed.

Specific examples indicate why the topic matters and show the author's awareness of his audience's values.

I don't think I'll ever quit working. I'm retired from the Army, but I'm still working to help people be prepared for disaster. And I may get to do a little farming someday, too. I'm not going to stop. I believe in my father's words. I believe in the blessing of work.

The author concludes by stating his position explicitly.

Listen to the audio essay at wwnorton.com/ write/everyonelinks. You'll hear someone who sounds like he grew up on a farm in Louisiana, a fact that contributes to Honoré's authority: this guy knows what he's talking about.

ANALYZE A SHORT PIECE OF WRITING on a website such as **Salon** *that takes a position on an issue you care about. Look at the list of characteristic features on p. 66 and annotate the text you have chosen to point out the ones that are represented in it, using Honoré's text as a model. Make a list of any features that are not included as well. (While not every effective position paper will include all of the features on p. 66, nearly all of them will.) Then consider whether including those features might have improved the text—and if so, how.*

ARGUING A POSITION / A Roadmap

Choose a topic that matters—to you, and to others

If you get to select your topic, begin by examining your own interests, values, and commitments in light of the context you are writing for. Global warming might be an appropriate topic for many courses in the life sciences or social sciences, but it's probably not going to serve you well in a course in medieval history unless you can find a direct link between the two topics. You might consider focusing on some issue that's being debated on campus (*Are those new rules for dropping classes fair?*), a broader political or ethical issue (*Is eating meat by definition unethical?*), or an issue in which you have a direct stake (*Does early admission penalize those who need financial aid?*).

Lynda Barry thinks arts education is really important. See how she makes us think the same in "The Sanctuary of School," p. 721.

If you've been assigned a topic, do your best to find an aspect of it that holds your interest. (If you're bored with your topic, you can be sure your readers will be.) If, for example, you're assigned to write about globalization in a required international studies course, you could tailor that topic to your own interests and write about the influence of American hip-hop on world music, or on whether community concern about a local factory outsourcing jobs to other countries is justified.

Be sure that your topic is one that is arguable—and that it matters. Short of astounding new evidence, it's no longer worth arguing that there is no link between smoking and lung cancer. It's a fact. But you can argue about what responsibility tobacco companies now have for tobacco-related deaths, as recent court cases demonstrate. One sure way to find out whether a topic is arguable is to see if it *is* being debated, and that is a good first step as you explore a topic. You can probably assume that any topic that's being widely discussed and debated matters—and for any topic, you'll want to know what's being said about it in order to write about it. Remember that your essay is part of an ongoing conversation about your topic: You need to become familiar with that conversation in order to contribute to it.

Consider your rhetorical situation

Looking at your audience, your purpose, and other aspects of your rhetorical situation will help you to think carefully about how to achieve your goals.

Focus on your AUDIENCE from start to finish. Begin by thinking about who the people are that you most want to reach, keeping in mind that there's always danger in speaking only to those who already agree with you. Remember, too, that especially on the web, you may not get to decide who your audience will be. If you keep audiences with differing viewpoints and levels of background knowledge in mind as you write, you will be much more likely to be able to represent all views fairly and hence to get others to consider your position seriously. In thinking about your audience, ask yourself questions like these:

- Who are you trying to reach, and why? What do you hope to persuade them to think or do?

- What convictions might they hold about the topic you are addressing?

- What do they likely know about your topic, and what background information will you need to provide?

- How sympathetic are they likely to be to the position you will take?

- How are they like or unlike you—or one another? Consider such factors as age; education; gender and sexual orientation; abilities and disabilities; regional, ethnic, cultural, and linguistic heritage; and so on. How will such factors influence the way you make your argument?

- Do you know anything about what they value, about what goals and aspirations they have? Will your topic matter to them, or will you need to persuade them that it matters?

Consider especially how any of your audience's goals or commitments relate to the argument you are constructing. If you're trying to convince your fellow business majors of the virtues of free-market capitalism, your task is quite different from if you're trying to convince members of the campus socialist organization. Both groups may be like you in terms of age or education, for example, but their value commitments differ from yours. In the first case, you would almost surely be preaching to the choir, whereas in the second, you would likely face a skeptical audience, at least initially.

Keeping audience in mind, then, means thinking in terms of who will be responding to your position, how they will be likely to respond, and why. In other words, let your understanding of your audience, especially those who might not immediately agree with your position, guide you as you construct your argument.

Think hard about your PURPOSE. Why are you arguing this position? What has motivated you to write on this topic? What do you hope to learn by writing about it? What do you want to convince your audience to think or do? How can you best achieve your purpose or purposes?

Think about your STANCE. Start by asking yourself where you are coming from in regard to this topic. What about the topic captured your interest, and how has that interest led you to the position you expect to take on it? Why do you think the topic matters? How would you describe your stance toward the topic: Are you an advocate, a critic, a mediator, an observer, an apologist, or something else? How do you want to be seen as an author—as forceful? thoughtful? curious? How can you establish your own authority in writing on this topic?

Consider the larger CONTEXT. What are the various perspectives on the issue, and what else has been said about it? If you intend to take a position on moving away from the use of ethanol as an alternative fuel source, for instance, you would need to look at what circumstances led to the use of ethanol, at who has supported and who opposed it (and why), and at the political and economic ramifications of continuing to produce ethanol for fuel rather than food as well as of abandoning this practice. As you come to understand the larger context, you'll become aware of various positions you'll want to consider, and you will be able to articulate and support whatever position you take clearly and forcefully. Understanding the context will also help you to see what reasons and evidence will appeal most to your audience and thus help you achieve your overall purpose.

Consider your MEDIUM. Will your writing take the form of a print essay? Will it appear as an editorial in a local paper? on a website? as an audio essay to be broadcast on a local radio station or posted as a podcast? as an oral or multimedia presentation for a class you are taking? The medium you choose should relate directly to your purpose and audience—and will affect the way you design your text.

Consider matters of DESIGN. Think about the "look" you want to achieve and how you can format your text to make it easy to follow. Do you need headings? illustrations? any other graphics? color? Does the discipline you're writing in have any conventions you should follow? A writer in psychology is much more likely to use headings and to include charts, tables, and other graphics than is one in literature.

Research your topic

Begin exploring the topic by looking at it from different points of view. Whatever position you take will ultimately be more credible and persuasive if you can show evidence of having considered other positions.

Begin by assessing what you know—and don't know—about the topic. What interests you about the topic, and why? What first got you interested in it? What more do you want or need to find out about it? What questions do you have about it? Why does it matter to you? To answer these questions, you might try **BRAINSTORMING** or other activities for **GENERATING IDEAS**.

What have others said? What are some of the issues that are being debated now about your topic, and what are the various positions on these issues? What other positions might be taken with respect to the topic?

Where you start your research—and what sources you consult—depends upon your topic. If you are focusing on a current issue, turn to news media and their coverage of the issue; to reputable online databases; to scholarly journals and books you can search by keywords; and to websites, listservs, or other online groups devoted to the issue. If you are investigating a topic that has been of interest for a decade or longer, many of the most useful sources will not be available online, so you will need to consult the library. For some issues you might want to interview experts.

Remember, too, that you may well need to look beyond national borders. If, for example, you're examining debates about NAFTA, the North American Free Trade Agreement, you'll find it especially useful to investigate what writers in Canada and Mexico, the United States' partners in this accord, have to say about the issue.

Do you need to cut your topic down to size? Few among us know enough to make strong general claims about global warming. While that fact does not and should not keep us from having opinions about the issue, it means that the existence of global warming is likely much too broad a topic to be appropriate for a five-page essay. Instead, you'll need to focus on some aspect of that topic for your essay. What angle you take will depend on the course you're writing for. For a geology class, you might focus on the effects of rising temperatures on melting glaciers; for an international relations course, you could look at climate shift and national security debates. Just remember that your goal is to take an informed position, one that you can support well.

Formulate an explicit position

Once you have sufficient information about your topic and some under-standing of the complexity of the issue, you'll need to formulate a position, one that you can state explicitly. Let's say you decide to take a position on a current controversy among scientists about climate change. Here's how one author formulated a position:

> Many scientists have argued that climate change has led to bigger and more destructive hurricanes and typhoons. Other researchers, how-ever, have countered by saying that climate change is not linked causally to an increase in hurricane strength. After reviewing both sides of this debate, I see two strong reasons why changes in our climate have not necessarily led to more severe hurricanes.
> —SOFI MINCEY, "On Climate Change and Hurricanes"

These three sentences articulate a clear position—that climate change is not necessarily to blame for bigger hurricanes—and frame that position as a response to a position the author disagrees with. Notice, however, that the writer does not claim definitively that climate change has not led to bigger hurricanes; rather, she promises to present reasons that argue for this view. In other words, she's taken a clear position while acknowledg-ing other positions on the issue. In short, she has qualified her claim.

By arguing that the claims of many scientists *may* be wrong, rather than saying they are necessarily wrong, the author greatly increases the likelihood that she can succeed in her argument, setting a much lower bar for what she must achieve than if she had not qualified her claim. Note that the writer still has an arguable position that requires support. The task she has set for herself is to present reasonable evidence to challenge the claim that climate change has necessarily meant bigger hurricanes.

State your position as a THESIS. Once you formulate your position, try stat-ing it several different ways and then decide which one is most compelling. Make sure the position is stated explicitly—no beating around the bush. Your statement should let your audience know where you stand and be in-teresting enough to attract their attention.

Then think about whether you should qualify your position. Should you limit what you claim—is it true only sometimes or under certain cir-cumstances? On the other hand, does it seem too weak or timid and need to be stated more forcefully?

Once you have come up with a statement of your position that satisfies you, use it as a tentative thesis to guide your drafting.

Come up with reasons and evidence. List all the REASONS supporting your thesis that you discovered in your research. Which ones will be most persuasive to your audience? Then jot down all the EVIDENCE you have to support those reasons—facts, quotations, statistics, examples, testimony, visuals, and so on. Remember that what counts as evidence varies across audiences and disciplines. Some are persuaded by testimonials, while others want statistical data. Finally, look for any weak reasons or evidence, and decide whether you need to do further research.

Identify other positions. Carefully consider other points of view on the topic and how you will account for them. At the very least, you need to acknowledge other positions that are prominent in the larger conversation about the topic and to treat them fairly. If you disagree with a position, you need to offer reasons why and to do so respectfully.

Organize and start writing

Once you have a fair sense of how you will present your position, it's time to write out a draft. If you have trouble getting started, it might help to think about the larger conversation about the topic that's already going on—and to think of your draft as a moment when you get to say what *you* think.

State your position as a THESIS. As you begin to organize, type it at the top of your page so that you can keep looking back to it to be sure that each part of your text supports the thesis.

Give REASONS for your position, with supporting EVIDENCE. Determine an order for presenting your reasons, perhaps starting with the one you think will speak most directly to your audience.

Don't forget to consider COUNTERARGUMENTS. Acknowledge positions other than your own, and respond to what they say.

Draft an OPENING. Introduce your topic, and provide any background information your audience may need. State your position clearly, perhaps as a response to what others have said about your topic. Say something about why the issue matters, why your audience should care.

Draft a **CONCLUSION**. You might want to end by summing up your position, and by answering the "so what" question: Why does your topic matter? Make sure you give a strong takeaway message. What are the implications of your argument? What do you want readers to remember or do as a result of reading what you've written?

Look critically at your draft, get response—and revise

Before you begin to revise your draft, go through it carefully, looking critically at the position you stake out, the reasons and evidence you provide in support of it, and the way you present them to your audience. For this review, play the "doubting game" with yourself by asking "Who says?" and "So what?" and "Can't you do better than that?" at every point. Being tough on yourself now will pay off by telling you where you need to find more evidence, where you need to qualify claims, and where else you need to shore up your arguments. Make notes on what you plan to do in your revision.

Next ask some classmates or friends to read and respond to your draft. Here are some questions that can help you or others read over a draft of writing that takes a position.

- *Is the position stated explicitly?* Is there a clear **THESIS** sentence—and if not, is one needed? Is it overstated, needing to be qualified, or does it need to be stated even more strongly?

- *What position are you responding to?* What is the larger conversation?

- *Is it clear why the topic matters?* Why do you care about the topic, and who else should care?

- *How effective is the **OPENING**?* How does the introduction capture your audience's interest? How else might you begin?

- *Is there sufficient background information?* What other information might the audience need?

- *How would you describe the **STANCE** and **TONE**—*and are they appropriate to your audience and purpose? Does the tone seem both authoritative and reasonable?

- *What good* REASONS *do you give for the position, and what* EVIDENCE *do you provide for those reasons?* What are the strongest reasons and evidence given? the weakest? What other reasons or evidence would support this position?

- *How trustworthy are the sources you've cited?* Are quotations, summaries, and paraphrases smoothly integrated in the text—and is it clear where you are speaking and where (and why) you are citing others?

- *What other positions do you consider, and do you treat them fairly?* Are there other COUNTERARGUMENTS you should address as well? How well do you answer possible objections to your position?

- *How is the draft organized?* Is it easy to follow, with clear and explicit TRANSITIONS from one point to the next? Are there headings—and if not, would they help? What about the organization could be improved?

- *Is the style—choice of words, kinds of sentences—appropriate to the audience and purpose?* Could the style be improved in any way?

- *How effective is your text design?* Have you used any visuals to support your position—and if so, have you written captions that explain how they contribute to the argument? If not, what visuals might be appropriate? Is there any information that would be easier to follow if it were presented in a chart or table?

- *How does the draft* CONCLUDE *?* Is the conclusion forceful and memorable? How else might you conclude?

- *Consider the title.* Does it make clear what the text is about, and does it arouse interest in reading it?

- *What is your overall impression of the draft*—does it persuade the audience to accept the position or not? Why? Even if you or others do not accept the position, do you consider it a plausible one?

Revise your draft in light of your own observations and any feedback from others—keeping your audience and purpose firmly in mind, as always.

REFLECT ON WHAT YOU'VE LEARNED. Once you've completed your essay, let it settle for a while and then take time to reflect. How well did you argue your point? What additional revisions would you make if you could? Research shows that such reflections help "lock in" what you learn for future use.

Our Schools Must Do Better

BOB HERBERT

I ASKED A HIGH SCHOOL KID walking along Commonwealth Avenue if he knew who the vice president of the United States was.

He thought for a moment and then said, "No."

I told him to take a guess.

He thought for another moment, looked at me skeptically, and finally gave up. "I'm sorry," he said. "I don't know."

The latest federal test results showed some improvement in public school 5 math and reading scores, but there is no reason to celebrate these minuscule gains. We need so much more. A four-year college degree is now all but mandatory for building and sustaining a middle-class standard of living in the U.S.

Over the next 20 or 30 years, when today's children are raising children of their own in an ever more technologically advanced and globalized society, the educational requirements will only grow more rigorous and unforgiving.

A one- or two-point gain in fourth grade test scores here or there is not meaningful in the face of that overarching 21st-century challenge.

What's needed is a wholesale transformation of the public school system from the broken-down postwar model of the past 50 or 60 years. The U.S. has not yet faced up to the fact that it needs a school system capable of fulfilling

---

BOB HERBERT was an op-ed columnist for the *New York Times* from 1993 to 2011, often focusing on issues of race and poverty in the United States. This column appeared in October 2007.

the educational needs of children growing up in an era that will be at least as different from the 20th century as the 20th was from the 19th.

"We're not good at thinking about magnitudes," said Thomas Kane, a professor of education and economics at the Harvard Graduate School of Education. "We've got a bunch of little things that we think are moving in the right direction, but we haven't stepped back and thought, 'O.K., how big an improvement are we really talking about?'" Professor Kane and I were discussing what he believes are the two areas that have the greatest potential for radically improving the way children are taught in the U.S. Both are being neglected by the education establishment.

The first is teacher quality, a topic that gets talked about incessantly. It has   10 been known for decades that some teachers have huge positive effects on student achievement, and that others do poorly. The positive effect of the highest performing teachers on underachieving students is startling.

What is counterintuitive, but well documented, is that paper qualifications, such as teacher certification, have very little to do with whatever it is that makes good teachers effective.

"Regrettably," said Professor Kane, who has studied this issue extensively, "we've never taken that research fact seriously in our teacher policy. We've done just the opposite."

Concerned about raising the quality of teachers, states and local school districts have consistently focused on the credentials, rather than the demonstrated effectiveness—or ineffectiveness—of teachers in the classroom.

New forms of identifying good teachers and weeding out poor ones—by carefully assessing their on-the-job performance—have to be established before any transformation of American schools can occur.

This can be done without turning the traditional system of teacher tenure on its   15 head. Studies have clearly shown that the good teachers and the not-so-good ones can usually be identified, if they are carefully observed in their first two or three years on the job—in other words, before tenure is granted.

Developing such a system would be difficult. But it's both doable and essential. Getting serious about teacher quality as opposed to harping on tiny variations in test scores would be like moving from a jalopy to a jet.

The second area to be mined for potentially transformative effects is the wide and varied field of alternative school models. We should be rigorously studying those schools that appear to be having the biggest positive effects on student achievement. Are the effects real? If so, what accounts for them?

The Knowledge Is Power Program (KIPP), to cite one example, is a charter school network that has consistently gotten extraordinary academic results from low-income students. It has worked in cities big and small, and in rural areas. Like other successful models, it has adopted a longer school day and places great demands on its teachers and students.

Said Professor Kane: "These alternative models that involve the longer school day and a much more dramatic intervention for kids are promising. If that's what it takes, then we need to know that, and sooner rather than later."

If American kids—all American kids, not just the children of the elite—are   20 to have a fair chance at a rewarding life over the next several decades, we've got to give them a school system adequate to the times. They need something better than a post–World War II system in a post-9/11 world.

Thinking about the Text

1. Write a one-paragraph **SUMMARY** of the position Bob Herbert argues here, including the reasons and evidence he offers in support of his position.

2. How would you describe Herbert's **TONE**? What passages best help to establish that tone?

3. How does Herbert establish the importance of his topic?

4. Point to at least two passages in which Herbert is appealing directly to his readers' values.

5. Op-ed essays like this one are often published online, where they invite reader response. Respond to Herbert in a paragraph or two. You might respond generally to what he says, agreeing or disagreeing (or both!)—or you could bring up a couple other points to add to what he says.

On Buying Local

KATHERINE SPRIGGS

AMERICANS TODAY can eat pears in the spring in Minnesota, oranges in the summer in Montana, asparagus in the fall in Maine, and cranberries in the winter in Florida. In fact, we can eat pretty much any kind of produce anywhere at any time of the year. But what is the cost of this convenience? In this essay, I will explore some answers to this question and argue that we should give up a little bit of convenience in favor of buying local.

"Buying local" means that consumers choose to buy food that has been grown, raised, or produced as close to their homes as possible ("Buy Local"). Buying local is an important part of the response to many environmental issues we face today (fig. 1). It encourages the development of small farms, which are often more environmentally sustainable than large farms, and thus strengthens local markets and supports small rural economies. By demonstrating a commitment to buying local, Americans could set an example for global environmentalism.

In 2010, the international community is facing many environmental challenges, including global warming, pollution, and dwindling fossil fuel resources. Global warming is attributed to the release of greenhouse gases such as carbon dioxide and methane, most commonly emitted in the burning of fossil fuels. It is such a pressing problem that scientists estimate that in the year 2030, there

KATHERINE SPRIGGS, a student at Stanford University, wrote this essay for a first-year writing course.

Fig. 1. Shopping at a farmers' market is one good way to support small farms and strengthen the local economy. Photograph from Alamy.

will be no glaciers left in Glacier National Park ("Global Warming Statistics"). The United States is especially guilty of contributing to the problem, producing about a quarter of all global greenhouse gas emissions, and playing a large part in pollution and shrinking world oil supplies as well ("Record Increase"). According to a CNN article published in 2000, the United States manufactures more than 1.5 billion pounds of chemical pesticides a year that can pollute our water, soil, and air (Baum). Agriculture is particularly interconnected with all of these issues. Almost three-fourths of the pesticides produced in the United States are used in agriculture (Baum). Most produce is shipped many miles before it is sold to consumers, and shipping our food long distances is costly in both the amount of fossil fuel it uses and the greenhouse gases it produces.

A family friend and farmer taught me firsthand about the effects of buying local. Since I was four years old, I have spent every summer on a 150-acre farm in rural Wisconsin, where my family has rented our 75 tillable acres to a farmer who lives nearby. Mr. Lermio comes from a family that has farmed the area for generations. I remember him sitting on our porch at dusk wearing his blue striped overalls and dirty white t-shirt, telling my parents about all of the changes in the area since he was a kid. "Things sure are different around here," he'd say. He told us that all the farms in that region used to milk about 30 head of cattle each. Now he and the other farmers were selling their herds to industrial-scale farms milking 4,000 head each. The shift came when milk started being processed on a large scale rather than at small local cheese factories. Milk is now shipped to just a few large factories where it is either bottled or processed into cheese or other dairy products. The milk and products from these factories are then shipped all across the country. "You see," Mr. Lermio would tell us, "it's just not worth shipping the milk from my 20 cows all the way to Gays Mills. You just can't have a small herd anymore." Farming crops is also different now. Machinery is expensive and hard to pay off with profits from small fields. The Lermio family has been buying and renting fields all around the area, using their tractors to farm hundreds of acres. Because they can no longer sell locally, Mr. Lermio and many other rural farmers have to move towards larger-scale farming to stay afloat.

Buying local could help reverse the trend towards industrial-scale farm- 5
ing, of which the changes in Wisconsin over Mr. Lermio's lifetime are just one

Fig. 2. A small polyculture farm. Photograph from iStockphoto.

example. Buying local benefits small farmers by not forcing them to compete with larger farms across the country. For example, if consumers bought beef locally, beef cattle would be raised in every region and their meat would be sold locally rather than shipped from a small number of big ranches in Texas and Montana. Small farms are often polycultures—they produce many different kinds of products (fig. 2). The Lermios' original farm, for example, grew corn, hay, oats, and alfalfa. They also had milking cattle, chickens, and a few hogs. Large farms are often monocultures—they raise only one kind of crop or animal (fig. 3). The Lermio family has been moving towards becoming a monoculture; they raise only three field crops and they don't have any animals. Buying local, as was common in the first half of the twentieth century, encourages small polyculture farms that sell a variety of products locally (McCauley).

For environmental purposes, the small polyculture farms that buying local encourages have many advantages over industrial-scale monoculture farms because they are more sustainable. The focus of sustainable farming is on minimizing waste, use of chemicals, soil erosion, and pollution ("Sustainable"). Small farmers tend to value local natural resources more than industrial-scale farmers do and are therefore more conscientious in their farming methods. Small

Fig. 3. A large monoculture farm. Photograph from iStockphoto.

farms are also intrinsically more sustainable. As mentioned, small farms are more likely to be polycultures—to do many different things with the land—and using a field for different purposes does not exhaust the soil the way continually farming one crop does. Rotating crops or using a field alternately for pasture and for crops keeps the land "healthy." On small farms, sometimes a farmer will pasture his cattle in the previous year's cornfield; the cattle eat some of the stubble left from last year's crop and fertilize the field. The land isn't wasted or exhausted from continuous production. I've even seen one organic farmer set up his pigpen so that the pigs plow his blueberry field just by walking up around their pen. This kind of dual usage wouldn't be found on a large monoculture farm. Most big farms use their fields exclusively either for crops or for pasture. Modern fertilizers, herbicides, and pesticides allow farmers to harvest crops from even unhealthy land, but this is a highly unsustainable model. Farming chemicals can pollute groundwater and destroy natural ecosystems.

Not only are small farms a more sustainable, eco-friendly model than big commercial farms, but buying local has other advantages as well. Buying local, for example, would reduce the high cost of fuel and energy used to transport food across the world and would bring long-term benefits as well. It is currently estimated that most produce in the United States is shipped about 1,500 miles before it is sold—it travels about the distance from Nebraska to New York ("Why Buy Local?"). Eighty percent of all strawberries grown in the United States are from California ("Strawberry Fruit Facts Page"). They are shipped from California all around the country even though strawberries can be grown in Wisconsin, New York, Tennessee, and most other parts of the United States. No matter how efficient our shipping systems, shipping food thousands of miles is expensive—in dollars, in oil, and in the carbon dioxide it produces (fig. 4). One of the main reasons that produce is shipped long distances is that fruits and vegetables don't grow everywhere all year around. Even though strawberries grow a lot of places during the early summer, they grow only in Florida in the winter, or in California from spring to fall (Rieger). Americans have become accustomed to being able to buy almost any kind of produce at any time of the year. A true commitment to buying local would accommodate local season and climate. Not everything will grow everywhere, but the goal of buying local should be to eliminate all unnecessary shipping by buying things from as close to home as possible and eating as many things in season as possible.

Some argue that buying local can actually have negative environmental effects; and their arguments add important qualifiers to supporting small local

Fig 4. Interstate trucking is expensive financially and ecologically. Photograph from iStockphoto.

farms. Alex Avery, the director of research and education at the Center for Global Food Issues, has said that we should "buy food from the world region where it grows best" (qtd. in MacDonald). His implication is that it would be more wasteful to try to grow pineapples in the Northeast than to have them shipped from the Caribbean. He makes a good point: trying to grow all kinds of food all over the world would be a waste of time and energy. Buying local should instead focus on buying *as much as possible* from nearby farmers. It has also been argued that buying locally will be detrimental to the environment because small farms are not as efficient in their use of resources as large farms. This is a common misconception and actually depends on how economists measure efficiency. Small farms are less efficient than large farms in the total output of one crop per acre, but they are more efficient in total output of all crops per acre (McCauley). When buying locally, the consumer should try to buy from these more efficient polyculture farms. Skeptics of buying local also say that focusing food cultivation in the United States will be worse for the environment because farmers here use more industrial equipment than farmers in the third world (MacDonald). According to the Progressive Policy Institute, however, only 13 percent of the American diet is imported ("98.7 Percent"). This is a surprisingly small percentage, especially considering that seafood is one of the top imports. It should also be considered that as countries around the world become wealthier they will industrialize, so exploiting manual labor in the third world would only be a temporary solution (MacDonald). The environmental benefits now, and in the long run, of buying local outweigh any such immediate disadvantages.

Critics have also pointed to negative global effects of buying local, but buying local could have positive global effects too. In the *Christian Science Monitor*, John Clark, author of *Worlds Apart: Civil Society and the Battle for Ethical Globalization*, argues that buying local hurts poor workers in third world countries. He cites the fact that an estimated fifty thousand children in Bangladesh lost their jobs in the garment industry because of the 1996 Western boycott of clothing made in third world sweatshops (qtd. in MacDonald). It cannot be denied that if everyone buys locally, repercussions on the global market seem unavoidable. Nonetheless, if the people of the United States demonstrated their commitment to buying local, it could open up new conversations about environmentalism. Our government lags far behind the European Union in environmental legislation. Through selective shopping, the people of the United States could demonstrate to the world our commitment to environmentalism.

Arguments that decentralizing food production will be bad for the national 10 economy also ignore the positive effects small farms have on local economies. John Tschirhart, a professor of environmental economics at the University of Wyoming, argues that buying locally would be bad for our national economy because food that we buy locally can often be produced cheaper somewhere else in the United States (qtd. in Arias Terry). This seems debatable since most of the locally grown things we buy in grocery stores today aren't much more expensive, if at all, than their counterparts from far away. In New York City, apples from upstate New York are often cheaper than the industrial, waxed Granny Smiths from Washington State or Chile; buying locally should indeed save shipping costs. Nonetheless, it is true that locally grown food can often be slightly more expensive than "industrially grown" food. Probably one of the biggest factors in the difference in price is labor cost. Labor is cheap in third world countries, and large U.S. farms are notorious for hiring immigrant laborers. It is hard to justify the exploitation of such artificially cheap labor. While the case for the economic disadvantages of buying local is dubious, buying local has clear positive economic effects in local communities. Local farms hire local workers and bring profits to small rural communities. One study of pig farmers in Virginia showed that, compared to corporate-owned farms, small farms created 10 percent more permanent local jobs, a 20 percent higher increase in local retail sales, and a 37 percent higher increase in local per capita income (McCauley).

Buying locally grown and produced food has clear environmental, social, and economic advantages. On the surface it seems that buying local could constitute a big personal sacrifice. It may be slightly more expensive, and it wouldn't allow us to buy any kind of produce at any time of the year, a change that would no doubt take getting used to. But perhaps these limitations would actually make food more enjoyable. If strawberries were sold only in the summer, they would be more special and we might even enjoy them more. Food that is naturally grown in season is fresher and also tends to taste better. Fresh summer strawberries are sweeter than their woody winter counterparts. Buying local is an easy step that everyone can take towards "greener" living.

Works Cited

Arias Terry, Ana. "Buying Local vs. Buying Cheap." *Conscious Choice: The Journal of Ecology and Natural Living.* Conscious Communications, Jan. 2007. Web. 27 Apr. 2011.

Baum, Michele Dula. "U.S. Government Issues Standards on Organic Food." *CNN.com.* Turner Broadcasting System, 20 Dec. 2000. Web. 25 Apr. 2011.

"Buy Local." *Sustainable Table.* Grace Communications Foundation, Jan. 2007. Web. 27 Apr. 2011.

"Global Warming Statistics." *Effects of Global Warming.* Effects of Global Warming, 2007. Web. 25 Apr. 2011.

MacDonald, G. Jeffrey. "Is Buying Local Always Best?" *Christian Science Monitor.* 24 July 2006: 13+. Print.

McCauley, Marika Alena. "Small Farms: The Optimum Sustainable Agriculture Model." *Oxfam America.* Oxfam America, 2007. Web. 27 Apr. 2011.

"98.7 Percent of Imported Food Never Inspected." *Progressive Policy Institute.* Progressive Policy Institute, 7 Sept. 2007. Web. 25 Apr. 2011.

"Record Increase in U.S. Greenhouse Gas Emissions Reported." *Environment News Service.* Environment News Service, 18 Apr. 2006. Web. 25 Apr. 2011.

Rieger, Mark. "Strawberry—*Fragaria X ananassa.*" *Mark's Fruit Crops.* U of Georgia, 2006. Web. 25 Apr. 2011.

"Strawberry Fruit Facts Page." *Grown in California*. Gourmet Shopping
    Network, LLC. Web. 25 Apr. 2011.
"Sustainable." *Paperback Oxford English Dictionary*. 6th ed. 2001. Print.
"Why Buy Local?" *LocalHarvest*. LocalHarvest, 2007. Web. 23 Apr. 2011.

Thinking about the Text

1. It's clear that this is a topic that matters to Katherine Spriggs. Has she convinced you that it matters—and if so, how? How does Spriggs establish the importance of her topic?

2. What **COUNTERARGUMENTS** or positions other than her own does Spriggs consider—and how does she respond in each case?

3. Choose a section of Spriggs' essay that you find especially effective or ineffective. Referring to the genre features discussed on p. 66, describe what makes this part of her argument persuasive—or not.

4. Spriggs includes several photos in her essay. How do they contribute to her argument?

5. Consider your own response to Spriggs' position. Write an essay in response to one of the issues she raises. State your position explicitly, and be sure to consider arguments other than your own.

EIGHT

"Here's What Happened"
Writing a Narrative

 O, TELL ME WHAT HAPPENED." Anytime we ask someone about an event at school or an incident at work, we are asking for a narrative: Tell us about what happened. Narratives are stories, and they are fundamental parts of our everyday lives. When we tell someone about a movie we saw or a basketball game we played in, we often do so using narrative. When we want someone to understand something that we did, we might tell a story that explains our actions. When we update our status on *Facebook*, we often write about something we've just done.

If you wrote an essay as part of your college applications, chances are that you were required to write a narrative. Here, for instance, are instructions from two colleges' applications:

> Describe a meaningful event or experience and how it has changed or affected the person you are. —HOFSTRA UNIVERSITY

> Describe a personal moral or ethical dilemma and how it impacted your life. —HAMPTON UNIVERSITY

Each of these prompts asks applicants to write a narrative about some aspect of their life. In addition, in each case the narrative needs to do more than just tell a good story; it needs to make a clear point.

Narrative is a powerful way to gain authority as a writer. Telling a good story helps us get an audience's attention and can even allow us a way to offer our own views. Take a look, for example, at the opening paragraphs from an obituary for Michael Jackson from the *Los Angeles Times:*

> Michael Jackson was fascinated by celebrity tragedy. He had a statue of Marilyn Monroe in his home and studied the sad Hollywood exile of Charlie Chaplin. He married the daughter of Elvis Presley.
>
> Jackson met his own untimely death Thursday [June 25, 2009] at age 50, and more than any of those past icons, he left a complicated legacy. As a child star, he was so talented he seemed lit from within; as a middle-aged man, he was viewed as something akin to a visiting alien who, like Tinkerbell, would cease to exist if the applause ever stopped.
>
> —GEOFF BOUCHER AND ELAINE WOO, "Michael Jackson's Life
> Was Infused with Fantasy and Tragedy"

The authors could have opened by saying simply that Michael Jackson had died, but they do more than that, providing details that grab our attention—and that promise a well-told narrative rather than just facts and figures about Jackson's life. The outlines of the story that they offer in these few lines make us want to keep reading.

Images, too, can tell stories, as the cover of *Rolling Stone* shows on the next page. The headline announces that it's a "special commemorative issue" celebrating the life of Michael Jackson, while the photograph shows someone with so much talent that "he seemed lit from within," leading readers to expect that what's inside will be more than just an obituary. All told, this cover captures our attention in a way that makes us want to read the stories inside and thus to buy the magazine. More specifically, this image itself—Jackson in mid–dance step with his signature ankle-high pants and glittering socks—tells a story about Jackson the entertainer.

Think about some of the powerful autobiographies that you've read, perhaps the *Narrative of the Life of Frederick Douglass* or Harriet Jacobs' *Incidents in the Life of a Slave Girl*. These are two of the most important narratives in American history, recounting the bondage of two former slaves and how they escaped from slavery. Barack Obama's *Dreams from My Father,* Andre Agassi's *Open,* and Sarah Palin's *Going Rogue* are other personal narratives that have captured the attention of many readers. We might read such books because we want to learn about the life and times of particular people. We could, of course, find that information on *Wikipedia,* but a good

Rolling Stone's tribute to Michael Jackson.

narrative provides more than just the facts; it gives us a well-told story that captures not only our attention but also our imagination.

So what exactly is a narrative? For our purposes, narrative is a kind of writing that presents events in some kind of time sequence with a distinct beginning, middle, and ending (but not necessarily in strict chronological order) and that is written for the purpose of making a point. That is, to write a narrative it is not enough to simply report a sequence of events ("this happened, then that happened"), which is often what children do when they tell stories. Narrative essays, especially in college, are meaningful ways of making sense of our experiences, of what's around us—and of illustrating a point, making an argument, or reporting information. And as the Michael Jackson example illustrates, we can use narratives to explore multiple topics that may have little or nothing to do with our personal lives.

THINK ABOUT some everyday narratives. Consider stories that are told in your favorite songs or music videos, or ones that you hear in sermons, or the ones that you and your friends share with each other over dinner or on Facebook. Make a list of the stories that you hear, read, see, or tell in one day and the subjects of those stories. By doing so, you'll begin to see the way that narratives are one important way that we communicate with each other.

Across Academic Fields

Visit the Digital Archive of Literacy Narratives, a site at Ohio State where you can read literacy narratives as well as post ones that you write. Go to wwnorton.com/write/everyonelinks.

The narrative essay is a common assignment in the humanities and increasingly in other academic fields as well. In a *composition* class, you may be asked to write a **LITERACY NARRATIVE** about how you learned to read or write or a personal narrative about an important person in your life. In a *history* class, you may be asked to take data from archives and transcripts from oral interviews and construct a narrative about a particular historical moment or event. (Many people think that historians focus on dates and facts about incidents in the past, but in fact, they are always constructing narratives, which provide a context for understanding what those dates and facts mean.) In *medicine,* narratives—in the form of medical histories and patients' accounts of symptoms—play an important role in diagnosis and treatment and provide important documentation for patients, medical professionals, insurance companies, and lawyers. In the *biological and physical sciences,* lab reports are narratives that tell the story of how researchers conducted an experiment and how they interpreted the data they collected. Since narratives take different forms across disciplines, one challenge you'll face will be to determine which narrative elements are valued or even required in a particular situation. Not all occasions or assignments call for a narrative, and you'll need to learn when one is appropriate.

Across Media

The medium you use makes a huge difference in what you can accomplish with narration. *Electronically,* for example, videos present a wide range of narrative possibilities. In early 2011, great political changes took place across the Arab world, and people used videos to share stories with one another about what was going on in various cities and countries. Videos of events in Tunisia, where an opponent of the government set himself on fire in protest, and Egypt, where demonstrators in Cairo demanded that President Hosni Mubarak resign, were posted to *YouTube* and *Facebook* and other sites, creating an information network for the protesters themselves and letting people around the globe see that the Middle East was changing drastically. The image below, originally posted on *Flickr,* shows a protest in Morocco.

These same stories about the Arab Spring were told differently in *print.* They were on the front page of most newspapers, with large headlines and photos showing crowds of demonstrators. The stories themselves were told

Young people turn out en masse to lobby for a role in Morocco's future, May 15, 2011.

with written words, and often with maps to show readers where the unrest was taking place. Radio coverage provided still other kinds of narratives that focused on *spoken* language along with background noise of chanting by demonstrators and sometimes even gunfire and explosions.

When you write narratives yourself, you'll often need to think carefully about what medium or media will help you tell your story in the way that's best suited to your audience and your purpose. You won't always have a choice, especially in academic writing, but whenever you do, remember to consider the full range of possibilities.

Across Cultures and Communities

What makes a good story often depends on who's telling the story and who's listening. Not only is that the case for individuals, but different communities and cultures also tell stories in unique ways and value particular things in them. In some communities, only the elders can tell a story. Or only the males. Or only the official storytellers. When someone who is not authorized to tell a story tries to do so, he or she runs the risk of offending. A good story also depends on what a community values. Some communities value stories that feature fictional characters and have a moral at the end. Others may value stories about real members of the community, though the stories themselves have no apparent moral. In some cultures, stories are the ways that history is passed down from generation to generation. Think about the ways that family histories are passed down in your family or community— through written stories? oral stories? photo albums? home movies?

Some cultures, in fact, consider narratives so important that the storyteller holds a place of honor. In much of *West Africa*, the griots are the official storytellers, entrusted with telling the history of a village or town through stories, which they share through recitation and song. In many *Appalachian communities*, storytelling functions both as entertainment and as a way to pass down family and community history. Storytelling is an event around which family members bond and from which they learn about ancestors, traditional folkways, and cultural values. As in West Africa, storytelling in Appalachia is an exalted art form, and the good storyteller enjoys high status in the community. So, too, in many *Native American tribes* is storytelling a highly valued tradition.

Many other communities have their own narrative conventions. The It Gets Better Project, featured in the example opposite, invites people to post their own stories to its site.

GO TO *itgetsbetter.org, the award-winning site of the It Gets Better Project, begun in 2010 to show LGBT youths that life will get better "if they can just get through their teen years." There you'll find thousands of videos, including many personal narratives from gay adults who tell about how their lives got better. There's also a button to add your story, in video or writing. Watch some of the videos and read some of the written stories. Which do you find more powerful, and why?*

THINK BEYOND WORDS

Across Genres

Narrative is often a useful strategy for writers working in other genres. For example, in an essay **ARGUING A POSITION**, you may use a narrative example to prove a point. In a **REVIEW** of a film, in which evaluation is the main purpose, you may need to tell a brief story from the plot to demonstrate how the film meets (or does not meet) a specific evaluative criterion. These are only two of the many ways in which narrative can be used to serve a larger purpose than the immediate narrative itself.

COMPARE NARRATIVES in different media. From the many kinds of narratives you encounter in one day—in books or magazines, on YouTube or in video games, in textbooks or discussions or conversations with friends, choose two from different media that you find most interesting. Think about the similarities and differences between the ways the two stories are told. How does the medium affect the storytelling in each case? What would change about each narrative if it were presented in a different medium?

CHARACTERISTIC FEATURES

There is no one way to tell a story. Most written narratives, however, have a number of common features, revolving around the following characteristics and questions:

- A clearly identified event: What happened? Who was involved?
- A clearly described setting: When and where did it happen?
- Vivid, descriptive details: What makes the story come alive?
- A consistent point of view: Who's telling the story?
- A clear point: Why does the story matter?

A Clearly Identified Event: What Happened? Who Was Involved?

Narratives are based on an event or series of events, presented in a way that makes audiences want to know how the story will turn out. Consider this paragraph by Mike Rose, in which he narrates how he, as a marginal high school student with potential, got into college with the help of his senior-year English teacher, Jack MacFarland:

> My grades stank. I had A's in biology and a handful of B's in a few English and social science classes. All the rest were C's—or worse. MacFarland said I would do well in his class and laid down the law about doing well in others. Still the record for my first three years wouldn't have been acceptable to any four-year school. To nobody's surprise, I was turned down flat by USC and UCLA. But Jack MacFarland was on the case. He had received his bachelor's degree from Loyola, so he made calls to old professors and talked to somebody in admissions and wrote me a strong letter. Loyola finally accepted me as a probationary student. I would be on trial for the first year, and if I did okay, I would be granted regular status. MacFarland also intervened to get me a loan, for I could never have afforded a private college without it. Four more years of religion classes and four more years of boys at one school, girls at another. But at least I was going to college. Amazing.   —MIKE ROSE, *Lives on the Boundary*

This paragraph tells about the series of events that led to Rose's acceptance to Loyola, particularly the assistance he received from MacFarland. As remarkable as it is to think that someone with lots of C's ("or worse") could get into college, it's not the actual facts that make this narrative worth reading but the way the facts are presented. The narrator grabs our attention with his first sentence ("My grades stank"), then lays out the challenges he faced ("turned down flat by USC and UCLA") and ends with a flourish ("Amazing"). He could have told us what happened much more briefly—but then it would have been just a sequence of facts; instead, he told us a story. As the author of a narrative, your challenge will be to tell about "what happens" in a way that gets your audience's attention and makes them care enough about what happens to keep on reading.

A Clearly Described Setting: When and Where Did It Happen?

Narratives need to be situated clearly within time and space. As authors, we usually want the audience to feel as if they are part of the story, to experience the events of the narrative as those events unfold. For that reason, you will generally arrange your story in chronological order. It is also usually easier for an audience to follow a narrative when it starts at the beginning and moves straight ahead to the end. There are times, though, when you may choose to present a narrative in reverse chronological order, starting at the end and looking back at the events that led up to it—or with a flashback or flashforward that jumps back to the past or ahead to the future. Whether you tell your story in chronological order or not, the sequence of events needs to be clear to your audience. Also important is that they get a clear idea of the place(s) in which the events occur. Time and space work together to create a scene that your audience can visualize and follow, as they do in the following example from an *ESPN.com* profile of a Rhodes scholar:

Michael Lewis' description of a setting adds flavor and interest to his simple narrative on p. 841.

> Oxford at first light is an ode to potential. The purple sky throws shadows off churches and their saw-blade spires, bringing definition to the gap-toothed smiles of crenellated walls. The ghosts come out in the dream of early morning. Twelve saints and seven British prime ministers walked these streets. So did Bill Clinton and John Donne, Sir Thomas More and Kris Kristofferson, plus the guy who invented the World Wide Web.
>
> That little list? It always happens. People construct a roster of famous yet diverse alumni when describing Oxford—the quirky sum even more fantastic than the successful parts—implying that greatness comes with the diploma. But a shadow lurks near those collections of names. Oxford

University is full of students who will one day change the world, yes, but it is also full of those who have the gifts to change it and will fail. In the hope of morning, though, let your focus fall on Clinton and Donne, More and Kristofferson and now, as the dreamy purple light burns off, as busses chug and belch down the ancient streets and another week of reality begins, Myron Rolle.

Rolle bounds down Banbury Road, long strides chewing up sidewalk, hurrying to his next lecture. Today's topic is "Pain and the Brain." He settles into a seat in the back of the room, the only student whose biceps strain against the fabric of his shirt. Around him, fellow Rhodes scholars open laptops, notebooks or leather-bound Moleskine journals. The professor, a world-renowned researcher, begins speaking, about Pavlov and the curious case of Phineas Gage. The students take notes furiously.

—WRIGHT THOMPSON, "The Burden of Being Myron Rolle"

Wright Thompson wants his readers to imagine this specific place, Oxford University in Oxford, England, at a specific time of day, "first light." He uses vivid details—"the purple sky throws shadows off churches," "busses chug and belch"—to create the scene that becomes an important part of his narrative about former Florida State University football player Myron Rolle. The specificity of place and time provides a way for readers to visualize

Myron Rolle photographed at the Bodleian Library in Oxford, England, in 2009.

the athletic Rolle ("biceps strain against the fabric of his shirt") in the early morning making his way to a lecture in this famous university. You should strive, in your narratives, for the same kind of specificity. You don't want to confuse your audience with a muddled timeline or an uncertain location.

Vivid, Descriptive Details: What Makes the Story Come Alive?

You may remember English teachers telling you that good writers "show rather than tell." It's an old adage that applies to narratives in particular. Vivid, descriptive detail makes the people and places and events in a narrative come alive for an audience, helping them see, hear, smell, taste, and feel "what happened." Add direct quotations and dialogue to bring the people in your narrative to life and to let them speak for themselves. See how the following example from a newspaper article *shows* us the devastation caused by the 2010 Haiti earthquake by focusing on the victims and describing their situation with vivid sensory detail.

> PORT-AU-PRINCE, Haiti—Survivors strained desperately on Wednesday against the chunks of concrete that buried this city along with thousands of its residents, rich and poor, from shantytowns to the presidential palace, in the devastating earthquake that struck late Tuesday afternoon. . . .
>
> And the poor who define this nation squatted in the streets, some hurt and bloody, many more without food and water, close to piles of covered corpses and rubble. Limbs protruded from disintegrated concrete, muffled cries emanated from deep inside the wrecks of buildings—many of them poorly constructed in the first place—as Haiti struggled to grasp the unknown toll from its worst earthquake in more than 200 years.
>
> In the midst of the chaos, no one was able to offer an estimate of the number of people who had been killed or injured, though there was widespread concern that there were likely to be thousands of casualties.
>
> "Please save my baby!" Jeudy Francia, a woman in her 20s, shrieked outside the St.-Esprit Hospital in the city. Her child, a girl about 4 years old, writhed in pain in the hospital's chaotic courtyard, near where a handful of corpses lay under white blankets. "There is no one, nothing, no medicines, no explanations for why my daughter is going to die."
>
> —SIMON ROMERO, "Haiti Lies in Ruins; Grim Search for Untold Dead"

A woman walks past bodies laid out on a sidewalk in Port-au-Prince, Haiti, on January 13, 2010. Huge swaths of Port-au-Prince lay in ruins one day after a 7.0 earthquake.

The vivid details, in both the article and the photo that accompanied it, give us a strong sense of the devastation, helping us see "limbs protrud[ing] from disintegrated concrete" and hear "muffled cries emanat[ing] from deep inside the wrecks of buildings." Direct quotations let us hear the desperate cries of a mother trying to get medical help for her child: "Please save my baby!" These are just some of the details that make this narrative powerful and memorable.

Think about how much detail and what kind of detail your narrative needs to "come to life" for your audience. Remember that you are likely writing for readers (or listeners) unfamiliar with the story you are telling. That means that you need to choose details that help them get a vivid picture of the setting, people, and events in the narrative. When deciding whether to include direct quotations or dialogue, ask yourself if the quotation or dialogue would paint a scene or create a mood more effectively than a summary would. As the Haiti article demonstrates, a well-placed quotation can illustrate or evoke an emotion in a way that a summary statement cannot. On the other hand, a descriptive statement may often be equally effective: "Her child, a girl about 4 years old, writhed in pain." Carefully choose appropriate quotations in the same way that you carefully choose other details.

A Consistent Point of View: Who's Telling the Story?

A good narrative is generally told from one consistent point of view. If you are writing about an event in which you are a participant, as in several of the examples in this chapter, then your narrative should be written in the first-person point of view (*I, we*). First person puts the focus of the narrative on the narrator, as Georgina Kleege does in the following example, which recounts the opening moments of one of her classes:

See how David L. Hoyt uses a first-person narrative to bring readers right into the action, p. 823.

> I tell the class, "I am legally blind." There is a pause, a collective intake of breath. I feel them look away uncertainly and then look back. After all, I just said I couldn't see. Or did I? I had managed to get there on my own—no cane, no dog, none of the usual trappings of blindness. Eyeing me askance now, they might detect that my gaze is not quite focused. My eyes are aimed in the right direction but the gaze seems to stop short of touching anything. But other people do this, sighted people, normal people, especially in an awkward situation like this one, the first day of class. An actress who delivers an aside to the audience, breaking the "fourth wall" of the proscenium, will aim her gaze somewhere above any particular pair of eyes. If I hadn't said anything, my audience might understand my gaze to be like that, a part of the performance. In these few seconds between sentences, their gaze becomes intent. They watch me glance down, or toward the door where someone's coming in late. I'm just like anyone else. Then what did I actually mean by "legally blind"? They wait. I go on, "Some people would call me 'visually challenged.'" There is a ripple of laughter, an exhalation of relief. I'm making a joke about it. I'm poking fun at something they too find aggravating, the current mania to stick a verbal smiley-face on any human condition which deviates from the status quo. Differently abled. Handicapable. If I ask, I'm sure some of them can tell jokes about it: "Don't say 'bald,' say 'follicularly challenged.'" "He's not dead, he's metabolically stable." Knowing they are at least thinking these things, I conclude, "These are just silly ways of saying I don't see very well."
>
> —GEORGINA KLEEGE, "Call It Blindness"

Notice how the first-person point of view—and the repetition of *I*—keep our attention focused on Kleege. Like the students in her class, we are looking right at her.

If your narrative is about someone else's experience or about events that you have researched but did not witness, then the narrative should probably be written in third person (*he, she, it, they*). Unlike a first-person narrative, a third-person narrative emphasizes someone or something other than the narrator. Historical and medical narratives are usually written in third person, as are newswriting and sportswriting. Look at the following account of the on-field actions leading up to the moment when quarterback Joe Theismann was tackled by Lawrence Taylor, suffering a devastating, career-ending broken leg.

> From the snap of the ball to the snap of the first bone is closer to four seconds than to five. One Mississippi: The quarterback of the Washington Redskins, Joe Theismann, turns and hands the ball to running back John Riggins. He watches Riggins run two steps forward, turn, and flip the ball back to him. . . . Two Mississippi: Theismann searches for a receiver but instead sees Harry Carson coming straight at him. It's a running down— the start of the second quarter, first and 10 at midfield, with the score tied 7–7—and the New York Giants' linebacker has been so completely suckered by the fake that he's deep in the Redskins' backfield. Carson thinks he's come to tackle Riggins but Riggins is long gone, so Carson just keeps running, toward Theismann. Three Mississippi: Carson now sees that Theismann has the ball. Theismann notices Carson coming straight at him, and so he has time to avoid him. He steps up and to the side and Carson flies right on by and out of the play. The play is now 3.5 seconds old. Until this moment it has been defined by what the quarterback can see. Now it—and he—is at the mercy of what he can't see.
>
> —MICHAEL LEWIS, *The Blind Side*

The opening sentence takes us right into the game, with the snap of the ball. The repetition of "one Mississippi . . . two Mississippi . . ." marches us one excruciating second at a time through the actions that led to an injury that became the lead story on every sports broadcast that evening and for days to come. The photograph and caption tell the story of how that play ended for Theismann.

Compare the points of view of Georgina Kleege's first-person narrative and Michael Lewis' third-person one. Notice that there is one consistent point of view in each example. As an author, you will have to determine whether your narrative is most effective told from the first-person or third-person point of view. No matter what you may have been taught in high school, the first person is acceptable in many (though not all) academic settings. Whatever point of view you use, however, do so consistently. That is, if you refer to yourself in the narrative, do not switch between first (*I, we*) and third (*he*,

Athletic trainers surround Joe Theismann after a tackle by Lawrence Taylor broke Theisman's leg.

she, they) person. (Rarely is a narrative told from second-person—*you*—point of view.)

Part of maintaining a consistent point of view is establishing a clear time frame. Notice Michael Lewis' use of present-tense verbs in the example from *The Blind Side*. By consistently narrating the actions in the game in the present tense, the narrator, much like a play-by-play announcer, places the reader in the moment of the story being told. Using a consistent verb tense situates the actions of the event within a clear time frame.

A clear time frame does not mean that every verb in the narrative has to be in the same tense, only that the writer establishes one primary tense—usually present or past—for the main action of the story. In the example by Mike Rose on p. 108, most of the verbs are in the past tense: *said, made, talked*. But other tenses are used to indicate events that, in relation to the main action of the narrative, occurred earlier (*He had received his bachelor's degree from Loyola*) or might occur later (*I would be granted regular status*).

A Clear Point: Why Does the Story Matter?

See how historical events can produce deep personal consequences in Michelle Cacho-Negrete's narrative on p. 733.

Good narratives tell a story that matters. In academic writing in particular, narratives are told to make a point, whether they begin by stating the point explicitly in a thesis or build toward a point that is expressed at the end. Wherever the main point is located, the purpose of the narrative needs to be clear to the audience. Nothing irritates an audience more than reading or listening to a story that has no point. Even if a story relates a series of interesting events, in an academic context, that story will most likely be deemed a failure if it does not have a clear point. Consider how the author and English professor bell hooks opens an essay about learning to value work:

> "Work makes life sweet!" I often heard this phrase growing up, mainly from old black folks who did not have jobs in the traditional sense of the word. They were usually self-employed, living off the land, selling fishing worms, picking up an odd job here and there. They were people who had a passion for work. They took pride in a job done well. My Aunt Margaret took in ironing. Folks brought her clothes from miles around because she was such an expert. That was in the days when using starch was common and she knew how to do an excellent job. Watching her iron with skill and grace was like watching a ballerina dance. Like all the other black girls raised in the fifties that I knew, it was clear to me that I would be a working woman. Even though our mother stayed home, raising her seven children, we saw her constantly at work, washing, ironing, cleaning, and cooking (she was an incredible cook). And she never allowed her six girls to imagine we would not be working women. No, she let us know that we would work and be proud to work.
>
> —BELL HOOKS, "Work Makes Life Sweet"

Hooks opens with her main point, that "work makes life sweet!" In the sentences that follow, she explains how she learned this lesson from members of her family, namely her aunt and mother. Through specific examples, she illustrates how these family members "took pride in a job well done" and passed on this pride in one's work to hooks and her sisters. The explicit restatement of the point in the final sentence—that hooks and her six sisters learned from their mother that they would "work and be proud to work"— recasts the notion of "working woman" in a unique and engaging way.

Now look at how a student at the University of Mary Washington introduces a literacy narrative—a story about her experience with reading or writing, which is a common assignment in college classes:

> I'm sitting in the woods with a bunch of Catholic people I just met yesterday. Suddenly, they ask me to name one of the talents God has given me. I panic for a split second and then breathe an internal sigh of relief. I tell them I'm a writer. As the group leaders move on to question someone else, I sit trying to mentally catch my breath. It will take a moment before the terror leaves my forearms, chest, and stomach, but I tell myself that I have nothing to fear. I am a writer. Yes, I most definitely am a writer. *Now breathe*, I tell myself . . . *and suppress that horrifying suspicion that you are actually not a writer at all.*
>
> The retreat that prepared me for my eighth grade confirmation was not the first time I found myself pulling out the old "I'm a writer" card and wondering whether I was worthy enough to carry this sacred card in the wallet of my identity. Such things happen to people with identity crises.
>
> —EMILY VALLOWE, "Write or Wrong Identity"

In contrast to bell hooks, Emily Vallowe plunges right into telling a story and uses it to lead up to her main point, which she makes at the end of the introduction and goes on to develop in the rest of her narrative. Even though she doesn't state it quite as directly as hooks does hers, it is no less clear: the idea of being a writer is central to her identity, but she's never sure if she's really entitled to call herself one.

As an author, don't assume that your audience will recognize the point you're trying to make. No matter how interesting you think your story is, your readers need to know why they should care. Why is the story important? Explicitly state your main point as both hooks and Vallowe do.

LOOK AT a narrative in a newspaper or magazine article or on a blog or other website to see what main point it makes and how it does so. Is the main point explicitly stated in a thesis, or is it only implied? Does the narrative make clear to readers why the story is important or why they should care about it?

ROMAN SKASKIW served as an infantry officer with the U.S. Army in Afghanistan and Iraq. He wrote this piece in 2010 for *Home Fires*, an online project that features the writing of men and women who have returned from wartime service in the U.S. military. Skaskiw now lives in Iowa City, Iowa.

Bidding Farewell to Arms
ROMAN SKASKIW

The author opens with a question that is at the heart of the dilemma his story is about.

FOR THE PAST YEAR, I could only provide a frustratingly long answer to the simple, frequently asked question, *Are you still in the Army?*

When I commissioned as an infantry officer in March, 2000, my contract specified four years of active service and four years in the inactive reserve (I.R.R.)—a name on a list. During graduate school, my answer was simple: *Sort of. I'm still a name on a list.*

At the eight year mark, I would have been allowed to resign my commission and irrevocably separate myself from the military, but my number came up at the seven year and two month mark, mobilizing me, as the letter said in all capital letters, "FOR 545 DAYS UNLESS EXTENDED."

Of course, the military had the right to do this according to the contract I signed back in 2000. I was not a victim of new policy. I either knew or should have known—can't remember which.

From here on, the story is told in chronological order.

The 545 days came and went and I returned safely and soundly from Afghanistan's Kunar Province to Iowa City where I began reassembling my life. I stayed with a friend, living from two suitcases for the couple weeks it took me to find an apartment, then paid a mover to transport my belongings from the "Garage-Mahaul."

I'd hardly begun unpacking my old life when another letter arrived. It read "SUBJECT: Election of Options after Fulfilling the Mandatory Military Service Obligation (MSO)," and asked me to select one of four boxes on the enclosed A.H.R.C. Form 4145.

One box requested transfer to a reserve unit—the guys who train one weekend a month and two weeks during the summer. Another was for retiring officers with twenty or more years of qualifying service.

The two others interested me. One read "I elect to remain a member of the I.R.R.," and the other, the choice I had been thinking about for a very long time, read "I hereby tender my unqualified resignation as a Reserve officer of the Army, USAR, under the provisions of Chapter 6, Section III of . . . . I understand that if my resignation is accepted, I am entitled to an honorable separation and will be furnished an Honorable Discharge Certificate."

Vivid details like these make the story come alive for readers.

I have no idea what to make of that ominous "if" in the last sentence.

Nevertheless, given my visceral opposition to our foreign, undeclared wars the choice should have been quick and easy. It was not. Partly out of nostalgia for the responsibility and fraternity I once enjoyed, and partly from wanting to keep my employment options open, the letter remained taped to my refrigerator for a full year, and the simple question *Are you still in the Army?* now drew a long-winded response.

The personal dilemma that prompts Skaskiw's narrative—his purpose for writing.

When friends followed up by asking if I could get recalled again, I repeated the rumor I'd heard that involuntarily mobilized service members could not be recalled again for a full two years. I told them, however, that when I tried to confirm the rumor with the many recruiters who rang my cell phone, they'd say the only sure way to avoid another call-up was to join their unit, because they have non-deployable slots available well suited for someone like me, and would I like to join them?

The Army provides. You get recession-proof employment, full medical and dental care, good schools for your kids, and an exquisitely defined role in the world. You can see paychecks and meals and a sense of purpose from here to the horizon.

Those first few mornings without your tribe or your uniform asserting your identity can be very lonely. They were for me. I realized how few people would miss me if I did nothing on any given day. I worried about money and about what I'd do next.

So, I kept the door open, just a crack, and felt comforted that the letter taped to my fridge might slam it shut at a moment's notice.

Day by day, the civilian world around me grew more familiar and comfortable. I taught a class at the University of Iowa. An Army buddy and I reunited to climb Africa's tallest mountain. Given how well we knew one another from our time in Afghanistan, it was hard for either of us to believe the Kilimanjaro adventure was our first interaction outside the military. We summited before sunrise on January 13, 2009.

I worked as a Web developer and technical editor, and in the summer, took my mother to visit the place of her birth near Lviv, Ukraine, where relatives I never knew of treated us lavishly. Over vodka, cognac, homemade wines, homegrown vegetables, freshly cured cheeses and fish from the nearby lake, they taught me family histories that made all my problems seem frivolous by comparison.

Climbing Kilimanjaro, day 4: morning summit from Barranco camp.

I rediscovered the mats of the Hawkeye Brazilian Jiu Jitsu Club, the crowded table of chess players in the pedestrian mall and friends I'd forgotten I had.

Life is a privilege. I now recognize that responsibility isn't gone when you leave the military, it is changed. Greater by far than the responsibility to comrades in arms is responsibility to friends, family and self, responsibility to the one life each of us gets to live. Such responsibility is harder to recognize because it is long and slow and unlikely to manifest itself in some violent sacrifice.

This paragraph and the 2 that follow express the main point of the story and why it matters.

I would also say that greater than the adventure of fighting our government's wars is the adventure of pursuing your own happiness in this world.

Such adventure and such responsibilities are truer because they originate not by decree, but from our humanity—from nature or nature's God, as it were. More is required to be successful and more is awarded when we are.

After about a year of waiting, I hereby tender my unqualified resignation.

The last sentence emphasizes the finality of Skaskiw's decision and provides an emphatic conclusion to the essay.

ANALYZE *a short nonfiction narrative that you find in a magazine or on a website. Look at the list of five characteristic features of narratives on p. 108 and annotate the essay to point out these features, using the Skaskiw essay as a model. Then look at your annotations and the parts of the text they refer to, and evaluate how well your chosen narrative illustrates the characteristic features. For example, is the setting clearly described? How vivid are the details?*

WRITING A NARRATIVE / A Roadmap

Choose a topic that matters—to you, and to others

Whether you write a narrative for personal reasons or in response to an assignment, choose your own topic or work with an assigned topic, try to write about something that matters to you, and try to make sure that it will matter to your audience as well.

If you are writing a personal narrative, choosing a topic is often difficult because you are deciding to share something personal about yourself or someone you know. You will need to choose an experience or event that you feel comfortable sharing, in some detail, with an audience. Be sure that the experience is not only important to you but is also of enough general interest to engage your audience.

If your narrative is not a personal one, you still want it to be compelling. Especially in narratives that do not have a personal focus, the story may be part of a larger conversation about an event or some topic that the event represents. For example, if you are writing a narrative about how specific students' academic performances changed when they enrolled in a charter school, you need to recognize that such stories are part of an ongoing educational and political debate about the effectiveness of charter schools as an alternative to traditional public schools. You may need to do some research to understand the background to this debate and how your narrative fits into it.

Consider your rhetorical situation

Whenever you write for someone other than yourself, you must consider the rhetorical situation. Writing a narrative is no different. You need to consider the following issues:

Think about your AUDIENCE. For whom and to whom are you writing? What's your relationship with these people? How will your answers to these questions affect your rhetorical choices, such as your method of organization, your TONE, or the amount of background information you provide?

- Are you writing for an audience with no knowledge of your topic? If so, you will need to provide some background information.

- Are you writing for an academic audience? If so, your language will almost certainly need to be more formal than if you were writing to a close friend.

- What characteristics do you share—or not share—with your audience? Consider anything from age and education to gender, cultural heritage, and religious and political beliefs. How will shared or differing background and values affect how you tell the story? If you're writing for an online audience, you'll often know almost nothing about who might read what you write. Whatever the case, you need to keep your audience in mind at every stage of the process and to provide sufficient vivid details so that they can follow your story, are engaged by it, and can see your point.

Think about your PURPOSE. Why are you writing this narrative? Maybe you want to tell a story about a fatal traffic accident to inform your audience about the dangers of texting while driving or to persuade lawmakers to make texting while driving illegal. Maybe the purpose of your narrative is to remind readers of a historical moment that is in danger of being forgotten—Hurricane Katrina, perhaps, or the first time humans walked on the moon. Remember that your narrative needs to do more than just tell a story, even an engaging story; it needs to make a point of some kind.

Think about your STANCE. Is the story you're telling a highly personal one that you have strong feelings about? Or is it one that you have some distance from and can think about in a calm, detached way? What about this story captures your interest, and why? Think about how your answers to these questions will affect the way you tell the story. How do you want to present yourself as the narrator? As witty and amusing, if you're telling a humorous family story? As knowledgeable but impersonal, if you're recounting historical events for a political science essay? Whatever your stance, how can you make your writing reflect that stance?

Consider the larger CONTEXT. What broader issues are involved in your narrative? If you are writing a narrative about your family's migration from Mexico to the United States, for example, you may need to consider questions like these: What economic, cultural, or other factors caused your family in particular and many others in general to want to leave Mexico? What drew them to the United States? How have the migration patterns from Mexico to the United States shifted over time, and why? What else has been said and written about this topic? Considering the larger context for your narrative can help you see it from perspectives different from your own—and present it in a way that is effective for your audience and purpose.

Consider your MEDIUM. Often you won't have a choice—but if you do, think about which one best fits the goals of your narrative. The kinds of details you include, the language and tone you use, the way you present material from sources, and many other rhetorical choices depend on the medium. The conventions of a print academic essay differ markedly from the conventions of an audio essay. If your purpose is to tell the story of how victims of a natural disaster in your area are doing years afterward, you may decide to do a documentary similar to Spike Lee's *When the Levees Broke,* about the aftermath of Hurricane Katrina. Such a medium allows you to feature specific people on camera telling their own stories. If you write a feature article for the local newspaper on the same topic, the medium of print will lead you to make different choices about how to tell stories about the victims. In this case, you might narrate more of the content yourself, using selected quotations from victims to add striking details.

Consider matters of DESIGN. Does your narrative need headings? Is there anything in the story that could be conveyed better with a photograph than with words alone? Will illustrations help you engage your audience? Often, and especially in academic writing, some aspects of design will be prescribed and thus beyond your control. For example, you may be expected to use a certain structure of headings or a specific font and type size. To whatever extent you can determine the look of your text, though, remember that design has a powerful impact on the impression your narrative makes.

Explore your topic and do any necessary research

If you are writing a personal narrative, write down all that you remember about your topic. Using **BRAINSTORMING**, **FREEWRITING**, or other activities for **GENERATING IDEAS**, write down as many specific details as you can: sounds, smells, textures, colors, and so on. What details will engage your audience? Not all the details that you jot down in this exploratory stage will make it into your essay. You'll need to choose the ones most relevant to your audience, purpose, and main point. In addition to sensory details, try to write down direct quotations or dialogue you can remember that will help bring your story to life.

If your narrative is not a personal one, you'll likely need to conduct RESEARCH so that you can provide accurate and sufficient details about the topic. It's especially important to get the "what, when, and where" of the narrative right, and consulting appropriate sources will help you do that. Depending on your topic, your research may involve using sources in the library or online, or conducting interviews, observations, or other FIELD RESEARCH. The point here is that when you write a narrative that is not personal, you will need to rely on more than your memory for the content— and you'll want to know what else has been said about your topic.

Decide on a point of view

The subject that you choose to write about will usually determine the point of view from which you write. If you're telling a story in which you are a central participant, you will usually use the first person *I*. In some cultures, however, bringing attention to oneself through a first-person narrative would be unacceptable. And in some academic disciplines, using the first person is rarely acceptable. So pay attention to the cultural and disciplinary conventions of the situation in which you are writing.

Related to point of view is your choice of verb tenses. When writing a narrative, think about what tense would be most effective for telling your story. Most personal narratives that are arranged in chronological order are written in the past tense ("When I *was* twelve, I *discovered* what I *wanted* to do for the rest of my life"). However, if you want the readers to feel like they are actually experiencing an event, you may choose to use the present tense, as Georgina Kleege and Wright Thompson do in examples earlier in this chapter. Notice how Kleege's and Thompson's use of present tense places their readers "in the moment" with the writers and their subjects.

Organize and start writing

Once you've chosen a subject and identified your main point, considered your rhetorical situation, come up with enough details, and decided on a point of view (not that you've necessarily done all these tasks in this order), you'll need to think about how to organize your narrative.

Remember that your story needs to have a point. As you begin to draft, type out that point as a tentative THESIS, something to keep your eye on as you organize your narrative; you can decide later whether you want to use it.

Organize your information. What happened? Where? When? Who was there? What details can you describe to make the story come alive? Decide whether to present the narrative in chronological order, reverse chronological order, or some other order.

Draft an OPENING. A good introduction draws your audience into the story and makes them want to know more. Sometimes you'll need to provide a context for your narrative—to describe the setting and introduce some of the people before getting on with what happened. Other times you might start in the middle of your story, or at the end—and then circle back to tell what happened.

Draft a CONCLUSION. If you organize your narrative chronologically, you'll likely conclude by telling how the story ends. But make sure your readers see the point of your story; if you haven't made that clear, you might end by saying something about the story's significance. Why does it matter to you? What do you want them to take away—and remember?

Look critically at your draft, get response—and revise

Read over your draft slowly and carefully. Try to see it as if for the first time: Does the story grab your attention, and can you follow it? Can you tell what the point is, and will your audience care? If at all possible, get feedback from others. Make an appointment at your school's writing center, meet with your instructor, ask a friend or classmate to read over the draft—or do all of these things. Following are some questions that can help you or others examine a narrative with a critical eye:

- *Does the OPENING capture the audience's interest?* How? How else might the narrative begin?

- *Is it clear why you're telling this story?* Have you made your audience care about what happened and who was involved?

- *Who's telling the story?* Have you maintained a consistent POINT OF VIEW?

- *Is the setting situated in a particular time and space?* Is it clear when and where the events in the story happened?

- *Are there enough vivid, concrete details?* Does it show rather than tell? Does it include any dialogue or direct quotations—and if not, would adding some help the story come alive?

- *Are there any visuals—and if not, should you add some?*

- *Is the story easy to follow?* If it's at all confusing, would TRANSITIONS help your audience follow the sequence of events? If it's a lengthy or complex narrative, would headings help?

- *How do you establish AUTHORITY and credibility?* How would you describe the STANCE and TONE—and are they appropriate for your audience and purpose?

- *Does the story have a clear point?* Is the point stated explicitly—and if not, should it be?

- *How satisfying is the CONCLUSION?* What does it leave the audience thinking? How else might the narrative end?

- *Does the title suggest what the narrative is about,* and will it make an audience want to read on?

Revise your draft in light of any feedback you receive and your own critique, keeping your purpose and especially your audience firmly in mind.

REFLECT ON WHAT YOU'VE LEARNED. Once you've completed your narrative, let it settle for a while and then take time to reflect. How well did you tell the story? What additional revisions would you make if you could? Research shows that such reflections help "lock in" what you learn for future use.

Lydia's Story

JAN BRIDEAU

JUST BEFORE LEAVING LOUISIANA I met a small, slender black woman. She was in her sixties, with her short gray hair neatly tucked up inside a kerchief. Let's call her Lydia. An internist and I had traveled to a rural town's shelter housed in the VFW hall, the temporary home of seventy-some people.

Entering the large VFW hall, we were struck by the chemical odor of a cleaning solution so strong that it seemed toxic. The hall had no windows; only fluorescent lighting illuminated the large space. Coming from the hot, humid weather outdoors, we found the inside uncomfortably cold from air conditioning. The cackle of a television set was the only sound. There were several rows of cots and mattresses with a few people lying on them. Most of the shelter residents had left for the day, to work or do errands, but they were expected to return later. A local official told us that two adult residents needed medical care.

One of these was Lydia, who had an abscessed tooth. Lydia was soft-spoken but eager to have her tooth examined. It turned out that she had been unable to chew on the affected side for several months. She hadn't been able to afford $25 for an x-ray, and she didn't have medical insurance; the pain, she told us, waxed and waned. Her cheek was quite tender, and it appeared that the tooth should be extracted. To address her immediate need, we started her on a course of antibiotics and made a note that a dentist should see her soon. The internist asked where she lived and if she knew how her family was doing.

JAN BRIDEAU is a pediatric nurse practitioner at Massachusetts General Hospital in Boston. She worked in Louisiana in 2005 as part of Operation Helping Hand, a group from Massachusetts General that provided care and assessed medical needs in the aftermath of Hurricane Katrina. Brideau's essay was originally published in 2006 in *Health Affairs*, an American journal about national and global health policy and research issues. The essay appeared in the "Narrative Matters" section of the journal that was devoted to stories about Hurricane Katrina. Unfortunately, we've been unable to locate a photograph of the author.

Lydia told us that she lived alone in her home, located in the Eighth Ward in New Orleans, adjacent to that city's devastated Ninth Ward. As the first storm raged, she knew to avoid windows. (Interestingly, she never used the names "Katrina" or "Rita" when speaking about the hurricanes. She, like many people I met, referred to them as the "first storm" and the "second storm.")

Lydia took a sleeping bag into her windowless hallway. She slept on the   5
floor for two nights. Then, one morning, she woke to find that her feet and the sleeping bag were soaking wet, and there was standing water throughout her house.

When she opened the front door, the whole street looked like a river, and water poured in. She described it as "rushing like the Colorado River." She knew that if she went outside, she would be swept up in the current and drown. There was no one in sight.

She was unable to shut the door against the brown rushing water. Horrified, she tried not to panic. Seeking higher ground, she climbed on top of her dining room table. It, like most of her furniture, had been handed down from her grandparents. The table was bulky and heavy; normally, it took three men

Rescue personnel searching for victims in New Orleans' Eighth Ward after Katrina struck in August 2005.

to move it. But as the water continued to rise, the table started moving, then rocking—and Lydia knew she was in trouble. She managed to climb up on her kitchen counter, but that soon became precarious as well. The water continued to rise quickly, and the water pressure was so strong that water spurted out of the kitchen sink like a fountain. Terrified of drowning, she kept reminding herself to think clearly.

The thing to do, she decided, was to find the highest spot in her one-story house. Lydia climbed off the kitchen counter and waded through the deep water, dragging a small kitchen stool behind her. She positioned the stool in front of her linen closet, propping one foot on the stool and the other on the doorknob; then she climbed to the top shelf of her linen closet. She described the shelf area as about three feet wide and about a foot and a half tall. Crouched there, she watched the water continue to rise. Her ceilings, she knew, were twelve feet tall. The water rose to above her height, then to above six feet, finally to about seven feet. (She could estimate numbers, she said, because she had gone to nursing school long ago. Eventually, she had to leave nursing because she cried over her patients' conditions too much, and they ended up consoling her.)

Lydia waited, cramped on the top shelf of the linen closet, until the water finally began to recede. When we asked if she got hungry or thirsty, she said that she didn't remember feeling that way. Her tongue became dry and her lips were cracked, but she only was aware of being terrified of the water. When the water receded to about five feet, it was five days later. She was finally able to come down from her perch. The water was up to her chin.

She tried to open the back door near the linen closet. But the wood had swollen from the water, and it wouldn't budge. She knew that the windows were probably swollen shut, too. Then she remembered that she'd never closed the front door because of the strong current. She moved through the water, out the front door, and onto her front porch. She couldn't recall how long she waited alone in the water, holding onto a porch post and screaming for help. Eventually, a far neighbor with a boat rescued her and took her to a larger rescue boat. Then that boat dropped her off at an overpass where, in the sun and the heat, she and a large group of other people waited without food or water.

At some point, a small van drove up and stopped directly in front of her. A female driver, dressed in scrubs, jumped out. The van was loaded with medical supplies, and there was room for only one person; she ordered Lydia to get in. The woman told Lydia that she worked in the emergency room of a local hospital and was soon to become a physician. She drove Lydia to a shelter.

As Lydia was telling us her story, I heard strength and resolve in her voice. She was proud that she had "kept her head," which had saved her life. She knew that she didn't have a home to return to, that everything in it was probably destroyed. There was, however, a reason for her to return home one last time. She needed to get back to that linen closet. There, on the top shelf, was her family photo album. It was the only thing Lydia thought might have survived the water. It would be the only thing from her past that she could take with her on her new journey.

For me, the enormity of the double hurricanes became clear only after witnessing so many people left without homes. Everywhere we traveled in Louisiana, there were countless people in shelters that had once been a hotel, convention center, sports arena, school, church, YMCA, and, yes, the VFW hall where I met Lydia. It was my privilege to meet and serve them. But it's Lydia's story that stays with me most, probably because it represents the essence of hope and determination in the face of terrible adversity.

Thinking about the Text

1. What is Brideau's main point, and where in the essay is it indicated?

2. What is the primary **POINT OF VIEW** from which Brideau narrates "Lydia's Story"? What impact does that point of view have on you as a reader?

3. How does Brideau make her narrative "come alive"? Make a list of words she uses to describe the setting and the characters. How do they appeal to readers' emotions?

4. This piece was first published in *Health Affairs,* a journal of health policy thought and research. Who would be the audience for this piece, and how does Brideau's **TONE** suit those readers? Point to specific words and phrases that create that tone.

5. Write a **NARRATIVE** in which you, like Brideau, tell a story about something that happened to someone else. Think about how to make your main point clear, whether or not you state it explicitly. Also, pay careful attention to how to sequence the events and the kinds of details that you need to include.

Literacy: A Lineage

MELANIE LUKEN

I T WOULD BE IMPOSSIBLE to discuss my path to literacy without talking about my literary guardian, the person who inspired and encouraged my love for reading and writing: my father. I spent a lot of time with my dad as a child, but one of the most important experiences we shared was our Sunday afternoon bike rides. We nearly always took the same route, down to the bike path by the river, circling around, and breaking at Carillon Park under the bell tower. We would just sit, rest, and think under the bells. Etched at the bottom of the bell tower was part of a poem by Henry Wadsworth Longfellow:

> It was as if an earthquake rent
> The hearth-stones of a continent,
> And made forlorn
> The households born
> Of peace on earth, good-will to men!
> And in despair I bowed my head;
> "There is no peace on earth," I said;
> "For hate is strong,
> And mocks the song

MELANIE LUKEN was a senior French and English major at The Ohio State University at the time that she wrote this literacy narrative for an English course in which she was being trained to be a writing tutor.

Of peace on earth, good-will to men!"
Then pealed the bells more loud and deep:
"God is not dead; nor doth he sleep;
The Wrong shall fail,
The Right prevail,
With peace on earth, good-will to men." (lines 21–35)

My dad would inevitably read it aloud, but we both knew it by heart; it is one of the many poems that have come to mean something to me. As I got older, my dad didn't come riding as often with me. He was older and more tired, but I still went by myself. Each time I arrived under the bells, I would recite the poem to myself, even when the weather was cold and my breath made the air foggy. It had become part of me, this poem, this tradition of riding and reading and thinking. In the same way, my passion for reading and writing developed in me through the influence of my father who has a deep love of literature himself. For this reason, my definition of literacy involves more than the ability to read and write; for me, it is also a tradition, an inheritance I received from my father, and an ability to appreciate language because of him and because of many other writers who came before me.

You could define my dad as a jack-of-all-trades artist. He has dabbled in almost every art: novel-writing, poetry-writing, songwriting, painting, sculpture, and acting. He was originally in graduate school for English with hopes of becoming a professor. After a couple of years, however, he tired of academia. His tendencies towards creativity and individuality did not mix well with the intense analysis and structure of university life. Eventually, he ended up as a stay-at-home dad, *my* stay-at-home dad, who continues to this day to work on his art and writing. Although our relationship has not always been simple and easy, I benefited greatly from having such an intelligent and imaginative father as my primary caretaker.

For my whole life, my father has quoted the "greats," the "classics," or at least the authors that he admired, in normal conversation. It has become a joke among me and my brothers because we can all recite from memory his favorite lines of books and his favorite poems. Because of him I can quote, "If you can keep your head when all about you / Are losing theirs and blaming it on you" (Kipling lines 1–2), "And early though the laurel grows / It withers quicker than the rose" (Housman lines 11–12), "I grow old . . . I grow old . . . / I shall wear the bottoms of my trousers rolled" (Eliot lines 120–21), and of course, "Call Me Ishmael" (Melville 3), among many others. Sometimes he will quote things far out of context, and yet I understand and enjoy it because these quotes evoke intense feelings of tradition and love. My father's love of literature pervaded my young mind the way it must pervade his own, and it has stayed with me.

From the time I could read and write, I wrote and acted out princess stories all on my own. I read vociferously, and I loved being told stories. I attribute all of this to my father, who taught me to read and to write, who put *Little Women* in my hands when I was ten years old, and who continued to introduce me to his favorite authors as I got older. The only reason I picked up books like *The Heart Is a Lonely Hunter* or Capote's *Other Voices, Other Rooms*, is because he suggested them or handed them to me. I realize that I did not have a particularly normal American childhood in terms of my relationship with books and literature (most of my friends preferred playing sports or watching TV to reading), but I am blessed to have a father who sees art in language and stories and who passed this gift to me. I have a greater understanding of the diversity of books, authors, and the ways in which language is used because of my father. He always pushed me to read literature other than what I read in school and particularly encouraged me to read female writers like Carson McCullers, Zora Neale Hurston, and Flannery O'Connor to empower me as a young girl and to expand my perspective. Now, everything I read is within this tradition that he and I have established.

Another thing that I vividly remember as a child is spending quite a bit of 5 time in public libraries. My brothers, my dad, and I would visit the library at least once a week, and more often in the summer when we were out of school. We were never allowed to play video games or watch much TV, so our entertainment consisted of what we could create ourselves or what we could gain from books. Our ability to use and understand language proficiently was very important to my father. Although I am the only child who has displayed a penchant for creative writing, I think my father has always held on to the hope that each of his children will spring into novel-writers. Since we were about twelve or thirteen, he has consistently demanded that we each write a story for him at Christmastime rather than buy him a gift. His favorite is a story I wrote for him in high school; it was my own personal version of *A Christmas Carol.*

I began seriously writing creatively towards the end of high school. I have kept journals since I was eight or nine, but in high school, I discovered my true capacity for poetry. I wrote poetry for English classes and for our high school literary magazine. When I got to college, I naturally began taking creative writing classes. I have taken Beginning Poetry, Intermediate Poetry twice, and the

Honors 598 seminar with a creative writing component. I improve constantly and with each class my relationship to language changes and grows. Anyone who has taken a workshop knows that, in these courses, you have to be able to stand criticism and to pick out which suggestions are beneficial and which are not. It was my father, the constant in my literacy narrative, who encouraged me through all of these classes, telling me that no matter what anybody thought, I was a poet, a better poet than he had ever been.

I believe that my choice to major in French is also rooted in this tradition of language and literature. Studying a foreign language can, at times, be just like learning how to read and write as a child. Studying French intensely became for me the perfect, impossible challenge: to read and write French like I read and write English. However, it seems that as long and hard as I study French, I will never be quite so comfortable nor quite so capable of understanding it or placing it within a context. I believe that this is partially because tradition plays no role in my study of French. It has nothing to do with my family or my background, and it cannot move me emotionally to the extent that English language can. Unlike French, I have a tradition of reading, speaking, and writing English, and I have a much vaster appreciation for English literature in general.

Because of my father and our shared love of literature, my definition of literacy is intimately linked to the idea of tradition. In a way, my literacy is part of my lineage, part of the legacy of my father. My love for literature and writing, my poetic tendencies, my passion for language are all gifts from him. I think that I tend to have more of an imagination than my peers, and I also love to write and create using words. The reason for these qualities is that my father once inspired in me his own creativity and instructed me on the understanding of human experience through writing. In turn, this literacy experience is something I want to pass on to my children someday.

Literacy is generally known as the ability to read and write. My definition of literacy is: the ability to read, write, and understand within a tradition. For me, this is a familial tradition that has permeated my literacy experience. Parents have an incredible power to influence their children through their own behaviors and attitudes, and it is certainly true that my father has impressed upon me his own attitudes towards literacy and literature. Now, every time we talk he asks me, "What are you reading? What do you think about it?" We talk about what each of us is reading, as well as our thoughts and impressions. In this way, the tradition continues.

Some daughters inherit a certain amount of money from their fathers. 10 Some inherit a car or a house. Others inherit jewelry. My father will never have much money or a nice car or many material goods at all. I have, however, received something from him that will last my whole life and will continue to give me joy as long as I live. He has passed on to me his love of language and literature. It is within this tradition that I understand literacy, a tradition that causes me to sometimes think "God is not dead; nor doth he sleep!" (Longfellow 32) when I hear bells ringing.

Works Cited

Eliot, T. S. "The Love Song of J. Alfred Prufrock." *Poets.org.* Academy of American Poets, n.d. Web. 12 Oct. 2009.

Housman, A. E. "To an Athlete Dying Young." *Poets.org.* Academy of American Poets, n.d. Web. 12 Oct. 2009.

Kipling, Rudyard. "If." *Poets.org.* Academy of American Poets, n.d. Web. 12 Oct. 2009.

Longfellow, Henry Wadsworth. "Christmas Bells." *Poets.org.* Academy of American Poets, n.d. Web. 12 Oct. 2009.

Melville, Herman. *Moby-Dick.* New York: Penguin Books, 1988. Print.

Thinking about the Text

1. What is Melanie Luken's main point, and how do you know? How does she support her main point?

2. How does Luken use PRIMARY SOURCES in her narrative? How did you react to her use of these sources?

3. Why does this story matter? To the author? To students like you?

4. Luken wrote this piece for a course in which she was learning to be a writing tutor. How do you think this CONTEXT helped her shape her narrative? In what ways might she have written this piece differently for a class focused on writing memoirs?

5. Write a LITERACY NARRATIVE in which you tell the story of one or two of your favorite moments related to reading or writing. Connect these individual moments to a larger discussion of what they taught you about the role of literacy in your life.

NINE

"Let's Take a Closer Look"
Writing Analytically

 ***NALYZE THIS. ANALYZE THAT.*** These are more than the titles of two movies starring Robert DeNiro and Billy Crystal. Analysis is a necessary step in much of the thinking that we do, and that we do every day. What should you wear today? T-shirt and hoodie? Sweatshirt? Your new red sweater? You look closely at the weather, what you will be doing, the people you will be with (and might want to impress, or not), and then decide based on those factors. You may not consciously think of it as analysis, but that's what you've done.

When you analyze something, you break it down into its component parts and think about those parts methodically in order to understand it in some way. Case in point: You want a new gaming system, but should you get a PlayStation 3? Nintendo Wii? Xbox 360? Or maybe something more portable, a Sony PSP-3000 or a Nintendo DSi? You might check websites like *TestFreaks*, which provide information based on expert analyses of each system, or you might conduct your own analysis. What kinds of games do you play? Party games? Arcade games? Online games? Which is more important to you: an easy-to-use interface or high-end HD graphics? big-name titles or an all-purpose entertainment center? These are some of the ways you might analyze the various systems, first to understand what they offer and then to decide which one you want to buy.

Since our world is awash in information, the ability to read it closely, examine it critically, and decide how—or whether—to accept or act on it becomes a survival skill. To navigate this sea of information, we rely on our ability to analyze.

You have probably analyzed literary texts in English classes; perhaps you've analyzed films or song lyrics. In many college classes, you'll be expected to conduct different sorts of analyses—rhetorical, causal, process, data, and more. Analysis is critical to every academic discipline, useful in every professional field, and employed by each of us in our everyday lives. It's essential to understanding and to decision making. This chapter provides guidelines for conducting an analysis and writing analytically.

THINK ABOUT your own use of analysis. How many decisions—large and small—have you made in the last week? in the last month? in the last year? From small (what to have for breakfast) to major (which college to attend), make a chart listing a representative sample of these decisions and what areas of your life they affected; then note the information you gathered in each case before you decided. What does this chart tell you about your interests, activities, and priorities? You've just completed an analysis.

Across Academic Fields

Some form of analysis can be found in every academic discipline. In a *history* class, you may be asked to analyze how Russia defeated Napoleon's army in 1812. In *biology*, you might analyze how the body responds to exercise. In *economics*, you might analyze the trade-off between unemployment and inflation rates. In a *technical communication* course, you might analyze a corporate website to understand how it appeals to various audiences. In your *composition* course, you'll analyze your own writing for many purposes, from thinking about how you've appealed to your audience to how you need to revise a draft. So many courses require analysis because looking closely and methodically at something—a text, a process, a philosophy—helps you discover connections between ideas and think about how things work, what they mean, and why.

Across Media

Your medium affects the way you present your analysis. In *print*, much of your analysis may be in paragraphs, but you might include photographs, tables, or graphs such as a flowchart to analyze a process. If you're analyzing something in an *oral presentation* you might show data in a handout or on presentation slides—and you would need to add some signpost language to

THINK BEYOND WORDS

WATCH THE VIDEO of a TED talk by statistician Nate Silver on whether race affects voting. He includes slides with lists, bar graphs, photos, and maps—and a space below the video invites readers to comment. How much do the visuals contribute to his analysis? TED talks are intended to focus on "ideas worth spreading." Write a tweet about something Silver said in his talk that you find thought-provoking: your challenge will be to make it clear and interesting in 140 characters. Go to wwnorton. com/write/everyonelinks to view the video.

200 years ago, there was some concern that the spread of literacy could cause civic unrest. Dennis Baron analyzes that history on p. 705.

help your audience follow your analysis. A *digital text* allows you to blend paragraphs, charts, images, audio, and video—and does so in a way that lets readers click on various parts as they wish. And some digital texts—blogs, listservs, tweets—allow readers to comment; in effect, to become authors themselves. You won't always be able to choose, but when you do, you'll want to choose the medium that enables you to most effectively make your point for the specific audience you are trying to reach.

Across Cultures and Communities

Human nature being what it is, communicating with people from other communities or cultures challenges us to examine our assumptions and think about our usual ways of operating. Analyzing something from (or for) another culture or community may require extra effort at understanding beliefs, assumptions, and practices that we are not familiar with. We need to be careful not to look at things only through our own frames of reference.

Sheikh Jamal Rahman, Pastor Don Mackenzie, and Rabbi Ted Falcon embody this extra effort. In their book, *Getting to the Heart of Interfaith: The Eye-Opening, Hope-Filled Friendship of a Pastor, a Rabbi and a Sheikh*, they have taken on the challenge of working toward interfaith understanding, saying that religion today "seems to be fuelling hatred rather than expanding love" and that in order to heal the divisions between us, we must "find ways of entering into conversation with those different from us." And they say that analysis—what they call "inquiring more deeply"—is essential to their ongoing journey toward understanding issues central to each faith.

All three agree it's critical to discuss the difficult and contentious ideas in faith. For the minister, one "untruth" is that "Christianity is the only way to God." For the rabbi, it is the notion of Jews as "the chosen people." And for the sheikh, it is the "sword verses" in the Koran, like "kill the unbeliever," which when taken out of context cause misunderstanding.

Their book embodies cultural sensitivity and describes the process of creating a text that's respectful of their different faiths. Reading a sentence that the sheikh had written about the security wall in Israel, the rabbi announced, "If that line is in the book, I'm not in the book." Then they analyzed the sentence, discussing it vigorously, and Sheikh Rahman revised the wording to be "respectful of [both] their principles."

Having respect for the principles, values, and beliefs of others means recognizing and respecting differences among cultures. The best way to demonstrate cultural sensitivity is to use precise language that avoids negative descriptions or stereotypes about age, class, gender, religion, race, ethnicity, and such—in short, by carefully selecting the words you use.

Across Genres

Seldom does any piece of writing consist solely of one genre; in many cases, it will contain multiple genres. You might use a short **NARRATIVE** as an introductory element in a process analysis. To **ARGUE A POSITION** on an issue, you'll need to analyze that issue before you can take a stand on it. You sometimes can't compose a **REPORT** until you have analyzed the data or the information that the report is to be based on. And a **REVIEW**—whether it's of a film, a website, a book, or something else—depends on your analysis of the material before you evaluate it.

LOOK FOR analysis in everyday use. Find two consumer-oriented websites that analyze something you're interested in—laptop computers, cell phones, cars, places you might like to go, things you might like to do. Study the analyses and decide which one is more useful, and then try to figure out what makes it better. Is it the language? the images? the amount of detail? the format? How might you change the other one to make it more effective?

CHARACTERISTIC FEATURES

While there are nearly as many different kinds of analysis as there are things to be analyzed, we can identify five common elements that analyses share across disciplines, media, cultures, and communities:

- A question that prompts you to take a closer look
- Some description of the subject you are analyzing
- Evidence drawn from close examination of the subject
- Insight gained from your analysis
- Clear, precise language

A Question That Prompts You to Take a Closer Look

Eric Schlosser poses a question that you've probably never considered: Why do McDonald's fries taste so good? To find the answer, Schlosser had to analyze; see what he came up with on p. 921.

If you look at the examples cited earlier in this chapter, you'll note that each is driven by a question that doesn't have a single "right" answer. Which gaming system best meets your needs? What should you wear? Which college offers the best education for the future you desire? How can we begin to achieve interfaith understanding? Each question requires some kind of analysis. While an author may not explicitly articulate such a question, it will drive the analysis—and the writing based on the analysis. In an essay about how partisan politics are driving opinions of President Obama, see how nationally syndicated columnist David Brooks starts by asking a question:

> Who is Barack Obama?
>
> If you ask a conservative Republican, you are likely to hear that Obama is a skilled politician who campaigned as a centrist but is governing as a big-government liberal. He plays by ruthless, Chicago politics rules. He is arrogant toward foes, condescending toward allies and runs a partisan political machine.
>
> If you ask a liberal Democrat, you are likely to hear that Obama is an inspiring but overly intellectual leader who has trouble making up his mind and fighting for his positions. He has not defined a clear mission. He has allowed the Republicans to dominate debate. He is too quick to compromise and too cerebral to push things through.
>
> You'll notice first that these two viewpoints are diametrically opposed. You'll observe, second, that they are entirely predictable. Political partisans always imagine the other side is ruthlessly effective and that the public would be with them if only their side had better messaging. And finally, you'll notice that both views distort reality. They tell you more about the information cocoons that partisans live in these days than about Obama himself.   —DAVID BROOKS, "Getting Obama Right"

To begin answering his opening question, Brooks offers brief summaries of both partisan opinions on Obama's leadership; then he takes a closer look, giving us a brief analysis of those opinions. You might not always start an analytical essay as Brooks does, by asking an explicit question, but your analysis will always be prompted by a question of some kind.

Some Description of the Subject You Are Analyzing

You need to describe what you are analyzing. How much description you need depends on your subject, your audience, and the medium you've chosen to compose in. For example, if you are analyzing the *Twilight* novels and movies for a class on vampires in film and literature, you can assume that most of your readers will be familiar with them, but you'll need to add extra details for readers who may not have seen or read the specific texts you refer to. If you are writing a paper for a psychology class on the impact of the film on those who are *"Twilight* addicted," however, you will have to describe that impact, as Christine Spines does in a piece written for the *Los Angeles Times* in 2010:

> Chrystal Johnson didn't think there was anything unhealthy about her all-consuming fixation with *The Twilight Saga*—until she discovered it was sucking the life out of her marriage.
>
> "I found poems my husband had written in his journal about how I had fallen for a 'golden-eyed vampire,'" says Johnson, a 31-year-old accountant from Mesa, Arizona, who became so enthralled by the blockbuster series of young adult novels and movies that she found herself staying up all night, re-reading juicy chapters and chatting about casting news and the are-they-or-aren't-they romance between the stars of the films, Kristen Stewart and Robert Pattinson.
>
> "*Twilight* was always on my mind, to the point where I couldn't function," Johnson says.
>
> —CHRISTINE SPINES, "When *Twilight* Fandom Becomes Addiction"

Robert Pattinson as the "golden-eyed vampire."

After this introduction, Spines adds more descriptive detail about the addictive behavior. She cites a professor of communication studies who says that "getting up at 4 a.m." to read or watch movies is "sacrificing marriage . . . [and] sounds like addictive behavior." She also quotes one of the fans who slept for days outside the Nokia Theatre in Los Angeles, just hoping to see the stars at the premiere of *Twilight*: "This is the first time I've been this passionate about anything. . . . I've read each of the books at least eight or nine times and I've watched each of the movies over 300 times."

Spines provides this detail because she is writing for a newspaper whose readers may know little or nothing about her subject and need it described in some detail in order to understand her analysis. Citing an academic expert and someone who has firsthand experience with the behavior gives her credibility. In a similar situation, when you're composing a text that will be read by an audience that you don't know well, you'll also need to provide necessary description and details. If your analysis is going to appear on the internet, you might provide an image or graphic, embed a video, or include a link to a site offering more information on your subject.

Evidence Drawn from Close Examination of the Subject

Examining the subject of your analysis carefully and in detail and then thinking critically about what you find will help you discover key elements, patterns, and relationships in your subject—all of which provide you with the evidence on which to build your analysis. For example, if you are analyzing a poem, you might examine word choice, rhyme scheme, figurative language, repetition, and imagery. If you are analyzing an ad in a magazine, you might look at the placement of figures or objects, the use of color, and the choice of fonts. Each element contributes something significant to the whole; each carries some part of the message being conveyed. Following are discussions and examples of four common kinds of analysis: rhetorical analysis, process analysis, causal analysis, and data analysis.

Rhetorical analysis. This kind of analysis can focus on a written text, a visual text, an audio text, or one that combines words, images, and sound. All of these are rhetorical analyses; that is, they all take a close look at how an author, designer, or artist communicates a message to an audience. Whether they are using words or images, adjusting font sizes or colors, they all are trying to persuade a particular audience to have a particular reaction to a particular message—theirs.

See how the following example from an article in the online magazine *Macworld* analyzes the core of Apple's "exceptional advertising . . . that indefinable element of cool," something that "Dell, Microsoft, and Hewlett-Packard lack":

> Despite their differences, Apple ads have in common at least one major advantage over many competitors' commercials: regardless of whether you love or hate the spots, you'll likely *remember* them, and that's the first step to building a successful image. . . .

Apple's current campaign for the Mac, "Get a Mac," conveys just as simple and straightforward a message as the name would suggest. It's a deliberate attempt to appeal to the vast majority of computer users who, as Apple sees it, are using a Windows machine either because they aren't aware they have an alternative or because they're nursing some erroneous preconceptions about Macs.

The ads, which first began airing in May 2006, feature actors Justin Long and John Hodgman as the Mac and PC, respectively—anthropo-morphized versions of the long-warring computer platforms.

Aside from a brief shot at the end of the spots, you won't see any actual computers in the "Get a Mac" ads. And there's a good reason for that—computer features are hard to show off in a small space in 30-second segments. Instead, Apple illustrates features by putting the characters into humorous situations. For example, when the PC sports a leg cast due to someone tripping over his power cord, it gives the Mac a chance to bring up the detachable MagSafe adapter.

The result: The ad spells out the Mac's advantages in a way that's both accessible and memorable for the average user. . . .

Because of the "Get a Mac" campaign's reliance on dialogue, Apple has also localized them for other markets. Both the U.K. and Japan now have their own version of the "Get a Mac" ads, with native actors and situations tuned to the nuances of those cultures. It's all part of the at-tention to detail that Apple knows it needs in order to compete globally.
—DAN MOREN, "Analysis: The Many Faces of Apple Advertising"

In the rest of his article, Moren takes us methodically through the ad cam-paigns for other Apple products to provide more evidence for his opening claim that Apple's ads are inherently memorable. And because this article was written for an online publication, he can use multiple media to demon-strate his points. He includes hyperlinks to the online ads, so we can actu-ally listen to the dialogue and see for ourselves that round-faced, balding, pudgy PC is a bit stodgy, dressed in a brown blazer and slacks with white shirt and tie, while lean, shaggy-haired Mac is quintessentially cool, in jeans and a casual shirt, hands tucked into his pockets. Moren also points out an example of how using actors allows for a humorous demonstration of an appealing gadget that's available with a Mac: "When the PC sports a leg cast due to someone tripping over his power cord, it gives the Mac a chance to bring up the detachable MagSafe adapter."

John Hodgman and Justin Long as PC and Mac in Apple's "Get a Mac" campaign.

Note how the author moves from a broad statement—"Apple ads have in common at least one major advantage over many competitors' commercials: regardless of whether you love or hate the spots, you'll likely *remember* them, and that's the first step to building a successful image"—to the supporting evidence, discovered by looking closely at the ads and identifying their essential components and the way each one contributes to make the ads "one of the best campaigns of all time."

To see the ads, go to wwnorton.com/write/everyonelinks and check out the "'Get a Mac' Collection" link.

Process analysis. The following example analyzes a process—how skaters make high-speed turns. This is the most critical element in speed skating, for being able to consistently make fast turns without slipping and losing ground can be the difference between winning and losing. This analysis from *Science Buddies,* a website for students and parents, closely examines the key steps of the process. Note how the author provides some information about the basic physics of speed and turns and then systematically explains how each element of the action—speed, angle, push back force from the surface—contributes to the total turn.

Check out the link to the entire piece at wwnorton.com/write/everyonelinks.

Whether it's ice, wood, or a paved surface, the science that governs a skater's ability to turn is essentially the same. It's based on a couple of basic laws of physics that describe speed and the circular motion of turns. The first is Newton's *law of inertia* that says a body in motion will stay in motion unless there is some outside force that changes it. To skaters hoping to make a turn after they speed down the straightaway, that means the force of inertia would tend to keep them going straight ahead if there wasn't a greater force to make them change direction and begin turning.

The force that causes the change in direction comes from the skater's blades or wheels as they cross over at an angle in front of the skater leaning to make a turn. Newton's *law of reaction* explains that the push from the skater's skates generates an equal but opposite push back from the ice or floor. This push back force draws the skater in towards the track and is described as a "center seeking" or *centripetal* type of force. It's the reason why turns are possible in any sport. The wheels of a bicycle, for example, also angle into the road surface when the cyclist leans to begin a turn. As the road pushes back on both bike and rider, it supplies the inward centripetal force to generate the turning motion.

The more a skater leans into a turn, the more powerful the push from the skate, and the greater centripetal force produced to carry the skater

Lee Jung-su, Lee Ho-suk, and Apolo Anton Ohno skate for the finish line during the last turn of the men's 1,000-meter short track speed skating finals at the Vancouver 2010 Winter Olympics.

through the turn. Leaning in also creates a smaller arc, or tighter turn, making for a shorter distance and a faster path around the turn. However, there's a catch. As the skater leans more and more into the track, the balancing point of the body, or the skater's *center of gravity*, also shifts more and more to the side. If it shifts too far, the skater no longer can maintain balance and ends up splayed out onto the rink rather than happily heading round the turn to the finishing line.

So success in turns, especially fast ones, means skaters must constantly find their center of gravity while teetering on the edge of their skates. To make the turn at all requires that the skater push the skates against the ice with sufficient power to generate enough inward centripetal force to counter the inertia of skating straight ahead. And to keep up speed in a race, a skater must calculate and execute the shortest, or tightest, turns possible around the track.

—DARLENE JENKINS, "Tightening the Turns in Speed Skating:
Lessons in Centripetal Force and Balance"

This kind of close examination of the subject is the heart of analysis. Darlene Jenkins explains the key elements in the process of making a high-speed turn—speed, angle, push back force—and also examines the relationships among these elements as she describes what happens in minute detail, revealing how they all combine to create the pattern of movement that leads to a successful high-speed turn. By including a photograph that shows skaters leaning into a turn, blades and bodies angled precariously, Jenkins emphasizes visually what her words convey, and readers actually see what she's describing.

Causal analysis. You'll often have occasion to analyze causes, to figure out why something occurs or once occurred. Why did the U.S. financial system almost collapse in 2008? What caused the 2011 NBA lockout?

Behavioral ecologist Karen McComb, who studies communication between animals and humans, wanted to understand why cat owners so often respond to purring cats by feeding them. To answer the question of what the cats do to solicit food this way, McComb and a team recorded a number of domestic cats in their homes and discovered what the team termed "solicitation purring"—an urgent high-frequency sound, similar to an infant's cry, that is embedded within the cats' more pleasing and low-pitched purring and that apparently triggered an innate nurturing response in their owners. In an article presenting their findings, the team provided numerical data about the pitch and frequency of different kinds of purring, along with their conclusion about what the data showed: that the similarities in pitch and frequency to the cries of human infants "make them very difficult to ignore."

Using data like these to support an analysis would be common in science classes, while in the humanities and social sciences, you're more likely to write about causes that are plausible or probable than ones that can be measured. In a literature class, for example, you might be asked to analyze the influences that shaped F. Scott Fitzgerald's creation of Jay Gatsby in *The Great Gatsby*—that is, to try to explain what caused Fitzgerald to develop Gatsby the way he did. In a sociology class, you might be asked to analyze what factors contributed to a population decline in a certain neighborhood. In both cases, these causes are probabilities—plausible but not provable.

Go to wwnorton. com/write/ everyonelinks to link to the full article, "The Cry Embedded within the Purr."

Data analysis. Some subjects will require you to analyze data, as in the example below, in which blogger Will Moller analyzes the performances of ten major league baseball pitchers to answer the question of whether New York Yankees pitcher Andy Pettitte is likely to get into baseball's Hall of Fame.

> I prefer to look at Andy versus his peers, because simply put, it would be very odd for 10 pitchers from the same decade to get in (though this number is rather arbitrary). Along that line, who are the best pitchers of Andy's generation, so we can compare them? . . .

	Wins	Win%	WAR	ERA+	IP	K	K/BB	WAR/9IP
Martinez	219	**68.7%**	89.4	154	2827	3154	4.15	0.28
Clemens	354	65.8%	**145.5**	143	4917	4672	2.96	0.27
Johnson	303	**64.6%**	114.8	136	4135	**4875**	3.26	0.25
Schilling	216	59.7%	86.1	128	3261	3116	**4.38**	0.24
Maddux	**355**	61.0%	120.6	132	5008	3371	3.37	0.22
Mussina	270	63.8%	85.6	123	3563	2813	3.58	0.22
Smoltz	213	57.9%	82.5	125	3473	3084	3.05	0.21
Brown	211	59.4%	77.2	127	3256	2397	2.66	0.21
Pettitte	240	63.5%	66.9	117	3055	2251	2.34	0.20
Glavine	305	60.0%	67.1	118	4413	2607	1.74	*0.14*

	Postseason Wins	Postseason Losses	Saves
Martinez	6	4	
Clemens	12	8	
Johnson	7	9	
Schilling	11	2	
Maddux	11	14	
Mussina	7	8	
Smoltz	15	4	158
Brown	5	5	
Pettitte	19	10	
Glavine	14	16	

The above table tells the story pretty well. I've bolded the numbers that are particularly absurd, and italicized one in particular which should act as a veto. Though I imagine most of the readers of this blog know full well what these statistics mean at this point, for those of you who don't, a primer:

WAR stands for Wins Above Replacement, and is a somewhat complicated equation which estimates the true value of a pitcher, taking into account league, ERA, park effects, etc. For instance, a pitcher that wins a game but gives up 15 earned runs has probably lost value in their career WAR, even though they get the shiny addition to their win-loss record. We like WAR around these parts.

ERA+ is a normalized version of ERA centered on 100, basically showing how much better or worse a pitcher was compared to their

Andy Pettitte pitching against the Kansas City Royals in April 2009.

league average (by ERA). 110, for example, would indicate that the pitcher's ERA was 10% better than average. 95, on the other hand, would be roughly 5% worse than average. This is a good statistic for comparing pitchers between different time periods—a 4.00 ERA in 2000 doesn't mean the same thing as a 4.00 ERA in 1920, for example.

K/BB is how many strikeouts a pitcher had per walk. More is better, less is worse.

As you can see, the above table doesn't do Andy any favors. He's 6th in wins and 5th in winning percentage, but he's 9th in ERA+ and dead last in WAR. His K/BB beats only Tom Glavine, who comes off looking pretty bad on this list. The only thing he has going for him is his playoff record—and frankly, the team he was on won a whole bunch of playoff games while he was on the team, even when he wasn't pitching. Besides, we're pretty much past the point of taking W/L record as a good indication of pitcher skill—why is it that when we slap the word "postseason" onto the statistic, we suddenly devolve 10 years to when such things seemed to matter?   —WILL MOLLER, "A Painful Posting"

Link to Moller's entire piece at wwnorton.com/ write/everyonelinks.

Moller's guiding question, "Should Andy Pettitte be in the Hall of Fame?" is unstated in this excerpt, but it is made clear earlier in the piece. He presents the data in a table for readers to see—and then walks us through his analysis of that data. It's critical when using numerical data like these not only to present the information but also to say what it means. That's a key part of your analysis. Using a table to present data is a good way to include numerical evidence, but be careful that you don't just drop the table in; you need to explain to readers what the data mean, as Moller does. Though he does not state his conclusions explicitly here, his analysis makes clear what he thinks—as does his URL: http://itsaboutthemoney .net/archives/2011/02/04/sorry-andy/. Just as Moller defines abbreviations some readers may not know, you should be careful to explain anything that your audience might not understand.

Insight Gained from Your Analysis

Like all rhetorical acts, analysis has a purpose. One key purpose is to give your audience insight into what you are analyzing. As you examine your subject, you come up with facts, data, and other specific information drawn from the subject—which will lead you to some insight, a deeper understanding of the subject you're analyzing. The insight that you gain will lead you to your thesis. When the "interfaith amigos" mentioned earlier in this chapter analyzed a sentence in their book that offended the rabbi, each gained insight into the others' principles that led them to further understanding. In "Getting Obama Right," these concluding lines make clear the insight David Brooks derived from analyzing the perceptions of Obama expressed by both liberal Democrats and conservative Republicans:

> In a sensible country, people would see Obama as a president trying to define a modern brand of moderate progressivism. In a sensible country, Obama would be able to clearly define this project without fear of offending the people he needs to get legislation passed. But we don't live in that country. We live in a country in which many people live in information cocoons in which they only talk to members of their own party and read blogs of their own sect. They come away with perceptions fundamentally at odds with reality, fundamentally misunderstanding the man in the Oval Office.   —DAVID BROOKS, "Getting Obama Right"

From Brooks' insight that both Republicans and Democrats are misreading the facts and presenting a biased view, we get his message: Such misperception is counterproductive to effective government.

Summarizing the study of the way cats manipulate humans noted earlier in this chapter, Karen McComb and her team note parallels between the isolation cry of domestic cats and the distress cry of human infants as a way of understanding why the "cry embedded within the purr" is so successful in motivating owners to feed their cats. They conclude that the cats have learned to communicate their need for attention in ways that are impossible to ignore, ways that prompt caring responses from people. Thus, their work suggests that much can be learned by focusing on animal-human communication from both directions, from animals to humans as well as the reverse.

Remember that any analysis you do needs to have a purpose. In an analysis, your purpose—to discover how cats motivate their owners to provide food on demand, to understand how partisan misperceptions create roadblocks in government, to explain why a favorite baseball player's statistics won't get him into the Hall of Fame—needs to generate a clear point that you make for your audience; in most cases, that point will be the insight you gain from the analysis.

Clear, Precise Language

Since the point of an analysis is to help an audience understand something, you need to pay extra attention to the words you use and the way you explain your findings. You want your audience to follow your analysis easily and not get sidetracked. In presenting your findings, you need to demonstrate that you know what you are talking about. You have studied your subject, looked at it closely, thought about it—*analyzed* it; therefore, you know it well, but most important, you know what you want to say about it and why. Now you have to craft your analysis in such a way that your audience will follow that analysis and understand what it shows.

Analyzing the elements in a text or explaining an intricate process requires you to use precise language that your audience will understand, to describe anything that may be unfamiliar to them, to define terms they may not be familiar with, and to lay out the exact steps in a process.

The analysis of speed skating turns earlier in this chapter was written for an audience of young people and their parents who are interested

In his report on the geopolitics of *Google Maps*, John Gravois makes a careful, precise analysis of *Google*'s policies and the complex issues involved. See how he did it on p. 793.

in science and creating projects for science fairs. The language used to describe the physics that govern the process of turning is appropriate for such an audience—specific and precise but not technical. When the author refers to Newton's law of inertia, she immediately defines *inertia* and then explains what it means for skaters. The important role of centripetal force is explained as "the more a skater leans into turns, the more powerful the push from the skate." Everything is clear because the writer uses simple, everyday words—"tighter turn," "teetering on the edge of their skates"—to convey complex science in a way that is concrete and to the point.

Look also at the analysis of baseball statistics presented earlier in this chapter. Even though it was written for a blog targeting Yankees fans, the author includes a "primer" for those readers who may not understand the kinds of statistics he presents.

You need to consider what your audience knows about your topic and what information you'll need to include to be sure they'll understand what you write. You'll also want to be careful about how you present information. In U.S. academic writing, you are expected to state your conclusions explicitly—in clear, specific language.

WRITING ANALYTICALLY / An Annotated Example

ROBERT CONNORS (1951–2000), rhetoric and composition scholar at the University of New Hampshire, wrote this essay about his encounter with a trapped wild animal for *Yankee* magazine in 1991. It's a deceptively simple account of the process he uses to free the animal—but look closer, and you'll see how Connors skillfully weaves his analysis of the process he used to free the skunk into the narrative account of the event. Look for the characteristic features of analysis; they're all here—question, description, explicit evidence drawn from close examination of the subject, insight, and precise language.

How in the World Do You Get a Skunk Out of a Bottle?

ROBERT J. CONNORS

The question that prompts the author to "take a closer look"—and invites the audience to do the same.

THE SANDY DIRT OF CANTERBURY ROAD is just right as I pant my way past Johnson's hayfield. The air cool enough for delight but not cold enough for long johns and stocking cap, the early sun slanting low. No sound but my labored breathing and the chunking noise of sneakers on dirt. Just another morning. Or so I think.

Specific sensory details, combined with the twist in the last sentence, engage readers' interest.

Then I see him, off to my right. Twenty-five feet or so from the road in a cut-over hayfield. A skunk. One of the kind that are mostly white, with the black mainly on their sides. From the cor-

"Then I see him, off to my right. Twenty-five feet or so from the road in a cut-over hayfield. A skunk. One of the kind that are mostly white, with the black mainly on their sides."

ner of my eye I watch him turn, move. I detour to the other side of the road.

But something seems wrong, in the way he moves or the way that he looks. Some glint of strangeness. I slow my pace, looking over my right shoulder. The skunk moves through the stubble toward the road. I stop and shade my eyes against the low sunlight. The skunk comes closer. And then I see it.

A glass jar. About 4½ inches long, about 3 inches in diameter, with a pinched-in neck—a large baby-food jar, perhaps. It is jammed over the skunk's head, completely covering it past the ears. Unable to hear or smell, the skunk raises his head in a clumsy, unnatural way. His dim eyes catch sight of my bright purple warm-up jacket. He begins, slowly but unmistakably, to come toward me.

As you probably know, this is not what skunks or any wild animals typically do. But as I stand on the bright, hard-packed road, this skunk is clearly coming toward me. More, I can't help but feel that he is coming *to* me.

I begin to talk to him. Only later does it occur to me that he is

The first four paragraphs provide the detail readers need to understand the process analysis that follows.

Clear, precise language: We see the skunk moving in "a clumsy, unnatural way" as his "dim eyes" catch the "bright purple" of the author's jacket.

This paragraph begins the systematic analysis of the situation, taking us through the encounter step-by-step.

probably unable to hear anything with the jar on his head, but the talk is more for my sake anyway.

"Oh, boy," I say, as the skunk trundles closer, "if you aren't a textbook case in conservation ethics, I've never seen one." I back away a step. What if he's rabid? He lifts his head, feebly, to the right, to the left. I can see the long white silky hairs of his back, the fogged translucence of the glass jar.

Here the author signals that this analysis is about more than just how to get a skunk out of a bottle.

I have a sudden desire to turn, go, keep running, get home.

By this time, the skunk has reached the high grass at the edge of the road. And there he stops. His sides heave; the tight neck of the jar can hardly admit any air, and each breath is a struggle of seven or eight seconds' duration. The skunk is shivering as well, slight tremors running through his whole body as he crouches, watching me. Clearly, the skunk is going to die and not of starvation. He is suffocating as I watch.

Narrative details show us what was happening.

"What do you want me to do?" I say. "You've got to come to me. I can't come to you. Who knows what mental state you're in?" The skunk looks at me. "Look, I'd love to help you. But the covered end of you isn't the end I'm worried about." The skunk wags his head slightly, tries to breathe. "What were you looking for in there anyway, you dumb-head? That jar's been out here empty for years."

By now I realize that the skunk is my responsibility. The police would probably kill him in order to save him. Getting someone from Fish and Game would take hours. I am the one here, now.

This sentence marks the point in the analysis where the author starts to have insight into the larger significance of the situation.

Maybe I can throw a big rock and break the jar. Not get close enough to be sprayed, but break the glass. Let the skunk breathe.

No. Any rock heavy enough to break the glass from a distance couldn't be thrown accurately. It might hit the skunk and injure him. Even if the glass broke, the edges might slash the skunk's face or get into his eyes. And with that kind of jar, the neck might not break with the bottle part, leaving the skunk with a jagged necklace of razor-edged glass that would sooner or later kill him. No, the rock idea is out.

Perhaps I can find something to throw over him—a coat or a blanket so he can't spray me—and grab the jar. But all I have is this warm-up jacket—too small to cover him and too light to keep him from turning.

"I don't know, old skunkoid," I say, moving slightly closer to where he sits, motionless except for the shivering. "There's no way that I'm just going to go over to you and pull that jar off." One step closer. I have no idea what I *am* going to do. Hunkering down, I keep on talking. "You understand my position. I have to go teach today. If you spray me, you will seriously undercut my efficiency." He is still not moving. Stand up, move one step closer. Squat down again.

"I'm not going to hurt you. I present no threat. I'm scared to death of you and you probably are of me." Stand up, one step closer, squat down.

I can see the bloody scratches along the skunk's neck where he tried with claws to free himself from the jar. I keep on talking, just to make noise, piling nonsense on nonsense.

Stand, step, squat, and I am three feet from the skunk. He regards me. Deep breath. Then, very slowly, I reach out with my right hand. "Don't worry now, bubba. I'm not here to hurt you. This jar is the problem." Slowly, slowly, reaching, the skunk still quiet, then *got it!* My hand clamps down on the warm rigidity of the jar.

Suddenly the skunk, until now motionless, is galvanized. He pulls back in panic, his paws scrabbling at the grass, at my hand. I pull hard on the jar. Now it will come off and he will run away. One way or another, this is it.

But this is not it. Pulling hard, I find I am dragging the skunk, who pushes frantically backward, onto the dirt road. His head is *impacted* into the jar. It will not come out.

"Oh, boy, come *on*." The skunk is now completely in the road, struggling furiously to get away, twisting and turning, as I hold the jar tight. The one good thing at this point is that he is so completely wedged that he can't turn and fire, although there is little doubt that he regrets this keenly. As long as I have his head, I'm safe. I pull again and am only able to drag the skunk farther. "Oh, *great*. Now I get to take you home." He grunts audibly, pulls again, scrabbling up packed dirt.

There's nothing for it. I have to grab him with one hand and try to pull the jar off with the other. With my left hand, I grasp him around the shoulder blades. His hair is soft. He would be nice to stroke. "Come on come on come on. . . ." I twist the jar hard to the left, and his head inside assumes a crazy angle, but he stops struggling. I pull hard on the jar. It does not move. "Come on, you . . . ." The jar is *really* socked onto his neck, which has swollen in some way. Grabbing hard at his shoulder blades, I twist and pull harder.

I am exerting all my strength now. And I see the threads of the jar turn, slowly, then more quickly. "Okay, something moving, heads up," then more movement, an upward sliding, and then with an audible *pop* the jar is off.

Without any thought except *escape*, I jump up, whirl, run. Unscathed. Unsprayed. At a safe distance, I stop and look back. The skunk stands in the middle of the road. He breathes deeply, several times, shakes himself from stem to stern, takes a few tottering steps across the road.

On the other side, he halts, then turns to look at me. I look back. For perhaps 30 seconds, we regard each other with great benignity. Then I hold up my index finger in a tutorial fashion.

"Next time you see me," I say, "don't spray me." He watches me gravely a moment more, then turns and plods off into a cemetery across the road.

There is something in my hand. An empty jar. Starting to run up the long hill to Main Street, I pitch it as hard as I can, sidearm, way out into a swamp. I hear it splash as I run up the hill into a sunny morning whose colors are joy, joy, joy.

Instead of running away from the skunk, the author runs into the morning with a joy that gives readers insight into why this encounter between a man and a skunk matters—to him and to all of us.

FIND a short analytical article in a newspaper or magazine or on a website. Look at the list of five characteristic features of analysis on p. 141 and, using the Connors essay as a model, annotate the article to point out these features. Then evaluate how successful the article's analysis is. For example, can you identify the question that drove the analysis? Has the author provided enough description for you to follow the analysis? Is the language clear and precise? Has the author clearly stated the insight the analysis led to? Does he or she provide evidence to support that insight?

WRITING ANALYTICALLY / A Roadmap

Find a topic that matters—to you, and to others

Whether you can choose your topic or have to respond to a specific assignment, make the project interesting—to you and your audience. Find an angle that appeals to your interests, that engages you. No audience will want to hear about something you are not interested in writing.

If you can choose your topic, begin by considering your own interests. What do you like to do? What issues catch your interest? What do you value? If you value courage, you might want to analyze how a particular literary character manifests that trait: Is Harry Potter courageous when he repeatedly confronts Voldemort alone, or is he foolhardy? An interest in sports could lead you to analyze statistical data on a favorite athlete (as Will Moller does) or to analyze the process of doing something in a particular sport (as Darlene Jenkins does). Concern about climate change could lead you to analyze the costs and benefits of alternative energy sources. Whatever your interests, you'll be sure to find some way of conducting rhetorical, process, causal, or data analysis.

If you've been assigned a topic, say to analyze the Gettysburg Address, you might consider the way President Lincoln appealed to his audience. To make the analysis more interesting, you might imagine that Lincoln was giving this speech to an audience of college students today. What advice would you give him about revising in order to reach such an audience? Or perhaps you've been assigned to analyze a physical process—the process of sleeping, for example. You might examine your own sleep habits and see how they compare with the norm for your age group.

Make your topic matter to your audience. Some topics matter to everyone, or nearly everyone; you might be able to identify such topics by checking the media for what's being debated and discussed. But when you're writing about something that may not automatically appeal to a wide audience, it's your responsibility as the writer to make the topic matter to them. Think about Robert Connors' essay on the skunk—not an inherently interesting topic or one that matters widely—but he involves us by showing how he came to care and by analyzing the situation in a way that engages our interest and makes us care, too.

Consider your rhetorical situation

Keep in mind the elements of your particular situation—your audience, your specific purpose, your stance, and so on—and how they will or should influence the choices you make in your writing.

Identify your AUDIENCE. Who do you want to reach, and how can you shape your analysis so that you get through to them? Karen McComb's analysis of cats purring was for an audience of scientific peers, whereas Robert Connors wrote his piece for *Yankee*, a New England "lifestyle" magazine with articles on travel, home, and food. Very different audiences, very different purposes, very different analyses. In each case, the author could target a specific audience.

However, if you are writing for the web, you will likely reach a broader audience than either of these, and one whose characteristics you can't predict, so you need to keep in mind what additional information you might need to provide—just as Will Moller does in his blog about Andy Pettitte. Even though his primary audience is Yankees fans, he knows that many of them won't know much about statistics, so he provides the definitions they need to understand his analysis. To identify your target audience, you might consider the following questions:

- Who are you trying to reach? And what do you know about them—their age, gender, cultural and linguistic background? Anything else?

- What are they likely to know about your subject, and what background information will you need to provide?

- How will they benefit from the analysis and insight you hope to offer?

- Will your subject matter to them—and if not, how can you make them care about it?

Keeping your likely audience firmly in mind will help you craft an analysis that connects with them.

Articulate your PURPOSE. In all likelihood, you won't be the first or only one to write on your topic, so one broad purpose for writing will be to add your voice to a larger conversation. Following are some questions that can help you narrow your focus and articulate more specific purposes:

- What are you analyzing? A text? A process? Causes? Data?

- What has motivated you to write? Are you responding to some other text or author?

- What do you want to accomplish by analyzing this subject? How can you best achieve your goals?

- What do you want your audience to take away from your analysis?

Think about your STANCE. What is your attitude toward the subject, and how do you want to come across as an author? Objective? Passionate? Something else? How can your writing reflect that stance? If your subject is surfing and you're writing on a surfers' blog about how to catch a wave, for an audience of beginners, your stance might be that of an experienced surfer, or a former beginner. Your language would probably be informal, with little or no surfing jargon. If, on the other hand, you're writing an article for *Surfing Magazine* analyzing the process Laird Hamilton developed to ride fifty-foot waves, your stance might be that of an objective reporter, and your language would need to be more technical for that well-informed audience. No matter what your stance or target audience, you need to consider what kind of language is appropriate, what terms need to be defined, and how you can establish your authority as an author.

Consider the larger CONTEXT. If you are analyzing an ad for a composition class, you will want to look at relevant information about the original context. When was the ad created, and who was the target audience? What were the social, economic, and political conditions at the time? All of that is contextual information. If you are preparing a load analysis for an engineering class, you'll need to consider such factors as how, when, and where the structure will be used. Much of the contextual information comes from what others have said about your subject, and your analysis adds to the conversation.

Consider MEDIA. Will your analysis be delivered in print? on a website? in an oral presentation? Are you writing for the opinion pages in your campus newspaper? Or are you assigned to give an oral presentation incorporating audio and images? If you get to choose your medium, the choice should depend on how you can best present your subject and achieve your purpose with your intended audience. Whether you have a choice or not, the media you use will affect how you organize and design your analysis.

Consider matters of DESIGN. Think about how to best present your information and whether you need to follow any disciplinary conventions. Does your information include data that is easiest to understand in a chart or graph? Would headings help readers follow your analysis? Does your subject require illustrations? What fonts are most appropriate for your subject, your medium, and your audience? Like all of your other writing choices, the design decisions you make can help you achieve your goals.

Analyze your subject

What kind of analysis is needed for your subject and purpose? You may be assigned to conduct a certain kind of analysis, or you may be inspired by a question, as Will Moller was in analyzing data to determine whether Andy Pettitte is likely to be elected to the Hall of Fame. But sometimes you may be asked simply to "analyze x"—an ad, a game, a historical event, several hedge funds—and then you'll need to determine what kind of analysis you'll do. The kind of analysis you need to do—*rhetorical analysis, process analysis, causal analysis, data analysis*—will determine the way you study your subject.

If you're analyzing rhetoric, you need to look at what the text you're examining says and how it supports its claims.

- What question has led you to analyze this text? What specifically are you looking for?

- What CLAIM is the text making—and how does it support that claim?

- If you're analyzing a written text, what REASONS and EVIDENCE does the author provide for the claim—and do they convince you?

- Does the writer acknowledge or respond to COUNTERARGUMENTS or other opinions? If so, are they presented fairly?

- If you're analyzing a visual text, how does it make its point? Where does your eye go first? What's in the foreground, and what's in the background?

- Are there any words that indicate what the author thinks—or wants you to think?

- How does the author establish **AUTHORITY** to address the topic?

- Does the text appeal to your **EMOTIONS**? If so, how?

If you're analyzing a process, you'll need to decide whether your analysis will be *informational* or *instructional*. An informational analysis tells how something works; an instructional one tells how to do something. Writing about how solar panels convert sunshine to energy would be informational, whereas writing about how to install solar panels would be instructional— and would need to explicitly identify all materials and conditions needed and then tell readers step-by-step exactly how to carry out the process. Once you've determined what kind of process you're analyzing, you might then consider questions like these:

- What question is prompting your analysis?

- If the process is instructional, what materials are needed?

- What are the steps in the process?

- What order do the steps follow?

Some processes follow a set order (throwing a curve ball, parallel parking a car), whereas others have no fixed order (playing sudoku). Remember that whatever the process, you'll need to present the steps in some kind of order.

If you're analyzing causes, you're looking for answers to why something happened. Why, for instance, did the Penn State University Board of Trustees fire legendary football coach Joe Paterno? Questions about causes can rarely be answered definitively, so if you're writing a causal analysis, you'll usually be **ARGUING** that certain causes are the most plausible or the primary ones, and that other possible causes are secondary or less likely. In addition, although an *immediate cause* may be obvious, less obvious *long-term causes* may also have contributed.

In the Paterno case, the Penn State trustees initially said only that they felt it "was necessary to make a change in leadership." At the time, however, some people speculated that Paterno was being blamed for not having done more in light of the sexual assault accusations about a former coach. Others argued that the immediate cause was damage control, that in light of the accusations the trustees felt they needed to "protect the brand" (football brings in $72 million a year to Penn State). Still others pointed out that Penn State had been trying to get Paterno to retire for many years—perhaps a contributing cause. Months later, the trustees named additional reasons, but the initial speculations serve as a good example of the kind of analysis that goes on when people want to know why something happened.

You also need to keep two other considerations in mind when analyzing causes. First, don't confuse coincidence with causation. That two events—such as a new police-patrol policy in a city and a drop in the crime rate—occurred more or less simultaneously, or even that one event preceded the other, does not prove that one *caused* the other. Second, you need to consider all possible causes and provide evidence to support the ones you identify as most plausible. If the city also experienced an economic boom around the same time that the new policy and the drop in crime began, for example, you would need to show (perhaps using evidence from other cities) that good economic conditions do not usually seem to reduce crime rates.

As the preceding example suggests, you'll often need to do some RE-SEARCH to be sure you understand all the possible causes and whether they are primary or contributing causes, immediate or long-term causes. Here are some questions that can guide your analysis:

- What question is prompting your analysis?

- List all the causes you can think of. Which ones seem like the primary causes? Which seem to be contributing or secondary causes?

- Is there an immediate cause, something that directly set off whatever happened?

- Think about long-term causes, ones that originated long ago but are ultimately responsible for what happened.

- Might any of the causes on your list be merely coincidences?

- Which are the most plausible causes—and why?

- Do you need to do research to help answer any of these questions?

If you're analyzing data, you're trying to identify patterns in information that you or someone else has gathered. The information collected by the U.S.

Census is data. Social scientists might classify that data according to certain criteria, such as numbers of families with children in urban areas, and then analyze those data looking for patterns on which to make claims or predictions about population trends.

In his piece on Andy Pettitte, Will Moller provides readers with numerical data on ten pitchers' performances, data he analyzes to determine whether Pettitte is likely to be nominated to the Hall of Fame. Moller's analysis expressly states his guiding question—"Who are the best pitchers of [Andy Pettitte's] generation, so we can compare them?"—and then answers it by considering each element of the data as it relates to the pitchers' performances.

Although the mathematical nature of some data analysis can often make it more straightforward than other kinds of analysis, identifying statistical patterns and figuring out their significance can be challenging. Here are some questions to consider when analyzing data:

- What question are you trying to answer?

- Are there any existing data that can help you find your answer? If so, will they provide sufficient information, or do you need to find more?

- Is the data up-to-date? trustworthy? Who collected the data, and why?

- Are there other data that tell a different story?

- Do you need to conduct any RESEARCH of your own to generate the data you need?

- Can you identify patterns in the data? If so, are they patterns you expected, or are any of them surprising?

Determine what your analysis shows

Once you've analyzed your subject, you need to figure out what your analysis shows. What was the question that first prompted your analysis, and how can you now answer that question? What have you discovered about your subject? What have you discovered that interests you—and how can you make it matter to your audience? Write out a tentative THESIS, noting what you've analyzed and why, and what conclusions or insights you want to share. Your thesis is your point, the claim you want to make about your subject. Let's say you're writing a rhetorical analysis of the Gettysburg Address. Here's how one author analyzed that speech:

> Following Edward Everett's two-hour oration, President Lincoln spoke eloquently for a mere two minutes, deploying rhetorical devices like repetition, contrast, and rhythm in a way that connected emotionally with his audience.

This sentence tells us that the writer will describe the event, say something about the length of the speech, and explain how specific words and structures resulted in an eloquently simple but profoundly moving speech.

As you formulate your thesis, begin by stating it several different ways and then look for the one that is most interesting to you. Think about your audience and how you can make your analysis most compelling to them. Then list the evidence you found that supports your analysis—examples, quotations, quantitative or qualitative data, and so forth. Which ones will be most persuasive to your audience? Consider other analytical perspectives and how you can account for them. Do you have everything you need, or do you need to do any further research?

Organize and start writing

Once you've carried out your analysis, it's time to start drafting.

Type out your tentative THESIS, and keep checking back to be sure that you are supporting it as you draft.

Give EVIDENCE that supports your thesis. The kind of evidence will depend on the kind of analysis—examples, statistics, and other data taken from the subject itself as well as from other sources you've consulted.

Cite other sources, but remember that this is *your* analysis. Your audience wants to hear your voice and learn from your insights. At the same time, don't forget to acknowledge other perspectives.

Draft an OPENING. You might begin by describing *what* you're analyzing and *why*, explaining what question prompted you to take a closer look at your topic. Provide any background information your audience might need. State your thesis: What are you claiming about your subject?

Draft a **CONCLUSION**. You might end by reiterating what you've learned from your analysis and what you want your audience to understand about your subject. Make sure they know why your analysis matters, both to them and to you.

Look critically at your draft, get response—and revise

Read your draft slowly and carefully to see whether you've made your guiding question clear, described your subject sufficiently, offered enough evidence to support your analysis, and provided your audience with some insight about your subject.

Then ask some others to read and respond to your draft. If your school has a writing center, try to meet with a tutor, taking along any questions you have. Here are some questions that can help you or others read over a draft of analytic writing:

- *Is the guiding question behind your analysis clear?* Is it a question worth considering?

- *How does the* **OPENING** *capture the audience's interest?* Does it indicate why this analysis matters? How else might you begin?

- *Is the subject described in enough detail for your intended audience?* Is there any other information they might need to follow your analysis?

- *What insights have you gained from the analysis?* Have you stated them explicitly? How likely is it that readers will accept your conclusions?

- *Is the point of your analysis clear?* Have you stated the point explicitly in a **THESIS** —and if not, do you need to?

- *What* **EVIDENCE** *do you provide to support your point?* Is it sufficient?

- *If you've cited any sources, are they credible and convincing?* Have you integrated them smoothly into your text—is it clear what *you* are saying and where (and why) you are citing others? And have you **DOCU-MENTED** any sources you've cited?

- *Have you addressed other perspectives?* Do you need to acknowledge possible **COUNTERARGUMENTS**?

- *How would you describe your* **TONE**, and does it accurately convey your **STANCE**? Is it an appropriate tone for your audience and purpose? If not, how could it be improved?

- *How effectively is the analysis designed?* Have you included any images or other visual data—and if so, how do they contribute to the analysis? If not, is there any information that might be easier to understand if presented in a table or chart or accompanied by an image?

- *How is the analysis organized?* Is it easy to follow, with explicit **TRANSITIONS** from one point to the next? Are there headings—and if not, would they help? If you're analyzing a process, are the steps in an order that your audience will be able to follow easily?

- *Consider style*—is it appropriate for the audience and purpose? Look at the choice of words and kinds of sentences—are they appropriately formal (or informal)? Could the style be improved in any way?

- *How does the draft conclude?* Is the **CONCLUSION** forceful and memorable? How else might the analysis conclude?

- *Consider the title.* Does it make clear what the analysis is about, and will it make your intended audience interested in reading on?

Revise your draft in light of your own observations and any feedback you get from others, keeping your audience and purpose firmly in mind. But remember: *You* are the analyst here, so you need to make the decisions.

REFLECT ON WHAT YOU'VE LEARNED. Once you've completed your analysis, let it settle for a while and then take time to reflect. How well did you analyze your subject? What insights did your analysis lead to? What additional revisions would you make if you could? Research shows that such reflections help "lock in" what you learn for future use.

Mad Men: Stillbirth of the American Dream
HEATHER HAVRILESKY

AMERICANS ARE CONSTANTLY in search of an upgrade. It's a sickness that's infused into our blood, a dissatisfaction with the ordinary that's instilled in us from childhood. Instead of staying connected to the divine beauty and grace of everyday existence—the glimmer of sunshine on the grass, the blessing of a cool breeze on a summer day—we're instructed to hope for much more. Having been told repeated stories about the fairest in the land, the most powerful, the richest, the most heroic (Snow White, Pokémon, Ronald McDonald, Lady Gaga), eventually we buy into these creation myths and concede their overwhelming importance in the universe. Slowly we come to view our own lives as inconsequential, grubby, even intolerable.

Meanwhile, the American dream itself—a house, a job, a car, a family, a little lawn for the kids to frolic on—has expanded into something far broader and less attainable than ever. Crafty insta-celebrities and self-branding geniuses and social media gurus assert that submitting to the daily grind to pay the mortgage constitutes a meager existence. Books like *The 4-Hour Work Week* tell us that working the same job for years is for suckers. We should be paid handsomely for our creative talents, we should have the freedom to travel and

HEATHER HAVRILESKY is the television critic at *Salon*. She wrote this piece for *Salon* in 2010, at the start of a new season of *Mad Men*, a TV series set in a New York advertising agency in the 1960s.

live wherever we like, our children should be exposed to the wonders of the globe at an early age.

In other words, we're always falling short, no matter what our resources, and we pass this discontent to our offspring. And so millions of aspiring 3-year-old princesses hum "Someday my prince will come!" to themselves, turning their backs on the sweetness of the day at hand.

Maybe this is why AMC's hit series *Mad Men* . . . resonates so clearly at this point in history, when the promise of the boom years has given way to two wars, a stubborn recession and a string of calamities that threaten to damage our way of life irreparably. Somehow *Mad Men* captures this ultra-mediated, postmodern moment, underscoring the disconnect between the American dream and reality by distilling our deep-seated frustrations as a nation into painfully palpable vignettes. Even as the former denizens of the Sterling Cooper advertising agency unearth a groundswell of discontent beneath the skin-deep promises of adulthood, they keep struggling to concoct chirpy advertising messages that provide a creepily fantastical backdrop to this modern tragedy. Don (Jon Hamm) sighs deeply and unlocks the door to his lonely apartment, Peggy (Elisabeth Moss) whiles away her waking hours trading casual quips with

Don Draper (Jon Hamm) packages the American dream for mass consumption.

co-workers, but happiness is still just a shiny kitchen floor or a sexy bikini or a cigarette away.

As the American dream is packaged for mass consumption, these isolated   5 characters find themselves unnerved by its costs. Alternating between be-fuddled breadwinner and longing lothario, Don has finally put his ambivalence toward Betty (January Jones) behind him: He's leaving his marriage and focus-ing on the new ad firm as his true passion, just as we saw at the end of the third season. But can someone as conflicted as Don commit wholeheartedly to anything? Not surprisingly, the premiere seems to suggest that Don may not feel comfortable yielding his entire life to his career. And now that he's free to pursue any woman he wants, instead of focusing on a woman whose intellect matches his own (like so many of his lovers, from Midge to Rachel to Abigail the schoolteacher), Don appears likely to be drawn in by the same manipula-tive style of femininity that Betty embodied.

Of course, Roger Sterling (John Slattery) has always provided a sort of an omen of where Don was headed, hence their volatile relationship. Roger also has a somewhat childish habit of falling for anyone who makes him feel pow-erful. First there was Joan (Christina Hendricks), whose standoffish charms sometimes obscure the fact that she's the most adaptive, resilient and person-ally effective character on the show, and next there was Jane (Peyton List), a character who could just as easily be called That Crying Girl, who's developed into more of a high-maintenance daughter to Roger than a real partner.

Roger and Don may represent the wildly fluctuating fortunes bequeathed to the masters of the universe: Told that they can have everything they want, these two are haunted by a constant desire for *more*. But what variety of *more* will suit them this time? The answer typically—and somewhat tragically—seems to spring out of impulse and ego and fear more often than any real self-reflection or wisdom.

Betty represents the female version of this lack of foresight, and as the fourth season develops, the arbitrary nature of her recent decisions starts to become more apparent. Showing her usual startling lack of insight, Betty smoothes over bumps in the road with Henry Francis (Christopher Stanley) while lashing out at her daughter, Sally (Kiernan Shipka). Betty has always had a life that's built around men, but she entirely lacks Joan's wisdom, survival instincts and compassion, and instead tends to resort to the foot-stomping of a petulant child. But what else can you expect from someone whose closest relations—overbearing father, paternal but deceitful husband—have consis-tently rewarded her for quietly, obediently playing along with their games?

Joan Holloway (Christina Hendricks) is the most resilient character on the show.

Having taken the opposite path in life, Peggy represents the victories (and defeats, and insults) of the single career girl. At the start of Season 4, Peggy appears more committed to this path than ever, and she's growing much more resilient and unflappable in the face of her co-workers' personal slights. Nonetheless, we'll surely see many of the fairy tales Peggy has been forced to give up along the way. Likewise, selling a kittenish flavor of femininity and sex while asserting your own power can't be an easy tightrope to walk for Peggy, and it's this uncomfortable spot that makes her one of the show's most riveting characters.

The ambition and conflicted desires of these characters in their pursuit of   10
happiness is what makes *Mad Men* such a singular and resonant reflection of a particularly American puzzle. But even as it strains to capture the transformation of the American dream into a commodity that can be bought and sold, *Mad Men* itself is the ultimate, endlessly marketable über-brand: Everyone and everything is gorgeous to the point of luminosity, a pitch-perfect reflection of the times that's been polished to such a high gloss that it upstages our hazy memories of that era completely. The terse exchanges, the sly banter, even the lighthearted quips dance over the mundane drudgery of workplace interactions like mean-spirited sprites. Bourbon glistens among ice cubes in immaculate glasses, fire engine red lipstick frames heartbreakingly white teeth, fingers tap perkily on typewriters as young men amble by, their slumped shoulders hidden behind the heroic cut of their tailored suits. Don Draper's unmoving cap of hair gleams like a beacon, sending some Morse code straight to female brain stems, stirring long-buried childhood notions about one day having a husband who looks just like a Ken doll.

Behind the impeccable facade, of course, we see the longing in Pete Campbell's (Vincent Kartheiser) tired face, we see the fear in Betty's eyes as she sits down to dinner with her brand-new mother-in-law. The lovely details of this fantasy—the hairstyles, the costumes and the props that come with the dream—occasionally fail to obscure the confused humans who straighten their shoulders and dry their eyes and take the stage day after day, dutifully mouthing lines about the thrills of work and family, all of it the invented, peppy rhetoric of laundry detergent jingles.

This is the genius of *Mad Men,* its dramatic reenactment of the disconnect between the dream of dashing heroes and their beautiful wives, living in style among adorable, adoring children, and the much messier reality of struggling to play a predetermined role without an organic relationship to your surroundings or to yourself. We're drawn to *Mad Men* week after week because each and every episode asks us, *What's missing from this pretty picture?*

What's missing on both a personal and a broader scale is empathy, of course—embodied most gruesomely in the lawn mower accident last season, but also wrapped up in the sharp edicts Don and Betty issue to their children, in the distracted insults Don aims at Peggy, in the self-involved funk of Joan's doctor fiancé, in the cruelty that springs from Pete's existential desperation. While *Mad Men*'s detractors often decry the empty sheen of it all, claiming that it has no soul, clearly that's the point. The American dream itself is a carefully packaged, soulless affair. *This is the automobile a man of your means should drive. This is the liquor a happy homemaker like yourself should serve to your husband's business guests.* As absurd as it seems to cobble together a dream around a handful of consumer goods, that's precisely what the advertising industry did so effectively in the 50s and 60s, until we couldn't distinguish our own desires from the desires ascribed to us by professional manipulators, suggesting antidotes for every real or imagined malady, supplying escapist fantasies to circumvent the supposedly unbearable tedium of ordinary life. In show creator Matthew Weiner's telling, the birth of the advertising age coincides directly with the birth of our discontent as a nation—and what got lost in the hustle was our souls.

Thinking about the Text

1. What is Heather Havrilesky's main insight about *Mad Men*? How can you tell? Point to specific passages that reflect this conclusion.

2. How does Havrilesky establish her **AUTHORITY** to write about this show?

3. How does she appeal to readers' emotions? Identify specific passages where she does so.

4. If you were familiar with *Mad Men* before you read this essay, is this an accurate description of the show and of its impact on viewers? If you weren't familiar with it, do you now understand its basic premise—and has Havrilesky made you want to watch it? Explain.

5. Write an **ANALYSIS** of Havrilesky's own argument about *Mad Men*. What question guides her analysis, what insights does she offer, and what evidence does she provide to support her conclusions?

Advertisements R Us

MELISSA RUBIN

ADVERTISEMENTS ARE WRITTEN to persuade us—to make us want to support a certain cause, buy a particular car, drink a specific kind of soda. But *how* do they do it? How do they persuade us? Since the beginning of modern consumer culture, companies have cleverly tailored advertisements to target specific groups. To do so, they include text and images that reflect and appeal to the ideals, values, and stereotypes held by the consumers they wish to attract. As a result, advertisements reveal a lot about society. We can learn a great deal about the prevailing culture by looking closely at the deliberate ways a company crafts an ad to appeal to particular audiences.

This ad from the August 1950 *Coca-Cola Bottler* magazine, a trade magazine for Coca-Cola bottlers (fig. 1), features a larger-than-life red Coca-Cola vending machine with the slogan "Drink Coca-Cola—Work *Refreshed*" (Coca-Cola). Set against a bright blue sky with puffy white clouds, an overlarge open bottle of Coke hovers just to the right and slightly above the vending machine, next to the head of "Sprite Boy," a pixie-ish character and onetime Coke symbol, who sports a bottle cap for a hat. Sprite Boy's left hand gestures past the floating Coke bottle and toward a crowd congregating before the vending machine. The group, overwhelmingly male and apparently all white, includes blue-collar workers in casual clothing, servicemen in uniform, and

MELISSA RUBIN, an English major at Hofstra University, wrote this analysis using an early draft of this chapter.

Fig. 1. 1950 ad from *Coca-Cola Bottler* magazine (Coca-Cola).

businessmen in suits in the foreground; the few women displayed are in the background, wearing dresses. The setting is industrialized and urban, as indicated by the factory and smokestacks on the far left side of the scene and by the skyscrapers and apartment building on the right.

Practically since its invention, Coca-Cola has been identified with mainstream America. Born from curiosity and experimentation in an Atlanta pharmacy in 1886, Coke's phenomenal growth paralleled America's in the industrial age. Benefiting from developments in technology and transportation, by 1895 it was "sold and consumed in every state and territory in the United States" (Coca-Cola Company). In 2010, Diet Coke became the second-most-popular carbonated drink in the world . . . behind Coca-Cola (Esterl). In the immediate post-war world, Coke became identified with American optimism and energy, thanks in part to the company's wartime declaration that "every man in uniform gets a bottle of Coca-Cola for 5 cents, wherever he is, and whatever it costs the Company" (Coca-Cola Company). To meet this dictate, bottling plants were built overseas with the result that many people other than Americans first tasted Coke during this war that America won so decisively, and when peace finally came, "the foundations were laid for Coca-Cola to do business overseas" (Coca-Cola Company).

Given the context, just a few years after World War II and at the beginning of the Korean War, the setting clearly reflects the idea that Americans experienced increased industrialization and urbanization as a result of World War II. Factories had sprung up across the country to aid in the war effort, and many rural and small-town Americans had moved to industrial areas and large cities in search of work. In this advertisement, the buildings surround the people, symbolizing a sense of community and the way Americans had come together in a successful effort to win the war.

The ad suggests that Coca-Cola recognized the patriotism inspired by the 5 war and wanted to inspire similar positive feelings about their product. In the center of the ad, the huge red vending machine looks like the biggest skyscraper of all—the dominant feature of the urban industrial landscape. On the upper right, the floating face of Coca-Cola's Sprite Boy towers above the scene. A pale character with wild white hair, hypnotic eyes, and a mysterious smile, Sprite Boy stares straight at readers, his left hand gesturing toward the red machine. Sprite Boy's size and placement in the ad makes him appear god-like, as if he, the embodiment of Coca-Cola, is a powerful force uniting—and refreshing—hardworking Americans. The placement of the vending machine in the center of the ad and the wording on it evoke the idea that drinking

Coca-Cola will make a hardworking American feel refreshed while he (and apparently it was rarely she) works and becomes part of a larger community. The text at the bottom of the ad, "A welcome host to workers—*Inviting you to the pause that refreshes with ice-cold Coca-Cola*"—sends the same message to consumers: Coke will refresh and unite working America.

The way that Coca-Cola chooses to place the objects and depict men and women in this ad speaks volumes about American society in the middle of the twentieth century: a white, male-dominated society in which servicemen and veterans were a numerous and prominent presence. The clothing that the men in the foreground wear reflects the assumption that the target demographic for the ad—people who worked in Coca-Cola bottling plants—valued hard workers and servicemen during a time of war. White, uniformed men are placed front and center. One man wears an Army uniform, the one next to him wears a Navy uniform, and the next an Air Force uniform. By placing the servicemen so prominently, Coca-Cola emphasizes their important role in society and underscores the value Americans placed on their veterans at a time when almost all male Americans were subject to the draft and most of them could expect to serve in the military or had already done so. The other men in the foreground—one wearing a blue-collar work uniform and the other formal business attire—are placed on either side of and slightly apart from the soldiers, suggesting that civilian workers played a valuable role in society, but one secondary to that of the military. Placing only a few women dressed in casual day wear in the far background of the image represents the assumption that women played a less important role in society—or at least in the war effort and the workforce, including Coke's.

The conspicuous mixture of stereotypical middle-class and working-class attire is noteworthy because in 1950, the U.S. economy had been marked by years of conflict over labor's unionization efforts and management's opposition to them—often culminating in accommodation between the two sides. The ad seems to suggest that such conflict should be seen as a thing of the past, that men with blue-collar jobs and their bosses are all "workers" whom Coca-Cola, a generous "host," is inviting to share in a break for refreshments. Thus all economic classes, together with a strong military, can unite to build a productive industrial future and a pleasant lifestyle for themselves.

From the perspective of the twenty-first century, this ad is especially interesting because it seems to be looking backward instead of forward in significant ways. By 1950, the highly urban view of American society it presents was starting to be challenged by widespread movement out of central cities to the suburbs, but nothing in the ad hints at this profound change. At the time, offices and factories were still located mostly in urban areas and associated in Americans' minds with cities, and the ad clearly reflects this perspective. In addition, it presents smoke pouring from factory smokestacks in a positive light, with no sign of the environmental damage that such emissions cause, and that would become increasingly clear over the next few decades.

Another important factor to consider: everyone in the ad is white. During the 1950s, there was still a great deal of racial prejudice and segregation in the United States. Coca-Cola was attuned to white society's racial intolerance and chose in this ad to depict what they undoubtedly saw as average Americans, the primary demographic of the audience for this publication: Coca-Cola employees. While Coke did feature African Americans in some ads during the late 1940s and early 1950s, they were celebrity musicians like Louis Armstrong, Duke Ellington, Count Basie, or Graham Jackson (the accordion player who was a huge favorite of Franklin Delano Roosevelt's) or star athletes like Marion Motley and Bill Willis, the first men to break the color barrier in NFL football ("World of Coca-Cola"). The contrast between these extremes underscores the prejudice: "ordinary" people are represented by whites, while only exceptional African Americans appear in the company's ads.

In 1950, then, the kind of diversity that Coke wanted to highlight and appeal 10
to was economic (middle-class and working-class) and war-related (civilian and military). Today, such an ad would probably represent the ethnic diversity missing from the 1950 version, with smiling young people of diverse skin colors and facial features relaxing with Cokes, probably now in cans rather than bottles. But the differences in economic, employment, or military status or in clothing styles that the 1950 ad highlighted would be unlikely to appear, not because they no longer exist, but because advertisers for products popular with a broad spectrum of society no longer consider them a useful way to appeal to consumers.

While initially the ads for Coca-Cola reflected the values of the time, their enormous success eventually meant that Coke ads helped shape the American identity. In them, Americans always appear smiling, relaxed, carefree, united in their quest for well-deserved relaxation and refreshment. They drive convertibles, play sports, dance, and obviously enjoy life. The message: theirs is a life to be envied and emulated, so drink Coca-Cola and live that life yourself.

Works Cited

Coca-Cola. Advertisement. *The Coca-Cola Bottler* 41.6 (1950): n. pag. Web. 5 May 2011.

Coca-Cola Company. "The Coca-Cola Company Heritage Timeline." *Coca-Cola History*. Coca-Cola Company, n.d. Web. 26 June 2011.

Esterl, Mike. "Diet Coke Wins Battle in Cola Wars." *Wall Street Journal*. 17 Mar. 2011: B1. Print.

"The World of Coca-Cola Self-Guided Tour for Teachers. Highlights: African-American History Month." *World of Coca-Cola*. World of Coca-Cola at Pemberton Place, n.d. Web. 26 June 2011.

Thinking about the Text

1. What insight does Melissa Rubin offer about the Coca-Cola ad she analyzes, and what **EVIDENCE** does she provide to support her analysis? Has she persuaded you to accept her conclusions—and if not, why not?

2. How does she incorporate historical context, and what does that information contribute to her analysis?

3. Rubin's analysis is driven by this question: What can we learn about the culture in which a given ad is created by closely examining how that ad appeals to particular audiences? What other questions might you try to answer by analyzing an ad?

4. This Coca-Cola ad reflects the values of its era. Can you think of a contemporary ad that projects the values of the era we live in? How do the two ads compare?

5. Write an **ANALYSIS** of a current ad, looking specifically at how it reflects American values in the twenty-first century. Be sure to include the ad in your essay.

TEN

"Just the Facts, Ma'am"
Reporting Information

MANY AMERICANS ASSOCIATE THE LINE "Just the facts, ma'am" with *Dragnet*, a 1950s TV crime drama that had a profound effect on America's understanding of the police and how they work, and more specifically with Sgt. Joe Friday, played by Jack Webb, who used this expression when interviewing women as part of an investigation. Or so people think. In fact, Sgt. Friday never uttered these exact words. He sometimes said, "All we want are the facts, ma'am" or "All we know are the facts," but the expression "Just the facts, ma'am" actually had its origins in a 1953 comedy routine that parodied the show. In the end, however, this line is linked forever with Sgt. Friday and *Dragnet* in the American popular imagination.

This story can be seen as a kind of very short report, and it demonstrates an important aspect of reports: They present information to audiences made up of individuals with varying degrees of knowledge. Perhaps you've heard the phrase "Just the facts, ma'am" but had no idea where it came from. Perhaps you've never heard of *Dragnet*. Now you have, and you know a few things about it: Jack Webb played Sgt. Friday, and many people (incorrectly) think he often said, "Just the facts, ma'am." Perhaps you were familiar with both the program and the expression. If so, you now likely have a new bit of information: The assumption that the expression came directly from the program is not borne out by fact.

Sgt. Joe Friday (Jack Webb) in *Dragnet*, a TV series that ran in the 1950s.

Thus, this very short report demonstrates how reports are written with a range of readers in mind.

It also reminds us of one of our favorite bumper stickers:

> ## You are entitled to your own opinions—but not your own facts.

Reports serve a documentary function; they are built of information that is factual in some way. As you no doubt realize, separating what is factual from what is opinion can be a challenge, especially when the topic is controversial. Whatever Sgt. Friday may have said, as a police investigator he was trying to establish factual information so that he could write an effective police report, one that would help solve a case and document how he had done so.

In fact, the defining quality of reports is that they present factual information with the primary goal of in some sense educating an audience. The stance of those who write them is generally objective rather than argumentative. Thus, newspaper and television reporters—note the word—in the United States have traditionally tried to present news developments in a neutral way. Writers of lab reports describe as carefully and objectively as they can how they conducted their experiments and what they found. Perhaps to an even greater extent than authors in other genres, therefore, writers of reports aim to create an **ETHOS** of trustworthiness and reliability.

This chapter offers guidelines for composing reports—and also profiles, a kind of report. As you'll see, writing effective reports requires you to pay careful attention to your purpose, audience, and stance as well as to whatever facts you're reporting.

THINK ABOUT REPORTS you've read, heard, seen, or written recently, and make a list of them. Your list may include everything from a lab report you wrote for a biology class, to a documentary film, to a PowerPoint *presentation you and several classmates created for a course. What similarities do these reports share—and in what ways do they differ?*

Across Academic Fields

Reports are found everywhere in academic life. You're certainly familiar with book reports, and you're probably familiar with lab reports from science courses. Students and practitioners in *biology, psychology, engineering,* and most fields in the *physical sciences, social sciences,* and *applied sciences* regularly write reports, generally based on experiments or other kinds of systematic investigation.

These scientific reports share a common format—often labeled IMRAD (introduction, methods, results, and discussion)—and a common purpose: to convey information. The format mirrors the stages of inquiry: You ask a question, describe the materials and methods you used to try to answer it, report what you found, and try to make sense of it in light of what you and others already know. In this regard, these reports are part of ongoing conversations—both actual conversations among those studying a particular topic and conversations across times and places as humans build on the knowledge of earlier generations.

Another kind of report students often write, especially in courses that focus on contemporary society in some way, is the **PROFILE**, a firsthand report on an individual, an event, a group, or an institution. A typical profile might be based on an interview, with an American soldier who fought in Vietnam, for example, or the first female professor to receive tenure in your college's economics department. In a field like marketing, a profile might describe a specific segment of the population representing a potential target market. Similarly, a profile of an institution might report on the congregation of a specific house of worship, an organization, or a company; such reports often have a specific audience in mind, whether it is donors, investors, members, or clients.

Across Media

When reporting information, you'll find that different media offer you radically different resources. Throughout this chapter, we'll refer to reporting by the *New York Times* on the "double-full-full-full," an especially challenging Olympic aerial skiing event involving a triple back flip that requires four body twists. Just before the 2010 Winter Olympics, the *Times* reported on this event in three media. It was the subject of a *news article* that appeared in print and online, "Up in the Air, and Down, with a Twist," by science writer Henry Fountain. It was also the basis of a *video* feature on the *Times'* website illustrating the physics of the flip, "Inside the Action: Aerial Skiing," showing U.S. Olympic skier Ryan St. Onge as he performed this move while Fountain described what St. Onge was doing from the perspective of physics. Finally, it was the focus of part of a science *podcast* featuring interviews with both St. Onge and Fountain. Two of these reports use images, two use spoken words, and one relies primarily on written words.

In studying these three reports, you'll get a clear idea of how medium influences not only how information is reported but also what kinds of information can be covered. (For another example of how much media affects the message, consider *Twitter*: Imagine what Fountain could have reported about the double-full-full-full in 140 characters.)

Some of the information remains the same across media, but at the same time the media influence which aspects of the information that might have been covered are in fact reported. As a writer, you'll want to choose your medium carefully and consider how best to exploit the resources it offers to help you report information clearly.

WATCH THE VIDEO of U.S. Olympic skier Ryan St. Onge performing a double-full-full-full, a triple back flip with four body twists. Then listen to the podcast on the physics of skiing. Pay attention to how some of the technical terms are defined (and keep in mind that in the video, definitions may include images as well as words.) Describe the double-full-full-full using words alone. Then add an image. Do you need to alter your original description once you add the image? Go to wwnorton.com/write/everyonelinks to access the video and podcast.

Across Cultures and Communities

Wherever you find formal organizations, companies, and other institutions, you'll find reports of various kinds. For example, a school board trying to maintain the quality of education in a time of shrinking budgets will surely rely on information in reports written by *parents' organizations, community groups, teachers' unions,* or *outside consultants.* Odds are that the reports from each of these groups would differ in focus and perhaps even tone. Some of these reports might be based primarily on quantitative data while others might feature personal testimonies. Those created by outside consultants would likely be very formal and might include a PowerPoint presentation to the school board followed by a question-and-answer period. In contrast, a report from a parents' group could include a homemade video consisting primarily of conversations with schoolchildren.

As a student, you'll be working in various academic communities, and you will need to pay attention to the way information is reported across disciplines—and to the expectations they have for any reports that you write.

Across Genres

While reports are a common genre of writing, you'll also have occasion to report information in other genres. **NARRATIVES**, **ANALYSES**, **REVIEWS**, **ARGUMENTS**, and many other genres contain factual information often presented as neutrally as possible—and you will often report factual evidence to support your claims.

On the other hand, some documents that are called reports present more than "just the facts" and cross the line to analyze or interpret the information presented, to make a **PROPOSAL**, and so on. For example, a report on economic development in Austin, Texas, concludes with recommendations for the future. Those recommendations follow pages and pages of careful reporting (as well as considerable analysis of the reported information). And in a report written for a college writing class about three roommates in her dorm, the author moves beyond merely reporting to analyzing and even evaluating their situation. As these examples illustrate, when you're assigned to write a report, you will want to determine exactly what the person who assigned it has in mind: text that only reports information or one that is called a report but requires you to analyze the information, make some kind of argument, and so on.

Sometimes the genre itself becomes part of the story. The humor of the *Onion* article on p. 881 is that such trivial information could even be reported.

ANALYZE THE PURPOSES of the reports that you made on p. 184. Who is the intended audience for each? To what degree does each simply report information, and to what degree does it use information to serve some larger goal, for example, to take a position on an issue? Can you distinguish clearly between "factual" information and the information used to argue a point?

CHARACTERISTIC FEATURES

While you can expect differences across media and disciplines, most of the reports you will write share the following characteristics:

- A topic carefully focused for a specific audience
- Definitions of key terms
- Trustworthy information
- Appropriate organization and design
- A confident, informative tone

A Topic Carefully Focused for a Specific Audience

The most effective reports have a focus, a single topic that is limited in scope by what the audience already knows and what the author's purpose is. For example, in 2008, Liveable City, a nonprofit organization that works to protect the quality of life in Austin, Texas, released a report on economic development in Austin. Liveable City's website offers this summary of the report's content and structure:

> [T]he report [looks at] where Austin's economic development strategy comes from, how it is implemented, and what institutions shape our economic development policies and programs. Focusing on tax incentives and how they fit into broader economic development activities, the study examines why incentives are used, how much the city is giving, and what the taxpayers are getting from the public investment. The study also identifies reforms needed to create a unified, sustainable economic strategy, embraced by the community, to better position Austin for future economic challenges and opportunities.
>
> —MICHAEL ODEN, "Building a More Sustainable Economy"

The title page of Michael Oden's report includes three images that capture the essence of his plan for the city of Austin: green industries, transportation, and arts and culture.

Notice how the report's author, Michael Oden, a local professor of urban planning, focuses and limits the topic of his report, examining broader issues of economic development strategies and tax incentives and then three related topics: "why incentives are used, how much the city is giving, and what the taxpayers are getting." In addition to informing readers about how the present policies came to be, this report also looks forward to the future, a common feature of reports that focus on an issue.

Oden assumes that he is writing for people who care about Austin (notice that he refers to "our" policies and programs). His intended readers would have included members of the board of Liveable City as well as individual and corporate donors. Because such reports are often cited in news stories and opinion pieces in the local media, we can assume that the intended readers also included Austinites more broadly. But Oden is also writing for audiences beyond Austin, especially those interested in how tax incentives fit into "broader economic development activities." Although the report was distributed as a print document, likely to selected local members of the intended audience, it is available to anyone with internet access.

In their twelve-page 2008 annual report for Proud Ground, a nonprofit group that seeks to provide affordable housing for first-time home buyers in Portland, Oregon, the anonymous authors have a very different purpose: to show the achievements of the organization over the past year. They do so with minimal text—a brief description of the organization along with lists of board members, advisors, staff, and major donors; a "snapshot" page listing information about Proud Ground's accomplishments during 2008 and since it was founded in 1999; and two pie charts showing 2008 revenues and expenses. Most of the report is devoted to profiles of new

"I can't believe this is my place."

That was Michelle's first thought as she walked in the front door of the home she now owns.

Tired of moving every time her rent increased, tired of asking for permission to paint or fix things up, tired of living without pets, and ready to have place of her own, Michelle was ready to become a home owner.

Michelle attended a Proud Ground orientation class hosted by her employer, New Seasons Market. Thanks to a great partnership, Michelle is one of four households who learned about Proud Ground's program through New Seasons.

But her favorite part about being in her home isn't inside at all.

"I love to garden," Michelle explains. "I like knowing I can plant a biannual and know I will be around to see it bloom."

MICHELLE

A page from Proud Ground's 2008 annual report.

homeowners, like the one of Michelle that appears above. Here we see a color image of Michelle with her cat that appeals to readers' emotions, along with information about who she is, how she became a homeowner, and why she looks forward to owning her own place. The report also mentions that she works for New Seasons Market, a Portland grocery chain that carries local produce; by noting this detail, the report acknowledges the participation of one of Proud Ground's donors and also appeals to Port-landers' sense of local pride.

In composing this report, the authors were obviously thinking about their primary audience: those individuals, groups, and corporations that have donated to Proud Ground in the past and those who might do so in the future, provided they are informed about the work the organization does—what it accomplishes and how economically it does so. Other likely audi-ences include staff and supporters of other nonprofit groups in Portland and those interested in affordable housing in Portland and elsewhere.

In both the Liveable City and Proud Ground reports, the topic is care-fully focused, and the authors approach their task with a keen eye toward the intended audiences and their own goals. You'll want to do the same in the reports that you write: to consider carefully whom you're addressing, what they know about your topic, and what information they expect.

Definitions of Key Terms

Effective reports always define key terms explicitly. These definitions serve several functions. Some audience members may not understand some of the terms used in the report, especially technical terms. And even those famil-iar with the terms pay attention to the definitions for clues about the writ-er's stance or assumptions. Here's an example of a definition from Michael Oden's report for Liveable City:

> **What Are Economic Incentives?** In addition to . . . general economic strategies, Austin—like most other cities—provides financial incentives designed to encourage specific economic outcomes, such as a desired company locating its headquarters here. Incentives may take many forms including tax abatements or rebates, fee waivers, expedited site approv-al process, up-zoning, or other types of grants or guarantees. Direct incentives are used to change the economic landscape by attracting new economic activities or new types of physical development that would not be generated by the private sector without specific inducements. In Austin, incentives can be generally categorized in one of two ways: "firm-based" or "project-based."

Notice how Oden explains the purpose of financial incentives ("to encour-age specific economic outcomes, such as a desired company locating its headquarters here"), gives examples ("tax abatements or rebates, fee waivers, expedited site approval process, up-zoning, or other types of grants or guarantees"), defines "direct incentives" (those "used to change the economic landscape by attracting new economic activities or new types of physical development that would not be generated by the private sector without specific inducements"), and finally divides incentives into two subcategories ("firm-based" and "project-based"). He then devotes a paragraph to defining and illustrating each of these subcategories of incentives.

It's also worth noting how Oden introduces his definitions. Partly because his report is lengthy, he uses headings to help structure it. Here he introduces his definition by posing a direct question—"What are economic incentives?"—and then answers that question in a paragraph.

In the article on aerial skiing mentioned on p. 186 for the Science section of the *New York Times*, Henry Fountain uses a number of strategies to provide readers with definitions they might need. As a newspaper journalist, Fountain writes for a general audience, but he can safely assume that at least some readers of the Science section will have a great deal of knowledge about physics. He can likewise assume that at least some readers will know something about aerial skiing. Here's one definition Fountain offers:

> The first time you watch skiers hurtle off a curved ramp at 30 miles per hour, soaring six stories in the air while doing three back flips and up to five body twists, you can't help but think: These people are crazy. . . .
>
>   Freestyle aerialists, as these athletes are known, are not actually throwing caution, along with themselves, to the wind.
>
>   —HENRY FOUNTAIN, "Up in the Air, and Down, with a Twist"

Here the short phrase "as these athletes are known" refers back to the skiers Fountain has described earlier, and this explains the term "freestyle aerialists."

A few paragraphs later, Fountain explains *torque*, the concept in physics that allows freestyle aerialists to do somersaults, without explicitly defining it:

> "The forces are pretty simple," said Adam Johnston, a physics professor at Weber State University in Ogden, Utah. . . . "There's the force of the ramp on his skis, and the force of gravity on him," Dr. Johnston said, after Ryan St. Onge, the reigning world champion in men's aerials and a member of the Olympic team, zipped down a steep inrun, leaned back as he

entered the curved ramp until he was nearly horizontal and flew off at a 70-degree angle. "That's all there is."

But it is enough to create *torque* that sends Mr. St. Onge somersaulting backward as he takes to the air, arcing toward a landing on a steep downslope that the skiers and coaches have chopped and fluffed for safety.

Later in the article, Fountain writes: "In this training jump, Mr. St. Onge adds a full twist in both the second and third flips—a lay-full-full in the language of the sport." Here Fountain provides a technical term used by experts—a "lay-full-full"—immediately after explaining what the term means. In a subsequent paragraph, Fountain uses another strategy, providing a definition of a "double-full-full-full" in a **SUBORDINATE CLAUSE** (italicized here): "And when doing a double-full-full-full, *which requires four full twists, including two in the first flip*, he will use all three methods at takeoff." Note that none of the definitions shown here quote a dictionary, nor do they use the formula "the definition of X is Y"—and that each of the experts offers memorable examples that help readers understand the subject.

Trustworthy Information

Effective reports present information that readers can trust to be accurate. In some cases, writers provide documentation to demonstrate the verifiability of their information, including citations of published research, the dates of interviews they have conducted, or other details about their sources.

See how an article in *Vanity Fair* is written in a style that enables a general audience to understand and trust relatively technical information, p. 683.

In a report for a writing class at Chapman University, Kelley Fox presents information in ways that lead readers to trust the details she presents and, ultimately, the author herself. The report describes how Griffin, Simon, and Andy, three roommates in Room 115 of her dorm, create their identities. Beginning with Muhammad Ali's line "Float like a butterfly, sting like a bee," which is the caption on a large poster of Ali on Griffin's wall, Fox seeks to characterize Griffin as someone who floats to "the top of the pecking order" and who seems "invincible":

In a sense, Griffin is just that: socially invincible. A varsity basketball athlete, Griffin has no shortage of friends, or of female followers. People seem to simply gravitate toward him, as if being around him makes all their problems trivial. Teammates can often be found in his room, hanging out on his bed, watching ESPN. Girls are certainly not a rarity, and they usually come bearing gifts: pies, CDs, even homework answers. It happens often, and I have a feeling this "social worship" has been going on for a while, although in myriad other forms. Regardless, the constant and excessive positive attention allows Griffin to never have to think about his own happiness; Griffin always seems happy. And it is because of this that, out of the three roommates, it is easiest to be Griffin.

—KELLEY FOX, "Establishing Identities"

Fox's description demonstrates to readers that she has spent considerable time in or around Room 115 and that she knows what she is writing about. Her use of specific details convinces us that Griffin is real and that the things she describes in fact occur—and on a regular basis.

In the following example from a report for a course on music and language at Columbia University, Jonathan Payne writes about Iannis Xenakis, an influential and experimental composer and architect who tried to change Western conceptions of classical music:

The connection between music and other disciplines is what Xenakis found to be missing from his music education, as he explains in his 1987 interview in *Perspectives in New Music,* "Xenakis on Xenakis," saying that in school, "things were scattered. Each subject was a domain. I wasn't trying to make any connection." He felt that without connections to other disciplines, he had not sufficiently been taught music; "if my professors had really taught me, in the true sense of the word," he writes, "they would have made the connection. . . . They didn't do it. They were speaking as musicians."[1] Throughout his career, Xenakis therefore devoted himself to making those connections by developing a musical language and compositional tool accessible to the musically untrained and by making compositions that combine music, architecture, science, history, and many other fields.

—JONATHAN PAYNE, "Xenakis, Cage, and the Architecture of Music"

Here Payne uses paraphrases and direct quotations from a published interview with Xenakis to demonstrate the trustworthiness of the information he presents; the footnote number leads readers to the notes and bibliography at the end of the report, all of which add to the credibility of Payne and the information he provides. Readers with any doubt can verify the quotation and the context in which it occurs.

Iannis Xenakis makes a recording in the Camargue near Arles, France.

Although Fox and Payne use different techniques, both of them convince readers that the information being presented and the writers themselves can be trusted.

Appropriate Organization and Design

There is no single best strategy for organizing the information you are reporting. In addition to **DEFINING** (as Henry Fountain does), you'll find yourself **DESCRIBING** (as Kelley Fox does), offering specific **EXAMPLES** (as the report from Proud Ground does), explaining (as Jonathan Payne does when he uses quotations to explain Xenakis' perspective on his own education), **ANA-LYZING CAUSES AND EFFECTS** (as Michael Oden does), **COMPARING** (as Fox does later in her report when she compares and contrasts the three roommates), and so on. The specific techniques you'll use will grow out of the information you want to report and your understanding of which techniques will help you do it most effectively.

Sometimes the way in which you organize and present your information will be prescribed. If you're writing a report for the social or physical sciences and following a version of the **IMRAD** format described on p. 184, for instance, you will have little choice in how you organize and present information. Everything from the use of headings to the layout of tables to the size of fonts may be dictated. Some disciplines specify certain format details. Students of psychology, for example, are expected to follow **APA STYLE**, that specified in the *Publication Manual of the American Psychological Association*. On the other hand, a report for a composition class may have fewer constraints. For example, you may get to decide whether you will need headings and whether to use personal examples.

In many cases, you'll want to include visuals of some sort, whether photographs, charts, figures, or tables. See, for example, the two pie charts from the Proud Ground annual report. The information they convey would be much harder to understand and thus far less effective if it were presented in a paragraph or even as a table. And as noted on p. 190, Proud Ground also

The Pew Research report on p. 885 incorporates definitions and graphs and tables to make the report clear and concise.

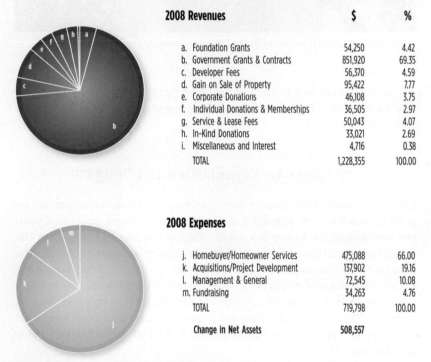

2008 Revenues		$	%
a.	Foundation Grants	54,250	4.42
b.	Government Grants & Contracts	851,920	69.35
c.	Developer Fees	56,370	4.59
d.	Gain on Sale of Property	95,422	7.77
e.	Corporate Donations	46,108	3.75
f.	Individual Donations & Memberships	36,505	2.97
g.	Service & Lease Fees	50,043	4.07
h.	In-Kind Donations	33,021	2.69
i.	Miscellaneous and Interest	4,716	0.38
	TOTAL	1,228,355	100.00

2008 Expenses			
j.	Homebuyer/Homeowner Services	475,088	66.00
k.	Acquisitions/Project Development	137,902	19.16
l.	Management & General	72,545	10.08
m.	Fundraising	34,263	4.76
	TOTAL	719,798	100.00
	Change in Net Assets	**508,557**	

Pie charts from Proud Ground's 2008 annual report.

uses color photos to make the report more interesting and appealing. Similarly, see on pp. 192–93 the way that Henry Fountain relies on visual images in his discussion of aerial skiing.

A Confident, Informative Tone

Effective reports have a confident tone that assumes the writer is just presenting reliable information rather than arguing or preaching. Michael Oden and Henry Fountain both sound like they know what they're writing about. In both these cases, we as readers are by and large getting just "the facts," though it is clear that Oden has strong convictions about what the city of Austin should be doing in the future and that Fountain delights in both the beauty and the science of what freestyle aerialists can achieve.

The line between informing and arguing can become fuzzy, however. If you read reports on any number of hot-button issues—climate change, the economy, gay marriage, abortion—you'll find that they often reflect some kind of position or make recommendations that betray a position. But the authors of such reports usually try to create an informative tone that avoids indicating their own opinions.

You may sometimes find yourself struggling with this line, working to present information while stopping short of telling readers what to think about or how to feel about a topic. Here we can offer two pieces of advice. First, keep in mind that you're aiming to explain something to your audience clearly and objectively rather than to persuade them to think about it a certain way. You'll know you've succeeded here if someone reading a draft of your report can't tell exactly what your own opinion about the topic is. Second, pay special attention to word choice because the words you use give subtle and not-so-subtle clues about your stance. Referring to "someone who eats meat" is taking an objective tone; calling that person a "flesh eater" is not.

REPORTING INFORMATION / An Annotated Example

WIKIPEDIA, the free online encyclopedia that "anyone can edit," has become one of the most-visited sites on the web since it was launched in 2001. Below is the opening section of the entry on same-sex marriage, as it appeared on August 14, 2010. This article offers a good example of how authors negotiate the challenges of reporting information. Wikipedia also provides interesting examples of reporting on controversial topics, for the site has explicit policies about the writing of entries and even offers an entry on writing from a "neutral point of view." Readers can also consult "Discussion," "View Source," and "View History" pages for information about which aspects of an article have been controversial and why. Finally, Wikipedia explicitly warns users about problematic aspects of an entry, noting when the neutrality of an article has been disputed and pointing out sections that need "additional citations for verification."

Same-sex Marriage

WIKIPEDIA

A definition of the topic, followed by a description of the controversy surrounding it.

SAME-SEX MARRIAGE (also called gay marriage)[1] is a legally or socially recognized marriage between two persons of the same biological sex or social gender. Same-sex marriage is a civil rights, political, social, moral, and religious issue in many nations. The conflict arises over whether same-sex couples should be allowed to enter into marriage, be required to use a different status (such

Underlining signals links to more information.

as a civil union, which either grants equal rights as marriage, or limited rights in comparison to marriage), or not have any such rights. A related issue is whether the term "marriage" should be applied.[2][3][4]

Financial, psychological, and physical well-being is enhanced by marriage, and children of same-sex couples benefit from being raised by two parents within a legally recognized union supported by society's institutions.[5][6][7] State policies that bar same-sex couples from marrying are based solely on sexual orientation, and they are both a consequence of the stigma historically attached to homosexuality, and a structural manifestation of that stigma.[6]

Support for same-sex marriage is often based upon what is regarded as a universal human rights issue, mental and physical health concerns, equality before the law,[8] and the goal of normalizing LGBT relationships.[9][10][11] Opposition to same-sex marriage arises from a rejection of the use of the word "marriage" as applied to same-sex couples or objections about the legal and social status of marriage itself being applied under any terminology. Other stated reasons include direct and indirect social consequences of same-sex marriages, parenting concerns, religious grounds,[12] and tradition. Supporters of same-sex marriage often attribute opposition to it as coming from homophobia[13][14][15][16] or heterosexism and liken prohibitions on same-sex marriage to past prohibitions on interracial marriage.[17]

Note the organization: definitions first, a statement of the issues, the controversy, and a review of the major arguments offered by each side.

Footnotes link to evidence that demonstrates the trustworthiness of the information. Go to wwnorton/write/everyone links to see the footnotes and read the full article.

The tone is confident and avoids taking a stance on this controversial topic.

Later in this entry readers encountered a message box asking whether one section strayed from the topic and inviting them to discuss the topic on a discussion page.

ANALYZE *a* Wikipedia *entry on a topic of your choice to see how focused the information is, how key terms are defined, and how the entry is organized. How trustworthy do you find the information—and what makes you trust it (or not)? How would you characterize the tone—informative? informative but somewhat argumentative? something else? Point to words that convey that tone.*

PROFILES

Profiles provide firsthand accounts of people, places, events, institutions, or other things. Newspapers and magazines publish profiles of interesting subjects; college websites often include profiles of the student body; investors may study profiles of companies before deciding whether or not to buy stock. If you're on *Facebook*, you have likely created a personal profile saying something about who you are and what you do. Profiles take many different forms, but they generally have the following characteristic features.

A Firsthand Account

In creating a profile, you're always writing about someone or something you know firsthand, not merely something you've read about. You may do some reading for background, but reading alone won't suffice. You'll also need to talk with people or visit a place or observe an event in some way. Keep in mind, however, that while a profile is a firsthand account, it should not be autobiographical. In other words, you can't profile yourself.

Detailed Information about the Subject

Profiles are always chock-full of details—background information, descriptive details (sights, sounds, smells), anecdotes, and dialogue. Ideally, these details help bring the subject to life—and persuade your audience that whatever you're writing about matters and is worth reading.

An Interesting Angle

The best profiles present a new or surprising perspective on whatever is being profiled. In other words, a good profile isn't merely a description; rather, it captures something essential about its subject from an interesting angle, much like a memorable photo does. For instance, many American college students study abroad in their junior year; writing a profile of one of them might not sound so interesting. But if you could find a student who was in London in 2011 who experienced some of the excitement about the royal wedding, then you've got a good subject for a profile. He or she will likely have stories to tell and memories to share that will get an audience's attention, provided you do your job well. Odds are that this student will also have photos, something else you might include in your profile.

KAISA McCROW writes for *Street Roots*, a biweekly street newspaper published in Portland, Oregon. Street newspapers are published in many U.S. cities and are often sold by people who are homeless. They provide regular employment for people who may find it difficult or impossible to find other work; and a voice for a segment of urban communities that is often the subject of public debate but is rarely heard. In fact, *Street Roots'* motto is "For those who can't afford free speech."

In this profile, McCrow takes readers into the life of Dymar Blanton, who regularly sells *Street Roots* on the corner near Voodoo Doughnut, a popular Portland landmark.

Hard Work, High Energy Means a Ticket Home

KAISA McCROW

DYMAR BLANTON SELLS *Street Roots* outside of Voodoo Doughnut, a spacious corner on Second Avenue and Burnside, a mini–downtown center. Groups of people, mainly tourists and Saturday marketgoers, can spend a serious chunk of their Saturday in line for these famous doughnuts. For Dymar, this means that instead of people coming and going, maybe stopping for a second to buy a *Street Roots* on their way to the grocery store, he sells to a slowly creeping line of the same hungry, fried-dessert-seeking faces. With a crowd this tough, he has to stay on his game, as people are likely to hear him trying to sell a paper three or more times while they wait. Luckily, Dymar is short on neither energy nor information. He is slight in stature, and wears

The profile opens with many details that provide important information about the subject.

The typical line outside Voodoo Doughnut in downtown Portland.

thick glasses that he has needed since birth. Recently, he spent six months without his glasses, living life on the streets virtually blind, which for most is an unfathomable feat. He circles the periphery of the doughnut line offering tidbits about the paper, singing songs, and good-naturedly heckling people when appropriate.

Here and elsewhere the author quotes what Blanton actually says as he sells newspapers.

"*Street Roots*, only a dollar. Help the homeless get off the streets and into the community. We have stories, art, and poetry, written by the people, for the people," calls out Dymar. He is the self-proclaimed Most Energetic Vendor, and he says that he never finishes a day of work until he has sold every paper.

He has to. "Only 6 papers left to sell, and I can finally go home. Ain't no nation like a donation. Get yourself a *Street Roots*—it's the new edition," he sings to the crowd. No one jumps to buy a paper this time, but maybe they are wondering what he means by, "home." At the end of the night "home" for Dymar is a hostel, but only if he has sold enough papers. Otherwise, it is a shelter.

Here the author provides background information about Blanton's life.

The path that led Dymar to where he is now is full of loss and abuses. When he was only 6 years old, Dymar's stepfather shot and killed his mother. He makes a motion to explain this, rather than saying it out loud. It seems unreal, so it takes a moment to sink in. After the death of his mother, the remainder of his youth was spent bounced between different homes and family members; often the experiences were traumatic. Dymar spent two years as a young teen living with his biological father, which he says was abusive and horrific from start to finish.

Things reached a breaking point when Dymar began dating a boy at school. Letters passed between the boys were brought to the attention of a school counselor who in turn told Dymar's father. The result of being outed without his consent to a homophobic father resulted in one of the worst beatings of his life. At that point, neither he nor his father wanted him to stay, so he left to live with an aunt, and eventually went back with his grandmother, which brought its own set of challenges.

Despite the intensity with which he is sharing about himself, Dymar cuts himself off to make sure he is approaching each new person in line before a panhandler does. If these folks are going to be in line for a while, they can only be approached once or twice, so Dymar wants to get there first.

After a few more songs to the crowd, Dymar goes back to talking about his teen years. He ended up on the streets after continuing to bounce between living in a group home and at his grandmother's. On the streets he was introduced to heroin. His boyfriend, Stitches, was a user and introduced Dymar to the drug. He overdosed the first time. "Ambulance, hospital, everything," Dymar explains with animation, highlighting the drama of a scenario that he himself does not remember. Citing a lack of familial support after his overdose, Dymar felt that he had no choice but to stay on the streets.

The author weaves together details about Blanton's past life with his words and actions in the present—and later in the profile with his hopes for the future.

Dymar and Stitches continued their relationship, and worked together to get clean. Stitches gave Dymar an engagement ring. They were in love and Dymar even brought him home for Thanksgiving to meet his grandmother. Only a month later, though, four days before Christmas, Stitches died of a drug overdose right in front of Dymar. Dymar makes no move to hide the pain that he still feels over the loss; he says it is with him every moment.

"*You don't need to be here, you don't need to be dead yet. Wake up,*" he hears them say to him. "They've been there protecting me, they are my guardian angels, and I know every day that I'm out here, they are right next to me. I feel their presence."

Dymar is now clean, and he is focused on continuing to stay

that way. He works hard and is bent in a positive direction. Still, listening to Dymar talk about his past hits hard, and could soften even the most focused Voodoo pilgrimagers.

Dymar wants to go back home to see his grandmother soon. He's waiting on a family member's tax return to purchase a bus ticket to her home in Colorado. When he makes the trip, the Voodoo Doughnut corner, teeming with life and people, will miss his energetic presence and funny quips. "Anybody have a chair they can give me?" he jokes to the crowd after mentioning how exhausted he is. Then he gets a little more serious, "Or, give me enough money so I can go buy a chair?" Some people laugh now, they are entertained by his sass. What is lost on most of them is the reality of the joke—Dymar isn't looking for a chair, he's out working, for a place to stay, for a meal, for a trip home. "*Street Roots*, it's only a dollar, folks."

The profile ends where it began—with Blanton selling newspapers outside the doughnut store.

NOTICE THE WAY *the author uses direct quotations from Dymar Blanton, weaving his words in with hers. Which other details, if any, might have been more effective had she conveyed them in Blanton's own words? How might you approach this same story if your medium were a podcast, or a video? What part of the story would you tell, and what would you try to get the subject to tell himself?*

WRITING A REPORT / A Roadmap

Choose a topic that matters—to you, and to others

If you get to select your topic, begin by considering topics that you know something about or would like to learn more about. Whether you're assigned to do a report on an individual, an event, an institution, or something else, choose one that you find intriguing and that you will be able to help your readers find intriguing, too. Consider how Henry Fountain got his readers interested in the physics of the double-full-full-full.

Be sure to choose a topic you can be objective about. If you're a devout Catholic and firmly believe that the church is wrong—or right—in its stance on birth control or abortion, those may not be the best topics for a report because you're likely to have trouble maintaining the "just the facts" stance necessary for good reporting. Remember that the more controversial a topic, the more challenging it may be to report fairly and accurately on it because the facts themselves likely will be the subject of controversy. If you are going to write about a controversial topic, you might consider reporting on the controversy itself: the major perspectives on the issue, the kinds of evidence cited, and so on. For example, one of our students found it difficult to write a report on the 2010 Gulf oil spill without taking a position on who was responsible; it was easier to report on the controversy over who should be held responsible for the spill.

If you've been assigned a topic, find an aspect of it that is both interesting and focused. Unless you've been specifically instructed to address a broad topic (for example, the consequences of World Bank policies for third-world economies), focus on a narrower aspect of the topic (take a single developing country that interests you and report on the consequences of World Bank policies for that economy). Even when you are asked to report on a broad topic, see if it is possible to start out with a specific case and then move to the broader issue.

Consider your rhetorical situation

Analyzing your audience, purpose, and other elements of your rhetorical situation will help you to make the decisions you'll face as you write.

Focus on your AUDIENCE from start to finish. If you're writing a report that only your instructor will read, you can sometimes assume that she or he will know a lot about your topic. But if you're writing for a broader audience—your classmates, fellow readers of a blog—you'll need to think about the kinds of knowledge your audience might already have. Part of writing an effective report for an audience whose members have different levels of knowledge is being sure to provide them with enough information but not to include irrelevant details. For example, Henry Fountain didn't explain what skiing is or waste his readers' time by including information that was not directly relevant to his topic. Here are some questions that might guide you in considering your audience:

- What do you know about your audience? To what extent are they like or unlike you—or one another? Consider such factors as age; education; gender and sexual orientation; abilities and disabilities; regional, ethnic, cultural, and linguistic heritage; economic background; and so on.

- What background information will your audience likely need? Will they all know roughly the same amount about your topic, or will they have differing assumptions and levels of knowledge about it?

- Which terms need to be defined or illustrated with examples? What sorts of examples will be most effective?

- Do you know anything about what your audience values, about what interests they have? How can you get them interested in the topic—or at least see that it matters?

Be clear about your PURPOSE. Spend some time focusing on the reasons you are writing a report on this topic for this particular audience. Odds are that you want your report to do more than merely convey information. If you're writing it for a course, you likely want to learn something and to get a good grade. If you're a new employee and the report is your first assignment, you want to demonstrate that those who hired you made a good choice. If the report is part of a large project—a campaign to encourage composting on campus, for example—a lot may be riding on the quality of your work. What short-term goals do you have in writing, and do they relate to any longer-term goals?

Consider your STANCE. Think about your own attitudes toward your topic and your audience: What about this topic captured your interest? Why do you think it matters—or should matter—both in general and to your audience? What do you want to learn about the topic as you research and write? What do you want your audience to learn from the report? How can you establish your authority on the topic and get your audience to trust you and the information you provide? How do you want them to see you? As a fair, objective reporter? As thoughtful? serious? curious? something else?

Consider the larger CONTEXT. What are the various perspectives on the topic, and what else has been said about it? What larger conversations, if any, is this topic a part of? For a report that's part of a campaign to encourage composting, for example, you'd need to become familiar with how such campaigns have been conducted elsewhere, which techniques have worked best and which have not worked, and what the main challenges and problems are that composting programs encounter. Understanding the larger context will help you decide what aspects of your topic you need to cover and in how much detail, and how best to demonstrate your authority to say something about the topic.

Think about MEDIA. As the three reports on aerial skiing make clear, Marshall McLuhan was on to something when he argued that "the medium is the message." (In other words, the way you say something, including the medium itself, becomes the message you convey.) If you have a choice, will your text be presented in print? on the web? as an oral report? Which will be most effective for your subject and audience? If you plan to conduct interviews, what is the best way to present your findings? In summaries? quotations? full transcripts? If you have video or audio data, can you embed them in an online report or incorporate them into a live oral report? If your report will be in print, can you use images captured from the videos or transcripts of any audio data? If your report will be oral, should you prepare PowerPoint slides to help your audience follow your main points?

Think about DESIGN. Consider what design elements are available to you and will help you convey your information in the clearest, most memorable way. For example, much of the effectiveness of Proud Ground's annual report comes from the large color photos and narratives of new homeowners and their homes that take up most of the report. Black-and-white images or plain headshots would have been far less effective. Think about whether your report will include any elements that need to be designed—anything needing to be set off or highlighted, for example. Do you need headings? Would photos, charts, tables, or other visuals help you convey information more effectively than words alone? Do you have the option of using color in your text—and if so, how might it help you achieve your purpose?

Research your topic

Your goal in researching your topic is first to get a broad overview of what is known about it and second to get a deeper understanding of the topic than you now have. While most high school research reports discuss the research of others, the reports you'll write in college will often call on you to gather data yourself or as part of a group and then write about the data in light of existing research. **LAB REPORTS**, for example, describe the results of experiments in engineering and the natural sciences. Reports based on ethnographic observation grow out of extended experience in a place or with a group. Even reports that are based on **SECONDARY SOURCES** require careful analysis and synthesis of the information you find.

Thus, your first task is to read broadly enough to get a feel for the various issues and perspectives on your topic so that you know what you're talking about and can write about it authoritatively.

Begin by assessing what you know—and don't know—about the topic. What do you already know about your topic, and what more do you need to find out about it? What questions do you have about it? What questions will your audience have? To answer these questions, you might try **BRAINSTORMING** or other activities for **GENERATING IDEAS**. Such activities may help you focus your topic and also discover areas you need to research further.

Find out what others say. Depending on your topic, you can research it in many different ways. If your topic is a local one, such as binge drinking at your college, you may want to conduct a student survey, interview administrators or counselors who deal with campus drinking problems, or do a search of local newspapers for articles about binge drinking. But it would also be a good idea to look for material on the topic beyond your own community, in order to gain perspective on how the situation at your school fits into national patterns. You could consult books and periodicals; online databases; or websites, listservs, or other online groups devoted to your topic. If your topic doesn't have a local focus, you will likely start out by consulting sources like these. You may also find that a professor at your school has scholarly expertise in your topic and is willing to be interviewed.

Decide whether you need to narrow your topic. What aspect of your topic most interests you, and how much can you cover given the constraints of your assignment? If your political science professor has assigned a five-minute oral report on climate-change legislation, for example, you will need to find a more specific focus than you would for a twenty-page written report on the same general topic. In the first case, you might (with your teacher's permission) focus on one specific bill and its fate in Congress rather than try to cover all of the legislation that falls into this category.

Organize and start writing

Once you've narrowed your topic and have some sense of what you want to say about it, you need to think about how you can frame your topic to appeal to your audience and how you can best organize the information you have collected. As you draft, you'll likely discover that you need to do some additional research, to dig deeper into your topic and find more information. But for now just get started.

Come up with a tentative thesis. What do you want to say about your topic, and why? Write out a tentative **THESIS** statement, trying to make it broad enough to cover the range of information you want to share with your audience but limited enough to be manageable—and keeping in mind that your goal is to report information, not to argue a position. A good thesis lays out the main parts of what you plan to say and often gives some sense of how your text will be structured. Expect to have to revise your thesis as you develop your text; rarely is an author's working thesis the one that ends up in the final draft.

Organize your information. Make a list of the information that supports your thesis, and think about what details you want to include. You'll find that you need various strategies for presenting information—you'll want to **DESCRIBE** this, **DEFINE** that, **ANALYZE** the causes or effects of something else. Then consider how to arrange your material. Some topics call for a **CHRONOLOGICAL** structure, moving from past to present, maybe even projecting into the future, as the report on economic development in Austin does.

But there are many other ways to organize a report. You just need to work out a structure that will help your audience understand your topic in a systematic way. If you are writing about something whose physical characteristics are important for your audience to understand, such as a new kind of environmentally friendly car, you may find that a spatial organization works well—moving from exterior to interior or from top to bottom. In a report on the effects of an earthquake, you might organize your draft chronologically or spatially, or perhaps you'll find that an organization that focuses on the effects of the earthquake—physical effects, economic effects, political effects, and so on—works best for your purposes.

Don't be surprised if you find that you do not need to use all of the information that you have collected. Authors often gather far more information than they finally use; your task is to choose the information that is most relevant to your thesis and present it as effectively as possible. It's no surprise that writers are told to "marshal" their evidence, a military term that means to arrange troops for exercise, review, or battle.

Draft an **OPENING**. How can you get your audience interested in your topic? Why do you care about it, and how can you make them care? While there's no one way to begin a report, you basically want to announce your subject and make your audience want to know more about it. Consider opening with an intriguing example or a provocative question. Perhaps you have a good anecdote. Or you could start by stating your thesis. In any case, it's usually a good idea to include the thesis somewhere in the introduction so that your audience can follow from the outset where your report is heading and don't have to figure it out for themselves along the way.

Draft a **CONCLUSION**. What do you want your audience to take away from your report? What do you want them to remember? You could end by noting the implications of your report, reminding them why your topic matters. You could summarize your main points, or you could end with a question, leaving them with something to think about.

Look critically at your draft, get response—and revise

Try rereading your draft several times from different perspectives. For example, you might pretend to be a reader who knows very little about the topic—and then a reader who is an expert. Imagine how each will experience your text. Will readers new to the topic follow what you are saying, and will those who know about the topic think that you have represented it accurately and fairly? If possible, get feedback from a classmate or a tutor at your school's writing center. Following are some questions that can help you and others examine a report with a critical eye:

- *How does the report* OPEN*?* Will it capture your audience's interest? How else might it begin?

- *Is the topic clear and well focused?* Are the scope and structure of the report set out in its opening paragraphs? Is there an explicit THESIS statement—and if not, would it help to add one?

- *Is it clear why the topic matters*—why you care about it and why others should?

- *What medium or media will the report be presented in,* and how does that affect the way it's written? If it will be in print, for instance, you could include photos; on the web, you would be able to include videos. You might quote or paraphrase source materials in print—but on the web, you might be able to link directly to the sources.

- *How does the draft appeal to your audience?* Will they be able to understand what you say, or do you need to provide more background information or define any terms?

- *How do you establish your* AUTHORITY *on the topic?* Does the information presented seem trustworthy? Are the sources for your information credible, and have you provided any necessary DOCUMENTATION?

- *Is the* TONE *appropriate for your audience and purpose?* If it seems tentative or timid, how could you make it more confident? If it comes across as argumentative, how could you make it focus on "just the facts"?

- *How is the information organized?* What STRATEGIES have you used to present information—comparison, description, narration? How is the whole piece organized—past to present? simple to complex? some other way?—and does the structure suit your topic and medium?

- *Is the report easy to follow?* If not, try adding TRANSITIONS or headings. If it's an oral report, you might put your main points on a PowerPoint.

- *If you've included illustrations,* are there captions that explain how they relate to the written text? Have you referred to the illustrations in your text? Is there information in your text that would be easier to follow as a chart or table?

- *Is the style appropriate* for your audience and purpose? Consider choice of words, level of formality, and so on.

- *How effective is your* CONCLUSION*?* How else might you end?

- *Does the title tell readers what the report is about,* and will it make them want to know more?

Revise your draft in response to any feedback you receive and your own analysis, keeping in mind that your goal is to present "just the facts."

REFLECT ON WHAT YOU'VE LEARNED. Once you've completed your report, let it settle for a while and then take time to reflect. How well did you report on your topic? How successful do you think you were in making the topic interesting to your audience? What additional revisions would you make if you could? Research shows that such reflections help "lock in" what you learn for future use.

Selling the Farm
BARRY ESTABROOK

L AST FRIDAY, for the first time in 144 years, no one at the Borland family farm got out of bed in the pre-dawn hours—rain, shine, searing heat, or blinding blizzard—to milk the cows. A day earlier, all of Ken Borland's cattle and machinery had been auctioned off. After six generations on the same 400 acres of rolling pastures, lush fields, and forested hillsides tucked up close to the Canadian border in Vermont's remote Northeast Kingdom, the Borlands were no longer a farm family.

It was not a decision they wanted to make. A fit, vigorous 62-year-old, Borland could have kept working. His son, who is 35 and has two sons of his own, was once interested in taking over. But the dismal prices that dairy farmers are receiving for their milk forced the Borlands to sell. "We've gone through hard times and low milk prices before," said Borland's wife, Carol, a retired United Methodist minister. "This time there doesn't seem to be any light at the end of the tunnel. There's no sense working that hard when you're 62 just to go into debt."

For several months I'd been reading headlines and following the statistics behind the current nationwide dairy crisis. The math is stark. Prices paid to farmers per hundredweight (about 12 gallons) have fallen from nearly $20 a

BARRY ESTABROOK, a journalist who concentrates on food politics, writes for the *New York Times*, the *Washington Post*, and a variety of publications. This article appeared in *Gourmet* magazine in August 2009.

year ago to less than $11 in June. Earlier this month, the Federal government raised the support price by $1.25, but that is only a drop in the proverbial bucket. It costs a farmer about $18 to produce a hundredweight of milk. In Vermont, where I live, that translates to a loss of $100 per cow per month. So far this year, 33 farms have ceased operation in this one tiny state.

Meanwhile, the price you and I pay for milk in the grocery store has stayed about the same. Someone is clearly pocketing the difference. Perhaps that explains why profits at Dean Foods—the nation's largest processor and shipper of dairy products, with more than 50 regional brands—have skyrocketed. The company announced earnings of $75.3 million in the first quarter of 2009, more than twice the amount it made during the same quarter last year ($30.8 million). (Dean countered that "current supply and demand is contributing to the low price environment.")

But rote statistics have a way of masking reality. So last week, I drove up to ⁵ the village of West Glover for a firsthand look at the human side of the dairy crisis by attending the Borland auction. "You will be witnessing what is going to be the fate of all heritage farms," Carol Borland told me.

It was a breathtakingly clear morning in one of the most stunning settings imaginable. The Northeast Kingdom is an undulating patchwork of fields,

Nearly 900 farmers from across the Northeast attended the auction that marked the end of the 144-year-old Borland family farm.

woodlots, streams, lakes, barns, and white clapboard houses, set against the jagged, blue-gray backdrop of distant mountaintops. I didn't need a sign to direct me to the Borland place: For more than a mile before I crested a hill and saw the barns and silos, the gravel road leading to the farm was lined with dusty, mud-splattered pickup trucks. A crowd of close to 900 had gathered, in part because a country auction is always a major social event, a festive excuse for bone-weary farmers to take a day off, bring the kids, catch up with the gossip, and grumble about the weather, costs, and prices. That made it easy to overlook the sad, serious nature of the business at hand: selling off every last item there (and with any luck, providing the Borlands with a retirement nest egg). Among other things to go on the auction block was a massive amount of equipment, much of which had been shared with neighbors in loose, mutually beneficial arrangements stretching back generations. The demise of one family farm can affect similar small operators for miles in all directions. The auctioneer had to sell a half-dozen tractors, a dump truck, a couple of pickup trucks, manure spreaders, hay balers, wagons, seeders, mowers, milking machines, and assorted antique farm implements. There was feed that Borland had harvested but would no longer have any use for, 50 tons of shelled corn, 800 bales of hay. And, last in the photocopied catalogue, 140 prime Holsteins, a herd known for its excellence, having earned Borland 16 quality awards over the previous two decades. Unlike the cows that pass their lives in complete confinement on the factory farms that are replacing farms like his, Borland's cows went out on those hilly pastures every day, strengthening their bodies and feeding on grass. Borland worried that with most other farmers as financially strapped as he was, or worse, the cows might not sell. "I didn't spend my whole life breeding up a good herd to see them beefed" (meaning slaughtered for hamburger meat), he said.

Items were sold at a nerve-rattling pace as the auctioneer chanted his frenzied, mesmerizing, "I've got five. Give me ten, ten, ten. Five, gimme ten, ten, ten. A ten dollar bill. Five gimme ten, ten ten." Three "ringmen" worked the crowd, waving their canes to cajole bids, and whooping when the price rose. A John Deere tractor started at $25,000 and was dizzily bid up to $30,000, $40,000, $50,000, and finally $60,000, in a matter of three minutes. Lesser machines sometimes sold in half that time. All morning long, there was no let-up.

Just after the Deere was sold, I asked Borland's son Nathan how he thought things were going. "Online, that tractor would be listed for $75,000, if you can find one half that good, which you can't," he said. "But I guess you can't complain, given how hard it is for everybody."

Making maple syrup a century ago at the sugarhouse built by Borland's great-grand-father in 1898.

After attending college and working out of state for a few years, Nathan came home and joined his father on the farm. But he left to become a paramedic. "I like the work, but it got so bad financially that I felt guilty taking a paycheck," he said. "My sons, they're young. It'd be nice if they wanted to farm one day, but there's not a living to be made in dairy farming."

Carol, who was beside us, added, "The reality of farming is that as a parent, even if you'd like to and they want to, you can't encourage a child to go into something where he won't be able to earn a decent living." 10

Once the last piece of machinery was gone, the throng moved to folding chairs set up around a fenced ring inside the barn. Borland, who had been taciturn and shy most of the day, stood before the crowd to deliver a short speech. After thanking everybody for coming and expressing his gratitude for the efforts of the auction crew, he said, "I just want to say that these are a good bunch of cows. This auction wasn't their fault. They've always done their part. They have produced well."

Then he told a sad joke. "There was this farmer's son who left the farm and found work as a longshoreman in the city. The first ship that came in carried a cargo of anvils. To impress his new workmates, the boy picked up two anvils, one under each arm. But the gangplank snapped under the weight. He fell

The Borlands still sugar the old-fashioned way, insisting it makes for better-tasting maple syrup.

into the water and sank. He came up one time and shouted for help. No one moved. He went down and came up a second time. Still no help. The third time he came up he hollered, 'If you guys don't help me soon, I'm going to have to let go of one of these anvils.'"

There was nervous laughter. Borland went on, "That's what farming's been these last six months, trying to stay afloat with anvils. This is the day that I let go of mine."

The herd sold well. As an emotional bonus, 20 went to local farmers and would still be grazing on nearby pastures. Borland and Carol were pleased with the overall proceeds of the auction, and doubly pleased because they had been fortunate enough to find a buyer for the property and buildings who would take good care of the land that had supported their family through the generations. The Borlands severed off a piece of land where they will build a house. In the spring, they still plan to tap some maples. The sap will be boiled in the sugarhouse that Borland's great-grandfather built in 1898.

Before the auction, Borland had told his son that he planned to sleep until noon the day afterwards. Fat chance. He was up at 3:30 in the morning, as always. A few cows that had been sold had yet to be picked up, and cows, even ones that now belong to another man, need to be milked. He finished 15 that chore and drove the full milk cans over to a neighbor who was still in the business and had a cooling tank. Borland offered him a lift back to a hayfield he wanted to cut that day. As they rode along in the cab of the truck with the early morning sun streaming over the mountains, the neighbor said, "Ken, do you know how many farmers around here would give anything to be in your shoes? We have to keep struggling. You had a way out."

Thinking about the Text

1. How does Barry Estabrook make this profile of the Borland auction interesting? What details does he provide to show the "human side of the dairy crisis"?

2. "Selling the Farm" is a **PROFILE**, a firsthand account written for *Gourmet* magazine. How would his **AUDIENCE**, readers interested in food and wine, have affected the details he included?

3. How does Estabrook establish his **AUTHORITY** to write on this topic? How does he convince readers that the information he's providing is trustworthy?

4. Imagine Estabrook had written about the Borland auction for a newspaper, as an objective **REPORT** rather than a profile. How would it have been different?

5. Write a profile of a person or event, following the guidelines on p. 200. To come up with an interesting angle for your profile it might help to identify the audience you want to reach: What angle would likely interest them?

The Future of Food Production

SAM FORMAN

THE PROCESS THAT food consumed in America goes through to make its way to our mouths is like a Rube Goldberg contraption. The seemingly straightforward process of growing, raising, harvesting, and slaughtering goes on every day, completely hidden from consumers. Very few Americans are aware of the highly complicated, mechanized, and convoluted journey that any given bite of food takes from its origins in nature (or some manipulated approximation of it) to its destination on our plates. Although some people criticize the state of our food system, it is clear that it grew to be the international machine that it is because of demand. More than 300 million Americans want lots of food, meat especially, and they want it cheap. So like every other production process in this country, our food system has been industrialized to produce maximum food calories for the American people at minimum cost. This industrialization of our food system has allowed for population increase and higher standards of living.

But there are significant problems with the industrial food system. Caught up in a drive to maximize production and profit, the industrial food system has grown to an unsustainable size. As food production has become increasingly industrialized, concern for the environment and the animals we eat has taken

SAM FORMAN wrote this report for a first-year tutorial at Grinnell College. The name of the class was "Our Town: The World at Our Doorstep," and the assignment was to assess the impact of food production on the environment.

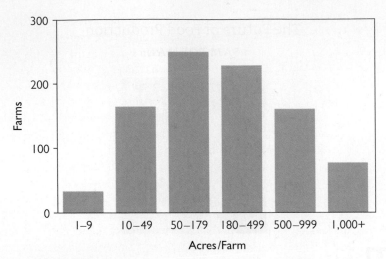

Fig. I. Range of farms by size in Poweshiek County, Iowa. United States, Dept. of Agriculture.

a backseat to expansion. Specialization, rather than integration, has become the hallmark of America's farms. Rather than having chickens, hogs, corn, and hay all on one farm, all these things now reside on separate, much larger farms. There is, however, another, very separate food system that supplements the industrial food system: the local food system. Local food systems cater to people who believe that it is better to "buy local" or from a smaller, usually family-owned farm rather than from a supermarket with less expensive mass-produced food.

There are few places where the two food systems are as visible and distinguishable as in Grinnell, Iowa. Poweshiek County has a range of farms in terms of size, as illustrated by fig. I, taken from the *2002 Census of Agriculture, County Profile: Poweshiek, Iowa*. As a resident of Grinnell, I have become very familiar with the faces of the two food systems. Wal-Mart, Hy-Vee, Monsanto Seed, and Fremont Farms are the incarnations of our industrial food system, while Café Phoenix, the farmers' market, and the various family farmers who participate in Community Supported Agriculture programs represent our local food system here in Grinnell.

Through both reading and personal interactions and interviews, I have come across all kinds of opinions and arguments from proponents of both small-scale and large scale agriculture. One theme that everyone agrees on is that our world is changing. Serious economic and environmental challenges are on the horizon. The current state of our food system in the United States is key to how well the industry will adapt when change comes. The American food system needs significant modification in order to guarantee that we can both eat healthfully and protect the natural workings of the planet. The most important change that could be made is a return to methods of food production that resemble nature's traditional processes, rather than methods that manipulate nature in an effort to make it work like a factory.

In Grinnell, as has been the case across the country, there has been a strong   5
trend in agriculture toward larger farms, fewer farms, and fewer farmers on each farm. According to the most recent county census of agriculture (taken in 2002), the number of farms in Poweshiek County has fallen 8 percent since 1997 and the average size of farms has grown 8 percent during the same time period. While growing bigger and industrializing, farms have also changed the nature of their operations to maximize efficiency and profit at all costs. Examples of this trend would be maximizing cropland by demolishing buildings on the farm that used to house livestock or by planting on hilly ground that is prone to erosion. In effect, too much farmland is used to grow crops, and not enough of it is left for livestock to graze on, throwing off the natural ecosystem. This is supported by the *2002 Census of Agriculture of Poweshiek County*, which shows that 85 percent of all farmland in Poweshiek County is used to grow crops while only 5.5 percent is open pasture. This great discrepancy begs the question, if so little land is used for pasture and so much is used to grow crops on, where and what do the livestock of Poweshiek County eat?

For the most part, livestock, especially those commonly consumed like hogs, beef, and poultry, have been taken off the farm and now reside in an invention of the industrial food system: the Concentrated Animal Feeding Operation, or CAFO for short. In a CAFO hundreds of thousands of animals live together, eating the grain (corn for the most part) that is grown on the land where they used to graze. These CAFOs are a prototypical example of how the industrial food system has rearranged nature to provide the ultimate value-added service: turning cheap, government-subsidized corn into protein and calories, in this case meat. During a phone interview, Professor Mark Honeyman of Iowa State University pointed out to me that by definition agriculture is the manipulation of nature to turn solar energy into caloric energy for our consumption. This logical assertion forced me to stop and ask myself why, if agriculture was by nature manipulating plants and animals, is there anything wrong with the way food is mass-produced in our country today? I quickly re-minded myself that there are different degrees of manipulation. The environ-mental impact of Barney Bahrenfuse, the owner of a 500-acre farm in Grinnell, keeping goats on his farm because they like to eat weeds is minimal because he is not changing anything about the goats' natural habits. Goats like to eat weeds. Greater degrees of manipulation often thwart the animals' natural in-stincts, reducing their existence to little more than converting grain into meat.

It should be added that small farms are not all good and big farms are not all bad. CAFOs recycle their animals' waste, just as Bahrenfuse does on his farm. The only difference is that while Bahrenfuse hauls his animals' waste across his smallish farm, CAFOs do not usually have farmland of their own and some-times (because they do not depend on the soil in any way) are not even located anywhere near farmland, and thus have to truck the manure to a buyer, using precious fossil fuels in the process. In a paper entitled "Sustainability Issues of U.S. Swine Production," Professor Honeyman points out that to optimize sustainability, "the relationship of swine population to arable land is important. Large swine production units [CAFOs] built on small acreages or not part of farms that also produce feed grains can have manure utilization problems" (1415). This is certainly not a problem in Iowa, where fecund soil is every-where. The CEO of Fremont Farms, Steve George, whose farm in Malcolm, Iowa, holds about 9 million hens that lay eggs for liquid egg products, does not have to look far to find a farmer in need of the waste his hens create. Animal waste is usually well dealt with by CAFOs; after all, it is not only environmen-tally conscious but also profitable to sell your animals' waste as fertilizer.

There are, however, ways in which CAFOs are clearly less earth-friendly than traditional farming. First, they are generally farther from farmland that needs fertilizer, and so the animal manure needs to be transported, a consid-erable waste of fossil fuel. This also contributes to pollution and global warm-ing, problems we all pay for. Another problem with CAFOs is the health of the animals they produce. Separating the animals from their natural habitat and constantly feeding them subtherapeutic levels of antibiotics weaken the ani-mals' natural robustness. In addition, these practices create antibiotic-resistant bacteria, a threat to the health of humans as well as to the animals that host the resulting super-bacteria. There is much debate about what is the healthi-est and safest environment for an animal. Steve George told me in a phone interview that he wouldn't want his chickens roaming around outside, because of all the dangerous pathogens that lurk outdoors. By keeping his hens indoors, he is able to protect them from disease and keep them big and productive by

Fig. 2. Not-so-concentrated accommodations at B&B Farms. Photograph by author.

giving them feed with growth-promoting antibiotics in it. In the other camp are Barney Bahrenfuse and Suzanne Costello, who run B&B Farms in Grinnell (see fig. 2). According to Bahrenfuse, they raise 600 chickens each year. They let their chickens peck around outside in addition to giving them feed that Barney grows and produces himself. As Costello put it, "One way of looking at it is there's this horrible world out there that we're all at war with," and then there's the way Bahrenfuse and Costello handle their chickens: "If [the chickens] are getting fresh air, and they're getting greens . . . they're healthier beings and they're less susceptible. So the way we view it is, you beef up their health and you don't have to worry about it." Based on direct observation I would have to say they are right. It just so happened that on a drive-by tour of Fremont Farms (shown in fig. 3), I observed a truck full of dead hens being covered for highway transport. Apparently about 10 percent of laying hens in CAFOs simply can't endure their situation and die, a fact that is built into the cost of production (Pollan 318). In the close confinement that CAFO-bound laying hens exist in, "Every natural instinct [is] thwarted, leading to a range of behavioral vices that can include cannibalizing [their] cage mates and rubbing [their] breast[s] against the wire mesh until [they are] completely bald and bleeding" (Pollan 317). Bahrenfuse mentions no such problems among his

Fig. 3. Fremont Farms in Malcolm, Iowa. Photograph by author.

chickens. Obviously there are many hundred thousand more chickens living at Fremont than at B&B, but that truckload stands in stark contrast to the three chickens at B&B that "crapped out," as Bahrenfuse put it.

There is also evidence that CAFOs are as bad for the people who live around them as for the animals that live in them. According to Honeyman:

> More than 20 years of studies have consistently shown the negative influences of large-scale specialized farming on rural communities (Allen, 1993). Lobao (1990) found that "an agricultural structure that was increasingly corporate and non-family-owned tended to lead to population decline, lower incomes, fewer community services, less participation in democratic processes, less retail trade, environmental pollution, more unemployment, and an emerging rigid class structure." (1413)

In addition to these findings, large CAFOs, especially hog or beef operations, create public nuisances in other ways. Because there can be hundreds of thousands if not millions of animals living in a densely populated environment, their waste becomes a problem. CAFOs pool the animals' feces in vast open cesspools that can cause huge environmental issues, in addition to attracting clouds of flies that plague anyone living nearby. It is clear that there are major drawbacks to the current industrial method of raising animals. But what choices do we have? There are more than 300 million people living in the United States who need to eat, and eat on a budget.

Proponents of large-scale agriculture argue that it is cheaper and more effi-   10 cient to produce food following an industrial model. Judging by price tags, they may be right. Often vegetables at a farmer's market fetch a higher price than those sitting in the supermarket do. But the supermarket is not the only place we pay for our industrially produced goods. Mark Honeyman pointed out to me, citing work by J. E. Ikerd, a professor emeritus of agricultural economics at the University of Missouri, Columbia, that many of the costs of mass-produced agriculture are hidden. For instance, we all pay taxes to the government, which in turn spends billions of tax dollars a year subsidizing the industrial food system. Between 2003 and 2005 the government spent an average of $11.5 billion per year on crop subsidies, 47 percent of which went to the top 5 percent of beneficiaries ("Crop Subsidy"). This means we are subsidizing a lot, and mostly the biggest agri-businesses. Family farmers, for the most part, receive no government subsidies. So when I told Bahlenfuse and Suzanne that I repeatedly heard from people involved in large-scale agriculture that family farming is nice, but ultimately not very profitable if even viable at all, Suzanne was quick to respond: "You take away [the industrial farms'] government subsidies— they don't work. We don't take any government subsidies, so who's viable?" In fact, Steve George of Fremont Farms pointed out to me that they receive no government subsidies, which I verified online; according to the Environmental Working Group's website, which gets its statistics from the United States Department of Agriculture, except for a paltry $5,361 in corn subsidies between 1999 and 2000, Fremont Farms gets no government subsidies at all. No direct subsidies, that is. It is important to remember, however, that their operation is indirectly subsidized by the artificially low price of corn in their chickens' feed. By subsidizing the largest producers, the government encourages large-scale agriculture to organize itself along the lines of a machine, operated with chemical inputs and minimal human management, and measured by output.

It is much harder to offer a solution to our increasingly problematic food system than it is to point out its flaws. Some experts, like Bill McKibben, point to local food systems as a more earth-friendly and sustainable solution (2007). Others, like Mark Honeyman, propose many "modest-sized" diversified family farms. Both are plausible solutions, but critics claim that an industrial food system is the only way to feed a country with the size and appetite of the United States. Yet smaller farms do not necessarily mean less food. The solution is integration. Rather than having one huge corn farm and another huge pig farm, we should have several smaller integrated farms that would produce the same number of hogs and acres of corn. Instead of agriculture existing in enormous monocultures, farms would resemble independent ecosystems. This would simplify and reinforce the nutrient cycle and the health of the farms as a whole. Some might say that this would just be backtracking several decades in agricultural history. But really any change made to improve sustainability would be progress.

The key to implementing a more sustainable future for our food system is a multilateral effort by both government and consumers. To reshape our food system, there needs to be a concerted effort by the government to refocus subsidies along with greater awareness on the part of consumers; ultimately, the consumers have the greatest effect on what the food system produces while the government influences how they do it. Many of the individuals I interviewed noted a growing movement toward local, fresh, chemical-free foods. Tom Lacina of Pulmuone Wildwood noted the continual increase in sales of organic foods in the United States. Mark Honeyman observed the proliferation of niche pork markets such as antibiotic-free and grass-fed pork. Locavore, a noun that means "one who seeks out locally produced food" ("locavore"), was the New Oxford American Dictionary's 2007 Word of the Year ("Oxford"). The local food movement is clearly alive at Grinnell. Many professors and students are conscious of what they eat, and during the growing season local foods are plentiful. From May until October there is a fledgling farmers' market in town. Some local restaurants, most notably Café Phoenix, make a point of buying local whenever possible. But there are also strong signs of the entrenched industrial food system. Wal-Mart and Hy-Vee supply cheap, mass-produced food, mostly to the townspeople of Grinnell, who generally do not have the economic means that people at the college do. This trend is not unique to Grinnell. As Tom Lacina put it, "The top half of the society is willing to pay for local, pure, organic. They have the time to shop; they have the education to shop." But fresh, chemical-free food should not be limited to those with the money and awareness needed to shop locally. Government subsidies to encourage more smaller farms to produce goods for smaller regions could effectively strengthen local food systems and perhaps even result in the kind of affordable prices that supermarket shoppers enjoy today.

There is a clear set of goals for our food industry that Americans must collectively work to achieve. Our food system must achieve sustainability, meaning it should be able to operate indefinitely in its current state. Our food must be produced in a manner that respects the plants and animals that we consume, and the system must reward the farmers as well. The key is to re-create a system of farming that mimics nature rather than a factory. But there are still daunting obstacles in the way of progress. Most Americans enjoy the quantity of cheap food available in supermarkets across the country. To ensure change, Americans have to cast off the myopia that allows us to enjoy the state of our food system without worry for the future. As a country we must plan ahead for a time when cheap fossil fuel, antibiotics, and government subsidies will not keep a grossly unnatural food system running smoothly.

Acknowledgments

I would like to formally thank everyone who spent his or her valuable time talking to me for this paper. Steve, Tom, Barney, Suzanne, and Mark, your knowledge and perspectives were all invaluable and greatly influenced me as well as my paper. Thank you so much.

Works Cited

Allen, Patricia, ed. *Food for the Future: Conditions and Contradictions of Sustainability.* New York: Wiley, 1993. Print.

Bahrenfuse, Robert ("Barney"), and Suzanne Costello. Personal interview. 14 Dec. 2007.

"Crop Subsidy Program Benefits." *Environmental Working Group Policy Analysis Database.* Environmental Working Group, 2008. Web. 5 Jan. 2008.

George, Steve. Telephone interview. 27 Nov. 2007.

Honeyman, Mark. "Sustainability Issues of U.S. Swine Production." *Journal of Animal Science* 74 (1996): 1410-17. Print.

---. Telephone interview. 18 Dec. 2007.

Lacina, Tom. Personal interview. 7 Dec. 2007.

Lobao, Linda M. *Locality and Inequality: Farm and Industry Structure and Socioeconomic Conditions.* Albany: State U of New York P, 1990. Print.

"Locavore." *The New Oxford American Dictionary.* 2nd ed. 2005. Print.

McKibben, Bill. *Deep Economy: The Wealth of Communities and the Durable Future.* New York: Holt, 2007. Print.

"Oxford Word of the Year: Locavore." *OUP blog*. Oxford U P, 12 Nov. 2007.
      Web. 5 Jan. 2008.
Pollan, Michael. *The Omnivore's Dilemma*. New York: Penguin, 2006. Print.
United States. Dept. of Agriculture. *2002 Census of Agriculture, County Profile:
      Poweshiek, Iowa. United States Department of Agriculture, National
      Agricultural Statistics Service*. United States Dept. of Agriculture, 2008.
      Web. 5 Jan. 2008.

Thinking about the Text

1. This is a **REPORT**, providing information about two different kinds of farming in Iowa. At the same time, however, Sam Forman makes his own **POSITION** clear. What is his position, and how do you know? Does he state it explicitly—and if so, what does he say?

2. Forman wrote this report for a college class, where his **AUDIENCE** included his professor and classmates. How might he have written this report differently for an audience of farmers?

3. Forman's **TONE** is quite confident. Remembering that when he wrote this report, he was a college student like yourself, can you identify what he does here to convey that confidence?

4. How does Forman demonstrate that the information he reports is trustworthy?

5. Identify a topic that you want to find out more about. Narrow the topic enough so that you can research it sufficiently in the time you have for this assignment. Identify an audience who knows something about the topic, and write a report providing information that will interest them.

ELEVEN

"Two Thumbs Up"
Writing a Review

 **OOKS, MOVIES, CONCERTS,** TV shows, cars, cell phones, toaster ovens, hotels, restaurants, employees—just about anything can be reviewed. If a friend asks you how you liked the movie *Avatar*, your response—"It was beautiful and the 3-D was cool, but really the acting was so-so and the plot was unoriginal, so in the end it wasn't all that interesting"—constitutes a quick and brief review, including as it does

A still from *Avatar* (2009).

two basic elements of all reviews: a judgment ("beautiful," "cool," "so-so") and the criteria you used to arrive at that judgment, in this case the quality of the cinematography, the acting, and the script. In that sense, you—and everyone who sees movies or shops for a cell phone—regularly read and author reviews. Reviews can vary a good deal, however, as you can see in these examples from other reviews of *Avatar*:

> Watching *Avatar*, I felt sort of the same as when I saw *Star Wars* in 1977. That was another movie I walked into with uncertain expectations. James Cameron's film has been the subject of relentlessly dubious advance buzz, just as his *Titanic* was. Once again, he has silenced the doubters by simply delivering an extraordinary film. There is still at least one man in Hollywood who knows how to spend $250 million, or was it $300 million, wisely.
>
> *Avatar* is not simply a sensational entertainment, although it is that. It's a technical breakthrough. It has a flat-out Green and anti-war message. It is predestined to launch a cult. It contains such visual detailing that it would reward repeating viewings. It invents a new language, Na'vi, as *Lord of the Rings* did, although mercifully I doubt this one can be spoken by humans, even teenage humans. It creates new movie stars. It is an Event, one of those films you feel you must see to keep up with the conversation.
> —ROGER EBERT, *Chicago Sun-Times*

Turn to p. 755 to see what Roger Ebert has to say about another topic—3-D movies.

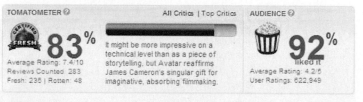

> TOMATOMETER ⊘   All Critics | Top Critics   AUDIENCE ⊘
>
> **83**%
> Average Rating: 7.4/10
> Reviews Counted: 283
> Fresh: 235 | Rotten: 48
>
> It might be more impressive on a technical level than as a piece of storytelling, but Avatar reaffirms James Cameron's singular gift for imaginative, absorbing filmmaking.
>
> **92**%
> liked it
> Average Rating: 4.2/5
> User Ratings: 622,949

—*RottenTomatoes.com*

Roger Ebert's review was written for a newspaper, one that was published both in print and on the web. His text was written as an essay that judges *Avatar* to be "an extraordinary film," using two specific criteria: It's a "technical breakthrough" and offers "visual detailing" worth seeing again and again. *RottenTomatoes.com*, on the other hand, measures the percentage of critics who recommend a film—here, 82 percent of 252 reviews—and includes excerpts and links that enable us to read their full reviews. Here's an excerpt from Richard Knight's *Windy City Times* review, just one of the 252 *Avatar* reviews collected on *RottenTomatoes.com*.

Richard Knight
Windy City Times

Entertaining enough and stunning to look at but essentially an
exceedingly detailed three hour video game -- without the benefit
of remote controls

February 8, 2010

Full Review ☒ | Comments (2)

— *RottenTomatoes.com*

Notice, by the way, that readers are invited to comment on the reviews, to say what they think—and thus to join in the conversation. On *RottenTomatoes.com*, everyone can be a reviewer.

This chapter provides guidelines for writing reviews—whether an academic book review for a political science class or a review of a new album that you want to post on a blog or on Amazon.

THINK ABOUT REVIEWS you've read. All reviews evaluate something—a product, a performance, a text—and they do so using relevant criteria. Someone reviewing a movie, for instance, would generally consider such factors as the quality of the script, acting, directing, and cinematography. Think about a product you are familiar with or a performance you have recently seen. Develop a list of criteria for evaluating it, and then write an explanation of why these criteria are appropriate for your subject. What does this exercise help you better understand about reviews?

Across Academic Fields

Reviews are written in many academic disciplines. One typical academic review is the book review, in which a student summarizes and critically evaluates a text. Writing a book review is a particularly common assignment in the *humanities* and *social sciences*. In the *creative arts*—from music to visual art to dance—reviews focus on artistic works and performances. Students in *family and consumer sciences* often write reviews of various products, as do students in *business*. When writing an academic review, you need to take particular care to develop appropriate criteria for your evaluation and to support that evaluation with substantial evidence. The kind of evidence you show will vary across disciplines. If you're evaluating a literary work, you'll likely need to show evidence from the text (quotations, for example), whereas if you are evaluating a proposed tax policy for

Alissa Wilkinson's review of a movie provides her an opportunity to add social commentary as well. See how she blends the two strands on p. 949.

an economics class, you're probably going to be required to show numerical data (such as statistics demonstrating projected outcomes).

Across Media

Reviews can appear in many media—from print to digital, online to television and radio. Each medium offers different resources and challenges. A *television* film critic reviewing a new movie can intersperse clips from the

**THINK
BEYOND
WORDS**

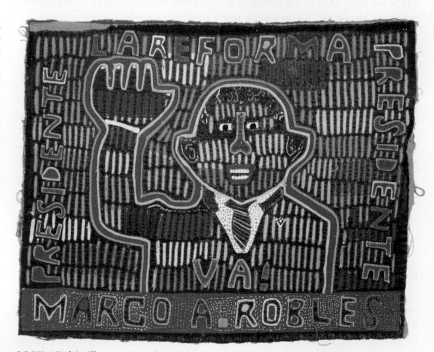

LOOK AT this illustration of a mola, an appliqué panel made in Panama, from a review of Testimonios: 100 Years of Popular Expression, *an exhibit at New York's El Museo del Barrio in 2012. The same review on the web includes a slideshow of art; see it at* wwnorton.com/write/everyonelinks. *The article on the site includes links to further information, but it's otherwise identical to the print version. How else could the web version take advantage of the medium—with maps? music? video? interviews? What else?*

film to back up her points, but her own comments must be brief. A different critic, writing about the same film for a *print magazine*, can develop a fuller, more carefully reasoned review—but with still images rather than video clips. (Take a look at the illustration from an art review in a newspaper on the facing page; go to the same article on the web, and you'll find a whole slide show.) As a college student, you will often be assigned to write an essay reviewing something—a book, a work of art, a musical performance—and you might well have occasion to use various media. For instance, if you give an *oral presentation* reviewing an art show, you might create slides that show some of the art you will discuss and that summarize your evaluation. Sometimes you'll be assigned to use a particular medium, but if you get to choose, you'll need to think about which medium (or media) will allow you to best cover your subject and reach your audience.

Across Cultures and Communities

The conventions for reviewing vary across communities and cultures. In most U.S. academic contexts, reviews are quite direct, explicitly stating whether something is good or bad, and why; in other contexts, reviews might be more guarded. When the *Detroit News* reviews a new car, for instance, its writers have to keep in mind the sensitivities of the community, many of whom work in the auto industry, and of the company that produces that car, a major advertiser in the newspaper. *Consumer Reports* might review the same car very differently, since it is supported not by advertisers (it has none) but by subscribers, consumers who want impartial data that will help them decide whether or not to purchase that car.

Read a review from an edgy pop culture blog on p. 915 and think about what the author might have had to change for publication in a national magazine.

Reviews are routine in the workplace, where employees receive annual written evaluations by their supervisors. There are often explicit criteria for evaluating workers, but they vary across professional communities: the criteria for someone who works at a hospital (a *medical community*) will be different from those for college instructors (an *academic community*).

At school, when you're assigned to write a review, one challenge will be to figure out what's expected. If you're reviewing a magazine for a journalism class, your goals will be different from what they would be if you were reviewing a draft by a friend who's writing an article for that magazine. As with any rhetorical situation, you'll need to figure out what's customary—and what's expected of you as a reviewer.

Across Genres

Writers will often use evaluation as a strategy in other genres. **PROPOSALS** offer solutions to problems, for example, and thus they must consider—and review—various solutions. Evaluation and **ANALYSIS** often go hand in hand, as when *Consumer Reports* analyzes a series of smart phones in order to evaluate and rank them for their readers.

LOOK FOR several reviews of a favorite movie. First, consult some print reviews. Then try to find one of those in its online version: How does it change from one medium to the next? What, if anything, does the online version have that the print version does not? Then check out some fan sites or messages on Twitter *about the same movie: How does the medium affect the decisions that a reviewer makes about content, length, style, and design?*

CHARACTERISTIC FEATURES

Whatever the audience and medium, the most successful reviews share most of the following features:

- Relevant information about the subject
- Criteria for the evaluation
- A well-supported evaluation
- Attention to the audience's needs and expectations
- An authoritative tone
- Awareness of the ethics of reviewing

Relevant Information about the Subject

The background information needed in a review may entail anything from the plot summary of a novel to items from a restaurant menu to a description of the graphics of a video game. How much information to include depends on your rhetorical situation. In the case of an academic review, your teacher may specify a length, which will affect how much information you can provide. Nonacademic reviews vary depending on the audience and publication. Someone reviewing a new album by an indie group for *Rolling Stone*, a magazine devoted to music, politics, and pop culture, may not need to provide much background information since readers are already likely to be familiar with the group. This would not be the case, however, if the same author were writing a review for a general-interest magazine, such as *Time*.

See how a review of the Nintendo 3DS device opens with background information to help readers appreciate how the new device improves on other 3-D devices:

> Nintendo's new 3DS device is quite literally like nothing you have seen before.
>
> Have you ever watched full-motion 3-D video without wearing those annoying special glasses? Didn't think so. With the 3DS, set to make its debut on Sunday, you will.
>
> In the guise of a hand-held game machine that costs about $250, Nintendo has produced a most astonishing entertainment device. In an age of technical wonders, Nintendo's only competition in innovating personal electronics is Apple.
>
> Though the DS has sold substantially more units than the iPhone (about 145 million DS's worldwide by the end of last year, to about 90 million iPhones), it generally eludes the attention of the technology and media elite because so many of its users are children.
>
> That will change very quickly now. Just about every child in America who likes video games is going to want a 3DS; the clamor will reach a fever pitch this weekend and will continue straight through the summer and into the holiday season. And millions of adults, who previously paid little attention to their kids' game machines, are going to look at it just once and say, "Wow."
>
> —SETH SCHIESEL, "Nintendo's New World of Games"

Nintendo 3DS

This example comes from a review written for the *New York Times;* the author assumes that his readers have some familiarity with 3-D images but that they may not have paid much attention to video game machines. Notice the three underscored words: In the web version, readers can click on these links to read all about (and purchase) each of the products.

Joaquin Phoenix as Johnny Cash in *Walk the Line* (2005).

Reviews of films (and other narratives) often provide background information about the story, as does the following example from a newspaper review of *Walk the Line*, the film about the singer Johnny Cash:

> Arkansas, 1944. Two brothers walk the long, flat corridor of earth between one corn field and another. Jack Cash, the elder, is memorizing the Bible. His little brother prefers the music of the hymnals and worries that Jack's talent for stories is the nobler enterprise. Jack wants to be a preacher. "You can't help nobody," he explains, "if you don't tell them the right story." Yet we already know it is his little brother, Johnny, who will grow up to tell the memorable stories, the kind you sing, the kind that matter most. In their own generic way, musical biopics are always the right story: the struggle towards self-actualization. With songs. They are as predictable and joyful as Bible stories: the Passion of Tina Turner, the Ascension of Billie Holiday. It is a very hard-hearted atheist indeed who does not believe that Music Saves. —ZADIE SMITH

This review was written for the *Daily Telegraph*, a British newspaper, by the well-known novelist Zadie Smith. She opens with a summary of the story as the film begins and quotes some dialogue that catches our interest—but she also tells us something about musical "biopics," the film's genre. In short, this review's opening gives us information we will need, and that makes us want to read on.

Criteria for the Evaluation

Underlying all good reviews are clear criteria—things that matter in deciding whether your subject succeeds or doesn't succeed, is strong or weak, or good in some respects and poor in others. As an author, then, you'll need to establish the criteria for any review you write. Sometimes the criteria are obvious or can be assumed: Criteria for reviewing cars, for example, would include price, style, comfort, performance, safety, gas mileage, reliability, and so on. Often, however, you may want to shape the criteria for specific purposes and audiences. In reviewing a concert for your composition class, you probably can't assume that your teacher, a primary audience for the review, is necessarily familiar with the performance you're reviewing, so you'll need to state your criteria explicitly: the program, the venue, the performers and musicians, the acoustics, and any special effects. If you're posting a quick review of the same concert on *Facebook* or *Twitter,* you may be able to assume that your followers are familiar with most of these criteria and skip straight to the evaluation.

One well-known source for evaluating colleges and universities is the annual rankings published by *U.S. News & World Report,* whose criteria are stated explicitly. Here's how one college, Texas A&M University, fared in this ranking system in 2012, coming in at number 63:

Tuition	Total Enrollment Fall 2009	Acceptance Rate	Average Freshman Retention Rate	6–year Graduation
In-state: 8,387 Out of state: 22,817	48,703	67%	92%	80%

In addition to these stated criteria, *U.S. News & World Report* includes brief reviews written by students, like this one:

> I love Texas A&M for all of its quirks and traditions. There is no other school this large where you will not feel like just another number to the faculty and staff. In fact, I rarely notice that the school is big at all. I love that everything seems to have a tradition to go along with it. While it takes a while to learn them all, and a lot of them seem kind of hokey, the traditions will enrich your college experience, and make you feel a kinship with your fellow schoolmates. Everyone you meet on campus is not a stranger, but merely a friend you've yet to meet! It's so true. Aggies are the friendliest bunch you will encounter. We are always willing to lend a hand, give directions, and answer any question you might have. We would welcome anyone with open arms. And while A&M is in many ways a great school, we do have our quirks, but you learn to live with and love them, to embrace them as your own.   —K'LEE, senior at Texas A&M

Note that the first set of criteria for ranking schools call for quantitative data, whereas K'Lee uses qualitative criteria such as the campus atmosphere ("you will not feel like just another number") and values ("everything seems to have a tradition to go along with it").

A Well-Supported Evaluation

At the center of every review is a clear evaluation, a **CLAIM** that something is good or bad, right or wrong, useful or not. Whatever you're reviewing, you need to give reasons for what you claim and sufficient evidence to support those reasons. And because rarely is anything all good or all bad, you also need to acknowledge any weaknesses in things you praise and any positives in things you criticize. Also, remember to anticipate reasons that others might evaluate your subject differently than you do. In other words, you need to acknowledge and respond to other views.

Journalist Amy Goldwasser approached a number of passengers on a New York subway and asked them for impromptu reviews of what they were reading. She then collaborated with the illustrator Peter Arkle to compose graphic reviews for the *New York Times Book Review*. Here's what two readers had to say:

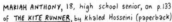

MARIAH ANTHONY, 18, high school senior, on p.133 of THE KITE RUNNER, by Khaled Hosseini (paperback)

I read every day. Every. Day. I'm not a novel-reader. I'm more self-help and psychology. But this is an amazing book. You should read it. The author went way into depth. Where I'm at, the main character's 18. He and his father moved to San Francisco from Kabul...they were refugees who had to be smuggled into the States. He had to travel *inside an oil tank* to be here. I don't think I can exactly relate, but it's about how people go through things. It's beautiful.

DON SHEA, 70, fiction writer, on p.214 of LIT, by Mary Karr (paperback)

This is her third book. I've read the first two. She's a poet.... I've been struck by the **wonderful** metaphors. I'm always surprised when poets really write superb prose. It gets a little draggy in the rehab part. She just keeps **slipping and slipping**. But it's good—all her stuff is good.

Both readers clearly stated what they thought of the books they were reading ("an amazing book," "it's good"). And then they gave reasons ("the author went way into depth," "all her stuff is good") and evidence to support those reasons ("he had to travel *inside an oil tank* to here," "wonderful metaphors"). Note as well that one of the readers, Don Shea, acknowledges one weakness in Mary Karr's book ("It gets a little draggy in the rehab part").

When you're writing a review for a college class, you'll need to be more systematic and organized than these off-the-cuff reviews—with an explicitly stated evaluation, for one thing. See how a more formal review opens with a clear evaluation of a documentary film about a cave in southern

France that contains paintings thought to have been done more than 30,000 years ago:

> What a gift Werner Herzog offers with *Cave of Forgotten Dreams*, an inside look at the Cave of Chauvet-Pont d'Arc—and in 3-D too.
> —MANOHLA DARGIS, "Herzog Finds His Inner Man"

The reviewer states her evaluation explicitly: The film is so good it is "a gift." As the review continues, she gives her readers background information on the cave and provides good reasons for her evaluation: "It's a blast . . . to see these images, within 3-D grabbing reach"; "Herzog is "an agreeable, sometimes . . . funny guide, whether showing you the paintings or talking with the men and women who study them"; and he "also has a talent for tapping into the poetry of the human soul." At the same time, though, she acknowledges that the film has some shortcomings, though nothing that changes her overall assessment:

> *Cave of Forgotten Dreams* is . . . an imperfect reverie. The 3-D is sometimes less than transporting, and the chanting voices in the composer Ernst Reijseger's new-agey score tended to remind me of my last spa massage. Yet what a small price to pay for such time traveling!

In addition, the reviewer provides an image from the film, visual evidence of the "inside look" the *Cave of Forgotten Dreams* offers:

A still from *Cave of Forgotten Dreams* (2010).

This review appeared in the *New York Times;* the print version includes the photo shown here, but the web version also includes four video clips from the film, along with several reviews posted by readers.

Attention to the Audience's Needs and Expectations

All authors need to consider what their audience expects from them. But this consideration plays a particularly important role in the case of reviews. Some audiences will be familiar with what you're reviewing, whereas others will need a detailed summary or description; some will expect an explicit statement of the criteria for the evaluation, while others will know what the criteria are without being told.

Audience considerations can also influence the criteria that reviewers identify as most crucial for their evaluation. Consider, for instance, the video game *Grand Theft Auto: San Andreas*. Gamers might expect one set of criteria of a review, perhaps focusing on the game's playability and entertainment value. Parents and teachers might want entirely different criteria, those that call attention to the game's violence and strong language or reflect concerns about the personal and social consequences of extended video game playing.

Here, for instance, is the introduction to a review of *Grand Theft Auto* from the website *Inside Mac Games*. This review is clearly written from the perspective of someone concerned primarily with the art and craft—and playability—of video games.

> October 25, 2004—I'm not going to beat around the bush. *Grand Theft Auto: San Andreas* is the single best PlayStation 2 title I have ever played. It's larger than the biggest RPG, has more story than the heftiest adventure game, and has almost as many mini-games as Nintendo's *Mario Party*. Additionally, it has a production value that's second to none, boasts a faithfulness to '90s source material with an eerie accuracy, and provides more hours of entertainment than all the previous *Grand Theft Autos* combined. In short, it's a terrific unending masterpiece of a game—and one that will never fall victim to an over-exaggeration of its lofty status. It's *the* defining piece of software for Sony's successful sophomore system, and it's almost impossible to imagine a PlayStation 2 library without it.

Now I realize that with a statement like that, I leave a lot of expectations on the table. Immediate questions from longtime *GTA* players (and haters) will no doubt surface regarding what kind of problems *San Andreas* must have. Does the frame rate still stutter? Is pop-in and draw distance still an issue? Are there any collision quandaries or other graphics-related bugs? Are the sound effects still tame by other action game standards? Does the AI ever have stupid moments or not perform the way you'd want it to? And is it true that there's absolutely no form of online play whatsoever? To be honest, the answer to all those questions is a definite yes. But an even better question to ask (and one that has a lot more direct impact) is, "Do any of the issues explored above really detract from the overall experience?" In a word: No.

—JEREMY DUNHAM, *Inside Mac Games*

Not only are the criteria that the author uses to evaluate the video game clear—size, production value, a faithfulness to the source material, and so on—but they reflect the values of those in the gaming community. Dunham also assumes his readers know the language of gamers and thus uses abbreviations and terms like "RPG" (for role-playing game), "frame rate," "pop-in," and "draw distance" without taking the time to define them (which, by the way, would position him as an outsider to the gaming community and thus diminish his credibility with readers). He signals his respect for his readers' knowledge by acknowledging weaknesses that they will be concerned about, such as stuttering frame rate, "graphics-related bugs," and tame sound effects.

THINK ABOUT how audiences affect reviews. Find two reviews of the same subject (such as a movie you've seen recently or a band you know well) in two different publications—Entertainment Weekly and Vibe, perhaps, or Rolling Stone and Time. Look over the two magazines, considering both the articles and ads, and decide what kind of audience each one seems to address. Young? Female? Male? Affluent? Hip? Intellectual? A broad general audience? Now study each magazine's review. How long is it? How much space is devoted to describing the subject and how much to evaluation? How much prior knowledge does each reviewer expect on the part of readers? What about the criteria each reviewer uses—are they the same, and if not, what might account for the difference? What does this analysis tell you about the role that audience plays in the way that reviews are written?

An Authoritative Tone

As the above review of *Grand Theft Auto* suggests, reviewers often make strong assertions but have only limited space to make and support their claims. Given this constraint, how can a reviewer come across as authoritative and worth listening to?

Authors of reviews have multiple ways of establishing their authority and credibility, and introductions are often crucial to doing so. Here, for instance, is the first paragraph of a lengthy review of several histories of American whaling that appeared in the *New Yorker:*

"Moby Dick swam swiftly round and round the wrecked crew."

> If, under the spell of *Moby-Dick,* you decided to run away to the modern equivalent of whaling, where would you go? Because petroleum displaced whale oil as a source of light and lubrication more than a century ago, it might seem logical to join workers in Arabian oil fields or on drilling platforms at sea. On the other hand, firemen, like whalers, are united by their care for one another and for the vehicle that bears them, and the fireman's alacrity with ladders and hoses resembles the whaler's with masts and ropes. Then, there are the armed forces, which, like a nineteenth-century whaleship, can take you around the world in the company of people from ethnic and social backgrounds unfamiliar to you. All these lines of work are dangerous but indispensable, as whaling once was, but none seems perfectly analogous. Ultimately, there is nothing like rowing a little boat up to a sixty-ton mammal that swims, stabbing it, and hoping that it dies a relatively well-mannered death.
>
> —CALEB CRAIN, "There She Blew: The History of American Whaling"

This introduction not only catches readers' attention with a series of arresting examples, but it also demonstrates how thoroughly and carefully the reviewer has thought about his subject, thus making readers trust him and want to hear what he has to say.

Here is the introduction to an essay published in *Harper's Magazine* reviewing a number of works by Egyptian novelists Albert Cossery and Sonallah Ibrahim:

> Egypt is hard on its novelists. Their audience is tiny, their rewards few, their risks considerable. This is true in most if not all Arab countries, but

> Egypt is notable in having a long and astonishingly varied novelistic tradition, some of which is now becoming available in translation.
>
>   —ROBYN CRESWELL, "Undelivered"

The broad generalizations at the start of this review make clear that this reviewer has considerable knowledge about Egyptian novels and Arab literature more generally.

Finally, here is the introduction to a review of Tim Burton's film version of *Alice in Wonderland,* broadcast on National Public Radio on March 4, 2010:

> To enjoy Tim Burton's *Alice in Wonderland,* you'll need to accept that it's not by any stretch Lewis Carroll's *Alice's Adventures in Wonderland* or its follow-up, *Through the Looking Glass,* but a fancy Hollywood hybrid. Yes, it uses *Alice*'s characters and motifs, but the plot is one part C.S. Lewis [the author of *The Chronicles of Narnia*] to one part *The Wizard of Oz.* You could call it "C.S. Lewis Carroll's *Alice in Narnia* with Johnny Depp as the Mad Scarecrow."
>
>   —DAVID EDELSTEIN, "Burton's 'Alice': A Curious Kind of Wonderful"

This introduction shows that the reviewer is knowledgeable about the original novel and also about other children's adventure stories and Hollywood

Johnny Depp as the Mad Hatter in *Alice in Wonderland* (2010)

films. Moreover, his use of humor establishes his voice as one you want to listen to. (And note as well that this text was written to be heard on the radio.)

See how Alex Horton's use of the pronouns *I*, *you*, and *we* bring readers into the action of his analysis on p. 817 and enhance his authority at the same time.

If you get to choose your subject, be sure to select a topic that you know something about and, ideally, that you care about—and share some of what you know in your introduction. Telling your audience something interesting about your subject and giving some sense that it matters will make them want to hear and read more.

Awareness of the Ethics of Reviewing

Depending on context and purpose, a review can have substantial—or minimal—consequences. When the widely syndicated film reviewer Roger Ebert gives a Hollywood movie a thumbs-up or thumbs-down, his judgment can influence whether the movie is shown in theaters across America or goes immediately to DVD. Those reviewing Broadway plays for publications like the *New York Times* hold similar powers. Reviews in *Consumers Reports* can significantly influence the sale of the products they evaluate.

By comparison, a review of a local high school musical will not determine how long the musical will run or how much money it will make, but a negative review will certainly wound the feelings of those involved in the production. And a customer review on Amazon or the *Internet Movie Database (IMDb)* that gives away key elements of a plot will spoil the film for some of the audience.

So an ethical reviewer will always keep in mind that a review has power—whether economic, emotional, or some other kind—and take care to exercise that power responsibly. It's not that you should hold back criticism (or praise) that you think the subject deserves, but you do need to think about the effect of your judgments before you express them. How you express them is also important. In academic contexts, remember this responsibility especially when reviewing other students' drafts. Don't avoid mentioning problems just because you might make the writer feel bad, but be sure that any criticisms are constructive.

STEVEN JOHNSON, the author of several books, including *Everything Bad Is Good for You* (2005) and *Where Good Ideas Come From: The Natural History of Innovation* (2010), and the cofounder and editor-in-chief of *Feed,* one of the earliest webzines, wrote "Mind Matters" for the *New York Times Book Review* in 2009.

Mind Matters

STEVEN JOHNSON

The author gets readers' attention with examples of well-known decisions and establishes an authoritative tone with references to other books and research.

Most great stories revolve around decisions: the snap brilliance of Captain Sullenberger choosing to land his plane in the Hudson, or Dorothea's prolonged, agonizing choice of whether to forsake her husband for true love in *Middlemarch*, or your parents' oft-told account of the day they decided to marry. There is something powerfully human in the act of deliberately choosing a path; other animals have drives, emotions, problem-solving skills, but none rival our capacity for self-consciously weighing all the options, imagining potential outcomes and arriving at a choice. As George W. Bush might have put it, we are a species of deciders.

Tells readers what the book is about (decision-making skills).

Jonah Lehrer's engaging new book, *How We Decide*, puts our decision-making skills under the microscope. At 27, Lehrer is something of a popular science prodigy, having already published, in 2007, *Proust Was a Neuroscientist*, which argued that great artists anticipated the insights of modern brain science. *How We Decide* tilts more decisively in the thinking-person's self-help direction, promising not only to explain how we decide, but also to help us do it better.

This is not exactly uncharted terrain. Early on, Lehrer introduces his main theme: "Sometimes we need to reason through our options and carefully analyze the possibilities. And sometimes we need to listen to our emotions." Most readers at this point, I suspect, will naturally think of Malcolm Gladwell's mega-bestseller *Blink*, which explored a similar boundary between reason and intuition. But a key difference between the two books quickly emerges: Gladwell's book took an external vantage point on its subject, drawing largely on observations from psychology and sociology, while Lehrer's is an inside job, zooming in on the inner workings of the brain. We learn about the nucleus accumbens, spindle cells and the prefrontal cortex. Many of the experiments he recounts involve fMRI scans of brains in the process of making decisions (which, for the record, is a little like making a decision with your head stuck in a spinning clothes dryer).

Introduces book's main focus and how its author approaches the topic.

Demonstrates knowledge of similar books and related research.

Explaining decision-making on the scale of neurons makes for a challenging task, but Lehrer handles it with confidence and grace. As an introduction to the cognitive struggle between the brain's "executive" rational centers and its more intuitive regions, *How We Decide* succeeds with great panache, though readers of other popular books on this subject (Antonio Damasio's *Descartes' Error* and Daniel Goleman's *Emotional Intelligence,* for example) will be familiar with a number of the classic experiments Lehrer describes.

A clear statement of his evaluation.

In part, the neuroscience medicine goes down so smoothly because Lehrer introduces each concept with an arresting anecdote from a diverse array of fields: Tom Brady making a memorable pass in the 2002 Super Bowl; a Stanford particle physicist nearly winning the World Series of Poker; Al Haynes, the Sully of 1989, making a remarkable crash landing of a jetliner whose hydraulic system had failed entirely. The anecdotes are, without exception, well chosen and artfully told, but there is something in the structure of this kind of nonfiction writing that is starting to feel a little formulaic: startling mini-narrative, followed by an explanation of What the Science Can Teach Us, capped by a return to the original narrative with some crucial mystery unlocked. (I say this as someone who has used the device in my own books.) It may well

One reason for his evaluation, supported by evidence from the book.

be that this is simply the most effective way to convey these kinds of ideas to a lay audience. But part of me hopes that a writer as gifted as Lehrer will help push us into some new formal technique in future efforts.

A book that promises to improve our decision-making, however, should be judged on more than its narrative devices. The central question with one like *How We Decide* is, Do you get something out of it? It's fascinating to learn about the reward circuitry of the brain, but on some basic level, we know that we seek out rewards and feel depressed when we don't get them. Learning that this process is modulated by the neurochemical dopamine doesn't, on the face of it, help us in our pursuit of those rewards. But Lehrer's insights, fortunately, go well beyond the name-that-neurotransmitter trivia. He's insightful and engaging on "negativity bias" and "loss aversion": the propensity of the human brain to register bad news more strongly than good. (Negativity bias, for instance, explains why in the average marital relationship it takes five compliments to make up for a single cutting remark.) He has a wonderful section on creativity and working memory, which ends with the lovely epigram: "From the perspective of the brain, new ideas are merely several old thoughts that occur at the exact same time."

For this reader, though, the most provocative sections of *How We Decide* involve sociopolitical issues more than personal ones. A recurring theme is how certain innate bugs in our decision-making apparatus led to our current financial crisis. We may be heavily "loss averse," but only in the short run: a long list of experiments have shown that completely distinct parts of the brain are activated if the potential loss lies in the mid- or long-term future, making us more susceptible to the siren song of the LCD TV or McMansion. So many of the financial schemes that led us astray over the past decade exploit precisely these defects in our decision-making tools. "Paying with plastic fundamentally changes the way we spend money, altering the calculus of our financial decisions," Lehrer writes. "When you buy something with cash, the purchase involves an actual loss—your wallet is literally lighter. Credit cards, however, make the transaction abstract." Proust may have been a neuroscientist, but so were the subprime mort-

Identifies a criterion for the evaluation.

Another criterion.

gage lenders. These are scientific insights that should be instruc- •— *Notes ethical consider-*
tive to us as individuals, of course, but they also have great import   *ations.*
to us as a society, as we think about the new forms of regulation
that are going to have to be invented in the coming years to prevent another crisis.

How We Decide has one odd omission. For a book that plumbs •— *Notes a flaw in the book,*
the mysteries of the emotional brain, it has almost nothing to say   *though one that doesn't*
                                                                        discount his overall evalu-
about the decisions that most of us would conventionally describe   *ation.*
as "emotional." We hear about aviation heroism and poker strategies, and we hear numerous accounts of buying consumer goods.
But there's barely a mention of a whole class of choices that are
suffused with emotion: whether to break up with a longstanding
partner, or to scold a disobedient child, or to let an old friend
know that you feel betrayed by something he's said. For most of
us, I suspect, these are the decisions that matter the most in our
lives, and yet *How We Decide* is strangely silent about them. Perhaps Jonah Lehrer will use his considerable talents to tackle these
most human of decisions in another volume. Until then, we've still
got *Middlemarch*.

✎ *STUDY A REVIEW on a subject that interests you and analyze it, using
the list of characteristic features of reviews on p. 234. Annotate the text you have
chosen as we have done here, noting which of the characteristic features of reviews
are included and which are not. Then consider whether including those features might
have improved the review.*

WRITING A REVIEW / A Roadmap

Choose something to review and find an interesting angle

Even if your subject is assigned, find a way to make it interesting—both for you and your audience.

If you get to choose your topic, begin by identifying a subject in which you already have some interest and expertise. Perhaps you're an avid fan of *Harry Potter*. Reviewing the final novel or film in the series might be a good choice. Or maybe you love mountain biking, in which case you could review the three best-selling bikes. Remember that many things can be reviewed—snowboards, restaurants, books, music. If your assignment is open, consider the full range of your interests before you decide.

If your topic is assigned, try to tailor it to your interests and to find an angle that will engage your audience. For instance, if your assignment is to review a specific art exhibit, ask if you can focus on some aspect of the work that intrigues you, such as the use of color or the way the artist represents nature. If you are assigned a particular book, you can center your review on themes that you find compelling, and that might interest your audience.

Consider your rhetorical situation

Once you have a tentative topic, thinking about your audience and the rest of your rhetorical situation will help you focus on what you need to do next.

Think about what your AUDIENCE knows and expects. If your review is for a class assignment, consider your instructor to be your primary audience unless he or she specifies otherwise. In this situation, it is important to remember that an academic review should be a substantial, well-supported essay.

　　If, however, you're writing for a specific publication or audience, you'll have to think about what's appropriate—or expected. Here are some things to consider:

- Who are you trying to reach, and why?

- How are they like or unlike you? How likely are they to agree with you?

- What do they likely know about your subject? What background information will you need to provide?

- Will the subject matter to them, or will you have to persuade them that it matters?

- What will they be expecting to learn from your review?

Think about your PURPOSE. Why are you writing this review? If it's for a class, what motivations do you have beyond getting a good grade? To recommend a book or film? evaluate the latest iPhone? introduce your classmates to a new musical group? What do you expect your audience to do with the information in your review? Do you want them to go see something? buy something (or not)? just appreciate something? How can you best achieve your purpose?

Consider your STANCE. Think about your overall attitude about the subject and how you want to come across as an author. If you're extremely enthusiastic about your subject, how can you communicate your feelings? What about the subject captured your interest, and how can you get your audience interested in it? How do you want your audience to see you? As well informed? thoughtful? witty? skeptical? How can your review reflect that stance, and how can you gain your audience's trust and respect?

Think about the larger CONTEXT. Is there any background information about your subject that you should consider—other books on the same subject or by the same author? movies in the same genre? similar products made by different companies? What else has been said about your subject? If you're writing for a course assignment, your instructor may specify whether you should (or should not) consider other perspectives and whether you need to acknowledge them in your review.

Consider MEDIA. Whether or not you have a choice of medium—print, spoken, or electronic—you need to think about how your medium will affect what you can do in your review. If you're presenting it online or to a live audience, you may be able to incorporate video and audio clips—for example, of a film or a concert. If your review will appear in print, can you include still photos? And most important of all: If you get to choose your medium which one will best reach your audience?

Consider matters of DESIGN. If you are writing an academic review essay, you will want to follow the format requirements of the discipline you're writing in. If you're writing for a particular publication, you'll need to find out what design options you have. But if you have the option of designing your text, think about what it needs. Should you include any illustrations? Is there any information that would be best presented in a list or a graph? Product reviews, for example, often display data in table form so that readers can compare several products. As always, keep in mind the needs and expectations of your audience.

Evaluate your subject

You need to be knowledgeable about a subject in order to evaluate it. Your subject will be your primary source of information, though you may need to consult other sources to find background information or to become aware of what else has been written about your subject.

Think about your own first impressions. What about the subject got your interest? What was your own first reaction, and why? Do you care enough about the subject to tell others about it?

Examine your subject closely. If you're reviewing a performance, take notes as you're watching it; if you're reviewing a book, read it more than once. Look for parts of your subject that are especially powerful (or weak) to mention in your review.

Do any necessary research. Consider whether learning more about a book's author or a film's director would help you evaluate your subject and put it in context for your audience. If you're writing a review for an academic assignment, do you need to find out what else has been said about your subject?

Determine the criteria for your evaluation. Sometimes these CRITERIA are obvious: Film reviews, for instance, tend to focus on widely shared criteria like acting, directing, script, cinematography, and so forth. At other times, you'll need to establish the criteria that will guide your review. Make a list of criteria that are appropriate for the genre you're reviewing—film, novel, smartphone, whatever—and then decide which criteria are ones that matter to you—and will matter to your audience.

Make a judgment about your subject. Based on the criteria you've established, evaluate your subject. Remember that few things are all good or all bad; you will likely find some things to praise, and others to criticize. Whatever you decide, use your criteria to examine your subject carefully, and look for specific evidence you can cite—**EXAMPLES**, **COMPARISONS**, images, and so on.

Anticipate other points of view. Not everyone is going to agree with your evaluation, and you need to acknowledge what others have said or might say, including **COUNTERARGUMENTS** to what you think. Even if you don't persuade everyone in your audience to accept your judgment, you can demonstrate that your opinion is worth taking seriously.

Think about your mix of summary and evaluation. If you are writing an academic review, you'll need to **DESCRIBE** or summarize your subject fully enough to show that you understand it well. However, be careful to strike an appropriate balance between **DESCRIPTION** or **SUMMARY** and evaluation. If you are writing for a magazine, you should look at other reviews published there to get a sense of their general approach. Some reviews are designed primarily to give a thumbs-up or thumbs-down, for instance, to let readers know whether they should see a movie—or not. In other cases, reviews are occasions for writing about an issue—one newspaper review of the new Martin Luther King Jr. memorial in Washington, D.C., for instance, devoted more space to describing the controversy about the quotes on the monument than to assessing the actual monument. The point is to figure out what's appropriate or expected in any reviews that you write.

Organize and start writing

Once you've determined your general evaluation of your subject, a list of its strengths and weaknesses, and **EVIDENCE** you can draw upon to support your evaluation, it's time to organize your materials and start writing. To organize your review, think about how you want to start, what your evaluation of your subject is, and why.

Come up with a tentative THESIS . What major point do you want to make about your subject? Try writing this point out as a tentative thesis. Then think about whether the thesis should be stated explicitly or not. Also consider whether to put the thesis toward the end of your introduction or save it for the conclusion.

Using the CRITERIA you identified for your review, list your subject's strengths and weaknesses, in order of importance. Provide REASONS and specific EVIDENCE to back them up. Don't forget to acknowledge other points of view.

DESCRIBE or SUMMARIZE your subject fully enough to show you understand it well, but be careful that your evaluation isn't overwhelmed by description or summary.

Draft an OPENING. Describe the subject you're reviewing, and provide any background information your audience may need. Make clear that you know what you're talking about!

Draft a CONCLUSION. Wrap up your review by summarizing your evaluation. If you have any recommendations, here's where to make them known.

Look critically at your draft, get response—and revise

Once you have a complete draft, read it over carefully, focusing on your evaluation, the reasons and evidence you provide as support, and the way you appeal to your audience. If at all possible, ask others—a writing center tutor, classmate, or friend—to read it over, too. Be sure to give your readers a clear sense of your assignment and your intended audience. Here are some questions that can help you or others respond:

- *Is the evaluation stated explicitly?* Is there a clear THESIS —and if not, is one needed?

- *How well does the introduction capture the audience's interest?* How well does it establish your AUTHORITY as a reviewer? How else might the review OPEN ? If there's a *title*, does it make clear what the review is about and engage your interest in reading it?

- *Is the subject DESCRIBED or SUMMARIZED sufficiently?* Is any additional information needed—and will the intended audience need more?

- *How much of the review is* DESCRIPTION *and how much is* EVALUA-TION —and does the balance seem right for the subject?

- *What are the* CRITERIA *for the evaluation?* Are they stated explicitly— and if not, should they be? Do the criteria seem appropriate for the sub-ject and audience? Are there other criteria that should be considered?

- *What good* REASONS *and* EVIDENCE support the evaluation? Will your audience be persuaded?

- *What other viewpoints do you consider,* and how well do you respond to these views? Are there other views you should consider?

- *How would you describe the* STANCE *and* TONE *?* Are they appropriate to the audience and purpose? Is the tone authoritative? If not, what par-ticular words or details make the review seem less than authoritative?

- *How is the draft organized?* Is it easy to follow, with clear TRANSITIONS from one point to the next?

- *What about design?* Should any material be set off as a list or chart or table? Are there any illustrations—and if not, should there be?

- *Is the style*—choice of words, kinds of sentences, level of formality— appropriate for the intended audience?

- *How does the draft conclude?* Is the CONCLUSION decisive and satisfy-ing? How else might it conclude?

- *Is this a fair review?* Even if readers do not agree with the evaluation, will they consider it fair?

⚶ *REFLECT ON WHAT YOU'VE LEARNED. Once you've completed your review, let it settle for a while and then take time to reflect. How well did you argue for your evaluation? How persuasive do you think your readers found your review? Would those who do not agree with your evaluation consider it fair? What additional revisions would you make if you could? Research shows that such reflections help "lock in" what you learn for future use.*

Out of the West: Clint Eastwood's Shifting Landscape

DAVID DENBY

ON A BEAUTIFUL DAY in Wyoming, in 1880, three men gather on a slight rise behind some rocks, ready to do a bit of killing. Two of them—William Munny (Clint Eastwood) and Ned Logan (Morgan Freeman)—are retired professional assassins, disgusted with their past but broke and therefore willing to shoot a couple of cowhands, unknown to either of them, for cash. The third is the excitable "Schofield Kid" (Jaimz Woolvett), who has read Western dime fiction all his life and is hot to plug someone—pretty much anyone will do. Logan is the best shot, and he raises his Spencer rifle, aiming at one of the men, who are rounding up cattle with some others below. But, after hitting the man's horse, Logan can't pull the trigger again; he just can't kill anymore. As the Schofield Kid loudly complains that no one's dead yet, Munny takes the rifle and mortally wounds the cowhand, who howls so persistently for water that Munny shouts at his companions, "Will you give him a drink of water, for Christ's sake? We ain't gonna shoot."

The scene, which appears more than halfway through Clint Eastwood's 1992 Western, *Unforgiven,* is excruciatingly long—nearly five minutes—and, watching it for the first time, you sense almost immediately that the episode is

---

DAVID DENBY is a film critic for the *New Yorker*. This essay, first published in the *New Yorker* in 2010, reviews Clint Eastwood's *Invictus* in the context of his long career.

Clint Eastwood in *For a Few Dollars More (1965), Dirty Harry (1971),* and *Million Dollar Baby (2004).*

momentous. The awkwardly insistent realism has a cleansing force: at least for that moment, ninety years of efficient movie violence—central to the Western and police genres—falls away. Old myths dissolve into the messy stupidity of life, which, as rendered by Eastwood, becomes the most challenging kind of art. It's idiotic to kill a stranger for money, and, not only that, it's hard. Particularly hard on the stranger, but hard on you, too. The Schofield Kid, it turns out, gets to shoot the other cowhand a bit later, as the guy is sitting in the crapper. But, afterward, the Kid is sickened and scared. Everything about the two killings feels wrong, which is all the more surprising since the creator of this sobering spectacle is an actor-director who became famous playing men who killed without trouble, and sometimes with pleasure.

Being underestimated is, for some people, a misfortune. For Eastwood, it became a weapon. Certainly, no one meeting him in his twenties, before his movie career began, would have seen much more than a good-looking Californian who loved beer, women, cars, and noodling at the piano—a fun guy to hang out with. Since those unprepossessing days, he has done the following: starred in a hit TV show, *Rawhide;* appeared in more than fifty movies and directed thirty-one, often acting, directing, and producing at the same time; added several menacingly ironic locutions to the language, such as "Make my day," which Ronald Reagan quoted in the face of a congressional movement to raise taxes; become a kind of mythic-heroic-redemptive figure, interacting with public desire in a way that no actor has done since John Wayne; served as the mayor of Carmel; won four Oscars and received many other awards, including a hug from Nicolas Sarkozy while becoming commander of the Légion d'Honneur, last November. Those who were skeptical of Eastwood forty years ago (I'm one of them) have long since capitulated, retired, or died. He has outlasted everyone.

Early on, his outsider heroes operated with an unshakable sense of right. Such men were angry enforcers of order defined not by law but by primal notions of justice and revenge. "Nothing wrong with shooting as long as the right people get shot," Eastwood's Dirty Harry said in *Magnum Force* (1973). Removed from normal social existence, these low-tech terminators eliminated "the right people" and withdrew into bitter isolation again. Noblesse oblige— or, perhaps, vigilante oblige. Yet by mid-career, in the late nineteen-seventies and early eighties, even as films in the Dirty Harry series were still coming out, Eastwood began showing signs of regret, twinges of doubt and self-reproof, along with a broadening of interest and a stunning increase of aesthetic ambition. He made comedies, bio-pics, and literary adaptations (and twice starred with an orangutan). The movies shifted from stiff, stark, enraged fables, decisive to the point of patness, to something more relaxed and ruminative and questioning. In *Unforgiven,* he holds scenes a few extra beats, so that characters can extend their legs, scratch behind their ears, air some issue of violence or honor. The movie comments on itself as it goes along.

It's now obvious that *Unforgiven* was less an end point than a significant way 5 station on an uninterruptible career path. Eastwood's latest film, *Invictus,* a celebration of the shrewd and noble way that Nelson Mandela united South Africa in 1995, is not one of his best movies—it's a little too simple—but it's devoted to a man who is the opposite of isolated, a man whose sense of right changes an entire society. (Eastwood, a moderate libertarian Republican, has acknowledged parallels with the Presidency of Barack Obama, and expressed his annoyance with the "morbid mood" of America and the "teen-age twits" in Washington.) In all, Eastwood has had an incredibly productive long run, and, in honor of it, Warner Bros. recently issued a DVD boxed set of thirty-four movies that Eastwood starred in or directed for the studio. There is also a recent biography, *American Rebel,* by Marc Eliot, although Richard Schickel's 1996 biography, despite the fact that it reflects Eastwood's views throughout, remains the shrewdest accounting of the director's films and character. At the end of May, rich, garlanded, and exceptionally busy, Eastwood will turn eighty.

Thinking about the Text

1. **SUMMARIZE** in a paragraph or so David Denby's evaluation of Clint Eastwood's long career.

2. How does Denby establish his own **AUTHORITY** and credibility?

3. Denby assumes that some readers know a lot about Eastwood, whereas others know only a little. How does he go about appealing to both **AUDIENCES**?

4. This review begins with an extended description of a scene in one of Eastwood's movies. What does this introduction do to frame what Denby goes on to say about Eastwood?

5. Choose someone you admire—maybe an athlete, writer, actor, or chef—and write a **REVIEW** that evaluates what that person has accomplished.

Undocumented Lives: Migrant Latinos in America

CHRISTINE BOWMAN

T O READ *BETWEEN THE LINES* is to begin to understand the *lives* of undocumented migrant Latinos in America. I emphasize the word *lives* to
avoid the singular, as though all migrant workers were alike. In this book, a
collection of letters between immigrants to the United States and their families
and friends in Mexico and Central America, multiple stories emerge. These
stories—and this book—provide powerful insights into the complex lives of
undocumented immigrants and those they leave behind.

The letters collected in *Between the Lines* are from husbands and wives,
daughters and sons, in-laws, nieces, uncles, sisters, fathers, and mothers.
Friends write to friends. Priests write for those who cannot write themselves.
Surprisingly, the letters from illiterate Latinos—letters that, in the case of
those who speak indigenous languages, have been translated twice—have a
refreshingly emotional style that sounds like conversation. But whether the
authors wrote or dictated their thoughts, almost every letter evokes a sense
of love and longing for those who are far away.

In many letters, writers implore their loved ones to write, send photos,

---

CHRISTINE BOWMAN wrote the following essay for an ethnic studies class at Oregon State University. Bowman's assignment was to review a book related to the
subject matter of the class. The book Chris reviewed is *Between the Lines: Letters
between Undocumented Mexican and Central American Immigrants and Their Families and Friends.* This book was edited by Larry Siems and published in 1992 by the
University of Arizona Press.

send news. To encourage response, the writers send their own news—about health, children, finance. They also share gossip, advice, and hopes for the future. In this respect, these migrants and their families are like any other ordinary "American" family. And yet they are clearly not ordinary. These writers lead difficult lives, more difficult than those of many Americans. In the very first letter, the writer tells of his deep sadness when he realized how much he would have to endure to get to America. Another letter writer describes her disappointment when friends give her a chilly reception when she arrives in the United States: friends were both sad and angry because they knew about the hardships she would now endure.

As these examples indicate, the letters in *Between the Lines* are powerful. And they are also powerfully arranged by editor Larry Siems. Siems has chosen compelling letters and organized them to tell an important story that takes readers behind scary anti-immigrant headlines. Together, they paint a picture of all that the immigrants, those left behind, friends, families, go through—and why in spite of those difficulties they continue to come. The first letters, from those who have recently arrived in this country, speak of hardship but with an underlying tone of hopefulness. The next section comprises letters from those who have been left behind. These letters convey faith in and encouragement for the migrants, as well as fears and advice about how to negotiate new situations. The next three sections, from close friends, spouses, and families, show that while the writers have been apart for some time, they continue to nurture their relationships. The final section includes a mix of letters that emphasize the complexity and difficulty of the lives of immigrants and also remind readers why they continue to risk these difficulties to come to the United States.

Between the Lines contributes to an understanding of the lives of Latino im-   5 migrants in America by telling a story different from those in the media that are told from the perspective of American taxpayers. In contrast, these letters are told from the perspective of the immigrants themselves, who make heart-wrenching decisions to leave family and friends. One man writes poignantly about how he actually hid when his friend came to tell him goodbye because he could not bear the parting. Many apologize to their families for leaving but feel that doing so is the only way that they can help their families.

Between the Lines also corrects many popular misconceptions about the lives of undocumented Latino migrants. These are not people on public assistance. These are workers who are sending money home to loved ones and saving what little they can for their future. The letters tell stories of migrants who are exploited by employers who refuse to pay them after a job has been completed, knowing full well that the undocumented worker has no recourse in such a situation. Letters also tell (time and time again) of migrants being scared because they do not speak English. One writer describes how "here one feels like a sad lost dog" (200).

Clearly, as Larry Siems indicates in his comments on the letters in this collection, these are individuals attempting to lead ordinary lives. They are also people who are deeply misunderstood and shamelessly abused. It's heartbreaking to read of vigilante groups who look on border crossings as opportunities for target practice. How ironic that many citizens in the United States are concerned about such practices as bilingual education but can't see the many ways that Latino migrants are mistreated in our country.

Between the Lines tells the story of human beings who are striving to provide for themselves and for their families. This should be a familiar story—but in this case it is not. These people know what it's like for their families to go hungry. Many know the horrors of war. And all know what it's like to be forced to leave the ones they love in order for them (and their families) to survive. Read this book if you want to know the other side of the story.

Thinking about the Text

1. How does Christine Bowman establish her **AUTHORITY** and credibility? What role, if any, does her use of the first-person *I* play?

2. What is her **EVALUATION** of the book she's reviewing, and what **EVIDENCE** does she offer in support of her views?

3. What **CRITERIA** does she use as a basis for her evaluations? How do you know?

4. Bowman wrote this review for an assignment in an ethnic studies class. How does this **RHETORICAL SITUATION** affect the way she wrote the review? Imagine that she wrote a review of the same book for an anti-immigrant blog. What changes would she have to make to reach that audience?

5. Choose a book, performance, game, or film that you like—or do not like. Then write a **REVIEW**, taking care to establish the criteria for your evaluation and to show evidence from the subject you're reviewing to support what you say.

TWELVE

Choosing Genres

COMICS HAVE MANGA, superheroes, and fantasy. Music has hip-hop, country, and folk. Video games? Think shooters, simulation, or role-playing. How about restaurants? Try Italian, Vietnamese, Tex-Mex, vegan, or southern soul food. Or movies: westerns, thrillers, drama, anime. These are all genres, and they are one important way we structure our world.

Genres are categorizations, ways of classifying things. The genres this book is concerned with are kinds of writing, but you'll find genres everywhere you look.

In fact, rhetorician and researcher Carolyn Miller has been tracking the use of the word *genre* and has found it everywhere, including on many of the sites you visit every day. *Netflix* lists 21 genres, from anime to sci-fi, thriller, and documentary—and many subgenres within each of these. *Wikipedia*'s entry on video games provides an extensive list of game genres, and *Podcast Alley* features a column that invites visitors to "pick a podcast genre." You can even see new genres developing on *YouTube,* including microgenres like "cute babies" or "cats being mean." And *iTunes* lists so many genres of media and apps—135 as this book goes to press—that a *Google* search for "*iTunes* genres" turned up sites offering advice on how to deal with them all. Indeed, there is now such a proliferation of genres that they've become the subject of parody, as in the cartoon on the next page.

In this cartoon, Roz Chast comes up with her own new movie genres: sci-fi/western, musical/self-help, sport/horror, and documentary/romance.

What You Need to Know about Genres of Writing

Genres are kinds of writing that you can use to accomplish a certain goal and reach a particular audience. As such, they have well-established features that help guide you, but they're not fill-in-the-blank templates; you may often need to stretch and adapt them to your own rhetorical situations.

Genres have features that can guide you as a writer and a reader. Argument essays, for instance, take a position supported by reasons and evidence, consider a range of perspectives, and so on. These features help guide you as an author in what you write—and they also set up expectations for you as a reader, affecting the way you interpret what you read. If something's called a report, for instance, you are likely assume that it presents information—that it's in some way factual.

This book covers those genres that are most often assigned in school: **ARGUMENTS**, **ANALYSES**, **PROFILES**, **REPORTS**, **NARRATIVES**, **REVIEWS**, **PROJ-**

ECT PROPOSALS, and **ANNOTATED BIBLIOGRAPHIES**. These are kinds of writing that have evolved over the years as a useful means of creating and sharing knowledge. As you advance in a major, you will become familiar with the most important genres and subgenres in that field. Especially when you are new to a genre, its features can serve as a kind of blueprint, helping you know how to approach an assignment. Knowing these features helps you organize a text and guides your choices in terms of content.

Genres can be flexible. Keep in mind that genres can be both enabling and constraining. Sometimes you'll have reason to adapt genre features to suit your own goals. One student who was writing an analysis of a sonnet, for example, wanted to bend the analysis genre just a little to include a sonnet of his own. He checked with his teacher, got approval, and it worked. You probably wouldn't want to stretch a lab report in this way, however. Lab reports follow a fairly set template, covering purpose, methods, results, summary, and conclusions to carry out the goals of the scientific fields that use them; they would not be appropriate (or effective) in a creative writing class.

Gerald Graff includes a personal narrative that describes how he and his friends analyzed sports teams in an essay that argues a position on p. 787.

You may also have occasion to combine genres—to tell a story in the course of arguing a position or to conclude a report with a proposal of some kind. If ever you decide to adapt or combine genres, think hard about your rhetorical situation: What genres will help you achieve your purpose? reach the audience you're addressing? work best in the medium you're using?

Genres evolve. While it is relatively easy to identify some characteristic genre features, such features are not universal rules. Genres are flexible, and they evolve across time and in response to shifting cultural contexts. Letters, for example, followed certain conventions in medieval Europe (they were handwritten, of course, and they were highly formal); by the twentieth century, letters had developed dozens of subgenres (complaint letters, congratulatory letters, application letters). Then, in the 1990s, letters began to morph into email, adapting in new and different ways to online situations. Today, text messages and tweets both may be seen as offshoots of the letter genre.

Or think of *Facebook*. In the early twentieth century, partygoers entertained themselves by drawing caricatures of each other and compiling them in collections they called "face books." Later, some colleges and boarding schools extended this practice by creating more formal face books, directories containing the name and photo of every student in a class. And then, in 2004, *Facebook* entered the world of social media.

And as with all genres and subgenres, letters, email, text messages, and

Facebook pages have developed their own conventions and features, ones that guide you as a writer and a reader.

⁓◎ *THINK ABOUT a favorite song, movie, or game, and then decide what genre it is. How do you know? List the features that help you identify it as belonging to a particular genre. What do you know about that genre? Name a few other examples of that genre, and then think about what features they have in common.*

Deciding Which Genres to Use

Sometimes you'll be assigned to write in a particular genre, but other times your assignments won't make the genre perfectly clear. The following advice can help determine which genre(s) to use when the choice is yours. In all cases, remember to consider your **PURPOSE** for writing and the **AUDIENCE** you want to reach in deciding which genres would be most appropriate.

If an assignment specifies a genre, think about what you know about the genre, about what it expects of you as a writer, and turn to the appropriate chapter in this book for details about its characteristic features and a roadmap to writing something in that genre.

If an assignment doesn't specify a genre, are there any keywords that suggest one? *Discuss*, for example, could indicate a **REPORT** or an **ANALYSIS**; you would want to ask your instructor which it is. And you might also need to consider how such a keyword is used in the discipline the assignment comes from—*analyze* in a philosophy assignment doesn't likely mean the same thing as in a literature assignment. In either case, you should ask your instructor for clarification.

Consider this assignment from an introductory communications course: "Look carefully at letters to the editor in one newspaper over a period of two weeks, and write an essay describing what you find. Who are the letter writers? What issues are they writing about? How many different perspectives are represented?" Though this assignment doesn't name a genre, it seems to be asking students for a **REPORT**: to research a topic and then report on what they find.

But what if this were the assignment: "Look carefully at letters to the editor in one newspaper over a period of two weeks, and write an essay describing what you find. Who are the letter writers? What issues are they writing about? How many different perspectives are represented? What rhetorical strategies do the writers use to get their points across? Draw some conclusions based on what you find." This assignment also asks students to research a topic and report on what they find. But in asking them to draw some conclusions based on their findings, it is also prompting them to do some **ANALYSIS**. As you look at your own assignments, look for words or other clues that will help you identify which genres are expected.

If an assignment doesn't include any clues, here are some questions to ask in thinking about which one may be most appropriate:

- *What discipline is the assignment for?* Say you're assigned to write about obesity and public health. If you're writing for a political science course, you might write an essay **ARGUING** that high-calorie sodas should not be sold in public schools. If, on the other hand, you're writing for a biology class, you might **REPORT** on experiments done on eating behaviors.

- *What is the topic?* Does it suggest that a specific genre is called for? If you are asked, for example, to write about the campaign speeches of two presidential candidates, that topic suggests that you're being asked to **ANALYZE** the speeches (and probably **COMPARE** them). You can then follow the guidelines for writing analytically and comparing in Chapters 9 and 14 in this book.

- *What is your purpose in writing?* If you want to convince your readers that they should "buy local," for example, your purpose will likely call for an **ARGUMENT**. If, however, you want to explain what buying local means, your purpose will call for a **REPORT**.

- *Who is the audience?* What interests and expectations might they have? Say you're assigned to write about the collective-bargaining rights of unions for a first-year seminar. There your audience would include other first-year students, and you might choose to write a **NARRATIVE** about the father of a friend who lost his job as a high school teacher. Imagine, however, writing on the same topic for a public policy course; there you would be more likely to write an essay **ANALYZING** the costs and benefits of unionized workers in the public sector.

- *What medium will you use?* Are there certain genres that work well—or not—in that medium? If you are assigned to give an oral presentation, for example, you might consider writing a **NARRATIVE** because listeners can remember stories better than they are able to recall other genres. Even if you decide to write an analysis or a report, you might want to include some narrative.

If the assignment is wide open, draw on what you know about genres. Sometimes you may receive a very broad assignment, one that leaves the topic and genre up to you. Consider, for example, an assignment one of the authors of this book got in college: In an exam for a drama class, the professor came into the room, wrote "Tragedy!" on the blackboard, and said, "You have an hour and a half to respond." We hope you don't run into such a completely open-ended assignment, especially in a timed exam. But if you do, your knowledge of genre can help out. If this assignment came in a Shakespeare course, for example, you might **ARGUE** that *Hamlet* is his most powerful tragedy. Or you might **ANALYZE** the role of gender in one of his tragedies.

Luckily, such wide-open assignments are fairly rare. It's more likely that you will encounter an assignment like this one: "Choose a topic related to our course theme and carry out sufficient research on that topic to write an essay of eight-to-ten pages. Refer to at least six sources and follow MLA citation style." In this instance, you know that the assignment calls for some kind of research-based writing and that you need a topic and thesis that can be dealt with in the length specified. You could write an *argument*, taking a position and supporting it with the research you have done. Or you could write a *report* that presents findings from your research. At this point, you would be wise to see your instructor to discuss your choices. Once you have decided on a genre, turn to the appropriate chapter in this book to guide your research and writing.

When an assignment is wide open, you can also try using what you know about genre as a way to explore your topic:

- What are some of the **POSITIONS** on your topic? What's been said or might be said? What controversies or disagreements exist? What's your own perspective?

- What stories— **NARRATIVES** —could you tell about it?

- What information might be important or interesting to **REPORT** on?

- How can your topic be evaluated, or **REVIEWED**?

- How might you **ANALYZE** your topic? What are its parts? What caused it—or what effects might it have? Does it follow a certain process?

LOOK AT THREE ASSIGNMENTS you have done for any of your classes. Did the assignment specify a genre? If so, what was it? If not, what genre would you say you were being asked to use—and how can you tell?

PART III

The Role of Argument

CHANCES ARE that your first attempt to communicate was an argument. Your first cry, that is, argued that you were hungry or sleepy or wanted to be held. Later, you could use words to say what you wanted: "More!" "No!" "Candy!" All arguments. So if you think that argument is just about disputes or disagreements, think again. In rhetorical terms, *argument* refers to any way that human beings express themselves to try to achieve a certain purpose—which, many would argue, means any way that people express themselves at all.

If you think about the kinds of writing covered in this book, for example, it is easy to understand that an op-ed taking a position on a political issue or a TV critic's rave review of a new movie is "arguing" for or against something. An editorial cartoon about the issue or an ad for the movie is making an obvious argument, too. But even when you post an update on *Facebook* about something you did yesterday, you're implicitly arguing that it will be intriguing or important or perhaps amusing to your audience, those who follow you on *Facebook*. Likewise, when you write a lab report, you'll describe and interpret the results of an experiment, arguing that your findings have certain implications.

In fact, we are immersed in argument. Try counting the number of arguments you either make or encounter in just one day, starting perhaps with the argument you have with yourself over what to wear, moving on to the barrage of posters asking you to support certain causes or attend various concerts, to a biology lecture where the professor explains the conflicting arguments about climate change, and ending only when you and a friend agree to disagree about who's the better quarterback, Eli Manning or his brother Peyton. We bet you'll be surprised by how many arguments you encounter in a day.

The point we want to make is simple: You are the author of many arguments and the target of many more—and you'll be better at making your own arguments if you understand how they work.

It's important to mention as well that arguments today often consist of more than just words, from the signs admonishing you to fasten your seat belt, to a big "thumbs up," to an ad for McDonald's. These familiar images demonstrate the way words and pictures and graphics can all make strongly visual arguments.

It's also worth noting that arguments today are more seductive than ever. A fifteen-second TV sound bite sways millions of voters; a song you loved as a twelve-year-old now boosts sales of soft drinks; celebrities write op-ed essays in newspapers on issues they care about. Even your school mounts arguments intended to attract prospective students and their parents—and, later, to motivate alumni to give generously. Check out your school's homepage and you'll probably find announcements intended to attract applications and contributions.

Perhaps you think that such arguments are somewhat manipulative, intended to trick you into buying a product or contributing to a cause. But arguments are always trying to achieve some purpose, so it is up to you both as a reader and writer to distinguish the good from the bad. And arguments can, of course, be used for good (think of the powerful arguments for human rights) or ill (think of Hitler's hypnotic arguments). They can be deceptive,

Words and images can make strong visual arguments.

even silly—does that gorgeous woman holding a can of cleanser really mean to claim that if you buy the cleanser you'll look just like her?

In fact, argument is about many things and has many purposes. Of the many purposes we might name, here are just a few:

To understand

To explore

To inform

To convince or persuade

To make decisions

To reach consensus

Keep in mind that arguments are always embedded in particular contexts—and that what is persuasive can vary from one context to another, or from one culture to another. The most persuasive evidence in one community might come from religious texts; in another, from personal testimony; in another, from facts or statistics. Especially now that arguments so often take place in cyberspace, reaching people all around the world, it's important to be aware of such differences.

In 1998 Madonna appeared at the MTV Video Music Awards with Hindu markings on her forehead and hands, performing a song whose lyrics were in Sanskrit—the sacred language of Hinduism—in front of a curtain depicting Hindu deities.

For her next song, though, she shifted radically, wearing a transparent top and performing a highly sexualized dance. What do you think the reac-

Madonna at the 1998 Video Music Awards.

tions were from the live (U.S.) audience at the time? And how do you think people in other countries, particularly in India, may have reacted? What are your reactions? Madonna's performance made an argument, all right, but cultural context played a large part in determining what that argument was—an appreciation of multiculturalism? of Hinduism in particular? Or was her performance a sacrilegious attack on Hinduism? on religious tradition in general? Whatever argument she intended to make may not have been the argument that those watching—both at the live performance and on television across the world—perceived. In the age of the internet, writers, speakers, and performers always need to remember that their intended arguments may be interpreted in multiple ways depending on audience and context.

    During his lifetime, Martin Luther King Jr. did not have the benefit of the internet, but the arguments he made eventually reverberated around the world. In "Letter from Birmingham Jail," King responds to a statement written in 1963 by eight white Alabama clergymen who had urged him to stop his campaign of civil disobedience to protest racial discrimination. This particular context—the U.S. South at the height of the civil rights struggle—

informs his argument throughout. And while King's argument remains the same in some ways, having been republished countless times, its interpretation varies across time and cultures. Thus when the letter first appeared, it responded point by point to the statement by the eight clergymen, and it was read in that time and place as an answer to their particular charges.

Martin Luther King Jr. in a jail cell in Birmingham, Alabama.

Today, however, it is read as a much more general statement about the importance of civil rights for all people. King's famous conclusion to this letter sums up his argument and consciously addresses an audience that extends far beyond the eight clergymen:

> Let us all hope that the dark clouds of racial prejudice will soon pass away and the deep fog of misunderstanding will be lifted from our fear-drenched communities, and in some not too distant tomorrow the radiant stars of love and brotherhood will shine over our great nation with all their scintillating beauty.   —MARTIN LUTHER KING JR., "Letter from Birmingham Jail"

As with all arguments, the effectiveness of King's argument has always varied according to the context in which it is read and, especially, to the audience that is reading it. In most of his letter, King addresses eight specific people, and they are clearly part of his primary audience. But his use of "us" and "our" in the passage above works to broaden that audience and reaches out beyond the current time and place to readers and listeners far beyond.

Because arguments are so central to our lives, it's important to understand how they work—and to learn how to make effective arguments of your own, remembering that you can only do so by paying very careful attention to your rhetorical situation and especially to your purpose and your intended audience. The next two chapters focus on how good arguments work and on strategies for supporting the arguments that you make.

THIRTEEN

Analyzing Arguments

Those You Read,
and Those You Write

 **HE CLOTHES YOU CHOOSE TO WEAR** argue for your own sense of style; the courses your college requires argue for what educators consider important; the kind of transportation you take, the food you eat (or don't eat)—almost everything represents some kind of argument. So it is important to understand all these arguments, those you encounter and those you yourself make. Consider a couple of everyday examples.

What's in an email address? You may not have thought much about the argument that your email address makes, but it certainly does make a statement about who you are. One student we know chose the email address maximman123@yahoo.com, an allusion to the men's magazine. But when it came time to look for meaningful employment, he began to think about what that address said about him. As a result, he chose an address he felt was more appropriate to the image he wanted to convey: whmiller@gmail.com.

If you need to think about what arguments you may be making yourself, it's even more important to understand the arguments that come from others. Take a look, for example, at the two images on the following page, both of which appeared in 2011 after NATO began bombing Libya in support of the forces there rebelling against the regime of

Two 2011 protests: anti-Gaddafi demonstrator in Libya (*left*); demonstrators in front of the White House calling for a stop to the NATO bombing of Libya (*right*).

Moammar Gaddafi. The first image shows a demonstrator against Gaddafi, accusing him of murder; the second takes a very different approach, condemning the bombing.

These two images make radically different arguments about the uprising in Libya, arguments that call on us to think very carefully before we respond. Should we accept one over the other—or reject both of them? On what basis should we make such a decision?

These examples suggest that it's worth your time to think carefully about the arguments you encounter, whether they are embedded in an email address or in an image you see in the news. They also demonstrate that arguments always exist in a larger context, that they always involve more than just the one making the argument. Arguments, in short, don't appear out of thin air: Every argument begins as a response to some other argument—a statement, an event, an image, and so on. That goes for arguments you read, and the ones you yourself write. Either way, all arguments are part of a larger conversation. Whether you're responding to something you've read, discussing a film you've seen, or writing an essay that argues a position, you enter a dialogue with the arguments of others.

This chapter provides guidance to help you analyze an argument—those you encounter, and those you yourself make.

You can tell by the brevity and the directness of his language that Brent Staples is jumping right into an ongoing conversation. See what he's done on p. 935.

WHO'S ARGUING—
AND WHERE ARE THEY COMING FROM?

Pay special attention to the source of an argument—literally to where it is coming from. It makes a difference, in short, whether an argument appears in the *New York Times* or a school newspaper, in *Physics Review* or on the blog of someone you know nothing about, in an impromptu speech by a candidate seeking your vote or in an analysis of that speech done by the nonpartisan website *FactCheck.org*. And even when you know the basic fact of who's putting forward the argument, you may well need to dig deeper to find out where—what view of the world—that source itself is "coming from."

For example, here's the homepage of the website of Public Citizen, a nonprofit organization founded in 1971 by consumer advocate and social critic Ralph Nader. So what can we tell about where this argument is coming from? We might start with the image in the upper-left corner of Lady Liberty holding up her torch right next to the headline "PUBLIC CITIZEN Celebrating 40 Years of Progress." Below that we see a series of rotating images and a sketch of the group's goals.

> Defending democracy. Resisting corporate power. Public Citizen advo-
> cates for a healthier and more equitable world by making government
> work for the people and by defending democracy from corporate greed.
> You can help.

We can surmise, then, that Public Citizen is coming from a viewpoint that
supports the rights of ordinary citizens and liberal democratic values and
that opposes the influence of corporations on government. Indeed, if we
look a bit further, to the "About Public Citizen" page, we will read:

> For four decades, we have proudly championed citizen interests before
> Congress, the executive branch agencies and the courts. We have suc-
> cessfully challenged the abusive practices of the pharmaceutical, nuclear
> and automobile industries, and many others. We are leading the charge
> against undemocratic trade agreements that advance the interests of
> mega-corporations at the expense of citizens worldwide.

Together, these images and statements tell us a lot about Public Citizen's
stance, where the organization is coming from. As savvy readers, we then
have to assess the claims it makes on its homepage (and elsewhere) in light
of this knowledge: Where it's coming from affects how willing we are to accept what it says.

Or consider a more lighthearted example, this time from a column in
the *New York Times* written by political pundit David Brooks:

> We now have to work under the assumption that every American has a
> tattoo. Whether we are at a formal dinner, at a professional luncheon,
> at a sales conference or arguing before the Supreme Court, we have to
> assume that everyone in the room is fully tatted up—that under each
> suit, dress or blouse, there is at least a set of angel wings, a barbed wire
> armband, a Chinese character or maybe even a fully inked body suit. We
> have to assume that any casual anti-tattoo remark will cause offense,
> even to those we least suspect of self-marking.
>
> —DAVID BROOKS, "Nonconformity Is Skin Deep"

What can we know about where Brooks is coming from? For starters, it's
easy to find out that he is a conservative journalist whose work appears
in many publications across the political spectrum and who often appears
as a television commentator on the *PBS NewsHour*. We also know that this

passage comes from one of his regular columns for the *New York Times*. His photo presents him as a professional, in coat and tie.

What more can we tell about where he's coming from in the passage itself? Probably first is that Brooks is representing himself here as somewhat old-fashioned, as someone who's clearly an adult and a member of what might be called "the establishment" in the United States (note his off-handed assumption that "we" might be "at a formal dinner" or "arguing before the Supreme Court"). He's someone who almost certainly does not have a tattoo himself. He's also comfortable using a little sarcasm ("everyone in the room is fully tatted up") and exaggeration ("every American has a tattoo") to make a humorous point. Finally, we can tell that he is a self-confident—and persuasive—author and that we'll need to be on our toes to understand the argument that he's actually making.

David Brooks

As an author, you should always think hard about where *you* are coming from in the arguments you make. What's your **STANCE**, and why? How do you want your audience to perceive you? As reasonable? knowledgeable? opinionated? something else? How can you convey your stance?

WHAT'S AT STAKE?

Figuring out the answer to this question takes you to the heart of the argument. Rhetoricians in ancient Rome developed what they called **STASIS THEORY**, a simple system for identifying the crux of an argument—what's at stake in it—by asking four questions in sequence:

1. What are the facts?
2. How can the issue be defined?
3. How much does it matter, and why?
4. What actions should be taken as a result?

Together these questions help determine the basic issues at stake in an argument. A look at the arguments swirling around Hurricane Katrina and its effects can illustrate how these questions work.

What are the facts? Certainly the hurricane hit the Gulf coast squarely, resulting in almost unimaginable damage and loss of life, especially in New Orleans, where levees failed along with the city's evacuation plan. Many arguments about the disaster had their crux (or stasis) here, claiming that the most important aspect of "what happened" was not the hurricane itself but the lack of preparation for it and the response to it.

How can the issue be defined? In the case of Katrina, the question of definition turned out to be crucial for many arguments about the event: It was easy enough to define the storm itself as a "category 4 hurricane" but much more difficult to classify the disaster beyond that simple scientific tag. To what extent was it a national disaster and to what extent a local one? To what extent was it a natural disaster and to what extent a man-made one? Was it proof of corruption and incompetence on the part of local and state officials? Of FEMA and the Bush administration? Something else?

How much does it matter, and why? In addition to questions of fact and definition, ones about how serious it was also produced many arguments in the wake of Katrina. In the first week or so after the storm hit, the mayor of New Orleans argued that it was the most serious disaster ever to strike that city and that up to 10,000 lives would be lost. Others argued that while the storm represented a huge setback to the people of the region, they could and would overcome their losses and rebuild their cities and towns.

What actions should be taken as a result? Of all the stasis questions, this one was the basis for the greatest number of arguments about Katrina. From those arguing that the federal government should be responsible for fully funding reconstruction, to those arguing that the government should work in concert with insurance agencies and local and state officials, to those arguing that the most damaged neighborhoods should not be rebuilt at all— literally thousands of proposals were offered and debated.

Such questions can help you understand what's at stake in an argument—to help you figure out and assess the arguments put forth by others, to identify which stasis question lies at the heart of an argument—and then to decide whether or not the argument answers the question satisfactorily.

As an author, you can use these questions to identify the main point you want to make in an argument of your own. In the Katrina example, for instance, working through the four stasis questions would help you see the disaster from a number of different perspectives and then to develop a cogent argument related to them.

WHAT'S THE CLAIM?

You probably run into dozens of claims every day. Your brother says the latest Spiderman film is the best one ever; your news feed says that Michigan State will be in the Final Four; a friend's *Facebook* update says it's a waste of time and money to eat at Power Pizza. Each of these statements makes a claim and argues implicitly for you to agree. The arguments you read and write in college often begin with a claim, an arguable statement that must then be supported with good reasons and evidence.

The sign in this photo of a Shell station certainly makes a clear claim: The cost of gasoline is causing great pain to consumers. The station owner, wanting to acknowledge both the fact of high gas prices and how it's affecting customers, has found a concise, amusing way to do it. But note that the claim is made indirectly rather than stated explicitly—and the indirectness is an essential part of its effectiveness as humor, and as advertising.

The easiest claims to identify are those that are stated directly as an explicit **THESIS**. Look, for instance, at the following paragraph from a journal article by civil rights activist W. E. B. Du Bois in 1922. As you read each sentence, ask yourself what Du Bois' claim is.

> Abraham Lincoln was a Southern poor white, of illegitimate birth, poorly educated and unusually ugly, awkward, ill-dressed. He liked smutty stories and was a politician down to his toes. Aristocrats—Jeff Davis, Seward and their ilk—despised him, and indeed he had little outwardly that compelled respect. But in that curious human way he was big inside. He had reserves and depths and when habit and convention were torn away there was something left to Lincoln—nothing to most of his contemners. There was something left, so that at the crisis he was big enough to be inconsistent—cruel, merciful; peace-loving, a fighter; despising Negroes and letting them fight and vote; protecting slavery and freeing slaves. He was a man—a big, inconsistent, brave man.
>
> —W. E. B. DU BOIS, "Abraham Lincoln"

We think you'll find that the claim is difficult to make out until the last sentence, which lets us know in an explicit thesis that the contradictions Du Bois has been detailing are part of Lincoln's greatness, part of what made him "big" and "brave." Take note as well of where the thesis appears in the text. Du Bois holds his claim for the very end.

Here is a very different example, from journalist Maria Hinojosa's 2011 syndicated newspaper column about legendary dancer Judith Jamison. Note that it begins with an explicit thesis stating a claim that the rest of the passage expands on—and supports:

> Judith Jamison is my kind of American cultural icon. . . . She has many accolades and awards—among them the National Medal of Arts, the Kennedy Center Honors and an Emmy. . . .
>
> But when I met her . . . she said with a huge smile, "Yes, honey, but you know I still have to do the laundry myself, and no one in New York parts the sidewalk 'cause I am comin' through!"
>
> I like icons who are authentic and accessible. I think our country benefits from that. It can only serve to inspire others to believe that they can try to do the same thing.
>
> —MARIA HINOJOSA, "Dancing Past the Boundaries"

Judith Jamison dancing at Alvin Ailey City Centre Dance Theater.

Notice that although Hinojosa's claim is related to her own personal taste in American cultural icons, it is not actually about her taste itself. Her argument is not about her preference for cultural icons to be "authentic and accessible." Instead, she's arguing that given this criterion, Judith Jamison is a perfect example.

As an author making an argument of your own, remember that a claim shouldn't simply express a personal taste: If you say that you feel lousy or that you hate *Twitter*, no one could reasonably argue that you don't feel that way. For a claim to be *arguable*—worth arguing—it has to take a position that others can logically have different perspectives on. Likewise, an arguable claim can't simply be a statement of fact that no one would disagree with ("Violent video games earn millions of dollars every year"). And remember that in most academic contexts claims based on religious faith alone often cannot be argued since there are no agreed-upon standards of proof or evidence.

In most academic writing, you'll be expected to state your CLAIM explicitly as a THESIS and to position the thesis near the beginning of your text, often at the end of the introduction or the first paragraph. In most academic contexts in the United States, authors are expected to make their claims directly and get to the point fairly quickly.

Roger Ebert states his claim right in the title—no waiting, no guessing. Check it out on p. 755.

When your claim is likely to challenge or surprise your audience, though, you may want to build support for it more gradually and hold off stating it explicitly until later in your argument, as Du Bois does. The same is true in many speeches and narratives, where a speaker or writer deliberately creates suspense or stimulates curiosity by withholding the thesis until a dramatic point in the text. In other situations, including some narratives and reports, you may not need to make a direct statement of your claim at all. But always make sure in such cases that your audience has a clear understanding of what the claim is.

EMOTIONAL, ETHICAL, AND LOGICAL APPEALS

While every argument appeals to audiences in a wide variety of ways, it's often convenient to lump such appeals into three basic kinds: *emotional* appeals (to the heart), *ethical* appeals (about credibility or character), and *logical* appeals (to the mind).

Emotional Appeals

Emotional appeals stir feelings and often invoke values that the audience is assumed to hold. The paragraph on Lincoln on p. 282, for example, offers a strong appeal to readers' emotions at the end when it represents Lincoln as "big" and "brave," invoking two qualities Americans traditionally value. Images can make especially powerful appeals to our hearts, such as these about the earthquake, tsunami, and nuclear meltdown that devastated Ja-

HOPEHELPHEAL
JAPAN

An image of submerged cars from Japanese TV coverage of the earthquake that jolted Honshu, Japan's main island, in March 2011 (*left*). Many groups offered aid, from governments and international organizations to small local groups that united under the slogan "Hope Help Heal Japan" (*right*).

pan in 2011. The first image captures the staggering destruction unleashed on Japan by forces of nature, and the second argues that the world must now provide hope, help, and healing to the stricken country. As the first example suggests, images can appeal very strongly to emotions: In this sense, a picture truly is worth a thousand words. But words too can make a powerful emotional appeal, as the second example shows. As a reader, you'll want to consider how any such emotional appeals support the author's claim.

As an author, you should consider how you can appeal to your audience's emotions and whether such appeals are appropriate to your claim, your purpose, and your audience. And be careful not to overdo emotional appeals, pulling at the heartstrings so hard that your audience feels manipulated.

Ethical Appeals

Ethical appeals evoke the credibility and good character of whoever is making the argument. See how the blog kept by Lawrence Lessig, an advocate for reform of copyright laws and a critic of institutional corruption, includes information intended to establish his credibility and integrity. Here is part of his "bio" page:

Lawrence Lessig is the Director of the Edmond J. Safra Foundation Center for Ethics at Harvard University, and a Professor of Law at Harvard Law School. . . .

For much of his academic career, Lessig has focused on law and technology, especially as it affects copyright. He is the author of five books on the subject—*Remix* (2008), *Code v2* (2007), *Free Culture* (2004), *The Future of Ideas* (2001) and *Code and Other Laws of Cyberspace* (1999)—and has served as lead counsel in a number of important cases marking the boundaries of copyright law in a digital age, including *Eldred v. Ashcroft,* a challenge to the 1998 Sonny Bono Copyright Term Extension Act, and *Golan v. Holder.* . . .

Lessig has won numerous awards, including the Free Software Foundation's Freedom Award, and was named one of *Scientific American's Top 50 Visionaries.* He is a member of the American Academy of Arts and Sciences, and the American Philosophical Society.

—*Lessig 2.0*

Lawrence Lessig

All of this information, including his position as director of a prestigious center at Harvard and his numerous awards, helps establish Lessig's credibility and helps readers decide how much stock they can put in his blog entries.

Citing scholarly positions and awards is only one way of establishing credibility. Here Lessig uses another approach in a keynote address to a 2002 convention devoted to discussion of free and open-source software:

I have been doing this for about two years—more than 100 of these gigs. This is about the last one. One more and it's over for me. So I figured I wanted to write a song to end it. But then I realized I don't sing and I can't write music. But I came up with the refrain, at least, right? This captures the point. If you understand this refrain, you're gonna' understand everything I want to say to you today. It has four parts: Creativity and innovation always builds on the past. The past always tries to control the creativity that builds upon it. Free societies enable the future by limiting this power of the past. Ours is less and less a free society.

—LAWRENCE LESSIG, Keynote Address, 2002 Open Source Convention

In this brief opening, Lessig lets listeners know that he has a lot of experience with his topic—in fact, he has spoken on it more than a hundred times. His very informal tone suggests that he is a down-to-earth person who has a simple, direct message to give to the people in his audience. In addition, his self-deprecating humor (he can't sing or write music) underscores his self-confidence: He knows he can create the equivalent of a "good song" on a topic about which he has spoken so frequently.

Building common ground. Lessig's use of simple, everyday language helps establish credibility in another way: by building common ground with his audience. He is not "putting on airs" but speaking directly to them; their concerns, he seems to say, are his concerns.

While building common ground cannot ensure that your audience is "on your side," it does show that you respect your audience and their views and that you've established, with them, a mutual interest in the topic. Each party cares about the issues that you are addressing. Thus, building common ground is a particularly important part of creating an effective argument: Especially if you are addressing an audience unlikely to agree with your position, finding some area of agreement with them, some common ground you can all stand on, can help give the argument a chance of being heard.

No global leader in recent history has been more successful in building common ground than Nelson Mandela, who became the first black president of South Africa in 1994 after the country's harsh apartheid system of racial segregation ended. In *Playing the Enemy: Nelson Mandela and the Game That Made a Nation*, the basis for the 2009 film *Invictus*, author John Carlin recounts hearing Mandela say that "sport has the power to change the world. . . . It has the power to unite people in a way that little else does. . . . It is more powerful than governments in breaking down racial barriers." Carlin uses this quotation as an example of Mandela's singular ability to "walk in another person's shoes" and to build common ground even where none seems possible. He goes on to detail the ways in which Mandela, employing one of the appeals, used white South Africans' fervent love of rugby to build common ground between them and the country's black majority, which had long seen the almost all-white national rugby team, the Springboks, as a symbol of white supremacy:

> He explained how he had . . . used the 1995 Rugby World Cup as an instrument in the grand strategic purpose he set for himself during his five years as South Africa's first democratically elected president: to reconcile blacks and whites and create the conditions for a lasting peace. . . . He told me, with a chuckle or two, about the trouble he had persuading his own people to back the rugby team. . . . Having won over his own people he went out and won over the enemy.
> —JOHN CARLIN, *Playing the Enemy*

President Nelson Mandela, wearing a Springboks cap and shirt, presents the Rugby World Cup to South African captain Francios Pienaar in June 1995.

Mandela understood, in short, that when people were as far apart in their thinking as black and white South Africans were when apartheid ended, the only way to move forward, to make arguments for the country's future that both groups would listen to, was to discover something that could bring them together. For Mandela—and for South Africa—rugby provided the needed common ground. His personal meetings with the Springboks players and his public support for the team, including wearing a Springboks jersey to their matches, paid off to such an extent that when they won a stunning upset victory in the 1995 World Cup final in Johannesburg, the multiracial crowd chanted his name and the country united in celebration. And establishing that common ground, through an emotional appeal, contributed to Mandela's extraordinary ethical appeal—which he put to good use in the difficult arguments he had to make in the transition to a post-apartheid South Africa.

In all the arguments you encounter, you'll want to ask yourself how much you can trust the author. Does he or she seem knowledgeable? represent opposing positions fairly (or at all)? do anything to build common ground?

As an author, you need to establish your own authority: to show you know what you're talking about by citing trustworthy sources; to demonstrate that you're fair by representing positions other than your own even-handedly and accurately; and to establish some kind of common ground with your audience.

Logical Appeals

Appeals to logic have long been regarded as the most important of all the appeals, following Aristotle's definition of humans as rational animals. Recent research has made it increasingly clear, however, that people seldom make decisions based on logic alone and that emotion might actually play a larger role in our decision making than does logic. Nevertheless, in academic contexts, logical appeals still count for a lot. Especially when we make an argument, we need to provide REASONS and EVIDENCE to support our claims. Such evidence takes many forms, including facts and statistics, data from surveys and questionnaires, direct observations, testimony, experiments, interviews, personal experience, visuals, and more.

Facts and statistics. Facts and statistics are two of the most commonly used kinds of evidence. Facts are ideas that have been proven to be true—and that an audience will accept without further proof. Statistics are numerical data based on research. See how the Nobel Prize–winning economist Joseph Stiglitz offers a number of facts and statistics as support for his argument that current levels of inequality are dangerous for the future of the United States:

> Although the United States has always been a capitalist country, our inequality—or at least at its current high level—is new. Some thirty years ago, the top 1 percent of income earners received *only* 12 percent of the nation's income.[13] That level of inequality should itself have been unacceptable; but since then the disparity has grown dramatically,[14] so that by 2007 the average after-tax income of the top 1 percent had reached $1.3 million, but that of the bottom 20 percent amounted to only $17,800.[15] The top 1 percent get in one week 40 percent more than the bottom fifth receive in a year; the top 0.1 percent received in a day and a half about what the bottom 90 percent received in a year; and the richest 20 percent of income earners earn in total *after* tax more than the bottom 80 percent combined.[16]
>
> For thirty years after World War II, America grew together—with growth in income in every segment, but with those at the bottom growing faster than those at the top. The country's fight for survival brought a new sense of unity, and that led to policies, like the GI Bill, that helped bring the country even closer together.
>
> But for the past thirty years, we've become increasingly a nation divided; not only has the top been growing the fastest, but the bottom has actually been declining. (It hasn't been a relentless pattern—in the 1990s, for a while, those at the bottom and in the middle did better. But then, as we've seen, beginning around 2000, inequality grew at an even more rapid pace.
>
> —JOSEPH STIGLITZ, *The Price of Inequality*

The facts and statistics Stiglitz presents about the increasing inequality in the United States are documented in endnotes that explain the methods he used to calculate the data and cite authoritative sources supporting his conclusions. Statistics can provide powerful support for an argument, but be sure they're accurate, up-to-date, from reliable sources—and relevant to the argument. And if you base an argument on facts, be sure to take into account all the relevant facts. Realistically, that's hard to do—but you should be careful not to ignore any important facts.

Surveys and questionnaires. You have probably responded to a number of surveys or questionnaires, and you will find them used extensively as evidence in support of arguments. When a college student wondered about the kinds of reading for pleasure her dormmates were doing, she decided to gather information through a survey. She distilled the information she gathered into a pie chart.

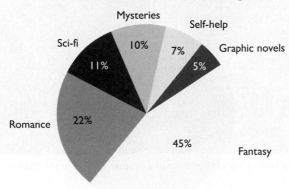

What Genres Students Are Reading

Mysteries

Self-help

Sci-fi   10%   7%   Graphic novels

11%   5%

Romance   22%

45%   Fantasy

The information displayed in the chart offers evidence that fantasy is the most-read genre, followed by romance, sci-fi, mysteries, self-help, and graphic novels. Before accepting such evidence, however, readers might want to ask some key questions: How many people were surveyed? What methods of analysis did the student use? How were particular works classified? (For example, how did she decide whether a particular book was a "romance" or a "mystery"?) Whether you're reacting to survey data in an essay or on a PowerPoint presentation, or conducting a survey of your own, you need to scrutinize the methods and findings. Who conducted the survey, and why? (And yes, you need to think about that if you conducted it.) Who are the respondents, how were they chosen, and are they representative? What do the results show?

Home is where the heart is, but look at p. 885 to see how the Pew Research Group employs questionnaires and statistics to define just what we mean when we say "home."

Observations. A study reported in 2011 in *Science News* demonstrates the way direct observations can form the basis for an argument. In this study, researchers in Uganda observed the way young chimpanzees play, and their findings support arguments about the relative importance of biology and socialization on the way boys and girls play.

A young chimp holds a stick in imitation of a mother caring for her child.

A new study finds that young females in one group of African chimpanzees use sticks as dolls more than their male peers do, often treating
pieces of wood like a mother chimp caring for an infant. . . .

Ape observations, collected over 14 years of field work with the
Kanyawara chimp community in Kibale National Park, provide the first
evidence of a nonhuman animal in the wild that exhibits sex differences
in how it plays, two primatologists report in the Dec. 21 *Current Biology.*
This finding supports a controversial view that biology as well as society
underlies boys' and girls' contrasting toy preferences.

—BRUCE BOWER, "Female Chimps Play with 'Dolls'"

As this study suggests, observations carried out over time are particularly
useful as evidence since they show that something is not just a onetime
event but a persistent pattern. As a college student, you won't likely have
occasion to spend 14 years observing something, but in most cases you'll
need to observe your subject more than once.

Interviews. Reporters often use information drawn from interviews to
add authenticity to their reports by providing evidence "from the horse's
mouth," so to speak. After Raúl Castro took over as leader of Cuba following

his brother Fidel's surgery in 2006, NPR reporter Tom Gjelten used material from an interview published in *Granma*, the Cuban Communist Party newspaper, to argue against the assumption that Castro would defer to his older brother and take few actions on his own:

> In fact, he's been busy. As Defense Minister, Raúl put the Cuban military on alert in the first hours after Fidel's surgery was announced. He also told the *Granma* editor that he had ordered the mobilization of tens of thousands of army reservists and militiamen because, he said, we could not rule out the risk of somebody going crazy within the U.S. government.
> —TOM GJELTEN, "Raúl Castro Reticent in Newspaper Interview"

Note that this interview, like many, depicts the subject largely as he wants to be seen. Reporters—and their audiences—would have had to look beyond the interview and track Raúl Castro's other actions to see whether they supported the claim Gjelten made on the basis of the interview. As an author, be sure that anyone you interview is an authority on your subject and will be considered trustworthy by your audience.

Testimony. Most of us depend on reliable testimony to help us accept or reject arguments: A friend tells us that *The Artist* is a great movie, and likely as not we'll go to see the film. Testimony is especially persuasive evidence when it comes from experts and authorities on the topic. When you cite authorities to support an argument, you help to build your own credibility as an author; readers know that you've done your homework and that you are aware of the different perspectives on your topic. In the example on p. 292 about gender-linked behavior among chimpanzees, for example, the *Science News* report notes testimony from the two scientists who conducted the research.

Experiments. Evidence based on experiments is especially important in the sciences and social sciences, where data is often the basis for supporting an argument. In arguing that multitaskers pay a high mental price, Clifford Nass, a professor of communications, based his claim on a series of empirical studies of college students, who were divided into two groups, those identified as "high multitaskers" and those identified as "low multitaskers." In the first studies, which measured attention and memory, the researchers were surprised to find that the low multitaskers outperformed high multitaskers in statistically significant ways. Still not satisfied that low multitaskers were more productive learners, the researchers designed a third test, hypothesizing that if high multitaskers couldn't do well in the earlier studies on attention and memory, maybe they would be better at shifting from task to task more quickly and effectively than low multitaskers.

> Wrong again, the study found.
>
> The subjects were shown images of letters and numbers at the same time and instructed what to focus on. When they were told to pay attention to numbers, they had to determine if the digits were even or odd. When told to concentrate on letters, they had to say whether they were vowels or consonants.
>
> Again, the heavy multitaskers underperformed the light multitaskers.
>
> "They couldn't help thinking about the task they weren't doing," the researchers reported. "The high multitaskers are always drawing from all the information in front of them. They can't keep things separate in their minds."   —ADAM GORLICK, "Media Multitaskers Pay Mental Price"

In writing up their results, these researchers had evidence to support their hypothesis; nevertheless, they realized the dangers of generalizing from one set of students to all students. Whenever you use data drawn from experiments, you need to be similarly cautious not to overgeneralize.

César Chávez

Personal experience can provide powerful support for an argument since it brings a kind of "eyewitness" evidence, which can establish a connection between author and audience. In an article for the *Atlantic* about the labor organizer César Chávez, Caitlin Flanagan—who grew up in the San Joaquin Valley, where Chávez's United Farm Workers movement began—recounts her mother's personal experience to support the argument that Chávez had a "singular and almost mystical way of eliciting not just fealty but a kind of awe."

> Of course, it had all started with Mom. Somewhere along the way, she had met César Chávez, or at least attended a rally where he had spoken, and that was it. Like almost everyone else who ever encountered him, she was spellbound. "This wonderful, wonderful man," she would call him, and off we went to collect clothes for the farmworkers' children, and to sell red-and-black UFW buttons and collect signatures.
>
> —CAITLIN FLANAGAN, "The Madness of César Chávez"

As an author, be careful that any personal experience you cite is pertinent to your argument and will be appropriate to your purpose.

Charts, images, and other visuals. Visuals of various kinds often provide valuable evidence to support an argument. Pie charts like the one of the literary genres favored in a college dorm, photographs like the one of the female chimpanzee cradling a stick, and many other kinds of visuals including drawings, bar and line graphs, cartoons, screenshots, videos, and advertisements—can sometimes make it easier for an audience to see certain kinds of evidence. Imagine how much more difficult it would be to take in the information shown in the pie chart about the genres read by students in the dorm had the data been presented in a paragraph. Remember, though, that visual evidence usually needs to be explained with words—photos may need captions, and any visuals need to be referenced in the accompanying text.

As an author, keep in mind that the MEDIUM you're using affects the kind of evidence you choose and the way you present it. In a print text, any evidence has to be in the text itself; in a digital medium, you can link directly to statistics, images, and other information. In a spoken text, any evidence needs to be said or shown on a slide or a handout—and anything you say needs to be simple and direct—and memorable (your audience can't rewind or reread data). And in every case any evidence drawn from sources need to be fully DOCUMENTED.

Are There Any Problems with the Reasoning?

Some kinds of appeals use faulty reasoning, or reasoning that some may consider unfair, unsound, or demonstrating lazy or simpleminded thinking. Such appeals are called fallacies, and because they can often be very powerful and persuasive, it's important to be alert for them in arguments you encounter—and in your own writing. Here are some of the most common fallacies.

Begging the question tries to support an argument by simply restating it in other language, so that the reasoning just goes around in circles. For example, the statement "We need to reduce the national debt because the government owes too much money" begs the question of whether the debt is actually too large, because the parts of the sentence before and after *because* say essentially the same thing.

Either-or arguments, also called *false dilemmas,* argue that only two alternatives are possible in a situation that actually is more complex. A candidate who declares, "I will not allow the United States to become a defenseless, bankrupt nation—it must remain the military and economic superpower of the world," ignores the many possibilities in between.

Ad hominem (Latin for "to the man") arguments make personal attacks on those who support an opposing position rather than address the position itself: "Of course council member Acevedo doesn't want to build a new high school; she doesn't have any children herself." The council member's childlessness may not be the reason for her opposition to a new high school, and even if it is, such an attack doesn't provide any argument for building the school.

Faulty causality, the mistaken assumption that because one event followed another, the first event caused the second, is also called *post hoc, ergo propter hoc* (Latin for "after this, therefore because of this"). For example, a mayor running for reelection may boast that a year after she began having the police patrol neighborhoods more frequently, the city's crime rate has dropped significantly. But there might be many other possible causes for the drop, so considerable evidence would be needed to establish such a causal connection.

Bandwagon appeals simply urge the audience to go along with the crowd: "Join the millions who've found relief from agonizing pain through Weleda Migraine Remedy." "Everybody knows you shouldn't major in a subject that doesn't lead to a job." "Don't you agree that we all need to support our troops?" Such appeals often flatter the audience by implying that making the popular choice means they are smart, attractive, sophisticated, and so on.

Slippery slope arguments contend that if a certain event occurs, it will (or at least might easily) set in motion a chain of other events that will end in disaster, like a minor misstep at the top of a slick incline that causes you to slip and eventually to slide all the way down to the bottom. For example, opponents of physician-assisted suicide often warn that making it legal for doctors to help people end their lives would eventually lead to an increase in the suicide rate, as people who would not otherwise kill themselves find it easier to do so, and even to an increase in murders disguised as suicide. Slippery slope arguments are not always wrong—an increasingly catastrophic chain reaction does sometimes grow out of a seemingly small beginning.

But the greater the difference is between the initial event and the predicted final outcome, the more evidence is needed that the situation will actually play out in this way.

Setting up a straw man misrepresents an opposing argument, characterizing it as more extreme or otherwise different than it actually is, in order to attack it more easily. The misrepresentation is like an artificial figure made of straw that's easier to knock down than a real person would be. For example, critics of the 2010 federal Affordable Care Act often attacked it as a "government takeover of health care" or a "government-run system." In fact, although the legislation increased government's role in the U.S. health-care system in some ways, it still relied primarily on private systems of insurance and health-care providers.

Hasty generalizations draw sweeping conclusions on the basis of too little evidence: "Both of the political science classes I took were deadly dull, so it must be a completely boring subject." "You shouldn't drink so much coffee—that study that NPR reported on today said it causes cancer." Many hasty generalizations take the form of stereotypes about groups of people, such as men and women, gays and straights, and ethnic and religious groups. It's difficult to make an argument without using some generalizations, but they always need to be based on sufficient evidence and appropriately qualified with words like *most, in many cases, usually, in the United States, in recent years*, and so on.

Faulty analogies are comparisons that do not hold up in some way crucial to the argument they are used to support. Accusing parents who home-school their children of "educational malpractice" by saying that parents who aren't doctors wouldn't be allowed to perform surgery on their children on the kitchen table, so parents who aren't trained to teach shouldn't be allowed to teach their children there either makes a false analogy. Teaching and surgery aren't alike enough to support an argument that what's required for one is needed for the other.

WHAT ABOUT OTHER PERSPECTIVES?

In any argument, it's important to consider perspectives other than those of the author's, especially those that would not support the claim or would

Camels ad, 1946.

argue it very differently. As a reader, you should question any arguments that don't acknowledge other positions, and as a writer, you'll want to be sure that you represent—and respond to—perspectives other than your own. Acknowledging other arguments, in fact, is another way of demonstrating that you're fair and establishing your credibility—whereas failing to consider other views can make you seem close-minded or lazy, at best, and unfair or manipulative, at worst. Think of all those advertisements you've seen that say, in effect, "Doctors recommend drug X."

The cigarette ad included here is one of the most infamous of these advertising arguments. Of course, this ad doesn't claim that all doctors smoke Camels, but it implies that plenty of them do and that what's good for a doctor is good for other consumers. But what if the ad had been required to consider other viewpoints? The result would have been a more honest and more informative, though perhaps a less successful, argument. Today, cigarette ads are required to carry another point of view: a warning about the adverse effects of smoking. So if an argument does not take other points of view into consideration, you will be right to question it, asking yourself what those other viewpoints might be and why they would not have been taken into account.

Compare the misleading Camels ad to the following discussion of contemporary seismology:

Jian Lin was 14 years old in 1973, when the Chinese government under Mao Zedong recruited him for a student science team called "the earthquake watchers." After a series of earthquakes that had killed thousands in northern China, the country's seismologists thought that if they augmented their own research by having observers keep an eye out for anomalies like snakes bolting early from their winter dens and erratic well-water levels, they might be able to do what no scientific body had managed before: issue an earthquake warning that would save thousands of lives.

In the winter of 1974, the earthquake watchers were picking up some suspicious signals near the city of Haicheng. Panicked chickens were squalling and trying to escape their pens; water levels were falling in wells. Seismologists had also begun noticing a telltale pattern of small quakes. "They were like popcorn kernels," Lin tells me, "popping up all over the general area." Then, suddenly, the popping stopped, just as it had before a catastrophic earthquake some years earlier that killed more than 8,000. "Like 'the calm before the storm,'" Lin says. "We have the exact same phrase in Chinese." On the morning of February 4, 1975, the seismology bureau issued a warning: Haicheng should expect a big earthquake, and people should move outdoors.

At 7:36 p.m., a magnitude 7.0 quake struck. The city was nearly leveled, but only about 2,000 people were killed. Without the warning, easily 150,000 would have died. "And so you finally had an earthquake forecast that did indeed save lives," Lin recalls. . . .

Lin is now a senior scientist of geophysics at Woods Hole Oceanographic Institution, in Massachusetts, where he spends his time studying not the scurrying of small animals and fluctuating electrical current between trees (another fabled warning sign), but seismometer readings, GPS coordinates, and global earthquake-notification reports. He and his longtime collaborator, Ross Stein of the U.S. Geological Survey, are champions of a theory that could enable scientists to forecast earth-quakes with more precision and speed.

Some established geophysicists insist that all earthquakes are random, yet everyone agrees that aftershocks are not. Instead, they follow certain empirical laws. Stein, Lin, and their collaborators hypothesized that many earthquakes classified as main shocks are actually aftershocks, and they went looking for the forces that cause faults to fail.

Their work was in some ways heretical: For a long time, earthquakes were thought to release only the stress immediately around them; an earthquake that happened in one place would decrease the possibility of another happening nearby. But that didn't explain earthquake sequences like the one that rumbled through the desert and mountains east of Los Angeles in 1992. . . .

Lin and Stein both admit that [their theory] doesn't explain all earth-quakes. Indeed, some geophysicists, like Karen Felzer, of the U.S. Geological Survey, think their hypothesis gives short shrift to the impact that dynamic stress—the actual rattling of a quake in motion—has on neighboring faults.

—JUDITH LEWIS MERNIT, "Seismology: Is San Francisco Next?"

As this excerpt shows, Lin and Stein's research supports the claim that earthquakes can be predicted some of the time, but they—and the author of the article about them—are careful not to overstate their argument or to ignore those who disagree with it. And the author responds to other perspectives in three ways. She *acknowledges* the "all random" theory that is held by "[s]ome established geophysicists"; she provides evidence (including details not shown here) to *refute* the idea that "earthquakes release only the stress immediately around them." And in the last paragraph she *accommodates* other perspectives by qualifying Lin and Stein's claim and mentioning what some critics see as a weakness in it.

As an author, remember to consider what **COUNTERARGUMENTS** someone might have to your position—and what other perspectives exist on your topic. You may not agree with them, but they might give reason to qualify your thesis—or even to change your position. In any case, they will help you to sharpen your own thinking, and your writing can only improve as a result.

Whatever you think about other viewpoints, be sure to acknowledge them fairly and respectfully in your writing—and to accommodate or refute them as possible.

WHAT ABOUT ORGANIZATION?

Arguments can be organized various ways. You may decide to approach a controversial or surprising argument slowly, building up to the claim but withholding it until you have established plenty of evidence to support it— as W. E. B. Du Bois does in his argument about Abraham Lincoln on p. 282. On the other hand, you may choose to start right off with the claim and then build support for it piece by piece by piece, as in this opening from a 2011 essay in *Wired* on the power of product tie-ins in today's world.

> Cartoon characters permeate every aspect of our children's existences. We serve them Transformers Lunchables and have them brush with SpongeBob-branded toothpaste. We tuck them in on branded sheets,

The Harry Potter brand: Baby Norbert dragon, Potions Class activity set, Hagrid and Hedwig dolls, and notecards, backpack, t-shirt, and hat.

fix their owies with branded bandages, and change their branded diapers because we know, or at least we think, that the characters will
make them happy. Whether our kids are sleeping, bleeding, or pooping,
Spider-Man is there. Even if you operate one of those rarefied TV-free
households, the brands will penetrate, assuming your children go to pre-
school, have friends, or eat food.

—NEAL POLLACK, "Why Your Kids Are Addicted to *Cars*"

One common pattern for starting with a claim comes from ancient Greek
and Roman orators. Such arguments begin with an introduction that gains
the audience's attention, provides any necessary background information, establishes the writer's credibility, and announces the central **CLAIM**.
The writer then presents good **REASONS** (including **EMOTIONAL**, **ETHICAL**,
and **LOGICAL** ones) in support of the claim, considers other perspectives
carefully and fairly, and concludes with a summary of the argument that
points out its implications and makes clear what the writer wants the audience to think or do. This structure tells your audience everything you
want them to know—and that they need to know.

One very common way to organize academic writing is to begin by noting what others say about your topic and then to present your own ideas—
your claim—as a response. Whether you agree, disagree, or both, you'll be
adding your voice to the larger conversation. See how libertarian journalist
Radley Balko uses this framework to begin a 2004 essay on *Cato.org*:

> This June, *Time* magazine and ABC News will host a three-day summit
> on obesity [that] promises to be a pep rally for media, nutrition activ-
> ists, and policy makers—all agitating for a panoply of government anti-
> obesity initiatives. . . . In other words, bringing government between you
> and your waistline. . . .
>
> This is the wrong way to fight obesity. Instead of manipulating or in-
> tervening in the array of food options available to American consumers,
> our government ought to be working to foster a sense of responsibility
> in and ownership of our own health and well-being.
>
> —RADLEY BALKO, "What You Eat Is Your Business"

As with all rhetorical choices, you will want to select an organizational
structure that will be most appropriate for your audience, purpose, and the
rest of your **RHETORICAL SITUATION**.

WHAT ABOUT STYLE?

An argument's style usually reinforces its message in as many ways as possible. The ancient Roman orator Cicero identified three basic styles, which he termed "high," "middle," and "low." Today, we can see a wider range of styles, from the highly formal language of U.S. Supreme Court opinions to the informal style of everyday written communication such as memos and email, to the colloquial style of spoken language, to the highly informal shorthand characteristic of texting and *Twitter*.

You can learn a lot by looking closely at the stylistic choices in an argument—the use of individual words and figurative language, of personal pronouns (or not), of vivid images (verbal and visual), of design and format. In 2005, the *Los Angeles Times* announced an experiment it called its "Wikitorial," in which the newspaper cautiously invited readers to log on to its website and rewrite editorials:

> Plenty of skeptics are predicting embarrassment; like an arthritic old lady who takes to the dance floor, they say, the *Los Angeles Times* is more likely to break a hip than to be hip. We acknowledge that possibility. Nevertheless, we proceed.

The skeptics turned out to be right, and after three days the paper ended the experiment, saying:

> Unfortunately, we have had to remove this feature, at least temporarily, because a few readers were flooding the site with inappropriate material. Thanks and apologies to the thousands of people who logged on in the right spirit.   —"*LA Times* Shuts Reader-Editorial Website"

Savvy readers will be alert to the power of stylistic choices in these messages. The description of closing down *Wikitorial* as "unfortunate" and the equally careful choice of "a few readers," "flooding," and "inappropriate material" mark this as a formal and judicious message that stands in sharp contrast to the breezy, slightly self-deprecating style of the first announcement, with its casual use of "plenty of " and its play on "hip." How does the sober style of the second announcement influence your response as a reader? How different might your response be if the paper had declared, "We're pulling the plug on this page since a few creeps loaded it with a bunch of crap"?

Now let's look at a visual argument. This spoof ad was created by Adbusters, whose website identifies it as a "global network of artists, activ-

Adbusters spoof ad.

Find other examples of Adbusters' arguments at www.adbusters.org.

ists, writers, pranksters, students, educators and entrepreneurs" and proclaims that its aim is "to topple existing power structures and forge a major shift in the way we will live in the 21st century." The ad satirizes the belief that drugs can be used to alleviate unhappiness, in this case presenting Prozac as an everyday necessity—like laundry detergent. Note especially the retro style, which evokes "the happy housewife" and "the good life" of the 1950s.

As an author, you will need to make similar important stylistic choices, beginning—as is almost always the case—with the overall effects you want to create. Try to capture that effect in a word or two (concern, outrage, sympathy, direct action, and so on), and then use it to help you choose words, images, and design that will create that effect and convey it most effectively to your audience.

FOURTEEN

Strategies for Arguing

Comparisons, Examples, Humor, and More

RGUMENTS ARE ONLY AS STRONG as the evidence that supports them. Just as flawed data entered into a computer system will yield flawed results, so it is with arguments. As an author arguing a point, then, you will always be searching for good, strong, reliable evidence. Ancient Greek rhetoricians developed strategies for finding such support, strategies that continue to serve us well today. This chapter introduces you to those strategies arranged alphabetically from **ANALOGY** to **REITERATION**.

Analogy

Analogies are comparisons that point out similarities between things that are otherwise very different. Authors often use them to create vivid pictures in a reader's mind and make abstract ideas more concrete. Analogies can be especially powerful in an **ARGUMENT**, demonstrating that what is true in one case is true in another, usually more complicated, case. Here Annie Dillard draws an analogy between a writer's words and various tools:

> When you write, you lay out a line of words. The line of words is a miner's pick, a wood-carver's gouge, a surgeon's probe. You wield it,

and it digs a path you follow. Soon you find yourself deep in new territory. Is it a dead end, or have you located the real subject? You will know
tomorrow, or this time next year.   —ANNIE DILLARD, *A Writing Life*

Dillard uses this analogy to suggest that writers can use words as tools for
exploring a topic—to "probe" or "dig a path" into whatever subject they're
writing about.

Now see how President Obama used an analogy in his 2012 State of the
Union address to support his argument that the nation needs to put aside its
differences to solve the serious problems that it faces:

> Those of us who've been sent here to serve can learn a thing or two from
> the service of our troops. When you put on that uniform, it doesn't mat-
> ter if you're black or white; Asian, Latino, Native American; conserva-
> tive, liberal; rich, poor; gay, straight. When you're marching into battle,
> you look out for the person next to you, or the mission fails. When
> you're in the thick of the fight, you rise or fall as one unit, serving one
> nation, leaving no one behind. . . .
>
> So it is with America. Each time I look at that flag, I'm reminded
> that our destiny is stitched together like those 50 stars and those 13
> stripes. No one built this country on their own. This nation is great
> because we built it together. This nation is great because we worked
> as a team. This nation is great because we get each other's backs.
> And if we hold fast to that truth, in this moment of trial, there is no
> challenge too great; no mission too hard. As long as we are joined in
> common purpose, as long as we maintain our common resolve, our
> journey moves forward, and our future is hopeful, and the state of our
> Union will always be strong.
>
> —BARACK OBAMA, 2012 State of the Union address

Obama's argument rests on an analogy he draws between the teamwork
that characterizes the "service of our troops"—like those who successfully
carried out the mission to capture bin Laden—and the teamwork that characterizes a great nation: "This nation is great because we get each other's
backs." He ends by calling on Americans to be true to the ideals his analogy
invokes and to remember that when we "get each other's backs," no challenge or mission is too difficult for us. If we live up to these ideals, "our Union
will always be strong."

Classification

When you classify, you group items into categories according to their similarities. Tomatoes, for example, can be classified according to their varieties: cherry, plum, grape, heirloom, and so on. Authors often turn to classification in order to organize and elaborate on a topic. If you were writing about women's attitudes about child rearing, for example, you might classify women into various categories in order to show that they do not all have the same attitudes. Writers of **REVIEWS** sometimes use classification when they're focusing on more than one work, as Adam Gopnik does in evaluating a number of new books about the internet:

> The Never-Betters believe that we're on the brink of a new utopia, where information will be free and democratic, news will be made from the bottom up, love will reign, and cookies will bake themselves. The Better-Nevers think that we would have been better off if the whole thing had never happened, that the world that is coming to an end is superior to the one that is taking its place, and that, at a minimum, books and magazines create private space for minds in ways that twenty-second bursts of information don't. The Ever-Wasers insist that at any moment in modernity something like this is going on, and that a new way of organizing data and connecting users is always thrilling to some and chilling to others—that something like this is going on is exactly what makes it a modern moment. One's hopes rest with the Never-Betters; one's head with the Ever-Wasers; and one's heart? Well, twenty or so books in, one's heart tends to move toward the Better-Nevers, and then bounce back toward someplace that looks more like home.
> —ADAM GOPNIK, "How the Internet Gets Inside Us"

Classification is an essential feature of all websites, starting with the menus on most homepages, which classify what's on the site by categories that visitors can then click on. Take a look at *Bleacher Report*, an award-winning site created by sports fans who contribute articles, videos, wacky lists, and more, and which delivers "entertaining content about all the teams and topics in sports." The homepage classifies that content by sports leagues—NFL, CFB, MLB, NBA, NHL, and so on. If you explore the site, you'll also find other classifications, from the 100 Most Amazing Sports Pictures to the Best Super Bowl Ads. As you'll see, the use of classification makes a

A "Cool List" on *Bleacher Report*, 2012.

complex site usable—and helps accommodate the many different kinds of texts that are regularly posted.

Comparison / Contrast

See how Nicholas Carr compares today's older adults, who remember life before computers, with those of an earlier era who remember life before electric lights. You'll find his article on p. 741.

When you compare things, you focus on their similarities, and when you contrast them, you look at their differences. Both strategies can be very useful in developing an argument, helping to explain something that is unfamiliar by comparing (or contrasting) it with something more familiar. In a book **REVIEW**, for example, you might compare the *Twilight Saga* series to the *Harry Potter* series, or in a **REPORT** on the decline of the euro, you might compare the situations in France and Spain.

There are two ways you can organize a comparison: block and point by point. Using the *block* method, you present the subjects you're comparing one at a time, as in the following paragraphs:

> Most men, I believe, think of themselves as average-looking. Men will think this even if their faces cause heart failure in cattle at a range of 300

yards. Being average does not bother them; average is fine, for men. This is why men never ask anybody how they look. Their primary form of beauty care is to shave themselves, which is essentially the same form of beauty care that they give to their lawns. If, at the end of his four-minute daily beauty regimen, a man has managed to wipe most of the shaving cream out of his hair and is not bleeding too badly, he feels that he has done all he can, so he stops thinking about his appearance and devotes his mind to more critical issues, such as the Super Bowl.

Women do not look at themselves this way. If I had to express, in three words, what I believe most women think about their appearance, those words would be: "not good enough." No matter how attractive a woman may appear to be to others, when she looks at herself in the mirror, she thinks: woof. She thinks that at any moment a municipal animal-control officer is going to throw a net over her and haul her off to the shelter.

—DAVE BARRY, "Beauty and the Beast"

Or you can organize your comparison *point by point*, discussing your subjects together, one point at a time, as David Sedaris does in the following paragraph comparing his own childhood in Raleigh, North Carolina, with that of his partner Hugh, a diplomat's son who grew up in Africa:

Certain events are parallel, but compared with Hugh's, my childhood was unspeakably dull. When I was seven years old, my family moved to North Carolina. When he was seven years old, Hugh's family moved to the Congo. We had a collie and a house cat. They had a monkey and two horses named Charlie Brown and Satan. I threw stones at stop signs. Hugh threw stones at crocodiles. The verbs are the same, but he definitely wins the prize when it comes to nouns and objects. An eventful day for my mother might have involved a trip to the dry cleaner or a conversation with the potato-chip deliveryman. Asked one ordinary Congo afternoon what she'd done with her day, Hugh's mother answered that she and a fellow member of the Ladies' Club had visited a leper colony on the outskirts of Kinshasa. No reason was given for the expedition, though chances are she was staking it out for a future field trip.

—DAVID SEDARIS, "Remembering My Childhood
on the Continent of Africa"

Here's Ashley Highfield, managing director of Microsoft UK, drawing a comparison in a 2005 speech to the Royal Television Society of Britain as part of an argument that the "digital revolution is only just beginning":

I was reading an article the other day called "The Dangers of Wired Love," about a teenage girl called Maggie, who helped her dad run a newspaper stand in Brooklyn. Business was booming, so Maggie's dad, George McCutcheon, decided to get wired up, to help him process electronic orders. Being a total technophobe, Mr. McCutcheon got Maggie to operate the thing, but soon found out she was using it to flirt with a number of men, particularly one married man she had met online called Frank. Breaking all the known rules of cyber dating, she invited Frank to visit her in the real world, and of course he accepted. McCutcheon found out, went mad and forbade his daughter to meet up with Frank. But Maggie nevertheless continued to meet him in secret. Her furious father found out and one day followed her to one of the couple's rendezvous. He threatened to blow her brains out. She later had him arrested and charged with threatening behaviour.

An everyday story of modern times maybe? McCutcheon's fathering skills perhaps a bit severe, and Maggie perhaps a little naive? The striking thing about this story is that it was published in a magazine called *Electrical World* in 1886. The Victorian network that McCutcheon got wired to, and Maggie got hooked on, was of course the telegraph.

Those of us in technology like to think we're breaking new ground, that we're creating history through the latest revolution, when we're quite clearly not as the very modern Maggie McCutcheon illustrates. The telegraph and the internet are perhaps more evolution than revolution: but in a way that means the seismic shifts in society that they cause creep up on us unnoticed. But these cycles of change come round again and again—and people tend to see them as momentous and more often than not scary.   —ASHLEY HIGHFIELD, "Why the Digital Revolution
Is Only Just Beginning"

Comparisons of data can often be easier to understand in a chart or graph than in paragraphs. Why spend pages describing changes in demographics over the last fifty years, for example, when a bar graph can make the comparison in a half page? See how the graph on the following page from an article in the *Atlantic* compares the number of college graduates in fourteen American cities, helping to support the article's argument that "America's educated elite is clustering in a few cities—and leaving the rest of the country behind."

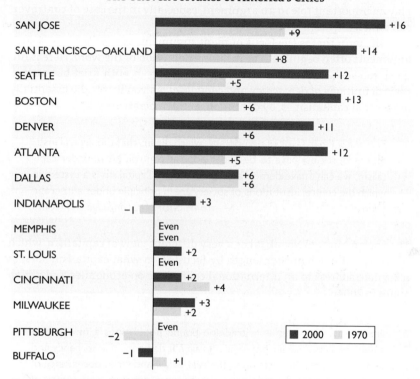

The Uneven Fortunes of America's Cities

Number of college graduates per 100 people, relative to the national average.

—RICHARD FLORIDA, "Where the Brains Are"

Definition

Definitions often lie at the heart of an argument: If readers don't agree with your definition of "the good life," for example, they aren't likely to take your advice on how to achieve such a life. Whether you're writing an **ANALYSIS**, a **REPORT**, or using some other genre, you'll often have reason to include definitions in all the writing you do. Good definitions provide a clear explanation of a word, concept, or idea, often by listing their characteristic features, noting any distinguishing details, and perhaps providing an example or illustration as well. It's important to remember,

Mike Rose takes on the way *intelligence* is defined and demonstrated in our culture. Check out what he says on p. 905.

however, that definitions themselves are rhetorical choices, ones that can play an important role in an argument, especially in the case of controversial topics.

One term that is the focus of many arguments is *capitalism,* and such arguments often begin with or include a definition of the word. Here is linguist and social critic Noam Chomsky weighing in with brief but memorable definitions of *democracy* and *capitalism.* As you'll note, he essentially argues that capitalism is, by definition, antidemocratic:

> Personally I'm in favor of democracy, which means that the central institutions of society have to be under popular control. Now, under capitalism, we can't have democracy by definition. Capitalism is a system in which the central institutions of society are in principle under autocratic control.   —NOAM CHOMSKY, *Language and Politics*

Theologian Michael Novak takes a very different view of capitalism, which he defines at much greater length by focusing on what capitalism *does,* in a keynote address to an international conference on economies and nation states in 2004:

> Finally, capitalism instills in tradition-bound populations a new and in some respects a higher personal morality. It demands transparency and honest accounts. It insists upon the rule of law and strict observance of contracts. It teaches hard work, inventiveness, initiative, and a spirit of responsibility. It teaches patience with small gains, incremental but steady and insistent progress. During the 19th century, Great Britain achieved an average of one-and-a-half percent of GDP growth every year, with the happy result that the average income of the ordinary laborer in Britain quadrupled in a single century. The moral habits of invention, discovery, hard work, persistence, saving, investment, and moral seriousness brought about the single greatest transformation in the condition of the poor of all time—the greatest advances in hygiene, medicine, longevity, and physical well-being in all recorded history.
>
> Capitalism brings in its train immense transformation, and the root of this transformation is moral. Those peoples and nations that neglect the moral ecology of their own cultures will not enjoy the fruits of such a transformation—or, having tasted them, will fall into rapid decline.   —MICHAEL NOVAK, "The Spirit of Capitalism"

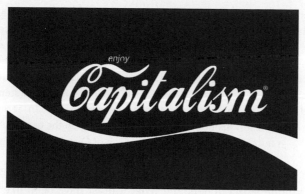

Image from *Daily Wallpapers* blog.

Visuals can help in making arguments that hinge on definition. Above is a case in which the way the word *capitalism* is designed argues for yet another definition of that word. What argument(s) do you find in this illustration?

Description

When you describe something, you explain how it looks (or sounds, smells, tastes, or feels). Good descriptions focus on distinctive features and concrete details that add up to some **DOMINANT IMPRESSION** and help readers or listeners imagine what you are describing. You'll have occasion to use description in most of the writing you do—in a **PROFILE** of a neighborhood, you might describe the buildings and people; in a **NARRATIVE**, you'll likely describe scenes and people.

In writing about atomic testing in Utah in the epilogue to her 1991 book *Refuge: An Unnatural History of Family and Place*, writer and activist Terry Tempest Williams uses description to set the scene for the facts, which she then presents about the high incidence of breast cancer in that state. She tells her father of a recurring dream she has, of a flash of light in the desert. When her father hears this story, he has a sudden realization:

> "You did see it," he said.
> "Saw what?"
> "The bomb. The cloud. We were driving home from Riverside, Cali-

Check out how many of the five senses Penelope Green includes in her article "The Year without Toilet Paper," on p. 801.

fornia. You were sitting on [your mother's] lap. . . . In fact, I remember the day, September 7, 1957. We had just gotten out of the Service. We were driving north, past Las Vegas. It was an hour or so before dawn, when this explosion went off. We not only heard it, but felt it. I thought the oil tanker in front of us had blown up. We pulled over and suddenly, rising from the desert floor, we saw it, clearly, this golden-stemmed cloud, the mushroom. The sky seemed to vibrate with an eerie pink glow. Within a few minutes, a light ash was raining on the car."

—TERRY TEMPEST WILLIAMS, "The Clan of One-Breasted Women"

Williams' description lets readers see the "golden-stemmed cloud" and feel the sky "vibrate"—and understand what it must have been like when the bomb exploded.

Description is often made visually. Compare her description with a photograph of the atomic bomb test. In this case, which do you find more powerful—the description of what it was like to be there when the bomb exploded or the photograph of the actual explosion? Would adding the photo have made Williams' description—and her argument—even more forceful?

Fiery mushroom cloud rising above Nevada atomic bomb test site, 1957.

Williams eventually testified before Congress about the effects of nuclear testing and has also worked as an environmental advocate. In 1995, aghast at a federal wilderness bill that would protect only a tiny fraction of Utah's wilderness areas, she spoke at a public hearing. In this passage from an interview, see how her description of the hearing helps her make the case that the governmental officials were openly dismissive of her arguments:

> Congressman Jim Hansen and his colleagues sat on a riser above us. I remember how his glasses were perched on the end of his nose, how when I began to speak he was shuffling his papers, yawning, coughing, anything to show his boredom and displeasure. I was half-way through reading the citizens' testimonies—speaking on behalf of those who were at the Indian Walk-In Center the night before. He wasn't even listening—that was clear. Finally, I stopped mid-sentence and said something to the effect, "Congressman Hansen, I have been a resident of Utah all of my life. Is there anything I could say to you that will in some way alter your perspective so that you might consider wilderness in another way?"
>
> What I remember is how he leaned over his elbows and looked down on me over the tops of his glasses and said simply, "I'm sorry, Ms. Williams, there is something about your voice I cannot hear." It was chilling—personal. I don't think he was referring to the quality of the microphone. And then, it was over.
>
> —TERRY TEMPEST WILLIAMS, interview with David Sumner

Williams could have simply told us who said what and what was decided, but her description helps us picture the congressman "shuffling his papers" and "yawning," hear him "coughing," and sense "his boredom and displeasure."

Example

If a picture is sometimes worth a thousand words, then a good example runs a close second: Examples can make abstract ideas more concrete and understandable and can provide specific instances to back up a claim. See how novelist Gretel Ehrlich uses two examples to support her **ANALYSIS** of what courage means in a cowboy context:

In a rancher's world, courage has less to do with facing danger than with acting spontaneously—usually on behalf of an animal or another rider. If a cow is stuck in a boghole, he throws a loop around her neck, takes his dally (a half hitch around the saddle horn), and pulls her out with horse-power. If a calf is born sick, he may take her home, warm her in front of the kitchen fire, and massage her legs until dawn.

—GRETEL EHRLICH, "About Men"

You can sometimes draw on personal experience for powerful ex-amples, provided that the experience you cite is pertinent to your point. In a commencement address to Stanford University's graduating class of 2005, Apple founder Steve Jobs used the example of his experience with cancer in **ARGUING** that the graduates should make the most of every moment:

Steve Jobs

About a year ago I was diagnosed with cancer. I had a scan at 7:30 in the morning, and it clearly showed a tumor on my pancreas. I didn't even know what a pancreas was. The doctors told me this was almost cer-tainly a type of cancer that is incurable, and that I should expect to live no longer than three to six months. My doctor advised me to go home and get my affairs in order, which is doctor's code for prepare to die. It means to try to tell your kids everything you thought you'd have the next 10 years to tell them in just a few months. It means to make sure every-thing is buttoned up so that it will be as easy as possible for your family. It means to say your goodbyes.

I lived with that diagnosis all day. Later that evening I had a biopsy, where they stuck an endoscope down my throat, through my stomach and into my intestines, put a needle into my pancreas and got a few cells from the tumor. I was sedated, but my wife, who was there, told me that when they viewed the cells under a microscope the doctors started cry-ing because it turned out to be a very rare form of pancreatic cancer that is curable with surgery. I had the surgery and I'm fine now. . . .

Your time is limited, so don't waste it living someone else's life. Don't be trapped by dogma—which is living with the results of other people's thinking. Don't let the noise of others' opinions drown out your own in-ner voice. And most important, have the courage to follow your heart and intuition. They somehow already know what you truly want to be-come. Everything else is secondary.

—STEVE JOBS, Stanford University commencement address

Examples can often be presented visually. See how the following blog posting from *Boing Boing* about the Occupy Wall Street library uses a minimum of words but provides a snapshot that shows a few of the "awesome librarians."

"NYPD & Brookfield have taken the People's Library again. and we love you all," tweet the Occupy Wall Street librarians of Zuccotti Park.

They also raided all the energy bars, waters, and snacks from the re-created library, and threw them away, too. This is not the first time.

Then, shortly after: "A few of our awesome librarians holding up new donations just after NYPD and Brookfield workers took our books tonight."

The librarians are restocking, in case you'd like to donate.

—XENI JARDIN, "NYPD Hates Books: Police and Brookfield
Properties Workers Destroy #OWS Library. Again."

Humor

Humor can sometimes be used to good effect to support an argument—as long as the humor is appropriate to the context and audience. Of course, humor comes in many forms—from a self-deprecating story you might tell about yourself to a gentle parody or satire, from biting ridicule to a well-worn joke. While few of us are talented enough to write an argument based entirely on humor, it's possible to learn to use it judiciously. Doing so can often help you to connect with your audience, to provide some relief from a serious topic, or just to vary the tone of your argument.

The late journalist Molly Ivins was famous for the way she used humor in arguing serious positions in her op-ed columns. In the following example from an interview on *Nightline,* Ivins is arguing in favor of gun regulation, but she uses humorous exaggeration—and a bit of real silliness—to help make her point:

> I think that's what we need: more people carrying weapons. I support the [concealed gun] legislation but I'd like to propose one small amendment. Everyone should be able to carry a concealed weapon. But everyone who carries a weapon should be required to wear one of those little beanies on their heads with a little propeller on it so the rest of us can see them coming.   —MOLLY IVINS

We're all familiar with the way cartoons use humor to make arguments—as in this one, which argues that perhaps airport security has gone just a little overboard:

The 5th Wave   By Rich Tennant

AIRPORT SECURITY

"They won't let me through security until I remove the bullets from my Word document."

The *Onion* is a satirical weekly newspaper that regularly uses humor to make its arguments. This article makes an indirect argument that at too many colleges and universities, athletics outweigh academics:

See what *The Onion* has to say about how we read on p. 881.

> SARASOTA, FL—Bowing to pressure from alumni, students, and a majority of teaching professors of Florida State University, athletic director Dave Hart Jr. announced yesterday that FSU would completely phase out all academic operations by the end of the 2010 school year in order to make athletics the school's No. 1 priority. "It's been clear for a while that Florida State's mission is to provide the young men and women enrolled here with a world-class football program, and this is the best way to cut the fat and really focus on making us No. 1 every year," Hart said. "While it's certainly possible for an academic subsidiary to bring a certain amount of prestige to an athletic program, the national polls have made it clear that our non-athletic operations have become a major distraction." FSU's restructuring program will begin with the elimination of the College of Arts and Sciences, effective October 15.
>
> —THE ONION, "Florida State University to Phase Out Academic Operations"

Narration

A good story well-told can almost always help to support an argument, and writers and speakers use narratives often—in **REPORTS**, **MEMOIRS**, and many other genres. Be sure, however, that any story you tell supports your point, and that it not be the only evidence you offer as support. In general, you shouldn't rely only on stories to support your argument, especially personal stories. In the following example, award-winning author Bich Minh Nguyen writes about her experiences becoming "The Good Immigrant Student." In this essay, she uses narration to capture the tension she felt between wishing to fit in and be obedient, and wanting to rebel:

Roger Lathbury selects detail carefully to add drama in his narrative of a simple business deal. See how he did it on p. 827.

> More than once, I was given the assignment of writing a report about my family history. I loathed this task, for I was dreadfully aware that my history could not be faked: it already showed on my face. When my turn came to read out loud the teacher had to ask me several times to speak louder. Some kids, a few of them older, in different classes, took to pressing back the corners of their eyes with the heels of their palms while they

chanted, "Ching-chong, ching-chong!" during recess. This continued until Anh [Bich's sister], who was far tougher than me, threatened to beat them up.

I have no way of telling what tortured me more: the actual snickers and remarks and watchfulness of my classmates, or my own imagination, conjuring disdain. My own sense of shame. At times I felt sickened by my obedience, my accumulation of gold stickers, my every effort to be invisible.　　　　—BICH MINH NGUYEN, "The Good Immigrant Student"

Advertisements use narrative to appeal to viewers in many ways, such as in this ad campaign for animal adoption. Using just three frames and eight words, this cartoon tells a story that argues for adopting an animal.

Narrative is often used to OPEN an argument. In arguing that national policies had left great parts of Utah and other states toxic and extremely hazardous to human health, Terry Tempest Williams opens the epilogue to *Refuge: An Unnatural History of Family and Place* with a narrative based on her own life:

I belong to a clan of one-breasted women. My mother, my grand-mothers, and six aunts have all had mastectomies. Seven are dead. The two who survive have just completed rounds of chemotherapy and radiation.

I've had my own problems: two biopsies for breast cancer and a small tumor between my ribs diagnosed as a "borderline malignancy."

This is my family history.

　　　　—TERRY TEMPEST WILLIAMS, "The Clan of One-Breasted Women"

Problem / Solution

Some kinds of **PROPOSALS** call on writers to articulate a problem that needs to be solved. The proposal, then, becomes a way of addressing that problem. The following brief passage from a National Institutes of Health press release sets out a clear problem (drinking among college students) and identifies three elements that must be addressed in any solution:

> The consequences of college drinking are larger and more destructive than commonly realized, according to a new study supported by the National Institute on Alcohol Abuse and Alcoholism (NIAAA). Commissioned by the NIAAA Task Force on College Drinking, the study reveals that drinking by college students age 18–24 contributes to an estimated 1,400 student deaths, 500,000 injuries, and 70,000 cases of sexual assault or date rape each year. It also estimates that more than one-fourth of college students that age have driven in the past year while under the influence of alcohol. . . .
>
> "Prevention strategies must simultaneously target three constituencies: the student population as a whole; the college and its surrounding environment; and the individual at-risk or alcohol-dependent drinker," says [task force co-chair Dr. Mark] Goldman. "Research strongly supports strategies that target each of these factors."
>
> —"College Drinking Hazardous to Campus Communities
> Task Force Calls for Research-Based Prevention Programs"

Often writers will **OPEN** with a statement of the problem, as Rhoi Wangila and Chinua Akukwe do in their article on HIV and AIDS in Africa:

> Simply stated, Africans living with H.I.V./AIDS and the millions of others at high risk of contracting H.I.V. are not benefiting significantly from current domestic, regional, and international high profile remedial efforts.
>
> —RHOI WANGILA AND CHINUA AKUKWE, "H.I.V. and AIDS
> in Africa: Ten Lessons from the Field"

Wangila and Akukwe's article includes a photograph of African children affected by AIDS, which enhances their statement of the problem.

The remainder of their essay then tackles the staggering complexities involved in responding to this problem.

Reiteration

A form of repetition, reiteration helps support an argument through emphasis: Like a drumbeat, the repetition of a key word, phrase, image, or theme can help drive home a point, often in very memorable ways. Reiterating is especially powerful in spoken texts—think "Yes, we can!" and "Ain't I a Woman?" Martin Luther King Jr. was a master of effective repetition, as is evident in the famous speech he delivered on the steps of the Lincoln Memorial in Washington, D.C., in 1963. Just think for a moment what would be lost in this speech without the power of that repeated phrase, "I have a dream."

> I have a dream that one day this nation will rise up and live out the true meaning of its creed: "We hold these truths to be self-evident, that all men are created equal." I have a dream that one day on the red hills of Georgia, the sons of former slaves and the sons of former slave owners will be able to sit down together at the table of brotherhood. I have a dream that one day even the state of Mississippi, a state sweltering with the heat of injustice, sweltering with the heat of oppression, will

be transformed into an oasis of freedom and justice. I have a dream that my four little children will one day live in a nation where they will not be judged by the color of their skin but by the content of their character.

I have a *dream* today!

I have a dream that one day, down in Alabama, with its vicious racists, with its governor having his lips dripping with the words of "interposition" and "nullification"—one day right there in Alabama little black boys and black girls will be able to join hands with little white boys and white girls as sisters and brothers.

I have a *dream* today!

I have a dream that one day every valley shall be exalted, and every hill and mountain shall be made low, the rough places will be made plain, and the crooked places will be made straight; "and the glory of the Lord shall be revealed and all flesh shall see it together."

This is our hope, and this is the faith that I go back to the South with.

—MARTIN LUTHER KING JR., "I Have a Dream"

Reiteration also works in visual texts and is a hallmark of graphic novelist Marjane Satrapi's work. Born and raised in Iran before being sent abroad in 1984 to escape what became the country's Islamic revolution, Satrapi tells the story of her childhood in *Persepolis I,* arguing implicitly that repressive

A frame from *Persepolis*.

regimes squelch individuality. In the frame shown here, Satrapi depicts a class of female students, using reiteration to make her point: All these girls look exactly the same.

A little reiteration can go a long way. In an article published in *Ebony* magazine about the future of Chicago, see how it drives an argument that Chicago is still a home of black innovation and creativity:

> [Chicago]'s the place where organized Black history was born, where gospel music was born, where jazz and the blues were reborn, where the Beatles and the Rolling Stones went up to the mountaintop to get the new musical commandments from Chuck Berry and the rock 'n' roll apostles.　　　　　　　—LERONE BENNETT JR., "Blacks in Chicago"

Here the reiteration of "where" creates a kind of drumbeat, and the parallel "where" clauses help establish a rhythm of forward movement that drives the argument.

CHOOSE ONE OF THE EXAMPLES in this chapter that's all words. Think about whether the same argument could be made visually—in a chart, with a photo and caption, and so on. If that doesn't seem possible, how might you illustrate the example?

PART IV

Research

RESEARCH IS AN EVERYDAY MATTER. You gather information from reliable sources to help you make decisions, support arguments, solve problems, become more informed, and a host of other reasons. How would you go about choosing a new smartphone? If you compare prices and service plans for different phones, read reviews, and talk to friends who have used them, you are doing research. When you review team records, player profiles, and statistics before filling out your March Madness basketball brackets, you're doing research. Do you check websites such as *Rotten Tomatoes* or the *Internet Movie Database* before heading to the movies? look at online restaurant guides like *UrbanSpoon* or *Yelp* to find a place to eat? speak with a family friend to find information about possible summer jobs? All research.

When you do research, you engage in a process of inquiry—that is, you are guided by questions for which you want answers. You might use a variety of methods—fieldwork, lab experiments, database searches—and you'll find information in books, articles, news reports, online databases, statistics, archives, opinion polls, family photographs, land deeds or other historical records, and elsewhere. However you approach it, research is a process of seeking answers to questions that matter to you. More than simply a matter of compiling information, the most meaningful research can be a process of discovery and learning.

Research plays an essential role in just about everyone's life. As a student, you'll engage in research in a variety of disciplines and in many of the courses you take. Research is likely to be part of your work life as well—people working in business, government, and industry all need to follow research in order to make important decisions and keep up with new developments in their fields. Restaurant owners need to do research, for instance, to discover how to maximize profits from menu options and portion sizes. Engineers constantly do research to find equipment and suppliers. When a group of U.S. senators argued for a federal ban on texting while driving, they cited research from a Virginia Tech study as evidence to show the dangers of texting while driving.

Even artists rely on research—for inspiration and also to gather information and materials to use in their artwork. In an interview from the PBS show *Art in the Twenty-First Century*, photographer Laurie Simmons discusses the role research plays in the work that artists do:

> I think that artists are always doing research on their own behalf and for their work. For some artists, it's reading. For some, it's shopping. For some, it's traveling. And I think that there's always this kind of seeking quality that artists have where they're looking for things that will jog them and move them in one direction or another. For me, movies and books have always been research.
> —"Laurie Simmons: Photography, Perfection, and Reality"

When you research something to present to others, your purpose, audience, and the rest of your rhetorical situation will inform both the kind of information you look for and the way you present your findings. And

From *The Boxes,* by Laurie Simmons, who researched dollhouses, paper dolls, and interior decorating books to create the scenario that she then photographed.

when you do academic research, you'll almost always be studying a topic that many scholars before you have already studied. You'll want to start by learning what has been written about your topic and then thinking carefully about questions you want to—and are able to—pursue in your research. In this way, you'll be engaging with the ideas of others and participating in conversations about topics that matter—to you and others. You'll be joining the larger academic conversation. The following chapters can help you do so.

THINK ABOUT activities you have engaged in during the past couple of weeks that called for research of some kind. List the different kinds of information you've sought and the different ways you went about that process. How did you use the information or data that you gathered?

FIFTEEN

Starting Your Research

Joining the Conversation

HAT DO YOU FIND MOST DIFFICULT about doing research? Gathering data? Writing it up? Documenting sources? For most students, the hardest part is just getting started. Researchers from Project Information Literacy, an ongoing study at the University of Washington's Information School, have found that U.S. students doing course-related research have the most difficulty with three things: getting started, defining a topic, and narrowing a topic. This chapter will help you to tackle these tricky first steps—and also to identify specific questions that will drive your research and make a schedule to manage the many tasks that go along with a research project.

At the same time, we aim to show you that doing research means more than finding sources. Doing research means learning about something you want to know more about. It means finding out what's been said about that topic, listening in on a larger conversation (where you will no doubt encounter many varying viewpoints)—and then, when you write about that topic, adding your own ideas to that conversation.

And so while this chapter suggests a sequence of activities for doing research, keep in mind that you won't necessarily move through these stages in a fixed order. As you learn more about your topic, you may want to change your focus or even your topic. But first of all, you have to get started, which this chapter will help you do.

Find a Topic That Fascinates You

At its best, research begins as a kind of treasure hunt, an opportunity for you to investigate a subject that you care or wonder about. And so finding that topic might be the single most important part of the research process.

If you've been given a specific assignment, study it carefully so that you understand exactly what you are required to do. Does it specify the **RESEARCH METHODS**? number and kinds of sources? And what about the writing? Does it name a specific **GENRE**? number of pages? **DOCUMENTATION** system? Do you need to write a **RESEARCH PROPOSAL**? an **ANNOTATED BIBLIOGRAPHY**? And does it assign a particular topic? If so, you'll likely still need to decide what aspect of the topic you'll focus on. Consider the following assignment:

> Identify a current language issue that's being discussed and debated nationally or in your local community. Learn as much as you can about this issue. Then write a 5-to-7-page informative essay, using both print and online sources and following MLA documentation style. And remember, your task is to inform your readers about the issue, not to pick one side over others.

This assignment identifies a genre (a report) and a general topic (a current language issue), but it leaves the specific issue up to the author. You might investigate how your local school district handles bilingual education for recent immigrants in the public schools or how several state systems approach bilingual education. You could research why proficiency in speaking English has become a controversial issue on the Ladies Professional Golf Association tour. Or you could report on the debate about how texting and social media have affected students' writing.

This particular assignment is broad enough to allow you to choose a particular issue, but even assignments that are more specific can be approached in a way that will make them interesting to you.

If you get to choose your topic, think of it as an opportunity to learn about something that intrigues you. Consider topics related to your personal interests, your major, or your professional interests. Are you a hunter who is concerned about potential legislation that impacts water and land rights in your hometown? Do the restrictions on downloading files from the internet affect you such that you'd like to understand the multiple sides of the issue? Is there a topic related to your major that you'd like to look into? Even if you've been given a general topic, try to find an aspect of it that relates to your own interests. For example, for the assignment above, a political science major might research court cases about the teaching of African American Vernacular English in schools. A biology major might focus on how the wording of legislation regarding stem-cell research could affect future grants in the field.

Think about doing research as an invitation to explore a topic that really matters to you. If you're excited about your topic, that excitement will take you somewhere interesting, lead you to ideas that will in turn inform what you know and think.

For ideas and inspiration, visit *TED.com*, a site devoted to "ideas worth spreading." While there, check out Steven Johnson's talk on "Where Good Ideas Come From."

Analyze Your Rhetorical Situation

As you get started, it's a good idea to do some thinking about your audience and purpose and the rest of your rhetorical situation. You may not yet know your genre, and you surely won't know your stance, but thinking about those things now will help you when you're narrowing your topic and figuring out a research question.

- **AUDIENCE**. Who will be reading what you write? What expectations might they have, and what do they likely know about your topic? What kinds of sources will they consider credible?

- **PURPOSE**. What do you hope to accomplish by doing this research? Are you trying to inform your audience about the topic? argue a position? something else?

- **GENRE**. Have you been assigned to write in a particular genre? Will you **ARGUE A POSITION**? **NARRATE** a historical event? **ANALYZE** some kind of data? **REPORT** information? something else?

- **STANCE**. What is your attitude toward the topic—and toward your audience? How can you establish your authority with them, and how do you want them to see you? As a neutral researcher? an advocate for a cause? something else?

- **CONTEXT**. Do you have any length requirements? Is there a due date? What other research has been done on your topic, and how does that affect the direction your research takes?

- **MEDIUM**. Are you required to use a certain medium? If not, what media will be most appropriate for your audience? What media will best suit your topic and what you expect to write? Will you want or need to include images? audio? video?

- **DESIGN**. Will you include photos or other illustrations? present any data in charts or graphs? highlight any parts of the text? need to include headings? Are you working in a discipline with any format requirements?

Don't worry if you can't answer all of these questions at this point or if some elements change along the way. Just remember to keep these questions in mind as you work.

Narrow Your Topic

A good academic research topic needs to be substantive enough that you can find adequate information but not so broad that you become overwhelmed by the number of sources you find. The topic "women in sports," for example, is too general; a quick search on *Google* will display hundreds of subtopics, from "Title IX" to "women's sports injuries." One way to find an aspect of a topic that interests you is to scan the subtopics listed in online search results. Online news sites like *Google News* and *NPR Research News* can give you a sense of current news or research related to your topic. Your goal is to move from a too-general topic to a manageable one, as in the following example:

General topic: women in sports

Narrower topic: injuries among women athletes

Still narrower: injuries among women basketball players

Even narrower: patterns of injuries among collegiate women basketball players compared with their male counterparts

Thinking about what you already know about your topic can also help identify a preliminary research focus. Have you had any experiences related to your topic? read about it? heard about it? chatted with friends about it? If, for example, you've been assigned to write about a language issue, write down everything that occurs to you based on your own experience, as well as your knowledge about any issues that are being discussed. Say you're studying a new language or questioning the foreign language requirement in your major. In a discussion with your teacher, you hear that a former president of Harvard has set off a national debate by saying that American students don't really need to learn another language since English has become "the global language."

Write down what you know about this issue and what you think. Do some brainstorming or some of the other activities for **GENERATING IDEAS**. And since it's an issue that's being debated, you could use your favorite search engine to find out what's being said. Exploring your topic in this way can give you an overview of the issue and help you find a focus that you'd like to pursue.

Just as a topic that is too broad will yield an overwhelming number of sources, one that is too narrow will yield too little information. Consider the topic "shin splints among women basketball players at the University of Tennessee." This topic is so narrow that there is probably not enough information available to you. Sometimes changing a few details can help. Changing "shin splints" to "kinds of injuries" and adding "current trends" may lead you to interesting information.

Do Some Background Research

Becoming familiar with some existing research on your topic can provide valuable background information—and give you an overview of the topic before diving into more specialized sources. It can also help you discover issues that have not been researched or perhaps even identified. At this point your goal should be to see your topic in a larger context and begin formulating questions to guide your research.

You may want to take a look at some encyclopedias, almanacs, and other **REFERENCE WORKS**, which can provide an overview of your topic and point you toward specific areas where you might want to follow up. Subject-specific encyclopedias provide more detail, including information about scholarly books you might want to check out. If you don't have access to a university library, visit the *Internet Public Library*.

Though online encyclopedias may not be considered appropriate to cite as authoritative sources, *Wikipedia* can be a helpful resource in the early stages of research because it links to additional resources and to information about the discussions that have taken place among those who've contributed to each article, alerting you to controversies about the topic.

Articulate a Question Your Research Will Answer

Once you have sufficiently narrowed your topic, you will need to turn it into a question that will guide your research. Start by asking yourself what you'd like to know about your topic. A good research question should be simple, be focused, and require more than a simple "yes" or "no" answer. Ask an open-ended question that will lead you to plenty of data. For example:

> *Topic:* injuries among women soccer players
>
> *What you'd like to know:* What are the current trends in injuries among women soccer players, and how are athletic trainers responding?

> *Topic:* disappearing languages
>
> *What you'd like to know:* What causes a language to disappear?

Keep your RHETORICAL SITUATION in mind as you work to be sure your research question is manageable in the time you have and narrow enough to cover in the number of pages you plan to write. Consider also any GENRE requirements. If you're assigned to argue a position, for example, be sure your research question is one that will lead to an argument. Notice how each question below suggests a different genre:

> *A question that would lead to a* REPORT: What are the current trends in injuries among women soccer players?

> *A question that would lead to an* ANALYSIS: Why do women soccer players suffer so many injuries during training?

> *A question that would lead to an* ARGUMENT: At what age should young girls interested in soccer begin serious athletic training?

Once you've settled on a research question, you should do some more research. Your goal at this point is to be looking for possible answers to your question and to get some sense of the various perspectives on the issue.

Plot Out a Working Thesis

When you've decided on a possible answer to your research question, you are ready to turn it into a working thesis, which will be a brief statement of what you claim in your essay. Basically, a working thesis is your hypothesis—your best guess about the claim you will make based on your research—and articulating it will help you focus the rest of the research you will need to do. Here are three working theses on the question about why women soccer players experience so many injuries during training:

> One reason that women soccer players sustain a large number of injuries during training is that they use training methods originally developed for men; developing training methods to suit female physiology would reduce the incidence of injuries.

> Some say that women soccer players are prone to more injuries than ever, especially during preseason training; however, the data show that injury rates are not increasing but are being reported and discussed much more than they once were.

> Increasing agility drills in the training regimens of women athletes would significantly decrease the risk of injuries.

Keep in mind that your working thesis may well change as you learn more about your topic. So stay flexible, and expect to revise it as your ideas develop. The more open your mind, the more you'll learn.

Establish a Schedule

Establishing a schedule will help you break your research into manageable tasks, stay organized and on task—and meet all your deadlines along the way. Following is a template that can help you make a plan:

Working title:

Working thesis:

	Due Date
Choose a topic.	_____
Analyze your rhetorical situation.	_____
Do some preliminary research.	_____
Narrow your topic and decide on a research question.	_____
Plot out a working thesis.	_____
Do library and web research.	_____
Start a working bibliography.	_____
Turn in your research proposal and annotated bibliography.	_____
Plan and schedule any field research.	_____
Do any field research.	_____
Draft a thesis statement.	_____
Write out a draft.	_____
Get response.	_____
Do additional research if you need to.	_____
Revise.	_____
Prepare your list of works cited.	_____
Edit.	_____
Write your final draft.	_____
Proofread.	_____
Turn in the final draft.	_____

SIXTEEN

Finding Sources, Considering Research Methods

OW DO YOU PICK A GOOD RESTAURANT to take relatives to when they visit? Would you check local blogs or websites for reviews or just ask your friends for a recommendation? How do you find information to help you decide which tablet computer to buy? Would you test-drive different models at different stores? go to trusted websites or technology publications that provide neutral reviews? talk to tech-savvy friends? consult a manufacturer's website? How would you find information on the East Coast Women's Roller Derby Week for an article you're writing for the school paper? Would you search the internet for women's roller derby leagues? contact a league administrative office and request printed materials? interview women who play on the local team? These are all matters of finding sources, the subject of this chapter.

Considering What Kinds of Sources You'll Need

Any time that you search for information, the decisions you make about what types of sources you look for, where you look for them, and how authoritative you need them to be will be guided by your **PURPOSE**,

Research sources vary by topic and discipline: interviews, observations (both in the outdoors and in the lab), library databases and printed resources, and archives can all prove valuable to your research project.

AUDIENCE, and other elements of the **RHETORICAL SITUATION**. For the research you do in college, an important part of the rhetorical situation may be the discipline you are working in; for example, scientists tend to value research done through observation and experimentation whereas historians tend to value research done in libraries and archives. For academic research, you'll also want to keep several other kinds of distinctions in mind in looking for sources: the differences between primary and secondary sources, between scholarly and popular sources, and between older and more current sources.

Primary and secondary sources. **PRIMARY SOURCES** are original documents or materials, firsthand accounts of events, or field research like interviews or observations. **SECONDARY SOURCES** are texts that analyze and interpret primary sources; they offer background and context that can help you gain perspective on your topic. Secondary sources on a subject might include scholarly books and journal articles about the topic, magazine and newspaper reviews, government research reports, or annotated bibliographies.

Whether a particular source is considered primary or secondary often depends on what the topic is. If you are analyzing an artistic work, say a film, the film itself is obviously a primary source, while A. O. Scott's review of the film is a secondary source. But if you are researching Scott's work as a critic, then his review would be a primary source.

This distinction between primary and secondary sources leads to a similar one between primary and secondary research. *Primary research* calls on you to engage personally and directly with your topic, whether by working in laboratories; by conducting interviews, observations, case studies, and surveys; or by doing your own analyses of literary or artistic works, other kinds of documents, or physical artifacts. *Secondary research* is when you study research done by others, usually through the library or on the internet.

Scholarly and popular sources. Popular, nonacademic, sources such as magazine articles or websites you find by running a search on your topic can play an important role at the start of your research project. For instance, you might consult *Wikipedia* while figuring out your **RESEARCH QUESTION** to see if a topic you're interested in but know little about seems viable. But for most academic assignments, you will quickly want to turn to scholarly sources, such as books and journal articles, for your secondary research.

Such research sources usually have been peer-reviewed—critically read and evaluated by established experts in the discipline.

Older and more current sources. You will need to determine whether older or more current sources are appropriate for your purpose. Although you will always want to investigate the latest news and research about your topic, sometimes older works will serve as essential sources of information. Your purpose and your discipline may dictate the use of older or more current sources.

Analyzing your assignment and the rest of your rhetorical situation can help you make appropriate decisions about the kinds of sources that will work best for your project. For academic projects, you'll need to think particularly about the level of credibility your sources need to have. Your professors may expect you to search for sources available only in the library, read books and articles published by scholars in your discipline, interview experts or conduct surveys on your topic, or rely primarily on academic research that is published in scholarly journals.

For some projects, however, the best research strategy may involve culling sources from various places—scholarly journals and popular magazines, the library and the web, books and individuals. For a report on the impact of recent floods on small farms in your area, for example, you may need to conduct background research via the library on the local climate and agriculture; search online for news reports, photographs, and videos that document the floods; and conduct interviews with local farmers affected by the floods. This chapter provides guidance that will help you to search for sources on the internet and through the library, and also to conduct research in the field.

USING KEYWORDS AND
ADVANCED SEARCH FUNCTIONS

When looking for sources on the internet or through the library, you'll need to know how to use keywords and search functions effectively in order to identify useful, relevant sources among the vast amount of information that's likely available on your topic. Following are some guidelines for conducting searches using search sites, library catalogs, and electronic indexes and databases.

Keyword Searches

Most search sites, library catalogs, and databases will allow you to conduct keyword searches. In catalogs and databases, keyword searches usually cover multiple fields, including authors, titles, and descriptions of each source. Keyword searches allow you to use words and phrases you've identified to locate sources—but keep in mind that you may need to adjust your keywords or use synonyms if your initial searches don't yield useful results. If searching for *women's sports injuries* doesn't yield much, try *female athlete injuries.* You may also need to try broader keywords (*women sports medicine*). If your search returns too many results, try narrowing your term (*women's sports injuries soccer*).

Following are some advanced search techniques that can help focus your search. *Google* and many search sites provide their own advanced-search options—allowing you to limit searches, for example, to items published only during a particular time period.

Quotation marks can be used around terms to search for an exact phrase, such as "International Monetary Fund" or "obesity in American high schools." Using quotation marks may exclude useful results, however—for example, searching for "factory farms" may omit results with "factory farming" in a library search.

Wildcard searches allow you to insert a symbol (usually *?* or ***) in the middle or at the end of a word to retrieve multiple forms of that word. For example, typing in *wom?n* would retrieve both *woman* and *women.*

Truncation allows symbols such as *?* or *** to stand in for missing letters: for example, typing in *ethnograph** would retrieve *ethnography, ethnographic, ethnographer,* and so on.

Boolean operators (AND, OR, and NOT) let you refine your search by combining keywords in different ways to include or exclude certain terms.

Using AND narrows a search to include all terms joined by AND; using OR broadens a search to include items with any of the terms joined by OR; and using NOT limits a search to exclude items with any term preceded by NOT. For example, if you're researching solar energy, typing in *alternative energy* will bring up many more options than *alternative energy AND solar,* which reduces the number to only those that include the term *solar.* Typing in *alternative energy NOT wind* narrows the search to results that exclude the term *wind.*

Parentheses allow you to combine Boolean searches in a more complex way. For example, a search for *alternative energy AND (solar OR wind)* yields only those items that contain both *alternative energy* and *solar* or both *alternative energy* and *wind.* And *alternative energy NOT (solar OR wind)* yields only items that contain *alternative energy* but do not contain either *solar* or *wind;* this kind of search might be useful, for example, if you are specifically researching forms of alternative energy other than solar or wind energy.

Plus and minus signs are used by some search sites instead of AND and NOT. Using a plus sign (+) in front of words and phrases indicates that those exact words must appear, so *+"alternative energy" +solar* will bring up results that include both terms. The minus sign (a hyphen) excludes results, so *+"alternative energy" -solar* brings up sources in which *alternative energy* is included but *solar* is not. Searching for *+"alternative energy" -solar -biofuel* excludes results with both *solar* and *biofuel.*

Author, Title, and Subject Searches

Most library catalogs and many databases are searchable by author, title, and subject as well as by keyword. Using the author and title fields allows you to go directly to a source when you know its title or author. To do an effective subject search, it helps to know what cataloging system the library uses—most commonly the Library of Congress Subject Headings (LCSH) or the National Library of Medicine's Medical Subject Headings (MeSH). Subject heading searches use what is called "left-hand truncation," which means that you can access a list of headings by entering the first term. These types of searches require terms that are specific to their lists. For example, if you're searching for material on the American Civil War, and you search for the subject *civil war*, you'll get a long list that begins with your term and branches to the right, like this:

NUM	MARK	SUBJECTS (1-43 OF 43)	YEAR	ENTRIES 105 FOUND
1		Civil War -- See Also the narrower term Insurgency		1
2	☐	Civil War		42
3	☐	Civil War Africa	2000	1
4	☐	Civil War Africa Case Studies	c2006	1
5	☐	Civil War Africa Sub Saharan		2
6	☐	Civil War Africa Sub Saharan Case Studies	2002	1
7	☐	Civil War Africa Sub Saharan History 20th Century		3
8	☐	Civil War Africa Sub Saharan History 20th Century Congresses	2000	1
9	☐	Civil War Africa West	2002	1

These results are too broad for your topic. If you then go back to the subject search page and type in *American Civil War,* you'll get this result.

> **" American Civil War 1861 1865 "** is not used in this library's catalog.
> **United States History Civil War, 1861-1865** is used instead.
> Try a search for United States History Civil War, 1861-1865 .

Subject searches allow an overview of your library's holdings on a topic. To get help in narrowing the topic more specifically, check with a reference librarian or consult the LCSH manuals (sometimes available on the search page). Once you know that the LCSH list uses "United States History" to begin subject headings in this field, then you'll be on the right track and may get this search result.

NUM	MARK	SUBJECTS (1-50 OF 272)	YEAR	ENTRIES 2422 FOUND
1		United States History Civil War 1861 1865 -- See Also the narrower term Northwestern Conspiracy, 1864		1
2	☐	United States History Civil War 1861 1865		293
3	☐	United States History Civil War 1861 1865 19th Century		3
4	☐	United States History Civil War 1861 1865 African American Troops Sources	1982	1
5	☐	United States History Civil War 1861 1865 African Americans		25
6	☐	United States History Civil War 1861 1865 African Americans Juvenile Fiction	c2002	1
7	☐	United States History Civil War 1861 1865 African Americans Juvenile Literature		4
8	☐	United States History Civil War 1861 1865 African Americans Sources		5
9		United States History Civil War 1861 1865 Afro Americans -- See United States History Civil War, 1861-1865 African Americans		1

SEARCHING ON THE INTERNET

Many students turn to the internet to begin their research, and understandably so; you can quickly and easily use it to locate an array of sources from home, from school, from just about anywhere. As convenient and useful as the internet may be for research, however, information you find there poses risks for academic projects. Because almost anyone can post material on the internet, it's especially important to EVALUATE your sources carefully to determine how credible they are and to think carefully about whether your audience will consider them persuasive. *Wikipedia* or a blog by someone who's not an expert on the topic you're researching may be sufficient to satisfy your personal curiosity, but they are probably not suitable or reliable for academic work. Also, material on the internet may be less stable than electronic material available through the library, so you'll need to DOCUMENT your internet sources especially carefully, including bookmarking pages and noting the date you accessed them. Following are some general tips and guidelines for locating appropriate sources on the internet:

- *Use a reliable, speedy browser* that allows you to have multiple related pages open at the same time and that makes using bookmarks simple and easy, like Firefox or Google Chrome.

- *Identify which search sites will be most relevant and useful* for your search. For academic searches, try *Google Scholar* or *JURN*. *Google Scholar* locates peer-reviewed articles, books, abstracts, and technical reports by searching the websites of academic publishers, professional societies, and universities, as well as sites elsewhere on the web that make scholarly articles available. When these searches yield only an abstract, there may be a charge to access the full text; check to see whether you may be able to access it for free via your library. *Google Scholar* tends to produce more results in the sciences than in the humanities. *JURN* searches free, open-access electronic journals from academic publishers; it focuses on the arts and humanities. There are also a variety of search engines that can be useful for specific types of searches, including those devoted to maps or image searches (*Google Maps, Bing Images*), news (*Yahoo! News*), and so on. You can also use metasearch engines such as *Dogpile* and *MetaCrawler* to collect results from several search engines at once.

- *Move from general concepts to more specific ones* by configuring short, increasingly narrowed combinations of keywords. Most search engines also allow advanced searches that help you limit results by date, type of source, or other criteria; check the search tips (sometimes you'll need to click on Help or About) for guidelines that are specific to the search engine you're using.

Keep in mind that some search engines allow websites to pay for higher placement or ranking in search results, which means that what comes up first in a search may not be the most useful or relevant to your topic. If you have a good idea of what kind of material you're looking for or what kind of resources you need, you may find it's easier to go directly to specific sites or resources. Here are just a few of the kinds of online tools and sources that may prove helpful to you:

Open-access archives and databases. A variety of archives and databases that do not require a library subscription provide free access to books, articles, images, and other resources. For example, like *JURN*, the *Directory of Open Access Journals* is a database that allows you to search research journals that are freely available on the web. At the *Project Gutenberg* website, you can access over 36,000 ebooks and digitized texts that are freely available in the public domain. *InfoMine*, curated by librarians, collects a variety of useful information for academic research, including databases, directories, and ebooks and electronic journals.

Open-access directories and indexes. General subject directories such as those provided by *Google* and *Yahoo!* may be helpful in narrowing your topic or directing you to relevant sites. Additionally, many curated directories and indexes collect and evaluate online resources. For example, *ipl2* includes resources from the *Internet Public Library* and the *Librarians' Internet Index* and is maintained by librarians, provides subject directories, and allows keyword searches of websites.

Government sources. Official reports, legislative records, texts of laws, maps and photos, census data, and other information from federal, state, and local governments are available for free online. Check the websites of government departments and agencies for these resources; you can access such resources for the U.S. government through *USA.gov*. In addition to government reports and documents, the *Library of Congress* website provides a large archive of photographs, maps, and other U.S. historical and cultural materials.

News sources. News organizations usually have websites that provide access to current and archived articles, photos, podcasts, videos, and streaming audio of broadcasts, as well as other resources. Some sites, like that of the *New York Times,* provide only limited access or require subscriptions, but much is available for free. News aggregators like *Google News* and *Bing News* collect articles on major stories and current events from a range of international or local news sources; often you can personalize such aggregators to track news on specific subjects.

Forums, discussion lists, and social media. You may be able to use online forums, discussion lists, and social media to communicate with groups of people who share an interest or expertise in specific topics. Many forums and discussion lists archive past posts and threads that you can search for material relevant to your topic; you can also join current discussions and post questions or requests for information. Check *Google Groups* to find forums and lists relevant to your topic. You may also be able to connect to such groups through social media tools like *Facebook* and *Twitter;* such connections allow you to stay updated about current events, media or press releases, commentary, and so on that are related to your topic. Because many forums, discussion lists, and social media allow users to participate anonymously, be sure to evaluate carefully any information you receive from such sources and try to confirm it elsewhere.

Blogs and wikis. Because blogs can include information that has not been reviewed, checked, or evaluated, many professors do not consider them reliable as academic sources. But they can be useful as starting points. Blogs that include comments posted by readers can reveal alternative perspectives on your topic; they may also direct you to events or other news not extensively covered by major news organizations. You can use blog directories such as *Technorati* to locate blogs relevant to your topic.

Similarly, because wikis allow any user to post and edit material and may have little or no editorial oversight, they may not be considered credible for academic work. But they can be useful for quick overviews and often include links to additional sources. *Wikipedia*, for example, often includes references and links to sources for its articles at the end of the article.

SEARCHING IN THE LIBRARY

Libraries provide access to a wealth of resources, many of them not easily available in other ways, ranging from reference works and bibliographies to **PRIMARY SOURCES** like letters, historical documents, rare books, and presidential papers to **SECONDARY SOURCES** such as books based on research, scholarly journals, and magazines. You can visit most college libraries online, and you can often access electronic resources such as indexes, databases, and the library catalog remotely. If you haven't already done so, take some time to familiarize yourself with the library resources available to you. Knowing what's available in the library and how to access it is crucial to conducting effective academic research. There are several possible ways to find out this information, including visiting the library website, taking a tour of the building(s), and—most useful of all—meeting with a librarian.

Library Websites

In addition to information about hours, location, and holdings, library websites often provide useful guides or tutorials to using the library, including specialized online sources to which it provides free access. You may also find out about special events, opportunities for tours or training sessions, and ways to use services such as course reserves—in which an instructor places materials on reserve for a class, thus assuring students in the class access to them. Another valuable service is interlibrary loan, which enables you to access materials in other libraries. (The time involved varies depending on whether your request involves books that must be delivered physically or files that can be delivered electronically.) Many college libraries also provide online research guides that list databases, references, websites, organizations, and other discipline- or subject-specific resources. The following image shows the homepage of Hofstra University's library system.

These   screens show subject-related resources that help with subject searches discussed on pp. 342–43.

If you click on Subject Resource Guides (LibGuides), the sixth item under "Finding Information," you'll get the screen below, the library's discipline-specific subject list.

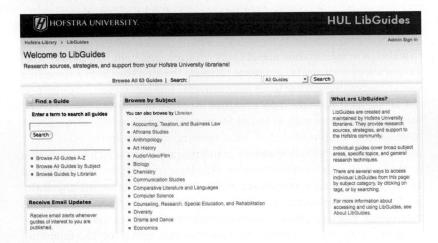

Library Tours

Because each school library is physically different, sign up to take a tour of yours; you'll learn the location of key materials and spaces, including electronic library catalogs, special collections, computer rooms, computers designated for searching databases, screening and other media rooms, meeting rooms, and so on. If there are no guided tours available, pick up a library map at the information desk and spend a little time exploring on your own.

Librarians as Resources

All college libraries provide reference librarians whose major responsibility is to help faculty and students with their research inquiries. While they will not do the research for you, reference librarians will help you identify where you can find materials specific to your research question or topic and how you can search for them most efficiently. Their advice can save you considerable time and frustration from looking in the wrong places or using search techniques that take longer than necessary.

In addition to reference librarians, many libraries have librarians who specialize in specific academic disciplines. Discipline (or subject) librarians work closely with academic departments to make sure that the appropriate journals, databases, and books for that discipline are in the library or quickly available to students and faculty; some disciplines may have their own library buildings separate from the main library.

Arrange a meeting with a reference or discipline librarian, and come to the meeting prepared to discuss your research question or topic. Also bring specific questions about library resources available on your topic.

Reference Works

Reference works available through your library, whether in print, online, or both, include encyclopedias, handbooks, bibliographies, atlases, directories of biographical information, and others. Such works can be helpful for gathering background information and understanding the larger context of your topic—or narrowing it if need be—as well as for getting leads to more specific sources.

General reference sources include general encyclopedias (*Encyclopaedia Britannica, Columbia Encyclopedia*), dictionaries (*Merriam-Webster's, Oxford English Dictionary*), almanacs (*The World Almanac and Book of Facts*), and atlases (*The National Atlas of Canada*), among others. Besides brief overviews of your topic, such sources can provide definitions of concepts and terms and geographic and historical background.

Specialized encyclopedias can give information more specifically related to your topic or discipline than general reference works, including not only overviews and definitions but also biographical information about key figures and bibliographies of sources related to your topic. Ask your reference or subject librarian to help you find specialized encyclopedias that might be useful to you.

Bibliographies, also called lists of references or works cited, are lists of books, articles, and other publications that you can use to locate further sources on a topic. These appear at the end of books or scholarly articles; if you've located a useful source, check its bibliography to find additional sources related to your topic. Book-length, topic-specific bibliographies may be available for popular or widely researched subjects; ask your librarian about availability. Many bibliographies also include descriptive annotations for listed sources.

Library Catalogs

Most libraries have electronic catalogs that account for all their holdings; searching the catalog is the best method for locating books and other materials, such as audio and video recordings, that you can check out from or access through the library. The record for each item includes the author, title, and publication information (publisher, location, and year) and a physical description of the item; the record also shows where the item is located in the library (or a networked library) and whether or not it is currently available to be checked out. The electronic catalog also provides call numbers, which are necessary for physically locating the item in the library stacks and sometimes gives summaries or overviews of the contents of items.

You can search a library catalog by author, title, subject, or keyword. Here is an example of the results of a keyword search in the Hofstra University Library catalog for *women writers Ireland*. The first image shows the library search page; the second image shows the first book chosen from the short list of search results, the book's cover, and a link to the table of contents and other information about the book.

LEXICAT
Hofstra University Libraries

Search   My Library Account   Help   Interlibrary Loan   Interlibrary Loan: Law Library   Law Library   Libraries Homepage

Keyword   Guided Search   Title   Author   Subject   Numbers   Reserves

Keyword Search

Search the catalog for word(s):
Women Writers Ireland

[View Entire Collection ⬍]

[Any Location ⬍]

[Any Material Type ⬍]

(Submit)

Tips:

Phrases
Search for complete phrases by enclosing them in quotation marks.
Example: *"world health organization"*

Wildcards
Words may be right-hand truncated using an asterisk.
Example: *environment* polic**

Boolean Operators
Use AND or OR to specify multiple words in any field, any order. Use AND NOT to exclude words.
Example: *stocks and bonds*
(indian or pacific) and (ocean life and not mammals)

Proximity
Use NEAR to specify words close to each other, in any order.
Example: *fractal near geometry*

* * *

Women, writing, and language in early modern Ireland / by Marie-Louise Coolahan. Coolahan, Marie-Louise.
Oxford ; New York : Oxford University Press, 2010.
1 copy available at Axinn - Stacks

Location	Call No.	Note	Status
Axinn - Stacks	PR8733 .C68 2010		AVAILABLE

TOC and
More

Library-Based Indexes and Databases

Articles from newspapers, magazines, and scholarly journals are available in your library in print or online or both, depending on the library and the periodical; you can locate such articles through indexes and databases to which the library subscribes. If you can't access an index electronically through your library, ask a reference librarian to help you locate the print version on the library shelves.

Indexes are listings by topic of popular and scholarly articles published in print and online. Because computerized indexing of most U.S. and international magazines and newspapers did not begin until around 1980, to find magazine and newspaper articles published before then, you'll most likely need to search print indexes such as the following:

- *The Readers' Guide to Periodical Literature*
- *Magazine Index*
- *National Newspaper Index*

Databases organize and provide access not only to listings (bibliographic citations) of articles but also, in many cases, to abstracts (brief summaries) and full texts. Your library likely has subscriptions to a number of general and subject-specific databases that you can access through its website.

General databases that cover a range of disciplines and topics and include scholarly articles, popular magazines, and news stories may be a good place to start. Here are a few of the most widely used:

- *Academic OneFile* (InfoTrac) provides access to more than 9,000 peer-reviewed journals, including full text for more than 6,000 of them. This database also offers the full text of the *New York Times* from 1985 on as well as podcasts and transcripts from CNN, CBC, and NPR.

- *Academic Search Complete* (EBSCO) includes more than 8,600 full-text periodicals from the humanities, arts, and sciences, of which more than 7,500 are peer-reviewed. It also offers indexing and abstracts for another 12,500 journals.

- *ArticleFirst* (OCLC) is an index of the items listed in the tables of contents of over 12,000 journals. It covers articles, news stories, letters, and items on many other topics. For most items, the database also provides a list of libraries that hold the journal.

- *JSTOR* is an archive of scanned copies of scholarly journals from many disciplines. It includes issues from further back in time than most other scholarly databases, but it does not include the most recent issues.

- *LexisNexis Academic* collects full-text documents from over 10,000 news, government, business, and legal sources. *Like Academic OneFile*, this database includes transcripts of broadcast news sources.

- *C Q Researcher* offers issue-focused reports, analyzing issues in the news and from business, the social sciences, and sciences.

Subject-specific databases are useful when you have a focused topic and research question. For example, if you are conducting research on sustainable farming efforts in urban areas, you might begin by searching databases that focus on food and nutrition, such as the *Food Science and Technology Abstracts*. If you are searching for information on trends in sports injuries among women athletes, you might search a sports research database like *SPORTDiscus with Full Text*. Below are a few more examples of subject-specific databases; ask a subject or reference librarian to direct you to those most relevant to your topic.

- *AGRIS,* from the UN Food and Agricultural Organization, provides bibliographic information and full text for a range of agricultural sources, including government and technical reports and conference papers.

- *IEEE Explore* provides access to more than 3 million full-text documents in computer science, electronics, and electrical engineering.

- *PsycINFO* provides indexes and abstracts for peer-reviewed sources in psychology and the behavioral sciences.

- *MLA International Bibliography* indexes scholarly books and articles related to literature, languages, linguistics, and folklore from around the world.

- *ERIC* (Educational Resource Information Center) provides bibliographic records for over 1.3 million journal articles, books, and other materials related to education.

- *SocINDEX,* a sociology-specific research database provided by EBSCO, includes over 2 million bibliographic records, a sociology-specific thesaurus, author profiles, indexing, and abstracts of journal articles.

CONDUCTING FIELD RESEARCH

Journalists who interview eyewitnesses, researchers who spend months observing the behavior of a particular population, historians who gather oral histories, and pollsters who conduct surveys on the general public's attitudes about current government policies are all engaging in field research. Depending on your research question, you may need to go "into the field" to conduct research, using data-gathering methods that rely on firsthand accounts. The three most common discovery methods for field research are observation, interviews, and surveys or questionnaires.

Keep in mind that conducting field research on human subjects may require prior approval from your college. Observing what kinds of clothing people wear to the mall may not need permission, but observing interactions in a private space like a doctor's office or doing any kind of field research with children probably will. Check with your instructor to find out if your project requires approval. If it does, be sure you understand the approval process and the time required to complete it.

Observations

Using observation as a field research method is more than casual people watching; you should have a clear sense of your purpose in observing and how doing so will best help you answer your research question. You'll need to concentrate and remain focused. Be sure to record your observations carefully, using notes, photographs, and other recording devices that are appropriate for the setting. Here are some guidelines for conducting effective observations:

1. Determine your purpose for observing. Is observation an appropriate method to pursue your research question? Do you expect to use the data to test your working thesis?

2. Plan ahead. Decide where you will observe, what materials you'll need, and make sure your equipment is ready and working. Also determine whether you'll need permission to observe, photograph, and/or record in a particular location; if so, secure appropriate permissions ahead of time, because you may need agreements from more than one person. Keep in mind that some sites, like church services, may not be appropriate places to take photographs or record video.

3. Record your observations. Take detailed descriptive notes, even if you are also recording audio or video; your notes will add necessary texture to any tape. Note who is present, any activities they engage in, and the details of the setting (such as the physical design of the space and the position of participants). Be sure to record the date, time, and location. As you observe, focus on recording and describing; save the interpretation and analysis for later when you go back and review your notes and recordings.

4. Be guided by your purpose for observing, but don't let that purpose restrain you—be open. Sometimes in the process of looking for one thing, you find something else that is equally interesting or important. On the other hand, don't always look for extraordinary behavior. The goal of observations is generally to look for the routine or the pattern, something that happens over and over again.

5. After your observation, take a moment to flesh out what you've recorded with notes about any additional thoughts or reflections you have. In particular, consider whether those you observe have changed their behavior because they are being monitored and, if so, how these changes may affect your data.

Interviews

You may find that the best way to answer your research question is to interview people who have a valuable perspective on your topic, such as experts on it or witnesses to or key participants in an event. Interviews can provide information that may not be available elsewhere; they can also complement other data-gathering methods, such as observations. Just as with observations, you'll need to consider your purpose for an interview and how the information you gain from it will speak to your research question. Will one interview provide the needed data, or will you need several? You'll also need to consider how qualified the potential interviewee is to address your research question. As a veteran of the war in Afghanistan, a friend or relative may not be the most credible source for a detailed analysis of the history of U.S. involvement in the region; print sources may be a better starting place for that type of background information. But your friend or relative probably *would* be a valuable, reliable source for a firsthand account of the combat experience and could likely provide details based on his or her personal experience that you would never get from a book or an article. Following are a few guidelines for conducting successful interviews.

1. Plan to conduct your interviews well before your research project is due in case you have to do follow-up interviews. Contact interviewees early to set up appointments; remember that you will need to schedule interviews at their convenience.

2. Do some background research on your topic before the interview so that you can ask informed questions.

3. Write out a list of questions that you will ask in the interview. These questions should be directly related to your research. Avoid questions that are too general or encourage one-word answers like "yes" or "no" when you really want specific, detailed, extended answers. For example, don't ask, "Do you like music?" when you want specific details. Try asking "What kind of music do you like?" instead. Also avoid leading questions, ones that encourage the interviewee to give the answer that you want. The question "Don't you think the Yankees need to trade for stronger relief pitching?" allows the interviewee to disagree, but it still tries to suggest a particular response. A better question would be "What kind of changes do you think the Yankees need to make?" This question is specific enough to provide a focus yet open enough to let the interviewee answer freely.

4. Decide how you'll record the interview. Will you rely solely on your own note-taking abilities, or will you combine note taking with audio or video recording? Remember that you must ask permission before you tape any part of an interview.

5. If your interview requires any kind of electronic equipment, test it before the interview to make sure that it is working. There's nothing more frustrating than finding out that you've lost the data from a wonderful interview because batteries died or you pushed the wrong button. Potential equipment malfunction is a good reason to have a backup plan.

6. Be polite during the interview. Interviewees are doing you a favor by agreeing to speak with you.

7. Record the date, time, and location of every interview that you conduct, and write down contact information for the interviewee.

8. Send a thank-you note to anyone whom you interview.

9. Check facts, dates, and other information the interviewee provides, especially about anything controversial. If any of the information seems questionable, try to interview others who can corroborate it or provide another perspective.

Surveys and Questionnaires

You've probably been asked to participate in marketing surveys that review products or services, or maybe you've completed questionnaires for course evaluations. Such surveys and questionnaires can be a useful method of soliciting information from a large number of people. Most often they aren't meant to poll an entire population; rather, surveys and questionnaires usually target a representative sampling of a group, such as a sampling of college students from several different schools across the country. And unlike interviews, most surveys or questionnaires do not solicit detailed information from individuals; generally, researchers use them to gauge large-group trends and opinions on a rather narrow topic. Here are some tips for deciding when to use surveys and how to design and administer them:

Consider your purpose. How will you use the results of your survey in the essay you are writing? Will they provide essential support for your argument or anecdotal detail to make your discussion more lively, interesting, and grounded? Imagine, for instance, that you are arguing that your school's library should extend its hours. For survey results to play a meaningful role as major evidence, you will need to survey a representative sample of students on your campus. If, however, you simply hope that your survey will provide some expressions of student opinion on this topic, then a smaller survey will be fine.

Will a survey be an effective method for collecting information you need to address your research question? Will you complement it with other data-gathering methods? If you are trying to find out how first-year medical residents negotiate the challenges of their demanding schedule, a survey is not likely to provide you with the level of detail that you will need; interviews might be more effective. However, if you are researching how the residents account for their time in a typical day, a survey would likely be your most expedient method.

Choose your sample. Consider whom you will contact for the survey; unless you are only after anecdotal information, you should aim to survey a representative sample of the targeted population—a small number of people who exhibit the characteristics of the larger population you want to gather information about. If you want to discover your college community's level of satisfaction with the campus dining services, for example, you'll need to solicit a sample that represents all the significant categories of people who use those services, including undergraduates, graduate students, faculty, administrative staff, and visitors, as well as the range of age, gender, ethnicity, and so on. To make your sample even more representative, you could categorize those who use the services according to when and where they eat on campus—for example, those who eat the majority of their meals in dormitory dining halls or those who occasionally eat in the student union cafeteria. Including only those who eat breakfast in the dining halls on weekends is not likely to give you a representative sample. Most important, decide *how many* people you will contact; generally, the larger proportion of the target population you sample, the more reliably you will be able to claim that your results represent trends in that population.

Choose your distribution method. Will you send a written survey through the mail? through email? Will you use an online service like *SurveyMonkey* or *KwikSurveys*? administer the survey over the phone or face-to-face? Choose a method that you think will yield the most results—and don't expect a 100 percent response rate. The acceptable response rate will depend on the size and quality of your sample. Researchers distribute surveys multiple times to get as many people in their targeted population to respond as they can.

Write the questions and an introduction, and test the survey. Respondents tend not to complete long or complicated surveys, so the best surveys include only a few questions and are easy to read. Use simple and unambiguous language, and avoid using jargon unless your survey is directed toward a specialized population who will understand it. Sequence questions from simple to complex unless there is a good reason not to do so. Also decide what kind(s) of questions are most likely to yield the information you're after. Below you can see four examples of typical survey questions: open-ended, multiple choice, agreement scale, and rating scale.

Open-ended

What genre of books do you like to read?

Where is your favorite place to read?

Multiple choice

Please select your favorite genre of book (check all that apply):
__ fiction   __ autobiography   __ self-help   __ histories   __ biography

Please indicate your favorite location for reading (check one):
__ coffee shop   __ library   __ home   __ office   __ other

Agreement scale

Indicate your level of agreement with the following statements.

	Strongly Agree	Agree	Strongly Disagree	Disagree
The library should provide both electronic and print versions of books whenever possible.	☐	☐	☐	☐
I am more likely to download a book electronically than I am to borrow a print book from the library.	☐	☐	☐	☐

Rating scale

How would you rate your satisfaction with materials available through the library?
__ Excellent   __ Good   __ Fair   __ Poor

Your questions should be focused on one specific topic related to your research question. For example, undergraduate researcher Steven Leone believes that solar energy provided by Copper Indium Gallium Selenium (CIGS) film could provide a serious alternative to fossil fuels as an energy source, but he understands the resistance many homeowners have to expensive solar installations. His project "The Likelihood of Homeowners to Implement CIGS Thin Film Solar Cells" is designed to discover the relationship between homeowners' socioeconomic status and their attitudes about alternative energy sources in order to gauge how likely they are to adopt this new technology. These are his survey questions. Notice that some call for short answers while others ask for more detailed responses.

1. What is your combined annual household income?

2. What is the highest level of education you have completed?
    __ high school   __ some college   __ college   __ graduate school

3. How is your home currently heated?

4. How much are you currently spending each year on home energy costs?

5. Which is more important to you—saving money or going green? Why?

6. How knowledgeable are you about solar energy technology?
    __ very knowledgeable   __ somewhat knowledgeable
    __ somewhat unfamiliar   __ very unfamiliar

7. Have you considered using solar energy as your home energy source? Why or why not?

8. Thin-film solar cells cost significantly less than conventional solar installations and offer an energy-cost payback that is twice as fast. Does this information make it more likely you would implement this technology? If so, how much more likely?
    __ very likely   __ somewhat likely
    __ somewhat unlikely   __ very unlikely

9. Thin-film solar cells will increase the resale value of your home. Does this information make it more likely you would implement the technology? If so, how much more likely?
    __ very likely   __ somewhat likely
    __ somewhat unlikely   __ very unlikely

10. If thin-film solar cells were cost-efficient and easy to install, would you consider them to be a good investment for your home? Why or why not?

Leone's questions will provide him with data that he can analyze to determine patterns (education, income, lifestyle) of attitudes on his topic.

Once you're satisfied with your questions, write a brief introductory statement that indicates the purpose of the survey and gives an estimate of how long it will take to complete. Then ask a small pilot group to take it before you distribute it widely. Use their responses to revise questions that they find confusing or otherwise problematic, and add or eliminate questions as necessary.

Manage your results. When you are done collecting data, be sure to carefully store your responses. Then analyze your results. If you are using a print survey, one simple method is to use a blank survey and tally responses next to each question. You can also use a spreadsheet or a similar program to track your findings. If your survey includes open-ended questions, you may want to designate some responses to use as quotations when you present your results.

Evaluate your survey. When you present your results, be sure to acknowledge any shortcomings of your survey. What topics were not covered? What populations were not surveyed? Was your sample too small to be truly representative?

SEVENTEEN

Keeping Track
Managing Information Overload

RESEARCH HAS ALWAYS BEEN A COMPLEX, often messy process, but in an age of information overload, it can easily spiral out of control. In fact, researchers today have so much information at their fingertips that just managing it has become a primary concern. This chapter aims to help you bring order out of potential chaos by offering tips for keeping track of your sources, taking notes, and maintaining a working bibliography.

Keep Track of Your Sources

The easiest way to keep track of your sources is to save a copy of each one. Especially when your research is spread out over several days or weeks, and when it turns up dozens of potential sources, don't even consider relying on your memory.

Electronic sources. Download and save files, or print them out. Be especially sure to make copies of materials on the web, which can change or even disappear: Print out what you might use, or make a screenshot. Some subscription database services let you save, email, or print citations and articles. Also, you might want to use one of the free online tools that allow

Your research may be spread over a period of weeks or months, with discoveries and epiphanies sprinkled among long hours poring over books or a computer screen. All the more reason, then, not to let your notes sprawl across your desk or your good ideas disappear among the couch cushions.

you to organize, store, and share articles, images, snapshots of web pages, even audio and video files; *CiteULike* and *Zotero* are two that we've used.

Once you've got copies, the challenge is to keep it all organized. Store all the files for a single project together in one folder, and use a consistent file-naming system such as the one that follows so it's all easy to identify.

ENG1102_research
    Arnovitz_Loneliness
    Ehrenreich_ServingFL
    Hoyt_MyBriefCareer
    Lathbury_Betraying
    Rose_BlueCollar
    Schlosser_Fries

Note the author(s), title, URL, and date of access on each item—and record all the other information needed in a **WORKING BIBLIOGRAPHY**. Be sure to back up your files regularly.

Print sources. Make photocopies, printouts, or scans of everything you think will be useful to your research. Keep a copy of the title and copyright pages of books, and of the table of contents or front page of periodicals. Label everything with the author(s), title, and page numbers, and file related materials together in a folder.

Take Notes

We cannot stress enough the importance of taking notes systematically *as you go*. Carefully select what details you note to be sure they are pertinent to your project.

Take notes in your own words—and be sure to indicate which words are yours and which ones come from a source. Label anything you QUOTE, PARAPHRASE, or SUMMARIZE as such so that you'll remember to acknowledge and document the original source if you use it—and so that you don't accidentally PLAGIARIZE. The sample notes below come from research into learning disabilities:

> Lyon, "Learning Disabilities" (54, 55)
> Summary: Focuses on problems with basic reading skills but cautions that early intervention with reading won't address all manifestations of LD.
> • Lyon is chief of Child Development and Behavior Branch within the National Institute of Child Health and Human Development at the National Institutes of Health.
> • LD is actually several overlapping disorders related to reading, language, and math (paraphrase, p. 54).
> • Lyon: "[L]earning disability is not a single disorder, but is a general category of special education composed of disabilities in any of seven specific areas: (1) receptive language (listening), (2) expressive language (speaking), (3) basic reading skills, (4) reading comprehension, (5) written expression, (6) mathematics calculation, and (7) mathematical reasoning" (direct quotation, p. 55).
> Comment: Lyon breaks down LD into more distinctive, precise categories. Defines each category. Will help me define LD.

If you copy any passages by hand, take care to do so accurately, paying attention to both words and punctuation and enclosing the entire passage in quotation marks. If you cut and paste any text from electronic sources, put quotation marks around it.

Label notes with the information you'll need to know about the source and where to find it—the author(s) and title, and the page numbers, date of access, URL, or DOI.

SUMMARIZE important points you want to remember in a sentence or two, especially if you'll be doing an **ANNOTATED BIBLIOGRAPHY**. Be very careful to write your summary using your own words and sentence patterns.

Record any of your own questions or reactions as you go. Do you see any interesting ideas? anything you question? What role might this source play in your own writing? Does it provide evidence? represent perspectives you should consider? show why the topic matters?

Maintain a Working Bibliography

Keep a record of all the sources you consult in a working bibliography. Maintaining a working bibliography will help you find sources if you need to— and to document any of them that you cite in your writing. Eventually this information will become your list of references, so it's a good idea to follow whatever **DOCUMENTATION** style you plan to use.

For books
- Author(s) and any editors or translators
- Title and subtitle
- Edition, volume number
- Publication information: city, publisher, year
- Medium of publication (e.g., Print, Web, Kindle)

For periodicals

- Author(s)
- Title and subtitle
- Name of periodical
- Publisher or sponsor (for online sources)
- Volume and issue numbers, date
- Page numbers
- Medium of publication (i.e., Print or Web)
- Date accessed (for online sources)

Additional items for articles accessed via database

- Name of database and any item number
- Name and URL of subscription service
- DOI, if there is one

For web sources

- Author(s) and any editors of source
- Title and subtitle of source
- Name and URL of site
- Sponsor of site
- Date published, posted, or last updated
- Page or paragraph numbers, if any
- Medium of publication (i.e., Web)
- Date accessed

EIGHTEEN

Evaluating Sources

 **OUR RESEARCH ASSIGNMENT:** Is it racism when a school uses American Indian mascots, symbols, or nicknames for its sports teams? To research this topic, you will need to consult reliable sources. Which would you trust more: the official "Statement of the U.S. Commission on Civil Rights on the Use of Native American Images and Nicknames as Sports Symbols," the *Wikipedia* page on the Native American mascot controversy, or a blog entry on the topic? Is it possible that they could all be useful? How will you know?

Your integrity as an author rests to some degree on the quality of the sources you cite, so your sources need to be appropriate and reliable. You can probably assume that an article or website recommended by a professor or an expert on your topic is a credible source of information—and one that you would be wise to consult. But in the absence of such advice, and given the overwhelming amount of information available, it can be difficult to know which sources will be useful, appropriate, and relevant for your purposes. This chapter provides advice for determining which sources are appropriate for your purposes, and then reading those that are with a critical eye.

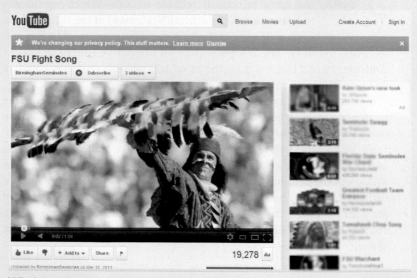

Which would you trust more: the official "Statement of the U.S. Commission on Civil Rights on the Use of Native American Images and Nicknames as Sports Symbols," the *Wikipedia* page on the Native American mascot controversy, or a *YouTube* video?

Is the Source Worth Your Attention?

A database search turns up fifty articles on your topic. The library catalog shows hundreds. *Google*? Think thousands. So how do you decide which sources are worth your time and attention? Here are some things to consider as you scan your search results:

- What's the title? Read it carefully. Does it sound relevant to your topic? If so, scan it for headings to get a fuller picture.

- What's covered? Look for clues. Is there an abstract? Are there details in the library catalog or on an internet search page?

- Who's the publisher? Is it an academic press? a commercial publisher? a news organization? a government agency? What kinds of sources does your research question call for?

- Who are the authors? Are they experts on your topic? journalists? something else?

- How current is it? Does that matter?

- How long is it? How thoroughly will it cover your topic?

- If it's a website, who's the sponsor? What's the purpose of the site?

Reading Sources with a Critical Eye

Once you've determined that a source is appropriate, you'll need to read it closely, thinking carefully about its author, its larger context, and the text itself.

Consider your own RHETORICAL SITUATION. Will the source help you achieve your **PURPOSE**? Look at introductory materials such as a preface or table of contents to determine how extensively and directly it addresses your topic. Scholarly articles often include an abstract summarizing the content. What about your **GENRE**? If you're writing a report, you'll be looking for facts and data; if you're arguing a position, you'll need sources that reflect a number of different viewpoints. Will your **AUDIENCE** consider the source reliable and credible? Are they expecting you to cite certain kinds of materials, such as historical documents or academic journals?

What are the author's qualifications to write on this subject? Is he or she recognized as an expert on the topic and cited in other reliable sources? Is the author affiliated with any organization or school of thought that would affect his or her viewpoint? If you can't answer these questions, check the source for biographical information, or do a search to see what else the author has written.

What is the author's STANCE? Does the title indicate a certain attitude or perspective? How would you characterize the TONE? Is it objective? argumentative? sarcastic? How does the author's stance affect its usefulness for your project?

Who is the publisher or sponsor? Whether it's a book or an article, online or in print, has it been reviewed or fact-checked? Scholarly books and journal articles are reviewed by experts, as are government publications. Some popular magazines and newspapers have fact-checkers on staff, but many do not and are not reliable sources for academic writing—unless they are relevant to your topic. If you were analyzing how a tabloid newspaper covered a national election, it would in fact be an important source, fact-checked or not. Consider also whether a publication has a particular political perspective: *The Nation* and *Mother Jones* reflect a liberal perspective, whereas the *Wall Street Journal* and the *American Spectator* have a more conservative angle.

If it's a website, who sponsors the site? An institution? A community group? A business? An individual? Look for this information on the homepage, sometimes next to the copyright date. The URL can also tell you something about what kind of organization is sponsoring the site: *com* is used by commercial organizations, *edu* by colleges and universities, *org* by nonprofits, *gov* by government agencies. Knowing the sponsor will tell you a lot—and if you can't identify who sponsors a site, don't consider it to be a trustworthy source.

Who is the AUDIENCE for this work? Is it aimed at the general public? members of a field? a special interest group? policy makers? Sources written for a general audience may provide useful overviews or explanations. Sources aimed at experts may be more authoritative and provide more detail—but they can be challenging to understand.

When was it published or last updated? If you're researching a current issue, you'll want sources that reflect current research, but it may be important to consult older works as well to get a sense of the larger context. And some topics call for older sources. If you were studying the history of censorship battles over *Adventures of Huckleberry Finn,* for instance, older sources would be essential. In cases when your topic calls for the most up-to-date sources, check to see if the citations in those sources are also up-to-date—and if your source is on a website, check to see that any links are still active.

What is the author's main point, and what has motivated him or her to write? Is he or she responding to someone else or to some other argument? What larger conversation is this source a part of? Is it clear why the topic matters?

What REASONS and EVIDENCE does the author provide as support? Is the evidence drawn from credible sources? How persuasive do you find the argument?

Does the author acknowledge and respond to other viewpoints? Look for sources that present multiple perspectives, not just their own. And be sure to consider how fairly any COUNTERARGUMENTS are represented. The most trustworthy sources represent other views and information fairly and accurately, even (especially) those that question their own.

Have you seen ideas given in this source in any other sources? Information found in multiple sources is more reliable than information you can find in only one place. Do other credible sources challenge the argument or information? If so, you should assume that what's said in this source is controversial.

How might you use this source? Remember that source materials can serve a variety of purposes in both your research and your writing. You might consult some sources for background information or to get a sense of the larger context for your topic. Other sources may provide support for your claims—or for your credibility as an author. Still others will provide other viewpoints, ones that challenge yours or that provoke you to respond. Most of all, they'll give you some sense of what's been said about your topic. Then, in writing up your research, you'll get your chance to say what *you* think— and to add your voice to the conversation.

NINETEEN

Writing a Project Proposal

HEN SOPHOMORE TENYIA LEE wanted to apply for a grant to research 9/11 memorials in New York City, she went to the undergraduate grants website at her college for guidelines to help her. Here's the one requirement she found: "Prepare a research proposal that describes the purpose of your research project, the steps you will take in pursuing it, what you hope to achieve by it, and what kinds of funding you need—and why." She wrote a proposal, with help from her writing center—and she got the grant.

You may need to write a proposal of this kind, to explain what you intend to research, how you'll conduct your research, and why your research is important. And, in fact, composing a proposal can help you think through the specific focus of your project and what sources you'll need in order to pursue it.

Characteristic Features

A research proposal should say clearly and succinctly what you want to research and how you'll go about doing so. You'll need to have done some preliminary background research first. Most of all, remember that a proposal is basically an **ARGUMENT**: Your goal is to demonstrate that your project is worth doing and feasible given the time and resources you have available. Unless your assignment names other specific requirements, your proposal should cover the following ground:

- A discussion of the topic
- An indication of your specific focus
- An explanation of why you're interested in the topic
- A research plan
- A schedule

A discussion of the topic. Explain what your topic is and give any necessary background information. Give some sense of any issues or controversies you want to investigate. Finally, say why the topic matters—so what, and who cares?

An indication of your specific focus. As much as you can at this point, say what your research focus will be, including the RESEARCH QUESTION you plan to pursue and a tentative THESIS.

An explanation of why you're interested in the topic. Briefly explain what you already know about your topic and why you've chosen to pursue this line of inquiry about it. You might describe any course work, reading, or work you've done that contributes to your knowledge and interest. Also note what you don't yet know but intend to find out through your research.

A research plan. Explain how you plan to investigate your research question: what types of sources you'll need and what your RESEARCH METHODS will be. Will you conduct library and internet research? If you plan to do FIELD RESEARCH, what do you have in mind?

A schedule. Break your project into tasks and sketch out a schedule, taking into account the writing you'll need to do. Include any specific tasks your instructor requires, such as handing in a rough draft or an ANNOTATED BIBLIOGRAPHY.

The Economic Impact on Major Cities of Investing Public Funds in Professional Sports Franchises

DAVID PASINI

SINCE THE 1960S, local governments have provided increased funding and subsidies for professional sports franchises. Taxpayer money has gone toward facilities like stadiums and arenas, and many cities have offered tax exemptions and other financial incentives to keep a team in town that has threatened to relocate. Proponents of public funding for privately owned sports franchises argue that cities gain more from the arrangement—namely jobs, status, and tourist dollars—than they lose. Opponents argue that using public funds for these purposes results in long-term financial drains on local governments and point out that many communities have been abandoned by teams even after providing substantial benefits, leaving the city or state holding the proverbial debt-heavy bag.

Writing in the *New York Times,* Ken Belson gives an example of one such government-funded project: "The old Giants Stadium, demolished to make way for New Meadowlands Stadium, still carries about $110 million in debt, or nearly $13 for every New Jersey resident, even though it is now a parking lot" (Belson). The image included here shows the governor of New Jersey look-

---

DAVID PASINI, an engineering major at The Ohio State University, wrote this research proposal for a first-year writing course on the theme of sports in contemporary American society.

Figure 1. Left to right: the governor of New Jersey, William T. Cahill; the owner of the Giants, Wellington Mara; and chairman of the New Jersey sports authority, Sonny Werblin admire a drawing of the new Giants Stadium. Though the stadium was eventually demolished, debt from its construction lives on. Photo by Neal Boenzi. (Belson A1)

ing over a drawing of the Giants Stadium, which was completed in 1976 and destroyed in 2010 (fig. 1).

Given the high stakes involved—and particularly the use of taxpayer dollars—it seems important, then, to ask what these sports franchises contribute (or do not contribute) to their cities and wider metropolitan areas. Do these teams "generate positive net economic benefits for their cities," or do they "absorb scarce government funds" that would be better spent on programs that have "higher social or economic payoff" (Noll and Zimbalist 55)? My research project will investigate these questions.

The question of public funding for sports is important to any resident of a community that has a professional sports franchise or is trying to lure one, as well as to any citizen, sports fan or not, who is interested in the economic and political issues surrounding this topic. I am in the latter group, a nonfan who is simply interested in how public monies are being used to support sports, and whose knowledge about the issues is primarily in the economic domain. At this point in the research process, I am neither a proponent nor an opponent of investing in sports, but I think that it's important to consider just how—and how much—professional sports contribute to the economic well-being of the government that funds them. How much of the money that teams generate supports local businesses, school districts, or other important entities that benefit all citizens? How much of it stays in the owners' pockets? Do the franchises "give back" to their communities in any other tangible or intangible ways? The franchises themselves should consider these questions, since the communities that helped to provide them with the amenities they require to be successful sports teams have a right to expect something in return.

To learn more about investment in sports teams and the teams' economic impact, I will consult business and sports management journals and appropriate news sources, both print and digital. I will also interview stakeholders on both sides of the debate as well as experts on this topic. In my research, I will consider the many factors that must be taken into account, such as the benefits of tourism and the costs of "creating extra demand on local services" (Crompton 33). As a result of my research, I hope to offer insight on whether public funds are in fact put to good use when they are invested in major sports franchises.

Preliminary Works Consulted

Belson, Ken. "As Stadiums Vanish, Their Debt Lives On." *New York Times* 8
    Sept. 2010: A1. Print.
Crompton, John L. "Economic Impact Analysis of Sports Facilities and Events:
    Eleven Sources of Misapplication." *Journal of Sport Management* 9.1
    (1995): 14–35. Print.
Noll, Roger G., and Andrew Zimbalist, eds. *Sports, Jobs, and Taxes: The
    Economic Impact of Sports Teams and Stadiums*. Washington: Brookings
    Inst., 1997. *Google Books*. Google, 1 Apr. 2011. Web.
Robertson, Robby. "The Economic Impact of Sports Facilities." *Sport Digest*
    16.1 (2008): n. pag. Web. 1 Apr. 2011.

Proposed Schedule

Do library and internet research	April 6–20
Submit annotated bibliography	April 20
Schedule and conduct interviews	April 21–25
Turn in first draft	May 10
Turn in second draft	May 18
Turn in final draft	May 25

TWENTY

Annotating a Bibliography

HEN WE ASSIGN RESEARCH PROJECTS, we often require our students to annotate a bibliography as part of the research process. Instructors do this for a variety of reasons, ensuring that you read sources carefully and critically, summarize useful information about them, and document how and why you expect to use particular sources. The rhetorical purpose of the annotated bibliography is to inform—and you are part of the audience. Conscientiously done, it will help you sort out the information you are collecting and gain a sense of the larger conversation about your topic.

In a formal annotated bibliography, you **DESCRIBE** each of the sources you expect to consult and what role each one will play in your research. Sometimes you will be required to **EVALUATE** sources as well—to assess their strengths and weaknesses in one or two sentences.

Characteristic Features

Annotations should be brief, but they can vary in length from a sentence or two to a few paragraphs. They also vary in terms of style: Some are written in complete sentences; others consist of short phrases. And like a works-cited or reference page, an annotated bibliography is arranged in alphabetical order. If you're assigned to write an annotated bibliography, you'll want to find out exactly what your instructor expects, but the following features are common in most annotated bibliographies.

Complete bibliographic information, using whatever documentation style you'll use in your essay—MLA, APA, or another style. This information will enable readers to locate your sources—and can also form the basis for your final works-cited or references list.

A brief SUMMARY or DESCRIPTION of each work, noting its topic, scope, and STANCE. The detail you include will depend on your own goals for your project. Whatever you choose to describe, however, be sure that it represents the source accurately and objectively.

Evaluative comments. If you're required to write evaluative annotations, decide on CRITERIA for determining how useful each source will be to your project—how AUTHORITATIVE it is, how up-to-date, whether it addresses multiple perspectives, and so on.

Some indication of how each source will inform your research: Describe how you expect to use each source. Does it present a certain perspective you need to consider? Is it written by an authority in the field? Does it report on important new research? Does it include a thorough bibliography that might alert you to other sources?

Consistency. Annotations should be presented consistently in all entries: If one is written in complete sentences, they all should be. The amount of information and the way you structure it should also be the same throughout.

Renewable and Sustainable Energy
in Rural India
SAURABH VAISH

Germany. German Energy Agency. "Renewable Energies." Deutsche Energie-
   Agentur GmbH (dena), n.d. Web. 12 Apr. 2011.

The German Energy Agency provides information on energy efficiency,
renewable energy sources, and intelligent energy systems. The website
contains some useful databases, including ones of energy projects in
Germany and of recent publications. It is a useful source of information on
the manufacturing and production of alternative energy systems.

   Though this site does not provide statistical data and covers only a
limited number of projects and publications, it includes links to much useful
information. It's a great source of publications and projects in both Germany
and Russia, and so it will help me broaden my research beyond the borders
of the United States.

SAURABH VAISH, a management and entrepreneurship major at Hofstra University, wrote this evaluative annotated bibliography for a research project on renewable and sustainable energy in rural India. The project reflects his interest in implementing green solutions for rural energy problems, a subject he'll pursue when he returns to India. Vaish briefly describes and summarizes each source in the first paragraph and then in the second paragraph explains how it will be useful in his research.

Moner-Girona, Magda, ed. "A New Scheme for the Promotion of Renewable Energies in Developing Countries: The Renewable Energy Regulated Purchase Tariff." *European Commission Joint Research Centre Publications Repository.* European Commission Joint Research Centre, 2008. Web. 12 Apr. 2011.

This report on a study by the PhotoVoltaic Technology Platform discusses how to promote the use of renewable energy in developing countries. The report proposes a new tariff scheme to increase the flow of money where it is most needed, suggests several business models, and estimates the potential success or failure of each.

   Though I question its assumption that its plans will eventually be feasible, this report contains useful data and models, including numerous graphs and charts. The detailed information it provides about business models, supply-chain setups, and financial calculations will be useful in my analysis, especially in the part of my project that deals with photovoltaic cells.

United States. Energy Information Administration. Renewable & Alternative Fuels Analysis Reports. U.S. Dept. of Energy, 1998–2010. Web. 2 Feb. 2012.

This site reports statistical and graphical data on energy production and consumption, including all major alternative energies. It provides access to numerous databases on energy consumption across the world.

   This website provides most of the statistical data I will need to formulate conclusions about the efficiency of alternative energies. Its data are reliable, current, and easy to understand—and the fact that it doesn't critique the data it presents will allow me to shape my own opinions regarding the research I undertake.

TWENTY-ONE

Synthesizing Ideas

Moving from What Your Sources Say to What You Say

IT'S **SUPER BOWL SUNDAY**, just before kickoff. You turn off your laptop, where DJ Schmolli's "Super Bowl Anthem" was playing, and turn on the TV to hear Kelly Clarkson singing the national anthem. So you've just heard two anthems—but what else, if anything, do these tunes have in common? Answer: Each is a mashup—a combination of material from a number of different sources. The "Star-Spangled Banner" combines a poem written by Francis Scott Key with the music of an old British club song. DJ Schmolli's effort combines clips from more than a dozen popular stadium anthems, from Madonna's "Celebration" to Queen's "We Will Rock You." And each smoothly integrates its sources into one seamless whole. In academic terms, the authors of these mash-ups have effectively engaged in **SYNTHESIS**, bringing together material from various sources in order to create something new.

Like a good mash-up artist, when you do research, you don't just patch together ideas from the various sources you've consulted. Instead, you synthesize what they say to help you think about and understand the topic you're researching—to identify connections among them and blend them into a coherent whole that at the same time articulates *ideas of your own*. When you synthesize print sources for a print text, you frame the synthesis with your own ideas and words; however, when you synthesize nonprint texts—maybe video and audio clips as DJ Schmolli does—the results of such blending represent your frame. Supplying your

An unlikely mash-up: Jane Austen's *Pride and Prejudice* and . . . zombies! With 85 percent Austen's original text and 15 percent zombie blood and gore, *Pride and Prejudice and Zombies* became an instant best-seller, setting off a slew of literary monster mash-ups.

own words or voice, or blending the clips to present the material in a new way, adds new ideas.

While you probably won't be following author Seth Grahame-Smith's example and bringing zombies into your academic writing, you will be bringing in plenty of ideas and information gathered from your sources. The result you are aiming for is a cohesive piece of writing that blends ideas from sources with your own ideas smoothly and effectively—just like a really great mash-up.

Synthesizing the Ideas in Your Sources

Here are some questions to help you synthesize information as you work with your sources:

- What central issues, problems, or controversies do your sources address?

- What else do your sources have in common? Are there any ideas found in more than one source? facts, examples, or statistics? Are any people or works cited in more than one source?
- What significant differences do you find among sources? Different **STANCES**? positions? purposes? kinds of **EVIDENCE**? conclusions?
- Do any of your sources cite or refer to one another? build on something said in another? Does one source provide details, examples, or explanations that illuminate the broader overview provided by another? Does any source respond specifically to something said in another?

Moving from What Your Sources Say to What You Say

As a researcher, you'll always be working to synthesize the ideas and information you find in your research. At the same time, you'll be striving to make sense of that research—and to connect the data you gather to your own ideas and to your research goals. You'll be learning a lot about what many others have discovered or said about your topic, and that will surely affect what you yourself think about it—and write. And then when you write, you'll want to weave in ideas from your sources with your own. Here are some questions that can help you move from the ideas you find in your sources to the ideas that you'll then write about:

- How do the ideas and information in your sources address your **RESEARCH QUESTION**? What answers do they give? What information do you find the most relevant, useful, and persuasive?
- How do they support your tentative **THESIS**? Do they suggest reasons or ways that you should expand, qualify, or otherwise revise it?
- What viewpoints in your sources do you most agree with? disagree with? Why?
- What conclusions can you draw from the ideas and information you've learned from your sources? What discoveries have you made in studying these sources, and what new ideas have they led you to?
- Has your research changed your own views on your topic? Do any of your sources raise questions that you can pursue further?

Laura Fraser weaves together literary and medical sources in her essay about women's bodies and beauty on p. 775.

- Have you encountered any ideas that you would like to build on—or challenge?
- From everything you've read, what is the significance of the topic you're researching? Who cares, and why does it matter?

When you work with your sources in this way, you can just about count on your ideas to grow—and maybe to change. As we've been saying, research is an act of learning and inquiry, and you never know quite where it will lead. But as soon as you sit down and write, no matter what you say or how you say it, you will be, as Kenneth Burke suggests, "putting in your oar," adding your voice *and your ideas* to the very conversation you've been researching.

THINK BEYOND WORDS

TAKE A LOOK at an award-winning documentary from the Las Vegas Sun *provided at wwnorton.com/write/everyonelinks and then scroll down to the story links below it on the same topic. See how all the authors synthesize material from several sources— interviews, government documents, public records, historical accounts—but note how they integrate these sources differently in different media. What conclusions can you draw from comparing the different versions?*

Entering the Conversation You've Been Researching

Let's look at how one writer synthesized ideas into her own writing. Julia Landauer wrote an essay tracing the changes in political cartoons in the United States between World War II and the Iraq War for her second-year writing course. As you read the excerpt from Landauer's introduction on pp. 386–87, note the way she not only cites sources in support of her argument but also weaves the sources together with her own ideas and opinions.

In the twelve pages that follow this introduction, Landauer examines a series of political cartoons from World War II (found through archival research) and from 2011, analyzing them for common themes and patterns. She then sums up her answers to the questions posed in her introduction and muses on just why these political cartoons have stayed pretty much the same when many other media have changed significantly.

Landauer begins her paper with an epigraph drawn from one of her sources to signal the importance of her topic and to provide some context for the essay to follow. She then introduces a cartoon (a primary source) that illustrates a point she is making—that editorial cartoons are known for stinging political critiques. She then refers to another source (McCloud) to provide some background information for readers before turning to still another (Becker) to provide additional history and description of the "modern editorial art" she intends to examine in her essay. At that point, Landauer raises questions her sources leave unaddressed—and says that answering them will be the work of her essay. Thus she integrates ideas drawn from her sources with her own ideas and weaves both together into a strong introduction. In the introduction and throughout her essay, Landauer is in control of her sources, using them to make a strong case for her own argument.

When Landauer began her research, she expected to find significant changes in editorial cartoons across time. But her working thesis shifted dramatically as she analyzed her data. Keeping an open mind and taking in all the information she could find—and engaging with the words, images, and ideas of others—led her to understand her subject in a new way.

In your college writing, you will have the opportunity to come up with a research question and to dig in and do some research in order to answer it. That digging in will lead you to identify key sources already in conversation about your topic, to read and analyze those sources, and to begin synthesizing them with your own ideas. Before you know it, you won't be just listening in on the conversation: You'll be an active participant in it.

War, Cartoons, and Society: Changes in Political Cartoons between World War II and the Iraq War

JULIA LANDAUER

To a news-hungry public, anxious about world affairs, it was the cartoon, with its immediacy and universal accessibility—even to the barely literate—that could speak the message mere words could never convey.

—MARK BRYANT

Gary Markstein shows carolers at the White House door making a choral argument to then president George W. Bush that "we gotta get out of this place," referring to America's involvement in the war in Iraq (fig. 1). Bush appears completely oblivious to their message.

   This cartoon offered a critique of America's continued presence in Iraq by criticizing the president's actions and attitudes towards the war, exemplifying how political cartoons have long been, and continue to be, a prominent part of wartime propaganda. Combining eye-catching illustrations with textual critique, such cartoons do more than merely convey messages about current events. Rather, political cartoons serve as a tool for shaping public opinion. In fact, since the 1500s, political cartoons have used satirical critiques to persuade the general public about matters large and small (McCloud 16–17).

JULIA LANDAUER, a science, technology, and society major at Stanford University, wrote this research essay for a second-year writing course.

Fig. 1. Gary Markstein, editorial cartoon criticizing war in Iraq (Copley News Service, 2006).

In the United States, the political (or editorial) cartoon is a form of editorializing that began as "scurrilous caricatures," according to Stephen Becker, author of *Comic Art in America*. His book looks, in part, at the social history of political cartoons and states that it was only after "newspapers and magazines came to be published regularly . . . that caricatures, visual allegories, and the art of design were combined to form . . . modern editorial art" (Becker 15). As all-encompassing as that description of "modern editorial art" seems to be, it suggests several questions that remain unanswered: Do cartoonists use common themes to send their critical messages? As society and regulations change from generation to generation, do the style and content of political cartoons change as well? Have political cartoons become "modernized" since World War II? The essay that follows aims to answer as well as draw out the implications of these questions.

TWENTY-TWO

Quoting, Paraphrasing, Summarizing

HEN YOU'RE TEXTING or talking with friends, you don't usually need to be explicit about where you got your information; your friends trust what you say because they know you. In academic writing, however, it's important to establish your credibility, and one way to do so is by consulting authoritative sources. Doing so shows that you've done your homework on your topic, gives credit to those whose

To quote? To paraphrase? Or summarize? That is the question.

ideas you've relied on, and helps demonstrate your own authority as an author. This chapter provides guidelines on the three ways you have for incorporating sources into your writing: quoting, paraphrasing, and summarizing.

A **QUOTATION** consists of someone's exact words, enclosed in quotation marks or set off as a block from the rest of your text. A **PARAPHRASE** includes the details of a passage in your own words and syntax. A **SUMMARY** contains the points of a passage that are important to your point, leaving out the other details.

Deciding Whether to Quote, Paraphrase, or Summarize

Quote

- Something that is said so well that it's worth repeating
- Complex ideas that are expressed so clearly that paraphrasing or summarizing could distort or oversimplify them
- Experts whose opinions and exact words help establish your own **CREDIBILITY** and **AUTHORITY** to write on the topic
- Passages that you yourself are analyzing
- Those whose views differ from those of others—quoting their exact words is a way to be sure you represent their opinions fairly

Paraphrase

- Passages where the details matter, but not the exact words
- Passages that are too technical or complicated for your audience to understand

Summarize

- Lengthy passages where the main point is important to your argument but the details are not

Whatever method you use for incorporating the words and ideas of others into your own writing, however, be sure that they work to support what *you* want to say. You're the author—and even as you weave the ideas of others in with your own, whatever they say needs to connect to what you say. Don't assume that your sources speak for themselves. Be sure to introduce any source information you cite, naming the author and identifying him or her in some way if your audience won't know who it is. In addition, be sure to follow any quotations with a comment that explains how they relate to *your* point.

And regardless of whether you decide to quote, paraphrase, or summarize, you'll need to credit each source. Even if what you include is not a direct quotation, the ideas are still someone else's, and failing to credit your source can result in plagiarism. Indicate the source in a **SIGNAL PHRASE** and include in-text documentation.

Quoting

See how direct quotations make the history of pizza interesting on p. 865.

When you include a direct quotation, be sure to use the exact words of the original. And while you don't want to include too many quotations—again, you are the author—quoting someone else's words is one way to incorporate the ideas of others in with your own ideas—and is sometimes the best way to ensure that you represent what they say fairly. But be sure to frame any quotation you include, introducing it and then explaining why it's important to the point that you are making.

Enclose short quotations in quotation marks within your main text. Such quotations should be no longer than four typed lines (in MLA style) or forty words (in APA style).

> Programmer and digital media pioneer Jaron Lanier describes the problems resulting from "lock-in" (in which software becomes difficult to change because it has been engineered to work with existing programs), arguing that lock-in "is an absolute tyrant in the digital world" (8). That is, according to Lanier, "lock-in" inhibits creativity and new development is constrained by old software

In MLA style, short quotations of poetry—no more than three lines—should also be enclosed in quotation marks within the main text. Include slashes (with a space on either side) between each line of verse.

> In his poem "When You are Old," William Butler Yeats advises Maud Gonne, the radical Irish nationalist whom he loved, that in her old age

when she reflects on her youth, she will need to consider "How many
loved your moments of glad grace, / And loved your beauty with love
false or true, / But one man loved the pilgrim soul in you." Yeats thus
suggests that he is the "one man" who has loved her so sincerely all
these years.

Set off long quotations as a block by indenting them from the left margin.
No need to enclose them in quotation marks, but do indent ten spaces (or
one inch) if you are using MLA style and five spaces (or one-half inch) if
you are using APA. Use this method for quotations that are more than four
lines of prose or three lines of poetry (in MLA) or longer than forty words
(in APA).

In her 1976 keynote address to the Democratic National Convention,
Texas congresswoman Barbara Jordan reflects on the occasion:

Listen to the full
text of Barbara
Jordan's speech at
wwnorton.com/
write/everyone
links.

> Now that I have this grand distinction, what in the world am
> I supposed to say? I could easily spend this time praising the
> accomplishments of this party and attacking the Republicans—
> but I don't choose to do that. I could list the many problems which
> Americans have. I could list the problems which cause people
> to feel cynical, angry, frustrated: problems which include lack of
> integrity in government; the feeling that the individual no longer
> counts; the reality of material and spiritual poverty; the feeling that
> the grand American experiment is failing or has failed. I could recite
> these problems, and then I could sit down and offer no solutions.
> But I don't choose to do that either. The citizens of America expect
> more. They deserve and they want more than a recital of problems.
> (189)

In this passage, Jordan resists the opportunity to attack the opposing
party, preferring instead to offer positive solutions rather than simply a
list of criticisms and problems.

Notice that with block quotations, the parenthetical citation falls *after* the
period at the end of the quotation.

Indicate changes to the text within a quotation by using brackets to enclose text that you add or change and ellipses to indicate text that you omit.

Use brackets to indicate that you have altered the original wording to fit grammatically within your text or have added or changed wording to clarify something that might otherwise be unclear. In this example, the author changed the verb *are* to the past tense *were:*

> Writing in 1987, Koepp described the rather surprising financial success of individual American investors who "[were] reaping lucrative profits during an era in which the big institutional players would seem to have all the advantages: research, resources, and speed" (15).

Use ellipsis marks in place of words, phrases, or sentences that you leave out because they aren't crucial or relevant for your purpose. Use three dots, with a space before each one and after the last, when you omit only words and phrases. If you leave out the end of a sentence or more, put a period after the last word before the ellipsis mark.

> In his article on the increase in the placebo response to drugs, Silberman claims that "products that have been on the market for decades . . . are faltering in more recent follow-up tests. In many cases, these are compounds that . . . made Big Pharma more profitable than Big Oil" (315).

> Discussing the declining role that handwriting plays in our culture, Trubek claims, "For many, the prospect of handwriting dying out would signal the end of individualism and the entrée to some robotic techno-future. . . . But when we worry about losing our individuality, we are likely misremembering our schooling, which included rote, rigid lessons in handwriting" (177).

When you use brackets or ellipses, make sure your alterations don't end up misrepresenting the author's original point, which would damage your own credibility. Mark Twain once joked that "nearly any invented quotation, played with confidence, stands a good chance to deceive." Twain was probably right—there are plenty of people who "invent" quotations or twist their meaning by taking them out of context, but you don't want to be among them! And of course be careful that you don't introduce any grammatical errors by altering the quotation.

Set off a quotation within a quotation with single quotation marks. In the following passage from an Associated Press article, the author quotes Susan Helper, who herself quotes hypothetical industry representatives and politicians:

> Susan Helper, a Case Western Reserve University professor who studies manufacturing issues, said industry job projections are suspect, in part because the estimate of natural gas reserves may be inflated. According to Helper, industry representatives and politicians have a self-interest in making rosy projections, pointing out that "it's a way of saying to environmentalists and others who say to slow down, 'Gee, you're preventing all this potential great job growth here'" ("Youngstown Reflects Revival of the Rust Belt").

Punctuate quotations carefully. Parenthetical documentation comes after the closing quotation mark, and any punctuation that is part of your sentence comes after the parentheses.

- *Commas and periods* always go inside the quotation marks. If there's parenthetical documentation, however, the period goes after the parentheses.

  "Everybody worships," said David Foster Wallace in a 2005 commencement speech. "There is no such thing as not worshipping" (8).

- *Colons and semicolons* always go outside closing quotation marks.

  Wallace warned as well that there are "whole parts of adult American life that nobody talks about in commencement speeches": sometimes, he says, we'll be bored (4).

- *Question marks and exclamation points* go inside closing quotation marks if they are part of the original quotation—but outside the quotation marks if they are part of your sentence.

Going on to explain the reasons for the early popularity of MSG, Jonah Lehrer says, "Besides, who had time to make meat stock from scratch?" (59).

So what, according to Kevin Kelly, is the cause of our "technophilia" (289)?

Paraphrasing

When you paraphrase, you restate information or ideas from a source using your words, your sentence structure, your style. A paraphrase should cover the same points that the original source does, so it's usually about the same length. And even though it's in your words, don't forget where the ideas came from: You should always name the author and include parenthetical documentation.

Here is a paragraph about the search for other life-forms similar to our own in the universe, followed by three paraphrases.

Original source

As the romance of manned space exploration has waned, the drive today is to find our living, thinking counterparts in the universe. For all the excitement, however, the search betrays a profound melancholy— a lonely species in a merciless universe anxiously awaits an answering voice amid utter silence. That silence is maddening. Not just because it compounds our feeling of cosmic isolation, but because it makes no sense. As we inevitably find more and more exo-planets where intelligent life *can* exist, why have we found no evidence—no signals, no radio waves—that intelligent life *does* exist?

        —CHARLES KRAUTHAMMER, "Are We Alone in the Universe?"

As the underlined words show, the following paraphrase uses too many words from the original.

Unacceptable paraphrase: wording too close to the original

Charles Krauthammer argues that finding our intelligent <u>counterparts</u> has become more important as the <u>romance of sending humans into</u>

space has declined. Even so, the hunt for similar beings also suggests
our sadness as a species waiting in vain for an acknowledgment that we
aren't alone in the cosmos. The lack of response, he says, just doesn't
make sense because if we keep finding planets that *could* support
life, then we should find evidence—like radio waves or signals—of
intelligent life out there (A19).

While the next version uses original language, the sentence structures are
much too similar to the original.

Unacceptable paraphrase: sentence structures too close to original

As the allure of adventuring into the unknown has receded, the desire
to discover beings like us has grown. The downside to the search,
however, is the sadness attending it—the calling out into empty space
that brings no response. Nothing but silence. That lack of response not
only emphasizes our solitary existence but increases our frustration.
How can we continue to discover potentially hospitable planets—
environments that could sustain life like ours—yet find no evidence that
such life exists (Krauthammer A19)?

When you paraphrase, be careful not to simply substitute words and phrases while replicating the same sentence structure. And while it may be necessary to use some of the key terms from the original in order to convey the
same concepts, be sure to put them in quotation marks—and not to use too
many (which would result in plagiarism).

Acceptable paraphrase

Syndicated columnist Charles Krauthammer observes that our current
quest to discover other intelligent life in the universe comes just as the
allure of space exploration is dimming. It's a search, he says, that reveals
a certain uneasiness (that we may in fact be all alone in the universe)
and a growing frustration: If scientists continue to discover more
planets where life like ours can be sustainable, why do we find no actual
signs that it does (A19)?

Summarizing

Like a paraphrase, a summary presents the source information in your words. However, a summary is dramatically condensed, covering only the most important points and leaving out the details. Summaries are therefore much briefer than the original texts, though they vary in length depending on the extent of the original and your purpose for summarizing; you may need only a single sentence to summarize an essay, or you may need several paragraphs. In any case, you should always name the author and include a source citation. The following example summarizes Krauthammer's passage in one sentence:

> Charles Krauthammer questions whether we will ever find other intelligent life in the universe—or whether we'll instead discover that we do in fact live in cosmic isolation (A19).

If we were to work the sentence into an essay, it might look like this:

> Many scientists believe that there is a strong probability, given the vastness of the universe and how much of it we have yet to explore, even with advances like the Hubble telescope—that there is life like ours somewhere out there. Syndicated columnist Charles Krauthammer, in a 2011 opinion piece, questions whether we will ever find other intelligent life in the universe—or whether we'll instead discover that we do in fact live in cosmic isolation (A19).

Incorporating Source Material

Whether you quote, paraphrase, or summarize source material, you need to be careful to weave it in smoothly with your own writing—and at the same time to distinguish what you say from what your sources say. In addition, you must make clear how the ideas you're citing relate to your own ideas. And of course you'll need to credit your source with in-text documentation.

Use signal phrases to introduce source materials, telling readers who said what you're quoting, paraphrasing, or summarizing and providing some context if need be. Don't just drop in a quotation or paraphrase or summary. You need to introduce it. And while you can always use a neutral signal phrase such as "he says" or "she claims," try to choose verbs that accurately reflect the **STANCE** of those you're citing. In some cases, "she says" reflects that stance, but usually you can make your writing livelier and more accurate with a more specific **SIGNAL VERB**.

Use a signal phrase and parenthetical documentation to clearly distinguish your own words and ideas from those of others. The following paraphrase introduces source material with a signal phrase that includes the author's name and closes with the page number from which the information is taken.

> As Ernst Mayr explains, Darwin's theory of evolution presented a significant challenge to then-prevalent beliefs about man's centrality in the world (9).

If you do not give the author's name in a signal phrase, include it in the parenthetical citation.

> Darwin's theory of evolution presented a significant challenge to then-prevalent beliefs about man's centrality in the world (Mayr 9).

Sometimes you'll want or need to state the author's credentials in the signal phrase, explaining his or her authority on the topic—and at the same time lending credibility to your own use of that source.

> According to music historian Ted Gioia, record sales declined sharply during the Great Depression, dropping by almost 90 percent between 1927 and 1932 (127).

Choose verbs that reflect the author's stance toward the material—or your own stance in including it. Saying someone "notes" means something different than saying he or she "insists" or "implies."

> Because almost anyone can create a blog, most people assume that blogs give average citizens a greater voice in public dialogue. Political scientist Matthew Hindman questions this assumption: "Though millions of Americans now maintain a blog, only a few dozen political bloggers get as many readers as a typical college newspaper" (103).

Signal phrases often come first, but to add variety to your writing, try positioning them in the middle or at the end of a sentence.

> The ancient Chinese philosopher Zhuangzi presented an alternate take on books: "Men of the world who value the Way all turn to books. But books are nothing but words. Words have value; what is of value in words is meaning" (152).

> "Attracting attention," observes Richard Lanham, "is what style is all about" (xi).

> "We've got to stop the debates! Enough with the debates!" pleaded John McCain last Sunday on *Meet the Press* (31).

> Noting the importance of literacy in American lives today, rhetorician Deborah Brandt argues, "Writing is at the heart of the knowledge economy" (117).

SOME USEFUL SIGNAL VERBS

acknowledges	contends	replies
adds	declares	reports
agrees	disagrees	responds
asserts	implies	says
believes	notes	suggests
claims	objects	thinks
concludes	observes	writes

Verb tenses. MLA style requires the present tense (*argues*) or the present perfect (*has argued*). If you give the date when the author wrote the source, however, use the past tense (*as Jaime Mejia argued in 1998*). APA style recommends the past tense (*argued*) or the present perfect (*has argued*). If, however, you are citing the results of an experiment or findings that have been clearly established, use the present tense (*a long-term study shows, researchers in the field agree*).

Parenthetical documentation. You'll also need to keep in mind the requirements of your documentation style. If you're following MLA, you'll need to include page numbers for all quotations, paraphrases, and summaries from print sources in your parenthetical documentation. If you're using **APA**, page numbers for paraphrases and summaries are recommended—but it's always a good idea to include them whenever possible.

Incorporating Visual and Audio Sources

Sometimes you will incorporate visual or audio elements from sources that you cannot literally weave into a paragraph. For example, you may include charts, tables, photographs, or drawings—and in online writing, you might include audio or video clips as well. Remember that any such materials that come from sources need to be introduced, explained, and documented just as you would for a quotation. If you're following MLA or APA style, refer to chapters 24 and 25 for specific requirements.

Tables. Label anything that contains facts or figures displayed in columns as a table. Number all tables in sequence, and provide a descriptive title for each one. Supply source information immediately below the table; credit your data source even if you've created the table yourself. If any information within the table requires further explanation (abbreviations, for example), include a note below the source citation.

Figures. Number and label everything that is not a table (photos, graphs, drawings, maps, and so on) as a figure. Unless the visual is a photograph or drawing you created yourself, provide appropriate source information after the caption; graphs, maps, and other figures based on information from other sources should always include a full credit. If the visual is discussed in detail within your text, like the Coca-Cola ad in Melissa Rubin's analysis on page 177, you can use an abbreviated citation and include full documentation in your **WORKS CITED** or **REFERENCES** list.

Captions. Create a clear, succinct caption for each visual: "Fig. 1: The Guggenheim Museum, Spain." The caption should identify and explain the visual—and should reflect your purpose. In an essay about contemporary architecture in Spain, your caption might say "Fig. 1: The Guggenheim Museum, Bilbao. Designed by Frank Gehry." If you're writing a blog post about your visit to Bilbao, your caption would almost surely be different, perhaps "Fig. 1: A roller coaster building: the Guggenheim!"

Guggenheim Museum Bilbao

Sizing and positioning visuals. Refer to every visual in your text: "(see fig. 1)," "as shown in Table 3." The visual may be on the same page where it's discussed, but it should not come before you introduce it to your readers. Think carefully about where you position each visual and what size it needs to be in order to be legible. Take a look at the Coca-Cola ad on p. 177. Because this ad is the subject of Melissa Rubin's analytical essay, she sized it large enough for readers to be able to see the details she's discussing.

Recorded materials (podcasts, video clips, audio recordings). If your medium allows it, provide a link to any recorded element and incorporate it into your discussion as you would for a visual. If you're working in a medium that won't allow for linking or embedding, discuss the recording in your text and provide **IN-TEXT DOCUMENTATION**. Supply a full citation in your **WORKS CITED** or **REFERENCES** list so your readers can track down the recording themselves.

TWENTY-THREE

Giving Credit,
Avoiding Plagiarism

HO OWNS WORDS AND IDEAS? Answers to this question differ from culture to culture: In some societies, they are shared resources, not the property of individuals. In others, using another person's words or ideas may be seen as a tribute or compliment that doesn't require specific acknowledgment. In the United States, however (as well as in much of the Western world), an elaborate system of copyright and patent law has grown up to protect the intellectual property (including texts, images, and sounds) of individuals and corporations. This system forms the foundation of the documentation conventions that are currently followed in U.S. schools. And while these conventions are being challenged today by the open-source movement and others who argue that "information wants to be free," the conventions still hold sway in the law and in the academy. Thus you, as a researcher and writer, need to understand these conventions and to practice them in your own writing. Put most simply, these conventions require you to give credit where credit is due by explicitly acknowledging what others contribute to your work and thereby avoiding plagiarism, the use of the words and ideas of others as if they were your own work.

But acknowledging your sources is not simply about avoiding charges of plagiarism (although if you document your sources properly, you will do just that). Rather, it helps establish your own **CREDIBILITY** and **AUTHORITY** as a researcher and an author. It shows that you have carefully read your sources and understand them well enough to openly engage with them in your work. Additionally, citing and documenting your sources allows readers to locate them for their own purposes if they wish; in effect, it anticipates the needs of your audience. There are some cases, however, in which you do not need to provide citations for information that you incorporate. This chapter will help you identify which sources you must acknowledge, explain the basics of documenting your sources, and provide strategies for avoiding plagiarism.

Knowing What You Must Acknowledge

As a general rule, material taken from specific outside sources—whether ideas, texts, images, or sounds—should be **CITED** and **DOCUMENTED**. But there are some exceptions.

INFORMATION THAT DOES NOT NEED ACKNOWLEDGMENT

- *Information that is "common knowledge."* Well-known historical events ("Neil Armstrong was the first person ever to walk on the moon"), facts ("All mammals are warm-blooded"), and quotations (Armstrong's "That's one small step for man, one giant leap for mankind") and uncontroversial information ("People today get more and more of their news and information from the internet") that is widely available in general reference sources do not need to be cited.

- *Information well known to your audience.* Keep in mind that what is common knowledge varies depending on your audience. While an audience of pulmonary oncologists would be familiar with the names of researchers who established that smoking is linked to lung cancer, for a general audience you might need to cite a source if you give the names.

- *Information from well-known, easily accessible documents.* You do not need to include the specific location where you accessed texts that are publicly available from a variety of sources and are widely familiar, such as the United States Constitution.

- *Your own work.* If you've gathered data or generated an idea or text (including images, multimedia texts, and so on) entirely on your own, then indicate that fact to your readers in some way—but it's not necessary to include a citation.

INFORMATION THAT MUST BE ACKNOWLEDGED

- *Direct quotations, paraphrases, and summaries.* Exact wording should always be included in quotation marks and cited. And always cite specific ideas taken from another source, even when you present them using your own words.

- *Controversial information.* If there is some debate over the information you're including, cite it.

- *Information given in only a few sources.* If only one or two sources make this information available (that is, it isn't common knowledge widely accessible in general sources), cite it.

- *Any materials that you did not create yourself*—including tables, charts, images, and sound. This includes any such material that you locate on the internet.

A word to the wise: It's always better to cite any information that you've taken from another source than to guess wrong about whether or not to cite it. If in doubt, err on the safe side and include a citation.

Fair Use and the Internet

In general, principles of fair use apply to the writing you do for your college classes. These principles allow you to use passages and images from the copyrighted work of others without their explicit permission as long as you fully cite what you use. When you post your writing online, however, where that image can be seen by all, then you must have permission from the copyright owner in order to post it.

Students across the country have learned about this limitation on fair use the hard way. One student we know won a prize for an essay she wrote, which was then posted on the writing prize website. In the essay, she included a cartoon that was copyrighted by the cartoonist and soon after the essay was posted, she received a letter from the copyright holder, demanding that she remove her essay and threatening her with a lawsuit. Another student, whose essay was published on a class website, was stunned when his instructor got an angry email from a professor at another university, saying that the student writer had used too much of her work in the essay and that, furthermore, it had not been fully and properly cited. The student, who had intended no dishonesty at all, was embarrassed, to say the least.

Many legal scholars and activists believe that fair use laws (or policies) should be relaxed and that making these laws more restrictive undermines creativity. While these issues get debated in public forums and law courts, however, you are well advised to be scrupulously careful not only in citing and documenting all your sources thoroughly but in getting permission in writing to use any text or image that you plan to use from someone else's posts to the web.

Avoiding Plagiarism

In U.S. academic culture, incorporating the words, ideas, or materials of others into your own work without giving credit through appropriate citations and documentation is viewed as unethical and considered plagiarism. The consequences of such unacknowledged borrowing are serious: Students who plagiarize may receive failing grades for assignments or courses, be subjected to an administrative review for academic misconduct, or even be dismissed from school.

Certainly, the deliberate and obvious effort to pass off someone else's work as your own, such as by handing in a paper purchased online or written by someone else, is plagiarism and can easily be spotted and punished. More troublesome and problematic, however, is the difficulty some students have using the words and ideas of others fairly and acknowledging them fully. Especially when you're new to a field or writing about unfamiliar ideas, incorporating sources without plagiarizing can be especially challenging.

In fact, researcher Rebecca Moore Howard has found that even expert writers have difficulty incorporating the words and ideas of others acceptably when they are working with material outside their comfort zone or field of expertise. What such difficulties most often lead to is what Howard calls **PATCHWRITING**, restating material from sources in ways that stick too close to the original language or syntax.

Some might wish to label patchwriting as plagiarism, even when it's documented, but Howard and other experts in writing studies (including the authors of this text) believe that it is instead a step in the developmental process of learning how to bring the words and thoughts of others seamlessly into your own work. Your college years offer the perfect opportunity to move beyond patchwriting and thus become a more skilled writer while maintaining your academic integrity—and Chapter 22 provides clear guidelines on **QUOTING**, **PARAPHRASING**, and **SUMMARIZING** appropriately.

Understand what constitutes plagiarism. Plagiarism includes any unacknowledged use of material from another source that isn't considered common knowledge; this includes phrases, ideas, and materials such as graphs, charts, images, videos, and so on. In a written text, it includes neglecting to put someone else's exact wording in quotation marks; leaving out in-text documentation for sources that you quote, paraphrase, or summarize; and borrowing too many of the original sources' words and sentence structures in paraphrases or summaries. Check to see if your school has any explicit guidelines for what constitutes plagiarism.

Take notes carefully and conscientiously. If you can't locate the source of words or ideas that you've copied down, you may neglect to cite them properly. So keep track of your sources; be sure to put any borrowed language in quotation marks and to clearly distinguish your own ideas from those of others.

Use caution with electronic sources. Technology makes it easy to copy and paste text and materials from electronic sources directly into your own work—and then to move on and forget to put such material in quotation marks or record the source. To avoid this problem, either print out the source material or copy it into a separate document, enclose it in quotation marks, note the documentation information, and then refer to that document while you are drafting.

Document sources carefully. Below you'll find an overview of the basics of documenting sources. More detail on using **MLA** and **APA** documentation is given in the next two chapters.

Plan ahead. Work can pile up in a high-pressure academic environment, and it may be tempting to resort to quick solutions by passing off someone else's work as your own. Stay on top of your projects by scheduling your work and sticking to the deadlines you set.

Consult your instructor if necessary. If you're uncertain about how to acknowledge sources appropriately, or are struggling with a project, talk with your instructor about finding a solution. Even taking a penalty for submitting an assignment late is better than being caught cheating or being accused of plagiarism that you didn't intend to commit.

Documenting Sources

When you document sources, you identify the sources you've used and giving information about their authors, titles, and publication. Documenting your sources allows you to show evidence of the research you've done and enables your readers to find those sources if they wish to. Most academic documentation systems include two parts: in-text documentation, which you insert in your text after the specific information you have borrowed, and an end-of-text list of WORKS CITED or REFERENCES, which provides complete bibliographic information for every work you've cited. This book covers two documentation systems—of the Modern Language Association (MLA) and the American Psychological Association (APA). MLA style is used primarily in English and other humanities subjects, and APA is used mostly in psychology and other social sciences. Chances are that you will be required to use either MLA or APA style or both in your college courses.

MLA and APA both call for the same basic information; you'll need to give the author's name (or sometimes the editor's name or the title) in the in-text citation, and your end-of-text list should provide the author, title, and publication information for each source that you cite. But the two systems differ in some ways. In APA, for example, your in-text documentation always includes the date of publication, but that is not generally done in MLA. You'll find detailed guidance on the specifics of MLA in Chapter 24 and of APA in Chapter 25, with color-coded examples to help you easily distinguish where the author and editor, title, and publication information appear for each type of work you document. Each of these chapters also includes a student paper that uses that style of documentation.

THINK ABOUT the kinds of information you'll need for your research. For your topic and your intended audience, what would be considered common knowledge? What on your list might not be common knowledge for a different audience? What kind of information will you need to have about your audience in order to make that decision?

TWENTY-FOUR

MLA Style

ODERN LANGUAGE ASSOCIATION style calls for (1) brief in-text documentation and (2) complete documentation in a list of works cited at the end of your text. The models in this chapter draw on the *MLA Handbook for Writers of Research Papers,* 7th edition (2009). Additional information is available at www.mla.org.

A DIRECTORY TO MLA STYLE

author   title   publication

Throughout this chapter, you'll find models and examples that are color-coded to help you see how writers include source information in their texts and lists of works cited: tan for author or editor, yellow for title, gray for publication information: place of publication, publisher, date of publication, page number(s), and so on.

IN-TEXT DOCUMENTATION

Brief documentation in your text makes clear to your reader what you took from a source and where in the source you found the information.

In your text, you have three options for citing a source: **QUOTING**, **PARA-PHRASING**, and **SUMMARIZING**. As you cite each source, you will need to decide whether or not to name the author in a signal phrase—"as Toni Morrison writes"—or in parentheses—"(Morrison 24)."

The first examples in this chapter show basic in-text citations of a work by one author. Variations on those examples follow. The examples illustrate the MLA style of using quotation marks around titles of short works and italicizing titles of long works.

1. Author named in a signal phrase

If you mention the author in a signal phrase, put only the page number(s) in parentheses. Do not write *page* or *p.*

> McCullough describes John Adams' hands as those of someone used to manual labor (18).

2. Author named in parentheses

If you do not mention the author in a signal phrase, put his or her last name in parentheses along with the page number(s). Do not use punctuation between the name and the page number(s).

> Adams is said to have had "the hands of a man accustomed to pruning his own trees, cutting his own hay, and splitting his own firewood" (McCullough 18).

Whether you use a signal phrase and parentheses or parentheses only, try to put the parenthetical citation at the end of the sentence or as close as possible to the material you've cited without awkwardly interrupting the sentence. Notice that in the example above, the parenthetical reference comes after the closing quotation marks but before the period at the end of the sentence.

3. Two or more works by the same author

If you cite multiple works by one author, include the title of the work you are citing either in the signal phrase or in parentheses. Give the full title if it's brief; otherwise, give a short version.

> Kaplan insists that understanding power in the Near East requires "Western leaders who know when to intervene, and do so without illusions" (*Eastward* 330).

Include a comma between author and title if you include both in the parentheses.

> Understanding power in the Near East requires "Western leaders who know when to intervene, and do so without illusions" (Kaplan, *Eastward* 330).

4. Authors with the same last name

Give the author's first name in any signal phrase or the author's first initial in the parenthetical reference.

> *Imaginative* applies not only to modern literature (E. Wilson) but also to writing of all periods, whereas *magical* is often used in writing about Arthurian romances (A. Wilson).

5. Two or more authors

For a work by two or three authors, name all the authors, either in a signal phrase or in the parentheses.

> Carlson and Ventura's stated goal is to introduce Julio Cortázar, Marjorie Agosín, and other Latin American writers to an audience of English-speaking adolescents (v).

For a work with four or more authors, either mention all their names or include just the name of the first author followed by *et al.*, Latin for "and others."

> One popular survey of American literature breaks the contents into sixteen thematic groupings (Anderson et al. A19–24).

6. Organization or government as author

Cite the organization either in a signal phrase or in parentheses. It's accept-able to shorten long names.

> The U.S. government can be direct when it wants to be. For example,
> it sternly warns, "If you are overpaid, we will recover any payments not
> due you" (Social Security Administration 12).

7. Author unknown

If you don't know the author, use the work's title or a shortened version of the title in the parentheses.

> A powerful editorial in last week's paper asserts that healthy liver
> donor Mike Hurewitz died because of "frightening" faulty postoperative
> care ("Every Patient's Nightmare").

8. Literary works

When referring to literary works that are available in many different edi-tions, cite the page numbers from the edition you are using, followed by in-formation that will let readers of any edition locate the text you are citing.

Novels. Give the page and chapter number.

> In *Pride and Prejudice*, Mrs. Bennet shows no warmth toward Jane and
> Elizabeth when they return from Netherfield (105; ch. 12).

Verse plays. Give the act, scene, and line numbers; separate them with periods.

> Macbeth continues the vision theme when he addresses the Ghost
> with "Thou hast no speculation in those eyes / Which thou dost glare
> with"(3.3.96–97).

Poems. Give the part and the line numbers (separated by periods). If a poem has only line numbers, use the word *line(s)* in the first reference.

Whitman sets up not only opposing adjectives but also opposing nouns in "Song of Myself" when he says, "I am of old and young, of the foolish as much as the wise, / . . . a child as well as a man" (16.330–32).

One description of the mere in *Beowulf* is "not a pleasant place!" (line 1372). Later, the label is "the awful place" (1378).

9. Work in an anthology

Name the author(s) of the work, not the editor of the anthology—either in a signal phrase or in parentheses.

"It is the teapots that truly shock," according to Cynthia Ozick in her essay on teapots as metaphor (70).

In *In Short: A Collection of Creative Nonfiction*, readers will find both an essay on Scottish tea (Hiestand) and a piece on teapots as metaphors (Ozick).

10. Encyclopedia or dictionary

Cite an entry in an encyclopedia or dictionary using the author's name, if available. For an entry in a reference work without an author, give the entry's title in parentheses. If entries are arranged alphabetically, no page number is needed.

Katz notes that before *Spartacus*, Kubrick went without work for two years ("Stanley Kubrick").

11. Legal and historical documents

For legal cases and acts of law, name the case or act in a signal phrase or in parentheses. Italicize the name of a legal case.

In 2005, the Supreme Court confirmed in *MGM Studios, Inc. v. Grokster, Ltd.* that peer-to-peer file sharing is illegal copyright infringement.

Do not italicize the titles of laws, acts, or well-known historical documents such as the Declaration of Independence. Give the title and any relevant articles and sections in parentheses. It's okay to use common abbreviations such as *art.* or *sec.* and to abbreviate well-known titles.

> The United States Constitution grants the president the right to make recess appointments *(US Const., art. 2, sec. 2).*

12. Sacred text

When citing sacred texts such as the Bible or the Qur'an, give the title of the edition used, and in parentheses give the book, chapter, and verse (or their equivalent), separated by periods. MLA style recommends that you abbreviate the names of the books of the Bible in parenthetical references.

> The wording from *The New English Bible* follows: "In the beginning of creation, when God made heaven and earth, the earth was without form and void, with darkness over the face of the abyss, and a mighty wind that swept over the surface of the waters" (Gen. 1.1–2).

13. Multivolume work

If you cite more than one volume of a multivolume work, each time you cite one of the volumes, give the volume *and* the page numbers in parentheses, separated by a colon.

> Sandburg concludes with the following sentence about those paying last respects to Lincoln: "All day long and through the night the unbroken line moved, the home town having its farewell" (4: 413).

If your works-cited list includes only a single volume of a multivolume work, give just the page number in parentheses.

14. Two or more works cited together

If you're citing two or more works closely together, you will sometimes need to provide a parenthetical citation for each one.

> Tanner (7) and Smith (viii) have looked at works from a cultural perspective.

If you include both in the same parentheses, separate the references with a semicolon.

> Critics have looked at both *Pride and Prejudice* and *Frankenstein* from a cultural perspective (Tanner 7; Smith viii).

15. Source quoted in another source

When you are quoting text that you found quoted in another source, use the abbreviation *qtd. in* in the parenthetical reference.

> Charlotte Brontë wrote to G. H. Lewes: "Why do you like Miss Austen so very much? I am puzzled on that point" (qtd. in Tanner 7).

16. Work without page numbers

For works without page numbers, including many online sources, identify the source using the author or other information either in a **SIGNAL PHRASE** or in parentheses.

> Studies reported in *Scientific American* and elsewhere show that music training helps children to be better at multitasking later in life ("Hearing the Music").

If the source has paragraph or section numbers, use them with the abbreviation *par.* or *sec.*: ("Hearing the Music," par. 2). If an online work is available as a PDF, cite its page numbers in parentheses.

17. An entire work or one-page article

If you cite an entire work rather than a part of it, or if you cite a single-page article, identify the author in a signal phrase or in parentheses. There's no need to include page numbers.

> At least one observer considers Turkey and Central Asia explosive (Kaplan).

NOTES

Sometimes you may need to give information that doesn't fit into the text itself—to thank people who helped you, provide additional details, refer readers to other sources, or to add comments about sources. Such information can be given in a *footnote* (at the bottom of the page) or an *endnote* (on a separate page with the heading *Notes* just before your works-cited list). Put a superscript number at the appropriate point in your text, signaling to readers to look for the note with the corresponding number. If you have multiple notes, number them consecutively throughout your paper.

Text

This essay will argue that small liberal arts colleges should not recruit athletes and, more specifically, that giving student athletes preferential treatment undermines the larger educational goals.[1]

Note

[1] I want to thank all those who have contributed to my thinking on this topic, especially my classmates and my teachers Marian Johnson and Diane O'Connor.

LIST OF WORKS CITED

A works-cited list provides full bibliographic information for every source cited in your text. See p. 444 for guidelines on preparing this list; for a sample works-cited list, see p. 462.

Books

For most books, you'll need to provide information about the author; the title and any subtitle; and the place of publication, publisher, and date. At the end of the citation provide the medium—Print.

author   title   publication

Important Details for Citing Books

- **AUTHORS:** Include the author's middle name or initials, if any.
- **TITLES:** Capitalize all principal words in titles and subtitles. Do not capitalize *a, an, the, to,* or any prepositions or coordinating conjunctions unless they are the first or last word of a title or subtitle.
- **PUBLICATION PLACE:** If there's more than one city, use the first.
- **PUBLISHER:** Use a short form of the publisher's name (Norton for W. W. Norton & Company, Yale UP for Yale University Press).
- **DATES:** If more than one year is given, use the most recent one.

1. One author

Author's Last Name, First Name. *Title*. Publication City: Publisher, Year
　　of publication. Medium.

Anderson, Curtis. *The Long Tail: Why the Future of Business Is Selling Less
　　of More.* New York: Hyperion, 2006. Print.

2. Two or more works by the same author(s)

Give the author's name in the first entry, and then use three hyphens in the author slot for each of the subsequent works, listing them alphabetically by the first important word of each title.

Author's Last Name, First Name. *Title That Comes First Alphabetically.*
　　Publication City: Publisher, Year of publication. Medium.

---. *Title That Comes Next Alphabetically.* Publication City: Publisher, Year
　　of publication. Medium.

Kaplan, Robert D. *The Coming Anarchy: Shattering the Dreams of the Post
　　Cold War.* New York: Random, 2000. Print.
---. *Eastward to Tartary: Travels in the Balkans, the Middle East, and the
　　Caucasus.* New York: Random, 2000. Print.

Documentation Map (MLA) / Book

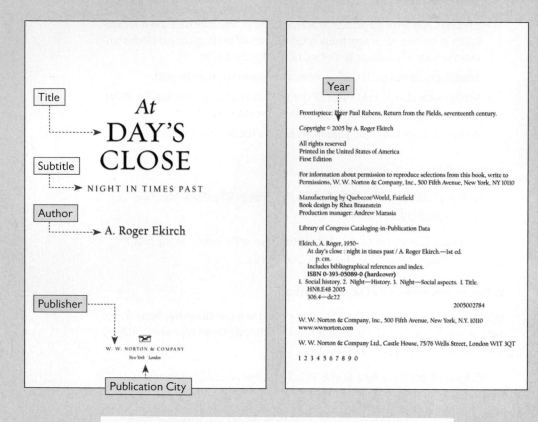

Title → *At* **DAY'S CLOSE**

Subtitle → NIGHT IN TIMES PAST

Author → A. Roger Ekirch

Publisher → W. W. NORTON & COMPANY
New York · London

Publication City

Year

Frontispiece: Peter Paul Rubens, Return from the Fields, seventeenth century.

Copyright © 2005 by A. Roger Ekirch

All rights reserved
Printed in the United States of America
First Edition

For information about permission to reproduce selections from this book, write to
Permissions, W. W. Norton & Company, Inc., 500 Fifth Avenue, New York, NY 10110

Manufacturing by Quebecor/World, Fairfield
Book design by Rhea Braunstein
Production manager: Andrew Marasia

Library of Congress Cataloging-in-Publication Data

Ekirch, A. Roger, 1950–
    At day's close : night in times past / A. Roger Ekirch.—1st ed.
        p. cm.
    Includes bibliographical references and index.
    ISBN 0-393-05089-0 (hardcover)
1. Social history. 2. Night—History. 3. Night—Social aspects. I. Title.
    HN8.E48 2005
    306.4—dc22
                                                            2005002784

W. W. Norton & Company, Inc., 500 Fifth Avenue, New York, N.Y. 10110
www.wwnorton.com

W. W. Norton & Company Ltd., Castle House, 75/76 Wells Street, London W1T 3QT

1 2 3 4 5 6 7 8 9 0

Ekirch, A. Roger. *At Day's Close: Night in Times Past*. New York:
    Norton, 2005. Print.

3. Two or three authors

First Author's Last Name, First Name, Second Author's First and Last Names, and Third Author's First and Last Names. *Title*. Publication City: Publisher, Year of publication. Medium.

Malless, Stanley, and Jeffrey McQuain. *Coined by God: Words and Phrases That First Appear in the English Translations of the Bible*. New York: Norton, 2003. Print.

Sebranek, Patrick, Verne Meyer, and Dave Kemper. *Writers INC: A Guide to Writing, Thinking, and Learning*. Burlington: Write Source, 1990. Print.

4. Four or more authors

You may give each author's name or the name of the first author only, followed by *et al.*, Latin for "and others."

First Author's Last Name, First Name, Second Author's First and Last Names, Third Author's First and Last Names, and Final Author's First and Last Names. *Title*. Publication City: Publisher, Year of publication. Medium.

Anderson, Robert, John Malcolm Brinnin, John Leggett, Gary Q. Arpin, and Susan Allen Toth. *Elements of Literature: Literature of the United States*. Austin: Holt, 1993. Print.

Anderson, Robert, et al. *Elements of Literature: Literature of the United States*. Austin: Holt, 1993. Print.

5. Organization or government as author

Organization Name. *Title*. Publication City: Publisher, Year of publication. Medium.

Diagram Group. *The Macmillan Visual Desk Reference*. New York: Macmillan, 1993. Print.

For a government publication, give the name of the government first, followed by the names of any department and agency (see p. 420).

United States. Dept. of Health and Human Services. Natl. Inst. of Mental Health. *Autism Spectrum Disorders*. Washington: GPO, 2004. Print.

6. Anthology

Editor's Last Name, First Name, ed. *Title*. Publication City: Publisher, Year of publication. Medium.

Hall, Donald, ed. *The Oxford Book of Children's Verse in America*. New York: Oxford UP, 1985. Print.

If there is more than one editor, list the first editor last-name-first and the others first-name-first.

Kitchen, Judith, and Mary Paumier Jones, eds. *In Short: A Collection of Brief Creative Nonfiction*. New York: Norton, 1996. Print.

7. Work(s) in an anthology

Author's Last Name, First Name. "*Title of Work*." *Title of Anthology*. Ed. Editor's First and Last Names. Publication City: Publisher, Year of publication. Pages. Medium.

Achebe, Chinua. "Uncle Ben's Choice." *The Seagull Reader: Literature*. Ed. Joseph Kelly. New York: Norton, 2005. 23–27. Print.

To document two or more selections from one anthology, list each selection by author and title, followed by the anthology editor(s)' names and the pages of the selection. Then include an entry for the anthology itself (see no. 6).

Author's Last Name, First Name. "Title of Work." Anthology Editor's Last Name Pages.

Hiestand, Emily. "Afternoon Tea." Kitchen and Jones 65–67.

Ozick, Cynthia. "The Shock of Teapots." Kitchen and Jones 68–71.

8. Author and editor

Start with the author if you've cited the text itself.

Author's Last Name, First Name. *Title*. Ed. Editor's First and Last
Names. Publication City: Publisher, Year of publication. Medium.

Austen, Jane. *Emma*. Ed. Stephen M. Parrish. New York: Norton, 2000.
Print.

Start with the editor to cite his or her contribution rather than the author's.

Editor's Last Name, First Name, ed. *Title*. By Author's First and Last
Names. Publication City: Publisher, Year of publication. Medium.

Parrish, Stephen M., ed. *Emma*. By Jane Austen. New York: Norton,
2000. Print.

9. No author or editor

Title. Publication City: Publisher, Year of publication. Medium.

2008 New York City Restaurants. New York: Zagat, 2008. Print.

10. Translation

Start with the author to emphasize the work itself.

Author's Last Name, First Name. *Title*. Trans. Translator's First and Last
Names. Publication City: Publisher, Year of publication. Medium.

Dostoevsky, Fyodor. *Crime and Punishment*. Trans. Richard Pevear and
Larissa Volokhonsky. New York: Vintage, 1993. Print.

Start with the translator to emphasize the translation.

Pevear, Richard, and Larissa Volokhonsky, trans. *Crime and Punishment*.
By Fyodor Dostoevsky. New York: Vintage, 1993. Print.

11. Graphic narrative

Start with the person whose work is most relevant to your research, and
include labels to indicate each collaborator's role (more on p. 422).

Pekar, Harvey, writer. *American Splendor*. Illus. R. Crumb. New York:
Four Walls, 1996. Print.

Crumb, R., illus. *American Splendor.* By Harvey Pekar. New York: Four
Walls, 1996. Print.

If the work was written and illustrated by the same person, format the entry
like that of any other book.

12. Foreword, introduction, preface, or afterword

Part Author's Last Name, First Name. Name of Part. *Title of Book.*
By Author's First and Last Names. Publication City: Publisher, Year
of publication. Pages. Medium.

Tanner, Tony. Introduction. *Pride and Prejudice.* By Jane Austen. London:
Penguin, 1972. 7–46. Print.

13. Multivolume work

If you cite all the volumes of a multivolume work, give the number of volumes after the title.

Author's Last Name, First Name. *Title of Complete Work.* Number of
vols. Publication City: Publisher, Year of publication. Medium.

Sandburg, Carl. *Abraham Lincoln: The War Years.* 4 vols. New York:
Harcourt, 1939. Print.

If you cite only one volume, give the volume number after the title.

Sandburg, Carl. *Abraham Lincoln: The War Years.* Vol. 2. New York:
Harcourt, 1939. Print.

14. Article in a reference book

Provide the author's name if the article is signed. If the reference work is
well known, give only the edition and year of publication.

Author's Last Name, First Name. "Title of Article." *Title of Reference
Book.* Edition number. Year of publication. Medium.

"Kiwi." *Merriam-Webster's Collegiate Dictionary.* 11th ed. 2003. Print.

If the reference work is less familiar or more specialized, give full publication information. If it has only one volume or is in its first edition, omit that information.

> Author's Last Name, First Name. "Title of Article." *Title of Reference Book*. Ed. Editor's First and Last Name. Edition number. Number of vols. Publication City: Publisher, Year of publication. Medium.

> Campbell, James. "The Harlem Renaissance." *The Oxford Companion to Twentieth-Century Poetry*. Ed. Ian Hamilton. Oxford: Oxford UP, 1994. Print.

15. Book in a series

> Editor's Last Name, First Name, ed. *Title of Book*. By Author's First and Last Names. Publication City: Publisher, Year of publication. Medium. Series Title abbreviated.

> Wall, Cynthia, ed. *The Pilgrim's Progress*. By John Bunyan. New York: Norton, 2007. Print. Norton Critical Ed.

16. Sacred text

If you have cited a specific edition of a religious text, you need to include it in your works-cited list.

> *The New English Bible with the Apocrypha*. New York: Oxford UP, 1971. Print.

> *The Torah: A Modern Commentary*. Ed. W. Gunther Plaut. New York: Union of Amer. Hebrew Congregations, 1981. Print.

17. Book with title within the title

When the title of a book contains the title of another long work, do not italicize that title.

> Walker, Roy. *Time Is Free: A Study of* Macbeth. London: Dakers, 1949. Print.

When the book title contains the title of a short work, put the short work in quotation marks, and italicize the entire title (see p. 424).

Thompson, Lawrance Roger. *"Fire and Ice": The Art and Thought of Robert Frost*. New York: Holt, 1942. Print.

18. Edition other than the first

Author's Last Name, First Name. *Title*. Name or number of ed. Publication City: Publisher, Year of publication. Medium.

Hirsch, E. D., Jr., ed. *What Your Second Grader Needs to Know: Fundamentals of a Good Second-Grade Education*. Rev. ed. New York: Doubleday, 1998. Print.

19. Republished work

Give the original publication date after the title, followed by the publication information of the republished edition.

Author's Last Name, First Name. *Title*. Year of original edition. Publication City: Current Publisher, Year of republication. Medium.

Bierce, Ambrose. *Civil War Stories*. 1909. New York: Dover, 1994. Print.

20. Publisher and imprint

Some sources may provide both a publisher's name and an imprint on the title page; if so, include both, with a hyphen between the imprint and the publisher.

Author's Last Name, First Name. *Title*. Publication City: Imprint-Publisher, Year of publication. Medium.

Rowling, J. K. *Harry Potter and the Goblet of Fire*. New York: Levine-Scholastic, 2000. Print.

Periodicals

For most articles, you'll need to provide information about the author, the article title and any subtitle, the periodical title, any volume or issue number, the date, inclusive page numbers, and the medium—Print.

author   title   publication

Important Details for Citing Periodicals

- **AUTHORS:** If there is more than one author, list the first author last-name-first and the others first-name-first.
- **TITLES:** Capitalize titles and subtitles as you would for a book. For periodical titles, omit any initial *A, An,* or *The.*
- **DATES:** Abbreviate the names of months except for May, June, or July: Jan., Feb., Mar., Apr., Aug., Sept., Oct., Nov., Dec. Journals paginated by volume or issue need only the year (in parentheses).
- **PAGES:** If an article does not fall on consecutive pages, give the first page with a plus sign (55+).

21. Article in a journal

Author's Last Name, First Name. "Title of Article." *Title of Journal*
    Volume.Issue (Year): Pages. Medium.

Cooney, Brian C. "Considering *Robinson Crusoe*'s 'Liberty of Conscience' in an Age of Terror." *College English* 69.3 (2007): 197–215. Print.

22. Article in a journal numbered by issue

Author's Last Name, First Name. "Title of Article." *Title of Journal* Issue
    (Year): Pages. Medium.

Flynn, Kevin. "The Railway in Canadian Poetry." *Canadian Literature*
    174 (2002): 70–95. Print.

23. Article in a magazine

Author's Last Name, First Name. "Title of Article." *Title of Magazine*
    Day Month Year: Pages. Medium.

Walsh, Bryan. "Not a Watt to Be Wasted." *Time* 17 Mar. 2008: 46–47. Print.

For a monthly magazine, include only the month and year.

Fellman, Bruce. "Leading the Libraries." *Yale Alumni Magazine* Feb. 2002:
    26–31. Print.

Documentation Map (MLA) / Journal Article

Pious Princes and Red-Hot Lovers: The Politics of ◄------- Title of Article
Shakespeare's Romeo and Juliet

Author -------► Jerry Weinberger
Michigan State University

Shakespeare's *Romeo and Juliet* is obviously a tragedy of impetuous young love. But it is also a play about politics, especially politics as conditioned by Christian morality and religion. The play's action is determined by the conflict between secular and priestly authority, and by the complex interaction among mercy, love, and punishment as practiced by Escalus, Prince of Verona, and Friar Laurence, the Franciscan. In the course of this action, the Veronese regime is transformed, and the common good determined, in ways more compatible with the friar's interests than with those of the Prince. *Romeo and Juliet* is one of Shakespeare's pictures of the unique problems that determined modern, as opposed to ancient, political life.

Critical opinion now agrees that Shakespeare presents a sophisticated teaching about politics, ancient as well as modern. While it was long thought that Shakespeare knew little about ancient politics, we now have a different view, for instance, of the Roman plays: *Coriolanus* depicts the Republic's subtle constitutional balance; *Julius Caesar* depicts the end of Republican liberty; *Antony and Cleopatra* describes the political, moral, and psychological conditions of the Empire (Cantor 1976). As regards modern politics, critics have long acknowledged that Shakespeare was a keen interpreter of the quintessential modern, Machiavelli. "It can hardly be doubted," said E. M. W. Tillyard in 1944, that Shakespeare knew well the doctrines of Machiavelli (Tillyard 1991, 28–30). More recent critics—from both ends of the ideological spectrum—agree. One conservative sees *Measure for Measure* as "a Machiavellian scheme to bring good government to a bad city" (Jaffa 1981, 189), while a leading cultural materialist tells us that "Shakespeare's Henry plays . . . can be seen to confirm the Machiavellian hypothesis of the origin of princely power in force and fraud even as they draw their audiences irresistibly toward the celebration of that power" (Greenblatt 1985, 20). Whereas Hume (1873, 357–58) once faulted Shakespeare for his indifference to English civil liberty (in the English history plays), we now know that

Volume

I thank Paul A. Cantor, Werner J. Dannhauser, Arthur Melzer, and Richard Zinman for their helpful criticism of this article's earlier drafts.

Issue

THE JOURNAL OF POLITICS, Vol. 65, No. 2, May 2003, Pp. 350–375 ◄-------------- Pages
© 2003 Blackwell Publishing, 350 Main St., Malden, MA 02148, USA, and PO Box 1354, 9600 Garsington Road, Oxford OX4 2DQ, UK.

Year

Title of Journal

Weinberger, Jerry. "Pious Princes and Red-Hot Lovers: The Politics of Shakespeare's *Romeo and Juliet*." *Journal of Politics* 65.2 (2003): 350–75. Print.

Documentation Map (MLA) / Magazine Article

Title of Article

The Wolf in Your Dog

By Michael W. Fox, DVM, PhD ◄-------- Author

Author

Though in their deep heart's core, there is a commonality of origin, spirit, emotional intelligence and empathetic sensibility, the wild wolf looks through us, while the dog looks to us.

OF ALL THE MYRIAD MEMBERS OF THE ANIMAL KINGDOM, the domesticated dog (*Canis lupus familiaris*) is closest to us. With individual exceptions in other species, this canine species is the most understanding, if not also the most observant, of human behavior—of our actions and intentions. This is why dogs are so responsive to us, even mirroring or mimicking our behavior. And it is why dogs are so trainable.

Fear in unsocialized and abused dogs interferes with their attentiveness to and interpretation of human behavior and intentions. This is one reason wild species like the coyote and wolf, even when born and raised in captivity, are difficult to train. The wolf "Tiny," whom I bottle-raised and intensely socialized during her formative early days, never really lost her fear and distrust of strangers.

Tiny did not start mirroring human behavior until she was close to nine years old. At this point, she began to mimic the human-to-human greeting grin, revealing her front teeth as she curled her lips into a snarly smile. In my experience, dogs

who can do this do so at a much earlier age, even as early as four to six months.

In comparing socialized (human-bonded) wolves and dogs in terms of how they have related to me as well as to my family members, friends and strangers, I would say that the main difference between the two species is the fear factor. Differences in trainability hinge on this; as I theorize in my new book (*Dog Body, Dog Mind*), domestication has altered the tuning of the dog's adrenal and autonomic nervous systems. This tuning (which dampens adrenal fright, flight and fight reactions and possibly alters brain serotonin levels), is accomplished through selective breeding for docility, and by gentle handling during the critical period for socialization. According to the earlier research of my mentors—Drs. John Paul Scott and John L. Fuller of the Jackson Laboratory in Bar Harbor, Maine—pups with no human contact during this critical socialization period (which ends around 12 to 16 weeks of age) are wild and unapproachable.

Month and Year ---► Mar/Apr 2008 | **Bark** 85 ◄---- Pages

Title of Magazine

Fox, Michael W. "The Wolf in Your Dog." *Bark* Mar.–Apr. 2008: 85–87. Print.

24. Article in a daily newspaper

Author's Last Name, First Name. "Title of Article." *Name of Newspaper*
Day Month Year: Pages. Medium.

Springer, Shira. "Celtics Reserves Are Whizzes vs. Wizards." *Boston
Globe* 14 Mar. 2005: D41. Print.

If you are citing a particular edition of a newspaper, list the edition (late ed.,
natl. ed., etc.) after the date. And if a section is not identified by a letter, put
the name of the section after the edition information.

Burns, John F., and Miguel Helft. "Under Pressure, YouTube Withdraws
Muslim Cleric's Videos." *New York Times* 4 Nov. 2010, late ed.,
sec. 1: 13. Print.

25. Unsigned article

"Title of Article." *Name of Publication* Day Month Year: Pages. Medium.

"Being Invisible Closer to Reality." *Atlanta Journal-Constitution* 11 Aug.
2008: A3. Print.

26. Editorial

"Title." Editorial. *Name of Publication* Day Month Year: Page. Medium.

"Gas, Cigarettes Are Safe to Tax." Editorial. *Lakeville Journal* 17 Feb.
2005: A10. Print.

27. Letter to the editor

Author's Last Name, First Name. "Title (if any)." Letter. *Name of
Publication* Day Month Year: Page. Medium.

Festa, Roger. "Social Security: Another Phony Crisis." Letter. *Lakeville
Journal* 17 Feb. 2005: A10. Print.

author   title   publication

28. Review

Reviewer's Last Name, First Name. "Title (if any) of Review." Rev. of
  Title of Work, by Author's First and Last Names. *Title of Periodical*
  Day Month Year: Pages. Medium.

Frank, Jeffrey. "Body Count." Rev. of *The Exception*, by Christian
  Jungersen. *New Yorker* 30 July 2007: 86–87. Print.

Online Sources

Not every online source gives you all the data that MLA would like to see
in a works-cited entry. Ideally, you will be able to list the author's name,
the title, information about print publication, information about electronic
publication (title of site, editor, date of first electronic publication and/or
most recent revision, name of the publisher or sponsoring institution), the
publication medium, date of access, and, if necessary, a URL.

Important Details for Citing Online Sources

- **AUTHORS OR EDITORS** and **TITLES:** Format authors and titles as you
  would for a print book or periodical.

- **PUBLISHER:** If the name of the publisher or sponsoring institution is unavailable, use *N.p.*

- **DATES:** Abbreviate the months as you would for a print periodical. Although MLA asks for the date when materials were first posted or most
  recently updated, you won't always be able to find that information; if
  it's unavailable, use *n.d.* Be sure to include the date on which you accessed the source.

- **PAGES:** If the citation calls for page numbers but the source is unpagi-
  nated, use *n. pag.* in place of page numbers.

- **MEDIUM:** Indicate the medium—Web, email, CD-ROM, and so on.

- **URL:** MLA assumes that readers can locate most sources on the Web by
  searching for the author, title, or other identifying information, so they
  don't require a URL for most online sources. When users can't locate the
  source without a URL, give the address of the website in angle brackets.
  When a URL won't fit on one line, break it only after a slash (and do not

add a hyphen). If a URL is very long, consider giving the URL of the site's home or search page instead.

29. Entire website

For websites with an editor, compiler, director, narrator, or translator, follow the name with the appropriate abbreviation (*ed., comp.*).

> Author's Last Name, First Name. *Title of Site.* Publisher or Sponsoring
> Institution, Date posted or last updated. Medium. Day Month Year
> of access.

> Zalta, Edward N., ed. *Stanford Encyclopedia of Philosophy.* Metaphysics
> Research Lab, Center for the Study of Language and Information,
> Stanford U, 2007. Web. 14 Nov. 2010.

Personal website

> Author's Last Name, First Name. Home page. Sponsor, Date posted or
> last updated. Medium. Day Month Year of access.

> Nunberg, Geoffrey. Home page. School of Information, U of California,
> Berkeley, 2009. Web. 13 Apr. 2009.

30. Work from a website

> Author's Last Name, First Name. "Title of Work." *Title of Site.* Ed.
> Editor's First and Last Names. Sponsor, Date posted or last
> updated. Medium. Day Month Year of access.

> Buff, Rachel Ida. "Becoming American." *Immigration History Research
> Center.* U of Minnesota, 24 Mar. 2008. Web. 4 Apr. 2008.

31. Online book or part of a book

Cite a book you access online as you would a print book, adding the name of the site or database, the medium, and the date of access.

> Anderson, Sherwood. *Winesburg, Ohio.* New York: B. W. Huebsch,
> 1919. *Bartleby.com.* Web. 7 Apr. 2008.

author   title   publication

Documentation Map (MLA) / Website

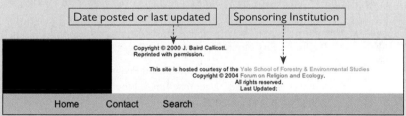

Callicott, J. Baird. "Environmental Ethics: An Overview." *Forum on Religion and Ecology*. Yale School of Forestry & Environmental Studies, 2000. Web. 17 Sept. 2008.

If you are citing a part of a book, put the part in quotation marks before the book title. If the online book is paginated, give the pages; if not, use *N. pag.*

> Anderson, Sherwood. "The Strength of God." *Winesburg, Ohio*. New
> York: B. W. Huebsch, 1919. N. pag. *Bartleby.com*. Web. 7 Apr. 2008.

To cite a book you've downloaded onto a Kindle, Nook, or other digital device, follow the setup for a print book, but indicate the ebook format at the end of your citation.

> Larson, Erik. *The Devil in the White City: Murder, Mayhem, and Madness at
> the Fair That Changed America*. New York: Vintage, 2004. Kindle.

32. Article in an online scholarly journal

If a journal does not number pages or if it numbers each article separately, use *n. pag.* in place of page numbers.

> Author's Last Name, First Name. "Title of Article." *Title of Journal*
> Volume.Issue (Year): Pages. Medium. Day Month Year of access.

> Gleckman, Jason. "Shakespeare as Poet or Playwright? The Player's
> Speech in *Hamlet*." *Early Modern Literary Studies* 11.3 (2006):
> n. pag. Web. 24 June 2008.

33. Article in an online newspaper

> Author's Last Name, First Name. "Title of Article." *Title of Newspaper*.
> Publisher, Day Month Year. Medium. Day Month Year of access.

> Banerjee, Neela. "Proposed Religion-Based Program for Federal
> Inmates Is Canceled." *New York Times*. New York Times, 28 Oct.
> 2006. Web. 24 June 2008.

34. Article in an online magazine

> Author's Last Name, First Name. "Title of Article." *Title of Magazine*.
> Publisher, Date of publication. Medium. Day Month Year of access.

> Lithwick, Dahlia. "Privacy Rights Inc." *Slate*. Washington Post–
> Newsweek Interactive, 14 Oct. 2010. Web. 25 Oct. 2010.

author   title   publication

35. Blog entry

> Author's Last Name, First Name. "Title of Entry." *Title of Blog.* Sponsor,
> Day Month Year posted. Medium. Day Month Year of access.

> Gladwell, Malcolm. "Enron and Newspapers." *Gladwell.com.* N.p., 4 Jan.
> 2007. Web. 26 Aug. 2008.

If the entry has no title, use "Blog entry" without quotation marks. Cite a whole blog as you would an entire website (see no. 29). If the publisher or sponsor is unavailable, use *N.p.*

36. Article accessed through a database

For articles accessed through a library's subscription services, such as Info-Trac and EBSCO, cite the publication information for the source, followed by the name of the database.

> Author's Last Name, First Name. "Title of Article." *Title of Periodical*
> Date or Volume.Issue (Year): Pages. *Database Name.* Medium.
> Day Month Year of access.

> Stalter, Sunny. "Subway Ride and Subway System in Hart Crane's 'The
> Tunnel.'" *Journal of Modern Literature* 33.2 (2010): 70–91. *Academic
> Search Complete.* Web. 28 May 2010.

37. Online editorial

> "Title of Editorial." Editorial. *Title of Site.* Publisher, Day Month Year of
> publication. Medium. Day Month Year of access.

> "Keep Drinking Age at 21." Editorial. *ChicagoTribune.com.* Chicago
> Tribune, 25 Aug. 2008. Web. 28 Aug. 2008.

38. Online film review

> Reviewer's Last Name, First Name. "Title of Review." Rev. of *Title of
> Work,* dir. First and Last Names. *Title of Site.* Publisher, Day Month
> Year posted. Medium. Day Month Year of access.

Documentation Map (MLA) / Database Article

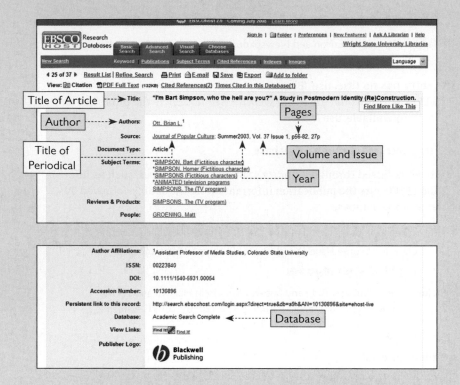

Ott, Brian L. "'I'm Bart Simpson, Who the Hell Are You?' A Study in
   Postmodern Identity (Re)Construction." *Journal of Popular Culture*
   37.1 (2003): 56–82. *Academic Search Complete*. Web. 24 Mar. 2008.

Edelstein, David. "Best Served Cold." Rev. of *The Social Network,* dir. David Fincher. *New York Magazine.* New York Media, 1 Oct. 2010. Web. 3 Nov. 2010.

39. Email

Writer's Last Name, First Name. "Subject Line." Message to the author. Day Month Year of message. Medium.

Smith, William. "Teaching Grammar—Some Thoughts." Message to the author. 19 Nov. 2007. Email.

40. Posting to an online forum

Writer's Last Name, First Name. "Title of Posting." *Name of Forum.* Sponsor, Day Month Year of posting. Medium. Day Month Year of access.

Mintz, Stephen H. "Manumission During the Revolution." *H-Net List on Slavery.* Michigan State U, 14 Sept. 2006. Web. 18 Apr. 2009.

41. Article in an online reference work

"Title of Article." *Title of Reference Work.* Sponsor, Date of work. Medium. Day Month Year of access.

"Dubai." *MSN Encarta.* Microsoft Corporation, 2008. Web. 20 June 2008.

42. Wiki entry

"Title of Entry." *Title of Wiki.* Sponsor, Day Month Year updated. Medium. Day Month Year of access.

"Pi." *Wikipedia.* Wikimedia Foundation, 28 Aug. 2008. Web. 2 Sept. 2008.

43. Podcast

Performer or Host's Last Name, First Name. "Title of Podcast." Host Host's First and Last Name. *Title of Program.* Sponsor, Day Month Year posted. Medium. Day Month Year of access.

Blumberg, Alex, and Adam Davidson. "The Giant Pool of Money." Host Ira Glass. *This American Life*. Chicago Public Radio, 9 May 2008. Web. 18 Sept. 2008.

44. Tweet

Author's Last Name, First Name (User Name). "Full tweet text." Day Month Year, Time. Medium.

Stern, Michael (Roadfood123). "Ice creamorama: Dr. Mike's is now open weekdays." 21 Mar. 2012, 5:21 p.m. Tweet.

Other Kinds of Sources (including online versions)

Many of the sources in this section can be found online, and you'll find examples here for how to cite them. If there is no Web model here, start with the guidelines most appropriate for the source you need to cite, omit the original medium, and end your citation with the title of the website, italicized; the medium (Web); and the day, month, and year of access.

45. Advertisement

Product or Company. Advertisement. *Title of Periodical* Date or Volume.Issue (Year): Page. Medium.

Empire BlueCross BlueShield. Advertisement. *Fortune* 8 Dec. 2003: 208. Print.

Advertisement on the web

Rolex. Advertisement. *Time*. Time, n.d. Web. 1 Apr. 2009.

46. Art

Artist's Last Name, First Name. *Title of Art*. Medium. Year. Institution, City.

Van Gogh, Vincent. *The Potato Eaters*. Oil on canvas. 1885. Van Gogh Museum, Amsterdam.

Art on the web

Warhol, Andy. *Self Portrait*. 1979. J. Paul Getty Museum, Los Angeles.
　　The Getty. Web. 29 Mar. 2007.

Cite photographs you find online by giving the photographer, title, and date
of the image, if available. If the date is unavailable, use *n.d.* For photographs
you take yourself, see no. 65.

Donnell, Ryan. *At a Pre-Civil War Railroad Construction Site Outside of
　　Philadelphia*. 2010. Smithsonian Institution. *Smithsonian.com*.
　　Web. 3 Nov. 2010.

47. Cartoon

Artist's Last Name, First Name. "Title of Cartoon (if titled)." Cartoon.
　　Title of Periodical Date or Volume.Issue (Year): Page. Medium.

Chast, Roz. "The Three Wise Men of Thanksgiving." Cartoon. *New
　　Yorker* 1 Dec. 2003: 174. Print.

Cartoon on the web

Horsey, David. Cartoon. *Seattle Post-Intelligencer*. Seattle
　　Post-Intelligencer, 20 Apr. 2008. Web. 21 Apr. 2008.

48. Dissertation

Treat a published dissertation as you would a book, but after its title, add the
abbreviation *Diss.*, the institution, and the date of the dissertation.

Author's Last Name, First Name. *Title*. Diss. Institution, Year.
　　Publication City: Publisher, Year. Medium.

Goggin, Peter N. *A New Literacy Map of Research and Scholarship in
　　Computers and Writing*. Diss. Indiana U of Pennsylvania, 2000.
　　Ann Arbor: UMI, 2001. Print.

For unpublished dissertations, put the title in quotation marks and end with
the degree-granting institution and the year (see p. 438).

Kim, Loel. "Students Respond to Teacher Comments: A Comparison of
Online Written and Voice Modalities." Diss. Carnegie Mellon U,
1998. Print.

49. CD-ROM or DVD-ROM

Title. Any pertinent information about the edition, release, or
version. Publication City: Publisher, Year of publication.
Medium.

Othello. Princeton: Films for the Humanities and Sciences, 1998.
CD-ROM.

If you are citing only part of the CD-ROM or DVD-ROM, name the part as you
would a part of a book.

"Snow Leopard." *Encarta Encyclopedia 2007*. Seattle: Microsoft, 2007.
CD-ROM.

50. Film, DVD, or video clip

Title. Dir. Director's First and Last Names. Perf. Lead Actors' First and
Last Names. Distributor, Year of release. Medium.

Casablanca. Dir. Michael Curtiz. Perf. Humphrey Bogart, Ingrid
Bergman, and Claude Rains. Warner, 1942. Film.

To cite a particular person's work, start with that name.

Cody, Diablo, scr. *Juno*. Dir. Jason Reitman. Perf. Ellen Page, Michael
Cera, Jennifer Garner, and Jason Bateman. Fox Searchlight,
2007. DVD.

Cite a video clip on *YouTube* or a similar site as you would a short work from
a website.

Director's Last Name, First Name, dir. "Title of Video." *Title of Site*.
Sponsor, Day Month Year of release. Medium. Day Month Year of
access.

PivotMasterDX, dir. "Bounce!" *YouTube*. YouTube, 14 June 2008. Web. 21 June 2008.

51. Broadcast interview

Subject's Last Name, First Name. Interview. *Title of Program*. Network. Station, City. Day Month Year. Medium.

Gates, Henry Louis, Jr. Interview. *Fresh Air*. NPR. WNYC, New York. 9 Apr. 2002. Radio.

52. Published interview

Subject's Last Name, First Name. Interview, or "Title of Interview." *Title of Periodical* Date or Volume.Issue (Year): Pages. Medium.

Stone, Oliver. Interview. *Esquire* Nov. 2004: 170. Print.

53. Personal interview

Subject's Last Name, First Name. Personal interview. Day Month Year.

Roddick, Andy. Personal interview. 17 Aug. 2008.

54. Unpublished letter

For medium, use MS for a hand-written letter and TS for a typed one.

Author's Last Name, First Name. Letter to the author. Day Month Year. Medium.

Quindlen, Anna. Letter to the author. 11 Apr. 2002. MS.

55. Published letter

Letter Writer's Last Name, First Name. Letter to First and Last Names. Day Month Year of letter. *Title of Book*. Ed. Editor's First and Last Names. City: Publisher, Year of publication. Pages. Medium.

White, E. B. Letter to Carol Angell. 28 May 1970. *Letters of E. B. White*. Ed. Dorothy Lobarno Guth. New York: Harper, 1976. 600. Print.

56. Map or chart

Title of Map. Map. City: Publisher, Year of publication. Medium.

Toscana. Map. Milan: Touring Club Italiano, 1987. Print.

Map on the web

"Portland, Oregon." Map. *Google Maps.* Google, 25 Apr. 2009. Web. 25
    Apr. 2009.

57. Musical score

Composer's Last Name, First Name. *Title of Composition.* Year of
    composition. Publication City: Publisher, Year of publication.
    Medium. Series Information (if any).

Beethoven, Ludwig van. *String Quartet No. 13 in B Flat, Op. 130.* 1825.
    New York: Dover, 1970. Print.

58. Sound recording

Artist's Last Name, First Name. *Title of Long Work.* Other pertinent
    details about the artists. Manufacturer, Year of release. Medium.

Beethoven, Ludwig van. *Missa Solemnis.* Perf. Westminster Choir and
    New York Philharmonic. Cond. Leonard Bernstein. Sony, 1992. CD.

Whether you list the composer, conductor, or performer first depends on
where you want to place the emphasis. If you are citing a specific song, put
it in quotation marks before the name of the recording.

Brown, Greg. "Canned Goods." *The Live One.* Red House, 1995. MP3 file.

For a spoken-word recording, you may begin with the writer, speaker, or producer, depending on your emphasis.

Dale, Jim, narr. *Harry Potter and the Deathly Hallows.* By J. K. Rowling.
    Random House Audio, 2007. CD.

59. Oral presentation

Speaker's Last Name, First Name. "Title of Lecture." Sponsoring
Institution. Site, City. Day Month Year. Medium.

Cassin, Michael. "Nature in the Raw—The Art of Landscape Painting."
Berkshire Institute for Lifetime Learning. Clark Art Institute,
Williamstown. 24 Mar. 2005. Lecture.

60. Paper from proceedings of a conference

Author's Last Name, First Name. "Title of Paper." *Title of Conference
Proceedings*. Date, City. Ed. Editor's First and Last Names.
Publication City: Publisher, Year. Pages. Medium.

Zolotow, Charlotte. "Passion in Publishing." *A Sea of Upturned Faces:
Proceedings of the Third Pacific Rim Conference on Children's
Literature*. 1986, Los Angeles. Ed. Winifred Ragsdale. Metuchen:
Scarecrow P, 1989. 236–49. Print.

61. Performance

Title. By Author's First and Last Names. Other appropriate details about
the performance. Site, City. Day Month Year. Medium.

Take Me Out. By Richard Greenberg. Dir. Scott Plate. Perf. Caleb
Sekeres. Dobama Theatre, Cleveland. 17 Aug. 2007.
Performance.

62. Television or radio program

"Title of Episode." *Title of Program*. Other appropriate information about
the writer, director, actors, etc. Network. Station, City, Day
Month Year of broadcast. Medium.

"Tabula Rasa." *Criminal Minds*. Writ. Dan Dworkin. Dir. Steve Boyum.
NBC. WCNC, Charlotte, 14 May 2008. Television.

Television or radio on the web

"Bush's War." *Frontline*. Writ. and dir. Michael Kirk. PBS, 24 Mar. 2008.
    PBS.org. Web. 10 Apr. 2009.

63. Pamphlet, brochure, or press release

Author's Last Name, First Name. *Title of Publication*. Publication City:
    Publisher, Year. Medium.

Bowers, Catherine. *Can We Find a Home Here? Answering Questions of
    Interfaith Couples*. Boston: UUA Publications, n.d. Print.

To cite a press release, include the day and month before the year.

64. Legal source

The name of a court case is not italicized in a works-cited entry.

Names of the First Plaintiff v. First Defendant. Volume Name Page
    numbers of law report. Name of Court. Year of decision. Source
    information for medium consulted.

District of Columbia v. Heller. 540 US 290. Supreme Court of the US.
    2008. *Supreme Court Collection*. Legal Information Inst., Cornell U
    Law School, n.d. Web. 18 Mar. 2009.

For acts of law, include both the Public Law number and the Statutes at Large
volume and page numbers.

Name of Law. Public law number. Statutes at Large Volume Stat. Pages.
    Day Month Year enacted. Medium.

Military Commissions Act. Pub. L. 109-366. 120 Stat. 2083–2521.
    17 Oct. 2006. Print.

65. MP3, JPEG, PDF, or other digital file

For downloaded songs, photographs, PDFs, and other documents stored on
your computer or another digital device, follow the guidelines for the type

of work you are citing (art, journal article, and so on) and give the file type as the medium.

> Talking Heads. "Burning Down the House." *Speaking in Tongues.* Sire, 1983. Digital file.

> Taylor, Aaron. "Twilight of the Idols: Performance, Melodramatic Villainy, and *Sunset Boulevard.*" *Journal of Film and Video* 59 (2007): 13–31. PDF file.

Citing Sources Not Covered by MLA

To cite a source for which MLA does not provide guidelines, look for models similar to the source you are citing. Give any information readers will need in order to find your source themselves—author; title, subtitle; publisher and/or sponsor; medium; dates; and any other pertinent information. You might want to try out your citation yourself, to be sure it will lead others to your source.

FORMATTING A RESEARCH ESSAY

Name, course, title. MLA does not require a separate title page. In the upper left-hand corner of your first page, include your name, your professor's name, the name of the course, and the date. Center the title of your paper on the next line after the date; capitalize it as you would a book title.

Page numbers. In the upper right-hand corner of each page, one-half inch below the top of the page, include your last name and the page number. Number pages consecutively throughout your paper.

Spacing, margins, and indents. Double-space the entire paper, including your works-cited list. Set one-inch margins at the top, bottom, and sides of your text; do not justify your text. The first line of each paragraph should be indented one-half inch from the left margin.

Long quotations. When quoting more than three lines of poetry, more than four lines of prose, or dialogue between two or more characters from a drama, set off the quotation from the rest of your text, indenting it one inch (or ten spaces) from the left margin. Do not use quotation marks, and put any parenthetical documentation *after* the final punctuation.

> In *Eastward to Tartary*, Kaplan captures ancient and contemporary
> Antioch for us:
>> At the height of its glory in the Roman-Byzantine age, when
>> it had an amphitheater, public baths, aqueducts, and sewage
>> pipes, half a million people lived in Antioch. Today the population
>> is only 125,000. With sour relations between Turkey and
>> Syria, and unstable politics throughout the Middle East,
>> Antioch is now a backwater—seedy and tumbledown, with
>> relatively few tourists. I found it altogether charming. (123)

> In the first stanza of Arnold's "Dover Beach," the exclamations make
> clear that the speaker is addressing a companion who is also present in
> the scene:
>> Come to the window, sweet is the night air!
>> Only, from the long line of spray
>> Where the sea meets the moon-blanched land,
>> Listen! You hear the grating roar
>> Of pebbles which the waves draw back, and fling. (6–10)

Illustrations. Insert illustrations in your paper close to the text that discusses them. For tables, provide a number (*Table 1*) and a title on separate lines above the table. Below the table, include a caption and provide information about the source. For figures (graphs, charts, photos, and so on), provide a figure number (*Fig. 1*), caption, and source information below the figure. If you give only brief information about the source (such as a parenthetical citation), or if the source is cited elsewhere in your text, include the source in your list of works cited. Be sure to discuss any illustrations, and make it clear how they relate to the rest of your text.

List of Works Cited. Start your list on a new page, following any notes. Center the title and double-space the entire list. Each entry should begin at the left margin, and subsequent lines should be indented one-half inch (or five spaces). Alphabetize the list by authors' last names (or by editors' or translators' names, if appropriate). Alphabetize works that have no identifiable author or editor by title, disregarding *A*, *An*, and *The*. If you cite more than one work by a single author, list them all alphabetically by title, and use three hyphens in place of the author's name after the first entry.

SAMPLE RESEARCH ESSAY

Walter Przybylowski wrote the following analysis for a first-year writing course. It is formatted according to the guidelines of the *MLA Handbook for Writers of Research Papers*, 7th edition (2009).

1"

½"

Walter Przybylowski

Professor Matin

English 102, Section 3

4 May 2009

Put your last name
and the page num-
ber in the upper-right
corner of each page.

Center the title.

Holding Up the Hollywood Stagecoach:

The European Take on the Western

Double-space
throughout.

    The Western film has long been considered by film scholars and
enthusiasts to be a distinctly American genre. Not only its subject
matter but its characteristic themes originate in America's own violent
and exciting past. For many years, Hollywood sold images of hard men
fighting savages on the plains to the worldwide public; by ignoring
the more complicated aspects of "how the West was won" and the true
nature of relations between Native Americans and whites, filmmakers
were able to reap great financial and professional rewards. In particular,
the huge success of John Ford's 1939 film *Stagecoach* brought about
countless imitations that led over the next few decades to American
Westerns playing in a sort of loop, which reinforced the same ideas and
myths in film after film.

1"

1"

    After the success of German-made Westerns in the 1950s, though,
a new take on Westerns was ushered in by other European countries.
Leading the Euro-Western charge, so to speak, were the Italians, whose
cynical, often politically pointed Westerns left a permanent impact
on an American-based genre. Europeans, particularly the Italians,
challenged the dominant conventions of the American Western by
complicating the morality of the characters, blurring the lines between

1"

Przybylowski   2

good and evil, and also by complicating the traditional narrative, visual, and aural structures of Westerns. In this way, the genre motifs that *Stagecoach* initiated are explored in the European Westerns of the 1950s, 1960s, and early 1970s, yet with a striking difference in style. Specifically, Sergio Leone's 1968 film *Once upon a Time in the West* broke many of the rules set by the Hollywood Western and in the process created a new visual language for the Western. Deconstructing key scenes from this film reveals the demythologization at work in many of the Euro-Westerns, which led to a genre enriched by its presentation of a more complicated American West.

  Stagecoach is a perfect example of almost all the visual, sound, and plot motifs that would populate "classic" Hollywood Westerns for the next few decades. The story concerns a group of people, confined for most of the movie inside a stagecoach, who are attempting to cross a stretch of land made dangerous by Apache Indians on the warpath. Little effort is made to develop the characters of the Indians, who appear mainly as a narrative device, adversaries that the heroes must overcome in order to maintain their peaceful existence. This plot, with minor changes, could be used as a general description for countless Westerns. In his book *Crowded Prairie: American National Identity in the Hollywood Western*, Michael Coyne explains the significance of *Stagecoach* to the Western genre and its influence in solidifying the genre's archetypes:

> [I]t was *Stagecoach* which . . . redefined the contours of the myth. The good outlaw, the whore with a heart of gold, the Madonna/Magdalene dichotomy between opposing female

Indent paragraphs 5 spaces or ½".

Quotations of more than 4 lines are set off from the main text and indented 10 spaces or 1".

leads, the drunken philosopher, the last-minute cavalry rescue, the lonely walk down Main Street--all became stereotypes from *Stagecoach*'s archetypes. *Stagecoach* quickly became the model against which other "A" Westerns would be measured. (18-19)

In a set-off quotation, the parenthetical source citation follows the closing punctuation.

Coyne is not exaggerating when he calls it "the model": in fact, all of these stereotypes became a sort of checklist of things that audiences expected to see. The reliance on a preconceived way to sell Western films to the public--where you could always tell the good characters from the bad and knew before the film ended how each character would end up-- led to certain genre expectations that the directors of the Euro-Westerns would later knowingly reconfigure. As the influential critic Pauline Kael wrote in her 1965 book *Kiss Kiss Bang Bang*, "The original *Stagecoach* had a mixture of reverie and reverence about the American past that made the picture seem almost folk art; we wanted to believe in it even if we didn't" (52).

Verb in signal phrase is past tense because date of source is mentioned.

Parenthetical reference following a quotation within the main text goes before the closing punctuation of the sentence.

There seemed to be a need not just in Americans but in moviegoers around the world to believe that there was (or had been) a great untamed land out there just waiting to be cultivated. More important, as Kael pointed out, Americans wanted to believe that the building of America was a wholly righteous endeavor wherein the land was free for the taking--the very myth that Europeans later debunked through parody and subversive filmmaking techniques. According to Theresa Harlan, author of works on Native American art, the myth was based in the need of early white settlers to make their elimination of American Indians more palatable in light of the settlers' professed Christian beliefs. In her article "Adjusting the Focus for an Indigenous Presence," Harlan writes that

> Eurocentric frontier ideology and the representations of
> indigenous people it produced were used to convince many
> American settlers that indigenous people were incapable
> of discerning the difference between a presumed civilized
> existence and their own "primitive" state. (6)

Although this myth had its genesis long before the advent of motion pictures, the Hollywood Western drew inspiration from it and continued to legitimize and reinforce its message. *Stagecoach*, with its high level of technical skill and artistry, redefined the contours of the myth, and a close look at the elements that made the film the "classic" model of the Western is imperative in order to truly understand its influence.

The musical themes that underscore the actions of the characters are especially powerful in this regard and can be as powerful as the characters' visual representation on screen. In *Stagecoach*, an Apache does not appear until more than halfway through the movie, but whenever one is mentioned, the soundtrack fills with sinister and foreboding drumbeats. The first appearance of Indians is a scene without dialogue, in which the camera pans between the stagecoach crossing through the land and Apaches watching from afar. The music that accompanies this scene is particularly telling, since as the camera pans between stagecoach and Apaches, the music shifts in tone dramatically from a pleasant melody to a score filled with dread. When the heroes shoot and kill the Apaches, then, the viewer has already been subjected to specific film techniques to give the stagecoach riders moral certitude in their annihilation of the alien menace. To emphasize this point, the music swells victoriously every time an Apache is shown falling from a horse. This kind of score is powerful stuff to accompany an image and does its best to tell the viewers how they should react. When Europeans start to make Westerns, the line of moral certitude will become less distinct.

In her essay "Of Mother Nature and Marlboro Men: An Inquiry into the Cultural Meanings of Landscape Photography," Deborah Bright argues that landscape photography has reinforced certain formulaic myths about landscape, and the same can be said of the Hollywood Western during the 1940s and 1950s. For example, in *Stagecoach*, when the stagecoach finally sets out for its journey through Apache territory, a fence is juxtaposed against the vast wide-open country in the foreground. The meaning is clear--the stagecoach is leaving civilized society to venture into the wilds of the West, and music swells as the coach crosses into that vast landscape (fig. 1). Ford uses landscape in this way to engender in the audience the desired response of longing for a time gone past, where there was land free for the taking and plenty to go around. Yet Bright suggests that "[i]f we are to redeem landscape photography from its narrow self-reflexive project, why not openly question the assumptions about nature and culture that it has traditionally served and use our practice instead to criticize them?" (141).

Figure number calls readers' attention to illustration.

Brackets show that the writer has changed a capital letter to lowercase to make the quotation fit smoothly into his own sentence.

Fig 1. In *Stagecoach*, swelling music signals the coach's passage through the Western landscape. Photograph from *Internet Movie Database*, www.imdb.com.

This is exactly what Europeans, and Italians in particular, seem to have done with the Western. When Europeans started to make their own Westerns, they took advantage of their outsider status in relation to an American genre by openly questioning the myths that have been established by *Stagecoach* and its cinematic brethren.

Sergio Leone's *Once upon a Time in the West* is a superior example of a European artist's take on the art form of the American Western. The title alone signals the element of storytelling: in a sublime stroke of titling, Leone makes the connection between Western films and fairy tales and announces that the genre myths that *Stagecoach* presented for audiences to revel in will now be questioned. In his book *Spaghetti Westerns*, Christopher Frayling observes that "*Once Upon a Time* is concerned with the 'language' and 'syntax' of the Western . . . an unmasking or 'display' of the terminology of the genre" (213). The "plot" of the film is flimsy, driven by the efforts of a mysterious character played by Charles Bronson to avenge himself against Henry Fonda's character, a lowdown gunfighter trying to become a legitimate businessman. Claudia Cardinale plays a prostitute who is trying to put her past behind her. All of these classic types from countless American Westerns are integrated into the "Iron Horse" plotline, wherein the coming of the railroad signifies great changes in the West. The similarities to American Westerns, on paper at least, seem to be so great as to make *Once upon a Time* almost a copy of what had long been done in Hollywood, but a closer look at European Westerns and at this film in particular shows that Leone is consciously sending up the stereotypes. After all, he needs to work within the genre's language if he is to adequately challenge it.

The opening scene of *Once upon a Time* runs roughly ten minutes and provides an introduction to many of the aesthetic and ideological changes made by the European Western to the American model. The viewer quickly notices how little dialogue is spoken during the whole ten minutes, since the requirements of post-synchronization (the rerecording of the movie's dialogue after filming in order to produce a clearer soundtrack) and country-specific dubbing into multiple languages resulted in a reliance on strong visual storytelling. Financial reasons made English the default language for most Euro-Westerns since it produced the largest market and, consequently, the greatest monetary rewards. Even cast members who could not speak it would sometimes mouth the words in English. However, the use of post-synchronization has an unsettling effect on any viewer, even an English-speaking one, who is used to the polished soundtracks of a Hollywood film. When viewers experience a post-synchronized film, the result is a distancing from the material; certain characters match the words coming out of their mouths better than others, so the movie takes on a surreal edge. This visual touch perfectly complements Leone's goal--to divorce the reality of the West from the myths encouraged by American Westerns.

During the opening of *Once upon a Time in the West*, the viewer is given a kind of audio and visual tour of Euro-Western aesthetics. Leone introduces three gunmen in typical Italian Western style, with the first presented by a cut to a dusty boot heel from which the camera slowly pans up until it reaches the top of the character's cowboy hat. During this pan, the gunman's gear and its authenticity--a major aspect of the Italian Western--can be taken in by the audience. A broader examination of the genre would show that many Euro-Westerns use this tactic of hyperrealistic attention to costuming and weaponry, which Ignacio Ramonet argues is intended to distract the viewer from the unreality of the landscape:

Extreme realism of bodies (hairy, greasy, foul-smelling), clothes or objects (including mania for weapons) in Italian films is above all intended to compensate for the complete fraud of the space and origins. The green pastures, farms and cattle of American Westerns are replaced by large, deserted canyons. (32)

   In the opening scene, the other two gunfighters are introduced by a camera panning across the room, allowing characters to materialize seemingly out of nowhere. Roger Ebert notes that Leone

established a rule that he follows throughout . . . that the ability to see is limited by the sides of the frame. At important moments in the film, what the camera cannot see, the characters cannot see, and that gives Leone the freedom to surprise us with entrances that cannot be explained by the practical geography of his shots.

No page number given for online source.

It is these aesthetic touches created to compensate for a fraudulent landscape that ushered in a new visual language for the Western. The opening of *Once upon a Time in the West* undercuts any preconceived notion of how a Western should be filmed, and this is exactly Leone's intention: "The director had obviously enjoyed dilating the audience's sense of time, exploiting, in his ostentatious way, the rhetoric of the Western, and dwelling on the tiniest details to fulfill his intention" (Frayling 197). By using jarring edits with amplified sounds, Leone informs the audience not only that he has seen all the popular Hollywood Westerns, but that he is purposely not going to give them that kind of movie. The opening ten-minute scene would be considered

When no signal phrase is used to introduce a quota-tion, the author's name is included in the parenthetical citation.

needlessly long in a typical Hollywood Western, but Leone is not making
a copy of a Hollywood Western, and the length of such scenes allows for
more meditation on the styling of the genre. In fact, it is this reliance on
the audience's previously established knowledge of Westerns that allows
Euro-Westerns to subvert the genre. Barry Langford, writing for *Film
History*, claims that

> *Once Upon a Time* strips bare the form's claims on historical
> verisimilitude and pushes its innately ritualized and stylized
> aspects to near-parodic extremes that evacuate the film of
> narrative credibility and psychological realism alike. (31)

Leone and other directors of Euro-Westerns are asking the public to open
their eyes, to not believe what is shown; they are attempting to take the
camera's power away by parodying its effect. When Leone has characters
magically appear in the frame, or amplifies the squeaking of a door hinge
on a soundtrack, he is ridiculing the basic laws that govern American
Westerns. The opening of *Once upon a Time* can be read as a sort of
primer for what is about to come for the rest of the film, and its power
leaves viewers more attuned to what they are watching.

Leone's casting also works to heighten the film's subversive effect.
Henry Fonda, the quintessential good guy in classic Hollywood Westerns
like *My Darling Clementine*, is cast as the ruthless Frank, a gunman
shown murdering a small child early in the film. In a 1966 article on
Italian Westerns in the *Saturday Evening Post*, Italian director Maurizio
Lucidi gave some insight into the European perspective that lay behind
such choices:

We're adding the Italian concept of realism to an old American

myth, and it's working. Look at Jesse James. In your country

he's a saint. Over here we play him as a gangster. That's what

he was. Europeans today are too sophisticated to believe in

the honest gunman movie anymore. They want the truth and

that's what we're giving them. (qtd. in Fox 55)

A citation of a source
the writer found
quoted in another
source.

Leone knew exactly what he was doing, and his casting of Fonda went a
long way toward confusing the audience's sympathies and complicating
the simple good guy versus bad guy model of Hollywood films. For this
reason, Fonda's entrance in the film is worth noting. The scene begins
with a close-up of a shotgun barrel, which quickly explodes in a series
of (gun)shots that establish a scene of a father and son out hunting near
their homestead. Here, Leone starts to move the camera more, with pans
from father to son and a crane shot of their house as they return home
to a picnic table with an abundance of food: the family is apparently
about to celebrate something. Throughout this scene, crickets chirp
on the soundtrack--until Leone abruptly cuts them off, the sudden
silence quickly followed by close-ups of the uneasy faces of three family
members. Leone is teasing the audience: he puts the crickets back on
the soundtrack until out of nowhere we hear a gunshot. Instead of then
focusing on the source or the target of the gunshot, the camera pans
off to the sky, and for a moment the viewer thinks the shot is from a
hunter. We next see a close-up of the father's face as he looks off into
the distance, then is rattled when he sees his daughter grasping the
air, obviously shot. As he runs toward her, tracked by the camera in a

startling way, he is quickly shot down himself.

The family has been attacked seemingly out of nowhere, with only a young boy still alive. During the massacre, there is no musical score, just the abstract brutality of the slayings. Then Leone gives us a long camera shot of men appearing out of dust-blown winds, from nearby brush. It is obvious to the viewer that these men are the killers, but there is no clear sight of their faces: Leone uses long camera shots of their backs and an overhead shot as they converge on the young boy. This is the moment when Leone introduces Henry Fonda; he starts with the camera on the back of Fonda's head and then does a slow track around until his face is visible. At this point, audience members around the world would still have a hard time believing Fonda was a killer of these innocent people. Through crosscutting between the young boy's confused face and Fonda's smiling eyes, Leone builds a doubt in the audience--maybe he will not kill the boy. Then the crosscutting is interrupted with a close-up of Fonda's large Colt coming out of its holster, and Ennio Morricone's score, full of sadness, becomes audible. The audience's fears are realized: Fonda is indeed the killer. This scene is a clear parody of Hollywood casting stereotypes, and Leone toys with audience expectations by turning upside down the myth of the noble outlaw as portrayed by John Wayne in *Stagecoach*.

During the late 1960s and the early 1970s, Europeans were at odds with many of the foreign policies of the United States, a hostility expressed in Ramonet's characterization of this period as one "when American imperialism in Latin America and Southeast Asia was

showing itself to be particularly brutal" (33). Morton, the railroad baron
who is Frank's unscrupulous employer in *Once upon a Time in the
West*, can easily be read as a critique of the sometimes misguided ways
Americans went about bringing their way of life to other countries.
Morton represents the bringer of civilization, usually a good thing in the
classic Western genre, where civilization meant doctors, schools, homes
for everyone. But the Europeans question how this civilization was built.
Leone, in a telling quotation, gives his perspective: "I see the history of
the West as really the reign of violence by violence" (qtd. in Frayling 134).

Leone's critique of the "civilizing" of the American West becomes
apparent in his depiction of Morton's demise at the hands of a bandit
gang that Frank has tried to frame for the murder of the family. As Frank
returns to Morton's train, wheezing and gasping resonates from the
track. In a long, one-take shot, the camera follows Frank as he looks for
Morton, and in the process dead and dying bodies in various poses are
revealed strewn about the ground. Many people have died for the dream
of "civilizing" the West, and there is nothing noble in their deaths. Frank
finally finds Morton crawling along outside the train in mud, striving to
reach a puddle; as he dies, the lapping waves of the Pacific Ocean--the goal
toward which the civilizing of the West always pushes--can be heard.

Instead of the civilizing myth and its representations, the concern
of *Once upon a Time*--and the Euro-Western in general--is to give voice
to the perspective of the marginal characters: the Native Americans,
Mexicans, and Chinese who rarely rated a position of significance in a
Hollywood Western. In *Once upon a Time*, Bronson's character Harmonica

Przybylowski   14

pushes the plot forward with his need to avenge. Harmonica can be
seen as either Mexican or Native American, though it matters little
since his character stands in for all the racial stereotypes that populated
the American Western genre. When he and Frank meet in the movie's
climactic duel, Frank is clearly perplexed about why this man wants
to fight him, but his ego makes it impossible for him to refuse (fig. 2).

Fig. 2. The climactic duel in *Once upon a Time in the West* between
Frank (Henry Fonda, foreground) and Harmonica (Charles Bronson,
background) challenges the casting and costuming stereotypes of the
Hollywood Western. Photograph from *Internet Movie Database*,
www.imdb.com.

They meet in an abandoned yard, with one character in the extreme
foreground and the other in the extreme background. The difference
between the two is thus presented from both physical and ideological
standpoints: Frank guns down settlers to make way for the railroad
(and its owner), whereas Harmonica helps people to fend for themselves.
Morricone's score dominates the soundtrack during this final scene, with
a harmonica blaring away throughout. The costuming of Frank in black
and Harmonica in white is an ironic throwback to classic Hollywood
costuming and one that suggests Harmonica is prevailing over the racial
stereotypes of American Westerns. Leone milks the scene for all it's
worth, with the camera circling Harmonica as Frank looks for a perfect
point to start the duel. Harmonica never moves, his face steadily framed
in a close-up. Meanwhile, Frank is shown in mostly long shots; his body
language shows that he is uncertain about the outcome of the duel,
while Harmonica knows the ending.

 As the two seem about to draw, the camera pushes into
Harmonica's eyes, and there is a flashback to a younger Frank walking
toward the camera, putting a harmonica into the mouth of a boy (the
young Harmonica), and forcing him to participate in Frank's hanging of
the boy's older brother. This brutal scene, in which Frank unknowingly
seals his own destiny, is set in actual American locations and is taken
directly from John Ford Westerns; Leone is literally bringing home the
violence dealt to minorities in America's past. As soon as the brother is
hanged, the scene returns to the present, and Frank is shot through the
heart. As he lies dying, we see a look of utter disbelief on his face as he

asks Harmonica, "Who are you?" At this moment, a harmonica is shoved into his mouth. Only then does recognition play over Frank's face; as he falls to the ground, his face in close-up is a grotesque death-mask not unlike the massacred victims of Morton's train. The idea of past misdeeds coming back to haunt characters in the present is a clear attempt to challenge the idea that the settlers had a moral right to conquer and destroy indigenous people in order to "win" the West.

The tremendous success of *Stagecoach* was both a blessing and curse for the Western genre. Without it, the genre would surely never have gained the success it did, but this success came with ideological and creative limitations. Both the popularity and the limitations of the American Western may have inspired European directors to attempt something new with the genre, and unlike American filmmakers, they could look more objectively at our history and our myths. Leone's demythologization of the American Western has proved a valuable addition to the Western genre. The effect of the Euro-Western can be seen in American cinema as early as *The Wild Bunch* in 1969--and as recently as the attention in *Brokeback Mountain* to types of Western characters usually marginalized. In this way, Italian Westerns forced a new level of viewing of the Western tradition that made it impossible to ever return to the previous Hollywood model.

List of works cited
begins on a new
page. Heading is
centered.

Each entry begins
at the left margin,
with subsequent lines
indented 5 spaces
or ½".

List is alphabetized
by authors' last
names or by title
for works with no
author.

Works Cited

Bright, Deborah. "Of Mother Nature and Marlboro Men: An Inquiry into
     the Cultural Meanings of Landscape Photography." *The Contest
     of Meaning: Critical Histories of Photography*. Ed. Richard Bolton.
     Cambridge: MIT P, 1993. 125-143. Print.

Coyne, Michael. *The Crowded Prairie: American National Identity in the
     Hollywood Western*. London: Tauris, 1997. Print.

Ebert, Roger. "The Good, the Bad and the Ugly." *Chicago Sun-Times*. Sun-
     Times Media, 3 Aug. 2003. Web. 25 Jan. 2012.

Fox, William. "Wild Westerns Italian Style." *Saturday Evening Post*. Nov.
     1966: 50-55. Print.

Frayling, Christopher. *Spaghetti Westerns: Cowboys and Europeans from
     Karl May to Sergio Leone*. New York: St. Martin's, 1981. Print.

Harlan, Theresa. "Adjusting the Focus for an Indigenous Presence."
     Overexposed: Essays on Contemporary Photography. Ed. Carol
     Squiers. New York: New P, 1999. Print.

Kael, Pauline. *Kiss Kiss Bang Bang*. New York: Bantam, 1965. Print.

Langford, Barry. "Revisiting the 'Revisionist' Western." *Film & History*
     33.2 (2003): 26-35. *Project Muse*. Web. 2 Feb. 2012.

Once upon a Time in the West. Dir. Sergio Leone. Perf. Henry Fonda,
     Claudia Cardinale, and Charles Bronson. Paramount, 1968. Film.

Ramonet, Ignacio. "Italian Westerns as Political Parables." *Cineaste* 15.1
     (1986): 30-35. Print.

Stagecoach. Dir. John Ford. Perf. John Wayne. United Artists, 1939. Film.

TWENTY-FIVE

APA Style

 **MERICAN PSYCHOLOGICAL ASSOCIATION** (APA) style calls for (1) brief documentation in parentheses near each in-text citation and (2) complete documentation in a list of references at the end of your text. The models in this chapter draw on the *Publication Manual of the American Psychological Association*, 6th edition (2010). Additional information is available at www.apastyle.org.

A DIRECTORY TO APA STYLE

In-Text Documentation   466

Throughout this chapter, you'll find models and examples that are color-coded to help you see how writers include source information in their texts and reference lists: tan for author or editor, yellow for title, gray for publication information: place of publication, publisher, date of publication, page number(s), and so on.

IN-TEXT DOCUMENTATION

Brief documentation in your text makes clear to your reader precisely what you took from a source and, in the case of a quotation, precisely where (usually, on which page) in the source you found the text you are quoting.

PARAPHRASES and **SUMMARIES** are more common than **QUOTATIONS** in APA-style projects. See Chapter 22 for more on all three kinds of citation. As you cite each source, you will need to decide whether to name the author in a signal phrase—"as McCullough (2001) wrote"—or in parentheses—"(McCullough, 2001)." Note that APA requires you to use the past tense or present perfect tense for verbs in **SIGNAL PHRASES:** "Moss (2003) argued," "Moss (2003) has argued."

1. Author named in a signal phrase

If you are quoting, you must give the page number(s). You are not required to give the page number(s) with a paraphrase or a summary, but APA encourages you to do so, especially if you are citing a long or complex work; most of the models in this chapter do include page numbers.

Author quoted

Put the date in parentheses right after the author's name; put the page in parentheses as close to the quotation as possible.

> McCullough (2001) described John Adams as having "the hands of a man accustomed to pruning his own trees, cutting his own hay, and splitting his own firewood" (p. 18).

Notice that in this example, the parenthetical reference with the page number comes *after* the closing quotation marks but *before* the period at the end of the sentence.

Author paraphrased

Put the date in parentheses right after the author's name; follow the date with the page.

> John Adams's hands were those of a laborer, according to McCullough (2001, p. 18).

2. Author named in parentheses

If you do not mention an author in a signal phrase, put his or her name, a comma, and the year of publication in parentheses as close as possible to the quotation, paraphrase, or summary.

Author quoted

Give the author, date, and page in one parenthesis, or split the information between two parentheses.

> One biographer (McCullough, 2001) has said John Adams had "the
> hands of a man accustomed to pruning his own trees, cutting his own
> hay, and splitting his own firewood" (p. 18).

Author paraphrased or summarized

Give the author, date, and page in one parenthesis toward the beginning or the end of the paraphrase.

> John Adams's hands were those of a laborer (McCullough, 2001, p. 18).

3. Authors with the same last name

If your reference list includes more than one person with the same last name, include initials in all documentation to distinguish the authors from one another.

> Eclecticism is common in modern criticism (J. M. Smith, 1992, p. vii).

4. Two authors

Always mention both authors. Use *and* in a signal phrase, but use an ampersand (&) in parentheses.

> Carlson and Ventura (1990, p. v) wanted to introduce Julio Cortázar,
> Marjorie Agosín, and other Latin American writers to an audience of
> English-speaking adolescents.

> According to the Peter Principle, "In a hierarchy, every employee tends
> to rise to his level of incompetence" (Peter & Hull, 1969, p. 26).

5. Three or more authors

In the first reference to a work by three to five persons, name all contributors. In subsequent references, name the first author followed by *et al.*, Latin for "and others." Whenever you refer to a work by six or more contributors, name only the first author, followed by *et al.* Use *and* in a signal phrase, but use an ampersand (&) in parentheses.

> Faigley, George, Palchik, and Selfe (2004, p. xii) have argued that where
> there used to be a concept called *literacy*, today's multitude of new
> kinds of texts has given us *literacies*.

> Peilen et al. (1990, p. 75) supported their claims about corporate
> corruption with startling anecdotal evidence.

6. Organization or government as author

If an organization name is recognizable by its abbreviation, give the full name and the abbreviation the first time you cite the source. In subsequent citations, use only the abbreviation. If the organization does not have a familiar abbreviation, always use its full name.

> **First citation**
>
> (American Psychological Association [APA], 2008)

> **Subsequent citations**
>
> (APA, 2008)

7. Author unknown

Use the complete title if it is short; if it is long, use the first few words of the title under which the work appears in the reference list.

> *Webster's New Biographical Dictionary* (1988) identifies William James as
> "American psychologist and philosopher" (p. 520).

> A powerful editorial asserted that healthy liver donor Mike Hurewitz
> died because of "frightening" faulty postoperative care ("Every Patient's
> Nightmare," 2007).

author   title   publication

8. Two or more works cited together

If you cite multiple works in the same parenthesis, place them in the order that they appear in your reference list, separated by semicolons.

> Many researchers have argued that what counts as "literacy" is not necessarily learned at school (Heath, 1983; Moss, 2003).

9. Two or more works by one author in the same year

If your list of references includes more than one work by the same author published in the same year, order them alphabetically by title, adding lowercase letters ("a," "b," and so on) to the year.

> Kaplan (2000a) described orderly shantytowns in Turkey that did not resemble the other slums he visited.

10. Source quoted in another source

When you cite a source that was quoted in another source, let the reader know that you used a secondary source by adding the words *as cited in*.

> During the meeting with the psychologist, the patient stated repeatedly that he "didn't want to be too paranoid" (as cited in Oberfield & Yasik, 2004, p. 294).

11. Work without page numbers

Instead of page numbers, some electronic works have paragraph numbers, which you should include (preceded by the abbreviation *para.)* if you are referring to a specific part of such a source. In sources with neither page nor paragraph numbers, refer readers to a particular part of the source if possible, perhaps indicating a heading and the paragraph under the heading.

> Russell's dismissals from Trinity College at Cambridge and from City College in New York City have been seen as examples of the controversy that marked his life (Irvine, 2006, para. 2).

12. An entire work

You do not need to give a page number if you are directing readers' attention to an entire work.

> Kaplan (2000) considered Turkey and Central Asia explosive.

When you are citing an entire website, give the URL in the text. You do not need to include the website in your reference list. To cite part of a website, see no. 20 on p. 481.

> Beyond providing diagnostic information, the website for the Alzheimer's Association includes a variety of resources for family and community support of patients suffering from Alzheimer's (http://www.alz.org).

13. Personal communication

Cite email, telephone conversations, interviews, personal letters, messages from nonarchived electronic discussion sources, and other personal texts as *personal communication,* along with the person's initial(s), last name, and the date. You do not need to include such personal communications in your reference list.

> L. Strauss (personal communication, December 6, 2006) told about visiting Yogi Berra when they both lived in Montclair, New Jersey.

NOTES

You may need to use *content notes* to give an explanation or information that doesn't fit into your text. To signal a content note, place a superscript numeral at the appropriate point in your text. Put the notes on a separate page with the heading *Notes*, after your text but before the reference list. If you have multiple notes, number them consecutively throughout your text. Here is an example from *In Search of Solutions: A New Direction in Psychotherapy* (2003).

Text with superscript

An important part of working with teams and one way mirrors is taking the consultation break, as at Milan, BFTC, and MRI.[1]

Content note

[1] It is crucial to note here that, while working within a team is fun, stimulating, and revitalizing, it is not necessary for successful outcomes. Solution-oriented therapy works equally well when working solo.

REFERENCE LIST

A reference list provides full bibliographic information for every source cited in your text with the exception of entire websites and personal communications. See p. 491 for guidelines on preparing such a list; for a sample reference list, see p. 508.

Books

For most books, you'll need to provide the author, the publication date, the title and any subtitle, and the place of publication and publisher.

Important Details for Citing Books

- **AUTHORS:** Use the author's last name but replace the first and middle names with initials (D. Kinder for Donald Kinder).
- **DATES:** If more than one year is given, use the most recent one.
- **TITLES:** Capitalize only the first word and proper nouns and proper adjectives in titles and subtitles.
- **PUBLICATION PLACE:** Give city followed by state (abbreviated) or country, if outside the United States (for example, Boston, MA; London, England; Toronto, Ontario, Canada). If more than one city is given, use the first. Do not include the state or country if the publisher is a university whose name includes that information.

- **PUBLISHER:** Use a shortened form of the publisher's name (Little, Brown for Little, Brown and Company), but retain *Association, Books,* and *Press* (American Psychological Association, Princeton University Press).

1. One author

Author's Last Name, Initials. (Year of publication). *Title.* Publication City, State or Country: Publisher.

Lewis, M. (2003). *Moneyball: The art of winning an unfair game.* New York, NY: Norton.

2. Two or more works by the same author

If the works were published in different years, list them chronologically.

Lewis, B. (1995). *The Middle East: A brief history of the last 2,000 years.* New York, NY: Scribner.
Lewis, B. (2003). *The crisis of Islam: Holy war and unholy terror.* New York, NY: Modern Library.

If the works were published in the same year, list them alphabetically by title, adding "a," "b," and so on to the year.

Kaplan, R. D. (2000a). *The coming anarchy: Shattering the dreams of the post cold war.* New York, NY: Random House.
Kaplan, R. D. (2000b). *Eastward to Tartary: Travels in the Balkans, the Middle East, and the Caucasus.* New York, NY: Random House.

3. Two or more authors

For two to seven authors, use this format.

First Author's Last Name, Initials, Next Author's Last Name, Initials, & Final Author's Last Name, Initials. (Year of publication). *Title.* Publication City, State or Country: Publisher.

Levitt, S. D., & Dubner, S. J. (2005). *Freakonomics: A rogue economist explores the hidden side of everything.* New York, NY: Morrow.

For a work by eight or more authors, name just the first six authors, followed by three ellipses, and end with the final author (see no. 21 for an example from a magazine article).

4. Organization or government as author

Sometimes a corporation or government organization is both author and publisher. If so, use the word *Author* as the publisher.

Organization Name or Government Agency. (Year of publication). *Title.* Publication City, State or Country: Publisher.

Catholic News Service. (2002). *Stylebook on religion 2000: A reference guide and usage manual.* Washington, DC: Author.

5. Author and editor

Author's Last Name, Initials. (Year of edited edition). *Title.* (Editor's Initials Last Name, Ed.). Publication City, State or Country: Publisher. (Original work[s] published year[s])

Dick, P. F. (2008). *Five novels of the 1960s and 70s.* (J. Lethem, Ed.). New York, NY: Library of America. (Original works published 1964–1977)

6. Edited collection

First Editor's Last Name, Initials, Next Editor's Last Name, Initials, & Final Editor's Last Name, Initials. (Eds.). (Year of edited edition). *Title.* Publication City, State or Country: Publisher.

Raviv, A., Oppenheimer, L., & Bar-Tal, D. (Eds.). (1999). *How children understand war and peace: A call for international peace education.* San Francisco, CA: Jossey-Bass.

Documentation Map (APA)/Book

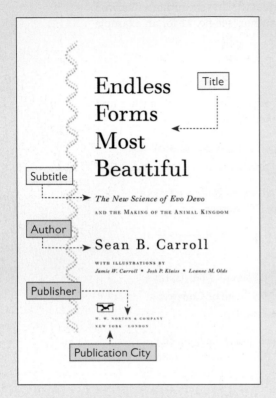

Carroll, S. B. (2005). *Endless forms most beautiful: The new science of evo devo and the making of the animal kingdom.* New York, NY: Norton.

7. Work in an edited collection

Author's Last Name, Initials. (Year of publication). Title of article or
    chapter. In Initials Last Name (Ed.), *Title* (pp. pages). Publication
    City, State or Country: Publisher.

Harris, I. M. (1999). Types of peace education. In A. Raviv, L.
    Oppenheimer, & D. Bar-Tal (Eds.), *How children understand war
    and peace: A call for international peace education* (pp. 46–70). San
    Francisco, CA: Jossey-Bass.

8. Unknown author

Title. (Year of publication). Publication City, State or Country: Publisher.

Webster's new biographical dictionary. (1988). Springfield, MA: Merriam-
    Webster.

If the title page of a work lists the author as *Anonymous,* treat the reference-
list entry as if the author's name were Anonymous, and alphabetize it accordingly.

9. Edition other than the first

Author's Last Name, Initials. (Year). *Title* (name or number ed.).
    Publication City, State or Country: Publisher.

Burch, D. (2008). *Emergency navigation: Find your position and shape your
    course at sea even if your instruments fail* (2nd ed.). Camden, ME:
    International Marine/McGraw-Hill.

10. Translation

Author's Last Name, Initials. (Year of publication). *Title* (Translator's
    Initials Last Name, Trans.). Publication City, State or Country:
    Publisher. (Original work published Year)

Hugo, V. (2008). *Les misérables* (J. Rose, Trans.). New York, NY: Modern
    Library. (Original work published 1862)

11. Multivolume work

Author's Last Name, Initials. (Year). *Title* (Vols. numbers). Publication
    City, State or Country: Publisher.

Nastali, D. P. & Boardman, P. C. (2004). *The Arthurian annals: The
    tradition in English from 1250 to 2000* (Vols. 1–2). New York, NY:
    Oxford University Press USA.

One volume of a multivolume work

Author's Last Name, Initials. (Year). *Title of whole work* (Vol. number).
    Publication City, State or Country: Publisher.

Spiegelman, A. (1986). *Maus* (Vol. 1). New York, NY: Random House.

12. Article in a reference book

Unsigned

Title of entry. (Year). In *Title of reference book* (Name or number ed., Vol.
    number, pp. pages). Publication City, State or Country: Publisher.

Macrophage. (2003). In *Merriam-Webster's collegiate dictionary* (10th ed.,
    p. 698). Springfield, MA: Merriam-Webster.

Signed

Author's Last Name, Initials. (Year). Title of entry. In *Title of reference
    book* (Vol. number, pp. pages). Publication City, State or Country:
    Publisher.

Wasserman, D. E. (2006). Human exposure to vibration. In *International
    encyclopedia of ergonomics and human factors* (Vol. 2, pp. 1800–
    1801). Boca Raton, FL: CRC.

Periodicals

For most articles, you'll need to provide information about the author; the
date; the article title and any subtitle; the periodical title; and any volume

author   title   publication

or issue number and inclusive page numbers. (APA also recommends including a DOI if one is available; for more on DOIs, see p. 481. For an example of a journal article that shows a DOI, see no. 21.)

Important Details for Citing Periodicals

- **AUTHORS:** List authors as you would for a book.
- **DATES:** For journals, give year only. For magazines and newspapers, give year followed by a comma and then month or month and day.
- **TITLES:** Capitalize article titles as you would for a book. Capitalize the first and last words and all principal words of periodical titles. Do not capitalize *a, an, the,* or any prepositions or coordinating conjunctions unless they begin the title of the periodical.
- **VOLUME AND ISSUE:** For journals and magazines, give volume or volume and issue, depending on the journal's pagination method. For newspapers, do not give volume or issue.
- **PAGES:** Use *p.* or *pp.* for a newspaper article but not for a journal or magazine article. If an article does not fall on consecutive pages, give all the page numbers (for example, 45, 75–77 for a journal or magazine; pp. C1, C3, C5–C7 for a newspaper).

13. Article in a journal paginated by volume

Author's Last Name, Initials. (Year). Title of article. *Title of Journal, volume,* pages.

Gremer, J. R., Sala, A., & Crone, E. E. (2010). Disappearing plants: Why they hide and how they return. *Ecology, 91,* 3407–3413.

14. Article in a journal paginated by issue

Author's Last Name, Initials. (Year). Title of article. *Title of Journal, volume*(issue), pages.

Weaver, C., McNally, C., & Moerman, S. (2001). To grammar or not to grammar: That is not the question! *Voices from the Middle, 8*(3), 17–33.

15. Article in a magazine

If a magazine is published weekly, include the day and the month. If there are a volume number and an issue number, include them after the magazine title.

> Author's Last Name, Initials. (Year, Month Day). *Title of article. Title of*
> *Magazine, volume(issue), page(s).*

> Gregory, S. (2008, June 30). Crash course: Why golf carts are more
> hazardous than they look. *Time, 171*(26), 53.

If a magazine is published monthly, include the month(s) only.

16. Article in a newspaper

If page numbers are consecutive, separate them with a dash. If not, separate them with a comma.

> Author's Last Name, Initials. (Year, Month Day). Title of article. *Title of*
> *Newspaper, p(p). page(s).*

> Schneider, G. (2005, March 13). Fashion sense on wheels. *The*
> *Washington Post, pp. F1, F6.*

17. Article by an unknown author

> Title of article. (Year, Month Day). *Title of Periodical, volume(issue), pages*
> *or p(p). page(s).*

> Hot property: From carriage house to family compound. (2004,
> December). *Berkshire Living, 1*(1), 99.

> Clues in salmonella outbreak. (2008, June 21). *New York Times*, p. A13.

18. Book review

> Reviewer's Last Name, Initials. (Date of publication). Title of review
> [Review of the book *Title of Work*, by Author's Initials Last Name].
> *Title of Periodical, volume(issue), page(s).*

Documentation Map (APA) / Magazine Article

Title of article

Author

Volume and Issue

Title of Magazine

Month, Day, and Year

Page

Cullen, L. T. (2008, March 24). Freshen up your drink: Reusing water
 bottles is good ecologically, but is it bad for your health? How to
 drink smart. *Time, 171*(12), 65.

Brandt, A. (2003, October). Animal planet [Review of the book
Intelligence of apes and other rational beings, by D. R. Rumb & D. A.
Washburn]. *National Geographic Adventure, 5*(10), 47.

If the review does not have a title, include the bracketed information about
the work being reviewed immediately after the date of publication.

19. Letter to the editor

Author's Last Name, Initials. (Date of publication). Title of letter [Letter
to the editor]. *Title of Periodical, volume*(issue), *or* p(p). page(s).

Hitchcock, G. (2008, August 3). Save our species [Letter to the editor].
San Francisco Chronicle, p. P-3.

Online Sources

Not every online source gives you all the data that APA would like to see in
a reference entry. Ideally, you will be able to list author's or editor's name;
date of first electronic publication or most recent revision; title of document;
information about print publication if any; and retrieval information: DOI
(Digital Object Identifier, a string of letters and numbers that identifies an
online document) or URL. In some cases, additional information about electronic publication may be required (title of site, retrieval date, name of sponsoring institution).

Important Details for Citing Online Sources

- **AUTHORS:** List authors as you would for a print book or periodical.
- **TITLES:** For websites and electronic documents, articles, or books, capitalize title and subtitles as you would for a book; capitalize periodical
titles as you would for a print periodical.
- **DATES:** After the author, give the year of the document's original publication on the Web or of its most recent revision. If neither of those years
is clear, use *n.d.* to mean "no date." For undated content or content that
may change (for example, a wiki entry), include the month, day, and
year that you retrieved the document. You don't need to include the retrieval date for content that's unlikely to change.

- **DOI OR URL:** Include the DOI instead of the URL in the reference whenever one is available. If no DOI is available, provide the URL of the home page or menu page. If you do not identify the sponsoring institution, you do not need a colon before the URL or DOI. When a URL won't fit on the line, break the URL before most punctuation, but do not break *http://*.

20. Work from a nonperiodical website

Author's Last Name, Initials. (Date of publication). Title of work. *Title of site*. DOI or Retrieved Month Day, Year (if necessary), from URL

Cruikshank, D. (2009, June 15). Unlocking the secrets and powers of the brain. *National Science Foundation*. Retrieved from http://www.nsf .gov/discoveries/disc_summ.jsp?cntn_id=114979&org=NSF

To cite an entire website, include the URL in parentheses in an in-text citation. Do not list the website in your list of references.

21. Article in an online periodical

When available, include the volume number and issue number as you would for a print source. If no DOI has been assigned, provide the URL of the home page or menu page of the journal or magazine, even for articles that you access through a database.

Article in an online journal

Author's Last Name, Initials. (Year). Title of article. *Title of Journal, volume*(issue), pages. DOI or Retrieved from URL

Corbett, C. (2007). Vehicle-related crime and the gender gap. *Psychology, Crime & Law, 13*, 245–263. doi:10.1080/10683160600822022

Article in an online magazine

Author's Last Name, Initials. (Year, Month Day). Title of article. *Title of Magazine, volume*(issue). DOI or Retrieved from URL

Documentation Map (APA) / Website

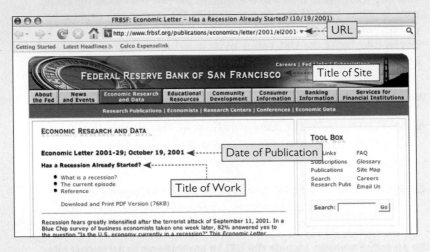

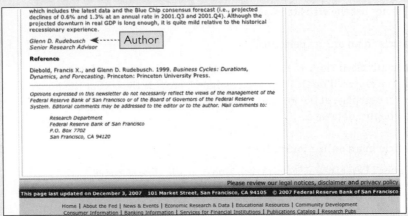

Rudebusch, G. D. (2001, October 19). Has a recession already started? *Federal Reserve Bank of San Francisco*. Retrieved April 3, 2008, from http://www.frbsf.org/publications/economics/letter/2001 /el2001-29.html

Documentation Map (APA) / Journal Article with DOI

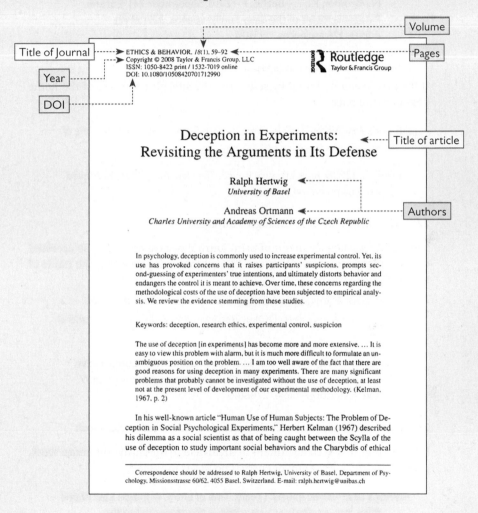

Volume

Title of Journal

Pages

Year

DOI

Title of article

Authors

ETHICS & BEHAVIOR, *18*(1), 59–92
Copyright © 2008 Taylor & Francis Group, LLC
ISSN: 1050-8422 print / 1532-7019 online
DOI: 10.1080/10508420701712990

Routledge
Taylor & Francis Group

Deception in Experiments: Revisiting the Arguments in Its Defense

Ralph Hertwig
University of Basel

Andreas Ortmann
Charles University and Academy of Sciences of the Czech Republic

In psychology, deception is commonly used to increase experimental control. Yet, its use has provoked concerns that it raises participants' suspicions, prompts second-guessing of experimenters' true intentions, and ultimately distorts behavior and endangers the control it is meant to achieve. Over time, these concerns regarding the methodological costs of the use of deception have been subjected to empirical analysis. We review the evidence stemming from these studies.

Keywords: deception, research ethics, experimental control, suspicion

The use of deception [in experiments] has become more and more extensive. ... It is easy to view this problem with alarm, but it is much more difficult to formulate an unambiguous position on the problem. ... I am too well aware of the fact that there are good reasons for using deception in many experiments. There are many significant problems that probably cannot be investigated without the use of deception, at least not at the present level of development of our experimental methodology. (Kelman, 1967, p. 2)

In his well-known article "Human Use of Human Subjects: The Problem of Deception in Social Psychological Experiments," Herbert Kelman (1967) described his dilemma as a social scientist as that of being caught between the Scylla of the use of deception to study important social behaviors and the Charybdis of ethical

Correspondence should be addressed to Ralph Hertwig, University of Basel, Department of Psychology, Missionsstrasse 60/62, 4055 Basel, Switzerland. E-mail: ralph.hertwig@unibas.ch

Hertwig, R., & Ortmann, A. (2008). Deception in experiments: Revisiting the arguments in its defense. *Ethics & Behavior*, *18*(1), 59–92. doi:10.1080/10508420701712990

Barreda, V. D., Palazzesi, L., Tellería, M. C., Katinas, L., Crisci, J. N., Bromer, K., . . . Bechis, F. (2010, September 24). Eocene Patagonia fossils of the daisy family. *Science, 329*(5949). doi:10.1126=sciences.1193108

Article in an online newspaper

If the article can be found by searching the site, give the URL of the home page or menu page.

Author's Last Name, Initials. (Year, Month Day). Title of article. *Title of Newspaper.* Retrieved from URL

Collins, G. (2008, June 21). Vice is nice. *The New York Times.* Retrieved from http://www.nytimes.com

22. Article available only through a database

Some sources, such as an out-of-print journal or rare book, can be accessed only through a database. When no DOI is provided, give either the name of the database or its URL.

Author's Last Name, Initials. (Year). Title of article. *Title of Journal, volume*(issue), pages. DOI or Retrieved from Name of database or URL

Simpson, M. (1972). Authoritarianism and education: A comparative approach. *Sociometry, 35*(2), 223–234. Retrieved from http://www.jstor.org/stable/2786619

23. Article or chapter in a web document or online reference work

For a chapter in a Web document or an article in an online reference work, give the URL of the chapter or entry if no DOI is provided.

Author's Last Name, Initials. (Year). Title of entry. In Initials Last Name (Ed.), *Title of reference work.* DOI or Retrieved from URL

Korfmacher, C. (2006). Personal identity. In J. Fieser & B. Dowden (Eds.), *Internet encyclopedia of philosophy.* Retrieved from http://www.iep.utm.edu/person-i/

author   title   publication

Documentation Map (APA) / Database Article with DOI

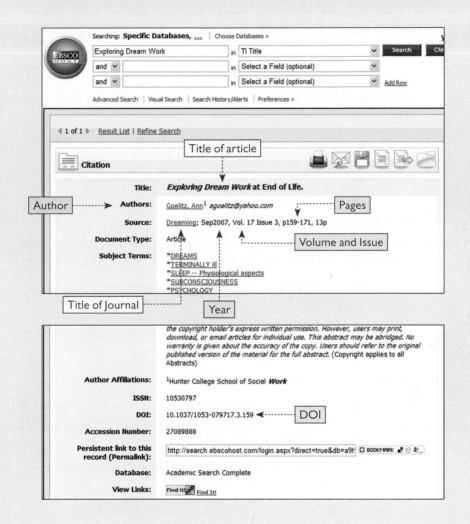

Goelitz, A. (2007). Exploring dream work at end of life. *Dreaming,*
17(3), 159–171. doi:10.1037/1053-079717.3.159

24. Electronic book

Author's Last Name, Initials. (Year). *Title of book*. DOI or Retrieved from
URL

TenDam, H. (n.d.). *Politics, civilization & humanity*. Retrieved from http://
onlineoriginals.com/showitem.asp?itemID=46&page=2

For an ebook based on a print version, include a description of the digital
format in brackets after the book title.

Blain, M. (2009). *The sociology of terror: Studies in power, subjection, and
victimage ritual* [Adobe Digital Editions version]. Retrieved from
http://www.powells.com/sub/AdobeDigitalEditionsPolitics
.html?sec_big_link=1

25. Wiki entry

Give the entry title and the date of posting, or *n.d.* if there is no date. Then
include the retrieval date, the name of the wiki, and the URL for the entry.

Title of entry. (Year, Month Day). Retrieved Month Day, Year, from Title
of wiki: URL

Discourse. (n.d.). Retrieved November 8, 2010, from Psychology Wiki:
http://psychology.wikia.com/wiki/Discourse

26. Online discussion source

If the name of the list to which to the message was posted is not part of the
URL, include it after *Retrieved from*. The URL you provide should be for the
archived version of the message or post.

Author's Last Name, Initials. (Year, Month Day). Subject line of message
[Descriptive label]. Retrieved from URL

Baker, J. (2005, February 15). Re: Huffing and puffing [Electronic
mailing list message]. Retrieved from American Dialect Society
electronic mailing list: http://listserv.linguistlist.org/cgi-bin
/wa?A2=ind0502C&L=ADS-L&P=R44

Do not include email or other nonarchived discussions in your list of references. Simply cite the sender's name in your text. See no. 13 on p. 470 for guidelines on identifying such sources in your text.

27. Blog entry

Author's Last Name, Initials. (Year, Month Day). Title of post [Blog post]. Retrieved from URL

Collins, C. (2009, August 19). Butterfly benefits from warmer springs? [Blog post]. Retrieved from http://www.intute.ac.uk/blog/2009/08/19/butterfly-benefits-from-warmer-springs/

28. Online video

Last Name, Initials (Writer), & Last Name, Initials (Producer). (Year, Month Day posted). *Title* [Descriptive label]. Retrieved from URL

Coulter, J. (Songwriter & Performer), & Booth, M. S. (Producer). (2006, September 23). *Code monkey* [Video file]. Retrieved from http://www.youtube.com/watch?v=v4Wy7gRGgeA

29. Podcast

Writer's Last Name, Initials. (Writer), & Producer's Last Name, Initials. (Producer). (Year, Month Day). Title of podcast. *Title of site or program* [Audio podcast]. Retrieved from URL

Britt, M. A. (Writer & Producer). (2009, June 7). Episode 97: Stanley Milgram study finally replicated. *The Psych Files Podcast* [Audio podcast]. Retrieved from http://www.thepsychfiles.com/

Other Kinds of Sources

30. Film, video, or DVD

Last Name, Initials (Producer), & Last Name, Initials (Director). (Year). *Title* [Motion picture]. Country: Studio.

Wallis, H. B. (Producer), & Curtiz, M. (Director). (1942). *Casablanca* [Motion picture]. United States: Warner.

31. Music recording

Composer's Last Name, Initials. (Year of copyright). Title of song. On *Title of album* [Medium]. City, State or Country: Label.

Veloso, C. (1997). Na baixado sapateiro. On *Livros* [CD]. Los Angeles, CA: Nonesuch.

32. Proceedings of a conference

Author's Last Name, Initials. (Year of publication). Title of paper. In *Proceedings Title* (pp. pages). Publication City, State or Country: Publisher.

Heath, S. B. (1997). Talking work: Language among teens. In *Symposium about Language and Society–Austin* (pp. 27–45). Austin: Department of Linguistics at the University of Texas.

33. Television program

Last Name, Initials (Writer), & Last Name, Initials (Director). (Year). Title of episode [Descriptive label]. In Initials Last Name (Producer), *Series title*. City, State or Country: Network.

Mundy, C. (Writer), & Bernaro, E. A. (Director). (2007). In birth and death [Television series episode]. In E. A. Bernaro (Executive Producer), *Criminal minds*. New York, NY: NBC.

34. Software or computer program

Title and version number [Computer software]. (Year). Publication City, State or Country: Publisher.

The Sims 2: Holiday edition [Computer software]. (2005). Redwood City, CA: Electronic Arts.

author   title   publication

35. Government document

Government Agency. (Year of publication). *Title*. Publication City, State
    or Country: Publisher.

U.S. Department of Health and Human Services, Centers for Disease Control
    and Prevention. (2009). *Fourth national report on human exposure to
    environmental chemicals*. Washington, DC: Government Printing Office.

Online government document

Government Agency. (Year of publication). *Title* (Publication No. [if
    any]). Retrieved from URL

U.S. Department of Health and Human Services, National Institutes of
    Health, National Institute of Mental Health. (2006). *Bipolar disorder*
    (NIH Publication No. 06-3679). Retrieved from http://www.nimh
    .nih.gov/health/publications/bipolar-disorder/nimh-bipolar-adults
    .pdf

36. Dissertation

Include the database name and accession number for dissertations that you
retrieve from a database.

Author's Last Name, Initials. (Year). *Title of dissertation* (Doctoral
    dissertation). Retrieved from Name of database. (accession
    number)

Knapik, M. (2008). *Adolescent online trouble-talk: Help-seeking in
    cyberspace* (Doctoral dissertation). Retrieved from ProQuest
    Dissertation and Theses database. (AAT NR38024)

For a dissertation that you access on the Web, include the name of the in-
stitution after *Doctoral dissertation*. For example: (Doctoral dissertation,
University of North Carolina). End your citation with *Retrieved from* and the
URL.

37. Technical or research report

Author's Last Name, Initials. (Year). *Title of report* (Report number). Publication City, State or Country: Publisher.

Elsayed, T., Namata, G., Getoor, L., & Oard., D. W. (2008). *Personal name resolution in email: A heuristic approach* (Report No. LAMP-TR-150). College Park: University of Maryland.

Citing Sources Not Covered by APA

To cite a source for which APA does not provide guidelines, look at models similar to the source you are citing. Give any information readers will need in order to find it themselves—author; date of publication; title; publisher; information about electronic retrieval (DOI or URL); and any other pertinent information. Try your citation to be sure it will lead others to your source.

FORMATTING A RESEARCH ESSAY

Title page. APA does not provide guidelines specifically for the title page of a paper written for a college course; check with your instructor about his or her preferences. Be sure to provide the full title; your name; the course and section number; your instructor's name; and the date. Center each element on a separate line.

Page numbers. Beginning with the title page, insert a shortened title in capital letters in the upper left-hand corner of each page; place the page number in the upper right-hand corner. Number pages consecutively throughout. Include the words "Running head:" before the shortened title on the title page.

Spacing, margins, and indents. Double-space the entire paper, including any notes and your list of references. Leave one-inch margins at the top, bottom, and sides of your text; do not justify the text. The first line of each paragraph should be indented one-half inch (or five-to-seven spaces) from the left margin. APA recommends using two spaces after end-of-sentence punctuation.

Headings. Though they are not required in APA style, headings can help readers follow your text. The first level of heading should be bold, centered, and capitalized as you would any other title; the second level of heading should be bold and flush with the left margin; the third level should be bold and indented, with only the first letter and proper nouns capitalized and with a period at the end of the heading.

First Level Heading

Second Level Heading
    Third level heading.

Abstract. An abstract is a concise summary of your paper that introduces readers to your topic and main points. Most scholarly journals require an abstract; check with your instructor about his or her preference. Put your abstract on the second page, with the word *Abstract* centered at the top. Unless your instructor specifies a length, limit your abstract to 120 words or fewer.

Long quotations. Indent quotations of more than forty words one-half inch (or five-to-seven spaces) from the left margin. Do not use quotation marks, and place the page number(s) in parentheses *after* the end punctuation.

> Kaplan (2000) captured ancient and contemporary Antioch for us:
>> At the height of its glory in the Roman-Byzantine age, when it had an amphitheater, public baths, aqueducts, and sewage pipes, half a million people lived in Antioch. Today the population is only 125,000. With sour relations between Turkey and Syria, and unstable politics throughout the Middle East, Antioch is now a backwater—seedy and tumbledown, with relatively few tourists. (p. 123)
>
> Antioch's decline serves as a reminder that the fortunes of cities can change drastically over time.

List of references. Start your list on a new page after any notes. Center the title and double-space the entire list. Each entry should begin at the left margin, and subsequent lines should be indented one-half inch (or five spaces). Alphabetize the list by authors' last names (or by editors' names, if appropriate). Alphabetize works that have no author or editor by title, disregarding *A, An,* and *The.* Be sure every source listed is cited in the text; do not include sources that you consulted but did not cite.

Illustrations. For each table, provide a number (*Table 1*) and a descriptive title on separate lines above the table; below the table, include a note with information about the source. For figures—charts, diagrams, graphs, photos, and so on—include a figure number (*Figure 1*) and information about the source in a note below the figure. Number tables and figures separately, and be sure to discuss any illustrations so that readers know how they relate to the rest of your text.

Table 1
Hours of Instruction Delivered per Week

	American classrooms	Japanese classrooms	Chinese classrooms
First Grade			
Language Arts	10.5	8.7	10.4
Mathematics	2.7	5.8	4.0
Fifth Grade			
Language Arts	7.9	8.0	11.1
Mathematics	3.4	7.8	11.7

Note. Adapted from "Peeking Out from Under the Blinders: Some Factors We Shouldn't Forget in Studying Writing," by J. R. Hayes, 1991, National Center for the Study of Writing and Literacy (Occasional Paper No. 25). Retrieved from National Writing Project website: http://www.nwp.org/

SAMPLE RESEARCH ESSAY

Amanda Baker wrote the following paper for a psychology course. It is formatted according to the guidelines of the *Publication Manual of the American Psychological Association,* 6th edition (2010).

Running head: THE PERCEPTION OF RISK 1

A shortened title in all capital letters is used as a running head in the upper left corner of each page; on the title page, it is preceded by the label "Running head" and a colon. Page numbers appear in the upper right corner.

The Perception of Risk in Medical Decision Making

The title is centered on the page, with your name, the course number, the instructor's name, and the date below.

Amanda Baker

Psychology H508

Professor Arkes

December 5, 2008

Abstract begins on a new page. Heading is centered.

Abstract text does not need a paragraph indent.

Use two letter spaces after each sentence.

Abstract

As patients increasingly share responsibility with their doctors for making medical decisions, it has become increasingly important for them to be able to understand the risks associated with particular decisions and to assess how these compare with the potential benefits. For a variety of reasons, however, including insufficient mathematical knowledge, problems with the presentation of information about risk, and distractions of various kinds, the average patient is poor at assessing risk. Methods that could potentially improve patient risk assessment include providing better mathematics instruction in schools, counseling patients about how to assess risks appropriately, and changing the ways in which risk information is presented to them.

The Perception of Risk in Medical Decision Making

Once upon a time, doctors knew everything there was to know about being well and getting well, and patients simply accepted the decisions of their doctors without question. That time has passed. Today, people are embracing the concept that decision making is something that should be shared between the doctor and the patient. In the perfect shared decision-making scenario, the doctor shares his or her expertise with a patient, who then takes that information and carefully considers both the risks and the benefits in order to make the optimal decision. As with all ideal situations, though, this one is not wholly realistic. The fact is that things can and will go wrong, especially given the complex human decision-making process. How can we make sure patients are fully equipped to make the best choices when it comes to their health?

Shared decision making includes everything that happens between a doctor and patient that leads to a medical decision. There are a number of factors that must be considered in making such a decision, and one major one is risk assessment. Often patients and doctors are faced with several treatment options that have varying levels of risk to the patient's health and, in some cases, his or her life. Both patients and doctors need to be able to assess and understand these risk levels in order to make a decision with good cost-to-benefit ratios. Just as a smart entrepreneur would not invest money in something without knowing how risky it was, so patients should not invest their health in something without knowing its risks as well as its potential rewards. The goals of this paper are first to assess the average patient's ability to understand risk,

Title is centered.

Essay is double-spaced.

1"

Indent each paragraph ½" (5–7 spaces).

THE PERCEPTION OF RISK   4

then to discuss some of the barriers that stand in the way of proper risk assessment, and finally to present some potential methods for eliminating this misunderstanding.

Because risk assessment is so important to shared decision making, it is very important to know to what extent the average patient is able to understand risk properly. Unfortunately, research suggests that the risk perceptions of the common patient are not very good. A recent study by van der Weijden, van Steenskiste, Stoffers, Timmermans, and Grol (2007) looked at patients aged 40-70 who discussed the risk of cardiovascular disease (CVD) with their doctor. All of the patients had received accurate risk information from the physician. Yet of those who were found to be at high risk for CVD, 4 out of 5 were overly optimistic and perceived themselves as having lower risk than they did.

> To our surprise, diabetes and a positive CVD family history were not determinants of high perceived risk, even though the patients with diabetes have a high actual risk by definition, and patients with a positive CVD family history often have a high actual risk. (van der Weijden et al., 2007, p. 759)

Meanwhile, of the low-risk patients, 1 in 5 were overly pessimistic and perceived themselves as being at higher risk for CVD than they actually were.

Causes of Poor Risk Assessment

So we know that even with a doctor's help, people are not so good at perceiving risk properly. What is causing this poor risk assessment? There is no one correct answer. Research has uncovered a number

---

Because this source has fewer than six authors, all authors are included in the signal phrase, with the year of publication given in parentheses after the names. The signal phrase uses past tense.

Set off any quote running 40 words or longer as block quotation. Begin the quote on a new line, indent all lines ½" from the left margin, and omit quotation marks.

Subsequent references to a work by three or more authors use the first author's name followed by et al.

First-level headings are centered, bold, and capitalized.

THE PERCEPTION OF RISK   5

of potential causes for the distortion of risk information, and no one of them seems more plausible than another. The leading candidates are simple mathematical misunderstanding, problems with the presentation of risk information, and just plain distractions that keep people from understanding the information accurately. This paper will explore each of these three types of risk-distorting phenomena, starting with mathematical misunderstandings.

Mathematical Misunderstanding ●————————————————

Second-level headings are flush left, bold, and capitalized.

Risk is often presented as probability or chance. That means that if people do not fully understand the mathematical principles involved in ratios and decimals or in proportions and probabilities, they will most likely struggle to understand risk information in even the simplest terms. Unfortunately, research suggests that many adults have issues with the math necessary to proper risk assessment. Theories such as fuzzy trace theory suggest that this is because people do not attend properly to numerical data; even if they remember it, in making decisions they tend to rely instead on the "vague gist" of what they recall (Reyna & Brainerd, 2008, p. 91). This tendency often prevents ●————

Because the authors are not named in a signal phrase, their names are given in parentheses, with an ampersand rather than and between them. A page number is provided for a direct quotation.

them from fully understanding the risk information they are given. A more basic problem is that some patients simply lack the mathematical knowledge of ratios, decimals, and fractions necessary to interpret these probabilities. Zikmund-Fisher, Smith, Ubel, and Fagerlin (2007) suggested that higher numeracy, or numerical aptitude, leads to better risk comprehension. A person with deficient numeracy skills will find it more difficult to make a good risk-based decision.

THE PERCEPTION OF RISK   6

Problems with Presentation

Mathematics is not the only thing preventing people from comprehending risk accurately. Often, people make different decisions about identical data just because the data are presented in different ways. Obviously, this is not a desirable way to make medical decisions. The only things that should factor into these decisions are risks (and/or costs) and benefits. However, research suggests that there are a number of ways in which presentation affects risk perception and shared decision making, including the presence of irrelevant anchors, framing effects, and graphing differences. Each of these is important and will be discussed in turn.

Third-level heading ⎯⎯⎯⎯• **Anchoring.** Anchoring refers to the phenomenon in which a person uses a numerical "anchor" as a mental starting or reference point for estimating something (such as benefits, risks, and so on) and then adjusts the anchor to arrive at what he or she considers an appropriate quantity. Anchoring becomes a problem when people use anchors that are irrelevant to the issue they are considering and do not adjust them sufficiently based on the information they know. Research done by Brewer, Chapman, Schwartz, and Bergus (2007) suggested that anchoring effects can change judgments of medical risks a good deal. In one experiment, they had HIV-positive men estimate the chances that their partner would be infected with HIV after sex with a failed condom. Before making their prediction, the men were asked whether they thought that chance was higher than 1% (low anchor) or whether it was lower than 90% (high anchor). The low-anchor condition produced an average estimate of 43% whereas the high-anchor condition produced an average of 64%--a huge 20-point difference in risk perception just from anchoring effects alone. They repeated this experiment, this time using doctors as participants and asking them to assess the risk of a pulmonary embolism. The anchoring effect in this case was even greater, increasing risk estimates from 23% for the low-anchor group to 53% for the high-anchor group. The experimenters also asked people from each anchoring group about treatment decisions based on their risk estimates and got some interesting results, which will be discussed later in this paper. The main point to take from this research, though, is that irrelevant anchors can destroy good risk assessments. This is naturally undesirable because anything keeping a person from knowing the true risk of his or her situation can lead to dangerously bad decision making.

Framing. Another aspect of presentation that can affect risk assessment is framing. Framing occurs when people react not to a set of statistics alone but to whether they are presented in a positive or a negative "frame valence"--for example, the difference between an 80% chance of survival (positive) or a 20% chance of death (negative). The statistics are the same; only their frame valence differs. Research by Ferguson and Gallagher (2007) suggested that the effects of frame valence on risk judgment depend on two aspects of perceived risk--personal outcome effectiveness, or how effective you think the outcome will be for you, and procedural risk. Meanwhile, Zikmund-Fisher, Fagerlin, Roberts, Derry, and Ubel (2008) suggested that merely framing a medication's risks as incremental risks or as total risks can change a person's risk assessment. Those receiving risk information framed in incremental terms (who were told, for example, that 5% of patients taking a placebo experience dizziness, whereas 10% of those taking the medication do) reported less worry about side effects than those receiving it framed as total risk (who were simply given the 10% figure). Clearly, the way in which risk information is framed holds a great deal of sway in medical judgments and decision making. Again, this is not desirable because it only detracts from the real risks and benefits that should be what a patient considers.

Graphing differences. Even small visual differences in the way probabilities are presented can make a good deal of difference in how people assess and understand them. For example, it has been found that there is a great deal of difference in how people perceive a certain treatment depending on whether it is described using graphs showing mortality rates after the treatment or survival rates after it and on whether the graphs show 5 years' worth of data or 15 years' worth. Ratings of effectiveness for survival graphs varied greatly based on whether there were more years' worth of data available, even though the data itself were very similar for the two periods. Meanwhile, effectiveness ratings were less varied with mortality graphs (Zikmund-Fisher, Fagerlin, & Ubel, 2007). This means that patients may see a treatment as more effective or less so depending on what type of graph a doctor gives them (survival vs. mortality) or how many data points it has. Although this study did not deal specifically with risk perception, it is plausible to imagine that such an effect of presentation could carry

THE PERCEPTION OF RISK   9

over to risk communication, in which case a person's assessment of the risks and benefits could vary based on small unconsidered visual differences.

Distractions

"Distractions," the last type of potential causes for distorted risk perceptions, are for the most part just things people should not base their medical decisions on but do anyway. In other words, as their name suggests, they distract patients from the valuable information that should be guiding their decisions and lead them to consider irrelevant factors that may skew their risk assessments. Distractions include prior probability estimation, comparative risk information, social and personal comparison information, and purpose-driven estimation.

Prior probability estimation. Prior probability estimation simply refers to a person having made his or her own estimate of risk before receiving risk information from medical authorities. Because prior probability estimations are not based on real data, they become worthless and should not be considered once real risk information becomes available. This idea sounds simple enough: Uninformed judgments no longer matter once information is provided. The problem is that people do not follow this rule. Fagerlin, Zikmund-Fisher, and Ubel (2005) demonstrated this statement with their study of women's attitudes toward the risk of breast cancer. They asked some women to estimate an average woman's risk of breast cancer, then gave them the actual statistics and asked for their reaction. Other women were simply given the statistical risk information and then asked whether the actual

THE PERCEPTION OF RISK   10

risk was higher or lower than they had expected and how they reacted to it. Women who estimated the risk before getting the statistics tended to overestimate it. Naturally, they were relieved to find that their original estimate was too high, and that relief led them to react to the real risk more positively than did women who had not made prior estimations; those women were much more likely to perceive it as high and to feel anxious about it. In other words, a prior risk assessment changed the "feel" of the actual risk by introducing relief, which led some women to actually underestimate their risk.

Comparative risk information. Another thing that can distract people from perceiving risk information appropriately is comparative risk information. In one study, women were told what their breast cancer risk was and also told that it was either "lower than average" or "higher than average," although the risk was actually the same for both groups. The "lower than average" women were less likely to accept a preventative treatment for breast cancer than were the "higher than average" group (Fagerlin, Zikmund-Fisher, & Ubel, 2007).

Social and personal comparison information. In addition to comparative risk information, social and personal comparison information can also detract from proper risk assessment. French, Sutton, Marteau, and Kinmonth (2004) had 970 adult participants respond to a series of vignettes involving risk perception. Some of the variables involved in the vignettes included using a "real world" analogue (a cardiac event such as a heart attack) versus none (a fictional

THE PERCEPTION OF RISK   11

pancreatic disease), telling participants that they had high or low
levels of personal risk, and telling them that their risk was high or low
compared to others of their age and sex. The researchers found that both
the respondents' emotional responses and their estimates of personal
risk were influenced by social comparison information (about risk
compared to that of others) and personal comparison information (about
high or low levels of personal risk). Furthermore, this influence was
found to be more prominent for the real-world condition.

    Purpose-driven estimation. Ideally, risk assessment should be
the determining factor for a patient's preferred choice of treatment. It
makes sense that information about risk should be gathered before the
decision is made. People do not, however, always work that way. Not
only do we not base our decisions on risks (and benefits) alone, but we
often inadvertently make decisions before we have much information
at all. Research suggests that this pattern could inadvertently lead
to distorting the risk information to fit with a previous preference.
One study done gave about 300 participants three different levels of
motivation to choose to undergo a particular treatment. The study
found that when people had more (or less) motivation to justify their
preference for (or against) treatment, they adjusted what they perceived
to be the probability of the treatment's success to match (Levy & Hershey,
2006). This adjustment, known as purpose-driven estimation, was not
apparently conscious or intentional. People simply like to justify their
preferences, and most likely their minds automatically adjust outcome
probabilities to match what they want.

Impact of Risk-Perception Assessment Research

Given the many factors that can distort risk assessment, it is easy to see that research into shared medical decision making has very serious real-life applications. The studies discussed in this paper alone address risk perception about such conditions as HIV infection and breast cancer (Brewer et al., 2007; Fagerlin et al., 2005, 2007). Specifically, Bonari et al. (2005) found that pregnant women are more likely to discontinue using antidepressants during pregnancy if their risk assessments are too high. This finding suggests the likelihood of a substantial number of women whose mental health has been needlessly put in jeopardy. Too-low risk assessments of a condition may lead to delay of treatment if a person does not feel that his or her condition is serious enough to warrant immediate attention. Meanwhile, too-low risk assessments of a treatment may lead to someone taking risks they aren't aware of. Too-high risk assessments of a condition can lead to unnecessarily risky treatments whereas too-high risk assessments of a treatment may lead to an avoidance of the treatment that is, in fact, the best decision.

So the research news regarding medical risk assessment so far is generally bleak. For a number of reasons, humans are basically not very good at evaluating risks. The good news, however, is that although risk perceptions are frequently incorrect, the extent to which they actually affect treatment decisions is unclear. When Brewer et al. (2007) did the study on the effects of anchoring, they found that although irrelevant anchors affected risk assessment drastically, they didn't seem to make any difference at all in the treatment choices for hypothetical HIV

Three sources are cited within the same parentheses; the two different author teams are arranged alphabetically and separated by a semicolon. A comma is used to separate the years of the two citations for the Fagerlin team.

THE PERCEPTION OF RISK   13

infection. This does not mean that risk assessment is not important,
given that studies such as Bonari et al. (2005) found that distorted risk
perceptions had a very real and immediate effect on women's decisions
to discontinue antidepressants during pregnancy. The link between risk
perception and decision making may, however, be less direct in some
instances than in others. Chances are that the Brewer et al. study points
to a greater complexity in the shared decision-making process than we
currently understand.

Possible Ways to Improve Risk Assessment

We have established how and why people are bad at risk
assessment, but one big question remains. What can we do to improve
risk communication so that people can make better medical decisions?
As of now, there is no one solution that will eliminate improper risk
assessment forever. However, a number of methods have been proposed
to help reduce some of the effects of taking extraneous variables into
account, and so increase the emphasis that is put on appropriate risk-to
benefit analysis.

The Subjective Numeracy Scale

The first method addresses the numeracy problem. It has
been established that higher mathematical aptitude leads to higher
achievement on risk comprehension tasks (Zikmund-Fisher, Smith, et
al., 2007). There are ways to improve a person's math skills, but first it
is necessary to know what his or her current skills are. The subjective
numeracy scale is designed to do just that. Created by Zikmund-Fisher,
Smith, et al. (2007), this scale was developed with the specific intention

Because the essay cites two sources from the same year with the same first author (Zikmund-Fisher), the citations in this paragraph include the second author's name as well to identify which source is meant.

of assessing the numeracy skills of the general population so that physicians will know what methods of communication about risk will be most effective. In addition, any improvement in the mathematical skills of the general population should, it would seem, lead to an improvement in numeracy skills. This is perhaps one more reason to encourage strong math instruction in the U.S. educational system, so that the number of adults who do not understand basic mathematical principles like decimals will go down.

Evidence-Based Counseling

In addition to improving the numerical aptitude of the general population, there is some suggestion that counseling a person to correctly assess risk levels could lead to better risk assessment and better overall shared decision making. Bonari et al. (2005) got mixed results with this approach. They found during the study on discontinuation of antidepressant use during pregnancy that evidence-based counseling was *somewhat* effective in reducing distorted risk perceptions. This success, however, was very limited. Despite evidence-based counseling that pregnancies were not harmed by antidepressants, a large number of women still chose to discontinue them during pregnancy, and some went so far as to avoid getting pregnant so they could continue taking them. These findings suggest that some inappropriate risk perceptions may be very robust. It seems likely that there are a number of "roadblocks" skewing risk perceptions, and counseling in this area would have to address a wide variety of issues in order to be effective in this particular area.

THE PERCEPTION OF RISK   15

Targeted Presentation Style

Finally, because a large number of inappropriate risk assessments seem to be caused by differences in presentation, understanding just which forms of presentation create which errors would allow medical professionals to carefully construct presentations that do not adversely affect shared decision making. The drawback to this approach is that having a greater understanding of how presentation affects risk assessment also opens up the process to manipulation. Would it be ethical for doctors to present risks in a certain way if they knew it would most likely lead to a certain result? This is a question that will need to be answered as we gain a deeper understanding of how risk perceptions are affected by things that can easily be manipulated, like presentation.

Conclusion

The study of shared decision making may occasionally present a bleak picture, but it also presents some opportunities. Yes, patients are very limited in their abilities to understand and account for risk in their medical decisions. But as the Brewer et al. (2007) study showed, doctors themselves are hardly immune to these limitations. The personal stake of patients in decisions offers additional incentive for them to improve. And although some causes of inappropriate risk assessments may be nearly impossible to eliminate (Bonari et al., 2005), others like numeracy may just require a little extra instruction. As in-depth studies of shared decision making and its difficulties continue, new and exciting solutions could be in the future.

List of references begins on a new page. Heading is centered.

References

Bonari, L., Koren, G., Einarson, T. R., Jasper, J. D., Taddio, A., & Einarson,
A. (2005). Use of antidepressants by pregnant women: Evaluation
of perception of risk, efficacy of evidence based counseling and
determinants of decision making. *Archives of Women's Mental
Health, 8*(4), 214-220. doi:10.1007/s00737-005-0094-8

DOI is provided for electronic source that has one. Do not add a period at the end of a DOI.

Brewer, N. T., Chapman, G. B., Schwartz, J. A., & Bergus, G. R. (2007). The
influence of irrelevant anchors on the judgments and choices
of doctors and patients. *Medical Decision Making, 27*(2), 203-211.
doi:10.1177/0272989X06298595

All lines except first line of each entry are indented 5 spaces or ½".

Use one letter space between parts of reference citations.

Fagerlin, A., Zikmund-Fisher, B. J., & Ubel, P. A. (2005). How making a risk
estimate can change the feel of that risk: Shifting attitudes toward
breast cancer risk in a general public survey. *Patient Education and
Counseling, 57,* 294-299. Retrieved from http://www.pec-journal
.com/home

URL of journal home page is provided for electronic source with no DOI. Do not add a period at the end of a URL.

Fagerlin, A., Zikmund-Fisher, B. J., & Ubel, P. A. (2007). "If I'm better than
average, then I'm ok?": Comparative information influences beliefs
about risk and benefits. *Patient Education and Counseling, 69*(1-3),
140-144. Retrieved from http://www.pec-journal.com/home

Entries with same author team are arranged chronologically by publication date.

Ferguson, E., & Gallagher, L. (2007). Message framing with respect to
decisions about vaccination: The roles of frame valence, frame
method and perceived risk. *British Journal of Psychology, 98*(4),
667-680. Retrieved from http://onlinelibrary.wiley.com/journal
/10.1111/%28ISSN%292044-8295

If a URL is too long to fit on one line, break it before punctuation.

THE PERCEPTION OF RISK   17

French, D. P., Sutton, S. R., Marteau, T. M., & Kinmonth, A. L. (2004). The
        impact of personal and social comparison information about health
        risk. *British Journal of Health Psychology*, *9*, 187-200. Retrieved from
        http://www.wiley.com/bw/journal.asp?ref=1359-107X&site=1

Levy, A. G., & Hershey, J. C. (2006). Distorting the probability of treatment
        success to justify treatment decisions. *Organizational Behavior and
        Human Decision Processes*, *101*(1), 52-58. Retrieved from http://www
        .journals.elsevier.com/organizational-behavior-and-human
        -decision-processes/

Reyna, V. F., & Brainerd, C. J. (2008). Numeracy, ratio bias, and
        denominator neglect in judgments of risk and probability. *Learning
        and Individual Differences*, *18*(1), 89-107. Retrieved from http://www
        .journals.elsevier.com/learning-and-individual-differences/

Van der Weijden, T., van Steenkiste, B., Stoffers, H. E. J. H., Timmermans,
        D. R. M., & Grol, R. (2007). Primary prevention of cardiovascular
        diseases in general practice: Mismatch between cardiovascular risk
        and patients' risk perceptions. *Medical Decision Making*, *27*(6), 754-
        761. doi:10.1177/0272989X07305323

Zikmund-Fisher, B. J., Fagerlin, A., Roberts, T. R., Derry, H. A., & Ubel,
        P. A. (2008). Alternate methods of framing information about
        medication side effects: Incremental risk versus total risk of
        occurrence. *Journal of Health Communication*, *13*(2), 107-124.
        doi:10.1080/10810730701854011

Zikmund-Fisher, B. J., Fagerlin, A., & Ubel, P. A. (2007). Mortality versus
        survival graphs: Improving temporal consistency in perceptions

Entries for which first two authors are the same are arranged alphabetically by names of third authors.

of treatment effectiveness. *Patient Education and Counseling, 66*(1),

100-107. doi:10.1016/j.pec.2006.10.013

Zikmund-Fisher, B. J., Smith, D. M., Ubel, P. A., & Fagerlin, A. (2007).

Validation of the subjective numeracy scale: Effects of low

numeracy on comprehension of risk communications and

utility elicitations. *Medical Decision Making, 27*(5), 663-671.

doi:10.1177/0272989X07303824

PART V

Style

ONCE UPON A TIME—and for a long time, too—style in writing meant ornamentation, "dressing up" your writing the way you might dress yourself up for a fancy dress ball. In fact, ancient images often show rhetoric as a woman in a gaudy flowing gown covered with figures of speech—metaphors, similes, alliteration, hyperbole, and so on—her stylish ornaments.

When we think of style today, however, we think not of ornamentation but of *how* a message is presented, whether that message is in writing, in speech, in images, or in another form. Think of a movie you like and then list all the things that go into creating its particular style, the *how* of its pre-

Dame Rhetorica, from Gregor Reisch's *Margarita Phylosophica (1525)*.

sentation: acting, musical score, camera angles, editing—and so on. All these elements interact to create the film's distinctive style.

What can you use to give your writing your own particular style? To begin with, you have what writers have always had: words, words, words. And choosing just the right word (diction) and putting it in just the right place (syntax) still matters a lot in developing style. Today, however, writers have many other tools to use for creating messages that have style. Think not just word choice and syntax—think also typography, punctuation, color, sound, images, and more. All these elements help you write with style.

Why is style so important to writers? For one thing, we all respond to style, even if unconsciously. When we see something pleasing or arresting, we're much more likely to pay attention to it or agree with it. Simply put, messages that can get and hold our attention are the ones we are most likely to tune in to, remember, and act on. Especially in an age of information overload, it's these messages that will win out in the competition for our attention. Style, then, is not something added on to what you write, like icing on a cake; rather, style is part of the substance of what you write.

That's why we take special care in this book to introduce you to issues of style: We want you to be a writer whose texts are distinctive, memorable, and persuasive. Getting and holding an audience's attention, however, is not the only thing that matters when it comes to style. You want to get that attention in ways that are *appropriate* to your topic, your purpose, your audience, and your entire rhetorical situation. If you're dressing for an important job interview, you choose clothes that are pleasing in a businesslike way; if you're dressing for another occasion—a rock concert, a game of Frisbee, a religious service, a funeral—you will dress very differently.

It's difficult, though—even impossible—to set hard-and-fast rules to be sure you're making the right choices for the particular situation. Consider a fascinating analogy—between the choices an athlete has to make and the choices we as authors have to make:

> Imagine . . . the relationship between the pitcher and the batter. It's a complicated relationship forged in a complex calculus of the probable, yet unknown. I love those close-up shots on television of the batter studying the pitcher, waiting for the ball. The batter is poised, bat over shoulder, feet planted just so, ready to nimbly meet whatever comes. In that moment, the batter is both *at the mercy of* the pitcher, the rules of game, the equipment, the umpire and also *a participant and creator of* the game.
>
> The ball leaves the pitcher's hand.

In that moment, the coach can't tell the batter exactly what to do at the plate. There's absolutely no way of knowing exactly where that ball is going to go prior to stepping into the situation. There's no way of knowing from which direction the wind will be blowing. There's no way of knowing exactly what the umpire is going to call a strike. The only thing the batter can do is to arrive at the plate poised and remain sensitive to the game unfolding.

Of course, the coach can make a pretty good guess about what will happen and how to react based on what has happened in the past and a myriad of other known factors. The batter can guess as well. And they can both prepare accordingly. But in that utterly kairotic moment when the ball is flying through the air, everything is in flux. . . . And the coach's line has to be: *do the right thing.*

That doesn't mean *do whatever you want.* It doesn't mean *anything goes.* Rather, it's an acknowledgment that . . . the terms of "rightness" are always shifting. . . . Do the *right* thing.

—BRENT SIMONEAUX, "Do the Right Thing"

The same goes for authors. But that's part of the great fun of writing with style. You get to analyze the rhetorical situation before you, like the batter and the pitcher do, and to think about how to seize the moment in order to get and hold the attention of your audience in the most appropriate ways. You even get something that the batter and pitcher don't have: the time to make your rhetorical decisions and to be an author who writes with a powerful and distinctive style.

The chapters that follow all aim to help you achieve that goal.

TWENTY-SIX

What's Your Style?

DOES THE TITLE OF THIS CHAPTER sound like a caption in a fashion ad? If so, it's no surprise: We often associate style with clothing, as we see fashions change from season to season or even week to week. What's hot right now will show up in outlet malls in a year or so—and in a decade or two, if you're lucky, those once-trendy clothes at the back of your closet may become retro-chic again. (Do you think there's any hope for these clothes from the 1990s on the left? How about those from the '70s on the right?)

Stars of the TV shows *Beverly Hills, 90210* (1990–2000) and the *Brady Bunch* (1969–1974) wear clothing typical of their times.

You might not be caught dead wearing these styles today. Style, after all, is about choices you do *not* make as well as those you do. Wearing a bikini to the beach might seem a perfectly good stylistic choice at twenty—but one you might well question at seventy or in a culture that puts a high value on personal modesty. Of course, there may be some things you would never choose to wear at any time because they just don't suit you at all—bright orange anything, for example, or cowboy boots. Most often, though, you choose your clothing to fit your own sense of yourself and to match the occasion: a business suit for an important interview; shorts and running shoes for the gym. Style, then, is both about creating your own "look" and making sure that look is appropriate to the particular situation.

Style in writing works the same way. As you write, you look for words and ways of using them that match the message you're trying to convey— including the impression of yourself that you want to project. To achieve this goal, you do certain things while not doing others. In this chapter, we aim to give you tools you can use to think about and shape the style of your writing. Specifically, we'll consider the issues of appropriateness, formality, and stance; as you'll see, they're all related.

Appropriateness and Correctness

Would you expect to see the word "yup" in the *Boston Globe*? See how that one carefully chosen word affects the style of the article on p. 783.

To understand style in writing, you need to think in terms of a key rhetorical term: appropriateness. Put most simply, an appropriate writing style is one in which your language and the way you arrange it suits your topic, your purpose, your stance, and your audience. But making appropriate stylistic choices in writing can be tricky, especially because we don't have a set of hard-and-fast rules to follow. You may have learned that it's never appropriate to start a sentence with *and* or *but* or to end a sentence with a preposition. But even those "rules" are far from universal—and change over time. In fact, much fine writing today breaks these "rules" to good effect (as we do in the preceding sentence!).

So it won't work to think about style simply as a matter of following the rules. In fact, when it comes to being "correct" or being "appropriate," being appropriate wins out in almost all cases. When *Star Trek* announced its mission "to boldly go where no man has gone before," that split infinitive ("boldly" splits the two words of the infinitive "to go") wasn't absolutely "correct," but it created just the emphasis the writers were after (say it out loud and see

The crew of the S.S. *Enterprise* split infinitives boldly, and with emphasis.

how different "to boldly go" and "to go boldly" sound!). Moreover, it was an appropriate choice for the time (the 1960s) and place (a TV show, not an academic paper). One mark of its stylistic appropriateness: It's still quoted, even in textbooks. Making appropriate stylistic choices, then, will almost always depend on your **RHETORICAL SITUATION** —what you're talking about, where you are, who the audience is, and how you're communicating with them.

Standard edited English: The default choice. In school and in many professional contexts, standard edited English is often seen as the most appropriate choice. Though there's plenty of debate over what standard edited English is, think of it as that variety of English most often used in education, government, and most professional contexts, especially in writing. Like the standard variety of any written language, standard edited English has changed across time—and will continue to change. If you read stories written by Flannery O'Connor, a twentieth-century fiction writer, you'll notice that she uses the words *man* and *he* to refer to people in general. Choices like this seemed appropriate at the time. But when many criticized the use of *he* to refer to both men and women, conventions changed, and writers looked for more appropriate choices. Were O'Connor, who died in 1964, writing today, it's likely that her use of language would reflect that change.

But the facts that standard languages emerge and change over time and that the appropriate use of a language most often depends on context don't mean that there are no rules at all. There are some rules, and following them—or not—has consequences. After all, the logic behind standard languages is that if users of a language all follow the same rules, then we can focus on content—on *what* is said—rather than being distracted by *how* it is said. When you don't follow these fairly basic rules, readers may end up focusing more on the how than on the what.

"You gotta know the rules to break the rules." This old saying still holds true in many situations. Take a look, for instance, at how linguist Geneva Smitherman breaks the rules of standard edited English brilliantly. In fact, had she stuck with those rules, the following paragraph would have been far less effective than it is.

> Before about 1959 (when the first study was done to change black speech patterns), Black English had been primarily the interest of university academics, particularly the historical linguists and cultural anthropologists. In recent years, though, the issue has become a very hot controversy, and there have been articles on Black Dialect in the national press as well as in the educational research literature. We have had pronouncements on black speech from the NAACP and the Black Panthers, from highly publicized scholars of the Arthur Jensen–William Shockley bent, from executives of national corporations such as Greyhound, and from housewives and community folk. I mean, really, it seem like everybody and they momma done had something to say on the subject!
>
> —GENEVA SMITHERMAN, *Talkin and Testifyin:*
> *The Language of Black America*

Geneva
Smitherman

Smitherman obviously knows the rules of standard edited English but breaks them to support her point and also to create a clear rhetorical stance, as a scholar, a skilled writer, and a proud African American. Writing in the late 1970s, she could assume that her readers would know that the NAACP is the National Association for the Advancement of Colored People, that the Black Panthers were a revolutionary social action group in the 1960s and 1970s, and that Arthur Jensen and William Shockley had made controversial claims about relationships between race and intelligence. She could also assume that readers of her book would expect her to write in standard edited English since the volume was published by a mainstream publisher and treated its subject from an academic perspective.

But Smitherman wasn't interested in writing a book about the vivid, energetic language of African Americans using only standard edited English. After all, one of her claims was that the language practices of African Americans were influencing American culture and language in many ways. Notice how her stylistic choices support that claim. She not only talks the talk of standard edited English but walks the walk of African American English as well. When she switches in her final sentence from standard edited English to African American English, she simultaneously drives home her point—that everyone at that time seemed to have an opinion about the language of African Americans—while demonstrating membership in that community by using the language variety associated with it. In short, she makes sound and appropriate stylistic choices.

Level of Formality

Being appropriate also calls on writers to pay attention to the levels of formality they use. In ancient Rome, Cicero identified three levels of style: low, or plain, style, which was used to teach or explain something; middle style, which was used to please an audience; and high, or grand, style, which was used to move or persuade the audience. Note how these classifications link style with a specific purpose and a likely audience.

Following the January 2011 tragedy in Tucson, Arizona, in which nineteen people, including Congresswoman Gabrielle Giffords, were shot and six died, President Obama delivered an address to the nation. The occasion was solemn and formal, and Obama, speaking as the nation's leader, offered a fine example of grand style, one that sought to move his audience by speaking from his heart to theirs as he sought to console the country.

Early in his speech, Obama quoted a passage from Psalm 46, part of the Hebrew Bible and the Christian Old Testament. He then offered short portraits of the victims of the shooting, those who had died and those who survived, as well as of people who had bravely intervened to limit the scope of the attack. Later in his remarks, he said:

You can find the speech by visiting wwnorton.com/write/everyone links.

> If this tragedy prompts reflection and debate—as it should—let's make sure it's worthy of those we have lost. . . . The loss of these wonderful people should make every one of us strive to be better. To be better in our private lives, to be better friends and neighbors and coworkers and

parents. And if, as has been discussed in recent days, their death helps usher in more civility in our public discourse, let us remember it is not because a simple lack of civility caused this tragedy—it did not—but rather because only a more civil and honest public discourse can help us face up to the challenges of our nation in a way that would make them proud.

Here Obama used repetition and complex sentence structure appropriate to the gravity of the occasion. If you listen to the speech, you'll also hear how he used pauses to great effect. Note, too, that even in the grand style he used contractions because their use helped lessen the distance between him and his audience of ordinary Americans; it humanized him in a moment when his focus was the common humanity of all present. In this case, the level of formality was perfectly appropriate to the occasion. But the president (or anyone else for that matter) doesn't use this level of formality all the time. In a news conference after the Democrats lost the 2010 congressional elections badly, for example, Obama used the slang term "shellacking" to refer to his party's defeat—a good example, we think, of shifting levels of formality to one that was appropriate to that occasion (a press conference) and that audience (Americans who were following the aftermath of the elections).

Stance

Stance refers to the attitude authors take toward their topic and audience. For example, you might write about immigration as an impassioned advocate or critic, someone with strong opinions about the inherent good or evil of immigration; or you might write as a dispassionate analyst, someone trying to weigh carefully the pros and cons of the arguments for and against a particular proposal. Either stance—and any possible stances in between—will affect what style you use, whether in speaking or in writing.

If your audience changes, your language will likely shift, too. Debating immigration issues with close friends whose opinions you're fairly sure of will differ in crucial ways from debating them with people you know less well or not at all because you'll be able to take less for granted. That you will likely shift all aspects of your message—from word choice and sentence structure to amount of background information and choice of examples—doesn't make you a hypocrite or a flip-flopper; instead, it demonstrates your skill at finding the most effective rhetorical resources to make your point.

In a posting titled "Same Food Planet, Different Food Worlds," blogger Rod Dreher calls attention to the drastically different stances taken by two restaurant reviewers. Here's an excerpt from one, a review of a new Olive Garden restaurant in Grand Forks, North Dakota, by eighty-five-year-old Marilyn Hagerty:

> It had been a few years since I ate at the older Olive Garden in Fargo, so I studied the two manageable menus offering appetizers, soups and salads, grilled sandwiches, pizza, classic dishes, chicken and seafood and filled pastas.
>
> At length, I asked my server what she would recommend. She suggested chicken Alfredo, and I went with that. Instead of the raspberry lemonade she suggested, I drank water.
>
> She first brought me the familiar Olive Garden salad bowl with crisp greens, peppers, onion rings and yes—several black olives. Along with it came a plate with two long, warm breadsticks.
>
> The chicken Alfredo ($10.95) was warm and comforting on a cold day. The portion was generous. My server was ready with Parmesan cheese. . . .
>
> All in all, it is the largest and most beautiful restaurant now operating in Grand Forks. It attracts visitors from out of town as well as people who live here.　　—MARILYN HAGERTY, "Long-awaited Olive Garden Receives Warm Welcome"

Hagerty's polite, unpretentious stance is evident in this review—and as it happens, the style of her writing attracted much attention when it went viral, with readers both celebrating and bashing that style.

Dreher contrasts Hagerty's stance with that of the following one by Dive Bar Girl (DBG), who writes for a newsletter in Baton Rouge, Louisiana. In fact, Dive Bar Girl starts right out by announcing her stance—that she's going to be "mean," not "informative"—and so after saying "a few nice things" about her topic, a restaurant called Twin Peaks, she writes the review that she assumes her readers "want to read":

> Admit it, you like it when DBG is mean. You only send her fan mail when she's mean. She never gets mail for being informative. . . . So she is going to write about the positive things first and then write the review you want to read. The smokehouse burger was above average. The patio

Marilyn Hagerty. Read the *LA Times*' take on the controversy—and Hagerty's son's response in the *Wall Street Journal*—via wwnorton.com/ write/everyone links.

was a nice space. The staff, while scantily clad, was professional. The salads even looked good. The place was miles above Hooters.

　　Here is the review you want: Twin Peaks has to be the brainchild of two 14-year-old boys who recently cracked the parental controls on the home computer. Waitresses are known as "Lumber Jills." In case you are missing the imagery—each Lumber Jill has been endowed with an epic pair of Twin Peaks.　　　　　　　　　　　—CHERRYTHEDIVEBARGIRL

These two reviews could hardly be more different in stance: The first is low key and even-handed, well suited to Hagerty's stance as a modest and sincere reviewer. The second is highly opinionated and sarcastic, true to the brash, in-your-face stance of Dive Bar Girl. So both are written in styles that suit (and reflect) their respective stances.

　　But what happens when that stance doesn't fit very well with a particular audience? That's what happened, in fact, when Hagerty's review went viral: Some writers immediately began making fun of her as inept and hopelessly out of it; others jumped in just as quickly to defend Hagerty's review, while still others read her review as an indirect parody of local restaurant reviews. Now imagine that Dive Bar Girl's review appeared in Hagerty's hometown newspaper. Chances are, it would attract some hefty criticism as well.

　　The takeaway lesson here: As a writer, you need to consider not only whether your stance is appropriate to your topic and audience but also to your mode of distribution. If what you write is going online, then you have to remember that your audience can be very broad indeed.

What do these photos say about an Olive Garden restaurant (*left*) and a Twin Peaks restaurant (*right*)?

Thinking about Your Own Style

As you've seen, style is all about making appropriate choices, choices that inevitably depend on all the elements of your rhetorical situation, including your stance, your purpose, your topic, and your audience. Have you written a review of something—a restaurant for the campus newspaper? A book on Amazon? A review of your school on *Collegeprowler.com*? If so, take a look at the choices you made there and then compare them to an essay you've written for your first-year writing class—or to a poster you've made for a school project on some subject like alcohol awareness. You'll see right away that you have instinctively used different styles for these different occasions. You may not, however, have paid much attention to the choices you were making to create these styles.

For an example of what we mean about making appropriate stylistic choices, take a look at a paragraph from this book, first as it appears on p. 511 and then as it is revised as a tweet, a report, and a flyer:

Original text

Once upon a time—and for a long time, too—style in writing meant ornamentation, or "dressing up" your writing the way you might dress yourself up for a fancy dress ball. In fact, ancient images often show rhetoric as a woman in a flowing gown covered with figures of speech—metaphors, similes, alliteration, hyperbole, and so on—her stylish ornaments.

Revised as a tweet

Writing style used to mean dressing up your words, like Cinderella getting ready for the ball. Not anymore. #rhetorictoday

Revised as a report

For more than 500 years, the definition of "style" held relatively stable: Style was a form of ornamentation that was added to texts in order to make them more pleasing or accessible to an audience. In ancient depictions, Rhetoric is often shown as a woman dressed in elegant attire and "ornamented" with dozens of stylish figures of speech.

Revised as a flyer

$\mathcal{O}$*nce upon a time . . .*

writing style was all about ornamentation.

ℰ𝒶 *Language* ℛℴ

in fancy dress

What do you know about writing style?

Join us in the Writing Center to learn how style has changed over time

and how your style can be *in* style.

Sterling C. Evans Library

Room 214

Note how the style changes to match each genre and audience: The tweet is short, of course, and very informal; it uses a sentence fragment and then uses a hashtag to link readers with others talking about rhetoric today. The report is much more formal and is written in standard edited English. The flyer uses a much more conversational style—ellipses to signal a pause, a sentence fragment, a question, and the use of italics for emphasis—and announces an event (the purpose of a flyer).

We hope this chapter has convinced you of the importance of paying attention to the stylistic choices you make—and has shown you that style is the key to getting and holding an audience's attention. As an author, you get to call the shots—and you need to do so with careful attention to your rhetorical situation. And though there may not be any simple do's and don't's for writing in an appropriate style, here are some questions that can help you think through the stylistic choices you'll need to make in your own writing.

- *What's appropriate?* In short, what word choice, sentence structure, images, punctuation, typography, and other elements of writing will get your message across in a way that is most fitting to your PURPOSE and AUDIENCE as well as the GENRE you are working in?

- *What level of formality should you use?* Think particularly of your topic and audience, and of your audience's expectations, as you decide whether to adopt a colloquial, informal, semiformal, or very formal level of language.

- *What stance should you take?* Again, think about matching your **STANCE** to your purpose and topic and audience. For a formal college essay, you will probably aim for a serious scholarly stance; for a letter of application, a businesslike, straightforward stance; and for a letter to the campus newspaper editor poking fun at a recent concert, a satiric, playful stance.

HAVE SOME FUN with style by choosing a writer you admire—or one you love to hate!—and then trying your hand at imitating that person's style. Cast a wide net in making your choice: Consider songwriters, editorialists, cookbook authors (Paula Deen? Julia Child?), novelists, poets, TV commentators (Stephen Colbert, maybe?). Gather a sample of this person's work, enough to give you a good sense of his or her style and stylistic choices in terms of language, sentence structure, rhythm, imagery, and so on. Then choose a well known story or song or other text: a children's story like "Little Red Riding Hood," a song like "Call Me Maybe," or a genre like a tweet or an ad. Now rewrite this text in the style of the author you chose—or ham it up a little by exaggerating the style! Your goal is to exercise your own authorial muscles and have some fun doing so.

TWENTY-SEVEN

Tweets to Reports

Moving from Social Media to Academic Writing

S *GOOGLE* MAKING US STUPID? Is texting destroying our ability to write? You're probably aware of the debate about whether the internet is undermining our ability to write well. The cartoon on the next page alludes to this debate; do you read it as a statement about the changes these questions refer to or as a spoof on the debate itself—or in some other way?

This cartoon is particularly funny because the two girls are using internet shorthand in *speech* when in fact it is used only in writing. In any case, the caption suggests that they are not quite ready for their transition back to school and "verbal communication." They aren't yet ready, that is, to shift from their informal online personas to their more formal academic ones.

We're betting that you, like the girls in the cartoon, are pretty comfortable with the writing you do on the web, especially on sites like *Facebook* and *Twitter*. Most often, you know who you are writing to, and you have a good sense of what's appropriate in terms of topic, language, and style. When it comes to academic writing, however, you may be a little less confident, wondering at times whether your writing is academic enough, formal enough, for your audience—usually a professor. If so, we have some good news: Our research shows that the informal writing you do on the internet uses many of the same strategies necessary in academic writing. This chapter aims to demonstrate how you can use what you already know

FIRST DAY BACK ᴛᴏ VERBAL COMMUNICATION

about effective communication in online settings to inform your academic writing. In short, this chapter will help you move between informal and formal writing, online or off.

Why is it important to be able to shift easily between informal and formal writing? The answer can be summed up in one word: appropriateness. You already know that what is appropriate for one situation (say, a college admissions essay) can be highly inappropriate in another situation (say, a party with good friends). And so you instinctively understand the rhetorical principle of appropriateness. In spite of claims about the internet destroying our ability to write, researchers who looked at thousands of pieces of writing done by students in first-year writing classes did not find even a single instance of anyone using acronyms like LOL or HBU or inserting "smilies." In other words, these students knew that abbreviations that are fine for communicating online are not *appropriate* for their college writing.

Of course, sometimes we slip up, as when someone laughs loudly at a somber occasion or follows up a job interview with a thank-you letter using slang or other inappropriate language. In these cases, the speaker or writer has failed to shift appropriately between informal and formal situations. We're hoping, however, that such slipups are few and far between for you and that this chapter will make you more aware of making appropriate choices in all the writing and speaking that you do.

To get more specific, let's look at several instances in which students have made some basic rhetorical moves on *Facebook, Twitter,* and other on-

David Crystal is one of those researchers, and he assures us that the English language is in no danger from texting abbreviations. Read what he says about it on p. 745.

line venues and at how you might make the same moves somewhat differently in academic writing.

Representing Yourself in Your Writing

Take a look at how some of your friends represent themselves on *Facebook:* What photos do they choose to say "this is who I am"? What personal information do they include? What facts about themselves run under their names? What kind of status updates do they generally create?

Here is Stephanie Parker, whose photo shows her with the words "laugh every day" inscribed on her face and hand, suggesting that she doesn't take herself too seriously, that she thinks laughter is good, as the old saying goes, "for what ails you," and that she wants us to think about how this motto might apply to us and our lives. She identifies herself as a student of media studies and lists some of her affiliations: with Stanford, with *TechSoup*, with Volunteers in Asia. In a recent post, she says:

> WOW!! Words cannot describe how happy I am that I got to see so many of you during my trip to Japan—you were all so kind and gracious to me, and made sure I had the best possible time. I will never forget, and look forward to your next visit to the U.S.!

Taken together, Parker's photo and this post depict her as a friendly, happy student who is engaged with friends, travel, and experiencing new things. The language of her posting is informal ("WOW!!") and a bit overstated ("words cannot describe," "best possible time"), and even her punctuation (multiple exclamation points) is more casual than she would use in a college essay. Her voice comes through here as a friend reaching out to say thanks and to issue an invitation to visit.

In her college writing, Parker could also represent herself as friendly and outgoing and enthusiastic, but her **TONE**, sentence structure, and punctuation would be more formal. As part of a presentation to the campus organization that funded her trip, she might say something like "Seeing many friends on my trip to Japan left me happy and very grateful for the kind and gracious way I was received. I will cherish these memories while I look forward to welcoming my hosts on a visit the United States." Note the more formal word choices ("cherish these memories" rather than "never forget," "United States" rather than "U.S.") and more formal punctuation—no use of all caps for emphasis, for example, and no exclamation points. This academic version is more restrained and formal, but it still conveys Parker's voice.

Note that first-person pronouns can be used in both formal and informal writing. You may have been told not to use first person in academic writing, and especially in the sciences doing so can sometimes be inappropriate. A researcher describing an experiment should, after all, put the emphasis on the experiment rather than on himself or herself. Thus that writer would appropriately say "The experiment revealed x" rather than "I conducted an experiment that revealed x." But in some academic writing, using the first person is perfectly acceptable. Consider the context: If your own experience is pertinent to the topic, saying *I* may be appropriate. But don't overdo it. Even in informal writing, overuse of the first person can get a little boring or sound a little too self-centered, as if everything is about ME.

Connecting to Audiences

On her popular lifestyle blog for women, *A Cup of Jo,* blogger Joanna Goddard posted "How to Talk to Little Girls," in which she links to other articles and poses questions about what's the most appropriate way to communicate with young girls. She ends her post with the following questions:

What's your take? Do you instinctively compliment little girls' looks too? What else do you talk about with little girls? Do you have any young girls in your life at the moment, or do you have a daughter? Do you think it's important or not that big of a deal? I'm curious to hear your thoughts.
—JOANNA GODDARD, "Motherhood Mondays: How to Talk to Little Girls"

Goddard's tone is casual and direct ("What's your take?") as she poses questions directly to her readers, and her confidence indicates that she knows her audience well—and has chosen questions designed to get them to speak up and respond to her posting. In fact, this post elicited 429 comments from readers, who responded to questions, thanked Goddard for commenting on the issue, and offered more advice and other links for exploring the topic.

In academic writing, attention to **AUDIENCE** is always important: You need to think carefully about who will read your writing and how best to connect to them. In courses that invite you to post comments to a course website, conduct peer reviews, or write regularly in a journal about what you read, the casual but direct tone used by this blogger can also serve you very well. In other instances, such as communicating with an instructor by email, a more formal approach is appropriate. Instead of using a series of direct questions as Goddard does in her blog post, an email to your instructor would more appropriately begin by saying, "I am writing to ask a question about the research I am doing on communicating effectively with young girls. Specifically, I wonder if it is appropriate to use a source I have found online in a blog. I would very much appreciate your advice on this issue."

Providing Context

When writing informally, you will often leave out a lot of information if you know that your readers are familiar with the context and don't need explicit cues. Especially online, writers often opt for brevity over clarity when writing to a group of friends or peers. Look, for instance, at this short piece of writing found on *Twitter*, a tweet about college football from Pat Bostick, a radio analyst and former quarterback for the Pitt Panthers.

What a great day for college football in the 'Burgh! Mid 60's and overcast for the Panthers vs. The Irish. Go #Pitt!!   —@PITTBOSTICK

This writer assumes that readers will understand a lot about the context for his post—that "the 'Burgh" is short for Pittsburgh (as is "Pitt"), for instance, and that the Panthers are the Pitt team and the Irish are Notre Dame. Readers will probably also know that the hashtag (#) is used here to link to others tweeting about the University of Pittsburgh—and if they don't know what a hashtag is, they'll just have to do some work to find out. In informal writing, readers are often expected to be able to understand the context or to figure out any context clues. And context clues are just that: *clues* that lead readers elsewhere and assume a lot about their prior knowledge, in this case, of the *Twitter* format. Informal writing—and especially brief messages like those on *Twitter*—allows you as an author to give readers quick context clues without detailed explanation.

In more formal writing, such as a newspaper article, a statement like this one would need to provide more explicit **CONTEXT**: to say when and where the game is taking place and why this particular game represents a "great day" for college football. So while you can learn from tweeting how to be succinct and make every word count, you can't count on readers to fill in the context in a news story—much less in formal academic writing—the way you can on *Twitter*. That's just one reason we don't see many 140-character responses to college assignments!

Organizing What You Write

The way you organize what you write or say plays a big role in making your words convincing. Even in your most informal writing, you probably intuitively structure what you write in a way that helps make your point. You state a claim, an idea, a thought—and then you offer reasons to support what you've stated. So organization is likely something you already utilize in your informal writing. Take a look at this concise review of a Chicago-area cooking school posted on *Yelp*. Note how the organization of the reviewer's message makes her point clear and convincing:

★★★★★ 8/10/2011

Ranjana's class in one of the best experiences I have had in Chicago. The class is insightful, cultural, and creative. It allows every attendee to explore both the simplicity and intricacies of Indian cooking. As a talented chef and teacher, Ranjana creates such a beautiful and comfortable space for learning that it is impossible to leave without a smile and fully belly

This writer uses a simple but effective structure in writing this review: First she offers an overall impression of the experience in the cooking school, and then she gives three reasons why the classes were the "best experience I have had in Chicago." Next, she provides a supporting statement and, finally, a concluding statement that reiterates her opening point.

Take a look at some of your own tweets or postings on *Facebook:* We bet they will show that you already have a pretty good idea of how to structure what you write, and this skill should transfer to your more formal and academic writing, too. Many college writing assignments will call for you to formulate a claim and then support it, just as the writer on *Yelp* does. In most of your college classes, however, you'll have more time and space to make your case: You'll be able (and expected) to introduce and explain your CLAIM and then to provide a number of good REASONS, examples, and other support for your claim; to consider and respond to COUNTERARGUMENTS; and to say something about its implications.

Using Images

As the cameras in smartphones get better and better, it's increasingly easy to snap a photo of almost anything. As a result, images are becoming a routine feature of much of our informal writing. Think about how often you've sent a photo along with a text message to show a friend something you've just seen. Writers now use images to make their writing more interesting or informative—or even to prove a point. One *Facebook* user had been posting status updates about a parrot (":D PEATRY THE TALKING PARROT! I saved him yesterday ♥"). One status update included this image along with the update:

He's beautiful. He was in a warehouse full of stuff from repo'd houses. In a corner, under a sheet. They were waiting for him to die so they could sell the cage.

Posting the photo of Peatry the talking parrot makes this message concrete, vivid, and memorable. In addition, the brightly colored bird with its rescuer adds emotional appeal, readers are glad to know Peatry has been saved! Note the informal language in the update: the heart at the end of the status update, "repo'd" instead of "repossessed," and the vague pronoun reference "they" that does not have a clear antecedent. Such informal language is welcome on *Facebook* but not in academic writing.

You can use images in your academic writing to very good effect as well. Adding a map, a diagram or pie chart, a photo, or even something you've drawn by hand is now easy to do and can make a point clear and concrete: Sometimes a picture really is worth a thousand words. In a college essay on buying and eating local, for instance, one writer found that adding a photograph of the fruit and vegetables on display at the local farmers' market helped make the point that locally produced food can offer plenty of variety. Of course, you need to be a little more careful about how you use images in your academic writing: Insert the image in the appropriate place, label it with a figure number (fig. 1), add an informative caption—and especially make sure readers know how the image supports your argument.

Dennis Baron sprinkles his presentation with images that work in concert with the text. Check it out on p. 705.

Sharing Information

In an email to her father and to her training partner, one student included a link to an article posted on *Active.com* titled "11 Major Marathon Mistakes." A runner herself, she wanted her running-fanatic dad and her training partner to read up on these common mistakes so all three of them could keep running without injury.

> Dad and Kendall,
>
> What do you think of this? http://www.active.com/running/Articles/ Eleven_major_marathon_mistakes.htm
>
> Guess we all better make sure we aren't making these mistakes before the race next month!

If you check out the link, you'll see that the article this student forwarded was written by Owen Davidson, PhD, an exercise scientist who presents only his own opinion about the mistakes runners make. Still, the student found it interesting and convincing enough to send it on to others, a decision that was perfectly appropriate in the informal context she was writing in. Browsing the web often leads to sources of information like this: interesting and informational but with no additional supporting sources or original research. Embedding links to sources—even if those sources may in some cases be questionable—is a useful way of sharing information and getting responses from others (who may write back challenging some of what the sources say). That is, it's a good way of joining in the conversation about a particular topic.

In more formal college writing, you will also be working with sources drawn from print as well as electronic media and also perhaps from field research you conduct yourself. You'll often be doing the same kind of browsing on the web that you do for informal purposes, and you can use the same strategies for identifying sources (through keyword searches, for example). You'll also be relying on the very same curiosity that drives your informal searches for information. In your more formal writing, however, you need to take another crucial step, which you can sometimes skip in informal contexts: to carefully evaluate the reliability of every source of information you want to use. So before citing that article on marathon runner mistakes in an academic writing assignment, you'd want to find out about the credentials of the doctor who wrote it (which, in this case, are included at the end of the article), check out other publications that he has written (preferably with secondary sources or original research), and evaluate the quality of the evidence he and any sources present before accepting it. And even then, you'd want to see if you could find other credible sources who agree with the doctor's arguments—or offer other viewpoints on the topic that you need to consider and acknowledge.

Citing Sources

Informal writing—whether it's on the internet or in your daily journal—allows you to skip some of the rules and requirements that formal writing requires. When you send someone a link, for example, you don't need to include a formal citation since readers can simply check out the information for themselves. You may make some reference to your sources: One student we know, a great fan of Bollywood films, tweets often about the latest ones he's seen and often includes a brief reference to reviews they've received. But when you send a tweet saying that you just heard about a great new movie, you probably don't take the time to say where you heard about it or who you heard it from, much less provide a formal citation.

Nevertheless, letting others know where you are getting your information can be very important. And giving others credit for their work is always important, whether you are writing a blog post or a college essay, even though the standards for citation are much more relaxed when you are writing for a nonacademic audience.

Take a look at Christina Hernandez Sherwood's post from her blog, *Spaghetti & Meatballs*, for example, which includes links to outside sources. Rather than relying on footnotes or in-text documentation (the kinds of citations you use in an academic essay), this blogger turned the words referring to the sources ("Gizmodo" and "small portion sizes") into links. She still gives the sources credit for the information she cites, but she does so in an appropriately informal way.

What would Italians think about Starbucks' Trenta?

There's been much hubbub this week over the newest, largest Starbucks drink size: Trenta.

The name means "thirty" in Italian, signifying the 30+ ounces of coffee the cup holds. That's more liquid than the average human stomach can handle, according to Gizmodo.

What would Italians think?

Italian diners, like other Europeans, are known for their  small portion sizes. Can you imagine Italians sipping a Big Gulp-sized cappuccino while nibbling on their biscotti?

—CHRISTINA HERNANDEZ SHERWOOD

So this blogger is aware of the need to provide information about sources. If this were an academic essay in print form, the writer would need to provide appropriate **DOCUMENTATION** for the linked references. Note, however, that some online academic journals, especially in the sciences, use links rather than in-text citations.

Establishing an Appropriate Tone

All of the writing you do—formal, informal, or in between—has a particular **TONE**. You may not think consciously about how to establish that tone, especially when commenting on a friend's *Facebook* photo or writing a text message, but even in the most informal writing, you are making choices about what attitude you want your text to convey. On *Facebook,* your readers are usually those friends and family members who read your postings regularly, so the tone you use there is probably pretty casual, like this status update posted by a student living in Washington, D.C.

> Note to self: avoid taking a train from union station out to the suburbs on a weekday morning. Going against the tide of aggressive commuters leaving the station is a major undertaking. Not fun.

In this piece of informal writing, the tone is one of tongue-in-cheek sarcasm ("Note to self") and frustration ("a major undertaking," "not fun"). Even in this very short snippet of writing, readers know the author's attitude.

If you were writing an essay instead of a *Facebook* status update on the commuter congestion problems in Washington, D.C., your tone would be different than the one used above: You would likely use the more serious tone of a reporter or researcher. But just like the status update, your writing would have some kind of a tone:

> Walking into the Metro station of Union Station on a weekday morning can be like going against a herd of stampeding cattle. Riders rush from the trains, swinging briefcases and computer bags, knocking over anything or anyone in the way. Looking at some usage statistics and videos will show just how unpleasant this experience is and how it affects those who regularly ride the Metro.

Here the tone is more serious: The writer opens by describing the scene in the congested station and then moves to introduce an analysis of usage statistics and videos. But even a serious tone doesn't need to be dry or dull. Note the lively description ("stampeding cattle," "swinging briefcases," and so on).

The examples in this chapter all aim to show that like the writers we cite here, you already know quite a bit about making appropriate choices in the informal writing you do—and that you can use this knowledge to help you move easily, and appropriately, between that informality and the more formal academic writing you need to do in school.

As we've tried to demonstrate, the internet is not only *not* destroying our ability to write, but in fact it is providing valuable, everyday practice that is teaching us how to represent ourselves, connect with audiences, and support our arguments—in writing. It's making us all writers, and it's one reason that today everyone's an author.

Alex Horton's article on p. 817 was originally published on his blog, *Army of Dude*. See how he sets a tone appropriate to his audience, his message, and his medium.

TWENTY-EIGHT

Meeting the Demands of Academic Writing

"It's Like Learning a New Language"

LLEN MacNAMARA ARRIVED AT COLLEGE excited but also anxious. She had grown up in a small town far from the college, had not taken calculus, and had never written more than a five-paragraph essay. So when she got her first college writing assignment—in a political science class, to write a ten-page essay on how the relationship among the three branches of the U.S. government has evolved—she felt a little panic. She had read all her assignments and done some research, and she had even met with her instructor during office hours. She had quite a bit of material. But when she started to write, it just didn't sound right. She wasn't sure what college writing sounded like, but this wasn't it. Following her instructor's advice, MacNamara studied several of the political science articles that were on her course reading list. Compared to her usual writing, they were much more formal, full of long words and complicated sentences. What she eventually came up with wasn't a particularly good paper (and she knew it), but it served its purpose: It had gotten her thinking about college-level writing. Looking back at the work she had done to get this far, she thought, "Wow, this is almost like learning a new language."

MacNamara had a point. Many students have experiences similar to hers, especially multilingual students who've grown up in other cultures. One Romanian student we know puts it this way:

In my country we care very much about the beauty of what we write. Even with academic and business writing, we try to make our texts poetic in some way. When I got to the U.S.A., I discovered that writing that I thought was beautiful struck my teachers as wordy and off task. I was surprised about this.

This student, like Ellen MacNamara, needed to set about learning a new language—in this case, the language of U.S. academic writing.

So Just What Is Academic Writing?

Academic writing is the writing you do for school. It follows a fairly strict set of conventions, such as using standard edited English, following logical patterns of organization, and providing support for the points you make. But academic writing reaches beyond the classroom: It's used in many journals, newspapers, and books as well as on the web, especially in many blogs. So "academic writing" is a broad category, one flexible enough to accommodate differences across disciplines, for example, while still remaining recognizably "academic." This chapter considers some of the assumptions that lie behind academic writing in the United States and describes some of the most common characteristics of that writing.

We're giving so much attention to academic writing for a couple of important reasons: First, becoming fluent in it will be of great help to you both in college and well beyond; and second, it poses challenges to both native and nonnative speakers of English. We want to acknowledge these challenges without making them sound like it takes a rocket scientist to meet them. Instead, we want to try to demystify some of the assumptions and conventions of academic writing and get you started thinking about how to use them to your advantage.

Joining U.S. Academic Conversations

If you are new to college, you need to learn to "talk the talk" of academic writing as soon as possible, so that you can join the conversations in progress all around you. Doing so calls for understanding some common expectations that most if not all of your instructors hold.

You're expected to respond. One important assumption underlying the kind of writing expected in American colleges is that reading and writing are active processes in which students not only absorb information but also respond to and even question it. Not all educational systems view reading and writing in this way. In some cultures, students are penalized if they attempt to read established texts critically or to disagree with authorities or insert their own views. If you are from such a background, you may find it difficult to engage in this kind of active reading and writing. It may feel rude, disrespectful, or risky, particularly if such engagement would result in a reprimand in your home culture.

Remember, however, that the kind of engagement your instructors want is not hostile or combative, not about showing off by beating down the ideas of others. Rather, they expect you to demonstrate your active engagement with the texts you read—and an awareness that in doing so you are joining an academic conversation, one that has been going on for a long time and that will continue. It's fine to express strong opinions, but it's also important to remember—and acknowledge—that there is almost surely some value in perspectives other than your own.

You're expected to ask questions. Because U.S. culture emphasizes individual achievement so much, students are expected to develop authority and independence, often by asking questions. In contrast to cultures where the best students never ask questions because they have already studied the material and worked hard to learn it, in American academic contexts, students are expected to ask questions. In other words, don't assume you have to figure everything out by yourself. Do take responsibility for your own learning whenever possible, but it's fine to ask questions, especially specific questions about assignments.

You're expected to say what *you* think. American instructors expect that students will progress from relying on the thoughts of others to formulating ideas and arguments of their own. One important way to make that move is to engage in dialogue with other students and teachers. In these dialogues, teachers are not looking for you to express the "right" position; instead, they're looking for you to say what *you* think and provide adequate and appropriate support for what you say.

You're expected to focus from the start. In contrast to many cultures, where writers start with fairly general background information for readers, American academic writing focuses in on the topic at hand from the start. Thus, even in the introduction of an essay, you begin at a relatively focused level, providing even greater detail in the paragraphs that follow. The point is not to provide evidence of how much you know but instead to provide as much specific information as is required for the audience to understand the point without having to work very hard.

Because American academic writers generally open their discussions at a fairly specific level, you wouldn't want to begin with a sentence like "All over the world and in many places, there are families," a thesis statement in an essay one of us once received from a native speaker of Arabic. (Translated into Arabic, this would make a beautiful sentence and an appropriate opening statement for a student essay.) Students educated in Spanish or Portuguese and, to an even greater extent, those educated in Arabic are accustomed to providing a great deal more background information than those educated in English do. If you are from one of these cultural backgrounds, do not be surprised if your instructor encourages you to delete most of the first few pages of a draft, for example, and to begin instead by addressing your topic more directly and specifically.

You're expected to state your point explicitly. In U.S. academic English, writers are expected to provide direct and explicit statements that lead readers, step by step, through the text—in contrast to cultures that value indirectness, circling around the topic rather than addressing it head-on. A Brazilian student we knew found it especially hard to state the major point of an essay up front and explicitly. From his cultural perspective, it made far more sense to develop an argument by building a sense of suspense and stating his position only at the end of the essay. As he said, "It took a lot of practice for me to learn how to write the very direct way that professors in the U.S.A. want."

All these expectations suggest that American academic discourse puts much of the burden for successful communication on the author rather than on members of the audience. So with these expectations in mind, let's take a close look at seven common characteristics of U.S. academic writing.

Academic writers at work in India, Chile, Italy, Burkina Faso, Thailand, and the United States.

CHARACTERISTIC FEATURES

Although no list of characteristics can describe all the kinds of texts you'll read or write in college, particularly given differences among disciplines, we can offer a list of conventional features that captures most, if not all, of what your professors will expect in the writing you do in their classes.

- Use standard edited English.
- Use clear and recognizable patterns of organization.
- Mark logical relationships between ideas.
- State claims explicitly and provide appropriate support.
- Present your ideas as a response to others.
- Express ideas clearly and directly.
- Be aware of how genres and conventions vary across disciplines.
- Document sources using the appropriate citation style.

Use Standard Edited English

Academic writing almost always follows the conventions of standard edited English in terms of spelling, grammar, and punctuation. In addition, it is more rather than less formal. Thus, the kind of abbreviations and other shortcuts you use all the time in text messaging or posting to social media sites usually aren't appropriate in academic writing: You'll have to write out "with respect to" rather than "wrt," and you'll also want to avoid ☺ and other emoticons. Likewise, slang isn't usually appropriate. In some contexts, you'll discover that even contractions aren't appropriate—although we use them in this book because we're aiming for a conversational tone, one that is formal to some degree but not stuffy. As you can probably tell, defining **STANDARD EDITED ENGLISH** is in many ways a matter of cataloging things you *shouldn't* do.

Additionally, however, thinking about the label itself—standard edited English—will give you some insights into the goal you are trying to accomplish. In general, the "standard" variety of any language is the one used in formal contexts, including academic ones, by people who are well educated; thus, the ability to use the standard variety of a language marks its user as educated.

The logic behind a standard language is simple and useful: If everyone can agree on and follow the same basic conventions, whether for spelling or subject-verb agreement, we'll be able to communicate successfully with a much broader range of people. It's a good principle in theory, but as you know if you have been to Canada or the United Kingdom, "standard" English varies from country to country. Moreover, standards change over time. So while having a "standard" set of conventions is valuable in many ways, it can't guarantee perfect communication.

"Edited," the second term of the label "standard edited English," reminds you that this variety of English is one that has been looked at very carefully. Many writers, especially those who grew up speaking a variety of English other than the standard and those whose first language is not English, reread their writing several times with great care before submitting it to ensure, for example, that every verb agrees with its subject. This is, of course, the role that good editors play: They read someone else's work and make suggestions about how to improve the quality, whether at the level of the sentence, the paragraph, or the text as a whole. Few of us pay such careful attention to our writing when we tweet, text, or email—but we *all* need to do so with our academic writing.

Use Clear and Recognizable Patterns of Organization

Academic writing is organized in a way that's clear and easy for readers to recognize. In fact, writers generally describe the pattern explicitly early in a text by including a **THESIS** sentence that states the main point and says how the text is structured.

At the level of the paragraph, the opening sentence generally serves as a **TOPIC SENTENCE**, which announces what the paragraph is about. Readers of academic writing expect such signals for the text as a whole and for each paragraph, even within shorter texts like essay exams. Sometimes you'll want to include headings to make it easy for readers to locate sections of text.

Readers of academic writing expect the organization of the text not only to be clear but also to follow some kind of logical progression. For example:

- Beginning with the simplest ideas and then moving step by step to the most complex ideas

- Starting with the weakest claims or evidence and progressing to the strongest ones
- Treating some topics early in the text because readers must have them as background to understand ideas introduced later
- Arranging the text chronologically, starting with the earliest events and ending with the latest ones

Some academic documents, including most journals in the sciences and social sciences, require a specific organization known as **IMRAD** for its specific headings: introduction, methods, results, and discussion. Although there are many possible logical patterns to use, readers will expect to be able to see that pattern with little or no difficulty. Likewise, they generally expect the **TRANSITIONS** between sections and ideas to be indicated in some way, whether with words like *first, next,* or *finally,* or even with full sentences like "Having considered three reasons to support this position, here are some alternative positions."

Finally, remember that you need to conclude your text by somehow reminding your readers of the main point(s) you want them to take away. Often, these reminders explicitly link the conclusion back to a thesis statement or introduction.

Mark Logical Relationships between Ideas

One more thing expected of academic writers is to make clear how your ideas relate to one another. Thus, in addition to marking the structure of the text, you need to mark the links between ideas and to do so explicitly. If you say in casual conversation, "It was raining, and we didn't go on the picnic," listeners will interpret *and* to mean *so* or *therefore.* In academic writing, however, you have to help readers understand how your ideas are related to one another. For this reason, you'll want to use **TRANSITIONS** like *therefore, however,* or *in addition.* Marking the relationships among your ideas clearly and explicitly helps readers recognize and appreciate the logic of your arguments.

State Claims Explicitly and Provide Appropriate Support

One of the most important conventions of academic writing is to present **CLAIMS** explicitly and support them with **EVIDENCE**, such as examples or statistics, or by citing authorities of various kinds. Notice the two distinct parts: presenting claims clearly and supporting them appropriately. In academic writing, authors don't generally give hints; instead, they state what is on their minds, often in a **THESIS** statement. If you are from a culture that values indirection and communicates by hinting or by repeating proverbs or telling stories to make a point, you'll need to work to be sure that you have stated your claims explicitly. Don't assume that readers will be able to understand what you're saying, especially if they do not have the same cultural background knowledge that you do.

Qualify your statements. It's important to note that being clear and explicit doesn't mean being dogmatic or stubborn. You'll generally want to qualify your claims by using **QUALIFYING WORDS** like *frequently*, *often*, *generally*, *sometimes*, or *rarely* to indicate how strong a claim you are making. Note as well that it is much easier to provide adequate support for a qualified claim than it is to provide support for an unqualified claim.

Choose evidence your audience will trust. Whatever your claim, you'll need to look for **EVIDENCE** that will be considered trustworthy and persuasive by your audience. And keep in mind that what counts as acceptable and appropriate evidence in academic writing often differs from what works in other contexts. Generally, for example, you wouldn't cite sacred religious texts as a primary source for academic arguments.

Consider multiple perspectives. Similarly, you should be aware that your readers may have a range of opinions on any topic, and you should write accordingly. Thus, citing only sources that reflect one perspective won't be sufficient in most academic contexts. Be sure to consider and acknowledge **COUNTERARGUMENTS** and viewpoints other than your own.

Organize information strategically. One common way of supporting a claim is by moving from a general statement to more specific information. When you see words like *for example* or *for instance*, the author is moving from a more general statement to a more specific example.

In considering what kind of evidence to use in supporting your claims, remember that the goal is not to amass and present large quantities of evidence but instead to sift through all the available evidence, choose the evidence that will be most persuasive to your audience, and arrange and present it all strategically. Resist the temptation to include information or **ANECDOTES** that are not directly relevant to your topic or contribute to your argument. Your instructor will likely refer to these as digressions or as "getting off topic" and encourage you to delete them.

Present Your Ideas as a Response to Others

The best academic writers do more than just make well-supported claims. They present their ideas as a response to what else has been said (or might be said) about their topic. One common pattern, introduced by Professors Gerald Graff and Cathy Birkenstein, is to start with what others are saying and then to present your ideas as a response. If, as noted earlier in this chapter, academic writing is a way of entering a conversation—of engaging with the ideas of others—you need to include their ideas in with your own.

In fact, providing support for your claims will often involve **SYNTHESIS** : weaving the ideas and even the words of others into the argument you are making. And since academic arguments are part of a larger conversation, all of us in some important ways are always responding to and borrowing from others, even as we develop our own ideas and present them to others.

Express Your Ideas Clearly and Directly

Another characteristic of academic writing is clarity. You want to be sure that readers can understand exactly what you are writing about. Have you ever begun a sentence by writing "This shows . . ." only to have your teacher ask, "What does *this* refer to?" Such a comment would be evidence that the teacher, as reader, wasn't sure what the author—you—was referring to: this argument? this evidence? this analysis? this figure? this claim? You'll also want to define terms you use, both to be sure readers will not be confused and to clarify your own positions—much as we defined "standard edited English" earlier in this chapter.

Clarity of expression in academic writing also means being direct and concise. Academic writers in the United States, for example, avoid highly elaborate sentence structures or flowery language, and they don't let the metaphors and similes they use get the best of them either, as this author did:

> Cheryl's mind turned like the vanes of a wind-powered turbine, chopping her sparrow-like thoughts into bloody pieces that fell onto a growing pile of forgotten memories.

In fact, this sentence was the winner of an annual "bad writing" contest in which writers try to write the worst sentence they possibly can. It's easy to see why this one was a winner: It has way too much figurative language—wind-powered turbines that chop, sparrows that bleed, thoughts in a pile, memories that are forgotten—and the metaphors get in the way of one another. Use metaphors sparingly in academic writing, and be very careful that they don't distract from what you're trying to say. Here's one way the prize-winning sentence might be revised to be clearer and more direct: "Cheryl's mind worked incessantly, thought after thought piling up until she couldn't keep track of them all."

Be Aware of How Genres and Conventions Vary across Disciplines

While we can identify common characteristics of all academic writing, it is important to note that some GENRES and conventions vary across disciplines. Thus, an analytic essay in psychology is similar to one in a literature class, but it is also different in crucial ways. The same will be true for lab reports or position papers in various fields. In this regard, different disciplines are like different cultures, sharing many things but unique in specific ways. Therefore, part of becoming a biologist or an engineer—or even an electrical engineer instead of a civil engineer—will require learning its particular rules and rituals as well as its preferred ways of presenting, organizing, and documenting information.

You'll also find that some rhetorical moves vary across genres. In the humanities, for example, writers often use a quotation to open an essay, as a way of launching an argument—or to close one, as a way of inspiring the audience. Such a move occurs far less often, if at all, in the sciences or social sciences.

Despite these differences in genres across academic disciplines, you'll also find there are some common rhetorical moves you'll make in much of the academic writing you do. Thus, you'll find that short essays and research articles generally open with three such moves:

- First, you give the **CONTEXT** or general topic of whatever you are writing; frequently, you will do this by discussing the existing research or commentary on the topic you are writing about.

- Second, you point out some aspect of this topic that merits additional attention, often because it is poorly understood or because there is a problem that needs to be solved—that is, you'll show there is a problem or gap of some kind in our understanding.

- Finally, you'll explain how your text addresses that problem or fills that gap. Notice that this often happens within the first paragraph or two of the text.

By contrast, in writing a response to a question on a timed exam, you might restate the question in some way, using it as the opening line of your response and a thesis statement or topic sentence. For example, if you get an essay exam question asking "How are West African influences evident in coastal southeastern areas of the United States today?" you might begin your response by turning the question into a statement like this: "West African influences to language, music, and food are still very visible in coastal areas of the southeastern United States." You should not spend several sentences introducing your topic while the clock ticks; to do so would be to waste valuable time.

With experience, you will learn the genres and conventions you need to know, especially within your major.

Document Sources Using the Appropriate Citation Style

Finally, academic writers credit and **DOCUMENT** all sources carefully. If becoming fluent in academic discourse is a challenge for all of us, understanding how Western academic culture defines intellectual property and plagiarism is even more complicated. Although you will never need to provide a source for historical events that no one disputes (for example, that the U.S. Declaration of Independence was signed on July 4, 1776, in Philadelphia), you will need to provide **DOCUMENTATION** for words, ideas, or organizational patterns that you get from others, including any information (words or images) you find on the internet.

What Else Do You Need to Learn about Academic Writing?

While we hope this brief list gives you a good idea of the major features of academic writing in the United States, you'll likely still find yourself asking questions. Just what does a direct and concise style look like? How much and what kinds of evidence are necessary to support a claim sufficiently? How much documentation is sufficient? Should a review of literature primarily describe and summarize existing research, or should it go one step further and critique this research? You will begin to learn the answers to these questions in time, as you advance through college, and especially when you choose your major. But don't be surprised that the immediate answer to all these questions will very often be, "It depends." And "it" will always depend on what your purpose is in writing and on the audience you wish to reach.

In the meantime, even as you work to become fluent in U.S. academic writing, it's worth returning to a note we have sounded frequently in this chapter: The U.S. way of writing academically is not the *only* way. Nor is it a *better* way. Rather, it is a *different* way. As you learn about and experience other cultures and languages, you may have an opportunity to learn and practice the conventions those cultures use to guide their own forms of academic writing. When you do so, you'll be learning yet another "new" language, just as you have learned the "academic writing" language of the United States.

TWENTY-NINE

How to Write Good Sentences

HEN A COLLEGE STUDENT asked author Annie Dillard, "Do you think I could become a writer?" Dillard replied with a question of her own: "Do you like sentences?" French novelist Gustave Flaubert certainly did, once saying that he "itched with sentences." We'll bet itching with sentences is not something you've experienced—and that liking or not liking sentences is not something you've ever thought about—but we'll also bet that you know something about how important sentences are. Anyone who has ever tried to write the perfect tweet or, better yet, the perfect love letter knows about choosing just the right words for each sentence and about the power of the three-word sentence "I love you"—or the even shorter sentence that sometimes follows from such declarations: "I do."

In his book *How to Write a Sentence,* English professor Stanley Fish declares himself to be a "connoisseur of sentences" and offers some particularly noteworthy examples. Here's one, written by a fourth grader in response to an assignment to write something about a mysterious large box that had been delivered to a school:

▶ I was already on the second floor when I heard about the box.

This reminded us of a favorite sentence of our own, this one the beginning of a story written by a third grader:

▶ Today, the monster goes where no monster has gone before: Cincinnati.

Here the student manages to allude to the famous line from *Star Trek*—"to boldly go where no man has gone before"—while suggesting that Cincinnati is the most exotic place on earth, and even using a colon effectively. It's quite a sentence.

Finally, here's a sentence that opens a chapter from a PhD dissertation on literacy among young people today:

▶ Hazel Hernandez struck me as an honest thief.

Such sentences are memorable: They startle us a bit and demand attention. They make us want to read more. Who's Hazel Hernandez? What's an honest thief, and what makes her one?

As these examples suggest, you don't have to be a famous author to write a great sentence. In fact, crafting effective and memorable sentences is a skill everyone can master with careful attention and practice. You may not come up with a zinger like the famous sentence John Updike wrote about Ted Williams' fabled home run in his last at bat at Fenway Park—"It was in the books while it was still in the sky"—but you can come close.

Just as certain effects in film—music, close-ups—enhance the story, a well-crafted sentence can bring power to a piece of writing. So think about the kind of effect you want to create in what you're writing—and then look for the type of sentence that will fit the bill. Though much of the power of the examples above comes from being short and simple, remember that some rhetorical situations call for longer, complex sentences—and that the kind of sentence you write also depends on its context, such as whether it's opening an essay, summing up what's already been said, or something else. This chapter looks at some common English sentence patterns and provides some good examples for producing them in your own work.

FOUR COMMON SENTENCE PATTERNS

We make sentences with words—and we arrange those words into patterns. If a sentence is defined as a group of words that expresses a complete thought, then we can identify four basic sentence structures: a SIMPLE SENTENCE (expressing one idea); a COMPOUND SENTENCE (expressing more than one idea, with the ideas being of equal importance); a COMPLEX SENTENCE (expressing more than one idea, with one of the ideas more important than the others); and a **COMPOUND-COMPLEX SENTENCE** (with more than one idea of equal importance and at least one idea of less importance).

Simple Sentences: One Main Idea

Let's take a look at some simple sentences:

▶ Resist!

▶ Consumers revolted.

▶ Angry consumers revolted against new debit-card fees.

▶ A wave of protest from angry consumers forced banks to rescind the new fees.

▶ The growth of the internet and its capacity to mobilize people instantly all over the world have done everything from forcing companies to rescind debit-card fees in the United States to bringing down oppressive governments in the Middle East.

As these examples illustrate, simple sentences can be as short as a single word—or they can be much longer. Each is a simple sentence, however, because it contains a single main idea or thought; in grammatical terms, each contains one and only one **MAIN CLAUSE**. As the name suggests, a simple sentence is often the simplest, most direct way of saying what you want to say—but not always. And often you want a sentence to include more than one idea. In that case, you need to use a compound sentence, a complex sentence, or a compound-complex sentence.

Compound Sentences:
Joining Ideas That Are Equally Important

Sometimes you'll want to write a sentence that joins two or more ideas that are equally important, like this one attributed to former President Bill Clinton:

▶ You can put wings on a pig, but you don't make it an eagle.

In grammatical terms, this is a compound sentence with two main clauses, each of which expresses one of two equally important ideas. In this case, Clinton joined the ideas with a comma and the coordinating conjunction *but*. But he had several other options for joining these ideas. For example, he could have joined them with only a semicolon:

▶ You can put wings on a pig; you don't make it an eagle.

Or he could have joined them with a semicolon, a conjunctive adverb like *however*, and a comma:

▶ You can put wings on a pig; however, you don't make it an eagle.

All of these compound sentences are perfectly acceptable—but which seems most effective? In this case, we think Clinton's choice is: It is clear and very direct, and if you read it aloud you'll hear that the words on each side of *but* have the same number of syllables, creating a pleasing, balanced rhythm—and one that balances the two equally important ideas. It also makes the logical relationship between the two ideas explicit; the version with only a semicolon, by contrast, indicates that the ideas are somehow related but doesn't show how.

Using *and, but*, and other coordinating conjunctions. In writing a compound sentence, remember that different coordinating conjunctions carry different meanings that signal different logical relationships between the main ideas in the sentence. There are only seven coordinating conjunctions.

COORDINATING CONJUNCTIONS

and	or	yet	nor
but	so	for	

▶ China's one-child policy has slowed population growth, *but* it has helped create a serious gender imbalance in the country's population.

▶ Most of us bike to work, *so* many of us stop off at the gym for a shower first.

▶ The champagne bottle crashed, the crowd cheered, *and* the ship slid down the ramp into the water.

See how the following sentences express different meanings depending on which coordinating conjunction is used:

▶ You could apply to graduate school, *or* you could start looking for a job.

▶ You could apply to graduate school, *and* you could start looking for a job.

Using a semicolon. Joining clauses with a semicolon only is a way of signaling that they are closely related without saying explicitly how. Often the second clause will expand on an idea expressed in the first clause.

▶ My first year of college was a little bumpy; it took me a few months to get comfortable at a large university far from home.

▶ The Wassaic Project is a multidisciplinary arts organization in Dutchess County, New York; artists go there to engage in "art, music, and everything else."

Adding a **CONJUNCTIVE ADVERB** can make the relationship between the ideas more explicit:

▶ My first year of college was a little bumpy; *indeed,* it took me a few months to get comfortable at a large university far from home.

Note that the conjunctive adverb in this sentence, *indeed,* cannot join the two main clauses on its own—it requires a semicolon before it. If you use a conjunctive adverb with only a comma before it, you've made a mistake called a **COMMA SPLICE**.

SOME CONJUNCTIVE ADVERBS

also	indeed	otherwise
certainly	likewise	similarly
furthermore	nevertheless	therefore
however	next	thus

〜☙ *READ THROUGH something you've written recently and identify compound sentences joined with* and. *When you find one, ask yourself whether it is the best word to use: Does it express the logical relationship between the two parts of the sentence that you intend? Would* but, or, so, for, nor, *or* yet *work better?*

Complex Sentences:
When One Idea Is More Important than Another

Many of the sentences you write will contain two or more ideas, with one more important than the other(s). So you need ways to indicate this difference: In grammatical terms, you want to show that a less important idea is subordinate to a more important one. Instead of putting the less significant idea in a **MAIN CLAUSE**, then, you put it in one of several kinds of **SUBORDINATE CLAUSES**:

▶ Most scientists believe *that global warming is caused by humans*.

▶ Those *who disagree* are a small minority of the scientific community.

▶ *If ocean levels rise significantly*, many cities *that are built at sea level* will be threatened.

As these examples show, the less important ideas—the ones in the subordinate clauses (italicized here)—can't stand alone as sentences: When we read "that global warming is caused by humans" or "who disagree," we know that something's missing. Subordinate clauses begin with words such as *if* or *because*— **SUBORDINATING CONJUNCTIONS**, words that signal the logical relationship between the subordinate clause and the rest of the sentence.

SOME SUBORDINATING CONJUNCTIONS

after	even though	until
although	if	when
as	since	where
because	that	while
before	though	who

Note that a subordinate clause can come at the end of a sentence, in the middle, or at the beginning. When it comes at the beginning, it is usually followed by a comma, as in the third example. If the opening clause in that sentence is moved to the end, there's no need for a comma: "Many cities that are built at sea level will be threatened if ocean levels rise significantly."

Grammatically, each of the three examples above is a complex sentence: It has one main idea and one or more ideas of less importance. In writing, you will often have to decide whether to combine ideas in a compound sentence, which gives the ideas equal importance, or in a complex one, which makes one idea more important than the other(s). Looking again at our sentence about the pig and the eagle, Bill Clinton could have written it as a complex sentence:

▶ Even though you can put wings on a pig, you don't make it an eagle.

Again, though, we think Clinton made a good choice in giving the two ideas in the sentence equal weight because doing so balances the sentence perfectly, telling us that both parts of the sentence are equally important. In fact, either part of this sentence isn't interesting in itself: It's the balancing and the contrast that make it interesting—and memorable.

Compound-Complex Sentences: Multiple Ideas—Some Less Important, Some More

When you are expressing three or more ideas in a single sentence, you'll sometimes want to use a compound-complex sentence, which gives some of the ideas equal importance and others less importance. Grammatically, such sentences have at least two **MAIN CLAUSES** and one **SUBORDINATE CLAUSE**.

▶   ⌐————— MAIN CLAUSE —————⌐⌐ SUBORDINATE CLAUSE⌐
We have experienced unparalleled natural disasters that have devastated

⌐————————⌐⌐————— MAIN CLAUSE —————⌐
entire countries, yet identifying global warming as the cause of these

⌐————————⌐
disasters is difficult.

▶   ⌐————— SUBORDINATE CLAUSE —————⌐⌐MAIN
Even after distinguished scientists issued a series of reports, critics

CLAUSE ————————⌐⌐————— SUBORDINATE CLAUSE————⌐
continued to question the findings because they claimed results were falsified;

⌐—— MAIN CLAUSE ——⌐
nothing would convince them.

As these examples show, English sentence structure is flexible, allowing you to combine groups of words in different ways in order to get your ideas across to your audience most appropriately and effectively. There's seldom only one way to write a sentence to get an idea across: As the author, you must decide which way works best for your **RHETORICAL SITUATION**.

WAYS OF EMPHASIZING
THE MAIN IDEA IN A SENTENCE

Sometimes you will want to lead off a sentence with the main point; other times, you might want to hold it in reserve until the end. **CUMULATIVE SENTENCES** start with a main clause and then add on to it, "accumulating" details. **PERIODIC SENTENCES** start with a series of phrases or subordinate clauses and save the main clause for last.

Cumulative Sentences: Starting with the Main Point

In this kind of sentence, the writer starts off with a **MAIN CLAUSE** and then adds details in phrases and **SUBORDINATE CLAUSES**, extending or explaining the thought. Cumulative sentences can be especially useful for describing a place or an event, operating almost like a camera panning across a room or landscape. The sentences below create such an effect:

▶ The San Bernardino Valley lies only an hour east of Los Angeles by the San Bernardino Freeway but is in certain ways an alien place: not the coastal California of the subtropical twilights and the soft westerlies off the Pacific but a harsher California, haunted by the Mojave just beyond the mountains, devastated by the hot dry Santa Ana wind that comes down through the passes at 100 miles an hour and whines through the eucalyptus windbreaks and works on the nerves.

—JOAN DIDION, "Some Dreamers of the Golden Dream"

▶ Public transportation in Cebu City was all about jeepneys: refurbished military jeeps with metal roofs for shade, decorated with horns and mirrors and fenders and flaps; painted with names, dedications, quotations, religious icons, logos—and much, much more.

▶   She hit the brakes, swearing fiercely, as the deer leapt over the hood and crashed into the dark woods beyond.

▶   The celebrated Russian pianist gave his hands a shake, a quick shake, fingers pointed down at his sides, before taking his seat and lifting them imperiously above the keys.

These cumulative sentences add details in a way that makes each sentence more emphatic. Keep this principle in mind as you write—and also when you revise. See if there are times when you might revise a sentence or sentences to add emphasis in the same way. Take a look at the following sentences, for instance:

▶   China has initiated free-market reforms that transformed its economy from a struggling one to an industrial powerhouse. It has become the world's fastest-growing major economy. Growth rates have been averaging 10 percent over the last decade.

These three sentences are clearly related, with each one adding detail about the growth of China's economy. Now look what happens when the writer eliminates a little bit of repetition, adds a memorable metaphor, and combines them as a cumulative—and more emphatic—sentence:

▶   China's free-market reforms have led to 10 percent average growth over the last decade, transforming it from a paper tiger into an industrial dragon that is now the world's fastest-growing major economy.

Periodic Sentences: Delaying the Main Point until the End

In contrast to sentences that open with the main idea, periodic sentences delay the main idea until the very end. Periodic sentences are sometimes fairly long, and withholding the main point until the end is a way of adding emphasis. It can also help create suspense or build up to a surprise or inspirational ending.

▶   In spite of everything, in spite of the dark and twisting path he saw stretching ahead for himself, in spite of the final meeting with Voldemort he knew must come, whether in a month, in a year, or in ten, he felt his heart lift at the thought that there was still one last golden day of peace left to enjoy with Ron and Hermione.   —J. K. ROWLING, *Harry Potter and the Half-Blood Prince*

▶ Unprovided with original learning, uninformed in the habits of thinking, unskilled in the arts of composition, I resolved to write a book.

—EDWARD GIBBON, *Memoirs of My Life*

▶ In the week before finals, when my studying and memorizing reached a fever pitch, came a sudden, comforting thought: I have never failed.

Here are three periodic sentences in a row about Whitney Houston, each of which withholds the main point until the end:

▶ When her smiling brown face, complete with a close-cropped Afro, appeared on the cover of *Seventeen* in 1981, she was one of the first African-Americans to grace the cover, and the industry took notice. When she belted out a chilling and soulful version of the "Star-Spangled Banner" at the 1991 Super Bowl, the world sat back in awe of her poise and calm. And in an era when African-American actresses are often given film roles portraying them as destitute, unloving, unlovable, or just "the help," Houston played the love interest of Kevin Costner, a white Hollywood superstar.

—ALLISON SAMUELS, "A Hard Climb for the Girl Next Door"

These three periodic sentences create a drumlike effect that builds in intensity as they move through the stages in Houston's career; in all, they suggest that Houston was, even more than Kevin Costner, a "superstar."

Samuels takes a chance when she uses three sentences in a row that withhold the main point until the end: Readers may get tired of waiting for that point. And readers may also find the use of too many such sentences to be, well, too much. But as the example above shows, when used carefully a sentence that puts off the main idea just long enough can keep readers' interest, making them want to reach the ending, with its payoff.

You may find times in your own writing when revising to create a periodic sentence can make your writing more emphatic. Take a look at the following sentence from an essay on the use of animals in circuses:

▶ The big cat took him down with one swat, just as the trainer, dressed in khakis and boots, his whip raised and his other arm extended in welcome to the cheering crowd, stepped into the ring.

This sentence paints a vivid picture, but it gives away all the action in the first six words. By withholding that action until the end, the writer builds anticipation and adds emphasis:

▶ Just as the trainer stepped into the ring, dressed in khakis and boots, his whip raised and his other arm extended in welcome to the cheering crowd, the big cat took him down with one swat.

OPENING SENTENCES

The opening sentences in your writing carry big responsibilities, setting the tone and often the scene—and helping draw your readers in by arousing their interest and curiosity. Authors often spend quite a lot of time on opening sentences for this very reason: Whether it's a business report or a college essay or a blog posting, the way it begins has a lot to do with whether your audience will stay with you and whether you'll get the kind of response you want from them. Here are three famous opening sentences:

▶ I am an invisible man.   —RALPH ELLISON, *Invisible Man*

▶ The sky above the port was the color of television, tuned to a dead channel.
                                        —WILLIAM GIBSON, *Neuromancer*

▶ They shoot the white girl first.   —TONI MORRISON, *Paradise*

Each of these sentences is startling, making us read on in order to find out more. Each is brief, leaving us waiting anxiously for what's to come. In addition, each makes a powerful statement and creates some kind of image in readers' minds: an "invisible" person, a sky the color of a "dead" TV channel, someone being shot. These sentences all come from novels, but they use strategies that work in many kinds of writing.

It usually takes more than a single sentence to open an essay. Consider, for example, how Michael Pollan begins a lengthy essay on animal liberation:

▶ The first time I opened Peter Singer's *Animal Liberation*, I was dining alone at the Palm, trying to enjoy a rib-eye steak cooked medium-rare. If this sounds like a good recipe for cognitive dissonance (if not indigestion), that was sort of the idea. Preposterous as it might seem to supporters of animal rights, what I was doing was tantamount to reading *Uncle Tom's Cabin* on a plantation in the Deep South in 1852.
                                —MICHAEL POLLAN, "An Animal's Place"

The first sentence presents an incongruous image that holds our attention (he's eating a steak while reading about animal liberation). Then the rest of the paragraph makes this incongruity even more pronounced, even comparing the situation to someone reading the antislavery novel *Uncle Tom's Cabin* while on a slave-owning plantation. It's an opening that makes us read on.

Here is the opening of a blog posting that begins with a provocative question:

▶ Have you ever thought about whether to have a child? If so, what factors entered into your decision? Was it whether having children would be good for you, your partner and others close to the possible child, such as children you may already have, or perhaps your parents? For most people contemplating reproduction, those are the dominant questions. Some may also think about the desirability of adding to the strain that the nearly seven billion people already here are putting on our planet's environment. But very few ask whether coming into existence is a good thing for the child itself.

　　　　　　　—PETER SINGER, "Should This Be the Last Generation?"

Singer's question is designed to get the reader's attention, and he follows it up with two additional questions that ask readers to probe more deeply into their reasons for considering whether or not to reproduce. In the fifth sentence, he suggests that the answers people give to these questions may not be adequate ones, and in the last sentence he lays down a challenge: Perhaps coming into existence is not always good for "the child itself."

Here's another example of an opening that uses several sentences, this one from a student essay about graphic memoirs:

▶ In 1974, before the Fall of Saigon, my 14-year-old father, alone, boarded a boat out of Vietnam in search of America. This is a fact. But this one fact can spawn multiple understandings: I could ask a group of students to take a week and write me a story from just this one fact, and I have no doubt that they would bring back a full range of interpretations.

　　　　　　　—BRANDON LY, "Leaving Home, Coming Home"

This opening passage begins with a vivid image of a very young man fleeing Vietnam alone, followed by a very short sentence that makes a statement and then a longer one that challenges that statement. This student writer is moving readers toward what will become his thesis: that memoirs can never tell "the whole truth, and nothing but the truth."

Finally, take a look at the opening of the speech Toni Morrison gave when she won the Nobel Prize for Literature:

▶ Members of the Swedish Academy, Ladies and Gentlemen:
Narrative has never been mere entertainment for me. It is, I believe, one of the principal ways in which we absorb knowledge. I hope you will understand, then, why I begin these remarks with the opening phrase of what must be the oldest sentence in the world, and the earliest one we remember from childhood: "Once upon a time . . ."

Here Morrison begins with a deceptively simple statement, that narrative is for her not just entertainment. In the next two sentences, she complicates that statement and broadens her claim that narrative is the way we understand the world, concluding with what she calls "the oldest sentence in the world."

You can use strategies similar to the ones shown here in opening your college essays. Here are just some of the ways you might begin:

- With a strong, dramatic—or deceptively simple—statement
- With a vivid image
- With a provocative question
- With an anecdote
- With a startling claim

Opening sentences online. If the internet lets us send messages to people all over the world, it also challenges us to get and keep their attention. And with limited space and attention (small screens; readers in a hurry, scanning for what they need), writers need to take care to craft opening sentences of any text posted online to be as attention getting and informative as possible.

In email, for instance, first sentences often show up in auto-preview lines, so it's a good idea to write them carefully. Here's the first line of an email sent recently to everyone at W. W. Norton:

▶ A Ping-Pong table has been set up on the 4th floor in loving memory of Diane O'Connor.

This email was sent by O'Connor's colleagues, honoring her efforts to persuade Norton to have an annual company Ping-Pong tournament. It might have said less ("Ping-Pong on 4," "Remembering Diane"), as email usually does—but there was more that they wanted to say.

And then there's *Twitter.* As if it weren't enough of a challenge to say what you want to say in 140 characters, you'd better begin with a sentence that will catch readers' attention. Here are two tweets that got ours:

▶ Steve Jobs was born out of wedlock, put up for adoption at birth, dropped out of college, then changed the world. What's your excuse?   —@JWMOSS

▶ It's so weird because Rush Limbaugh has been such an awesome human being until now.   —@BUCK4ITT

You'll want to think carefully about how you open any text that you post to the web—and to craft opening sentences that will make sense in a *Google* search list. Here are two that we like:

▶ Smith Women Redefine "Pearls and Cashmere."

This is the headline for an article in *Inside Higher Ed,* an online magazine read by educators, but it's also the line that comes up in a *Google* search. The article is about a controversy at Smith College—and we think you'll agree that the headline surely got the attention of those scanning the magazine's list of articles or searching *Google.*

▶ **The Art of Fielding** is a 2011 novel by former *n+1* editor Chad Harbach. It centers on the fortunes of shortstop Henry Skrimshander, and his career playing college baseball with the Westish College Harpooners, a Division III (NCAA) team.

This is the start of the *Wikipedia* entry for a novel, which comes up in a *Google* search. As you can see, it identifies the book, says who wrote it, and gives a one-sentence description of the story. Safe to say, the authors of this entry were careful to provide this information in the very first sentences.

CLOSING SENTENCES

Sentences that conclude a piece of writing are where you have a chance to make a lasting impact: to reiterate your point, tell readers why it matters, echo something you say in your opening, make a provocative statement, issue a call for action.

Here's Joe Posnanski, wrapping up an essay on his blog arguing that college athletes should not be paid:

> College football is not popular because of the stars. College football is popular because of that first word. Take away the college part, add in money, and you are left with professional minor league football . . . . See how many people watch that.   —JOE POSNANSKI, "The College Connection"

These four sentences summarize his argument—and the last one's the zinger, one that leaves readers thinking.

Now take a look at the conclusion to a scholarly book on current neurological studies of human attention, the brain science of attention:

> Right now, our classrooms and workplaces are structured for success in the last century, not this one. We can change that. By maximizing opportunities for collaboration, by rethinking everything from our approach to work to how we measure progress, we can begin to see the things we've been missing and catch hold of what's passing us by.
>
>   If you change the context, if you change the questions you ask, if you change the structure, the test, and the task, then you stop gazing one way and begin to look in a different way and in a different direction. You know what happens next:
>
>   *Now* you see it. —CATHY DAVIDSON, *Now You See It: How the Brain Science of Attention Will Transform the Way We Live, Work, and Learn*

Cathy Davidson uses two short paragraphs to sum up her argument and then concludes with a final paragraph that consists of just one very short four-word sentence. With this last sentence, she uses a tried-and-true strategy of coming full circle to echo the main idea of her book and, in fact, to reiterate its title. Readers who have worked their way through the book will take pleasure in that last sentence: *Now* they do see her point.

For another example, note how in the ending to a speech about language and about being able to use "all the Englishes" she grew up with, author Amy Tan closes with a one-sentence paragraph that quotes her mother:

> Apart from what any critic had to say about my writing, I knew I had succeeded where it counted when my mother finished reading my book and gave me her verdict: "So easy to read."   —AMY TAN, "Mother Tongue"

Tan's ending sums up one of her main goals as an author: to write so that readers who speak different kinds of English will find her work accessible, especially her mother.

Finally, take a look at how Toni Morrison chose to close her Nobel Prize acceptance speech:

> ▶ It is, therefore, mindful of the gifts of my predecessors, the blessing of my sisters, in joyful anticipation of writers to come that I accept the honor the Swedish Academy has done me, and ask you to share what is for me a moment of grace.   —TONI MORRISON, Nobel Prize acceptance speech

In this one-sentence conclusion, Morrison speaks to the past, present, and future when she says she is grateful for those writers who came before her, for those who are writing now (her sisters), and for those yet to come. She ends the sentence by asking her audience to share this "moment of grace" with her and, implicitly, with all other writers so honored.

You may not be accepting a Nobel Prize soon, but in your college writing you can use all the strategies presented here to compose strong closings:

- By reiterating your point
- By discussing the implications of your argument
- By asking a question
- By referring back to your beginning
- By recommending or proposing some kind of action

IDENTIFY two memorable openings and closings from a favorite novel, comic book, film, or blog. What makes them so good? Do they follow one of the strategies presented here?

VARYING YOUR SENTENCES

Read a paragraph or two of your writing out loud and listen for its rhythm. Is it quick and abrupt? slow and leisurely? singsong? stately? rolling? Whatever it is, does the rhythm you hear match what you had in mind when you were writing? And does it put the emphasis where you want it? One way to establish the emphasis you intend and a rhythm that will keep readers reading is by varying the length of your sentences and the way those sentences flow from one to the other.

A string of sentences that are too much alike is almost certain to be boring. While you can create effective rhythms in many ways, one of the simplest and most effective is by breaking up a series of long sentences with a shorter one that gives your readers a chance to pause and absorb what you've written.

Take a look at the following passage, from an article in the *Atlantic* about the finale of the *Oprah Winfrey Show*. See how the author uses a mix of long and short sentences to describe one of the tributes to Oprah, this one highlighting her support of black men:

▶ [Oprah's] friend Tyler Perry announced that some of the "Morehouse Men," each a beneficiary of the $12 million endowment she has established at their university, had come to honor her for the scholarships she gave them. The lights were lowered, a Broadway star began singing an inspirational song, and a dozen or so black men began to walk slowly to the front of the stage. Then more came, and soon there were a score, then 100, then the huge stage was filled with men, 300 of them. They stood there, solemnly, in a tableau stage-managed in such a way that it might have robbed them of their dignity—the person serenading them (or, rather, serenading Oprah on their behalf) was Kristin Chenoweth, tiniest and whitest of all tiny white women; the song was from *Wicked*, most feminine of all musicals; and each man carried a white candle, an emblem that lent them the aspect of Norman Rockwell Christmas carolers. But they were not robbed of their dignity. They looked, all together, like a miracle. A video shown before the procession revealed that some of these men had been in gangs before going to Morehouse, some had fathers in prison, many had been living in poverty. Now they were doctors, lawyers, bankers, a Rhodes Scholar—and philanthropists, establishing their own Morehouse endowment.

　　　　　　　—CAITLIN FLANAGAN, "The Glory of Oprah"

The passage begins with three medium-length sentences—and then one very long one (seventy-two words!) that points up the strong contrast between the 300 black men filling the stage and the "whitest of white" singer performing a song from the "most feminine" of musicals. Then come two little sentences (the first one eight words long and the second one, seven) that give readers a chance to pause and absorb what has been said while also making an important point: that the men "looked, all together, like a

The Morehouse Men surprise Oprah.

miracle." The remainder of the passage moves back toward longer sentences, each of which explains just what this "miracle" is. Try reading this passage aloud and listen for how the variation in sentences creates both emphasis and a pleasing and effective rhythm.

In addition to varying the lengths of your sentences, you can also improve your writing by making sure that they don't all use the same structure or begin in the same way. You can be pretty sure, for example, that a passage in which every sentence is a simple sentence that opens with the subject of a main clause will not read smoothly at all but rather will move along awkwardly. Take a look at this passage, for example:

▶ The sunset was especially beautiful today. I was on top of Table Mountain in Cape Town. I looked down and saw the sun touch the sea and sink into it. The evening shadows crept up the mountain. I got my backpack and walked over to the rest of my group. We started on the long hike down the mountain and back to the city.

There's nothing wrong with these sentences as such. Each one is grammatically correct. But if you read the passage aloud, you'll hear how it moves abruptly from sentence to sentence, lurching along rather than flowing smoothly. The problem is that the sentences are all the same: Each one is a simple sentence that begins with the subject of a main clause (*sunset, I, I, evening shadows, I, we*). In addition, the use of personal pronouns at the beginning of the sentences (three *I*'s in only six sentences!) makes for dull reading. Finally, these are all fairly short sentences, and the sameness of the sentence length adds to the abrupt rhythm of the passage—and doesn't keep readers reading. Now look at how this passage can be revised by working on sentence variation:

▶ From the top of Cape Town's Table Mountain, the sunset was especially beautiful. I looked down just as the fiery orb touched and then sank into the sea; shadows began to creep slowly up the mountain. Picking up my backpack, I joined the rest of my group, and we started the long hike down the mountain.

This revision reduces the number of sentences in the passage from six to three (the first simple, the second compound-complex, the third compound) and varies the length of the sentences. Equally important, the revision eliminates all but one of the subject openings. The first sentence now begins with the prepositional phrase ("From the top"); the second with the subject of a main clause ("I"); and the third with a participial phrase ("Picking up my backpack"). Finally the revision varies the diction a bit, replacing the repeated word "sun" with a vivid image ("fiery orb"). Read the revised passage aloud and you'll hear how varying the sentences creates a stronger rhythm that makes it easier to read.

This brief chapter has only scratched the surface of sentence style. But we hope we've said enough to show how good sentences can be your allies, helping you get your ideas out there and connect with audiences as successfully as possible. Remember: Authors are only as good as the sentences they write!

TAKE A LOOK at a writing assignment you've recently completed. Read it aloud, listening for rhythm and emphasis. If you find a passage that doesn't read well or provide the emphasis you want, analyze its sentences for length (count the words) and structure (how does each sentence begin?). Revise the passage using the strategies presented above.

THIRTY

Designing What You Write

DESIGN. **IT'S A WORD YOU HEAR ALL THE TIME,** one you use without thinking about it. "Kate Middleton's wedding dress was designed by Sarah Burton for Alexander McQueen." "Have you seen Apple's design for the new Nano?" "Frank Gehry's design of the Disney Concert Hall astonished critics with its waves of gleaming stainless steel." "My essay was designed to get the attention of the college admissions committee."

Fashion, technology, architecture, toys: Everything is designed, including writing. Whenever you write something—a slide presentation for a report, a blog post, an essay—you design it, whether you are conscious of doing so or not. You select a medium and tools: a lined notebook and a pencil, a text message and a smartphone, white paper and a laser printer. You choose fonts and colors: big red capital letters for a poster, 12-point black Times New Roman for an essay. You think about including visuals: a bar graph on a slide, a cartoon in a blog, a photo in an essay. You consider whether to use multiple columns and where to leave some white space. You decide what you want readers to notice first and put that in a prominent position.

This chapter discusses several key design elements: typography, color, visuals, and layout. Whatever fonts or images you use, though, remember that they are not mere decoration. However you design a text, you need to be guided by your purpose, your audience, and the rest of your rhetorical situation.

THINKING RHETORICALLY ABOUT DESIGN

Your design choices play a role in the way your audience receives your message and whether your text achieves its purpose. Look, for example, at the different ways that Coca-Cola was advertised in 1913 and 2010. In 1913, Coke was relatively new, and its ads relied on words to introduce it to an audience that was not yet familiar with it, telling them it had "character" and was "delicious," "refreshing," and "thirst-quenching." The ad shown here was designed so that these words would pop and be easy to read. To reach today's audiences, advertisers use today's media—in the case of the 2010 ad here, a video—to reach a mass audience. The cartoon characters Stewie Griffin and Underdog vie for control of the Coke bottle balloon, and the only word is the one on the bottle: "Coca-Cola." One thing the two ads have in common, though, is the logo: Whether it's in black ink on white paper or red and white pixels on a screen, the Coca-Cola logo was *designed* to be recognizable—and thus to get our attention.

In designing what we write, we need always to think about how we can best reach our audience and achieve our purpose. Given the deluge of words, images, and other data, readers today are less likely than they once were to read anything start to finish. Instead, they may scan for just the information they need. As an author, then, you need to design your documents to be user-friendly: easy to access, to navigate, to read—and to remember.

A print ad for Coca-Cola in Georgia Tech's 1913 yearbook and a video ad presented during the telecast of the 2010 Super Bowl.

Remember as well that your design can shape your audience's reaction before they read a word, so you'll want to start by thinking about that audience, your purpose, and your entire rhetorical situation.

- *What's your* GENRE*?* Does it call for certain design elements—a style or size of type, perhaps, or tables and graphs?

- *Who is your* AUDIENCE*,* and what design elements will appeal to them? Are there any elements that might *not* appeal to them—or cause them to question your authority as author?

- *What is your* PURPOSE*?* To provide information? To entertain? To persuade readers to take some kind of action? What design elements might help you achieve that purpose? Is there anything that would work against it—using a playful typeface in a business letter, for example?

- *What's your* STANCE *as an author,* and how do you want to come across to your audience? Do you want to seem businesslike? serious? ironic? practical and matter-of-fact? How can your design—fonts, color, images—reflect that stance?

- *Consider the larger* CONTEXT*.* Do you have any time constraints? What technology do you have available? Does your assignment have any design requirements?

- *What's your* MEDIUM —print? digital? spoken?—and what kinds of design elements are appropriate (or possible)? A print essay, for example, could include photographs but not video.

CHOOSING FONTS

We have hundreds of fonts to choose from today. The ones we use affect our message—what it looks like, and how it is received—so it's important to think carefully about what's appropriate for our medium, genre, and the rest of our rhetorical situation.

Serif fonts such as Times New Roman or Bodoni have a traditional look, whereas sans serif fonts such as Arial or Futura give a more modern look. Your instructors may require you to use a specific font, but if you get to choose, you'll want to think about what look you want for your text—and what will be most readable. Some readers find serif fonts easier to read in longer pieces of writing. Sans serif, on the other hand, tends to be easier to read in slide presentations. Save novelty or decorative fonts such as **Impact** or *Allegro Script* for your nonacademic writing—and even there, use them sparingly, since they can be difficult (or annoying!) to read.

Most fonts include **bold**, *italics,* and <u>underlining</u> options, which you can use to highlight parts of a text. In academic writing, bold is generally used for headings, whereas italics or underlining is used for titles of books, films, and other long works. If you're following MLA, APA, or another academic style, be careful that your use of fonts conforms to their requirements.

Readability matters. For most academic and workplace writing, you'll want to use 10-to-12-point type, and at least 18-point type for most presentation slides. Academic writing is usually double-spaced; letters and résumés are single-spaced.

Headings

Brief texts may need no headings at all, but for longer texts, headings can help readers follow the text and find specific information. Some kinds of writing have set headings that authors are required to use— IMRAD reports, for instance, require introduction, methods, research, and discussion headings. When you include headings, you need to decide on wording, fonts, and placement.

Wording. Make headings succinct and parallel. You could make them all nouns ("Energy Drinks," "Snack Foods"), all gerund phrases ("Analyzing the Contents of Energy Drinks," "Resisting Snack Foods"), or all questions ("What's in Energy Drinks?" or "Why Are Snack Foods So Hard to Resist?").

Fonts. If you're using more than one level of heading, distinguish them from one another typographically by using bold, italic, underlining, and capitalization. For example:

FIRST-LEVEL HEADING
Second-Level Heading
Third-Level Heading

When you get to choose, you may want to make headings larger than the main text or to put them in a different font or color (as we do throughout this book). But if you're following MLA or APA styles, be aware that they require headings to be in the same font as the main text.

Placement. You can center headings or set them flush left above the text or place them to the left of the text; but whatever you do, treat each level of heading consistently throughout the text. If you're following MLA or APA styles, be aware that first-level headings must be centered.

USING COLOR

Sometimes you'll be required to write in black type on a white background, but many times you'll have reason to use colors. In some media, color will be expected or necessary—on websites or presentation slides, for instance. Other times it may be inappropriate—in a thank-you note following a job interview at a law firm, or in an application essay to business school. As with any design element, color should be used to help you get a message across to an audience, never just to decorate your text.

Be aware that certain colors evoke specific emotional reactions: blue, like the sky and sea, suggests spaciousness and tranquility; red invokes fire and suggests intense energy and emotions; yellow, the color of our sun, generates warmth and optimism. Also remember that certain colors carry different associations across cultures—to Westerners, white suggests innocence and youth, but in China white is traditionally associated with death (which is why Chinese brides wear red).

Especially if you use more than one color in a text, you'll want to consider how certain colors work together. Look at the color wheel on p. 575 to see how the colors are related. *Primary colors* (red, blue, and yellow) create an effect of simplicity and directness. The more *secondary and tertiary colors* you use, the more sophisticated the design. *Complementary colors*, located opposite each other on the color wheel, look brighter when placed next to each other. (Black and white are also considered complementary colors.) *Cool and dark colors* appear to recede, whereas *warm and bright colors* seem to advance. So using both cool and warm colors can create a feeling of movement and energy.

Remember that any color scheme includes the type, the background, and any images or graphics that you use. If colorful photos are an important

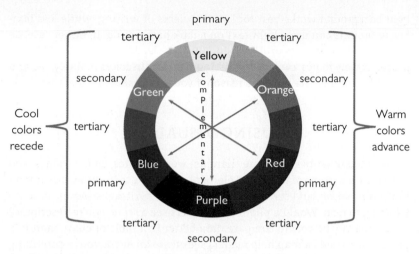

A color wheel.

part of your website, they'll stand out most strongly on a white background and with black type—both of which you may want to use for that reason alone. If you're writing a report that includes multicolored pie charts and want to have color headings, you wouldn't want to use primary colors in the headings and pastels in the charts. In short, if you use colors, make sure they work well with all the other design elements in the text.

Using color to guide readers. Like bold or italic type, color can help guide readers through a text. In fact, that's the way color is used in this book. The headings are all red to make them easy to spot, and key words are color-coded as a signal that they're defined in the glossary/index. In addition, we've color-coded parts of the book—genre roadmaps are on yellow pages, research chapters are on green, style chapters are on lavender—to help readers find them easily.

Color is an important navigational element on websites, sometimes used to indicate links and to highlight headings. For such uses of color, though, it's important to choose colors that are easy to see.

Considering legibility. Using color can make your writing easier—or harder—to read. Use type and background colors that are compatible. Dark type on a light background works best for lengthy pieces of writing, while less text-heavy projects can use a light text on a dark background. In either case, be sure that the contrast is dramatic enough to be legible. Keep in mind many people, largely males, can't see or distinguish certain colors (notably, red and green) so be sure to have a good reason if you use these colors together.

USING VISUALS

Authors today write with more than just words. Photos, charts, tables, and videos are just some of the visual elements you can use to emphasize important information, and sometimes to make your writing easier or more interesting to read. Would a photo help readers see a scene you're describing? Would readers be able to compare data better in a table or chart than in a paragraph? Would a map help readers see where an event you're describing takes place? Would an image help an audience at an oral presentation see what you're talking about? These are questions you should be asking yourself as you write.

Be sure that any visuals you use are relevant to what you have to say—that you use them to support your point, not just to decorate your text. And remember that even the most spectacular images do not speak for themselves: You need to refer to them in your text and to explain to readers what they are and how they support what you're saying.

Kinds of Visuals

You may be assigned to include visuals—but if not, a good way to think about what kinds of visuals to use (or not) is by considering your rhetorical situation. What visuals would be useful or necessary for your topic and **PURPOSE**? What visuals would help you reach your **AUDIENCE**? What kinds of visuals are possible in your **MEDIUM**—or expected in your **GENRE**?

Photographs can help an audience envision something that's difficult to describe or to explain in words. A good photo can provide powerful visual evidence for an argument, and can sometimes move readers in a way that words alone might not. Think of how ads for various charities use photos of hungry children to appeal to readers to donate.

Photos can be useful for many writing purposes, letting readers see something you're **DESCRIBING** or **ANALYZING**, for instance, or even something you're **REPORTING** on. (See how Melissa Rubin needed to include a photo of the ad that she analyzes on p. 177, and how Sam Forman included photos of two different kinds of farms in his report on pp. 223–24.) You can take your own photos, as Forman did, or use ones that you find in other sources, as Rubin did. Remember, however, to provide full documentation for any photos that you don't take yourself.

A photo of street art in a Texas parking lot demonstrates the layering effect of graffiti in a way that would be difficult to do with words alone.

Videos are useful for demonstrating physical processes or actions and for showing sequences. Your medium will dictate whether you can include videos in a text. The print version of a newspaper article about aerialist skiers, for instance, includes a still photo of a skier in mid-jump, whereas the same article on the newspaper's website and on a TV news report features videos showing the skier in action. Your topic and genre will affect whether or not you have reason to include video: If you were writing a **PROCESS ANALYSIS** to teach a skier how to perform a double-full-full-full, a video would be far more useful than a still photo.

A video of a public service announcement about the dangers of texting while driving created by the South Dakota Office of Highway Safety can be used as an example of the ways different states approach the issue.

Graphs, charts, and tables. Numerical and statistical data can be easier both to describe and understand when they are presented visually. You'll often have occasion to present data in bar graphs, pie charts, and the like, especially in **REPORTS** and **ANALYSES**. In many cases, you'll be able to find tables and graphs in your research and then to incorporate ones you find into your own writing. You can also use templates found in *Excel, Word, PowerPoint*, and other programs to create charts and tables yourself. Whether you find or create them, be sure to indicate in your text how they support your argument.

Line graphs are useful for illustrating trends and changes over time—how unemployment fluctuates over a period of time, for instance. By using more than one line, you can compare changes in different variables, such as unemployment for those with a college education and those with only a high school education. When comparing more than one variable, the lines should be in two different colors so that readers can easily see the comparison.

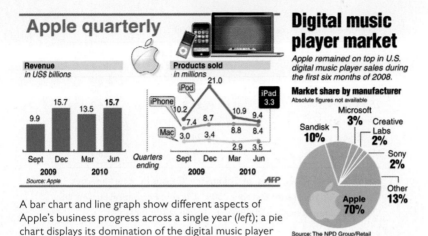

A bar chart and line graph show different aspects of Apple's business progress across a single year (*left*); a pie chart displays its domination of the digital music player market.

Bar graphs are useful for comparing quantitative data in different categories, such as for different age groups or different years. In the example shown on this page, see how the bars make it easy to compare sales of Apple products over the course of several months. It would be easy enough to convey this same information in words alone—but more work to read and harder to remember.

Pie charts give an overview of the relative sizes of parts to a whole, such as what share of a family budget is devoted to food, housing, entertainment, and so on. Pie charts are useful for showing which parts of a whole are more or less significant, but they are less precise (and less easy to read) than bar graphs. It's best to limit a pie chart to six or seven slices, since when the slices become too small, it's difficult to see how they compare in size.

Tables are efficient ways of organizing and presenting a lot of information concisely, in horizontal rows and vertical columns. Table 1 on the next page presents data about home internet access in the United States, information that is made easy to scan in a table.

Table 1
US Home Internet Access by Age Group, 2009

Age of Householder	No In-Home Internet (%)	In-Home Internet (%)
Under 25 years	33.0	67.0
25-34 years	25.8	74.2
35-44 years	22.2	77.8
45-55 years	24.2	75.8
55 years and older	41.8	58.2

Source: United States, Dept. of Commerce, Census Bureau; "Internet Use in the United States: October 2009," Current Population Survey; US Dept. of Commerce, Oct. 2009; Web; 11 June 2012; table 1.

Maps can provide geographic context, helping to orient your audience to places mentioned in your text. A report on the 2011 earthquake in New Zealand, for example, includes maps of the city of Christchurch showing where the earthquake was centered. Include a map when seeing a location is important to your point.

Diagrams are useful for illustrating details that cannot be shown in a photograph. A carefully drawn diagram can deliver a lot of information in a small amount of space.

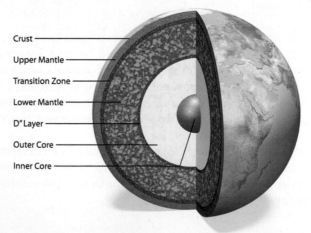

Crust
Upper Mantle
Transition Zone
Lower Mantle
D" Layer
Outer Core
Inner Core

A diagram of the earth's internal structure shows the various layers.

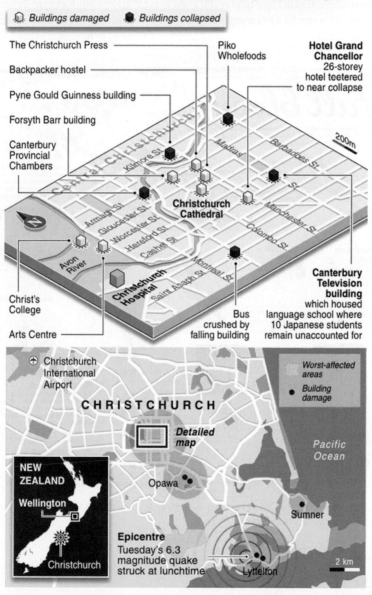

CHRISTCHURCH BUILDINGS DAMAGE

Buildings damaged   *Buildings collapsed*

The Christchurch Press

Backpacker hostel

Pyne Gould Guinness building

Forsyth Barr building

Canterbury
Provincial
Chambers

Piko
Wholefoods

**Hotel Grand
Chancellor**
26-storey
hotel teetered
to near collapse

200m

Central Christchurch

Kilmore St.

Matras

Barbadies St.

St.

Manchester St.

Armagh St.

Gloucester St.

Worcester St.

Hereford St.

Cashel St.

Colombo St.

**Christchurch
Cathedral**

Avon
River

Christchurch Hospital

Saint Asaph St.

Montreal St.

Christ's
College

Arts Centre

Bus
crushed by
falling building

**Canterbury
Television
building**
which housed
language school where
10 Japanese students
remain unaccounted for

Christchurch
International
Airport

CHRISTCHURCH

*Detailed
map*

*Pacific
Ocean*

Worst-affected
areas

Building
damage

**NEW
ZEALAND**

Wellington

Opawa

Sumner

Epicentre
Tuesday's 6.3
magnitude quake
struck at lunchtime

Christchurch

Lyttelton

2 km

Infographics incorporate several different types of visuals—charts, tables, photos—on a single topic to give detailed information about a topic. Because infographics can be so densely packed with information, make sure you can display them large enough for your audience to be able to read.

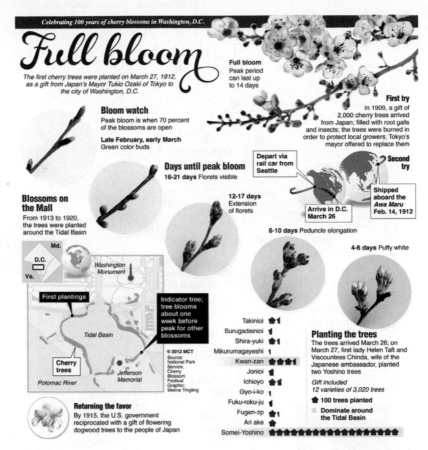

This infographic on the cherry blossom season in Washington, D.C., includes photos, diagrams, maps, and a bar chart.

Creating Visuals

You can find visuals online, scan them from print sources, or create them yourself using basic software or a digital camera. If you come across an illustration you think would be useful, make a copy. Scan or photocopy visuals from print sources; for a digital source, import a link or make a screen grab from digital sources. Label everything clearly. Be aware that visuals—and any data you use to compile them—need to be **DOCUMENTED** in a **CAPTION** or source note, so keep track of where you found everything as you go.

- *Photographs and videos.* If you plan to print an image, save each file in as high a resolution as possible. If a photo is only available in a very small size or low resolution, try to find a more legible option. Be careful about cropping, adjusting color, and altering images in other ways that could change the meaning; straying too far from the original is considered unethical.

- *Graphs, charts, and tables.* Be consistent in your use of fonts and colors, especially if you include more than one graph, chart, or table. Be sure that the horizontal (*x*) and vertical (*y*) axes are labeled clearly. If you use more than one color, add labels for what each color represents. When you have many rows or columns, alternating colors can make categories easier to distinguish.

- *Maps.* Provide a title and a key explaining any symbols, colors, or other details. If the original is missing these elements, add them. If you create the map yourself, include a key with different colors or other symbols to highlight notable locations or other important information.

- *Diagrams.* Use a single font for all labels, and be sure to make the diagram large enough to include all of the necessary detail.

Introducing and Labeling Visuals

Introduce visuals as you would any other source materials, explaining what they show and how they support your point. Don't leave your audience wondering how a photo or chart pertains to your project—spell it out, and be sure to do so *before* the visual appears ("As shown in fig. 3, population growth has been especially rapid in the Southwest.") Number visuals sequentially, numbering tables and figures separately. If you're following MLA, APA, or another academic style, be sure to follow their guidelines for how to label tables and figures.

MLA STYLE. For tables, provide a number ("Table 1") and a descriptive title ("Population Growth by Region, 1990–2010") on separate lines above the table; below the table, add a caption explaining what the table shows and including any source information. For graphs, charts, photos, and diagrams, provide a figure number ("Fig.1"), caption, and source information below the figure. If you give only brief source information in a parenthetical citation, include the source in your list of works cited.

APA STYLE. For tables, provide a number ("Table 1") and a descriptive title on separate lines above the table; below the table, include a note with information about the source. For charts, diagrams, graphs, and photos, include a figure number ("Figure 1") and source information in a note below the figure.

PUTTING IT ALL TOGETHER

Once you've chosen fonts, colors, and visuals, you need to think about how they all come together as a text. Look, for instance, at the homepage of TED, a nonprofit group devoted to disseminating "ideas worth spreading." It's easy to read with a sans-serif font and minimal text. The logo draws your eye because it's large, red, capitalized, and positioned in the upper left corner of the screen. The soft gray "ideas worth spreading" complements the red and leads your eye to the bold black text below—"Riveting talks by remarkable people, free to the world"—which defines the site's purpose and audience. Each of the cascading images is a link to a specific TED talk, and when you mouse over each image, a short summary pops up. Note how white space separates the parts and makes the page easy to read. No surprise that this site won a Webby Award, the online equivalent of an Oscar.

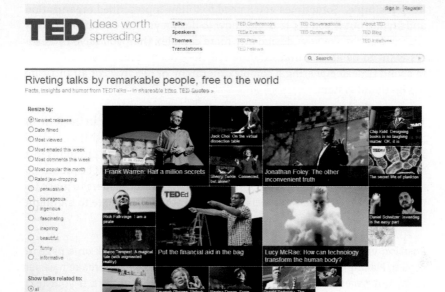

You may not have occasion to design anything as large or complex as a TED site, but the same design principles will apply for all the writing you do. Whether you're designing a report, a photo essay, or a slide presentation, chances are you'll be working with some combination of words, images, and graphs or charts, which you'll need to put on paper or screen in order to reach a certain audience for some purpose.

Look beyond the details and think about what you want your design to accomplish. To help your audience grasp a simple message as fast as possible? convey your identity as a hip and creative author? conform to the requirements of a certain academic style? be simple enough to implement by an approaching deadline? Taking such a perspective can help you determine how to "put it all together" in a way that achieves what you intend.

Keep it simple. Sometimes you'll need to follow a prescribed organization and layout, but if you get to decide how to design your document, take this advice: Don't make your design any more complex than you have to. Readers want to be able to find information they need—and they won't want to spend time deciphering a complex hierarchy of headings or an intricate navigational system.

Think about how to format your written text. Should it all be in the form of paragraphs, or is there anything that should be set off as a list? If so, should it be a bulleted list to make it stand out, or a numbered list to put items in a sequence? If your text includes numerical data, should any of it be presented in a graph, chart, or table? Would that make it easier for readers to grasp? Is there anything else that's especially important that you'd like to highlight in some way?

Position visuals carefully. Keep in mind how they will look on a page or screen. Placing them at the top or bottom of a print page will make it easier to lay out pages and will cause less interruption to your text. If your text will be online, you have more freedom to put them wherever you wish. Reproduce visuals large enough so that readers will be able to see all the pertinent detail; if you're using a file, be aware that digital images become fuzzier when they are enlarged. Downsave images to reduce file sizes; you don't want readers to have problems loading the image. Look over your text carefully to be sure that nothing is too small or blurry to read.

Use white space to separate the various parts of your text. Add some extra space above headings and around lists, images, graphs, charts, and tables.

Organize the text. Whether your text is a simple five-page report or a full website, readers will need to know how it's organized. In a brief essay, you might simply indicate that in a sentence in your introduction, but in lengthier pieces, you may need headings, both to structure your text and to make it easy for readers to navigate.

If you're creating a website, you'll need to figure out how you're dividing materials into pages and to make that clear on the site's homepage. Most homepages have a horizontal navigation bar across the top indicating and linking to the main parts, and often another navigation menu going down the left side of the screen, with links to specific materials on the site. The same navigation menus should appear in the same position on all the other pages of the site—and make sure that every page includes a link to take readers back to the homepage. Look at these examples from *National Geographic.* You can see the consistency from the homepage through the subsequent pages; note the elements that help readers navigate between pages: Colors, fonts, and navigational information are the same on all pages.

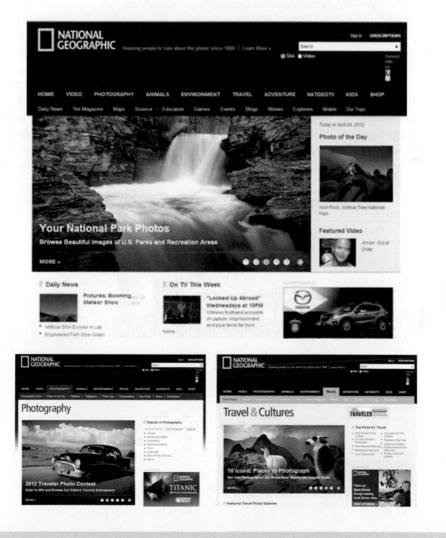

Creating Slide Presentations

When you give an oral report, slides can help make your main points clear and memorable. Presentation software such as *PowerPoint* or *Keynote* makes it fairly easy to design slides, providing templates and layouts to guide you.

Three principles to keep in mind when you're designing slide presentations: legibility, simplicity, and consistency. Remember that your slides are likely to be viewed from a distance, so make your fonts large enough for your audience to read, at least 18 points. Simple bold fonts are easiest to read; italics can be hard to read and are best avoided. Bulleted lists are easier to read than paragraphs.

Keep slides as simple as you can. Don't put too much information on a slide, and keep points in bulleted lists brief. Decorative backgrounds and animations can be distracting; don't include them unless they in some way support your points. And be consistent. Using one font or color for headings and making them parallel in structure will help your audience follow what you're saying.

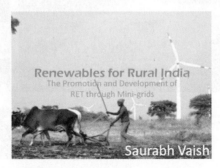

Examples from a slide presentation about renewable energy in India.

Prezi is a kind of presentation software in which the presenter has the ability to zoom in and out, looking at images in detail and from different perspectives. It's an approach that allows for some options in the way you arrange and format your text.

The opening slide for a *Prezi* on jazz bassists (*top*), along with a subsequent slide that appears halfway down the timeline (*middle*) and the following slide, which zooms in to allow readers to see details about the events of 1949 (*bottom*).

Pecha Kucha is a kind of slide presentation that features twenty slides, each onscreen for exactly twenty seconds. Presenters have a little over six minutes to make their point, and the fixed format requires you to be absolutely clear and concise—and prepared.

The first two slides from a Pecha Kucha about Toronto.

ANALYZE a design you find attractive (or not)—a book or magazine cover, a CD cover, a brochure, a poster, a blog, a website. Analyze its use of fonts, colors and visuals. What works, and what doesn't? How would you revise the design if you could?

THIRTY-ONE

Checking for Common Mistakes

POET **N**IKKI **G**IOVANNI ONCE SAID, "Mistakes are a fact of life. It is the response to the error that counts." Albert Einstein put a little different spin on the issue when he said, "Anyone who has never made a mistake has never tried anything new." We agree. Anyone who writes is going to make mistakes: That's a given. What matters is to know when something *is* a mistake, to learn from any mistakes we make, and sometimes even to use them, as Einstein might say, to try something new.

Most of all, it means understanding that what may be a mistake in one context may be perfectly appropriate in another, depending—as always—on your purpose, your audience, and the rest of your rhetorical situation. So when you're editing your writing, you need to think about what's appropriate for your particular rhetorical context.

As a college writer, you may sometimes decide to use a sentence fragment or something else that's typically seen as an error for special effect. In most of your academic writing, however, it's wise to play it safe and avoid anything that might be considered a mistake. This chapter offers tips and examples for checking and editing your writing for some common mistakes, arranged alphabetically from articles to verbs.

ARTICLES

WHAT'S THE DIFFERENCE between *a dog* and *the dog?* "A" dog could be any dog; it does not matter which one. "The" dog, by comparison, refers to one specific dog. *A, an,* and *the* are articles. Use *a* or *an* with **NOUNS** when their specific identity isn't known or doesn't matter: *I want a golden retriever.* Use *the* with nouns whose specific identity is known or has been mentioned: *I want the golden retriever I told you about last week.*

When to Use *A* or *An*

Use *a* or *an* with singular **COUNT NOUNS** that cannot be identified specifically. Count nouns are those referring to things you can count: *one egg, two chairs, three facts.* Use *a* before words beginning with a consonant sound: *a baby*; use *an* before words beginning with a vowel sound: *an apple.* (And be careful to consider sound rather than spelling: *a uniform, an uncle.*)

Do not use *a* or *an* before a **NONCOUNT NOUN**, one that refers to an abstract concept or something that cannot be counted or made plural such as *loyalty, knowledge,* or *gasoline.*

▶ The vacant apartment looked much better with *furniture* in it.

When to Use *The*

Use *the* with nouns that can be identified specifically—singular and plural, count and noncount.

▶ Many cities have passed laws that require restaurants to provide information about *the ingredients* in their food.

▶ Tyler Cowen criticizes *the eat-local movement* as expensive and snobbish.

When to Use No Article

When you're making a generalization, no article is needed with noncount or count nouns.

▶ Large *corporations* generally offer *health insurance* to *employees.*

▶ Most *Americans* like *ice* in their *drinks.*

WHEN TO USE *A* OR *AN*

▶ My parents see attending college as *an honor* and *a privilege*.

▶ Studying in another country can give you *a new perspective* on your home country.

▶ The chef added *a little water* to the stew because it was too thick.

▶ When I'm 16, I'm getting ~~the~~ $\overset{a}{\wedge}$ Chrysler because of their Super Bowl ads.

There's more than one kind of Chrysler, and the writer doesn't indicate which one he plans to get.

WHEN TO USE *THE*

▶ *The U.S. Supreme Court* has nine members, who are appointed by *the president*.

▶ After *the attacks* of September 11, 2001, on *the World Trade Center* and *the Pentagon*, Americans recognized *the need* for better security at airports.

▶ Bobby Thomson's home run against *the Brooklyn Dodgers* became known as "*the shot* heard 'round *the world*." Russ Hodges captured *the excitement* in his radio broadcast, shouting out, "*The Giants* win *the pennant! The Giants* win *the pennant! The Giants* win *the pennant!*"

WHEN TO USE NO ARTICLE

▶ *People* whose bodies are intolerant of *lactose* cannot digest *milk* easily.

▶ Many *people* have found that winning a lottery does not bring them *happiness*.

▶ Airline *passengers* now often have to pay fees to check *luggage*.

TO SEE HOW IMPORTANT COMMAS ARE, read the following sentence: *Let's eat Grandma!* Now see what a difference a comma can make:

▶ Let's eat, Grandma!

We found this sentence on *Facebook*, followed by this excellent advice: "Punctuation saves lives."

This section focuses on some of the ways that commas help authors and readers, from setting off introductory words to separating items in a series to making sure that Grandma gets to eat rather than being eaten.

To Set Off Introductory Words

Put a comma after any word, **PHRASE**, or **CLAUSE** that comes before the **SUBJECT** of the sentence. Some authors omit a comma after very short introductory elements, but you'll never be wrong to so include it.

▶ In 2012, the New York Giants defeated the New England Patriots in the Super Bowl.

▶ Gleefully, New Yorkers celebrated.

▶ Holding up the Vince Lombardi trophy, MVP Eli Manning waved to the fans.

▶ To honor the team, Mayor Bloomberg gave each player a key to the city.

▶ As he accepted his key, Victor Cruz did his signature salsa moves.

Be careful of sentences with inverted word order, where the subject comes after the verb; do not put a comma after a phrase that begins such a sentence.

▶ On the horizon appeared a plane.

▶ In the package were a box of chocolate-chip cookies and various salty snacks.

TO SET OFF INTRODUCTORY WORDS

▶ The marathon completed, the runners greeted their friends and family members.

▶ At the candidate's rally, her supporters waved signs and shouted encouragement.

▶ Because they are dissatisfied with both public and private schools, some parents homeschool their children.

▶ Joyfully, the Heat celebrated after defeating the Thunder in the NBA Finals.

▶ Distracted by a text message, the driver failed to see the stop sign.

▶ Frantically stacking sandbags, the volunteers tried to hold back the rising floodwaters.

▶ To write well, seek out responses to your draft and allow time to revise.

▶ Although many texters enjoy breaking linguistic rules, they also know they need to be understood.

To celebrate World Poetry day in 2007, T-Mobile tried to find the UK's first "Txt laureate" in a competition for the best romantic poem in SMS.

The most important finding is that texting does not erode children's ability to read and write. On the contrary, literacy improves.

In short, it's fun.

—DAVID CRYSTAL, "2b or Not 2b"

To Join Clauses in Compound Sentences

Put a comma before the **COORDINATING CONJUNCTION** (*and, but, for, nor, or, so,* or *yet*) that connects the **MAIN CLAUSES** in a compound sentence.

▶ A balanced budget amendment to the Constitution sounds like a good way to reduce spending, but the government needs more budgetary flexibility for varying economic conditions.

To Set Off Nonessential Elements

Parts of a sentence that are not essential to its meaning should be set off with commas. Parts that are essential to a sentence's meaning should not be set off with commas.

NONESSENTIAL CLAUSE Opera fans, who are notoriously fickle, loved Luciano Pavarotti throughout his long career.

ESSENTIAL CLAUSE Opera fans who love *The Magic Flute* would especially appreciate Ingmar Bergman's film version.

NONESSENTIAL PHRASE The wood, cut just yesterday, needs to cure before it can be burned in the fireplace.

ESSENTIAL PHRASE Wood cut from hardwood trees burns longer and hotter than wood cut from softwood trees.

NONESSENTIAL WORDS My sister, Laura, loves to make the cranberry sauce for Thanksgiving.

ESSENTIAL WORDS My sister Susan always brings her special mashed potatoes for Thanksgiving, while my sister Betty brings pumpkin pie.

In the first sentence, the author has only one sister, so her name is not essential to the meaning—and is thus enclosed in commas. In the second, the names of the sisters are essential to the meaning because there is more than one sister.

TO JOIN CLAUSES IN COMPOUND SENTENCES

▶ The tornado severely damaged the apartment building, but the residents all survived.

▶ Several residents were trapped for hours in the wreckage, and one was not rescued until two days later.

▶ I grew up in Kansas, so I take tornado warning sirens seriously.

TO SET OFF NONESSENTIAL ELEMENTS

▶ Members of the baby boom generation, who were born between World War II and the early 1960s, have started to become eligible for Medicare.

▶ The dramatic increase in childhood obesity in the United States, which public health officials have described as a crisis, has many possible contributing causes.

▶ Fast-food chains, blamed for encouraging fattening food, are trying to offer lower-calorie options.

▶ Daniel Radcliffe, famous for his lead role in the Harry Potter movies, starred on Broadway in *Equus* and *How to Succeed in Business without Really Trying.*

▶ *Glee,* the hit TV show about a high school glee club, has made many of its cast members into celebrities.

▶ Congress should increase access to medical and health savings accounts, which give consumers the option of rolling money reserved for health care into a retirement account.
　　　　　　　　　　—RADLEY BALKO, "What You Eat Is Your Own Business"

▶ Growing corn, which from a biological perspective had always been a process of capturing sunlight to turn it into food, has in no small measure become a process of converting fossil fuels into food.
　　　　　　　　　　—MICHAEL POLLAN, "What's Eating America"

To Separate Items in a Series

Use a comma to separate items in a series. Some authors omit the comma before the final item in the series, but you'll never be wrong to include it—and sometimes omitting the comma can confuse your readers.

▶ We're celebrating Cinco de Mayo with a special menu: tamales, refried beans, chicken and beef tacos, fresh salsa, and corn.

The final comma makes it clear that fresh salsa and corn are two separate items.

To Set Off Interjections, Direct Address, Tag Questions, and Contrasting Elements

INTERJECTIONS	Wow, that was a great film!
DIRECT ADDRESS	"Corporations are people, my friend."
	—MITT ROMNEY
TAG QUESTIONS	You're kidding, aren't you?
CONTRASTING ELEMENTS	Tai chi, unlike yoga, is practiced for its martial training as well as for its health benefits.

To Set Off Parenthetical and Transitional Expressions

▶ Umami, by the way, has recently been recognized as a fifth taste, along with sweet, bitter, sour, and salty.

▶ Homemade applesauce, in fact, is both tastier and healthier than store-bought applesauce.

▶ In other words, we're arguing that it makes no sense to build a large waste transfer station in a densely populated residential neighborhood.

TO SEPARATE ITEMS IN A SERIES

▶ My father told me I was going to college even if he had to beg, borrow, or steal the money.

▶ Americans today can eat pears in the spring in Minnesota, oranges in the summer in Montana, asparagus in the fall in Maine, and cranberries in the winter in Florida. —KATHERINE SPRIGGS, "On Buying Local"

▶ Students came to class in cars, on bicycles, on foot, and even on skateboards.

▶ The cat ran out the door, across the road, and into the woods.

TO SET OFF INTERJECTIONS, DIRECT ADDRESS, TAG QUESTIONS, AND CONTRASTING ELEMENTS

▶ "Oh, I think you know what I'm talking about," Samantha said.

▶ Mike laughed and said, "Dude, you need some help."

▶ Members of Congress have to file financial disclosure forms, don't they?

▶ The queen, not the king, is the most powerful piece in chess.

▶ The Penn State football program, unlike the programs of many other top-ranked schools, is known for the high graduation rate of its players.

TO SET OFF PARENTHETICAL AND TRANSITIONAL EXPRESSIONS

▶ Investment income, on the other hand, is taxed at a lower rate.

▶ Wind power, however, has environmental disadvantages as well as benefits.

▶ Ultimately, what's at stake is the health of everyone who lives or works in this neighborhood.

With Addresses, Place Names, and Dates

▶ Please send any contributions to The Oregon Cultural Trust, 775 Summer St. NE, Ste. 200, Salem, OR 97301-1280.

▶ Strasbourg, France, is the site of the European Parliament.

▶ No one who experienced the events of September 11, 2011, will ever forget that day.

To Set Off Quotations

▶ "In my view," said Junot Díaz, "a writer is a writer because even when there is no hope, even when nothing you do shows any sign of promise, you keep writing anyway."

▶ "Poetry is not a healing lotion, an emotional massage, a kind of linguistic aromatherapy," said Adrienne Rich in a speech to the National Book Foundation in 2006.

▶ "Don't compromise yourself," Janis Joplin advised. "You are all you've got."

Do not use a comma before quotations that are introduced with *that*.

▶ It was Virginia Woolf who said that "A woman must have money and a room of her own if she is to write fiction."

Do not use a comma to set off an indirect quotation, one that does not quote someone's exact words.

▶ In a commencement address at Harvard in 2008, J. K. Rowling spoke about failure, saying that failure teaches you who you are and who you can be.

▶ Tallulah Bankhead once said that if she had her life to live over again, she'd make the same mistakes, only sooner.

WITH ADDRESSES, PLACE NAMES, AND DATES

▶ The company's address is 500 Fifth Ave., New York, NY 10110.

▶ The performance venues in Branson, Missouri, have become popular tourist destinations.

▶ The movie director Ang Lee was born in Chaochou, Taiwan, and came to the United States to attend college.

▶ President Franklin Roosevelt said that December 7, 1941, was "a day that will live in infamy."

TO SET OFF QUOTATIONS

▶ The King James Bible warns, "Pride goeth before destruction."

▶ "Life can only be understood backward, but it has to be lived forward," wrote Søren Kierkegaard.

▶ "There have been only two geniuses in the world," insisted Tallulah Bankhead, "Willie Mays and Willie Shakespeare."

▶ When he was asked if Major League Baseball was ready for an openly gay player, Willie Mays was quick to respond, asking, "Can he hit?"

▶ Humphrey Bogart once declared that he'd "rather have a hot dog at the ballpark than a steak at the Ritz."

▶ Lauren Bacall was once quoted as saying that "Imagination is the highest kite that one can fly."

Unnecessary Commas

Do not put commas around essential elements

▶ The Galápagos Islands are home to many species of plants and animals, that are found nowhere else.

▶ Shirley Brice Heath's book, *Ways with Words*, is a study of children learning to use language in two communities in the Carolinas.

Since Heath has written more than one book, the title is essential information and should not be set off by commas.

Do not put commas between subjects and verbs

▶ What the original Occupy Wall Street protesters could not have anticipated, was the speed with which their movement would spread throughout the country.

▶ The only reason that the committee gave for its decision to end the program, was lack of funds.

Do not put commas between compound subjects or verbs

▶ People who live in "red" states, and those who live in "blue" states hold many mistaken beliefs about each other.

▶ The chef whisked the eggs and milk together in a bowl, and poured the mixture into the omelet pan.

Do not add a comma after a question mark or an exclamation point

▶ "Hi, may I help you?," shouted the manager at Gates Bar-B-Q.

▶ "Everybody out of the water!," yelled the lifeguard.

UNNECESSARY COMMAS

Around essential elements

▶ The painting, that was found in the abandoned house, sold for ten thousand dollars.

▶ The novelist, Jonathan Franzen, has been invited to speak at a campus writers' seminar next month.

▶ The article argues that children, raised in conditions of poverty, often suffer long-term damage to their cognitive development.

Between subjects and verbs

▶ One of the factors that make the health-care system in the United States so expensive, is the amount spent to extend the last few months of patients' lives.

In compound subjects or verbs

▶ Families looking for more affordable space, and hipsters looking for a cool cultural scene all flocked to Brooklyn.

▶ The earthquake and tsunami devastated the northeastern coast of Honshu, but mostly spared the densely populated Tokyo and Osaka areas.

After a question mark or an exclamation point

▶ "What can I possibly do about global warming?," ask many of my friends.

▶ "I want my money back!," the angry customer yelled.

A **COMMA SPLICE OCCURS** when you join two **MAIN CLAUSES** with only a comma. Leave out the comma, and it's a fused sentence. Writing like this might be perfectly appropriate in a tweet or a comment on a blog, but it's likely to be seen as a mistake in academic writing. This section shows four ways to edit comma splices and fused sentences.

COMMA SPLICE   Why build a new stadium, the existing one is just fine.

FUSED SENTENCE   She shoots she scores we win!

Make the Clauses into Two Separate Sentences

▶ Tropical Storm Irene caused major flooding in the Northeast .Hundreds ~~hundreds~~ of roads and bridges were damaged or destroyed.

Link Clauses with Comma + *And, But, Or, Nor, For, So,* or *Yet*

▶ Tropical Storm Irene caused major flooding in the Northeast ,and hundreds of roads and bridges were damaged or destroyed.

Link the Clauses with a Semicolon

▶ Tropical Storm Irene caused major flooding in the Northeast ; hundreds of roads and bridges were damaged or destroyed.

Adding a **TRANSITION** after the semicolon such as *therefore* or *however,* followed by a comma, can help make explicit how the two clauses relate.

▶ Tropical Storm Irene caused major flooding in the Northeast ; as a result, hundreds of roads and bridges were damaged or destroyed.

Revise One Clause as a Subordinate Clause

▶ When Tropical Storm Irene caused major flooding in the Northeast , hundreds of roads and bridges were damaged or destroyed.

MAKE THE CLAUSES INTO TWO SEPARATE SENTENCES

▶ The number of landline telephones is decreasing, *. More* ~~more~~ and more people have only a cell phone.

▶ Why build a new stadium, *? The* ~~the~~ existing stadium is just fine.

LINK CLAUSES WITH COMMA + *AND, BUT, OR, NOR, FOR, SO,* OR *YET*

▶ The 2011 Japanese tsunami produced five million tons of trash, *and* most of it stayed near the Japanese coastline.

▶ Some adoptees would like to find their birth parents *, but* they are often thwarted by laws protecting the privacy of the parents.

▶ Many jobs today are not tied to a particular physical location *, so* employees can work anywhere online.

LINK THE CLAUSES WITH A SEMICOLON

▶ Green tea has been gaining in popularity in recent years *;* it has less caffeine than black tea and is seen as a more healthful alternative.

▶ Global warming could have serious consequences *; for example,* many countries and cities might be threatened by rising ocean levels.

REVISE ONE CLAUSE AS A SUBORDINATE CLAUSE

▶ Small Midwestern towns have been losing population *because* young people go elsewhere to find jobs.

▶ *Although* *Moby-Dick* got terrible reviews when it was first published, many people now consider it the greatest American novel ever written.

PREPOSITIONS

ABOUT, AT, BY, FOR, FROM, IN, ON, TO—these are all prepositions, words that show relationships between other words. Imagine you've got a book *about* your mom, *by your mom*, *for your mom*, or *from your mom*; each means something different, and the difference is all in the prepositions. Not all languages use prepositions, and if English is not your primary language, they can be a challenge to learn. Following are some tips and examples that can help with three of the most widely used prepositions: *at, in,* and *on.* Remember, though, that are there are many exceptions; if in doubt, consult a dictionary.

Prepositions of Place

AT *a specific address:* the house *at* 54 Main Street

a general kind of place: at home, *at* work, *at* school

a general kind of event: at a concert, *at* a party

IN *an enclosed space: in* the closet, *in* my pocket, *in* a cup

a geographical area: in Brazil, *in* Chicago, *in* Africa

a printed work: an article *in* a journal, a chapter *in* a book

ON *a surface:* sitting *on* the bench, a fly *on* the wall, papers *on* a desk

a street: driving *on* Route 17, a restaurant *on* Maple Avenue

an electronic medium: on the web, *on* TV, *on* the radio

Prepositions of Time

AT *a specific point in time: at* 4:46 a.m., *at* noon, *at* sunrise

IN *a part of a day: in* the morning, *in* the evening (but *at* night)

a year, month, or season: in 2012, *in* January, *in* the spring

a period of time: graduated *in* three years, return *in* an hour

ON *a day of the week or month: on* Thursday, *on* March 13

a holiday: travel *on* Thanksgiving, a parade *on* Memorial Day

PREPOSITIONS OF PLACE

▶ Dylan Thomas once lived *in* New York, *at* the Chelsea Hotel *on* Twenty-third Street.

▶ People *in* the neighborhood often rent rooms *in* their homes to students.

▶ Dogs are not allowed *in* most grocery stores *in* the United States.

▶ The story *on* the radio was about the growth of Pentecostal religion *in* South America.

▶ The money *in* the tip jar was divided among the employees.

▶ An accident *on* Interstate 81 injured three people.

▶ Put your papers *in* the envelope *on* my office door.

PREPOSITIONS OF TIME

▶ The Beatles first came to the United States *in* 1964.

▶ Betsye takes classes *in* the evening.

▶ Jamaica Kincaid was the Grinnell College commencement speaker *on* May 21, 2012.

▶ The performance will be *on* July 25 *at* noon.

▶ The Occupy Wall Street movement began *in* 2011.

▶ Juliet Rose was born *on* April 15, 2012.

▶ The Kenyon Gospel Choir will perform *on* Martin Luther King Jr.'s birthday.

IF YOU'VE EVER BEEN READING SOMETHING and stumbled over a word like *he* or *which* because you couldn't tell what it referred to, you've discovered a problem with pronoun reference. Pronouns need to have a clear **ANTECED-ENT**, a specific word that they refer to—and to agree with that antecedent in gender and number, as the following example demonstrates:

▶ *Coffee shops* are good places to work because *they* offer quiet spaces and comforting beverages.

Clear Pronoun Reference

A pronoun should refer clearly to one and only one antecedent.

AMBIGUOUS   Although Lady Gaga and Madonna are often compared, she is more accomplished as a musician.

Who's more accomplished, Lady Gaga or Madonna? To eliminate the ambiguity, revise the sentence to use pronouns that refer clearly to one woman or the other or to eliminate the need for a pronoun.

EDITED   Although she is often compared to Madonna, Lady Gaga is more accomplished as a musician.

EDITED   Although often compared to Madonna, Lady Gaga is more accomplished as a musician.

This, That, Which

Be sure the pronouns *this*, *that*, and *which* refer to a specific antecedent rather than to an idea or a sentence. Because the context often makes the meaning obvious, this kind of vague reference is common in conversation, but in writing you should eliminate the pronoun or provide a clear antecedent.

▶ Cable television has consistently challenged the domination of the major
    a trend that
networks, ~~which~~ has benefited viewers.

▶ Cable provides many more programming options than the networks can,
    variety
and viewers appreciate this.

CLEAR PRONOUN REFERENCE

▶ In the climax of the play, the central character tells his brother
the brother
that ~~he~~ will never measure up to their father.
 ^

▶ The management representatives reached a tentative agreement on a new
                    management's
contract with the unions, but ~~their~~ tough negotiating stance on the details
                            ^
made a final settlement difficult.

▶ The management representatives reached a tentative agreement on a new
                    the unions'
contract with the unions, but ~~their~~ tough negotiating stance on the details
                            ^
made a final settlement difficult.

THIS, THAT, WHICH

▶ Most scientists believe that global warming is occurring at least partly
                                        idea
because of human activity, but most conservatives reject that.
                                                      ^

                drop in price
▶ Solar energy is becoming cheaper, and this will eventually make it
                                        ^
competitive with fossil fuels.

                        and therefore are
▶ Most Americans have to drive to work~~, which makes them~~ extremely
                                        ^
sensitive to gasoline prices.

                    a fact that
▶ Most Americans have to drive to work, ~~which~~ makes them extremely
                                            ^
sensitive to gasoline prices.

They, It, You

In informal contexts, we often use *they*, *it*, or *you* without any antecedent. In academic writing, however, *they* and *it* should always have a specific antecedent, and *you* should be used only to refer specifically to the reader.

▶ At some airports, ~~they~~ *TSA agents* do not ask passengers to remove belts to go through the security check.

▶ ~~On the~~ *The* website, ~~it~~ identifies the author as a former speechwriter for Stephen Colbert.

▶ ~~In many states, you must~~ *Many states require people to* go through a law enforcement background check before ~~you~~ *they* can work with children.

This use of you *could be appropriate in some rhetorical situations—in a manual for day-care workers, for instance—but is inappropriate in most academic writing.*

Implied antecedents

In informal contexts, we often use pronouns that refer to words clearly implied but not directly stated in a sentence. In academic writing, however, do not use such implied antecedents.

▶ I had planned to *ride my* bike to class yesterday, but it had a flat tire.

Although the pronoun it *implies that* bike *is a noun, it was used as a verb. The revision makes it into a noun.*

▶ In ~~Edward Ball's~~ *Edward Ball* *Slaves in the Family*, ~~he~~ writes about finding and interviewing the African American descendants of his white slave-owning ancestors.

THEY, IT, YOU

▶ At some airports, ~~they do not ask~~ passengers ‸ to remove belts *are not asked*

 to go through the security check.

▶ ~~On the website, it~~ identifies the author as a former speechwriter for *The "Contributors" link*

 Stephen Colbert.

▶ In many states, ~~you~~ must go through a law enforcement background check *job applicants*
 before ~~you~~ can work with children. *they*

▶ ~~On the~~ voter registration form ~~they ask you for your~~ home address *The* *asks for the voter's*

 and phone number.

▶ ~~In the~~ advertisement, ~~it~~ claims that the company will pay the shipping *The*

 charges for returning items for any reason.

IMPLIED ANTECEDENTS

▶ The children spent the afternoon sledding until a runner broke off of ~~it~~. *the sled*

▶ The contractor repaired several holes in the wall and did not charge for
 ~~them~~. *that part of the work*

▶ The inscription on Thomas Jefferson's tombstone does not mention that ~~he~~ *Jefferson*
 was president of the United States.

Pronoun-Antecedent Agreement

A pronoun has to agree with its antecedent in gender and number.

GENDER   As Speaker of the House of Representatives, *John Boehner* was known for *his* candor and for letting *his* emotions show, sometimes choking up during debates about issues that mattered a lot to *him.*

NUMBER   *Speakers* must often exert *themselves* to persuade *their* party's representatives to side with *them.*

Compound antecedents

Compound antecedents joined with *and* take a plural pronoun unless they are preceded by *each* or *every.*

▶ Because of security concerns, when *the president and vice president* travel to the same event, *they* rarely travel together.

▶ *Every* U.S. *president and vice president* has needed to decide how to define *his* political role.

When a compound antecedent is joined with *or* or *nor,* the pronoun should agree with the nearest antecedent. If the antecedents are different genders or numbers, you might want to edit the sentence to keep it from being awkward.

AWKWARD   Neither Serena Williams nor Roger Federer was at his best.

EDITED   Serena Williams wasn't at her best, and Roger Federer wasn't either.

AWKWARD   Either the teachers or the principal needs to use his authority.

EDITED   Either the principal or the teachers need to use their authority.

Collective nouns as antecedents

COLLECTIVE NOUNS such as *team* or *audience* or the others listed on the facing page take a singular pronoun when the pronoun refers to the unit as a whole but a plural pronoun when the pronoun refers to multiple parts of the unit.

SINGULAR   The *band* changed *its* name to try to attract a different fan base.

PLURAL   The band left *their* instruments in the music room.

PRONOUN-ANTECEDENT AGREEMENT

Compound antecedents

▶ *Every fruit and vegetable* labeled "organic" has to be certified by ~~their~~ *its* grower.

▶ *Each manager and salesperson* is required to set ~~their~~ *his or her* personal goals each year.

▶ Neither Angela Merkel nor François Hollande felt politically secure enough to risk offending *domestic* public opinion ~~in his own country~~ during the EU crisis.

▶ Under the Articles of Confederation, either the ~~states~~ *national government* or the ~~national government~~ *states* could issue ~~its~~ *their* own currency.

Collective nouns as antecedents

COMMON COLLECTIVE NOUNS

audience	herd	faculty	chorus
crowd	family	congregation	jury
team	couple	choir	panel

▶ The *committee* took *their* seats, and the meeting began.

▶ The judge told the *jury* to consider only the facts of the case in reaching *its* verdict.

Indefinite pronouns as antecedents

Most **INDEFINITE PRONOUNS** such as *anybody, everyone, nobody,* or *someone* take a singular pronoun.

▶ *Everyone* involved in the negotiations had *his or her* own agenda.

If you find *his or her* awkward, revise the sentence to make both pronouns plural or to eliminate the indefinite pronouns.

▶ *All* of those involved in the negotiations had *their* own agendas.

▶ The *individuals* involved in the negotiations all had *their* own agendas.

In informal conversation, words like *everybody, someone,* and *nobody* are often used with plural pronouns: *Somebody left their coat on the chair.* In academic writing, however, stick to the singular for such references.

Noun antecedents that could be either male or female

If an antecedent could be either male or female, do not use masculine pronouns such as *he* or *him* to refer to it. Use *he or she, her or his,* and so on, or edit the sentence to make the antecedent and pronoun both plural or to eliminate the pronoun.

▶ A *Speaker of the House* has to be good at enforcing party discipline; it is an important part of *his or her* job.

▶ *Speakers of the House* have to be good at enforcing party discipline; it is an important part of *their* job.

▶ A *Speaker of the House* has to be good at enforcing party discipline; it is an important part of *the* job.

Indefinite pronouns as antecedents

SINGULAR INDEFINITE PRONOUNS

another	each	much	one
any	either	neither	other
anybody	everybody	nobody	somebody
anyone	everyone	no one	someone
anything	everything	nothing	something

▶ ~~Anyone who uses~~ *Users of* *Facebook* ~~has~~ *have* to remember to set up their primary settings carefully.

▶ Everybody on the girls' volleyball team *was* expected to buy ~~their~~ *her* own uniform.

▶ *Someone* who has served in the military should not have to worry about losing *his or her* health insurance.

▶ *People* in my generation once thought that going to college would guarantee *their* financial security.

Noun antecedents that could be either male or female

▶ A college student often chooses his *or her* major on the basis of its expected financial rewards.

▶ A college student often chooses ~~his~~ *a* major on the basis of its expected financial rewards.

▶ ~~A college student often chooses his~~ *College students often choose their* major on the basis of its expected financial rewards.

SENTENCE FRAGMENTS

A SENTENCE FRAGMENT OCCURS when something less than a sentence is capitalized and punctuated as if it were a complete sentence. Fragments are common in advertising, where they serve to grab the attention of readers and sometimes to create memorable slogans. For example:

> ▶ A unique mix of clothing and accessories you don't even know you want yet!
> —Lizard Lounge ad, *Willamette Week*

As common as they are in many informal contexts, fragments are frowned upon in academic writing. In these contexts, they are considered errors because readers see them as violating the basic rules of sentence structure—and as evidence that the author doesn't know what those rules are.

A sentence fragment occurs when some essential element is missing, usually a **SUBJECT** or a **VERB**—or when it begins with a **SUBORDINATING WORD** like *which* or *because* and is merely a **SUBORDINATE CLAUSE**. To be a sentence, there must be at least one **MAIN CLAUSE**.

NO SUBJECT	Many people could not resist buying homes at very low interest rates. As a result, took on too much debt.
NO VERB	Bank loans available with little or no down payment.
SUBORDINATE CLAUSE	In Ireland, many new homes remain empty. Because the real estate bubble burst.

To edit most fragments, you need to do one of two things: (1) make the fragment into a complete sentence, or (2) attach it to a nearby sentence.

Make the Fragment into a Complete Sentence

ADD A SUBJECT	As a result, *they* took on too much debt.
ADD A VERB	Bank loans *became* available with little or no down payment.
DELETE THE SUBORDINATING WORD	In Ireland, many new homes remain empty. ~~Because~~ *because* the real estate bubble burst.

MAKE THE FRAGMENT INTO A COMPLETE SENTENCE

▶ *I had* ~~Had~~ an accident in my truck and had to spend a lot of money on repairs.

▶ U.S. companies have come under increasing pressure to cut costs. *Many of them have* ~~Have~~ outsourced jobs to China, India, and other Asian countries.

▶ The U.S. housing market still *is* extremely depressed. *The president and Congress need* ~~Need~~ to figure out a way to help millions of homeowners who cannot pay their mortgages.

▶ The program showed glaciers melting as a result of global warming. Many *are* disappearing faster than predicted a few years ago.

▶ My sister's room *was* always a mess, crammed with posters, athletic equipment, and clothes thrown on the floor.

▶ *It was* ~~Was~~ really exciting and stimulating to live in Tokyo.

▶ The Semester at Sea students and their instructors sailed around the world on the *MV Explorer*. *They visited* ~~Visiting~~ twelve countries in 106 days.

▶ *The Best Exotic Marigold Hotel* ~~starring~~ *starred* Judi Dench, Maggie Smith, Bill Nighy, and Tom Wilkinson in an extravagant Indian adventure.

▶ Dad explained how to write checks and balance my checkbook. *He also taught me* ~~Also~~ how to scramble eggs.

▶ Nick worked as an intern at a consulting firm for six months after graduating. *He did so to* ~~To~~ get experience and perhaps to get a permanent position there.

▶ He eventually decided to move to New York. *He thought he'd* ~~Because he~~ find more job opportunities there.

Attach the Fragment to a Nearby Sentence

▶ A growing number of "medical tourists" travel abroad to have cosmetic

　　　　or

surgery. ~~Or~~ other medical procedures that are much cheaper outside the
　　　　　^

United States.

▶ Michael Moore's movie *Sicko* made the American health-care system a topic

　　　　　　　　　　, although

of national conversation. ~~Although~~ even many who share his politics
　　　　　　　　　　　　^

criticized him for playing fast and loose with the facts.

　　　　　　　　　　　　　　　　　　　　nomination,

▶ In 1968, George Romney tried for the Republican presidential ~~nomination.~~
　　　　　　　　　　　　　　　　　　　　　　　　　　^

which

~~Which~~ his son Mitt won forty-four years later.
^

　　　　　　　　　　　　　　television, we decided

▶ Tired of the same old reality shows and reruns on ~~television. Decided~~
　　　　　　　　　　　　　　　　　　　　　　　^

to go to an a cappella concert on campus.

ATTACH THE FRAGMENT TO A NEARBY SENTENCE

▶ Older Americans are often nostalgic for the 1950s. *, when* ~~When~~ families and jobs seemed more stable.

▶ The average family size has dropped sharply. *because* ~~Because~~ people are marrying at later ages and having fewer children than in the baby boom era.

▶ In the 1970s, the United States began losing manufacturing jobs to overseas competitors. *, a trend that has* ~~Has~~ only recently been reversed.

▶ In recent years, India has begun to develop its own high-tech ~~economy.~~ *economy,* *which* ~~Which~~ is centered in the city of Bangalore.

▶ ABC is broadcasting the 2012 NBA finals. *with* ~~With,~~ a panel of experts breaking down the games afterward.

▶ The farmers market opens every Sunday morning at 9:00. *and* ~~And~~ closes at 1:00.

▶ Much of the country is suffering from a heat wave. *, which* ~~Which~~ makes many of us especially irritable.

You'll often have reason to shift gears when you write, as when you shift from one verb tense to another.

▶ The National Weather Service issued a freeze warning, saying that temperatures will dip into the 20s tomorrow.

This sentence refers to actions occurring at different times, so they require different tenses. But unnecessary shifts in tense—or point of view—can confuse readers.

Shifts in Tense

It's sometimes necessary to shift verb tenses to refer to actions that take place at different times.

▶ The play that *opened* yesterday *will be reviewed* in newspapers tomorrow.

Readers may be confused, however, if you shift from one tense to another in referring to things that happen in the same time frame.

SHIFT   The editorial *noted* the increases in college tuition this year and also *discusses* the causes of skyrocketing tuition costs over the last few decades.

This sentence starts out using the past tense (*noted*) and then switches to the present tense (*discusses*). To eliminate the shift, make both verbs either past tense or present:

▶ The editorial *noted* the increases in college tuition this year and also *discussed* the causes of skyrocketing tuition costs over the last few decades.

▶ The editorial *notes* the increases in college tuition this year and also *discusses* the causes of skyrocketing tuition costs over the last few decades.

Be careful to use the present tense when you're writing about a literary work—and not to accidentally shift to the past tense.

▶ Fitzgerald portrays Gatsby as a boy from a poor family who eventually becomes rich enough to buy a mansion, where he ~~threw~~ *throws* huge extravagant parties in the hope of impressing Daisy.

SHIFTS IN TENSE

▶ After Pearl Harbor, U.S. authorities wrongly suspected that Japanese

                                            were

  Americans living near the Pacific coast ~~are~~ a security risk.

▶ According to several studies, women are more likely than men to develop

                                  tend

  the disease, but their symptoms ~~tended~~ to be less severe.

▶ In many cities, the Occupy protesters came into conflict with police and

                    were

  in some cases ~~are~~ injured by pepper spray and other crowd-control tactics.

▶ In *Moneyball,* Brad Pitt plays Billy Beane, general manager of the Oakland A's,

          shows

  and ~~showed~~ how he uses statistics to find undervalued ball players.

▶ Only a few countries are major contributors to global warming, but this

                 affects

  phenomenon ~~affected~~ everyone in the world.

▶ Miguel was paddling swiftly to the pier deep in the Amazon rainforest; he

  missed   *fell*

  ~~misses~~ a stroke and almost ~~falls~~ overboard.

▶ Chen competed successfully for the women's Olympics semifinal in aerial

               failed

  acrobatics, but then she ~~fails~~ to attain the title in the end.

Shifts in Point of View

Sometimes you may have good reason to shift between first person (*I, we),* second person (*you*), or third person (*he, she, they*).

▶ *You* may think that you clearly remember the details of an event, but *scientists* who have studied eyewitness testimony in court cases have found that witnesses' memories are often extremely faulty.

In this sentence, the writer is contrasting readers' beliefs about something with research findings about the same topic, so a shift from second person (*you*) to third (*scientists*) is appropriate. Shifting from one point of view to another when referring to the same subjects, however, would be inconsistent—and could confuse your audience.

SHIFT   *Employees* were stunned by the huge increases in health-insurance premiums. *You* had no choice, though, but to pay or to lose coverage.

Here the point of view shifts from *employees* to *you,* even though both sentences refer to the same group of people. To eliminate the inconsistency, revise one of the sentences to use the same point of view as the other.

▶ *Employees* were stunned by the huge increases in health-insurance premiums. *They* had no choice, though, but to pay or to lose coverage.

Some shifts in number are actually problems in agreement between a **PRO-NOUN** and its **ANTECEDENT**. Such a shift is often the result of an effort to avoid using *he* to refer to both men and women—or to avoid the awkward *he or she* construction. Here's an example from this book, shown as it was in the first draft, then as it was edited to eliminate the confusing shift.

SHIFT   Today, *anyone* with access to a computer can publish what *they* write.

EDITED   Today, if you have access to a computer, you can publish what you write.

SHIFTS IN POINT OF VIEW

▶ *If you decide* *, you have*
  A̶ ̶p̶e̶r̶s̶o̶n̶ ̶w̶h̶o̶ ̶d̶e̶c̶i̶d̶e̶s̶ to become a vegetarian h̶a̶s̶ to pay careful attention
  to your diet to make sure you are getting essential nutrients.

▶ Many Americans want the government to provide services that benefit
  they
  them, but w̶e̶ do not want to pay for these services through taxes.

▶ The library is so quiet during exams week that one can hear a sheet of paper
  one's
  fall on the floor or y̶o̶u̶r̶ fingers tapping on a laptop.

▶ When you get to college, you have to grow up and do laundry, balance a
  you're on
  checkbook, and keep track of all your courses, so for the first time, I̶'̶m̶ ̶o̶n̶
  your
  m̶y̶ own.

▶ Students working on service-learning projects in Ghana or Kenya or South
  they have
  Africa are making a difference, even though a̶ ̶s̶t̶u̶d̶e̶n̶t̶ ̶h̶a̶s̶ little power to
  change the world.

▶ *economists*
  Even though a̶n̶ ̶e̶c̶o̶n̶o̶m̶i̶s̶t̶ may understand what's wrong with the economy,
  they don't necessarily know how to fix it.

▶ Teachers who speak more than one language are in great demand, and
  teachers who speak *have*
  a̶ ̶t̶e̶a̶c̶h̶e̶r̶ ̶w̶h̶o̶ ̶s̶p̶e̶a̶k̶s̶ Spanish in particular probably h̶a̶s̶ many job
  opportunities.

▶ Our relay team practiced passing the baton over and over and over again
  Runners need
  before the Penn Relays. A̶ ̶r̶u̶n̶n̶e̶r̶ ̶n̶e̶e̶d̶s̶ to hand the baton off very carefully
  so that no one drops it.

SUBJECT-VERB AGREEMENT

VERBS NEED TO AGREE (that is, match up) with their subjects in number (singular or plural) and person (first, second, or third): *I smile, you smile, he or she smiles, we smile, they smile.* Sometimes getting subjects and verbs to agree can be tricky, however, especially when other words come between them: *The best paintings in the show were watercolors.* Following are guidelines to help you check for subject-verb agreement in your writing.

When Other Words Come between Subject and Verb

Sometimes the subject is separated from the verb by other words. Be careful that the verb agrees with the subject, not with a word that falls in between.

▶ The *contents* of the old family photo album ~~has~~ *have* provided many clues in our genealogical research.

▶ The *mayor* as well as the taxpayers ~~support~~ *supports* the stadium proposal.

Compound Subjects

If two or more subjects are joined by *and,* they generally take a plural verb.

▶ My math textbook and workbook ~~costs~~ *cost* more than all my other books combined.

However, if two words joined by *and* are considered a single unit, like *fish and chips,* they take a singular verb.

▶ Fish and chips ~~are~~ *is* a dish found on menus everywhere in England.

If two or more subjects are joined by *or* or *nor,* the verb should agree with the closest subject.

▶ Neither the legislators nor the governor ~~were~~ *was* willing to take a stand.

A sentence like this, where the subject includes both singular and plural parts, may read more smoothly if you revise to put the plural part closest to the verb: *Neither the governor nor the legislators were willing to take a stand.*

WHEN OTHER WORDS COME BETWEEN SUBJECT AND VERB

▶ *Institutions* of higher education *continue* to think of creative ways to increase income.

▶ The *laughter* of the children watching the clowns *was* soothing.

▶ *Produce* grown using organic methods *is* more expensive.

▶ A bowl of ripe yellow pears, which created a delicious smell in the kitchen,
  was
  ~~were~~ part of the strategy to make the house more inviting to potential
  ^
  buyers.

COMPOUND SUBJECTS

▶ *Peanut butter and pizza are* my favorite foods.

▶ *Peanut butter and jelly*, however, *is* my favorite sandwich.

▶ I love Justin Bieber, but *neither "All around the World" nor "Boyfriend" lives up* to all the hype about his new album.

▶ *The president or the chancellor or the trustees have* the power to overturn decisions of the faculty senate.

  were
▶ *A blanket and a pillow* ~~was~~ *distributed* to each camper.
  ^

                                                              is
▶ Either the workers on the renovation project *or their supervisor* ~~are~~
  ^
  responsible for the damage.

▶ Neither she nor I knows the answer to your question.

Subjects That Follow Verbs

Although verbs usually follow their subjects in English sentences, sometimes this order is reversed. In a sentence that begins with *there is* or *there are,* the subject always follows the verb. In the following example, the subject is *problems.*

> ▶ There ~~is~~ ^{are} undoubtedly many unresolved problems with the current proposal.

Sentences that begin with a prepositional phrase followed by a verb may also cause problems. In the following sentence, the subject is *rights,* not *importance.*

> ▶ Of greatest importance ~~is~~ ^{are} the rights to the performers' videos.

Collective Nouns Such as *Audience* or *Team*

In American English, collective nouns like *audience, team,* and *crowd* are usually treated as singular. Sometimes, however, when they refer to individuals in a group rather than to the group as a unit, they take a plural verb.

SINGULAR The *team wins* convincingly each week.

PLURAL The *committee disagree* about the report's suggestions.

The members of the committee disagree with each other. If a sentence like this sounds awkward, you can revise to make it clear that you are referring to individuals, not the unit: *The committee members disagree about the report's suggestions.*

COMMON COLLECTIVE NOUNS

audience	herd	faculty	chorus
crowd	family	congregation	jury
team	couple	choir	panel
committee	board (of directors, of trustees, etc.)		

SUBJECTS THAT FOLLOW VERBS

▶ There *are a desk and a computer* for each of the temporary employees.

▶ Here ~~is~~ *are* *the plan* for the renovation *and a list* of items to buy.

▶ Behind the stage ~~was~~ *were* *a dressing room and storage space* for costumes.

COLLECTIVE NOUNS SUCH AS *AUDIENCE* OR *TEAM*

▶ In criminal cases, a *jury needs* to reach a unanimous verdict to convict or acquit; otherwise, a mistrial is declared.

▶ In criminal cases, the *members* of a jury *need* to reach a unanimous verdict to convict or acquit; otherwise, a mistrial is declared.

▶ The *audience were chatting* with one another as they waited for the performance to begin.

▶ The *cast* for the San Francisco production of *The Book of Mormon was* different from the one in New York.

▶ For the last few performances, the audience ~~were~~ *was* made up almost entirely of people who had gotten deeply discounted or even free tickets.

▶ The cast of a Broadway show sometimes agrees to reduce their salaries to try to keep the show running longer.

Indefinite Pronouns Such as *Everyone* or *Nobody*

Most **INDEFINITE PRONOUNS** —words like *anyone, anything, each, every-one, nobody, no one,* and *something*—take a singular verb, even those that seem to have plural meanings (and are often treated as plural in casual conversation).

▶ *Everyone* at the Academy Awards *likes* to make a fashion statement.

▶ *Each* of the nominees *prepares* an acceptance speech and *hopes* to use it.

A few indefinite pronouns, including *both, few, many, others,* and *several,* are plural and take plural verbs.

▶ *Many* of the athletes in the Ironman Triathlon *have trained* for years.

Some indefinite pronouns, including *all, any, none, some, more, most,* and *enough,* take a singular verb when they refer to a singular noun or a plural verb when they refer to a plural noun.

SINGULAR *None* of the information given on the site *identifies* the sponsor.

PLURAL *None* of the Greeks interviewed for the article *expect* the country's economic problems to improve in the next few years.

Words Such as *News* That Look Plural But Are Usually Singular

Words such as *news* and *athletics* look plural because they end in *–s,* but they are generally treated as singular. Some such words, notably *physics, mathematics, statistics, politics,* and *economics,* can be singular or plural, depending on the context.

SINGULAR Statistics *is* a required course for political science majors.

PLURAL Statistics *show* that texting while driving is extremely dangerous.

INDEFINITE PRONOUNS SUCH AS *EVERYONE* OR *NOBODY*

▶ *Everyone,* it seems, *wants* to be on a reality show.

▶ *All of the candidates were* nervous about having to take a position on the immigration reform issue.

▶ *All of the media attention was focused* on the female candidates' appearance and the male candidates' sex life.

▶ *Some of the service members* discharged under the "don't ask, don't tell" policy *have reapplied* to the military.

▶ *Some of the debate* over the issues involved *was* similar to the debate over racial integration of the military in the 1940s.

▶ *Each of the traditional neighborhoods* in Chicago contributes distinctive qualities to the city.

WORDS SUCH AS *NEWS* THAT LOOK PLURAL BUT ARE USUALLY SINGULAR

▶ *News travels* across the globe in a matter of seconds over the internet.

▶ German *measles* ~~are~~ is especially dangerous to pregnant women.

▶ *Economics* ~~have~~ has become one of the most popular majors at many colleges.

▶ The *economics* of higher education in the United States *puts* great financial pressure on families with average incomes.

Who, That, Which

The **RELATIVE PRONOUNS** *who, that*, and *which* take singular verbs when they refer to a singular noun and plural verbs when they refer to a plural noun.

SINGULAR   Solar energy *technology* that *is* cheap and easy to install is growing in popularity.

PLURAL   *Cows*, which *produce* methane gas, play a surprisingly important part in global warming.

Problems sometimes occur with the expressions *one of the* and *the only one of the*. Phrases beginning with *the only one of the* always take a singular verb. Those beginning with *one of the* usually take a plural verb.

▶   The *only one of the* candidates who *was* appealing to younger voters was Ron Paul.

▶   A lack of safe drinking water is *one of the* main factors that *reduce* life expectancy in some developing countries.

Subjects That Are Titles

Subjects that are titles of books, movies, and so on use a singular verb even if the title is plural in form.

▶   *The Chronicles of Narnia* ~~have~~ has been cited as an influence by J. K. Rowling, author of the Harry Potter series.

WHO, THAT, WHICH

▶ Walter Isaacson has written *biographies* of Albert Einstein, Henry Kissinger, Benjamin Franklin, and Steve Jobs that *have* brought him much acclaim.

▶ Makers of flooring are increasingly turning to *bamboo*, which *is* easy to grow and harvest and is environmentally sustainable.

▶ PETA is one of the organizations that opposes using animals in scientific experiments.

▶ Johnson is the only one of the presidential candidates who supports legalizing marijuana.

SUBJECTS THAT ARE TITLES

▶ *Friday Night Lights captures* perfectly the atmosphere of a small Texas town and its high school football team.

▶ Released in 1963, Alfred Hitchcock's thriller *The Birds is* still giving moviegoers nightmares half a century later.

▶ *Angry Birds* has become tremendously popular through what Wikipedia calls "its successful combination of addictive gameplay, comical style, and low price."

VERBS

WHAT'S THE DIFFERENCE between *lie* and *lay*? When would you say you remembered *to study*, and when would you say you remembered *studying*? Why would you say you'd do something *if you had time* when you know you won't have time? These are all questions about verbs, the subject of this section.

Verb Forms

Every English verb has four forms: base, past tense, past participle, and present participle. For regular verbs, the past tense and past participle are both formed by adding *-ed* or *-d* to the base (and sometimes dropping a silent *e* or doubling a final consonant): *worked, danced, chatted*. For all verbs, the present participle is formed by adding *–ing* to the base form (again, sometimes dropping an *e* or doubling a consonant): *working, dancing, chatting*.

The problems that some writers have with verb forms are mostly with the past tense and past participle of **IRREGULAR VERBS**, which do not follow the *-ed* or *-d* pattern and thus have to be memorized. A list of the forms of some common irregular verbs appears on the facing page.

Be careful not to confuse the past tense with the past participle. The past tense is used alone, whereas the past participle must be used together with one or more **HELPING VERBS** such as *have* or *be*.

▶ When the maple tree *fell* in the storm, it *broke* the kitchen window.

▶ If other trees *had fallen*, more damage *would have been done*.

Forms of **be.** The verb *be* is especially irregular, with eight forms that simply must be learned.

BASE FORM	be
PRESENT TENSE	am, is, are
PAST TENSE	was, were
PRESENT PARTICIPLE	being
PAST PARTICIPLE	been

Some Common Irregular Verbs

BASE FORM	PAST TENSE	PAST PARTICIPLE	PRESENT PARTICIPLE
begin	began	begun	beginning
broadcast	broadcast	broadcast	broadcasting
choose	chose	chosen	choosing
do	did	done	doing
eat	ate	eaten	eating
find	found	found	finding
fly	flew	flown	flying
give	gave	given	giving
go	went	gone	going
grow	grew	grown	growing
have	had	had	having
know	knew	known	knowing
lay	laid	laid	laying
lie (recline)	lay	lain	lying
make	made	made	making
prove	proved	proved, proven	proving
read	read	read	reading
rise	rose	risen	rising
set	set	set	setting
sit	sat	sat	sitting
show	showed	showed, shown	showing
think	thought	thought	thinking
win	won	won	winning
take	took	taken	taking
write	wrote	written	writing

Verb Tenses

English verbs have three tenses to indicate time: present, past, and future.

PRESENT	**PAST**	**FUTURE**
I smile	I smiled	I will smile
I speak	I spoke	I will speak

Each tense has progressive forms, which indicate continuing actions.

PRESENT PROGRESSIVE   I *am smiling* in my class photo.

PAST PROGRESSIVE   I *was smiling* when it was taken.

FUTURE PROGRESSIVE   We *will* still *be working* on this book next week.

In addition, each tense has perfect forms. The *present perfect* indicates actions that happened at an indefinite time in the past or that began in the past and continue in the present. The *past perfect* indicates actions that took place before another past action. The *future perfect* indicates actions that will occur in the future before some other action.

PRESENT PERFECT   We *have spoken* about this situation repeatedly.

PAST PERFECT   She *had finished* before I arrived.

FUTURE PERFECT   By this time next year, we *will have been* to Paris.

Verbs can also be both perfect and progressive: I *have been working* late for many months now. This section focuses on several issues with verbs that often cause confusion in academic writing.

Verb Tenses

PRESENT	We *work* hard and *play* hard.
PAST	He *worked* at Northern Trust many years ago.
FUTURE	I *will* never again *work* this hard!
PRESENT PROGRESSIVE	It's midnight, and we *are* just *eating!*
PAST PROGRESSIVE	When I saw her, she *was making* cupcakes.
FUTURE PROGRESSIVE	Our take-out food *will be arriving* soon.
PRESENT PERFECT	That building *has been* empty for many months.
PAST PERFECT	This house *had been* empty for months when we rented it.
FUTURE PERFECT	Tomorrow we *will have been married* a year.
PRESENT PERFECT PROGRESSIVE	She *has been talking* since age two.
PAST PERFECT PROGRESSIVE	I *had been hoping* to see you.
FUTURE PERFECT PROGRESSIVE	We *will be seeing* you soon.

Use the present tense for scientific or general facts, even if the main clause of the sentence is in the past tense.

▶ Magellan's voyage proved conclusively that the world *is* round.

Use the present perfect tense to indicate a past action that continues in the present or to specify an action that took place in an indefinite time in the past.

▶ According to the 2010 census, the United States *has become* a predominantly urban nation.

Use the past tense to indicate a specific time in the past.

▶ Once the children moved out, we *decided* to move back to the city.

If you're writing about literature, use the present tense to discuss a text and the past tense to discuss its historical context.

▶ In *Pride and Prejudice and Zombies,* Elizabeth Bennet and Mr. Darcy *defeat* a field of zombies and then *settle* down to live happily ever after.

▶ According to author Seth Grahame-Smith, *Pride and Prejudice was* "just ripe for gore and senseless violence" ("Zombies Literature").

If you're following MLA, use the present tense in SIGNAL PHRASES introducing sources. But if you mention the date of the source, use the past tense.

▶ In his book *Spaghetti Westerns,* Christopher Frayling *observes* that "*Once Upon a Time* is concerned with the 'language' and 'syntax' of the Western" (213).

▶ As Pauline Kael *wrote* in her 1965 book *Kiss Kiss Bang Bang,* "*Stagecoach* had a mixture of reverie and reverence about the American past that made the picture seem almost folk art; we wanted to believe in it even if we didn't" (52).

If you're following APA, use the past tense or the present perfect tense in identifying a source:

▶ Zikmund-Fisher, Smith, Ubel, and Fagerlin (2007) *suggested* that numerical aptitude leads to better risk comprehension.

▶ Research *has proven* that higher mathematical aptitude leads to higher achievement on risk comprehension tasks (Zikmund-Fisher et al., 2007).

Use the present tense for scientific or general facts

▶ Galileo demonstrated that the earth *revolves* around the sun.

Use the present perfect to indicate a past action that continues in the present

▶ Since she finished school, Carolina *has had* three different jobs.

▶ She *has received* a big promotion since we last saw her.

▶ Since we arrived in Hong Kong, rents *have* almost *doubled*.

If you're writing about literature

▶ In *Native Son,* Chang-rae Lee *tells* the story of Henry Park, a man of two worlds who fears he belongs to neither one.

▶ Published to great acclaim in 1995, it *was* Lee's first novel.

If you're citing sources MLA style

▶ In his book *Crowded Prairie: American National Identity in the Hollywood Western*, Michael Coyne *explains* the significance of *Stagecoach* to the Western genre and its influence in solidifying the genre's archetypes.

▶ In her 1993 essay on landscape photography, Deborah Bright *argued* that landscape photography has reinforced certain formulaic myths about landscape.

If you're citing sources APA style

▶ Bonari et al. (2005) *found* that pregnant women are more likely to discontinue using antidepressants during pregnancy if their risk assessments are too high.

Gerunds and Infinitives

A **GERUND** is the *-ing* form of a verb that functions as a **NOUN**: *walking, thinking.* An **INFINITIVE** is *to* + the base form of a verb that's also used as a noun: *to walk, to think.* Deciding when to use a gerund or an infinitive can be a challenge, but in general, use gerunds to state facts and use infinitives to state intentions, desires, or expectations.

Use gerunds after verbs that express facts

admit	enjoy	practice	suggest
consider	finish	recall	tolerate
discuss	imagine	resist	understand

▶ Susanna had always *enjoyed making* things, so none of us were at all surprised that she majored in art.

Use infinitives after verbs that express intentions, desires, or expectations

ask	decide	intend	plan
agree	expect	manage	promise
claim	hope	offer	want

▶ She *decided to major* in art.

A few verbs can be followed by either a gerund or an infinitive: *begin, continue, hate, like, love, prefer,* and *start.* In some cases—*forget, remember, stop, try*—the choice of a gerund or infinitive affects the meaning.

▶ He remembered *to call* his mom on her birthday.
   He intended to call, and he did.

▶ He remembered *calling* his mother for her birthday.
   He remembered that he had made the call.

Always use a gerund, not an infinitive, after a preposition

▶ She got college credit *for passing* the Advanced Placement calculus exam.

INFINITIVES

▶ Television *started to get* big in the US in 1948 with the incredible success of Milton Berle's show, which was so popular that the reservoir levels in Detroit dropped every Tuesday night at 9 p.m. because everyone *waited* until the show was over *to go* to the toilet.   —FRANK ROSE, *The Art of Immersion*

▶ The foods *I like to eat* the best, like pizza and hamburgers and ice cream, are not always things that I should eat.

▶ Most students at Grinnell *plan to study* abroad during their junior year. Some students *hope to learn* a new language, while others simply *want to travel.*

▶ Those with double majors usually can't *manage to take* a semester abroad.

▶ We *decided to get* Dad a shredder for Father's Day when we realized he was burning return-address labels in the barbecue.

▶ Environmentalists *hoped to convince* people that long-life fluorescent bulbs were a good investment.

GERUNDS

▶ Whatever a man's age may be, he can reduce it several years *by putting* a bright-colored flower in his button-hole.   —MARK TWAIN

▶ Roger Clemens never *admitted using* steroids, and the jury believed him.

▶ In her most stressful moments, she *imagined being* in Paris.

▶ Who doesn't *enjoy taking* time off every now and then to relax?

▶ *By comparing* the food served in Chinese restaurants in five different countries, Yunshu made progress *in answering* her question about why Chinese food is so universally popular.

▶ In high school, I *avoided taking* courses that *required* a lot of *writing.*

▶ Switzerland has many famous resorts *for skiing.*

Mood

English has three moods: indicative, imperative, and subjunctive. Use the indicative to state facts, opinions, or questions. Use the imperative to give commands. Use the SUBJUNCTIVE to express wishes, requests, and conditions that are hypothetical, unlikely, or contrary to fact. Use MODAL helping verbs such as *may, might,* or *would* to indicate likelihood or probability.

INDICATIVE   Megastores *have spread* across the country.

IMPERATIVE   *Shop* at Walmart to save money.

SUBJUNCTIVE   I would shop at Target if there *were* one in my hometown.

Writers are sometimes confused by conditional sentences, especially ones with a clause starting with *if.* Use the indicative if the condition in the *if* clause is possible; use the subjunctive if it's unlikely.

When the if *clause expresses a condition that is possible,* use the present tense in the *if* clause and a modal such as *may, might,* or *will* plus the base form of a verb in the other clause.

▶ If our school *wins* the conference championship, applications *will go* up.

When the if *clause expresses a condition that is unlikely, hypothetical, or contrary to fact,* use the past tense in the *if* clause and *would* or another modal such as *might* plus the base form of a verb in the other clause. Use *were* rather than *was* in the *if* clause.

UNLIKELY   If I *won* the lottery, I *would buy* a house.

CONTRARY TO FACT   If I *were* you, I *would* not *shop* at Target.

In clauses expressing a wish, use the past tense of the verb—use *were* for *be.*

▶ I *wish* I *were* three inches taller and twenty pounds lighter.

MOOD

Conditions that are possible

► If temperatures next winter *are* warmer than usual, we *will save* on heating bills.

► If I *have* time, I *will be* happy to help.

► According to the directions on the box, your teeth *will become* white if you *apply* the whitening strips for a half hour a day.

► If the company ~~will match~~ *matches* my other offer, I will stay.

Conditions that are unlikely or hypothetical

► If Costco *opened* a store here, my family's store *might not survive*.

► If our college *had* a larger endowment, it *could reduce* class sizes.

► I *wouldn't do* that if I *were* you!

► If it ~~wasn't~~ *weren't* against the law, we would visit Cuba.

Wishful thinking

► I *wish* that I *were* able to attend college full-time.

► My mother *wishes* my sisters and I *lived* closer to home.

► We *wish* that it *didn't cost* so much to live in Rio.

► "If wishes *were* horses, beggars *would ride*" is a nursery rhyme often used to suggest that it is better to act than to wish.

Authors' Resources

THIRTY-TWO

Assembling a Portfolio

OR HIS FIRST-YEAR WRITING CLASS, Julio Martinez was required to build a portfolio of his work to demonstrate how his writing had improved during the term. He included the drafts and final revision of a rhetorical analysis, along with two peer reviews he received from fellow students; an annotated bibliography; and the drafts and final revision of a research report. Finally, he wrote a cover letter to his instructor in which he described, evaluated, and reflected on his writing—and set out several goals to work on after the term was over. He submitted his portfolio in print.

Not so Susanna Moller, an art major, who created a website to host the portfolio of her artwork. She included only finished works, organized by subject and style. When she had her first solo show, she posted the review from the college newspaper. As graduation approached, she put her résumé on the site—and added the URL to résumés she sent to potential employers so they could see her work.

Deborah Burke began her portfolio with a first-year essay she was very proud of. The next year, she wrote a radio essay on the same topic, which became the second item in her portfolio. Continuing her research, she wrote a play and added the script to her portfolio, along with a video of herself performing a scene from the play. Finally, she added her résumé and a statement reflecting on her work in college. This portfolio helped her to get an internship—and later a job.

You may be required to keep a portfolio of your work for a writing course as a way of thinking about what you've learned, demonstrating to your instructor what you've done, and assessing your strengths and weaknesses as a writer. Even if you're not required to do so, keeping a portfolio is one of the best ways of demonstrating what you've learned and showcasing your best work. Portfolios can make powerful statements to prospective employers about your abilities and accomplishments, and they can be an important part of how your work is assessed. Whatever your purpose, assembling a portfolio offers an excellent opportunity to reflect on your writing and to chart future goals for yourself as a writer. This chapter provides guidelines to help you compile a portfolio for a writing class.

What to Include in a Writing Portfolio

Your portfolio should represent your best work and demonstrate your growth as a writer, so you'll probably include some of the following materials:

- A number of your best papers
- Writing in several genres and media
- Freewriting and other notes
- Various drafts, from first to final
- Response from readers
- A statement reflecting on your work

Your instructor may specify what you need to include, but often you'll get to choose. In that case, what you include will depend on what you're trying to show. If you're trying to show your best work, you might include three pieces that you like best; if, on the other hand, you're trying to show a range of what you've written, you would probably choose writing in various **GENRES** and **MEDIA**. If you're trying to show how you've improved, you'll want to include papers in several drafts. Just remember that your portfolio is an opportunity for *you* to evaluate and present your own writing: Choose work that demonstrates what you want to show.

Collecting Your Work

Start working on your portfolio early in the term. Organization is critical, so create a specific computer folder for the portfolio and save it with a file name (like "My Portfolio") where you can easily find it; inside the folder, create sub-folders, one for each piece of writing you include. Identify all drafts with a title and date, as shown in the following example.

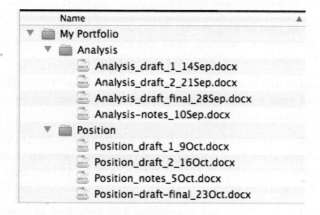

If you're required to include a statement reflecting on your writing, take notes on your process and your work *throughout the term*. If you receive any peer response, keep copies in your file.

Reflecting on Your Writing

An essential component is a statement that introduces and reflects on the work that's included in the portfolio. Such a statement should DESCRIBE your writing process, EXPLAIN what's included and why you included the pieces you did, and REFLECT on your development as a writer.

Writing such a statement gives you the opportunity to take a good look at your writing and to evaluate it on your own terms. Maybe the essay on which you received your lowest grade was one where you experienced a breakthrough in your writing process—even if the grade it earned doesn't reflect that. You may well want to discuss this breakthrough in your statement. Did you discover that freewriting worked better than outlining as a way to generate ideas? These are the kinds of insights you can weave into your statement, demonstrating to your instructor that you have thought carefully about both your writing and your writing process. Following are some prompts to help you think about your writing with a critical eye:

- **REVIEW** *each piece of writing in your portfolio.* What are the strengths and the weaknesses? Which is your best piece? Explain why it is the best and what it demonstrates about what you've learned. Which would you say is the weakest—and how would you change it if you could?

- **ANALYZE** *your writing process.* Study any drafts, responses, and other materials you're including. How did they help you revise? Which of them helped the most? Were any not helpful?

- **DESCRIBE** *the strategies and techniques you use.* Which ones have proved most helpful to you, and which have been less helpful? Are there any you really enjoy?

- **REFLECT** *on your work as an author.* What does the writing in your portfolio show about you? What do you do well—and less well? What kinds of writing do you like the most? Is there any kind of writing that you dislike—and if so, why?

- **DEFINE** *goals.* What has assembling and reflecting on your portfolio helped you better understand about yourself as a writer? What strengths or weaknesses do you see that you didn't see before? Based on this analysis, what do you now want to work on?

Budget plenty of time for writing and revising your statement, and try to get feedback from classmates or a tutor at the writing center. Ask them to read with an eye for what the statement says about you as a writer. Remember that the statement itself demonstrates your writing ability: Write it thoughtfully and carefully.

This statement is usually written either as a letter or an essay. Whatever form it takes, it should describe your work, reflect on your development as a writer, assess what you have learned, and perhaps establish goals for yourself. You may or may not have an explicit **THESIS**, but it needs to be clear what your portfolio demonstrates about you as a writer.

A Sample Portfolio Statement

December 7, 2011

Dear Reader,

Writing used to be one of those things I never gave much time to. I'd get it done but without thinking much about how to do it better. It wasn't until coming to Ball State and taking a class with Professor Clark-Upchurch that writing started to be more than just a nuisance. For the first time, I was forced to look at the inner workings of formal writing, picking it apart and examining each part, learning what each part is supposed to contribute and why it's important. Slowly over the course of this semester, I have moved beyond the simple five-paragraph style of writing I learned in high school. All in all, I have become a stronger writer.

Writing the first paper, the literacy narrative, came easily to me . . . or so I thought. When my paper came back to me with Professor Clark-Upchurch's questions about my thesis and organization, some irrelevant incidents I included, a lack of illustrations to support my points, and comments about my "repetitive and simplistic sentence structures," I knew I needed to work harder. On the second paper, an analysis of a magazine ad, my thesis was clear and my paragraphs "flowed, one into the next" with good examples from the ad as support, but I still needed to work on using a variety of sentences to "make the reader want to read on."

It was on my last paper, the research-based essay, that I finally pulled everything together: an engaging introduction, a clear thesis, logical organization, solid development with lots of supporting examples, and (finally!) varied sentences.

Although my writing style has improved and my understanding of all that goes into a paper is at an all-time high, I still struggle with writing a proposal. I'm not sure why, but for some reason writing an essay about writing a future essay leaves me confused. I'd rather just write the essay in the first place than waste time and effort proposing what I'm going to write about. As a result, I never really made a decent effort at the third writing project— the proposal for the research paper. Thus I have decided to exclude that paper from my portfolio as I am sure it is my weakest.

In addition to these three papers, I include drafts with peer responses and Professor Clark-Upchurch's suggestions in order to provide a clear picture of how much I learned this term. One of the most helpful parts of the class was the peer responding sessions, when we analyzed each other's essays. Doing this allowed me to see that writing in college is for more than just pleasing the teacher and getting a grade.

The essays you are about to read are just a stepping-stone, a sturdy base for me to continue developing my writing into something more. But now the seed has been planted, whether willingly or unwillingly. Now whenever I need to write a formal paper, I have some tools I have learned and can use instead of simply scraping by on whatever I can muster.

Sincerely,
Kameron Wiles

Organizing a Portfolio

The way you organize and present your portfolio is important, part of how you present yourself as a writer. There's no one way to organize a portfolio, but it needs to be carefully organized so that it's easy to read. Be sure you know if your instructor expects a certain format or system.

Print portfolios can go in a folder (for a small portfolio) or a binder (for a longer one). Begin with a title page that includes your name, the course title and number, the instructor's name, the date, and the portfolio's title. Follow the title page with a table of contents. Next comes your statement and then the writing. Organize the portfolio by assignments, putting all the materials from each assignment together, with the final draft on top. Label everything. If you're using a binder, add tabbed dividers, one for each assignment. Number the pages consecutively, and be sure each item is labeled.

E-portfolios can be as basic as uploading *Word* documents to *Blackboard* or some other online course management system. Or you might post texts to an e-portfolio platform such as *Digication*.

There are many other platforms where you can create an e-portfolio, from *Google Docs* or *Google Sites* to blogging sites like *WordPress*, *Scribd*, and

The homepage of Eda Charmaine V. Gimenez shows her careful organization of work by topic and type of writing.

Tumblr. Here are a few things to keep in mind when working on a portfolio that will be submitted online:

- Figure out exactly what you're going to put in your portfolio before uploading anything.

- Be sure you know what system your instructor expects you to use, and contact your school's IT help desk in case you need assistance.

- If you need to upload files, know what type of file you should use, *Word* documents or PDFs.

- Double-check that the version you are uploading is the final version.

- If you are working on an e-portfolio website, set up a homepage with your basic information and include links to your statement and to each piece of writing, each on its own page.

- To be sure all of the links work and everything looks the way you expect, check your site in different browsers and on different computers (laptops and desktops); you don't want to find out after you've submitted it that links don't work or some parts aren't visible.

- If you'd like to preserve your e-portfolio or continue to add to it, ask your instructor or IT help desk if it will remain online after the term ends. If you find it will be deleted, you will need to move it to a more permanent platform.

Portfolios are becoming increasingly necessary, both in school and on the job. Your portfolio is more than an archive of your writing—it's a way of looking systematically at your work. Keeping a portfolio of your work enables you to reflect on your development as a writer and to build connections between that self and your professional self after graduation. Working portfolios establish connections—between what you've learned and what you need to work on, and between your work as a student and your future as a professional.

THIRTY-THREE

Taking Advantage of the Writing Center

AVE YOU EVER been assigned to write an essay but couldn't quite get started? Perhaps you didn't feel ready to meet with your instructor to discuss your topic (or lack of one), but you wanted to speak with someone about the assignment. Or maybe you had a rough draft, but you weren't sure if your argument made sense. Maybe you're struggling with the conclusion to an essay now, or you don't quite understand the difference between MLA and APA documentation. Or maybe you just want to know how readers will react to your blog before you post it.

Where can you turn to for help? Chances are your school has a writing center—and that's the place to go. It may be in the English Department, in an academic skills center, in the library, or online. And if your school does not have a writing center, worry not: You can find help at other online writing centers. In this chapter, you'll learn about the kind of help you can get at a writing center, how to prepare for a tutoring session—and how to become a tutor yourself.

What Writing Centers Offer

All writers need good readers, and the writing center is a place where you can find good readers, generally graduate or undergraduate students who have been trained to tutor student writing. While you may go to the writing center for help on a particular piece of writing, you will usually find that the advice you receive is helpful for almost any kind of writing. In other words, writing centers are places where you can talk with someone else about your writing—and where you can try out ideas with a tutor without worrying about a grade. Keep in mind, though, that tutors will not edit your draft or predict what grade you'll get; they will, however, ask you questions, engage you in discussion about what your goals are, and work to help you meet those goals.

All writers, from all disciplines across campus, can benefit from receiving feedback from a writing tutor: undergraduates in their first year, honors students working on senior theses, graduate students working on dissertations, faculty working on academic articles. Some writers set up regular weekly appointments; others come to the writing center now and then. Check the website of your campus writing center to determine what options exist for making appointments. You don't even need to have a specific problem in mind when you visit the writing center; often it just helps to have another reader look at your work, someone with some distance from your project.

Visiting the writing center can be useful at any stage of the writing process. If you have an assignment and you're having a little trouble getting started, you can brainstorm ideas with a tutor. Or maybe you've written a draft of your essay, but you know the introduction needs work. Perhaps you're struggling to understand a particular grammatical concept or need help with MLA documentation style. Maybe you don't actually have an assignment due, but you're looking for help to strengthen your writing in general. Most writing centers do not require that their clients have specific assignments and will be happy to have you meet with a tutor. In short, writing centers are places where you can go to improve as a writer and not just to ace an important assignment.

Do remember, however, that when you visit the writing center you are the author. Be open to the guidance and advice that your tutor offers, but you should never relinquish control of your draft. You will be the one to implement any changes that you and your tutor discuss.

Remember as well that writing center tutors are not teachers. If you have questions about the specifics of an assignment, or about a grade, you should speak with your instructor. One of the great things about going to the writing center, in fact, is that when you are working with a tutor, you do not have to be concerned about a grade.

Preparing for a Tutoring Session

Before your first visit, check your writing center's website or call to find out its hours, location, and policies. For example, do you need to make an appointment, or is it a walk-in center? How long does a session last? Can you sign up for more than one session with the same tutor if you have a large writing project or want to work over time on improving your writing skills?

Think about what you need to take with you. If you're looking for help with a specific assignment, review the assignment and any written notes or drafting you've already done. Give some thought to what you most want to work on. Prioritize. Remember that you have a limited amount of time and that you can't do everything. It can be helpful to write down questions you have or points you want to cover and to take these notes with you to your tutoring session. If you're looking for help on an assigned piece of writing, be sure to bring the assignment—and if your assignment requires that you respond to something that you've read, bring that, too. If you are looking for help on a particular aspect of your writing, bring copies of your previous work. Doing so will ensure that you have a satisfying, productive conference with your tutor.

What If English Is Not Your Primary Language?

Writing centers can be especially helpful if English is not your primary language. Perhaps your first language is American Sign Language, or your family communicates primarily in Spanish, or you speak three languages. Or maybe you're an international student studying at an American school, and you don't have previous experience with the kind of explicit argumentation required in U.S. academic contexts. Whatever your situation, you may find it helpful to work with a tutor at the writing center. When you have your first conference, take the opportunity to talk with your tutor about any writing issues that are especially important to you.

Because most tutors are native speakers, they typically recognize when writing is correct or incorrect, idiomatic or nonidiomatic. But this knowledge is often intuitive, and they may not be able to explain just why something is right or wrong. You may need to be patient when a tutor says, "I'm sorry, but I can't explain it. This is just how we say it in English."

Tutors are generally trained not to correct or edit students' writing, but they can help you identify, understand, and correct common errors. They can also teach you about other resources, both print and online, that you can turn to for help. In other words, a good tutor can help you become a proficient editor of your own writing.

Some students find it especially helpful to meet regularly with the same tutor. If your writing center offers this option, you may want to take advantage of the opportunity to work with a tutor who will be familiar with you and the writing issues most important to you.

Visiting an Online Writing Center

At many schools, writing centers have both a physical site and an online site, whereas some schools have only an online site. If your school has an online writing center (often known as an OWL, for online writing lab), it likely conducts virtual tutoring sessions in one of two ways: synchronous or asynchronous. Like face-to-face sessions, synchronous tutoring sessions are conducted in real time, with tutor and client working together online, usually in a chat program. Synchronous tutorials generally require that you make an appointment and send in a draft sometime before your appointment. Asynchronous online tutoring does not take place in real time, so the tutor and client are not necessarily online at the same time. Usually, the writer sends a series of questions to the tutor along with the draft. The tutor then responds to those questions and may, in return, send the writer questions to think about. Just as face-to-face writing centers differ from school to school, so do online writing centers. You'll need to check the policies at your school's writing center before signing up for online tutoring.

What if your school does not have either a face-to-face or online writing center? You can still get help from school and commercial sites whose online writing centers offer writing help to the general public. Check out the following links to online writing centers:

> Purdue University's OWL—http://owl.english.purdue.edu/
>
> Colorado State's Writing Studio—http://writing.colostate.edu

The International Writing Center Association also keeps a list of online and face-to-face writing centers at http://writingcenters.org/links/writing-centers-online/

And most writing centers have links on their websites to help writers through the writing process—writing thesis statements, writing introductions and conclusions, using various styles of documentation, writing persuasive essays, understanding writing conventions in a variety of disciplines, and so on. Again, check out your writing center's website to see what online resources it offers, and broaden your search to OWLs at other schools, too.

Making the Most of a Tutoring Session

Arrive prepared and on time. It's important to be on time so that you can take full advantage of the allotted session.

Tell the tutor what you want to accomplish, and share any concerns. Don't be afraid to share your questions, ideas, and goals.

Set the agenda. If your tutor suggests that you focus on a different aspect of the assignment than you want, ask why. You may want to focus on your organization while the tutor thinks that you should first have a clearer, stronger thesis statement. The tutor may have a good reason for making such a suggestion, so listen and be open to suggestions—but also let him or her know what your concerns are and that you want to spend time on them. The session should be a collaboration between the two of you.

Take notes during the session. Write down changes you want to make to your text. If you do any revising or editing during the session, be sure to write it down then and there. If you see that you need to reorganize your draft, make specific notes about the reorganization—what goes where, and so on. Tutoring is usually a combination of talking and writing, so it's important to take notes during or immediately after your session. Sometimes the tutor may also take notes and share them with you at the end of the session.

Write down your plan of action. Do not leave your tutoring session without writing down a plan for what you'll do afterward. This plan will be your guide when you next sit down in front of your computer to work on your assignment.

Schedule your next appointment (if necessary). If you'd like another session, you may want to schedule a follow-up visit before you leave the writing center. By doing so, you can continue to work on items that you did not cover in the first session, receive feedback on other aspects of your writing, and plan for future writing assignments. You're also more likely to get your preferred time if you schedule in advance.

What about Becoming a Writing Tutor?

Do you enjoy talking with others about their writing? Do you like working with your peers on their writing? Do you find that your writing improves when you provide feedback to others about their writing? If you answered yes to any of these questions, you may want to consider becoming a writing tutor.

The first step to becoming a writing tutor is to contact your school's writing center to find out how it selects tutors. Most writing centers require that potential tutors go through an interview process and some kind of training.

Some writing centers, especially those staffed primarily by undergraduates, require that students take a tutor-training course or a one-time orientation or seminar. In such a course, you may be introduced to theories about how people learn to write, how writing centers work, and how writing tutors work. You will probably learn a great deal about practical ways to conduct tutoring sessions—nuts and bolts advice about how to begin, how to ask questions, what not to do, and so on.

Becoming a writing tutor may help you gain valuable experience working in an educational setting, provide you with an opportunity to meet new students from diverse backgrounds, and add an impressive accomplishment to your résumé. Best of all, working as a writing tutor nearly guarantees an improvement in your own writing and editing skills—and most tutors say that they really value the collaborative community that the writing center fosters.

THIRTY-FOUR

Joining a Writing Group

GOOD WRITERS NEED GOOD READERS. Most good writers know that receiving feedback on their writing, at any stage, makes them better writers. Showing our writing to others helps us see the effect that our writing has on an audience. Is our organization logical? Does that example in the third paragraph illustrate our point? Will that statement that we think is really clever and witty elicit a chuckle after all? There's one good way to find out: by joining a writing group.

Writing groups are small groups of people who meet regularly to read and give feedback on one another's work. While similar to peer response groups, they're not generally required for a class but instead are formed voluntarily outside of class. Writing can sometimes be solitary and lonely, so joining a writing group is an opportunity to be part of a community of writers who will respond to your writing—and will not be grading it. Consider the benefits that two writers cite:

> For me, the most valuable part of being in a writing group is getting a chance to talk out my ideas with a friendly audience who are not ultimately going to be evaluating my work. I often go into my writing group meeting confused—and come out with a sense of clarity about where my writing project needs to go next.
>
> —JASON PALMERI, Miami University–Ohio

My writing groups provide two essential elements to my writing life: a thoughtful audience that offers me feedback on my work in progress, and a structure that reinforces deadlines. Having that "other" who's expecting something from me by a set time keeps me from procrastinating.
—MARCIA DICKSON, The Ohio State University at Marion

Finding a Writing Group

You can find writing groups on and off campus: in dorms, community centers, and coffee shops; at work; among students, senior citizens, and professional writers. Three aspiring science fiction writers meet regularly at a coffee shop. Five fledging playwrights get together monthly after their drama class to give and receive feedback on their plays. Four friends at four different universities meet online every other week to comment on one another's work for their various writing-intensive courses. Writing groups take many forms, so find one that works for you.

Just make sure to find a group committed to meeting regularly and to reading and responding to one another's work. You may have heard the old saying that "two heads are better than one"; in the case of writing groups, it is more than a mere cliché. Whatever their perspective, members of a good writing group will be able to ask you questions about your text or make suggestions that you would not have thought of on your own. More than that, they'll provide an opportunity to talk out your ideas—and to try out your writing on a real audience before turning it in or making it public.

Starting a Writing Group

If you want to start your own writing group, talk to students in your dorm or classes, or to friends at work. If you don't know anyone interested in joining a group, post a notice in the writing center. Get names of potential members from instructors. Don't limit yourself to people at your school: With the internet, you can share documents, send comments, and even meet virtually with writers who aren't local. Following are some questions we're often asked by friends who want to start a writing group:

Should all of the members of a group be at the same writing skill level? Most writing groups have members with varying levels of expertise. Everyone brings different talents to the group, and the goal of the group is to support each member's growth as a writer. You do not need to be a great writer to be a valuable member of a writing group.

Do you all need to be in the same course or have the same interests? Some writing groups are made up of members who share interests, but many include writers from different backgrounds. When you're forming a group, this is something to discuss, but know that both kinds of groups can work. Those groups that fail usually do so because members are not willing to attend regularly or to read one another's work, not because of how much their members have in common.

How many members should a writing group have? There is no magic number. Your group should be big enough so that each piece of writing receives more than one set of comments but not so big that there are too many personalities, schedules, and texts to negotiate. Be careful that your group isn't so large that individual writers do not receive adequate attention. We've found that three to five members is generally a good number.

Making a Writing Group Successful

Writing groups are only successful if all members feel an equal responsibility to the group. Commitment is key.

Establish a schedule and procedures. Decide how often each group member will submit a piece of work to the others for feedback, how it will be distributed, and when. For example, your group may decide that each member will submit work every four weeks on a rotating basis. You'll also need to decide if work will be submitted electronically or by hard copy, and when—a week before a meeting or just a few days? These are things to be decided by the group. Be flexible, but if your group often calls off meetings or regularly allows members to avoid submitting their writing, then the writing group isn't doing what it should.

Attend all the meetings. It's important that everyone attend meetings whether their writing is being considered or not. When you join a writing group, you are committing to everyone in the group. Your contributions as both a writer and reader are equally important. Keep the meeting time sacred, but don't let it drag on.

Come prepared. You each need to come to meetings prepared, having read each submission carefully and ready to say what you like and what you have questions about. And it's not enough to say "I like it" or "I didn't really understand it." Come with specific comments about what the writer has done well and what concerns he or she needs to address. Maybe you like the way someone uses questions as an organizing tool, but you don't understand the thesis. Perhaps you're not quite sure what the point is. Whatever it is, the more detailed your response, the more helpful your feedback will be.

You may want to ask writers to circulate a list of concerns they'd like members of the group to consider when reading their drafts. Or for writing in any of the genres covered in this book— **ARGUMENTS**, **ANALYSES**, **RE-PORTS**, **NARRATIVES**, or **REVIEWS** —you could consult the reading guidelines in those chapters.

Find a group that makes you be a better writer. You want people who expect you to give them your best efforts—and who will read your work carefully, react to it honestly and thoughtfully, and provide you with direction and encouragement to continue. This requires respect for each other and for the craft of writing.

Work with people you know and trust. Members should be able to comfortably express frustration, confusion, anxiety, or whatever else about their writing. It might take some time to build this trust, but a good writing group will support you through your entire writing process.

Don't forget to laugh. While everyone needs to take writing group responsibilities seriously, also just enjoy the group. Don't forget to laugh. Relax. Have fun with it. But don't lose sight of the main goal: to be a resource for other writers.

Learning How to Critique

You'll likely need to work at being a good reader and providing helpful feedback. Here are some tips for responding to someone else's writing.

- *Respond as a reader, not a teacher.* Remember that your goal is not to evaluate a fellow group member's work but to respond as one potential reader. You're not grading it!

- *Prioritize your comments.* Don't try to comment on every single thing. Begin with your overall impression of the text. What stands out to you? Why? Comment first on larger elements like organization and how well the ideas are developed. Leave comments about sentence-level elements to the end.

- *Search for patterns.* If you are responding to a text that has many sentence-level errors, try to identify two or three major patterns of error.

- *Maintain a positive and civil tone.* Critique does not mean criticism. Be honest about your response to what you read, but do so in a positive way. Think about the feedback that has been most helpful to you. Most likely, it was detailed but not overwhelming, told you what you did well and what you needed to work on, and offered some kind of encouragement.

We conclude this chapter with some good advice we once got from a friend and fellow writing group member:

> Commit to always showing up even if you don't have writing to bring. Meet regularly but not so often that it becomes a burdensome obligation. Make it easy to participate by not requiring members to do a lot of preparation. If the writing group ain't fun, it won't last!
> —KATIE BRAUN, The Ohio State University at Marion

THIRTY-FIVE

Publishing Your Work

NCE UPON A TIME you had to get a newspaper, magazine, or book editor to read and accept your work in order to be published. Go back further, and talent (and a cooperative editor) weren't enough to get your work into print—you usually had to be a man as well. Even further back in time, writers who wanted to share their thoughts and ideas with others often had to hire a scribe to handwrite their work since writing was a specialized skill not everyone mastered. So getting published wasn't easy. But today things have changed. Got access to a computer? Then you're only a few clicks away from publishing your writing.

The internet not only allows writers to publish their work, but it has also changed how we define publishing, since being "published" no longer only means seeing your work distributed in print by an authoritative source. Today publishing your work means making it available to an audience, whether in print or online.

As a writer today, you have many ways to publish your writing. This chapter thus concludes our book with a list of print and online venues where you can publish your writing—and with an award-winning essay first written for an undergraduate writing course that went on to be published. We invite you to join the fun—and to publish what you write!

College publications. Most colleges and universities have newspapers and journals that publish the writing of its students. And don't be intimidated: It may be easier to get your work published than you think. Rutgers University's newspaper, the *Daily Targum,* is one of the oldest and largest college papers in the country, but it makes it easy for students to submit work for publication.

> Interested in writing, taking photos, editing, reporting or designing for the *Targum?* Drop by our editorial office at 26 Mine Street after 4 p.m., Sunday through Thursday. If you would like to write for the news section, attend our writers meetings: Every Wednesday at 9:30 p.m. in Suite 431 of the Rutgers Student Center. Or, send an email to the head of the respective department.   —*DailyTargum.com*

Many schools also have literary magazines and journals that publish fiction, poetry, essays, and visual art done by students. *Jabberwock Review,* a student-run journal at Mississippi State University, "welcomes all forms and styles of writing, from traditional to experimental," according to its submission guidelines. DeAnza Community College's literary magazine, *Red Wheelbarrow,* welcomes submissions of all kinds from students. And Penn State University lists over twenty campus publications that solicit student work on everything from food culture (*Penn Appétit*) to politics (*Penn Political Review*). If your school does not have a literary magazine, research national undergraduate literary magazines that accept work from students around the country. *Red Wheelbarrow,* for instance, publishes a national edition open to "everyone around the country and the world."

Essay competitions. Many schools have annual writing contests, often sponsored by the writing program or English department, and publish the winners' work. The University of California at Davis holds such a competition, inviting students to submit essays or scientific or technical writing done for a course at Davis. The winning works are then published in an annual collection they call *Prized Writing.*

W. W. Norton, the publisher of this book, sponsors an annual prize for an outstanding essay written by an undergraduate student. You'll find an essay written by one recent winner at the end of this chapter and can read all the winning essays at wwnorton.com/books/norton-writers-prize.

Some national organizations and publications sponsor writing competitions as well. The *New York Times* holds annual essay contests for college students. Recent prompts have included the question "What is love like for you as a student in the U.S. today?" and a call to respond to an article asking "What's the Matter with College?" Other publications hold essay contests that offer cash prizes and publication to the winners—the *Nation, Atlantic Monthly*, and *Rolling Stone* are just a few.

And some academic journals and associations hold annual contests for student work. The Children's Literature Association, for example, gives an award to the best undergraduate essay in its field, invites the author to present at the annual conference, and publishes the paper online.

These are just a few of the competitions to look into for publishing your work. With a little exploring, you'll surely find other opportunities like these.

Anthologies of student writing. In addition to sponsoring competitions, some publishers issue anthologies of student writing. Norton, for example, invites students to submit essays for publication in *The Norton Pocket Book of Writing by Students* and other Norton textbooks. (A form that you can use to submit an essay appears at the end of this book.) Other publishers offer student collections as well, and you'll find submission forms in some other writing textbooks.

Publish yourself! What if you pursue some of the options listed above but don't get the recognition or exposure you want? Or what if you want to be published in a book of your own? Print-on-demand and e-publishing technologies enable writers to publish their work, though most of them cost money. Still, there have been some notable works that were self-published. Ever heard of *The Joy of Cooking*? Irma Rombauer self-published that book in 1931—and it has since sold more than 18 million copies. More recently, Amanda Hocking, author of young adult paranormal romance and urban fantasies, self-published nine of her own novels, several of which made the *New York Times* best-seller list.

You can also try services like *Lulu* and *iUniverse,* which allow writers to publish their own books, even offering (for a price) editorial, marketing, and sales services as well as print-on-demand book distribution. And Kindle Direct Publishing makes it possible to self-publish works and then sell them in the Kindle store. John Locke, who writes contemporary crime fiction, sells his books there for ninety-nine cents each—and recently entered the elite "Kindle Million Club" of authors who have sold over 1 million ebooks for the Kindle, joining Stieg Larsson, author of *The Girl with the Dragon Tattoo.*

Blogs. If you're interested in writing about a particular topic, a blog can be a good site for publishing your writing. Many blogs focus on single themes or topics—politics, baseball, coffee, travel, science, whatever—and most of them are interactive, providing space for readers to comment. And comment they do, which often leads to a kind of back-and-forth where it's hard to tell who's the author and who's the reader. Free blogging platforms such as *Blogger, Tumblr,* and *WordPress* make it fairly easy to create and maintain a blog.

Social networks. Social networks, most notably *Facebook*, allow you to post your writing under your own name for your friends and family to see. Unlike blogs, which can be created anonymously and visited by readers who don't identify themselves, social networks take the anonymous aspect out of online publishing—you control your audience by controlling your network. *Facebook* offers a space for short writing via status updates and also for longer-form writing using the "notes" feature. Some writers use *Facebook* as a portal to all of their written work, posting links to writing they've done elsewhere. So not only can you use *Facebook* to publish writing directly, but you can also use it to direct your network of readers to other places where your work can be found.

Twitter. *Twitter* allows you to publish your writing, too, though in very short snippets. But if we understand a publication as work that reaches an audience, then *Twitter* certainly fits the bill: companies tweet about new products, conference goers tweet about presentations they've seen, reporters tweet about breaking news. And writers in Tahrir Square during the Egyptian revolution subverted the 140-character limit by becoming "serial tweeters" in order to get substantial amounts of information out to a worldwide audience.

Document-sharing websites. You may be familiar with sites like *Google Docs* for storing and managing written documents, but this site and some others can also be used for sharing those documents with an audience. Check out also *Scribd*, which bills itself as "the world's largest social reading and publishing company" aiming to "democratize the publishing process." Given that anyone can upload a file—PDF, *Word*, or *PowerPoint*—and turn it into a web document that will then be searchable, it's no wonder that its site claims to be a place "where your content finds an audience." Another way to share writing is *Reddit,* a link-sharing site that depends on its millions of

Read a *Wired* article about one writer's *Reddit* experience: wwnorton.com/ write/everyone links.

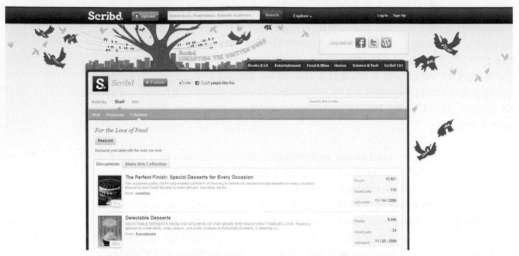

A typical *Scribd* collection.

users for both content and reviews. *Reddit* tracks what's most popular on the web through its users' up-or-down votes and comment threads; the more you participate, the more you gain from the site. And you never know where a *Reddit* thread can lead: One user, James Erwin, was offered a screenwriting deal based on his response to a post with a time-travel query.

Wikis. If you have ever visited *Wikipedia*, you've read a wiki. Wikis are written collaboratively, meaning anyone can post, update, or add to the information on a page. As a wiki writer, you can choose to be anonymous, and a wiki editor may remove or change what you add. But wikis are a good way to take part in a conversation on a topic you know something about. And wikis are generally visited by a large volume of readers, so you can be certain that if your contribution remains on the site, your writing is reaching an audience. *Wikipedia* offers the opportunity to write about anything that interests you, from Casas Grandes pottery to the South by Southwest festival to Taj Mahal (the palace or the musician). Whatever the topic, there's likely to be an entry on *Wikipedia* that you might consider contributing to as an author. And there are many wikis beyond *Wikipedia:* The *DavisWiki* is devoted to all things about the city of Davis, California; *Foodista* focuses on food and recipes; and *Wookieepedia* is an encyclopedia dedicated to *Star Wars*.

Comments. Many newspapers and magazines provide a space in their online versions inviting readers to post comments on articles and editorials, sometimes resulting in long and thoughtful discussions with other readers. It can be rewarding to post a response to an article and have others read and respond to what you say. *YouTube* also offers a space for commenting, as do many blogs.

Reviews. Amazon and other online stores provide space for readers to post reviews of books or other products sold there. Maybe you ordered some great (or horrible) take-out food from a new restaurant last night; publish a review on *Yelp* saying so! These are sites that allow you to reach a large audience — and to offer them some useful advice. Even though some of these venues are anonymous, they allow you to put your ideas out there, and as often as not to get responses to what you say.

Fan fiction websites. If you're unfamiliar with these sites, check out *FanFiction.net,* where you'll find forums to discuss favorite works, writing tips, and a place to write fiction of your own based on works you admire. Write a new ending to *Harry Potter*—or a story about when the heroines in *Pride and Prejudice* go to college (or when they encounter vampires). Most fan fiction sites include spaces where writers can discuss their work and also serve as editors critiquing one another's writing before it is published on the site.

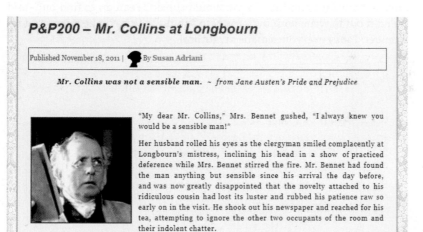

P&P200 – Mr. Collins at Longbourn

Published November 18, 2011 | By Susan Adriani

Mr. Collins was not a sensible man. ~ *from Jane Austen's Pride and Prejudice*

"My dear Mr. Collins," Mrs. Bennet gushed, "I always knew you would be a sensible man!"

Her husband rolled his eyes as the clergyman smiled complacently at Longbourn's mistress, inclining his head in a show of practiced deference while Mrs. Bennet stirred the fire. Mr. Bennet had found the man anything but sensible since his arrival the day before, and was now greatly disappointed that the novelty attached to his ridiculous cousin had lost its luster and rubbed his patience raw so early on in the visit. He shook out his newspaper and reached for his tea, attempting to ignore the other two occupants of the room and their indolent chatter.

A posting from *AustenAuthors*, a Jane Austen fan fiction site.

Fan fiction websites offer a good way to practice and find an audience and a community—readers who both write and read work like yours.

With the words that you scribble on the back of an envelope or poke out with your thumbs on a little device, you become part of something as big as the world, as near as your heart. Check out how an organization devoted to nothing more than the sharing of words and thoughts has influenced the course of history for nearly a century: http://www.pen-international.org/.

Almost all writers long to find an audience, and the internet has made it dramatically easier for writers and readers who share an interest to connect. Perhaps you want to start a blog about a favorite basketball team—or fan fiction to share with other devotees of Jane Austen's novels. Could be your aunt wants to publish a family history in honor of your grandmother's ninetieth birthday using *Lulu*. Or maybe you've written an essay for a college class that you're really proud of and have decided to submit it to the publisher of this book hoping it might be published in another writing textbook. These are just some of the ways that writers today can publish what they write, confirming again that in the twenty-first century everyone can be an author.

As promised, we conclude this chapter, and this book, with a student essay that began as an assignment for an undergraduate writing class and ended up winning the first Norton Writer's Prize and later being published in a book—this one! The essay "But Two Negatives Equal a Positive" was written by Carrie Barker when she was a student at Kirkwood Community College. Barker wrote her essay in response to an assignment from instructor Heal McKnight asking her to reflect on an important turning point in her life. She chose a crucial moment—an unexpected pregnancy when she already had three children. What should she do? Read on to find out—and then set out to write your own essay to submit to this competition. And remember: Today everyone can be an author!

But Two Negatives Equal a Positive

CARRIE BARKER

O H MY GOD. *Oh my God. OH MY GOD! This cannot be happening.* Tears surged down my face, pelting my bare thighs. Two different brands, two different stores, two different bathrooms. Same results. *Are you frickin' kidding me?!* The second one only confirmed the first, and the first only confirmed what I'd recently begun to suspect.

How? I kept demanding. *How could this happen?* Okay, the "how" wasn't the mystery. *This wasn't supposed to happen. Not now.*

I must have sat there for a long time, numb. My head and limbs felt far too heavy to get up, my brain incapable of forming intelligent thought, eyes closed, head tilted backward, positioned awkwardly against the tiled wall behind. At some point, my eyes flickered open to the glare of a recessed floodlight directly above.

Was this the Universe's idea of a sick joke? A test of some kind?

I stared into the white hot light. Mesmerized by the orb, I consented to it cauterizing the tears, scorching my corneas.

What words of wisdom might help here? I needed something. Anything. *When life hands you lemons, make lemonade? What doesn't kill you will only make you stronger?*

CARRIE BARKER is completing her final semester at Kirkwood Community College and plans on attending the University of Iowa in the fall. She lives in Cedar Rapids, Iowa, with her husband and four children.

A shoulder angel whispered, "No one ever has to know."

"There *are* options," the other chimed in.

Activity a few feet away briefly interrupted the conversation only I could hear.

"But could she go through with it? Could she live with herself afterward?" the first asked.

"Dunno. She never thought she'd be in this situation," the second answered.

I closed my eyes and gently rubbed the black blobs out of my vision. I dug the other contraption out from a small brown sack at the bottom of my purse and discarded them both in the receptacle mounted in the stall.

"A little different from the typical trash thrown in there," a shoulder angel observed.

"It is ironic," the other agreed.

Go away, I told my shoulder angels. *I don't like you anymore.*

I pulled myself together and made it to the sink. The reflection in the mirror wasn't kind; twin mascara ruts flanked each side of my face, eyelids swollen and naked, the whites bloodshot and raw. The splash of cold water stung my pores. Stalling, I wandered throughout the store and tried to come to terms with this new reality. My loitering terminated in the baby section.

How will Scott react? What will people think? What are we going to do? I tried to put myself in his shoes. *We . . . will there continue to be a "we"?* I just didn't know . . .

I slipped into the house and quickly scanned the rooms. Scott was alone in the kitchen, cleaning out the refrigerator. *Damn, I had bad timing.* I quietly crossed the room and erected myself alongside the sweaty Tupperware and condiment containers sitting on the counter.

I crossed my arms and erupted, "You were right."

He backed out of the fridge and shut the door, giving me his full attention. "About what?" he asked.

Be strong, I told myself, *and do not cry.*

The instant our eyes met, mine started to well up with tears; I looked down and away, focusing on a few stray dust bunnies gathering in the corner. I hesitated. Scott sighed impatiently; he hated to be interrupted in the middle of something. Briefly, my eyes met his arched brows, then darted back to the corner again. *For Christ's sake,* my brain screamed, *he's your husband, not your father!* I took a deep breath and purged, "You were right about me being pregnant." I stole another glance; his expression was impossible to read. I took another breath and elaborated. "When you suggested it earlier, I thought you'd lost your mind. But then I got to thinking . . . the dates, not feeling well. I still thought you were nuts, but I took a test. Two actually, and they were both positive."

Just then, the patter of footsteps getting louder interrupted my confession. "Mom, can I have some crackers?"

"Sure, buddy." I handed him the box, trying to buy us more time alone. "Share with your brother and sister, okay?"

"Okay. Thanks, Mom!" And back to the living room he went.

Scott's silence was unbearable. I forced myself to look directly into his deep blue eyes.

"I haven't cheated on you," I offered.

"I wasn't thinking you did," he countered calmly.

"You weren't?" My brain couldn't comprehend. *How does a man with two surgically cut vas deferens not suspect his knocked-up wife?*

"You remember the numbers the doctor told us," he said.

"Yeah, I remember joking about our odds of having another baby being greater than winning the lottery." *And asking if I could do the honors,* I recalled. (After all, dads were given the option of cutting the umbilical cord after a baby was born; it seemed like a perfectly reasonable request to me.)

"I can't believe I figured out you were pregnant before you did," he said. "What kind of woman are you?" He was teasing, but I failed to see humor in the situation.

"The kind of woman who is done with that part of her life," I belched, sounding defensive. "The kind that gave birth to three babies in thirty-three months and likes eight hours of sleep a night. The kind that is done changing diapers and washing bottles and already got rid of every bit of baby stuff we ever owned." I'm sure he was sorry he asked. "Why would being pregnant even cross my mind?"

If he answered I didn't hear him. My brain was busy cranking out reasons not to have this baby: *Because I was done with that part of my life, because I finally owned clothes that were stain-free, because I was a frazzled, overwhelmed mess when the kids were babies. And because I was tired of feeling like my sole purpose on this earth was to be someone's wife or mother. What about me? When was it my turn?* I stopped, realizing Scott was watching me shake my head back and forth.

"Scott, I can't start over. I don't want to. They're all finally in school." Guilt overwhelmed me. "And you know people are going to assume I had an affair. Everyone knows you got a vasectomy."

"I don't give a shit what they think," he said. "Ultimately, it's your decision and I'll support whatever you decide, but I think we're in a better position now than when we had the first three. Things are better now, right?"

It was true; we weren't exactly living the high life, but we weren't nearly as broke as during those early years. And I couldn't remember the last time we had an argument.

He continued, "I'd say I'm more mature now than at twenty-five. And more patient." I nodded. "Care, it's not like you're going to have three babies again. Just one."

Also good points. Wait a minute—what the hell just happened? Since when was he the voice of reason? That's always been my job!

"Come here," he said, gently pulling me into his protective embrace.

Wow, I thought, dissolving into a blubbering train wreck. *I had prepared for a whole slew of reactions, but that wasn't one of them.*

Exhausted and relieved, I agreed to let the idea of a fourth child marinate awhile.

I knew myself pretty well; I was capable of talking myself into or out of just about anything. I had been known to rationalize, justify, or just procrastinate until someone decided for me. But I wasn't a fan of indecision either, and the gravity of what Oprah called a "defining moment" weighed heavily on my mind and gnawed at my brain stem. During downtimes, my shoulder angels reappeared to duke it out; one would throw out a legitimate objection and the other would counter with an equally valid rebuttal.

In the shower: "She has no baby necessities; it would be absurd to start from scratch."

"She learned the difference between a necessity and a gadget the first time around."

"Has she looked at the prices of the stuff? This is going to cost a bundle."

"It doesn't have to be brand new; there are always garage sales and secondhand stores."

At a stoplight: "Another child is less than ideal in a three-bedroom home; the boys are already sharing a room."

"Maybe it's a girl. Her daughter has always wanted a little sister."

"Yeah, till she actually has one."

"People make do. Years ago, babies slept in dresser drawers."

In line at the grocery store: "A new baby will totally mess up the whole birth-order dynamic."

"It will. There will no longer be a middle child."

"The older kids may resent the baby."

"Maybe they'll be old enough to remember the experience of having a new little brother or sister—being helpers, teaching new things, reveling in all the firsts."

At night in bed: "She lives in a time where women can choose. She doesn't have to blindly accept whatever card life throws her."

"She considered all her options; she feels too often people try to control every aspect of their lives. That's not life, that's a spreadsheet. The bumps in the road are there to teach things—about life, about adversity, about herself."

"But she said she doesn't want this."

"Well, it's not always about getting what you want. She wants chocolate all the time. Wait, that's a bad example."

"But she said she was just starting to get her life back."

"It's true that the timing isn't convenient. But have you noticed that things have a way of working out pretty terrific when given the chance?"

"Wait, does this mean she's having a baby?"

"She's decided; they're having a baby."

"I still can't go to sleep."

"Maybe it's because you consume too much caffeine."

"Maybe. Or maybe it's because I can't turn off my brain. How is it that he can be lying next to her snoring, sixty seconds after his head hits the pillow? She's been lying here for more than an hour."

"She's gonna have to get up to pee soon anyway, so she may as well get used to it."

"Hey, what were all those girls' names we had picked out? Do you remember?"

"Oh, the girls' names were a piece of cake! We found lots of names that we loved. It was the boys' names that were tough. . . . They had to sound masculine, but not too macho. "

"Hmm, I wonder where she put that name book."

Shut up! I scolded them. *I'm trying to fall asleep. Maybe I'll look for the book tomorrow.*

IF EVERYONE'S AN AUTHOR, that includes you, too. So get busy. Now's the time to publish something you've written. We hope this book will help you do so.

Readings

IF EVERYONE'S AN AUTHOR, then we are all readers as well. All authors, in fact, learn constantly by engaging with what other authors have written. On the following pages you'll find an anthology of 36 readings, arranged alphabetically by author. And on the inside back cover of the book, we've added a menu that categorizes the readings by both genres and themes. And that's not all. We'll be posting additional essays, articles, cartoons, speeches, videos, and more regularly on everyonesanauthor.tumblr.com for you to read, analyze, reflect on—and respond to. So read on, enjoy, and see what you can learn.

Man in the Middle

KEVIN ARNOVITZ

NBA JOURNEYMAN JOHN AMAECHI'S coming out has already spawned hundreds of rote conversations about homophobia and sports. Beat writers have probed players about how they'd deal with a gay teammate, producing few revelations other than that Shavlik Randolph probably hasn't attended many LGBT barbecues. Whether it's a mark of progress or the triumph of collective cynicism, Amaechi's confession has mostly been seen as either an attempt to sell his memoir, *Man in the Middle*, or an irrelevant, self-indulgent gesture. Brian Schmitz of the *Orlando Sentinel*, for one, squawked that Amaechi's coming out was "so '90s"—a response that might've been appropriate if a former NBA player had proclaimed his love for MTV's *Real World-Road Rules* tandem. Then, on Wednesday, former NBA star Tim Hardaway finally

---

KEVIN ARNOVITZ is a basketball specialist for ESPN, where he edits and contributes to blogs about the game as well as presents radio and TV commentary. He often writes about the social dimensions of professional sports, including issues surrounding gay sports figures. This article is a review of *Man in the Middle*, a memoir by John Amaechi, who played in the NBA and European leagues from 1995 to 2003 and in 2007 became the first NBA player to come out as gay. Arnovitz's review first appeared in *Slate* in 2007 under the title "The Loneliness of the Gay Basketball Player"; as with most book reviews, one of its principal objectives is to introduce the book to the public and stimulate interest in reading it.

cut to the chase. "I hate gay people," he told radio host Dan Le Betard. "I am homophobic. I don't like it. It shouldn't be in the world or in the United States."

Amaechi responded by calling Hardaway's rant bigoted. "But it is honest," he continued. "And it illustrates the problem better than any of the fuzzy language other people have used so far." Hardaway's loud-and-proud prejudice is also a reminder that beat writers needn't bother asking straight players how they'd respond to a gay teammate. The more interesting question, and the one *Man in the Middle* tries to answer, is: How would a gay man react to a teammate like Hardaway?

Arnovitz' diction sets a friendly, informal tone. See pp. 515–25 on crafting the style of your work.

Most of the time, *Man in the Middle* reads like a conventional sports memoir. An awkward, fat, working-class kid finds refuge in basketball. After learning the fundamentals, he emerges from his shell. With the encouragement of his courageous single mother, Amaechi makes it big and sees the world.

In the latter half of the book, Amaechi tentatively delves into his own sexuality. Early in his career, the closest he comes to announcing he's gay is introducing his Orlando teammates to the wonders of Earl Grey tea. Little by little, he affords himself allowances in, of all places, Salt Lake City. During his final season with the Jazz, he invites queeny friends to the family room at the Delta Center and starts hanging out in the town's gay enclave.

John Amaechi (*left*) is boxed out for a rebound by three players from the San Antonio Spurs in a 2001 game at the TD Waterhouse Center in Orlando.

This leads to one of the book's most affirming moments, when young Jazz forward Andrei Kirilenko urges Amaechi to attend a party at his home: "You are welcome to bring your partner, if you have one, someone special to you."

Amaechi doesn't soft-pedal the NBA's homophobia, but he believes it's 5 more "a convention of a particular brand of masculinity than a genuine prejudice." A team bus ride past a billboard reading "SOMEONE YOU KNOW IS GAY," for example, launches a "cacophony of shock and horror." Rather than rant about his teammates, Amaechi points out the locker room's sexual ironies. "They checked out each other's cocks. They primped in front of the mirror. . . . They tried on each other's $10,000 suits and shoes. . . . And I'm the gay one. Hah!" While cocks were being checked out, Amaechi says, he "stood in the corner in baggy clothes or wrapped in an oversized towel."

That scene—Amaechi, standing alone, as his hetero teammates engage in homosocial behavior—is the book's lasting image. Unlike, say, *Juiced*— Jose Canseco's homoerotic steroids homage—*Man in the Middle* doesn't revel in titillating erotica. Other than a few anonymous encounters with a volleyballer in the locker room at Penn State and a short relationship when he played in the British Basketball League, he seems to have led one of the most celibate existences of any athlete since A. C. Green. (Amaechi self-deprecatingly ascribes this to personal incompetence as much as intolerance.)

Amaechi doesn't speculate what percentage of the league is gay, and he doesn't name any names. One gets the sense that this is partly by design— innuendo just isn't his style—and partly a consequence of the distance he keeps from his fellow jocks. Amaechi's alienation from the culture of the NBA was not merely sexual. Surprisingly, his disaffection seems to be as much a product of his literacy as of his homosexuality. In *Man in the Middle*, Amaechi comes out as an intellectual—a creature almost as alien in the NBA as a gay man. He frequents art galleries on his off days, loves poetry, and is one of the first pro athletes to author a blog. The guy is smart enough that he can make something as dull as a fondness for Twinkies—"I loved their spongy richness and I devoured them by the dozen"—into a thoughtful disquisition.

Twinkies are just one of many things that Amaechi loves more than basketball. He writes with the most zeal—and at the most length—about mentoring, a passion that culminated in his official adoption of two teenagers in Orlando. (In passing, he reminds us that it's illegal for gays and lesbians to adopt in the state of Florida.) The more involved he gets with his off-court charity work, the less he cares about hoops. "Nobody could make me love something I picked up more or less because I was tall," he says.

The most interesting revelation in *Man in the Middle* has nothing to do with homosexuality. The profoundly isolated Amaechi says he finds common cause with other players on at least one matter: seeing sports as a means to an end. He writes that the pros play the game for a lot of easons—money, fame, groupies, self-esteem—but that very few NBA players love basketball. "The fan sitting at home . . . wants us to love the game like he does," he writes. "If he knew why we really play the game, for the most part, he might not love the game. He might not even watch it." The average fan, gay or straight, will probably find that contention more troubling than a former player's homosexuality.

Thinking about the Text

1. Even though Kevin Arnovitz says that most of *Man in the Middle* "reads like a conventional sports memoir" (3) and briefly explains how, his **REVIEW** mostly discusses the ways that the book is *un*conventional. Why do you think he took this approach?

2. Most of this review is devoted to summary rather than evaluation of Amaechi's book, and the **CRITERIA** for evaluation are implied rather than stated explicitly. What do Arnovitz's criteria seem to be? Should he have been more explicit about them? Why or why not?

3. In his final paragraph, Arnovitz points out what Amaechi sees as the **CONTRAST** between fans' and players' attitudes, speculating that fans might find it very "troubling" to learn that "very few NBA players love basketball" (9). How do you feel about that revelation? Troubled? Angry? Saddened? Indifferent?

4. Arnovitz is a basketball aficionado writing about the memoir of a pro basketball player. How does he make his review interesting to a wider **AUDIENCE**?

5. Since Amaechi's book came out in 2007, the sports world has become somewhat more open to gay and lesbian pro athletes, and the topic is more widely discussed (a 2011 *Google* search for the term "gay pro athletes" returned 1,600,000 hits). What implications does "outness" in sports have for society in general? Do you care whether a particular athlete comes out publicly as gay? Why or why not? Write an essay that **REFLECTS** on your responses to these questions.

Monsanto's Harvest of Fear

DONALD L. BARLETT & JAMES B. STEELE

GARY RINEHART CLEARLY REMEMBERS the summer day in 2002 when the stranger walked in and issued his threat. Rinehart was behind the counter of the Square Deal, his "old-time country store," as he calls it, on the fading town square of Eagleville, Missouri, a tiny farm community 100 miles north of Kansas City.

The Square Deal is a fixture in Eagleville, a place where farmers and townspeople can go for lightbulbs, greeting cards, hunting gear, ice cream, aspirin, and dozens of other small items without having to drive to a big-box store in Bethany, the county seat, 15 miles down Interstate 35.

Everyone knows Rinehart, who was born and raised in the area and runs one of Eagleville's few surviving businesses. The stranger came up to the counter and asked for him by name.

"Well, that's me," said Rinehart.

As Rinehart would recall, the man began verbally attacking him, saying 5 he had proof that Rinehart had planted Monsanto's genetically modified (G.M.) soybeans in violation of the company's patent. Better come clean and settle with Monsanto, Rinehart says the man told him—or face the consequences.

DONALD L. BARLETT and JAMES B. STEELE have worked together as investigative journalists for more than three decades, winning two Pulitzer Prizes and many other awards. They are contributing editors at *Vanity Fair*, where this article was published in 2008.

Monsanto brought false accusations against Gary Rinehart—shown here at his rural Missouri store. There has been no apology.

The report kicks off with an attention-grabbing narrative —a good strategy, and not hard to do. See Ch. 8 and pp. 319–20.

Rinehart was incredulous, listening to the words as puzzled customers and employees looked on. Like many others in rural America, Rinehart knew of Monsanto's fierce reputation for enforcing its patents and suing anyone who allegedly violated them. But Rinehart wasn't a farmer. He wasn't a seed dealer. He hadn't planted any seeds or sold any seeds. He owned a small—a *really* small—country store in a town of 350 people. He was angry that somebody could just barge into the store and embarrass him in front of everyone. "It made me and my business look bad," he says. Rinehart says he told the intruder, "You got the wrong guy."

When the stranger persisted, Rinehart showed him the door. On the way out the man kept making threats. Rinehart says he can't remember the exact words, but they were to the effect of: "Monsanto is big. You can't win. We will get you. You will pay."

Scenes like this are playing out in many parts of rural America these days as Monsanto goes after farmers, farmers' co-ops, seed dealers—anyone it suspects may have infringed its patents of genetically modified seeds. As interviews and reams of court documents reveal, Monsanto relies on a shadowy army of private investigators and agents in the American heartland to strike fear into farm country. They fan out into fields and farm towns, where they secretly videotape and photograph farmers, store owners, and co-ops; infiltrate community meetings; and gather information from informants about farming activities. Farmers say that some Monsanto agents pretend to be surveyors. Others confront farmers on their land and try to pressure them to sign papers giving Monsanto access to their private records. Farmers call them the "seed police" and use words such as "Gestapo" and "Mafia" to describe their tactics.

When asked about these practices, Monsanto declined to comment specifically, other than to say that the company is simply protecting its patents. "Monsanto spends more than $2 million a day in research to identify, test, develop and bring to market innovative new seeds and technologies that benefit farmers," Monsanto spokesman Darren Wallis wrote in an e-mailed letter to *Vanity Fair*. "One tool in protecting this investment is patenting our discoveries and, if necessary, legally defending those patents against those who might choose to infringe upon them." Wallis said that, while the vast majority of farmers and seed dealers follow the licensing agreements, "a tiny fraction" do not, and that Monsanto is obligated to those who do abide by its rules to enforce its patent rights on those who "reap the benefits of the technology without paying for its use." He said only a small number of cases ever go to trial.

Some compare Monsanto's hard-line approach to Microsoft's zealous efforts to protect its software from pirates. At least with Microsoft the buyer of a program can use it over and over again. But farmers who buy Monsanto's seeds can't even do that.   10

The Control of Nature

For centuries—millennia—farmers have saved seeds from season to season: they planted in the spring, harvested in the fall, then reclaimed and cleaned the seeds over the winter for re-planting the next spring. Monsanto has turned this ancient practice on its head.

Monsanto developed G.M. seeds that would resist its own herbicide, Roundup, offering farmers a convenient way to spray fields with weed killer without affecting crops. Monsanto then patented the seeds. For nearly all of its history the United States Patent and Trademark Office had refused to grant patents on seeds, viewing them as life-forms with too many variables to be patented. "It's not like describing a widget," says Joseph Mendelson III, the legal director of the Center for Food Safety, which has tracked Monsanto's activities in rural America for years.

Indeed not. But in 1980 the U.S. Supreme Court, in a five-to-four decision, turned seeds into widgets, laying the groundwork for a handful of corporations to begin taking control of the world's food supply. In its decision, the court extended patent law to cover "a live human-made microorganism." In this case, the organism wasn't even a seed. Rather, it was a *Pseudomonas* bacterium developed by a General Electric scientist to clean up oil spills. But the precedent was set, and Monsanto took advantage of it. Since the 1980s, Monsanto has become the world leader in genetic modification of seeds and has won 674 biotechnology patents, more than any other company, according to U.S. Department of Agriculture data.

Farmers who buy Monsanto's patented Roundup Ready seeds are required to sign an agreement promising not to save the seed produced after each harvest for re-planting, or to sell the seed to other farmers. This means that farmers must buy new seed every year. Those increased sales, coupled with ballooning sales of its Roundup weed killer, have been a bonanza for Monsanto.

This radical departure from age-old practice has created turmoil in   15 farm country. Some farmers don't fully understand that they aren't supposed to save Monsanto's seeds for next year's planting. Others do, but ignore the stipulation rather than throw away a perfectly usable product. Still others say that they don't use Monsanto's genetically modified seeds, but seeds have been blown into their fields by wind or deposited by birds. It's certainly easy for G.M. seeds to get mixed in with traditional varieties when seeds are cleaned by commercial dealers for re-planting. The seeds look identical; only a laboratory analysis can show the difference. Even if a farmer doesn't buy G.M. seeds and doesn't want them on his land, it's a safe bet he'll get a visit from Monsanto's seed police if crops grown from G.M. seeds are discovered in his fields.

Most Americans know Monsanto because of what it sells to put on our lawns—the ubiquitous weed killer Roundup. What they may not know is that the company now profoundly influences—and one day may virtually control—what we put on our tables. For most of its history Monsanto was a chemical giant, producing some of the most toxic substances ever created, residues from which have left us with some of the most polluted sites on earth. Yet in a little more than a decade, the company has sought to shed its polluted past and morph into something much different and more far-reaching—an "agricultural company" dedicated to making the world "a better place for future generations." Still, more than one Web log claims to see similarities between Monsanto and the fictional company "U-North" in the movie *Michael Clayton,* an agribusiness giant accused in a multibillion-dollar lawsuit of selling an herbicide that causes cancer.

Monsanto's genetically modified seeds have transformed the company and are radically altering global agriculture. So far, the company has produced G.M. seeds for soybeans, corn, canola, and cotton. Many more products have been developed or are in the pipeline, including seeds for sugar beets and alfalfa. The company is also seeking to extend its reach into milk production by marketing an artificial growth hormone for cows that increases their output, and it is taking aggressive steps to put those who don't want to use growth hormone at a commercial disadvantage.

Even as the company is pushing its G.M. agenda, Monsanto is buying up conventional-seed companies. In 2005, Monsanto paid $1.4 billion for Seminis, which controlled 40 percent of the U.S. market for lettuce, tomatoes, and other vegetable and fruit seeds. Two weeks later it announced the acquisition of the country's third-largest cottonseed company, Emergent Genetics, for $300 million. It's estimated that Monsanto seeds now account for 90 percent of the U.S. production of soybeans, which are used in food products beyond counting. Monsanto's acquisitions have fueled explosive growth, transforming the St. Louis–based corporation into the largest seed company in the world.

In Iraq, the groundwork has been laid to protect the patents of Monsanto and other G.M.-seed companies. One of L. Paul Bremer's last acts as head of the Coalition Provisional Authority was an order stipulating that "farmers shall be prohibited from re-using seeds of protected varieties." Monsanto has said that it has no interest in doing business in Iraq, but should the company change its mind, the American-style law is in place.

To be sure, more and more agricultural corporations and individual   20
farmers are using Monsanto's G.M. seeds. As recently as 1980, no genetically modified crops were grown in the U.S. In 2007, the total was 142 million acres planted. Worldwide, the figure was 282 million acres. Many farmers believe that G.M. seeds increase crop yields and save money. Another reason for their attraction is convenience. By using Roundup Ready soybean seeds, a farmer can spend less time tending to his fields. With Monsanto seeds, a

farmer plants his crop, then treats it later with Roundup to kill weeds. That takes the place of labor-intensive weed control and plowing.

Monsanto portrays its move into G.M. seeds as a giant leap for mankind. But out in the American countryside, Monsanto's no-holds-barred tactics have made it feared and loathed. Like it or not, farmers say, they have fewer and fewer choices in buying seeds.

And controlling the seeds is not some abstraction. Whoever provides the world's seeds controls the world's food supply.

Under Surveillance

After Monsanto's investigator confronted Gary Rinehart, Monsanto filed a federal lawsuit alleging that Rinehart "knowingly, intentionally, and willfully" planted seeds "in violation of Monsanto's patent rights." The company's complaint made it sound as if Monsanto had Rinehart dead to rights:

> During the 2002 growing season, Investigator Jeffery Moore, through surveillance of Mr. Rinehart's farm facility and farming operations, observed Defendant planting brown bag soybean seed. Mr. Moore observed the Defendant take the brown bag soybeans to a field, which was subsequently loaded into a grain drill and planted. Mr. Moore located two empty bags in the ditch in the public road right-of-way beside one of the fields planted by Rinehart, which contained some soybeans. Mr. Moore collected a small amount of soybeans left in the bags which Defendant had tossed into the public right-of way. These samples tested positive for Monsanto's Roundup Ready technology.

Faced with a federal lawsuit, Rinehart had to hire a lawyer. Monsanto eventually realized that "Investigator Jeffery Moore" had targeted the wrong man, and dropped the suit. Rinehart later learned that the company had been secretly investigating farmers in his area. Rinehart never heard from Monsanto again: no letter of apology, no public concession that the company had made a terrible mistake, no offer to pay his attorney's fees. "I don't know how they get away with it," he says. "If I tried to do something like that it would be bad news. I felt like I was in another country."

Gary Rinehart is actually one of Monsanto's luckier targets. Ever since commercial introduction of its G.M. seeds, in 1996, Monsanto has launched thousands of investigations and filed lawsuits against hundreds of farmers and seed dealers. In a 2007 report, the Center for Food Safety, in Washington, D.C., documented 112 such lawsuits, in 27 states.

Even more significant, in the Center's opinion, are the numbers of　25 farmers who settle because they don't have the money or the time to fight Monsanto. "The number of cases filed is only the tip of the iceberg," says Bill Freese, the Center's science-policy analyst. Freese says he has been told of many cases in which Monsanto investigators showed up at a farmer's house or confronted him in his fields, claiming he had violated the technology agreement and demanding to see his records. According to Freese, investigators will say, "Monsanto knows that you are saving Roundup Ready seeds, and if you don't sign these information-release forms, Monsanto is going to come after you and take your farm or take you for all you're worth." Investigators will sometimes show a farmer a photo of himself coming out of a store, to let him know he is being followed.

Lawyers who have represented farmers sued by Monsanto say that intimidating actions like these are commonplace. Most give in and pay Monsanto some amount in damages; those who resist face the full force of Monsanto's legal wrath.

Scorched-Earth Tactics

Pilot Grove, Missouri, population 750, sits in rolling farmland 150 miles west of St. Louis. The town has a grocery store, a bank, a bar, a nursing home, a funeral parlor, and a few other small businesses. There are no stoplights, but the town doesn't need any. The little traffic it has comes from trucks on their way to and from the grain elevator on the edge of town. The elevator is owned by a local co-op, the Pilot Grove Cooperative Elevator, which buys soybeans and corn from farmers in the fall, then ships out the grain over the winter. The co-op has seven full-time employees and four computers.

In the fall of 2006, Monsanto trained its legal guns on Pilot Grove; ever since, its farmers have been drawn into a costly, disruptive legal battle against an opponent with limitless resources. Neither Pilot Grove nor Monsanto will discuss the case, but it is possible to piece together much of the story from documents filed as part of the litigation.

Monsanto began investigating soybean farmers in and around Pilot Grove several years ago. There is no indication as to what sparked the probe, but Monsanto periodically investigates farmers in soybean-growing regions such as this one in central Missouri. The company has a staff devoted to enforcing patents and litigating against farmers. To gather leads, the company maintains an 800 number and encourages farmers to inform on other farmers they think may be engaging in "seed piracy."

Once Pilot Grove had been targeted, Monsanto sent private investigators into the area. Over a period of months, Monsanto's investigators surreptitiously followed the co-op's employees and customers and videotaped them in fields and going about other activities. At least 17 such surveillance videos were made, according to court records. The investigative work was outsourced to a St. Louis agency, McDowell & Associates. It was a McDowell investigator who erroneously fingered Gary Rinehart. In Pilot Grove, at least 11 McDowell investigators have worked the case, and Monsanto makes no bones about the extent of this effort: "Surveillance was conducted throughout the year by various investigators in the field," according to court records. McDowell, like Monsanto, will not comment on the case.

Not long after investigators showed up in Pilot Grove, Monsanto subpoenaed the co-op's records concerning seed and herbicide purchases and seed-cleaning operations. The co-op provided more than 800 pages of documents pertaining to dozens of farmers. Monsanto sued two farmers and negotiated settlements with more than 25 others it accused of seed piracy. But Monsanto's legal assault had only begun. Although the co-op had provided voluminous records, Monsanto then sued it in federal court for patent infringement. Monsanto contended that by cleaning seeds—a service which it had provided for decades—the co-op was inducing farmers to violate Monsanto's patents. In effect, Monsanto wanted the co-op to police its own customers.

In the majority of cases where Monsanto sues, or threatens to sue, farmers settle before going to trial. The cost and stress of litigating against a global corporation are just too great. But Pilot Grove wouldn't cave—and ever since, Monsanto has been turning up the heat. The more the co-op has resisted, the more legal firepower Monsanto has aimed at it. Pilot Grove's lawyer, Steven H. Schwartz, described Monsanto in a court filing as pursuing a "scorched earth tactic," intent on "trying to drive the co-op into the ground."

Even after Pilot Grove turned over thousands more pages of sales records going back five years, and covering virtually every one of its farmer customers, Monsanto wanted more—the right to inspect the co-op's hard drives. When the co-op offered to provide an electronic version of any record, Monsanto demanded hands-on access to Pilot Grove's in-house computers.

Monsanto next petitioned to make potential damages punitive—tripling the amount that Pilot Grove might have to pay if found guilty. After a judge denied that request, Monsanto expanded the scope of the pre-trial investigation by seeking to quadruple the number of depositions. "Monsanto is doing its best to make this case so expensive to defend that the Co-op will have no choice but to relent," Pilot Grove's lawyer said in a court filing.

With Pilot Grove still holding out for a trial, Monsanto now subpoenaed 35 the records of more than 100 of the co-op's customers. In a "You are Commanded . . . " notice, the farmers were ordered to gather up five years of invoices, receipts, and all other papers relating to their soybean and herbicide purchases, and to have the documents delivered to a law office in St. Louis. Monsanto gave them two weeks to comply.

Whether Pilot Grove can continue to wage its legal battle remains to be seen. Whatever the outcome, the case shows why Monsanto is so detested in farm country, even by those who buy its products. "I don't know of a company that chooses to sue its own customer base," says Joseph Mendelson, of the Center for Food Safety. "It's a very bizarre business strategy." But it's one that Monsanto manages to get away with, because increasingly it's the dominant vendor in town.

Chemicals? What Chemicals?

The Monsanto Company has never been one of America's friendliest corporate citizens. Given Monsanto's current dominance in the field of bioengineering, it's worth looking at the company's own DNA. The future of the company may lie in seeds, but the seeds of the company lie in chemicals. Communities around the world are still reaping the environmental consequences of Monsanto's origins.

Monsanto was founded in 1901 by John Francis Queeny, a tough, cigar-smoking Irishman with a sixth-grade education. A buyer for a wholesale drug company, Queeny had an idea. But like a lot of employees with ideas, he found that his boss wouldn't listen to him. So he went into business for himself on the side. Queeny was convinced there was money to be made manufacturing a substance called saccharin, an artificial sweetener then imported from Germany. He took $1,500 of his savings, borrowed another $3,500, and set up shop in a dingy warehouse near the St. Louis waterfront. With borrowed equipment and secondhand machines, he began producing saccharin for the U.S. market. He called the company the Monsanto Chemical Works, Monsanto being his wife's maiden name.

The German cartel that controlled the market for saccharin wasn't pleased, and cut the price from $4.50 to $1 a pound to try to force Queeny out of business. The young company faced other challenges. Questions arose about the safety of saccharin, and the U.S. Department of Agriculture even tried to ban it. Fortunately for Queeny, he wasn't up against opponents as aggressive and litigious as the Monsanto of today. His persistence and the loyalty of one steady customer kept the company afloat. That steady customer was a new company in Georgia named Coca-Cola.

Monsanto added more and more products—vanillin, caffeine, and 40 drugs used as sedatives and laxatives. In 1917, Monsanto began making aspirin, and soon became the largest maker worldwide. During World War I, cut off from imported European chemicals, Monsanto was forced to manufacture its own, and its position as a leading force in the chemical industry was assured.

After Queeny was diagnosed with cancer, in the late 1920s, his only son, Edgar, became president. Where the father had been a classic entrepreneur, Edgar Monsanto Queeny was an empire builder with a grand vision. It was Edgar—shrewd, daring, and intuitive ("He can see around the next corner," his secretary once said)—who built Monsanto into a global powerhouse. Under Edgar Queeny and his successors, Monsanto extended its reach into a phenomenal number of products: plastics, resins, rubber goods, fuel additives, artificial caffeine, industrial fluids, vinyl siding, dishwasher detergent, anti-freeze, fertilizers, herbicides, pesticides. Its safety glass protects the U.S. Constitution and the *Mona Lisa*. Its synthetic fibers are the basis of Astroturf.

During the 1970s, the company shifted more and more resources into biotechnology. In 1981 it created a molecular-biology group for research in plant genetics. The next year, Monsanto scientists hit gold: they became the first to genetically modify a plant cell. "It will now be possible to introduce virtually any gene into plant cells with the ultimate goal of improving crop productivity," said Ernest Jaworski, director of Monsanto's Biological Sciences Program.

Over the next few years, scientists working mainly in the company's vast new Life Sciences Research Center, 25 miles west of St. Louis, developed one genetically modified product after another—cotton, soybeans, corn, canola. From the start, G.M. seeds were controversial with the public as well as with some farmers and European consumers. Monsanto has sought to portray G.M. seeds as a panacea, a way to alleviate poverty and feed the hungry. Robert Shapiro, Monsanto's president during the 1990s, once called G.M. seeds "the single most successful introduction of technology in the history of agriculture, including the plow."

By the late 1990s, Monsanto, having rebranded itself into a "life sciences" company, had spun off its chemical and fibers operations into a new company called Solutia. After an additional reorganization, Monsanto re-incorporated in 2002 and officially declared itself an "agricultural company."

In its company literature, Monsanto now refers to itself disingenu- 45 ously as a "relatively new company" whose primary goal is helping "farmers around the world in their mission to feed, clothe, and fuel" a growing planet. In its list of corporate milestones, all but a handful are from the recent era. As for the company's early history, the decades when it grew into an industrial powerhouse now held potentially responsible for more than 50 Environmental Protection Agency Superfund sites—none of that is mentioned. It's as though the original Monsanto, the company that long had the word "chemical" as part of its name, never existed. One of the benefits of doing this, as the company does not point out, was to channel the bulk of the growing backlog of chemical lawsuits and liabilities onto Solutia, keeping the Monsanto brand pure.

But Monsanto's past, especially its environmental legacy, is very much with us. For many years Monsanto produced two of the most toxic substances ever known—polychlorinated biphenyls, better known as PCBs, and dioxin. Monsanto no longer produces either, but the places where it did are still struggling with the aftermath, and probably always will be.

"Systemic Intoxication"

Twelve miles downriver from Charleston, West Virginia, is the town of Nitro, where Monsanto operated a chemical plant from 1929 to 1995. In 1948 the plant began to make a powerful herbicide known as 2,4,5-T, called "weed bug" by the workers. A by-product of the process was the creation of a chemical that would later be known as dioxin.

The name dioxin refers to a group of highly toxic chemicals that have been linked to heart disease, liver disease, human reproductive disorders, and developmental problems. Even in small amounts, dioxin persists in the environment and accumulates in the body. In 1997 the International Agency for Research on Cancer, a branch of the World Health Organization, classified the most powerful form of dioxin as a substance that causes cancer in humans. In 2001 the U.S. government listed the chemical as a "known human carcinogen."

On March 8, 1949, a massive explosion rocked Monsanto's Nitro plant when a pressure valve blew on a container cooking up a batch of herbicide. The noise from the release was a scream so loud that it drowned out the emergency steam whistle for five minutes. A plume of vapor and white smoke drifted across the plant and out over town. Residue from the explosion coated the interior of the building and those inside with what workers described as "a fine black powder." Many felt their skin prickle and were told to scrub down.

Within days, workers experienced skin eruptions. Many were soon di- 50
agnosed with chloracne, a condition similar to common acne but more severe, longer lasting, and potentially disfiguring. Others felt intense pains in their legs, chest, and trunk. A confidential medical report at the time said the explosion "caused a systemic intoxication in the workers involving most major organ systems." Doctors who examined four of the most seriously injured men detected a strong odor coming from them when they were all together in a closed room. "We believe these men are excreting a foreign chemical through their skins," the confidential report to Monsanto noted. Court records indicate that 226 plant workers became ill.

According to court documents that have surfaced in a West Virginia court case, Monsanto downplayed the impact, stating that the contaminant affecting workers was "fairly slow acting" and caused "only an irritation of the skin."

In the meantime, the Nitro plant continued to produce herbicides, rubber products, and other chemicals. In the 1960s, the factory manufactured Agent Orange, the powerful herbicide which the U.S. military used to defoliate jungles during the Vietnam War, and which later was the focus of lawsuits by veterans contending that they had been harmed by exposure. As with Monsanto's older herbicides, the manufacturing of Agent Orange created dioxin as a by-product.

As for the Nitro plant's waste, some was burned in incinerators, some dumped in landfills or storm drains, some allowed to run into streams. As Stuart Calwell, a lawyer who has represented both workers and residents in Nitro, put it, "Dioxin went wherever the product went, down the sewer, shipped in bags, and when the waste was burned, out in the air."

In 1981 several former Nitro employees filed lawsuits in federal court, charging that Monsanto had knowingly exposed them to chemicals that caused long-term health problems, including cancer and heart disease. They alleged that Monsanto knew that many chemicals used at Nitro were potentially harmful, but had kept that information from them. On the eve of a trial, in 1988, Monsanto agreed to settle most of the cases by making a single lump payment of $1.5 million. Monsanto also agreed to drop its claim to collect $305,000 in court costs from six retired Monsanto workers who had unsuccessfully charged in another lawsuit that Monsanto had recklessly exposed them to dioxin. Monsanto had attached liens to the retirees' homes to guarantee collection of the debt.

Monsanto stopped producing dioxin in Nitro in 1969, but the toxic 55 chemical can still be found well beyond the Nitro plant site. Repeated studies have found elevated levels of dioxin in nearby rivers, streams, and fish. Residents have sued to seek damages from Monsanto and Solutia. Earlier this year, a West Virginia judge merged those lawsuits into a class-action suit. A Monsanto spokesman said, "We believe the allegations are without merit and we'll defend ourselves vigorously." The suit will no doubt take years to play out. Time is one thing that Monsanto always has, and that the plaintiffs usually don't.

Poisoned Lawns

Five hundred miles to the south, the people of Anniston, Alabama, know all about what the people of Nitro are going through. They've been there. In fact, you could say, they're still there.

From 1929 to 1971, Monsanto's Anniston works produced PCBs as industrial coolants and insulating fluids for transformers and other electrical equipment. One of the wonder chemicals of the 20th century, PCBs were exceptionally versatile and fire-resistant, and became central to many American industries as lubricants, hydraulic fluids, and sealants. But PCBs are toxic. A member of a family of chemicals that mimic hormones, PCBs have been linked to damage in the liver and in the neurological, immune, endocrine, and reproductive systems. The Environmental Protection Agency (E.P.A.) and the Agency for Toxic Substances and Disease Registry, part of the

Department of Health and Human Services, now classify PCBs as "probable carcinogens."

Today, 37 years after PCB production ceased in Anniston, and after tons of contaminated soil have been removed to try to reclaim the site, the area around the old Monsanto plant remains one of the most polluted spots in the U.S.

People in Anniston find themselves in this fix today largely because of the way Monsanto disposed of PCB waste for decades. Excess PCBs were dumped in a nearby open-pit landfill or allowed to flow off the property with storm water. Some waste was poured directly into Snow Creek, which runs alongside the plant and empties into a larger stream, Choccolocco Creek. PCBs also turned up in private lawns after the company invited Anniston residents to use soil from the plant for their lawns, according to *The Anniston Star.*

So for decades the people of Anniston breathed air, planted gardens, drank from wells, fished in rivers, and swam in creeks contaminated with PCBs—without knowing anything about the danger. It wasn't until the 1990s—20 years after Monsanto stopped making PCBs in Anniston—that widespread public awareness of the problem there took hold.

Studies by health authorities consistently found elevated levels of PCBs in houses, yards, streams, fields, fish, and other wildlife—and in people. In 2003, Monsanto and Solutia entered into a consent decree with the E.P.A. to clean up Anniston. Scores of houses and small businesses were to be razed, tons of contaminated soil dug up and carted off, and streambeds scooped of toxic residue. The cleanup is under way, and it will take years, but some doubt it will ever be completed—the job is massive. To settle residents' claims, Monsanto has also paid $550 million to 21,000 Anniston residents exposed to PCBs, but many of them continue to live with PCBs in their bodies. Once PCB is absorbed into human tissue, there it forever remains.

Monsanto shut down PCB production in Anniston in 1971, and the company ended all its American PCB operations in 1977. Also in 1977, Monsanto closed a PCB plant in Wales. In recent years, residents near the village of Groesfaen, in southern Wales, have noticed vile odors emanating from an old quarry outside the village. As it turns out, Monsanto had dumped thousands of tons of waste from its nearby PCB plant into the quarry. British authorities are struggling to decide what to do with what they have now identified as among the most contaminated places in Britain.

"No Cause for Public Alarm"

What had Monsanto known—or what should it have known—about the potential dangers of the chemicals it was manufacturing? There's considerable documentation lurking in court records from many lawsuits indicating that Monsanto knew quite a lot. Let's look just at the example of PCBs.

The evidence that Monsanto refused to face questions about their toxicity is quite clear. In 1956 the company tried to sell the navy a hydraulic fluid for its submarines called Pydraul 150, which contained PCBs. Monsanto supplied the navy with test results for the product. But the navy decided to run its own tests. Afterward, navy officials informed Monsanto that they wouldn't be buying the product. "Applications of Pydraul 150 caused death in all of the rabbits tested" and indicated "definite liver damage," navy officials told Monsanto, according to an internal Monsanto memo divulged in the course of a court proceeding. "No matter how we discussed the situation," complained Monsanto's medical director, R. Emmet Kelly, "it was impossible to change their thinking that Pydraul 150 is just too toxic for use in submarines."

Ten years later, a biologist conducting studies for Monsanto in streams near 65
the Anniston plant got quick results when he submerged his test fish. As he reported to Monsanto, according to *The Washington Post,* "All 25 fish lost equilibrium and turned on their sides in 10 seconds and all were dead in 3½ minutes."

When the Food and Drug Administration (F.D.A.) turned up high levels of PCBs in fish near the Anniston plant in 1970, the company swung into action to limit the P.R. damage. An internal memo entitled "CONFIDENTIAL—F.Y.I. AND DESTROY" from Monsanto official Paul B. Hodges reviewed steps under way to limit disclosure of the information. One element of the strategy was to get public officials to fight Monsanto's battle: "Joe Crockett, Secretary of the Alabama Water Improvement Commission, will try to handle the problem quietly without release of the information to the public at this time," according to the memo.

Despite Monsanto's efforts, the information did get out, but the company was able to blunt its impact. Monsanto's Anniston plant manager "convinced" a reporter for *The Anniston Star* that there was really nothing to worry about, and an internal memo from Monsanto's headquarters in St. Louis summarized the story that subsequently appeared in the newspaper:

"Quoting both plant management and the Alabama Water Improvement Commission, the feature emphasized the PCB problem was relatively new, was being solved by Monsanto and, at this point, was no cause for public alarm."

In truth, there was enormous cause for public alarm. But that harm was done by the "Original Monsanto Company," not "Today's Monsanto Company" (the words and the distinction are Monsanto's). The Monsanto of today says that it can be trusted—that its biotech crops are "as wholesome, nutritious and safe as conventional crops," and that milk from cows injected with its artificial growth hormone is the same as, and as safe as, milk from any other cow.

The Milk Wars

Jeff Kleinpeter takes very good care of his dairy cows. In the winter he turns on heaters to warm their barns. In the summer, fans blow gentle breezes to cool them, and on especially hot days, a fine mist floats down to take the edge off Louisiana's heat. The dairy has gone "to the ultimate end of the earth for cow comfort," says Kleinpeter, a fourth-generation dairy farmer in Baton Rouge. He says visitors marvel at what he does: "I've had many of them say, 'When I die, I want to come back as a Kleinpeter cow.' "

Monsanto would like to change the way Jeff Kleinpeter and his family do business. Specifically, Monsanto doesn't like the label on Kleinpeter Dairy's milk cartons: "From Cows *Not* Treated with rBGH." To consumers, that means the milk comes from cows that were not given artificial bovine growth hormone, a supplement developed by Monsanto that can be injected into dairy cows to increase their milk output.   70

No one knows what effect, if any, the hormone has on milk or the people who drink it. Studies have not detected any difference in the quality of milk produced by cows that receive rBGH, or rBST, a term by which it is also known. But Jeff Kleinpeter—like millions of consumers—wants no part of rBGH. Whatever its effect on humans, if any, Kleinpeter feels certain it's harmful to cows because it speeds up their metabolism and increases the chances that they'll contract a painful illness that can shorten their lives. "It's like putting a Volkswagen car in with the Indianapolis 500 racers," he says. "You gotta keep the pedal to the metal the whole way through, and pretty soon that poor little Volkswagen engine's going to burn up."

Kleinpeter Dairy has never used Monsanto's artificial hormone, and the dairy requires other dairy farmers from whom it buys milk to attest that they don't use it, either. At the suggestion of a marketing consultant, the dairy began advertising its milk as coming from rBGH-free cows in 2005, and the label began appearing on Kleinpeter milk cartons and in company literature, including a new Web site of Kleinpeter products that proclaims, "We treat our cows with love . . . not rBGH."

The dairy's sales soared. For Kleinpeter, it was simply a matter of giving consumers more information about their product.

But giving consumers that information has stirred the ire of Monsanto. The company contends that advertising by Kleinpeter and other dairies touting their "no rBGH" milk reflects adversely on Monsanto's product. In a letter to the Federal Trade Commission in February 2007, Monsanto said that, notwithstanding the overwhelming evidence that there is no difference in the milk from cows treated with its product, "milk processors per-

Jeff Kleinpeter, of Baton Rouge, was accused by Monsanto of making misleading claims just for telling customers his cows are free of artificial bovine growth hormone.

sist in claiming on their labels and in advertisements that the use of rBST is somehow harmful, either to cows or to the people who consume milk from rBST-supplemented cows."

Monsanto called on the commission to investigate what it called the "deceptive advertising and labeling practices" of milk processors such as Kleinpeter, accusing them of misleading consumers "by falsely claiming that there are health and safety risks associated with milk from rBST-supplemented cows." As noted, Kleinpeter does not make any such claims—he simply states that his milk comes from cows not injected with rBGH. 75

Monsanto's attempt to get the F.T.C. to force dairies to change their advertising was just one more step in the corporation's efforts to extend its reach into agriculture. After years of scientific debate and public controversy, the F.D.A. in 1993 approved commercial use of rBST, basing its decision in part on studies submitted by Monsanto. That decision allowed the company to market the artificial hormone. The effect of the hormone is to increase milk production, not exactly something the nation needed then—or needs now. The U.S. was actually awash in milk, with the government buying up the surplus to prevent a collapse in prices.

Monsanto began selling the supplement in 1994 under the name Posilac. Monsanto acknowledges that the possible side effects of rBST for cows include lameness, disorders of the uterus, increased body temperature, digestive problems, and birthing difficulties. Veterinary drug reports note that "cows injected with Posilac are at an increased risk for mastitis," an udder infection in which bacteria and pus may be pumped out with the milk. What's the effect on humans? The F.D.A. has consistently said that the milk produced by cows that receive rBGH is the same as milk from cows that aren't injected: "The public can be confident that milk and meat from BST-treated cows is safe to consume." Nevertheless, some scientists are concerned by the lack of long-term studies to test the additive's impact, especially on children. A Wisconsin geneticist, William von Meyer, observed that when rBGH was approved the longest study on which the F.D.A.'s approval was based covered only a 90-day laboratory test with small animals. "But people drink milk for a lifetime," he noted. Canada and the European Union have never approved the commercial sale of the artificial hormone. Today, nearly 15 years after the F.D.A. approved rBGH, there have still been no long-term studies "to determine the safety of milk from cows that receive artificial growth hormone," says Michael Hansen, senior staff scientist for

Consumers Union. Not only have there been no studies, he adds, but the data that does exist all comes from Monsanto. "There is no scientific consensus about the safety," he says.

However F.D.A. approval came about, Monsanto has long been wired into Washington. Michael R. Taylor was a staff attorney and executive assistant to the F.D.A. commissioner before joining a law firm in Washington in 1981, where he worked to secure F.D.A. approval of Monsanto's artificial growth hormone before returning to the F.D.A. as deputy commissioner in 1991. Dr. Michael A. Friedman, formerly the F.D.A.'s deputy commissioner for operations, joined Monsanto in 1999 as a senior vice president. Linda J. Fisher was an assistant administrator at the E.P.A. when she left the agency in 1993. She became a vice president of Monsanto, from 1995 to 2000, only to return to the E.P.A. as deputy administrator the next year. William D. Ruckelshaus, former E.P.A. administrator, and Mickey Kantor, former U.S. trade representative, each served on Monsanto's board after leaving government. Supreme Court justice Clarence Thomas was an attorney in Monsanto's corporate-law department in the 1970s. He wrote the Supreme Court opinion in a crucial G.M.-seed patent-rights case in 2001 that benefited Monsanto and all G.M.-seed companies. Donald Rumsfeld never served on the board or held any office at Monsanto, but Monsanto must occupy a soft spot in the heart of the former defense secretary. Rumsfeld was chairman and C.E.O. of the pharmaceutical maker G. D. Searle & Co. when Monsanto acquired Searle in 1985, after Searle had experienced difficulty in finding a buyer. Rumsfeld's stock and options in Searle were valued at $12 million at the time of the sale.

From the beginning some consumers have consistently been hesitant to drink milk from cows treated with artificial hormones. This is one reason Monsanto has waged so many battles with dairies and regulators over the wording of labels on milk cartons. It has sued at least two dairies and one co-op over labeling.

Critics of the artificial hormone have pushed for mandatory labeling on all milk products, but the F.D.A. has resisted and even taken action against some dairies that labeled their milk "BST-free." Since BST is a natural hormone found in all cows, including those not injected with Monsanto's artificial version, the F.D.A. argued that no dairy could claim that its milk is BST-free. The F.D.A. later issued guidelines allowing dairies to use labels saying their milk comes from "non-supplemented cows," as long as the carton has a disclaimer saying that the artificial supplement does not in any way change the milk. So the milk cartons from Kleinpeter Dairy, for example, carry a label on the front stating that the milk is from cows not treated with rBGH, and the rear panel says, "Government studies have shown no significant difference between milk derived from rBGH-treated and non-rBGH-treated cows." That's not good enough for Monsanto.

The Next Battleground

As more and more dairies have chosen to advertise their milk as "No rBGH," Monsanto has gone on the offensive. Its attempt to force the F.T.C. to look into what Monsanto called "deceptive practices" by dairies trying to distance themselves from the company's artificial hormone was the most recent national salvo. But after reviewing Monsanto's claims, the F.T.C.'s Division of Advertising Practices decided in August 2007 that a "formal investigation and enforcement action is not warranted at this time." The agency found some instances where dairies had made "unfounded health and safety claims," but these were mostly on Web sites, not on milk cartons. And the F.T.C. determined that the dairies Monsanto had singled out all carried disclaimers that the F.D.A. had found no significant differences in milk from cows treated with the artificial hormone.

Blocked at the federal level, Monsanto is pushing for action by the states. In the fall of 2007, Pennsylvania's agriculture secretary, Dennis Wolff, issued an edict prohibiting dairies from stamping milk containers with labels stating their products were made without the use of the artificial hormone. Wolff said such a label implies that competitors' milk is not safe, and noted that non-supplemented milk comes at an unjustified higher price, arguments that Monsanto has frequently made. The ban was to take effect February 1, 2008.

Wolff's action created a firestorm in Pennsylvania (and beyond) from angry consumers. So intense was the outpouring of e-mails, letters, and calls that Pennsylvania governor Edward Rendell stepped in and reversed his agriculture secretary, saying, "The public has a right to complete information about how the milk they buy is produced."

On this issue, the tide may be shifting against Monsanto. Organic dairy products, which don't involve rBGH, are soaring in popularity. Supermarket chains such as Kroger, Publix, and Safeway are embracing them. Some other companies have turned away from rBGH products, including Starbucks, which has banned all milk products from cows treated with rBGH. Although Monsanto once claimed that an estimated 30 percent of the nation's dairy cows were injected with rBST, it's widely believed that today the number is much lower.

But don't count Monsanto out. Efforts similar to the one in Pennsylva-   85
nia have been launched in other states, including New Jersey, Ohio, Indiana, Kansas, Utah, and Missouri. A Monsanto-backed group called AFACT— American Farmers for the Advancement and Conservation of Technology— has been spearheading efforts in many of these states. AFACT describes itself as a "producer organization" that decries "questionable labeling tactics and activism" by marketers who have convinced some consumers to "shy away from foods using new technology." AFACT reportedly uses the same St. Louis public-relations firm, Osborn & Barr, employed by Monsanto. An Osborn & Barr spokesman told *The Kansas City Star* that the company was doing work for AFACT on a pro bono basis.

Even if Monsanto's efforts to secure across-the-board labeling changes should fall short, there's nothing to stop state agriculture departments from restricting labeling on a dairy-by-dairy basis. Beyond that, Monsanto also has allies whose foot soldiers will almost certainly keep up the pressure on dairies that don't use Monsanto's artificial hormone. Jeff Kleinpeter knows about them, too.

He got a call one day from the man who prints the labels for his milk cartons, asking if he had seen the attack on Kleinpeter Dairy that had been posted on the Internet. Kleinpeter went online to a site called StopLabelingLies, which claims to "help consumers by publicizing examples of false and misleading food and other product labels." There, sure enough, Kleinpeter and other dairies that didn't use Monsanto's product were being accused of making misleading claims to sell their milk.

There was no address or phone number on the Web site, only a list of groups that apparently contribute to the site and whose issues range from disparaging organic farming to downplaying the impact of global warming. "They were criticizing people like me for doing what we had a right to do, had gone through a government agency to do," says Kleinpeter. "We never could get to the bottom of that Web site to get that corrected."

As it turns out, the Web site counts among its contributors Steven Milloy, the "junk science" commentator for FoxNews.com and operator of junk-science.com, which claims to debunk "faulty scientific data and analysis." It may come as no surprise that earlier in his career, Milloy, who calls himself the "junkman," was a registered lobbyist for Monsanto.

Thinking about the Text

1. A good **REPORT** should have a confident **TONE** that informs rather than argues (see p. 197). Does Donald L. Barlett and James B. Steele's report satisfy this criterion? Cite examples from the article to support your answer.

2. Do the dairy products that you consume come from rGBH-fed cows? Has reading this article stimulated you to read food labeling more carefully? Should more information be available on labeling? Should it be required? Why or why not?

3. An extensive report about biotechnology, agribusiness, and large-scale litigation runs the risk of being dry and uninteresting to a general audience. Barlett and Steele provide many concrete **EXAMPLES** and cases to illustrate complex situations and stimulate interest in the topic. The case of Gary Rinehart is one such example. What are three other examples? Which was most interesting or surprising to you? Why?

4. Barlett and Steele say that Monsanto is moving ever closer to controlling the world's agricultural seeds, and they present a variety of **EVIDENCE** to support this conclusion. Do you feel that their evidence is convincing? Why or why not? Is any important kind of evidence lacking? If so, what would it be?

5. Are your food purchases influenced by the information available on packaging about the use of genetically modified organisms or growth hormones? Has Barlett and Steele's article prompted you to think differently about your food choices? Why or why not? Write an essay that explains your reasoning.

Should Everybody Write?

DENNIS BARON

SHOULD EVERYODY WRITE? That's the question to ask when looking at the cyberjunk permeating the World Wide Web. The earlier technologies of the pen, the printing press, and the typewriter, all expanded the authors club, whose members create text rather than just copying it. The computer has expanded opportunities for writers too, only faster, and in greater numbers. More writers means more ideas, more to read. What could be more democratic? More energizing and liberating? But some critics find the glut of internet prose obnoxious, scary, even dangerous. They see too many people, with too little talent, writing about too many things.

Throughout the 5,000-year history of writing, the privilege of authorship was limited to the few: the best, the brightest, the luckiest, those with the right connections. But now, thanks to the computer and the internet, anyone can be a writer: all you need is a laptop, a Wi-Fi card, and a place to sit at Starbucks. The internet allows writers to bypass the usual quality

DENNIS BARON is a professor of English and linguistics at the University of Illinois at Urbana-Champaign and is well known for his writing on language issues and contemporary everyday life. His essays and commentaries on such topics as language and gender and the English-only movement have appeared in newspapers and scholarly journals as well as on CNN, NPR, the Voice of America, and the BBC. This piece was first delivered as a lecture with an accompanying slide presentation; this version was published on Baron's blog, *Web of Language*, in 2010.

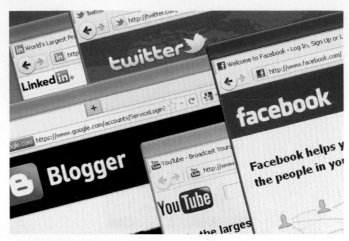

Today anyone can be a writer.

controls set by reviewers, editors and publishers. Today's authors don't even need a diploma from the Famous Writers School.[1] And they don't need to wait for motivation. Instead of staring helplessly at a blank piece of paper the way writers used to, all they need is a keyboard and right away, they've got something to say.

You may not like all that writing, but somebody does. Because the other thing the internet gives writers is readers, whether it's a nanoaudience of friends and family or a virally large set of FBFs,[2] tweeters, and subscribers to the blog feed. Apparently there are people online willing to read anything.

In the past, writing was restricted to a few diehards and adepts, and the question, "Should everybody write?" if it ever came up, was answered with a resounding, "No!"

Writing itself was a communication technology that came in for plenty of criticism in its early days. Socrates warned that writing was just a shadow of speech. Writing isn't interactive, he tells Phaedrus: you can't ask a text a question, because all it can do is repeat the same words back to you, over and over

5

---

1. *Famous Writers School:* A correspondence course in writing instruction that was advertised in many magazines in the 1960s and 70s. The school required an aptitude test that would be evaluated by celebrity authors; almost every student was accepted, and investigations revealed that the famous writers did not review any of the submitted tests. [Editor's note]
2. *FBFs:* Facebook friends. [Editor's note]

Visuals can contribute a lot to an argument. See Ch. 30 for tips on using them in your writing.

Socrates and Plato

again. At best, writing is nothing but a mnemonic, a device not to teach us new things but to remind us of what we already know. But paradoxically, its danger as a mnemonic is that we will come to rely on it, so that according to Socrates, the ultimate effect of writing will be to weaken memory, not strengthen it. We remember this because Plato wrote it down.

Henry David Thoreau made pencils for a living and sought endorsements for his writing instruments from the likes of Emerson. But in *Walden* Thoreau suggests that not everyone should write, because not everyone has something to say: "We are in great haste to construct a magnetic telegraph from Maine to Texas, but Maine and Texas, it may be, have nothing important to communicate."

Henry David Thoreau

Every new communication technology has the capacity to expand the set of who gets to write and talk, who gets to publish and be heard. But expanding the authors club tends to be a by-product of the technologies, not their intent.

When writing came on the scene, very few could read, and fewer still could write. If our interpretation of the Susa stones[3] is correct, writing comes on the scene 7,000–8,000 years ago as a device for Mediterranean traders to track their inventory. The first writers used the technology of shaping and

3. *Susa stones*: Stones bearing distinctive cup and ring markings (also known as cup-marked stones) that date to prehistoric times. It has been suggested that these markings were used to communicate information. The Susa Valley in Italy contains many examples, but similar markings have been found in coastal Europe and Mexico, Brazil, and India. [Editor's note]

A cup-marked stone from the Susa Valley.

marking stones as a memory device to represent jars of olive oil, goats, and sheep. It was the ancient world's equivalent of a bar tab.

Even after someone repurposed writing as a way to transcribe speech, and writers as we might think of them today came on the scene, only a few brave souls were tempted to try the technology, which came with a steep learning curve, required expensive or labor-intensive materials, and for most people, didn't seem to do anything that speech couldn't do better. In order for writing to spread, costs had to come down; materials had to be more easily accessible; writing technologies had to become more user-friendly; and writing itself had to offer something better than communicating the old-fashioned way, by word of mouth.

More and more people began to write, and the new technologies of writing enabled writers to create new genres. But even so, the rise of literacy was painfully slow. Harris reports the literacy rate in Greece during the 4th and 5th century BCE as below 10% (and that was the figure for urban males; literacy among women and in rural areas wasn't much better than 1%). And yet *letters* were everywhere in ancient Greece: inscriptions on public buildings, legal documents, commercial texts, and literary and scientific ones. Even with *arma virumque cano, Gallia est omnes divisa in partes tres*, and *et tu Brute*, literacy rates were no better at the height of Roman civilization. 10

In the Hellenistic period, the great library at Alexandria may have housed half a million scrolls at its peak, but still the average Egyptian didn't have a library card.

Greek coin
c. 6th-century BCE

By the 12th century, written documents were becoming *the* way to transact business in England, and scriptoria churned out copies of sacred texts. Still, not everybody wrote. The number of text creators remained small, as did the number of text copiers and the number of people who could sign their names. This late

11th-century Anglo-Norman charter transferring some English land to a French abbey is "signed" by Sir Ilbert de Lacy, his wife Hawise, and King William Rufus, the second son of William the Conqueror. It bears the earliest example of an English knight's seal as an authenticator. But none of the principals could write their names, and it's very likely that none of the signatories, who witnessed the document with three crosses, even made those crosses. The charter was probably created some time after the physical land transfer took place, with the scribe, not the author or the witnesses, filling in all the necessary details to commemorate the act.

Even though the age of print opened up publication opportunities for writers, the printing press is a copying technology, not a

Seal of Ilbert de Lacy

technology for text creation. Gutenberg copied Bibles, after all, and while the press eventually created a demand for reading materials—William Caxton was just one early English printer who commissioned original works—many early printed books were reprints of sacred or classical works, or translations, rather than original works.

Readers as well as writers encountered obstacles. Received wisdom praises Protestantism for spreading literacy as a way to encourage the faithful to read vernacular translations of sacred texts for themselves, but even Martin Luther warned in 1520 of the danger of too many books—in his view, you just need one good book, which you can read over and over—the gift that keeps on giving—not a lot of bad books that will fill your head with error or just confuse you.

Gutenberg's press

And later, in 17th-century England, a period known

Martin Luther

for the flowering of English letters, where even kings and queens composed poetry and the brand-new Royal Society promoted science writing, literacy in London remained a mere 10% for men, a shocking 1% for women. But who *should* write was not the same population as who *could* write. The route to publication wasn't simple or direct, and even William Shakespeare couldn't put on a play without first getting a license from the Stationers' Company.

Not until the 19th century did literacy in England reach about 70%. And in this period of "exploding" literacy we find explicit concerns being voiced over who gets to read and write, together with a sorting of the literate population into two groups: the functional literates and the literati. Functional literates used their literacy to work in offices, shops, factories. The writers in this group were the copiers, not the creators of text, like the Ruler of the Queen's Navy in Gilbert and Sullivan's *Pirates of Penzance,* a clerk who began his climb from office class to officer class by copying all the letters in a big round hand. The literati were a vastly smaller group whose station in life allowed them to appreciate and exploit a higher education, to create texts, and to consume texts with some sort of higher-order understanding that ordinary people lacked.

The Alphabet is the whole Order of the Letters in any Language,—from Alpha and Beta, the two first Letters in the Greek Tongue.—The English Alphabet contains twenty six Letters, but others differ—

Round-hand writing

Concerns arose that too much literacy would elevate people above their station in life, causing depression, discontent, or even civil unrest. Victorian essayist Thomas Carlyle complained that the explosion of reading matter made possible by the invention of the steam press in 1810 led to a decline in the quality of what there was to read. At the very least, literacy-controllers argued, reading too much exposed good citizens and the faithful to error and heresy.

Steam-powered printing press

Yes, writing expanded the authors club, and later, so did the printing press, and eventually, by the end of the 19th century, literacy levels rose over the 80% mark—in Western Europe and the U.S. But the question of who gets to write has always been a vexed one, and every writing technology came with limits on who gets to be in the authors club—who gets to create texts and not just copy them, and who gets to read—limits that were imposed and that continue to be imposed by governments, by religious authorities, and by social norms. The pencil, the printing press, the typewriter, all expanded opportunities for writers, so long as they could clear the hurdles imposed by publishers, government censors, or the church. In terms of raw numbers, however, all of these technologies benefited copyists more than they benefited the creators of texts.

With the typewriter, as with the press and the big round hand before it, everyone's a copyist. This 1875 ad in *The Nation* for the Remington "Type-Writer" reads, in part,

> a machine now superseding the pen. . . . anyone who can spell can begin to write with it. . . . It is worked without effort, and is not liable to get out of order. . . . Young persons acquire its use with wonderful ease and interest. . . . The benevolent can, by the gift of a "Type-Writer" to a poor, deserving young woman, put her at once in the way of earning a good living as a copyist.

Mark Twain wrote about this newest writing technology,

> I will now claim—until dispossessed—that I was the first person in the world to apply the typewriter to literature. . . . The early machine was full of caprices, full of defects—devilish ones. It had as many immoralities as the machine of today has virtues. After a year or two I found that it was degrading my character, so I thought I would give it to [William Dean] Howells. . . . He took it home to Boston, and my morals began to improve, but his have never recovered. ("The First Writing-Machines")

But to make this early celebrity endorsement of typing, Twain dictated to a typist rather than composing directly at the keyboard.

A 1930s experiment put portable typewriters on the desks of schoolchildren around the country and "proved" that typing students outperformed nontypists on standardized tests in all their subjects. According to teacher reports, typing students even had better handwriting than nontypists. But despite such positive results, two factors combined to keep typewrit-

Typewriters in the classroom, 1935.

ers off desks: it was the Depression, and schools couldn't afford to replace pencils with typewriters; plus it proved too difficult to train the teachers to use typewriters. So instead of a widescale adoption of typewriters to create knowledge, the machines were relegated to dedicated typing classrooms, where students were trained "to copy all the letters" in Courier 12 pt. so that they could eventually win jobs as office clerks.

Unlike other communication technologies, which effectively limited   20
who could read and write, the telephone immediately offered the opportunity for anyone to talk to anyone. Preservers of the social status didn't like this. They sniffed that all you had to have was a nickel for the pay phone, and you could cross social lines at will, entering homes over the wires where you had no hope of being admitted should you knock at the door. But telephones were for talking, not for writing. They might have destabilized so-

Dial M for Murder.

cial class (and despite complaints about this, it's not clear that they really did), but in the long run people didn't worry so much about the democratizing thrust of the phone, since access to speech was nowhere near as guarded as access to writing. Of course, as we see in this still from Alfred Hitchcock's *Dial M for Murder*, there are times when not everyone should make a call.

Enter the computer. People worked with text on mainframes, to be sure, but the machines' strength lay in number crunching; they weren't writing machines. The personal computer too was initially billed as a "work processor"—*word* processing, a phrase deployed widely by IBM in its advertising and training literature, was still the province of the typewriter. Like earlier communication technologies, the computer had to overcome some obstacles before it was widely adopted as a writing tool: costs had to come

Apple IIe, c. 1983.

down; the machine had to become user-friendly; and it had to allow writers to do what they used to do with older technologies (pen, typewriter) only better (faster, more efficiently, with a superior product). As word processing software was perfected and hardware improved, the PC replaced the typewriter as the text copying machine of choice in American offices. But along the way something unusual happened: once the PC was hooked up to the internet, copyists of text began to create text as well. And as the personal computer claimed its space in the writer's toolbox, it enabled the creation of new internet-enabled genres: email, web page, IM, blog, social network pages, tweets, and videos.

The computer combined with the internet affords writers something they never really had before, the ability to bypass traditional publication controls. To repeat, all you need is a computer, a Wi-Fi card, and a place to sit at Starbucks. Given that kind of access, more and more of us are finding something to write about, whether momentous or trivial, positive or negative. And while throughout history authors have wondered whether anyone would ever read what they had to say, on the internet there seem to be readers for every text. As a result the authors club is expanding in ways it never has before, and with that expansion comes new concerns about how to control this particular literacy explosion. Because in addition to all the good texts out there in cyberspace, there's pornography, fraud, and hate. And Wikipedia.

Wikipedia

In a 1999 *New York Times* op-ed, educational reformer Theodore Roszak complained that computers prevented us from writing. To him, "a child with a pencil in hand is ready to write. A child with a crayon in hand is ready to draw." But the pencil didn't turn us all into writers, and despite the promise of the Famous Artists School,[4] turning us loose with crayons didn't make us all artists either. In contrast, the computer facilitated exactly what Roszak warned that it would prevent, making children, and adults ready to write, and even Roszak admitted in his critique of the computer-processed word that he much preferred WordPerfect for DOS to the steel-tipped dip pen which had been a torture for him when he learned to write in school.

In any case, today the question, "Should everybody write?" is rendered moot by the fact that everybody appears to be using their computers, and their cell phones, for writing. And so the new question seems to have become, "How can we control these writers and their explosion of text?" Although linguist Geoffrey Nunberg has rightly pointed out that from the earliest days of writing there has always been too much to read, critics bemoan the internet's information glut, and they seek to control access to, or censor outright, the more dangerous parts of cyberspace. There are firewalls and filters to block prohibited topics or content; plus the tethering of devices—like smart phones or the soon-to-be-released iPad—to limit or control what writers can do. But there are other ways that we're controlling authorship that may be less traditional, and a bit more subtle.

As we write on our computers, we're giving up our privacy in ways that   25
writers never did before, not just exposing ourselves—or our personas—on Facebook, Twitter, or a blog, but also by leaving digital fingerprints that allow both businesses and the government to log our keystrokes and track our clicks. Back in 1890, lawyers Samuel D. Warren and Louis D. Brandeis, concerned about the intrusiveness of photographers and journalists, warned in an essay for the *Harvard Law Review,*

> Recent inventions and business methods call attention to the next step which must be taken for the protection of the person, and for securing to the individual . . . the right "to be let alone." Instantaneous photographs and newspaper enterprise have invaded the sacred precincts of private and domestic life; and

4. *Famous Artists School*: A correspondence course in painting, illustration/design, and cartooning that began in 1948. This course was the precursor to (and inspiration for) the Famous Writers School. [Editor's note]

numerous mechanical devices threaten to make good the prediction that "what is whispered in the closet shall be proclaimed from the house-tops." ("The Right to Privacy")

We used to think that the internet offered a kind of anonymity that would allow us to express ourselves more freely than ever, taking any pose or persona we want. But if everyone from Sun MicroSystems CEO Scott McNealy, who is supposed to have said back in 1999, "You have zero privacy anyway. Get over it," to Facebook founder Mark Zuckerberg, who insisted in an interview this year that his company is only trying to adapt to the needs of Facebook users, then privacy is indeed dead, even if only college students, Google, and the NSA[5] are willing to admit it. But now that everyone is writing, we're going beyond the simple invasions of privacy outlined by Warren and Brandeis to a more complex inversion of public and private. Putting

Mark Zuckerberg

ourselves online allows other users not just to watch our online behavior and send us context-motivated ads or pack us off to Guantanamo for a nice waterboarding session, but also to remix the posts they find or create mashups of our posts with theirs.

Helene Hegemann

Accompanying the "everyone is writing" phenomenon is a growing amateurization of online text, which is democratic in spirit but which also calls into question the nature of intellectual property, the writing, graphics, and music that we post online. Internet-published text means writers are easily ripped off, and plagiarism has become that much easier—as we see in everything from schoolsucks.com and the online term paper mills to the "creative" plagiarism of the award-winning teenage German novelist Helene Hegemann. But every communication technology brings with it opportunities for fraud and cheating, and eventually we

---

5. *NSA*: National Security Agency. [Editor's note]

manage to get enough safeguards in place so that any counterfeits that get past the controls can simply be chalked up to the cost of doing business.

Jonathan Zittrain, a professor of internet law and computer science at Harvard, warns that even with plagiarism and mashups, too strict an adherence to traditional notions of copyright may limit the generativity and inventiveness of the Web. *Wired* editor Kevin Kelly goes even further, simply announcing that writers will have to hang on to their day jobs, because royalties will simply dry up because law or no law, online text will inevitably be treated as communal property.

The late John Updike pushed back against Kelly, and historian Anthony Grafton suggests that the age of the seamless cybertext is far from a reality. But since most writers don't live off their royalties anyway, there's a bigger danger to the status of authorship than a revised economic model for writing. It's the growing centralization of online services, with Apple, Microsoft, Google, Amazon, and Wikipedia controlling larger and larger blocks of our information and what we can do with that information (and maybe Zappos controlling the shoes we buy). This represents a particular kind of monopolization of our data by for-profit corporations, who unlike most libraries or public utilities are responsible not to the people as a whole, but to shareholders and boards of directors. The mission of libraries is typically openness and accessibility, but Google & Co. are bastions of secrecy and digital rights management, renting you the privilege of reading online, but retaining ownership of text and limiting access by distributing it according to a carefully calculated business model.

Add to this corporatization of the data stream the trend toward cloud computing. With the spread of the next generation of computers—netbooks, smartphones, and tablets, all of them devices with limited storage space— we will be encouraged more and more to turn to software located not on our hard drives but on a remote server. For some users, that server will be at home or at their university or office. But for most, it will be a Google or Microsoft or other proprietary server, accessible by subscription. And we will be encouraged/forced to cede control of our data to these remote servers as well. The advantage of cloud computing is that all our digital files will be available to us, no matter where we are or what computer or computer-like device we're using to access it. The disadvantage is that our texts will slip from our control to the control of the for-profit corporation that manages the cloud.

Is that so bad? Just as we trade convenience for accuracy when we rely 30 on Wikipedia as our first resort for information, we'll trade convenience for

Cloud computing via remote server.

control, which may be worth the trade until Amazon decides it doesn't like what's on our Kindle and takes it back; until Facebook decides we've committed an illegal act and blocks us; until Google loses our data or turns it over to the government, or to our employer, or some other third party, with or without a subpoena or warrant. Or until I log on and instead of the draft of my next book I get the dreaded Error 404, file not found.

Of course there's always someone who objects to a new technology rollout. Critics of the first wheel probably argued that round technologies sped up the pace of life too much compared to the old way of doing things, preferring animals for locomotion or simply keeping their feet planted firmly on the ground. And of course, as we see from this 1956 ad for a Chrysler with in-dash record changer, not all new technologies catch on. But

HIGHWAY HI-FI PHONOGRAPH
. . . provides the music you want wherever you go

Within-dashboard record changer.

One Laptop per Child Program

the computer is now the writer's tool of choice, and even though pencils still sell in the billions annually, more and more people are joining the authors club and uploading text to the internet.

So, finally, again, I ask, should everybody write? More people are writing now than ever before, if by writing we mean creating text for readers—whether those readers consist of a nanoaudience of friends and family or a virally large set of FBFs, Twitter followers, or other denizens of cyberspace. More people are writing in North America, in Europe, and even in parts of the world where individuals have not typically had a public voice. Yet one critic of the One Laptop per Child Program[6] echoes Victorian concerns of educating people beyond their station when he argues that giving computers to masses of children will create discontent: "Access to eBay and YouTube isn't going to give them clean water and freedom from disease. But it may help breed resentment and discontent where it hasn't been before" (Gene Spafford, cited in Zittrain's *The Future of the Internet and How to Stop It*, 240). Functional literacy remains a goal, but creative literacy—putting the tools of meaning production into everyone's hands—is still seen as too destabilizing, and not just in China or Myanmar, but also in Silicon Valley.

For those who are already writing, the question is becoming: are they producing anything worth reading? We may not think so—to repeat, there's a lot of junk being cranked out. But then again, somebody seems to think so—there seems to be no lack of readers for even the most inane of cyberposts. Previous technologies of writing did not guarantee quality either. There are plenty of clay tablets, manuscripts, printed books, mimeographed screeds and Xeroxed memos, that should never have seen the light of day. To Nunberg's observation that there has always been too much to read, I might add that there has always been a lot of stuff that no one wants to read.

So, should everybody write? Sure, because it increases the chances that there will be something you will want to read, and you can just ignore the rest. Perhaps the more interesting question is, Will everyone *continue* to write? Cell phone users are texting more than they're talking, and computer

---

6. *One Laptop per Child*: A nonprofit organization that aims to distribute inexpensive but durable computers to children throughout the developing world. [Editor's note]

The iPad as entertainment.

users everywhere are creating and publishing text at growing rates. Most digital texts are short, and most aren't "keepers," even though it turns out to be difficult to wipe out a text once it's been uploaded. But there are explosions of fan fiction, online essays, blogs, extended chats and commentaries, and explorations of text, audio and video, and that sort of text production doesn't seem to be slowing down much.

Perhaps the predicted shift from PCs and laptops to tethered devices like the iPad, which really promise to be entertainment devices rather than text-production machines, could signal an eventual decline in internet-enabled authorship. These are machines that permit text entry, though they're billed as entertainment machines, not writing tools. I don't really think the iPad will prompt a decline in card-carrying authors. After all, the original PCs were not text-production machines either. What's more likely to happen is that writers will see the usefulness of tablets, as we once saw, a mere 30 years ago, the usefulness of PCs, for what we do. And developers will reengineer tablets so that, while they satisfy the needs of gamers and video watchers and the readers of ebooks and newspapers, they also allow us to key in and upload our textual, musical, and visual creations. 35

Maybe one day we'll all use *Star Trek*–like communicators pinned to our chests to create our texts—just tap and talk—but I think that speech-to-text software is still a long way off, and for the near term we'll be keyboarding, and doing so in growing numbers. No matter what you or I think of their products, writers gaining access to the internet seem to have no trouble finding a subject to write about, and no trouble finding readers to read their output. However new communication technologies destabilize the conditions of writers and readers, writers will continue to find ways to get the word out, and new genres to clothe the word in.

Thinking about the Text

1. Dennis Baron **ANALYZES** the very ordinary activity of writing from a historical perspective. A thorough history of the subject, of course, could not have been presented in such a brief article, so Baron carefully selects the information he presents and weaves it into a cohesive whole. **SUMMARIZE** the aspects of writing that Baron chose to trace through its history. What is the unifying theme that pulls them all together?

2. We generally take very much for granted all of the contemporary technologies of writing that Baron describes; many of us, in fact, have never lived in a world without them. How would your life be different if you could write only with a pen or pencil? In what ways would your social circle be different? How about your work and school life? What changes would need to take place in your daily routine?

3. Baron's article includes many **ILLUSTRATIONS**, not all of which are directly referred to in the text. How do these contribute to your comprehension of his argument? How important are they to it? Which of them do you find particularly effective? Do any just seem distracting? Why do you suppose that Baron included so many illustrations?

4. Baron mentions that in the nineteenth century, concerns were raised that "too much literacy" might cause "depression, discontent, or even civil unrest" (16). At first glance, this claim may seem amusing, even ridiculous, but it bears consideration, if only to be able to refute it. **REFLECT** as openly and as deeply as you can about your own life and the world around you. Depression and discontent certainly exist, as well as civil unrest. Has literacy made any contribution to them?

5. Most modern objects and activities don't have as obviously long a history as writing does, but a little research may reveal deeper roots than you'd realized. Choose a favorite object or activity that you consider very new (skateboards or nail art, perhaps) and do some historical research about it. Write an essay **REPORTING** on the social effects your topic has produced, incorporating the history that you discover.

The Sanctuary of School

LYNDA BARRY

I **WAS 7 YEARS OLD** the first time I snuck out of the house in the dark. It was winter and my parents had been fighting all night. They were short on money and long on relatives who kept "temporarily" moving into our house because they had nowhere else to go.

My brother and I were used to giving up our bedroom. We slept on the couch, something we actually liked because it put us that much closer to the light of our lives, our television.

At night when everyone was asleep, we lay on our pillows watching it with the sound off. We watched Steve Allen's mouth moving. We watched Johnny Carson's mouth moving. We watched movies filled with gangsters shooting machine guns into packed rooms, dying soldiers hurling a last

LYNDA BARRY is the creator of the comic strip *Ernie Pook's Comeek,* which was syndicated for more than two decades in many U.S. alternative weekly newspapers. She has also written several books that variously combine the genres of collage, memoir, novel, graphic novel, and workbook; these include *The Good Times Are Killing Me* (1988), which was staged as an off-Broadway musical in New York, and most recently *What It Is* (2008) and *Picture This: The Near-sighted Monkey Book* (2010). This essay was originally published in the *New York Times* in 1992, when public schools were suffering a recessionary crunch much like the ones that many schools are experiencing as this book goes to press.

grenade and beautiful women crying at windows. Then the sign-off finally came and we tried to sleep.

The morning I snuck out, I woke up filled with a panic about needing to get to school. The sun wasn't quite up yet but my anxiety was so fierce that I just got dressed, walked quietly across the kitchen and let myself out the back door.

It was quiet outside. Stars were still out. Nothing moved and no one was 5 in the street. It was as if someone had turned the sound off on the world.

I walked the alley, breaking thin ice over the puddles with my shoes. I didn't know why I was walking to school in the dark. I didn't think about it. All I knew was a feeling of panic, like the panic that strikes kids when they realize they are lost.

That feeling eased the moment I turned the corner and saw the dark outline of my school at the top of the hill. My school was made up of about 15 nondescript portable classrooms set down on a fenced concrete lot in a run-down Seattle neighborhood, but it had the most beautiful view of the Cascade Mountains. You could see them from anywhere on the playfield and you could see them from the windows of my classroom—Room 2.

I walked over to the monkey bars and hooked my arms around the cold metal. I stood for a long time just looking across Rainier Valley. The sky was beginning to whiten and I could hear a few birds.

In a perfect world my absence at home would not have gone unnoticed. I would have had two parents in a panic to locate me, instead of two parents in a panic to locate an answer to the hard question of survival during a deep financial and emotional crisis.

But in an overcrowded and unhappy home, it's incredibly easy for any 10 child to slip away. The high levels of frustration, depression and anger in my house made my brother and me invisible. We were children with the sound turned off. And for us, as for the steadily increasing number of neglected children in this country, the only place where we could count on being noticed was at school.

"Hey there, young lady. Did you forget to go home last night?" It was Mr. Gunderson, our janitor, whom we all loved. He was nice and he was funny and he was old with white hair, thick glasses and an unbelievable number of keys. I could hear them jingling as he walked across the playfield. I felt incredibly happy to see him.

He let me push his wheeled garbage can between the different porta-
bles as he unlocked each room. He let me turn on the lights and raise the
window shades and I saw my school slowly come to life. I saw Mrs. Holman,
our school secretary, walk into the office without her orange lipstick on yet.
She waved.

I saw the fifth-grade teacher, Mr. Cunningham, walking under the
breezeway eating a hard roll. He waved.

And I saw my teacher, Mrs. Claire LeSane, walking toward us in a red
coat and calling my name in a very happy and surprised way, and suddenly
my throat got tight and my eyes stung and I ran toward her crying. It was
something that surprised us both.

It's only thinking about it now, 28 years later, that I realize I was crying   15
from relief. I was with my teacher, and in a while I was going to sit at my
desk, with my crayons and pencils and books and classmates all around me,
and for the next six hours I was going to enjoy a thoroughly secure, warm
and stable world. It was a world I absolutely relied on. Without it, I don't
know where I would have gone that morning.

Mrs. LeSane asked me what was wrong and when I said "Nothing," she
seemingly left it at that. But she asked me if I would carry her purse for her,
an honor above all honors, and she asked if I wanted to come into Room 2
early and paint.

She believed in the natural healing power of painting and drawing for troubled children. In the back of her room there was always a drawing table and
an easel with plenty of supplies, and sometimes during the day she would
come up to you for what seemed like no good reason and quietly ask if you
wanted to go to the back table and "make some pictures for Mrs. LeSane." We
all had a chance at it—to sit apart from the class for a while to paint, draw
and silently work out impossible problems on 11×17 sheets of newsprint.

Drawing came to mean everything to me. At the back table in Room 2,
I learned to build myself a life preserver that I could carry into my home.

We all know that a good education system saves lives, but the people of
this country are still told that cutting the budget for public schools is necessary, that poor salaries for teachers are all we can manage and that art,
music and all creative activities must be the first to go when times are lean.

Before- and after-school programs are cut and we are told that public schools   20
are not made for baby-sitting children. If parents are neglectful temporarily

or permanently, for whatever reason, it's certainly sad, but their unlucky children must fend for themselves. Or slip through the cracks. Or wander in a dark night alone.

We are told in a thousand ways that not only are public schools not important, but that the children who attend them, the children who need them most, are not important either. We leave them to learn from the blind eye of a television, or to the mercy of "a thousand points of light"[1] that can be as far away as stars.

I was lucky. I had Mrs. LeSane. I had Mr. Gunderson. I had an abundance of art supplies. And I had a particular brand of neglect in my home that allowed me to slip away and get to them. But what about the rest of the kids who weren't as lucky? What happened to them?

By the time the bell rang that morning I had finished my drawing and Mrs. LeSane pinned it up on the special bulletin board she reserved for drawings from the back table. It was the same picture I always drew—a sun in the corner of a blue sky over a nice house with flowers all around it.

Mrs. LeSane asked us to please stand, face the flag, place our right hands over our hearts and say the Pledge of Allegiance. Children across the country do it faithfully. I wonder now when the country will face its children and say a pledge right back.

> Describing how one child was saved by art classes helps argue for funding school programs. See Ch. 14 for more about argument strategies.

1. *"A thousand points of light"*: An often-used phrase of then-President George H.W. Bush to refer to the many private, nonprofit community organizations that he hoped would step in to help people in need when his government-sponsored social programs were cut. [Editor's note]

Thinking about the Text

1. Lynda Barry begins her **NARRATIVE** by revealing some painful personal information, which leads to a damning criticism of the state of education in the United States. Does her personal anecdote enhance her political argument? Damage it? How well do these two elements of her essay complement one another? Explain your answer, citing evidence from the text.

2. It could easily be argued that the art-making opportunities in Barry's school were more beneficial to her than to other students because she was always artistically inclined and even went on to become a professional artist—or even that there is no reason to have art instruction in elementary schools at all be-

cause so few children actually become artists. How would you respond to that argument? Agree or disagree, presenting **EVIDENCE** from your own school experiences.

3. Barry uses the expression "the sound off" or "the sound turned off" three times in the essay (3, 5, 10). In which instances is it meant literally and in which figuratively? How does the repetition of this language help make the point of her narrative?

4. Barry concludes her essay with a call for the United States and its education system to make a "pledge" to children (24). Although her proposals are not spelled out, what can you infer about what Barry is asking the schools to do? Provide **EXAMPLES** from the text that indicate what she thinks is important.

5. Did you ever have a teacher who, in the course of simply doing her or his job, helped you get through a hard time or a tremendous struggle? Write a **NARRATIVE** about an experience you had with a memorable teacher, and relate your experience in some way to your adult life.

Compulsory Reading

ALISON BECHDEL

O KAY, I FEEL BAD FOR ELLEN O and anyone else who was out combing th' convenience store aisles for *Entertainment Weekly*. I got the go-ahead to post this essay I just did for their 1000th issue. I forgot to mention the best part—my memoir *Fun Home* is number 68 on their list of "new classic" books from the past 25 years. . . .

ALISON BECHDEL is a cartoonist and writer best known for her award-winning 2006 graphic memoir about her father, *Fun Home: A Family Tragicomic*. Her serialized comic strip, *Dykes to Watch Out For*, ran in dozens of periodicals from 1983 to 2008, when Bechdel suspended it to focus on graphic books.

Bechdel is originally from Lock Haven, Pennsylvania, and currently lives near Burlington, Vermont. Her latest book, *Are You My Mother? A Comic Drama*, centers on her relationship with her mother and involves painful remembering and reflection. Bechdel, in a 2012 interview in the *New Yorker*, states that "by looking inward deeply I'm trying to get outside myself and connect with other people." The following piece was written originally for *Entertainment Weekly*'s 1000th issue, in 2008. If you like it, you can find more of Bechdel's work in *Slate*, *McSweeney's*, and *Granta*—and on her blog, dykestowatchoutfor.com.

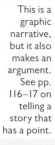

This is a graphic narrative, but it also makes an argument. See pp. 116–17 on telling a story that has a point.

OH, I READ FOR WORK.

ODD THINGS I'M RESEARCHING...

...STAYING CURRENT IN MY FIELD, ALL THAT.

BUT READING FOR **PLEASURE?** THE HALLOWED, RAPT ABSORPTION OF LIVING IN A FICTIONAL WORLD FOR **DAYS ON END?**

I HAVE TROUBLE FITTING THAT INTO MY SCHEDULE.

WHERE DID I GO ASTRAY? I WAS ONE OF THOSE MODEL CHILDREN! A HARDENED CHAIN-READER.

PALE

TORPID

BY SECOND GRADE, I WAS MAINLINING ANYTHING I COULD GET MY HANDS ON.

ANYTHING!

ENTIRE CHILDHOOD OF FAMOUS AMERICANS SERIES

IN THOSE DAYS, THERE WAS WORLD ENOUGH AND TIME. I ASSUMED I'D GET TO EVERYTHING EVENTUALLY. EVEN THE WEIRD BOOKS IN THE "AUTHORS" DECK.

ROBERT! *THE TALISMAN,* BY SIR WALTER SCOTT, PLEASE!

AAAGHH! CURSE YOU!

MY BROTHERS, MY FRIENDS, AND I HAD AN INORDINATE FONDNESS FOR THIS GAME—A HIGHFALUTIN VERSION OF "GO FISH."

AND *KENILWORTH* WHILE YOU'RE AT IT, MY GOOD MAN.

WE'D PLAY ENDLESS ROUNDS, WORKING OURSELVES INTO FRENZIES OVER ARCANE TEXTS WE KNEW NOTHING ABOUT.

WELL, WE'D HEARD OF SOME OF THEM, MAYBE EVEN SEEN THE MOVIES.

ALISON! TOM SAWYER.

ROMEO

LITTLE WOMEN

NOPE!

BUT MOSTLY WE GROUPED OUR CARDS BY FACIAL HAIR.

ALFRED, LORD TENNYSON

CHARLES DICKENS

EASILY CONFUSED

(THERE WERE ONLY THREE CLEAN-SHAVEN AUTHORS. COUNTING LOUISA MAY ALCOTT.)

ALISON! *CROSSING THE BAR, IDYLLS OF THE KING,* AND *THE CHARGE OF THE LIGHT BRIGADE!*

YOU RAT FINK!

STILL, THE GAME WAS MY FIRST EXPOSURE TO THE NOTION OF A CANON.

THESE WERE "CLASSICS" —AT LEAST ACCORDING TO PARKER BROTHERS— AND THAT MEANT YOU **HAD** TO READ THEM.

THIS COERCIVE PARADIGM BEGAN TO IMPINGE ON MY INNOCENT READING PLEASURE IN OTHER, LESS SUBTLE WAYS.

MY FATHER GREW UP IN A BOOKLESS HOME, AND LITERATURE HAD BEEN HIS SALVATION. BUT NOW HE'D BECOME AN ANNOYING MISSIONARY.

I DEVELOPED A SEVERE AVERSION TO READING ANYTHING ANYONE ELSE TOLD ME TO, EVEN MY FRIENDS.

ARE YOU READING THAT *AGAIN?*

HIGH SCHOOL ENGLISH TEACHER

SO?

READ THIS.

WHAT'S IT ABOUT?

A MAGICAL BIRD-GIRL WHO LIVES IN THE JUNGLE.

THAT'S THE MOST BORING THING I EVER HEARD OF.

GREEN MANSIONS

YOU'LL LOVE THESE! YOU SHOULD START WITH THIS ONE!

FIVE CHIL-DREN AND IT

THE WORKS OF E. NESBIT, LOST TO ME FOREVER.

ONE DAY WHEN I WAS 11 OR 12, DAD TRIED A NEW TACK.

I DIDN'T WANT TO GIVE HIM THE SATIS-FACTION, BUT FIVE BUCKS WAS A LOT OF MONEY IN THOSE DAYS.

AND WHEN I DID INDEED BEAT MY YOUNGER BROTHERS TO THE FINISH, I COULDN'T HELP FEELING A TWINGE OF SUSPICION.

FIVE DOLLARS TO THE FIRST ONE OF YOU WHO READS *HUCKLEBERRY FINN.*

GIMME ONE!

EIGHTH TIME

HARRIET THE SPY

I WAS RATHER ANNOYED TO FIND MYSELF SO CAUGHT UP IN THE STORY. FOR CHAPTERS ON END, I FORGOT ABOUT THE CONTEST.

HUCKLE-BERRY FINN

"I BEEN THERE BEFORE." DONE!

NO FAIR!

ALTHOUGH I'D NEVER READ *TOM SAWYER,* THE BOOK'S PREQUEL, EVERYONE KNOWS THE STORY ABOUT THE FENCE—HOW TOM TRICKS THE OTHER KIDS INTO WHITEWASHING BY PRETENDING IT'S FUN.

I WOULD SHOW MY FATHER. I WOULD FORCE **MYSELF** TO READ THINGS. WHEN I WAS 14, I BEGAN A GRIM LIST.

THE VARIOUSLY IMPRISONED AND DOOMED PROTAGONISTS REFLECTED MY OWN JOYLESS SELF-INCARCERATION.

I'LL GIVE YOU FIVE WHEN YOU FINISH IT, TOO.

THIS INCIDENT LEFT ME BITTER.

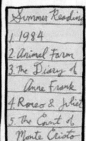

Summer Reading

1. 1984
2. Animal Farm
3. The Diary of Anne Frank
4. Romeo & Juliet
5. The Count of Monte Cristo

ONE IN A SERIES OF SECOND-DEGREE BURNS.

COUNT of MONTE CRISTO

I ACTUALLY LIKED ANNE FRANK. AND I GOT THROUGH ORWELL, THOUGH I MISSED ALL THE ALLEGORY. BUT THAT WAS AS FAR AS I GOT WITH MY LIST.

I CAN'T HELP BUT THINK OF MR. KNIGHTLEY'S DRY OBSERVATION ON A SIMILAR PROJECT UNDERTAKEN BY EMMA WOODHOUSE.

"Emma has been meaning to read more ever since she was twelve years old. I have seen a great many lists of her drawing up at various times of books that she meant to read regularly through – and very good lists they were – very well chosen, and very neatly arranged – sometimes alphabetically, and sometimes by some other rule. The list she drew up when only fourteen – I remember thinking it did her judgment so much credit, that I preserved it some time; and I dare say she may have made out a very good list now."

THANK **GOD** JANE AUSTEN WASN'T IN THE AUTHORS DECK OR I WOULD HAVE NO WAY OF KNOWING THIS.

I LEFT THE COUNT OF MONTE CRISTO LANGUISHING IN THE CHATEAU D'IF BECAUSE I HAD DISCOVERED A KIND OF READING THAT WAS INFINITELY MORE COMPELLING.

THE FORBIDDEN KIND.

MY PARENTS KEPT THE GOOD STUFF UP HERE.

"A MAN OUGHT TO READ JUST AS INCLINATION LEADS HIM; FOR WHAT HE READS AS A TASK WILL DO HIM LITTLE GOOD."

I ABSOLUTELY **MUST** GET TO BOSWELL'S *LIFE OF JOHNSON* ONE OF THESE DAYS.

THUP!

IF YOU REALLY WANT YOUR CHILDREN TO READ SOME-THING, FOR GOD'S SAKE, KEEP IT TO YOURSELF.

GUARD THAT BOOK LIKE A PRECIOUS SECRET.

SHELVE IT JUDICIOUSLY.

AND *UNDER NO CIRCUMSTANCES* PUT IT ON A LIST.

NOW, IF YOU'LL EXCUSE ME, I HAVE SOME READING TO DO.

OH... YOU'RE STILL HERE?!

I'M JUST CHECKING OUT THESE CLASSICAL ALLUSIONS.

WHAT!

Thinking about the Text

1. Alison Bechdel's narrative describes her relationship with reading throughout her life. What is the point of her narrative? What is her **ARGUMENT**?

2. Bechdel suggests that failing to read is sinful, and she writes of feeling guilty for not reading enough literary novels. Do you enjoy reading? Do you enjoy the reading that you have to do for school? Why or why not? Whatever your relationship to reading, what might make it better?

3. Bechdel's drawings aren't the only element of her narrative that creates images; she uses figurative language and allusions as well. Find two examples and explain what they contribute to the effect of the narrative.

4. Bechdel advocates the use of reverse psychology to get children to read, suggesting that restricting access to certain books will make them more attractive. Do you think this is an effective strategy? Why or why not? Have you ever read something just because you believed that you weren't supposed to?

5. Write a **NARRATIVE** of your lifelong experience with reading (it needn't be in graphic form). Make sure that your narrative has a clear point that readers can identify.

Tell Me Something

MICHELLE CACHO-NEGRETE

ON A SHELF IN MY HOME I have my brother's record albums, their covers worn with handling, sticky residue evidence of his fondness for candy. Johnny Mathis, Frankie Lyman, the Drifters, Martha and the Vandellas: "Oh, Jimmy Mack, when are you coming back?" On the dull black vinyl of Smokey Robinson and the Miracles, a fingerprint offers itself up like a message from the past. As I slide the record back into its jacket, a photograph tumbles into my lap: my brother, perhaps twelve, eyes closed, pretend microphone in hand, body leaning into the music. I can hear his off-key voice trying to be like Smokey's: "I'm on the outside looking in, and I don't want to be." Everything else in the picture is blurred, as though my brother were the only solid thing.

Everything of my brother's fits on a couple of shelves: boxes of records, books, a few photographs. When you're killed at eighteen, you don't leave much behind.

· · ·

MICHELLE CACHO-NEGRETE, a prizewinning nonfiction writer and trained psychotherapist, lives in Maine and teaches writing to local and online students. This piece was originally published in 2008 in the *Sun*, a publication that describes itself as an "ad-free monthly magazine that for more than thirty years has used words and photographs to invoke the splendor and heartache of being human."

In December 1968 I was recovering from the birth of my first child three months earlier. A hemorrhage during delivery had left me anemic, and the days had turned hallucinogenic, constructed of jagged shards of color. My brother had shipped out to Vietnam in October. My marriage was faltering. My mother was angry at me for not having married a Jew. My Cuban husband worked six twelve-hour days a week at Grumman Aircraft Engineering Corporation, a leading military contractor. The rent on our Queens apartment would be raised in January. He wanted to buy a house in an isolated section of Long Island, but I'd always lived in the city and had never learned to drive.

Vietnam permeated everything that Christmas. Even the carols seemed part of the national deception: "Peace on earth, goodwill to men."

My anger at my husband had deepened over his views on the war; his   5
cavalier attitude about working for Grumman; his support for the president's policies; his lack of support for me. I dragged myself through the gray-lit days in a stupor. We argued over Vietnam, my exhaustion, his late hours, the mutual hate between my mother and him, whether to have a Christmas tree or a menorah, to move or accept the rent increase. He said I was weak; his grandmother had had fourteen kids and after each birth had gone back to the fields to cut sugar cane. I paced, took iron pills, told him he was unfeeling. I snuck out of the apartment to smoke cigarettes. Finally we agreed to a temporary truce. We agreed to postpone the arguments until an easier time. We agreed to pretend.

It was just before dawn: The baby slept. My husband showered. I stared out the window at the Manhattan skyline ablaze with holiday lights, as if the city were on fire. A Christmas tree twinkled in front of our apartment complex. Dirty snow rimmed the streets, and pigeons rested on windowsills, casting ominous shadows against the panes. A chorus of salt-spattered cars backfired and honked below. The apartment air was oppressive, close. That sorrowful, pleading carol "Have Yourself a Merry Little Christmas" played on the radio: "We'll have to muddle through somehow."

The phone rang. A man with a husky voice gave a name I don't remember, confirmed who I was, then cleared his throat and recited by rote, "We regret to inform you . . ."

I remember little things: The coffee left brewing too long; its bitter, weary smell. Half-browned bread popped up in the toaster. How the streetlights flickered, then went out as the sun began to crack open the early-morning sky.

The man on the phone, who was calling from my mother's home after having delivered the news to her in person, advised me to "come now," as my mother screamed, "No! No! No!" in the background.

I hung up.   10

"My brother is dead!" I yelled into the recesses of the apartment. I drifted up from my seat, my body threatening to collapse. I was entering the baby's room to wake him when my husband stepped out of the bathroom, encircled by mist, and said, "What? I couldn't hear you."

My mother came to stay with us as we waited for the body to be brought back to the U.S. She and I fed the baby, played with him, took him on long walks. My husband went to work. ("Staying home isn't going to change anything.") Friends dropped by with deli sandwiches, baskets of fruit, cookies, chocolate. We received official documents from the military: commendations, explanations, letters of sympathy signed by generals: "A barrage of gunshots . . . mourned by his fellow marines . . . bravery . . . Purple Heart." In bed at night, I conjured a memory of my brother at my wedding: He's standing beside my husband's cousin, whom he has a crush on. His eyes are bright, and he's slimmed down from the chubby child he once was. He says something that makes the cousin laugh, sees me watching him, and winks.

My brother and I had lived much of our lives apart. After having battled with my mother over a phone bill as a teen, he'd gone to live with his father, my stepfather, somewhere in Brooklyn. I didn't know much about how he'd spent those years, but I kept reaching for the sparse memories I did have of him.

When my brother was twelve and I was eighteen, the police left a message that they'd arrested him for stealing a car. My mother wasn't home from work yet, and I ran the eight blocks to the station. The squad room was overheated and stank of sweat and some unidentifiable food. I remember cells, doors leading to shadowy rooms, accused men proclaiming their innocence. The police wouldn't let me see my brother. They stood over me menacingly and called me "street cunt." I went outside and sat on the front steps to wait for my mother. The cops walking in and out glanced at me, nightsticks swinging against their legs, their holstered guns passing me at eye level. A couple of men on the other side of the street shoved each other and screamed in Spanish. Gulls wheeled overhead on the winds off the East River.

When my mother arrived, she straightened her shoulders, said, "Wait   15
here," and went inside.

The first-person *I* provides a powerful focus. See pp. 113–15 for tips on using the first-person point of view.

My brother had been an unsuspecting passenger in the stolen car, but he was sent to a group home for a year anyway. I remember taking the train from Grand Central Station to Pleasantville, New York, to visit him, but I don't remember the visits.

My memories of my brother are disconnected, without contiguous flow: he is two, he is six, he is ten, he is twelve, he is fifteen, he is dead.

When his body finally arrived from Vietnam, they told us it was too perforated with bullet holes to be shown to family members. We stood before the closed coffin at the funeral parlor as if before a holy icon, though the coffin itself was nothing special: standard military issue, as common as M16s. Four marines in crisp blue uniforms and shining brass guarded the body. The proper time to have guarded it, I thought, would have been while it still breathed. As we stared at the coffin, a fantasy seized me: my brother was still alive somewhere in Vietnam; the marines had lost track of him and fabricated this cover story. That Christmas it was easy to disbelieve the government.

I wore a leftover black maternity dress, belted at the waist, and felt unwashed and gritty despite the two showers I'd taken that day. My feet were freezing in tights, wool socks, and scuffed boots. My mother sat crumpled on a chair, a loose arrangement of bent limbs and bowed head. My stepfather, whom I hadn't seen in years, greeted me by saying, "I'm still the handsomest man in Brooklyn, aren't I?" We hugged, and any animosity over his divorce from my mother, after he'd gambled away the rent and food money, was forgiven. A death accomplishes that.

My husband, handsome in the suit he'd worn for our wedding, whispered to his aunts and cousins in the back of the room. The cousin my brother had been attracted to sat in the front row, weeping silent tears beside my mother. I felt as if I were in a foreign movie, something Greek or Italian where everyone wore black and spoke too fast for me to understand. I stared at the coffin and thought about how I'd once had no idea where the Mekong Delta was.

I accepted my share of blame. I'd complained about the war but hadn't protested it. I had been too caught up in my marriage and finding temporary work (I'd been fired when my pregnancy had begun to show) and trying to push through the postpartum exhaustion. I hadn't written letters, gone to demonstrations, participated in sit-ins. I'd done nothing to try to end this war.

. . .

The snow was falling heavily when we left for the cemetery, wind whipping up white ghosts. The body was loaded into a hearse with pale satin curtains in the windows and a stealthy engine. Our car skidded and slipped all the way to Long Island National Cemetery, where we stepped onto a plain of squat white stones that must have been churned out by the hundreds. There were fewer of us here than at the funeral parlor: my mother; my husband; a handful of friends, aunts, and cousins; the rabbi assigned by the funeral home. We advanced toward a hole in the ground covered by a black tarp. A couple of men in heavy clothing stood at a distance, shivering. One, in a black wool hat and army jacket, nodded in sympathy to me. My stepfather was already standing over the grave, a slight figure in a skullcap.

As the rabbi moved between the rows, he looked carefully at each name as though making a list. He turned to my mother and said, "Out of the question."

Leaning on my husband's cousin's arm, she stepped around the rabbi the way you'd circle a rock or another nonsentient object in your path. The snow coated the rabbi's black coat and hat as if intending to bury him also.

I waved my husband on and stopped to talk to the rabbi alone. "What are you saying?" I asked. The wind blew the words back into my face. 25

"There are non-Jews buried here," he said. "How can I pray?" He asked this as though it were a reasonable question.

As I battled my desire to strike him, I thought of my husband's accusation that I would always be a hoodlum from the streets, that anybody could see it. At that moment, I hoped he was right.

I put my face close to the rabbi's, and he took an alarmed step backward. "You *will* pray here," I whispered close to his cheek. "You will pray here because God—the real God, not the one you've made up—mourns every dead child. You will pray here, because otherwise I won't let you leave." I put my hand on his wrist and smiled at him. My lashes were coated with snow, and my scarf flapped around me like a black flag.

The yeshiva had not prepared the rabbi for this threatening woman who would bend him to her will. He glanced from side to side. Nobody was watching. We could have been alone in an alley. Finally he nodded and walked to the graveside. His dark beard caught the pristine snow. He leaned over the coffin and prayed in a low voice, his eyes fixed on the hole in the ground.

. . .

News of the war dominated the papers. Rows of coffins covered with Ameri- 30
can flags flashed across the television screen. Every night I dreamed my
brother was alive, being tortured in a prison camp, running between dense
green palms, crawling through rivers, panting, screaming, leaving a trail of
blood that his enemies would follow. I'd wake covered with perspiration and
gasping for breath. Some friends said I was projecting my own anxiety onto
his death, others that I had a telepathic connection, a few that I was having
a nervous breakdown.

I prayed that my gentle brother had died instantly rather than suffered
pain. I remembered his pride when he'd received his very first paycheck
and had "adopted" a Korean war orphan, faithfully paying fifteen dollars a
month—until he'd lost his job and enlisted in an act of desperation, believing the military's promise to provide an education. I thought of his certainty
that someday he'd leave the city's tenements behind and move to a farm
and grow vegetables and flowers, a dream he'd picked up from a book we'd
read together as children. I had marveled at his decision, during our poverty-
stricken childhood, never to steal, whereas I'd had no problem shoplifting. I
wept that my brother—sensitive, good-natured, astonished by cruelty—had
been sent to Vietnam. I wanted to prevent the same from happening to any
other boy.

I began attending antiwar marches every week, bringing the baby with
me: bottles, blankets, diapers, toys. I didn't believe that it would make a difference. I knew it wasn't people protesting in the street that would end the
war; it would be over only when it was no longer profitable. But I wanted
that spirit of protest to seep into my son. I waved signs and chanted, "Hey,
hey, LBJ, how many kids did you kill today?" This became my penance for
my previous inertia. It would be five more years before the war ended, and
several more after that before my nightmares would be gone and I'd accept
that my brother was truly dead.

When the Bush administration decided to invade Iraq in 2003, I protested in
Washington, D.C., with a friend and later in New York City with my second
husband. Millions of us around the world demonstrated, but it didn't stop
the invasion. As I watched the bombs drop on Baghdad, I wondered if we are
infected with some malevolent virus that will not let us value peace.

It was nearly Christmas that year when my friend Sarah called to tell me, in a hesitant voice, "Jamie is dead."

The news was on in the background this time. No carols. 35

"They're bringing his body back from Iraq. No announcement yet on the funeral."

We hung up. What else was there to say?

I'd first met Jamie at a party Sarah had thrown for writers. His wife, Marika, was writing a novel about leaving Russia to seek freedom and opportunity in the U.S. They were newlyweds, both twenty-two, and had met in an English class. Kevin, my husband, spoke with Jamie about his decision to enlist in the National Guard for financial help with college tuition. Marika and I discussed her novel. She was concerned that Americans would be unable to relate to characters based on people she knew in Russia. "Americans seem to have little understanding about life in other countries," she told me. She shook her head and took a sip of her wine. "But I've made such good friends here."

A few weeks later I saw Jamie and Marika's picture in the newspaper above a story about National Guard members shipping out to Iraq. There they were, arms around each other, Marika's eyes full of love and dread, Jamie's smile tentative. (I thought of all the times his mother must have told him to "smile for the camera.") His arm was wound around his young wife, his military beret perched on his head.

He lasted one month in Iraq. 40

At the funeral Marika, weeping bitterly, said, "I thought this couldn't happen. He was in the National Guard, not the army."

Jamie's flag-draped coffin was not pictured in the paper. It is forbidden now for returning coffins to be shown in the news.

I recently went to a concert by Anaïs Mitchell, who sang a song called "Tell Me Something," about the invasion of Iraq: "Tell me something good about my country, tell me one good thing."

I have no answer for her, but the lyric still haunts me. It makes me think of my brother, dead in Vietnam, and Jamie, who died thirty-five years later in a different war, which is really the same war. To those who die, they are all the same war.

Thinking about the Text

1. Michelle Cacho-Negrete certainly wrote this narrative to express her pain about the death of her younger brother in Vietnam. What other **PURPOSE** might she have had? How can you tell? How successfully did she achieve this purpose? Provide evidence for your conclusions.

2. In the thematic table of contents in the back of this book, we've classified Cacho-Negrete's narrative in the theme of "Home." Why do you think we made that association? How do you relate the painful and compelling story that Cacho-Negrete tells to your ideas about home?

3. Cacho-Negrete narrates small descriptive details ("A Christmas tree twinkled in front of our apartment complex" [6]) and major revelations ("When you're killed at eighteen, you don't leave much behind" [2]) in the same low-key matter-of-fact **TONE**. Would her story have been more effective if it were told more dramatically? Explain why or why not.

4. There are eight distinct scenes in Cacho-Negrete's narrative. Which one had the most emotional impact for you? Why?

5. The title of this piece is "Tell Me Something," and it is not until the final two paragraphs that we learn how the title relates to the narrative. In making this request, is Cacho-Negrete looking to challenge and criticize, or is she instead looking for meaning? Think about what you would say to comply with such a request. Write your own **NARRATIVE** in which you answer her call to "[t]ell me something good about my country" (43).

Flame and Filament

NICHOLAS CARR

ONE OF MAN'S GREATEST INVENTIONS was also one of his most modest: the wick. We don't know who first realized, many thousands of years ago, that fire could be isolated at the tip of a twisted piece of cloth and steadily fed, through capillary action, by a reservoir of wax or oil, but the discovery was, as Wolfgang Schivelbusch writes in *Disenchanted Night*, "as revolutionary in the development of artificial lighting as the wheel in the history of transport." The wick tamed fire, allowing it to be used with a precision and an efficiency far beyond what was possible with a wooden torch or a bundle of twigs. In the process, it helped domesticate us as well. It's hard to imagine civilization progressing to where it is today by torchlight.

The wick also proved an amazingly hardy creation. It remained the dominant lighting technology all the way to the nineteenth century, when it was replaced first by the wickless gas lamp and then, more decisively, by Edison's electricity-fueled incandescent bulb with its glowing metal filament. Cleaner, safer, and even more efficient than the flame it replaced,

NICHOLAS CARR's best-selling books on technology, culture, and economics have sparked vigorous debate, won numerous awards, and been translated into seventeen other languages. Carr writes a blog, *Rough Type*, and is the author of *The Shallows: What the Internet Is Doing to Our Brains* (2010); he is also a member of the editorial board of advisors for *Encyclopaedia Britannica*. This piece is the epilogue to his 2008 book, *The Big Switch: Rewiring the World, from Edison to Google*.

the lightbulb was welcomed into homes and offices around the world. But along with its many practical benefits, electric light also brought subtle and unexpected changes to the way people lived. The fireplace, the candle, and the oil lamp had always been the focal points of households. Fire was, as Schivelbusch puts it, "the soul of the house." Families would in the evening gather in a central room, drawn by the flickering flame, to chat about the day's events or otherwise pass the time together. Electric light, together with central heat, dissolved that long tradition. Family members began to spend more time in different rooms in the evening, studying or reading or working alone. Each person gained more privacy, and a greater sense of autonomy, but the cohesion of the family weakened.

Cold and steady, electric light lacked the allure of the flame. It was not mesmerizing or soothing but strictly functional. It turned light into an industrial commodity. A German diarist in 1944, forced to use candles instead of lightbulbs during nightly air raids, was struck by the difference. "We have noticed," he wrote, "in the 'weaker' light of the candle, objects have a different, a much more marked profile—it gives them a quality of 'reality.'" This quality, he continued, "is lost in electric light: objects (seemingly) ap-

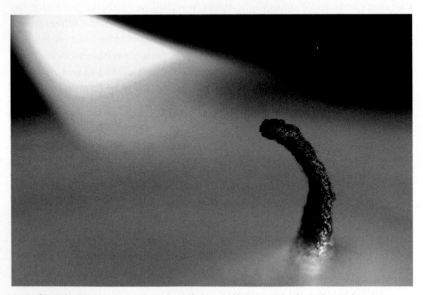

One of man's greatest inventions was also one of his most modest: the wick.

pear much more clearly, but in reality it *flattens* them. Electric light imparts too much brightness and thus things lose body, outline, substance—in short, their essence."

We're still attracted to a flame at the end of a wick. We light candles to set a romantic or a calming mood, to mark a special occasion. We buy ornamental lamps that are crafted to look like candleholders with bulbs shaped as stylized flames. But we can no longer know what it was like when fire was the source of all light. The number of people who remember life before the arrival of Edison's bulb has dwindled to just a few, and when they go they'll take with them all remaining memory of that earlier, pre-electric world. The same will happen, sometime toward the end of this century, with the memory of the world that existed before the computer and the Internet became commonplace. We'll be the ones who bear it away.

All technological change is generational change. The full power and consequence of a new technology are unleashed only when those who have grown up with it become adults and begin to push their outdated parents to the margins. As the older generations die, they take with them their knowledge of what was lost when the new technology arrived, and only the sense of what was gained remains. It's in this way that progress covers its tracks, perpetually refreshing the illusion that where we are is where we were meant to be.

5

Analysis is all about taking a closer look at something; Ch. 9 provides guidelines for doing so.

Thinking about the Text

1. Nicholas Carr argues that "all technological change is generational change" and that as older generations die, they take with them the "knowledge of what was lost when the new technology arrived" (5). Think about the changes brought about by current and in-the-works technological advances. What knowledge might become lost in the future once your generation has passed?

2. Carr cites Schivelbusch, who mentions that in pre-electricity times, the fire was "the soul of the house" (2). What is the soul of your house? Is there one? Is it a single one, or are there multiple points that draw household members together? If you have experience of an extended power outage, how did it change "the soul of your house"? How do your answers to these questions compare with those of your classmates?

3. When writing for a newspaper or magazine, authors generally have a rough idea of the readership, and they can direct their writing toward a particular

AUDIENCE. A book has a much broader potential audience. What seem to be the characteristics of Carr's intended audience? What knowledge does Carr assume his audience already has? Provide examples from the reading to support your conclusions.

4. Carr points out that "we're still attracted to a flame at the end of a wick," and he mentions the use of candles to set a romantic mood (4). What other **EVIDENCE** can you find in everyday life to support Carr's assertion?

5. What technologies that you have lived with are in the process of being replaced? Landline phones? Television sets with antennas? Component stereos? What will people of the future have missed? Write an essay with an intended audience of people who are forty or fifty years younger than you (they may not have been born yet). Tell them about life with a technology that they will likely never have known.

2b or Not 2b?

DAVID CRYSTAL

Last year, in a newspaper article headed "I h8 txt msgs: How texting is wrecking our language," John Humphrys argued that texters are "vandals who are doing to our language what Genghis Khan did to his neighbours 800 years ago. They are destroying it: pillaging our punctuation; savaging our sentences; raping our vocabulary. And they must be stopped."

As a new variety of language, texting has been condemned as "textese," "slanguage," a "digital virus." According to John Sutherland of University College London, writing in this paper in 2002, it is "bleak, bald, sad shorthand. Drab shrinktalk . . . Linguistically it's all pig's ear . . . it masks dyslexia, poor spelling and mental laziness. Texting is penmanship for illiterates."

Ever since the arrival of printing—thought to be the invention of the devil because it would put false opinions into people's minds—people have been arguing that new technology would have disastrous consequences for language. Scares accompanied the introduction of the telegraph, telephone, and broadcasting. But has there ever been a linguistic phenomenon that has

---

DAVID CRYSTAL is a linguist and a prolific author on themes as far-flung as Shakespearean English and language use in twenty-first-century contexts and technologies. He is currently an honorary professor of linguistics at Bangor University in Wales. In addition to his many academic books and articles, he is a frequent contributor to newspapers and magazines. This piece was published in the *Guardian*, a London-based daily paper, in 2008.

aroused such curiosity, suspicion, fear, confusion, antagonism, fascination, excitement and enthusiasm all at once as texting? And in such a short space of time. Less than a decade ago, hardly anyone had heard of it.

The idea of a point-to-point short message service (or SMS) began to be discussed as part of the development of the Global System for Mobile Communications network in the mid-1980s, but it wasn't until the early 90s that phone companies started to develop its commercial possibilities. Text communicated by pagers were replaced by text messages, at first only 20 characters in length. It took five years or more before numbers of users started to build up. The average number of texts per GSM customer in 1995 was 0.4 per month; by the end of 2000 it was still only 35.

The slow start, it seems, was because the companies had trouble working out reliable ways of charging for the new service. But once procedures were in place, texting rocketed. In the UK, in 2001, 12.2bn text messages were sent. This had doubled by 2004, and was forecast to be 45bn in 2007. On Christmas Day alone in 2006, over 205m texts went out. World figures went from 17bn in 2000 to 250bn in 2001. They passed a trillion in 2005. Text messaging generated around $70bn in 2005. That's more than three times as much as all Hollywood box office returns that year.

Vandalism? Teenagers texting on a mobile phone.

People think that the written language seen on mobile phone screens is new and alien, but all the popular beliefs about texting are wrong. Its graphic distinctiveness is not a new phenomenon, nor is its use restricted to the young. There is increasing evidence that it helps rather than hinders literacy. And only a very tiny part of it uses a distinctive orthography. A trillion text messages might seem a lot, but when we set these alongside the multi-trillion instances of standard orthography in everyday life, they appear as no more than a few ripples on the surface of the sea of language. Texting has added a new dimension to language use, but its long-term impact is negligible. It is not a disaster.

Although many texters enjoy breaking linguistic rules, they also know they need to be understood. There is no point in paying to send a message if it breaks so many rules that it ceases to be intelligible. When messages are longer, containing more information, the amount of standard orthography increases. Many texters alter just the grammatical words (such as "you" and "be"). As older and more conservative language users have begun to text, an even more standardised style has appeared. Some texters refuse to depart at all from traditional orthography. And conventional spelling and punctuation is the norm when institutions send out information messages, as in this university text to students: "Weather Alert! No classes today due to snow storm," or in the texts which radio listeners are invited to send in to programmes. These institutional messages now form the majority of texts in cyberspace—and several organisations forbid the use of abbreviations, knowing that many readers will not understand them. Bad textiquette.

Research has made it clear that the early media hysteria about the novelty (and thus the dangers) of text messaging was misplaced. In one American study, less than 20% of the text messages looked at showed abbreviated forms of any kind—about three per message. And in a Norwegian study, the proportion was even lower, with just 6% using abbreviations. In my own text collection, the figure is about 10%.

People seem to have swallowed whole the stories that youngsters use nothing else but abbreviations when they text, such as the reports in 2003 that a teenager had written an essay so full of textspeak that her teacher was unable to understand it. An extract was posted online, and quoted incessantly, but as no one was ever able to track down the entire essay, it was probably a hoax.

There are several distinctive features of the way texts are written that combine to give the impression of novelty, but none of them is, in fact, linguistically novel. Many of them were being used in chatroom interactions that predated the arrival of mobile phones. Some can be found in pre-computer informal writing, dating back a hundred years or more.

The most noticeable feature is the use of single letters, numerals, and symbols to represent words or parts of words, as with b "be" and 2 "to." They are called rebuses, and they go back centuries. Adults who condemn a "c u" in a young person's texting have forgotten that they once did the same thing themselves (though not on a mobile phone). In countless Christmas annuals, they solved puzzles like this one:

YY U R YY U B I C U R YY 4 ME
("Too wise you are . . .")

Similarly, the use of initial letters for whole words (n for "no," gf for "girl-friend," cmb "call me back") is not at all new. People have been initialising common phrases for ages. IOU is known from 1618. There is no difference, apart from the medium of communication, between a modern kid's "lol" ("laughing out loud") and an earlier generation's "Swalk" ("sealed with a loving kiss").

In texts we find such forms as msg ("message") and xlnt ("excellent"). Almst any wrd cn be abbrvted in ths wy—though there is no consistency between texters. But this isn't new either. Eric Partridge published his *Dictionary of Abbreviations* in 1942. It contained dozens of SMS-looking examples, such as agn "again," mth "month," and gd "good"—50 years before texting was born.

English has had abbreviated words ever since it began to be written down. Words such as exam, vet, fridge, cox and bus are so familiar that they have effectively become new words. When some of these abbreviated forms first came into use, they also attracted criticism. In 1711, for example, Joseph Addison complained about the way words were being "miserably curtailed"—he mentioned pos (itive) and incog (nito). And Jonathan Swift thought that abbreviating words was a "barbarous custom."

What novelty there is in texting lies chiefly in the way it takes further 15 some of the processes used in the past. Some of its juxtapositions create forms which have little precedent, apart from in puzzles. All conceivable types of feature can be juxtaposed—sequences of shortened and full words (hldmecls "hold me close"), logograms and shortened words (2bctnd "to be continued"), logograms and nonstandard spellings (cu2nite) and so on. There are no less than four processes combined in iowan2bwu "I only want to be with you"—full word + an initialism + a shortened word + two logograms + an initialism + a logogram. And some messages contain unusual processes: in iohis4u "I only have eyes for you," we see the addition of a plural ending to a logogram. One characteristic runs through all these examples: the letters, symbols and words are run together, without spaces. This is certainly unusual in the history of special writing systems. But few texts string together long sequences of puzzling graphic units.

There are also individual differences in texting, as in any other linguistic domain. In 2002, Stuart Campbell was found guilty of the murder of his 15-year-old niece after his text message alibi was shown to be a forgery. He had claimed that certain texts sent by the girl showed he was innocent. But a detailed comparison of the vocabulary and other stylistic features of his own text messages and those of his niece showed that he had written the messages himself. The forensic possibilities have been further explored by a team at the University of Leicester. The fact that texting is a relatively unstandardised mode of communication, prone to idiosyncrasy, turns out to be an advantage in such a context, as authorship differences are likely to be more easily detectable than in writing using standard English.

Texters use deviant spellings—and they know they are deviant. But they are by no means the first to use such nonstandard forms as cos "because," wot "what," or gissa "give us a." Several of these are so much part of English literary tradition that they have been given entries in the *Oxford English Dictionary*. "Cos" is there from 1828 and "wot" from 1829. Many can be found in literary dialect representations, such as by Charles Dickens, Mark Twain, Walter Scott, DH Lawrence, or Alan Bleasdale ("Gissa job!").

Sending a message on a mobile phone is not the most natural of ways to communicate. The keypad isn't linguistically sensible. No one took letter-frequency considerations into account when designing it. For example, key 7 on my mobile contains four symbols, pqrs. It takes four key-presses to access the letter s, and yet s is one of the most frequently occurring letters in English. It is twice as easy to input q, which is one of the least frequently occurring letters. It should be the other way round. So any strategy that reduces the time and awkwardness of inputting graphic symbols is bound to be attractive.

Abbreviations were used as a natural, intuitive response to a technological problem. And they appeared in next to no time. Texters simply transferred (and then embellished) what they had encountered in other settings. We have all left notes in which we have replaced an and by an &, a three by a 3, and so on. Anglo-Saxon scribes used abbreviations of this kind.

But the need to save time and energy is by no means the whole story   20
of texting. When we look at some texts, they are linguistically quite complex. There are an extraordinary number of ways in which people play with
language—creating riddles, solving crosswords, playing Scrabble, inventing
new words. Professional writers do the same—providing catchy copy for
advertising slogans, thinking up puns in newspaper headlines, and writing poems, novels and plays. Children quickly learn that one of the most
enjoyable things you can do with language is to play with its sounds, words,
grammar—and spelling.

The drive to be playful is there when we text, and it is hugely powerful. Within two or three years of the arrival of texting, it developed a ludic
dimension. In short, it's fun.

To celebrate World Poetry day in 2007, T-Mobile tried to find the UK's
first "Txt laureate" in a competition for the best romantic poem in SMS. They
had 200 entrants, and as with previous competitions the entries were a mixture of unabbreviated and abbreviated texts.

The winner, Ben Ziman-Bright, wrote conventionally:

> The wet rustle of rain
> can dampen today. Your text
> buoys me above oil-rainbow puddles
> like a paper boat, so that even
> soaked to the skin
> I am grinning.

The runner-up did not:

> O hart tht sorz
> My luv adorz
> He mAks me liv
> He mAks me giv
> Myslf 2 him
> As my luv porz

(The author of the latter was, incidentally, in her late 60s.)

The length constraint in text-poetry fosters economy of expression in
much the same way as other tightly constrained forms of poetry do, such as
the haiku or the Welsh englyn. To say a poem must be written within 160

characters at first seems just as pointless as to say that a poem must be written in three lines of five, seven, and five syllables. But put such a discipline
into the hands of a master, and the result can be poetic magic. Of course,
SMS poetry has some way to go before it can match the haiku tradition; but
then, haikus have had a head-start of several hundred years.

There is something about the genre which has no parallel elsewhere. 25
This is nothing to do with the use of texting abbreviations. It is more to do
with the way the short lines have an individual force. Reading a text poem,
wrote Peter Sansom, who co-judged a *Guardian* competition in 2002, is "an
urgent business . . . with a text poem you stay focused as it were in the now
of each arriving line." The impact is evident even in one-liners, whose effect
relies on the kind of succinctness we find in a maxim or proverb. UA Fan-
thorpe, Sansom's fellow judge, admired "Basildon: imagine a carpark." And
they both liked "They phone you up, your mum and dad."

Several competitions have focussed on reworking famous lines, titles,
or quotations:

> txt me ishmael
> zen & T @ f m2 cycl mn10nc

The brevity of the SMS genre disallows complex formal patterning—of, say,
the kind we might find in a sonnet. It isn't so easy to include more than a
couple of images, such as similes, simply because there isn't the space. Writers have nonetheless tried to extend the potential of the medium. The SMS
novel, for example, operates on a screen-by-screen basis. Each screen is a
"chapter" describing an event in the story. Here is an interactive example
from 2005, from an Indian website called "Cloakroom":

> Chptr 6: While Surching 4 Her Father, Rita Bumps In2 A Chaiwalla
> & Tea Spills On Her Blouse. She Goes Inside Da Washroom, & Da
> Train Halts @ A Station.

In Japan, an author known as Yoshi has had a huge success with his
text-messaging novel *Deep Love*. Readers sent feedback as the story unfold-
ed, and some of their ideas were incorporated into it. He went on to make a
film of the novel.

A mobile literature channel began in China in 2004. The "m-novel," as
it is called, started with a love story, "Distance," by writer and broadcaster

Xuan Huang. A young couple get to know each other because of a wrongly sent SMS message. The whole story is 1008 Chinese characters, told in 15 chapters, with one chapter sent each day.

Plainly, there are severe limits to the expressive power of the medium, when it is restricted to a screen in this way. So it is not surprising that, very early on, writers dispensed with the 160-character constraint, and engaged in SMS creative writing of any length using hard copy. Immediately there was a problem. By taking the writing away from the mobile phone screen, how could the distinctiveness of the genre be maintained? So the stylistic character of SMS writing changed, and texting abbreviations, previously optional, became obligatory.

Several SMS poets, such as Norman Silver, go well beyond text-messag- 30 ing conventions, introducing variations in line-shape, type-size, font, and colour that are reminiscent of the concrete poetry creations of the 1960s. They illustrate the way the genre is being shaped by the more powerful applications available on computers.

In 2007 Finnish writer Hannu Luntiala published *The Last Messages,* in which the whole 332-page narrative consists of SMS messages. It tells the story of an IT executive who resigns his job and travels the world, using text messages to keep in touch with everyone. And the growing independence of the genre from its mobile-phone origins is well illustrated by the French novelist Phil Marso, who published a book in 2004 written entirely in French SMS shorthand, *Pas Sage a Taba vo SMS*—a piece of word-play intended to discourage young people from smoking. The next year he produced *L,* an SMS retelling of French poetic classics.

An extraordinary number of doom-laden prophecies have been made about the supposed linguistic evils unleashed by texting. Sadly, its creative potential has been virtually ignored. But five years of research has at last begun to dispel the myths. The most important finding is that texting does not erode children's ability to read and write. On the contrary, literacy improves. The latest studies (from a team at Coventry University) have found strong positive links between the use of text language and the skills underlying success in standard English in pre-teenage children. The more abbreviations in their messages, the higher they scored on tests of reading and vocabulary. The children who were better at spelling and writing used the most textisms. And the younger they received their first phone, the higher their scores.

Children could not be good at texting if they had not already developed considerable literacy awareness. Before you can write and play with abbre-

See Ch. 27 on how you can use texting and other online conventions appropriately in your academic writing.

viated forms, you need to have a sense of how the sounds of your language relate to the letters. You need to know that there are such things as alternative spellings. If you are aware that your texting behaviour is different, you must have already intuited that there is such a thing as a standard. If you are using such abbreviations as lol and brb ("be right back"), you must have developed a sensitivity to the communicative needs of your textees.

Some people dislike texting. Some are bemused by it. But it is merely the latest manifestation of the human ability to be linguistically creative and to adapt language to suit the demands of diverse settings. There is no disaster pending. We will not see a new generation of adults growing up unable to write proper English. The language as a whole will not decline. In texting what we are seeing, in a small way, is language in evolution.

Thinking about the Text

1. David Crystal's **ANALYSIS** includes the results of a recent study of students in England that found a positive correlation between the use of texting abbreviations and scores on reading and vocabulary tests. Think about yourself and the friends you text with. Do your own experience and observations match the results of that study? How might you explain any differences you may find?

2. Crystal states, "There is no point in paying to send a message if it breaks so many rules that it ceases to be intelligible" (7). Are you able to decipher all of the text messages that you receive? Have you established any texting shorthand with your frequent text partners that other people would likely not understand? Are you always careful to text intelligibly for your addressee? Why or why not?

3. In writing this article for the *Guardian*, Crystal could be fairly certain that he and his credentials were known to that paper's audience, and he did not need to establish his **AUTHORITY**. If you were to write a similar article for your hometown newspaper, what could you include to give your writing an authoritative tone?

4. Crystal's **EVIDENCE** that texting conventions are no cause for alarm falls into two main categories: historical (that the abbreviation strategies used in texts have been around for a long time, with no ill effect) and cognitive (that the more such strategies students use, the better they do on reading and vocabulary tests). Which of these kinds of evidence do you find more convincing?

Why? Which would you be more likely to use with someone complaining that texting conventions are damaging to those who use them and to language it-self? Why?

5. Crystal presents a strong argument in support of texting conventions as a per-fectly normal use of the language. Still, many people prefer to use standard spelling and punctuation in their text messages (see Lynne Truss' article on p. 939). Write an essay in which you support or refute Crystal's position, using your own practices and those of your most frequent texting partners as evi-dence.

Why I Hate 3-D (And You Should Too)

ROGER EBERT

3-D **IS A WASTE** of a perfectly good dimension. Hollywood's current crazy stampede toward it is suicidal. It adds nothing essential to the moviegoing experience. For some, it is an annoying distraction. For others, it creates nausea and headaches. It is driven largely to sell expensive projection equipment and add a $5 to $7.50 surcharge on already expensive movie tickets. Its image is noticeably darker than standard 2-D. It is unsuitable for grown-up films of any seriousness. It limits the freedom of directors to make films as they choose. For moviegoers in the PG-13 and R ranges, it only rarely provides an experience worth paying a premium for.

That's my position. I know it's heresy to the biz side of show business. After all, 3-D has not only given Hollywood its biggest payday ($2.7 billion and counting for *Avatar*), but a slew of other hits. The year's top three films—*Alice in Wonderland, How to Train Your Dragon*, and *Clash of the Titans*—were all projected in 3-D, and they're only the beginning. The very notion of *Jackass* in 3-D may induce a wave of hysterical blindness, to avoid seeing

What a great opening sentence! Direct, to the point, forceful. Learn how to craft your own great openings on p. 294.

ROGER EBERT, the first film critic to win a Pulitzer Prize for criticism, is syndicated in more than 200 periodicals. He has been doing film criticism since 1967 and credits *Mad Magazine* as his first teacher in the field. Ebert's direct and outspoken criticism covers not only individual movies but the industry as a whole, including trends and practices within it. This article, published in *Newsweek* in 2010, is a good example of his unabashed voice.

Steve-O's you-know-what in that way. But many directors, editors, and cinematographers agree with me about the shortcomings of 3-D. So do many movie lovers—even executives who feel stampeded by another Hollywood infatuation with a technology that was already pointless when their grandfathers played with stereoscopes. The heretics' case, point by point:

1. It's the waste of a dimension. When you look at a 2-D movie, it's already in 3-D as far as your mind is concerned. When you see Lawrence of Arabia growing from a speck as he rides toward you across the desert, are you thinking, "Look how slowly he grows against the horizon"? Our minds use the principle of perspective to provide the third dimension. Adding one artificially can make the illusion less convincing.

2. It adds nothing to the experience. Recall the greatest moviegoing experiences of your lifetime. Did they "need" 3-D? A great film completely engages our imaginations. What would *Fargo* gain in 3-D? *Precious*? *Casablanca*?

3. It can be a distraction. Some 3-D consists of only separating the visual   5
planes, so that some objects float above others, but everything is still in 2-D. We notice this. We shouldn't. In 2-D, directors have often used a difference in focus to call attention to the foreground or the background. In 3-D the technology itself seems to suggest that the whole depth of field be in sharp focus. I don't believe this is necessary, and it deprives directors of a tool to guide our focus.

4. It can create nausea and headaches. As 3-D TV sets were being introduced at the Consumer Electronics Show in Las Vegas in January, Reuters interviewed two leading ophthalmologists. "There are a lot of people walking around with very minor eye problems—for example, a muscle imbalance— which under normal circumstances the brain deals with naturally," said Dr. Michael Rosenberg, a professor at Northwestern University. 3-D provides an unfamiliar visual experience, and "that translates into greater mental effort, making it easier to get a headache." Dr. Deborah Friedman, a professor of ophthalmology and neurology at the University of Rochester Medical Center, said that in normal vision, each eye sees things at a slightly different angle. "When that gets processed in the brain, that creates the perception of depth. The illusion that you see in three dimensions in the movies is not calibrated the same way that your eyes and your brain are." In a just-published article, *Consumer Reports* says about 15 percent of the moviegoing audience experiences headache and eyestrain during 3-D movies.

5. Have you noticed that 3-D seems a little dim? Lenny Lipton is known as the father of the electronic stereoscopic-display industry. He knows how films made with his systems should look. Current digital projectors, he writes, are "intrinsically inefficient. Half the light goes to one eye and half to the other, which immediately results in a 50 percent reduction in illumination." Then the glasses themselves absorb light. The vast majority of theaters show 3-D at between three and six foot-lamberts (fLs). Film projection provides about 15fLs. The original IMAX format threw 22fLs at the screen. If you don't know what a foot-lambert is, join the crowd. (In short: it's the level of light thrown on the screen from a projector with no film in it.) And don't mistake a standard film for an IMAX film, or "fake IMAX" for original IMAX. What's the difference? IMAX is building new theaters that have larger screens, which are quite nice, but are not the huge IMAX screens and do not use IMAX film technology. But since all their theaters are called IMAX anyway, this is confusing.

6. There's money to be made in selling new digital projectors. These projectors are not selling themselves. There was initial opposition from exhibitors to the huge cost of new equipment and infighting about whether studios would help share these expenses. Some studios, concerned with tarnishing the 3-D myth, have told exhibitors that if they don't show a movie in 3-D, they can't have it in 2-D. Although there's room in most projection booths for both kinds of projectors, theaters are encouraged to remove analog projectors as soon as they can. Why so much haste to get rid of them? Are exhibitors being encouraged to burn their bridges by insecure digital manufacturers?

7. Theaters slap on a surcharge of $5 to $7.50 for 3-D. Yet when you see a 2-D film in a 3-D-ready theater, the 3-D projectors are also outfitted for 2-D films: it uses the same projector but doesn't charge extra. See the Catch-22? Are surcharges here to stay, or will they be dropped after the projectors are paid off? What do you think? I think 3-D is a form of extortion for parents whose children are tutored by advertising and product placement to "want" 3-D. In my review of *Clash of the Titans*, I added a footnote: "Explain to your kids that the movie was not filmed in 3-D and is only being shown in 3-D in order to charge you an extra $5 a ticket. I saw it in 2-D, and let me tell you, it looked terrific." And it did. The "3-D" was hastily added in postproduction to ride on the coattails of *Avatar*. The fake-3-D *Titans* even got bad reviews from 3-D cheerleaders. Jeffrey Katzenberg, whose DreamWorks has moved wholeheartedly into 3-D, called it "cheeseball," adding: "You just snookered the movie audience." He told *Variety* he was afraid quickie, fake-3-D conversions would kill the goose that was being counted on for golden eggs.

8. I cannot imagine a serious drama, such as *Up in the Air* or *The Hurt* 10
***Locker,* in 3-D.** Neither can directors. Having shot *Dial M for Murder* in 3-D, Alfred Hitchcock was so displeased by the result that he released it in 2-D at its New York opening. The medium seems suited for children's films, animation, and films such as James Cameron's *Avatar*, which are largely made on computers. Cameron's film is, of course, the elephant in the room: a splendid film, great-looking on a traditional IMAX screen, which is how I saw it, and the highest-grossing film in history. It's used as the poster child for 3-D, but might it have done as well in 2-D (not taking the surcharge into account)? The second-highest all-time grosser is Cameron's *Titanic*, which of course was in 2-D. Still, *Avatar* used 3-D very effectively. I loved it. Cameron is a technical genius who planned his film for 3-D from the ground up and spent $250 million getting it right. He is a master of cinematography and editing. Other directors are forced to use 3-D by marketing executives. The elephant in that room is the desire to add a surcharge.

Consider Tim Burton, who was forced by marketing executives to create a faux-3-D film that was then sold as *Alice in Wonderland: An IMAX 3D Experience* (although remember that the new IMAX theaters are not true IMAX). Yes, it had huge grosses. But its 3-D effects were minimal and unnecessary; a scam to justify the surcharge.

Even Cameron plans to rerelease *Titanic* in 3-D, and it's worth recalling his 3-D documentary, *Ghosts of the Abyss*, which he personally photographed from the grave of the *Titanic*. *Titanic 3-D* will not be true 3-D, but Cameron is likely to do "fake 3-D" better than others have. My argument would nevertheless be: *Titanic* is wonderful just as it stands, so why add a distraction? Obviously, to return to the No. 2 cash cow in movie history and squeeze out more milk.

I once said I might become reconciled to 3-D if a director like Martin Scorsese ever used the format. I thought I was safe. Then Scorsese announced that his 2011 film *The Invention of Hugo Cabret*, about an orphan and a robot, will

be in 3-D. Well, Scorsese knows film, and he has a voluptuous love of its possibilities. I expect he will adapt 3-D to his needs. And my hero, Werner Herzog,
is using 3-D to film prehistoric cave paintings in France, to better show off the
concavities of the ancient caves. He told me that nothing will "approach" the
audience, and his film will stay behind the plane of the screen. In other words,
nothing will hurtle at the audience, and 3-D will allow us the illusion of being
able to occupy the space with the paintings and look into them, experiencing
them as a prehistoric artist standing in the cavern might have.

**9. Whenever Hollywood has felt threatened, it has turned to technology:
sound, color, widescreen, Cinerama, 3-D, stereophonic sound, and now 3-D
again.** In marketing terms, this means offering an experience that can't be
had at home. With the advent of Blu-ray discs, HD cable, and home digital
projectors, the gap between the theater and home experiences has been narrowed. 3-D widened it again. Now home 3-D TV sets may narrow that gap
as well.

What Hollywood needs is a "premium" experience that is obviously, 15
dramatically better than anything at home, suitable for films aimed at all
ages, and worth a surcharge. For years I've been praising a process invented
by Dean Goodhill called MaxiVision48, which uses existing film technology
but shoots at 48 frames per second and provides smooth projection that is
absolutely jiggle-free. Modern film is projected at 24 frames per second (fps)
because that is the lowest speed that would carry analog sound in the first
days of the talkies. Analog sound has largely been replaced by digital sound.
MaxiVision48 projects at 48fps, which doubles image quality. The result is
dramatically better than existing 2-D. In terms of standard measurements
used in the industry, it's 400 percent better. That is not a misprint. Those
who haven't seen it have no idea how good it is. I've seen it, and also a system of some years ago, Douglas Trumbull's Showscan. These systems are
so good that the screen functions like a window into three dimensions. If
moviegoers could see it, they would simply forget about 3-D.

I'm not opposed to 3-D as an option. I'm opposed to it as a way of life
for Hollywood, where it seems to be skewing major studio output away
from the kinds of films we think of as Oscar-worthy. Scorsese and Herzog
make films for grown-ups. Hollywood is racing headlong toward the kiddie
market. Disney recently announced it will make no more traditional films
at all, focusing entirely on animation, franchises, and superheroes. I have
the sense that younger Hollywood is losing the instinctive feeling for story

and quality that generations of executives possessed. It's all about the marketing. Hollywood needs a projection system that is suitable for all kinds of films—every film—and is hands-down better than anything audiences have ever seen. The marketing executives are right that audiences will come to see a premium viewing experience they can't get at home. But they're betting on the wrong experience.

Thinking about the Text

1. A **REVIEW** requires appropriate **CRITERIA** for evaluation. What are Roger Ebert's criteria? Are they appropriate? Why or why not?

2. Have you seen a 3-D film recently? Did you feel it was worth the surcharge? Why or why not? Apply Ebert's criticisms to the film that you saw. Do you agree with his assessment? Why or why not?

3. Ebert numbered his objections to 3-D. Was that an effective **DESIGN** strategy? Why or why not? In responding, consider that his article was published in *Newsweek*; might he have framed his nine arguments differently for *Rolling Stone*, for example? for a daily newspaper? Explain your reasoning and your conclusions.

4. Ebert is very careful to say that he doesn't oppose 3-D as an option but that it should not become "a way of life for Hollywood" (16). What kinds of films does he think are suitable for 3-D? Can you think of any other kinds or individual 2-D films that you think 3-D would enhance? What features do all these kinds and films have in common? Use your answers to establish a set of criteria for 3-D-worthy movies.

5. Ebert says the proliferation of 3-D movies grows out of Hollywood's need to provide a "premium" experience—something that is better than what people have at home (15). How important is this factor in your own moviegoing? What, if anything besides more income or closer theaters, might get you out to the movies more often? What kind of cinema experience would be worth paying for? Different seating options? Different refreshment options? Larger screens? Better sound? Something else? Write a **PROPOSAL** in which you suggest changes that would get you to the movies more often and/or get you to spend more when you go—or explain why no added "premium" would work in your case. Be precise and thorough in your proposal or explanation, and provide reasons for it.

Serving in Florida

BARBARA EHRENREICH

MOSTLY OUT OF LAZINESS, I decide to start my low-wage life in the town nearest to where I actually live, Key West, Florida, which with a population of about 25,000 is elbowing its way up to the status of a genuine city. The downside of familiarity, I soon realize, is that it's not easy to go from being a consumer, thoughtlessly throwing money around in exchange for groceries and movies and gas, to being a worker in the very same place. I am terrified, especially at the beginning, of being recognized by some friendly business owner or erstwhile neighbor and having to stammer out some explanation of my project. Happily, though, my fears turn out to be

---

BARBARA EHRENREICH holds a PhD in cell biology, and early in the course of her scientific work became involved in a nonprofit organization to improve health care for people with limited resources. The investigative reporting that she did with that organization directed her toward a path of journalism and political activism, which she has pursued ever since. "Sure, I could have had more stability and financial security if I'd stuck to science or teaching," she has written. "But I chose adventure and I've never for a moment regretted it." Ehrenreich is the author of twenty books on diverse topics as well as articles for *Ms.*, *Harper's*, the *New York Times*, the *Wall Street Journal*, and many other periodicals. This piece is an excerpt from her acclaimed 2001 book, *Nickel and Dimed: On (Not) Getting By in America*, a memoir of her experience living for three months on minimum wage earnings as a waitress, hotel maid, and other service jobs.

entirely unwarranted: during a month of poverty and toil, no one recogniz-
es my face or my name, which goes unnoticed and for the most part unut-
tered. In this parallel universe where my father never got out of the mines
and I never got through college, I am "baby," "honey," "blondie," and, most
commonly, "girl."

My first task is to find a place to live. I figure that if I can earn $7 an
hour—which, from the want ads, seems doable—I can afford to spend $500
on rent or maybe, with severe economies, $600 and still have $400 or $500
left over for food and gas. In the Key West area, this pretty much confines
me to flophouses and trailer homes—like the one, a pleasing fifteen-minute
drive from town, that has no air-conditioning, no screens, no fans, no television, and, by way of diversion, only the challenge of evading the landlord's
Doberman pinscher. The big problem with this place, though, is the rent,
which at $675 a month is well beyond my reach. All right, Key West is ex-
pensive. But so is New York City, or the Bay Area, or Jackson, Wyoming, or
Telluride, or Boston, or any other place where tourists and the wealthy compete for living space with the people who clean their toilets and fry their
hash browns. Still, it is a shock to realize that "trailer trash" has become, for
me, a demographic category to aspire to.

So I decide to make the common trade-off between affordability and
convenience and go for a $500-a-month "efficiency" thirty miles up a two-
lane highway from the employment opportunities of Key West, meaning
forty-five minutes if there's no road construction and I don't get caught behind some sun-dazed Canadian tourists. I hate the drive, along a roadside
studded with white crosses commemorating the more effective head-on col-
lisions, but it's a sweet little place—a cabin, more or less, set in the swampy
backyard of the converted mobile home where my landlord, an affable TV
repairman, lives with his bartender girlfriend. Anthropologically speaking,
the trailer park would be preferable, but here I have a gleaming white floor
and a firm mattress, and the few resident bugs are easily vanquished.

The next piece of business is to comb through the want ads and find a
job. I rule out various occupations for one reason or another: hotel front-desk
clerk, for example, which to my surprise is regarded as unskilled and pays
only $6 or $7 an hour, gets eliminated because it involves standing in one
spot for eight hours a day. Waitressing is also something I'd like to avoid,
because I remember it leaving me bone-tired when I was eighteen, and I'm
decades of varicosities and back pain beyond that now. Telemarketing, one
of the first refuges of the suddenly indigent, can be dismissed on grounds

of personality. This leaves certain supermarket jobs, such as deli clerk, or housekeeping in the hotels and guest houses, which pays about $7 and, I imagine, is not too different from what I've been doing part-time, in my own home, all my life.

So I put on what I take to be a respectable-looking outfit of ironed Ber- 5 muda shorts and scooped-neck T-shirt and set out for a tour of the local hotels and supermarkets. Best Western, Econo Lodge, and HoJo's all let me fill out application forms, and these are, to my relief, mostly interested in whether I am a legal resident of the United States and have committed any felonies. My next stop is Winn-Dixie, the supermarket, which turns out to have a particularly onerous application process, featuring a twenty-minute "interview" by computer since, apparently, no human on the premises is deemed capable of representing the corporate point of view. I am conducted to a large room decorated with posters illustrating how to look "professional" (it helps to be white and, if female, permed) and warning of the slick promises that union organizers might try to tempt me with. The interview is multiple-choice: Do I have anything, such as child care problems, that might make it hard for me to get to work on time? Do I think safety on the job is the responsibility of management? Then, popping up cunningly out of the blue: How many dollars' worth of stolen goods have I purchased in the last year? Would I turn in a fellow employee if I caught him stealing? Finally, "Are you an honest person?"

Apparently I ace the interview, because I am told that all I have to do is show up in some doctor's office tomorrow for a urine test. This seems to be a fairly general rule: if you want to stack Cheerios boxes or vacuum hotel rooms in chemically fascist America, you have to be willing to squat down and pee in front of a health worker (who has no doubt had to do the same thing herself.)[1] The wages Winn-Dixie is offering—$6 and a couple of dimes to start with—are not enough, I decide, to compensate for this indignity.

I lunch at Wendy's, where $4.99 gets you unlimited refills at the Mexican part of the Super-bar, a comforting surfeit of refried beans and cheese sauce. A teenage employee, seeing me studying the want ads, kindly offers me an application form, which I fill out, though here, too, the pay is

---

1. Eighty-one percent of large employers now require preemployment drug testing, up from 21 percent in 1987. Among all employers, the rate of testing is highest in the South. The drug most likely to be detected—marijuana, which can be detected weeks after use—is also the most innocuous, while heroin and cocaine are generally undetectable three days after use. Alcohol, which clears the body within hours after ingestion, is not tested for.

just $6 and change an hour. Then it's off for a round of the locally owned inns and guest houses in Key West's Old Town, which is where all the serious sightseeing and guzzling goes on, a couple of miles removed from the functional end of the island, where the discount hotels make their homes. At The Palms, let's call it, a bouncy manager actually takes me around to see the rooms and meet the current housekeepers, who, I note with satisfaction, look pretty much like me—faded ex-hippie types in shorts with long hair pulled back in braids. Mostly, though, no one speaks to me or even looks at me except to proffer an application form. At my last stop, a palatial B & B, I wait twenty minutes to meet "Max," only to be told that there are no jobs now but there should be one soon, since "nobody lasts more than a couple weeks."

Three days go by like this and, to my chagrin, no one from the approximately twenty places at which I've applied calls me for an interview. I had been vain enough to worry about coming across as too educated for the jobs I sought, but no one even seems interested in finding out how overqualified I am. Only later will I realize that the want ads are not a reliable measure of the actual jobs available at any particular time. They are, as I should have guessed from Max's comment, the employers' insurance policy against the relentless turnover of the low-wage workforce. Most of the big hotels run ads almost continually, if only to build a supply of applicants to replace the current workers as they drift away or are fired, so finding a job is just a matter of being in the right place at the right time and flexible enough to take whatever is being offered that day. This finally happens to me at one of the big discount chain hotels where I go, as usual, for housekeeping and am sent instead to try out as a waitress at the attached "family restaurant," a dismal spot looking out on a parking garage, which is featuring "Pollish sausage and BBQ sauce" on this 95-degree day. Phillip, the dapper young West Indian who introduces himself as the manager, interviews me with about as much enthusiasm as if he were a clerk processing me for Medicare, the principal questions being what shifts I can work and when I can start. I mutter about being woefully out of practice as a waitress, but he's already on to the uniform: I'm to show up tomorrow wearing black slacks and black shoes; he'll provide the rust-colored polo shirt with "Hearthside," as we'll call the place, embroidered on it, though I might want to wear my own shirt to get to work, ha ha. At the word *tomorrow*, something between fear and indignation rises in my chest. I want to say, "Thank you for your time, sir, but this is just an experiment, you know, not my actual life."

So begins my career at The Hearthside, where for two weeks I work from 2:00 till 10:00 P.M. for $2.43 an hour plus tips.[2] Employees are barred from using the front door, so I enter the first day through the kitchen, where a red-faced man with shoulder-length blond hair is throwing frozen steaks against the wall and yelling, "Fuck this shit!" "That's just Billy," explains Gail, the wiry middle-aged waitress who is assigned to train me. "He's on the rag again"—a condition occasioned, in this instance, by the fact that the cook on the morning shift had forgotten to thaw out the steaks. For the next eight hours, I run after the agile Gail, absorbing bits of instruction along with fragments of personal tragedy. All food must be trayed, and the reason she's so tired today is that she woke up in a cold sweat thinking of her boyfriend, who was killed a few months ago in a scuffle in an upstate prison. No refills on lemonade. And the reason he was in prison is that a few DUIs caught up with him, that's all, could have happened to anyone. Carry the creamers to the table in a "monkey bowl," never in your hand. And after he was gone she spent several months living in her truck, peeing in a plastic pee bottle and reading by candlelight at night, but you can't live in a truck in the summer, since you need to have the windows down, which means anything can get in, from mosquitoes on up.

At least Gail puts to rest any fears I had of appearing overqualified. 10 From the first day on, I find that of all the things that I have left behind, such as home and identity, what I miss the most is competence. Not that I have ever felt 100 percent competent in the writing business, where one day's success augurs nothing at all for the next. But in my writing life, I at least have some notion of *procedure:* do the research, make the outline, rough out a draft, etc. As a server, though, I am beset by requests as if by bees: more iced tea here, catsup over there, a to-go box for table 14, and where are the high chairs, anyway? Of the twenty-seven tables, up to six are usually mine at any time, though on slow afternoons or if Gail is off, I sometimes have the whole place to myself. There is the touch-screen computer-ordering system to master, which I suppose is meant to minimize server-cook contacts but in

2. According to the Fair Labor Standards Act, employers are not required to pay "tipped employees," such as restaurant servers, more than $2.13 an hour in direct wages. However, if the sum of tips plus $2.13 an hour falls below the minimum wage, or $5.15 an hour, the employer is required to make up the difference. This fact was not mentioned by managers or otherwise publicized at either of the restaurants where I worked.

practice requires constant verbal fine-tuning: "That's gravy on the mashed, OK? None on the meatloaf," and so forth. Plus, something I had forgotten in the years since I was eighteen: about a third of a server's job is "side work" invisible to customers—sweeping, scrubbing, slicing, refilling, and restocking. If it isn't all done, every little bit of it, you're going to face the 6:00 P.M. dinner rush defenseless and probably go down in flames. I screw up dozens of times at the beginning, sustained in my shame entirely by Gail's support—"It's OK, baby, everyone does that sometime"—because, to my total surprise and despite the scientific detachment I am doing my best to maintain, I *care*.

The whole thing would be a lot easier if I could just skate through it like Lily Tomlin in one of her waitress skits, but I was raised by the absurd Booker T. Washingtonian precept that says: If you're going to do something, do it well. In fact, "well" isn't good enough by half. Do it better than anyone has ever done it before. Or so said my father, who must have known what he was talking about because he managed to pull himself, and us with him, up from the mile-deep copper mines of Butte to the leafy suburbs of the Northeast, ascending from boiler-makers to martinis before booze beat out ambition. As in most endeavors I have encountered in my life, "doing it better than anyone" is not a reasonable goal. Still, when I wake up at 4 A.M. in my own cold sweat, I am not thinking about the writing deadlines I'm neglecting; I'm thinking of the table where I screwed up the order and one of the kids didn't get his kiddie meal until the rest of the family had moved on to their Key lime pies. That's the other powerful motivation—the customers, or "patients," as I can't help thinking of them on account of the mysterious vulnerability that seems to have left them temporarily unable to feed themselves. After a few days at Hearthside, I feel the service ethic kick in like a shot of oxytocin, the nurturance hormone. The plurality of my customers are hardworking locals—truck drivers, construction workers, even housekeepers from the attached hotel—and I want them to have the closest to a "fine dining" experience that the grubby circumstances will allow. No "you guys" for me; everyone over twelve is "sir" or "ma'am." I ply them with iced tea and coffee refills; I return, midmeal, to inquire how everything is; I doll up their salads with chopped raw mushrooms, summer squash slices, or whatever bits of produce I can find that have survived their sojourn in the cold storage room mold-free.

There is Benny, for example, a short, tight-muscled sewer repairman who cannot even think of eating until he has absorbed a half hour of air-conditioning and ice water. We chat about hyperthermia and electrolytes until he is ready to order some finicky combination like soup of the day, garden salad, and a side of grits. There are the German tourists who are so touched by my pidgin *"Wilkommen"* and *"Ist alles gut?"* that they actually tip. (Europeans, no doubt spoiled by their trade union–ridden, high-wage welfare states, generally do not know that they are supposed to tip. Some restaurants, the Hearthside included, allow servers to "grat" their foreign customers, or add a tip to the bill. Since this amount is added before the customers have a chance to tip or not tip, the practice amounts to an automatic penalty for imperfect English.) There are the two dirt-smudged lesbians, just off from their shift, who are impressed enough by my suave handling of the fly in the piña colada that they take the time to praise me to Stu, the assistant manager. There's Sam, the kindly retired cop who has to plug up his tracheotomy hole with one finger in order to force the cigarette smoke into his lungs.

Sometimes I play with the fantasy that I am a princess who, in penance for some tiny transgression, has undertaken to feed each of her subjects by hand. But the nonprincesses working with me are just as indulgent, even when this means flouting management rules—as to, for example, the number of croutons that can go on a salad (six). "Put on all you want," Gail whispers, "as long as Stu isn't looking." She dips into her own tip money to buy biscuits and gravy for an out-of-work mechanic who's used up all his money on dental surgery, inspiring me to pick up the tab for his pie and milk. Maybe the same high levels of agape can be found throughout the "hospitality industry." I remember the poster decorating one of the apartments I looked at, which said, "If you seek happiness for yourself you will never find it. Only when you seek happiness for others will it come to you," or words to that effect—an odd sentiment, it seemed to me at the time, to find in the dank one-room basement apartment of a bellhop at the Best Western. At Hearthside, we utilize whatever bits of autonomy we have to ply our customers with the illicit calories that signal our love. It is our job as servers to assemble the salads and desserts, pour the dressings, and squirt the whipped cream. We also control the number of butter pats our customers get and the amount of sour cream on their baked potatoes. So if you wonder why Americans are so obese, consider the fact that waitresses both express their humanity and earn their tips through the covert distribution of fats.

Ten days into it, this is beginning to look like a livable lifestyle. I like Gail, who is "looking at fifty," agewise, but moves so fast she can alight in one place and then another without apparently being anywhere between.

Ehrenreich's evidence comes from personal experience. See more examples of this strategy on pp. 294 and 316.

I clown around with Lionel, the teenage Haitian busboy, though we don't have much vocabulary in common, and loiter near the main sink to listen to the older Haitian dishwashers' musical Creole, which sounds, in their rich bass voices, like French on testosterone. I bond with Timmy, the fourteen-year-old white kid who buses at night, by telling him I don't like people putting their baby seats right on the tables: it makes the baby look too much like a side dish. He snickers delightedly and in return, on a slow night, starts telling me the plots of all the *Jaws* movies (which are perennial favorites in the shark-ridden Keys): "She looks around, and the water-skier isn't there anymore, then SNAP! The whole boat goes . . ."

I especially like Joan, the svelte fortyish hostess, who turns out to be a   15
militant feminist, pulling me aside one day to explain that "men run every-thing—we don't have a chance unless we stick together." Accordingly, she backs me up when I get overpowered on the floor, and in return I give her a chunk of my tips or stand guard while she sneaks off for an unauthorized cigarette break. We all admire her for standing up to Billy and telling him, after some of his usual nastiness about the female server class, to "shut the fuck up." I even warm up to Billy when, on a slow night and to make up for a particularly unwarranted attack on my abilities, or so I imagine, he tells me about his glory days as a young man at "coronary school" in Brooklyn, where he dated a knockout Puerto Rican chick—or do you say "culinary"?

I finish up every night at 10:00 or 10:30, depending on how much side work I've been able to get done during the shift, and cruise home to the tapes I snatched at random when I left my real home—Marianne Faithfull, Tracy Chapman, Enigma, King Sunny Adé, Violent Femmes—just drained enough for the music to set my cranium resonating, but hardly dead. Midnight snack is Wheat Thins and Monterey Jack, accompanied by cheap white wine on ice and whatever AMC has to offer. To bed by 1:30 or 2:00, up at 9:00 or 10:00, read for an hour while my uniform whirls around in the landlord's washing machine, and then it's another eight hours spent following Mao's central instruction, as laid out in the Little Red Book, which was: Serve the people.

I could drift along like this, in some dreamy proletarian idyll, except for two things. One is management. If I have kept this subject to the margins so far it is because I still flinch to think that I spent all those weeks under the surveil-lance of men (and later women) whose job it was to monitor my behavior for signs of sloth, theft, drug abuse, or worse. Not that managers and especially "assistant managers" in low-wage settings like this are exactly the class enemy. Mostly, in the restaurant business, they are former cooks still capable of pinch-hitting in the kitchen, just as in hotels they are likely to be former clerks, and paid a salary of only about $400 a week. But everyone knows they have crossed over to the other side, which is, crudely put, corporate as opposed to human. Cooks want to prepare tasty meals, servers want to serve them graciously, but managers are there for only one reason—to make sure that money is made for some theoretical entity, the corporation, which exists far away in Chicago or New York, if a corporation can be said to have a physical existence at all. Reflecting on her career, Gail tells me ruefully that she swore, years ago, never to work for a corporation again. "They don't cut you no slack. You give and you give and they take."

Managers can sit—for hours at a time if they want—but it's their job to see that no one else ever does, even when there's nothing to do, and this is why, for servers, slow times can be as exhausting as rushes. You start dragging out each little chore because if the manager on duty catches you in an idle moment he will give you something far nastier to do. So I wipe, I clean, I consolidate catsup bottles and recheck the cheesecake supply, even tour the tables to make sure the customer evaluation forms are all standing perkily in their places—wondering all the time how many calories I burn in these strictly theatrical exercises. In desperation, I even take the desserts out of their glass display case and freshen them up with whipped cream and bright new maraschino cherries; anything to look busy. When, on a particularly dead afternoon, Stu finds me glancing at a *USA Today* a customer has left behind, he assigns me to vacuum the entire floor with the broken vacuum cleaner, which has a handle only two feet long, and the only way to do that without incurring orthopedic damage is to proceed from spot to spot on your knees.

On my first Friday at Hearthside there is a "mandatory meeting for all restaurant employees," which I attend, eager for insight into our overall marketing strategy and the niche (your basic Ohio cuisine with a tropical twist?) we aim to inhabit. But there is no "we" at this meeting. Phillip, our top manager except for an occasional "consultant" sent out by corporate headquarters, opens it with a sneer: "The break room—it's disgusting. Butts in the ashtrays, newspapers lying around, crumbs." This windowless little room, which also houses the time clock for the entire hotel, is where we stash our bags and civilian clothes and take our half-hour meal breaks. But a break room is not a right, he tells us, it can be taken away. We should also know that the lockers in the break room and whatever is in them can be searched at any time. Then comes gossip; there has been gossip; gossip (which seems to mean employees talking among themselves) must stop. Off-duty employees are henceforth barred from eating at the restaurant, because "other servers gather around them and gossip." When Phillip has exhausted his agenda of rebukes, Joan complains about the condition of the ladies' room and I throw in my two bits about the vacuum cleaner. But I don't see any backup coming from my fellow servers, each of whom has slipped into her own personal funk; Gail, my role model, stares sorrowfully at a point six inches from her nose. The meeting ends when Andy, one of the cooks, gets up, muttering about breaking up his day off for this almighty bullshit.

Just four days later we are suddenly summoned into the kitchen at 3:30 20 P.M., even though there are live tables on the floor. We all—about ten of us— stand around Phillip, who announces grimly that there has been a report of some "drug activity" on the night shift and that, as a result, we are now to be a "drug-free" workplace, meaning that all new hires will be tested and possibly also current employees on a random basis. I am glad that this part of the kitchen is so dark because I find myself blushing as hard as if I had been caught toking up in the ladies' room myself: I haven't been treated this way—lined up in the corridor, threatened with locker searches, peppered with carelessly aimed accusations—since at least junior high school. Back on the floor, Joan cracks, "Next they'll be telling us we can't have *sex* on the job." When I ask Stu what happened to inspire the crackdown, he just mutters about "management decisions" and takes the opportunity to upbraid Gail and me for being too generous with the rolls. From now on there's to be only one per customer and it goes out with the dinner, not with the salad. He's also been riding the cooks, prompting Andy to come out of the kitchen and observe—with the serenity of a man whose customary implement is a butcher knife—that "Stu has a death wish today."

Later in the evening, the gossip crystallizes around the theory that Stu is himself the drug culprit, that he uses the restaurant phone to order up marijuana and sends one of the late servers out to fetch it for him. The server was caught and she may have ratted out Stu, at least enough to cast some suspicion on him, thus accounting for his pissy behavior. Who knows? Personally, I'm ready to believe anything bad about Stu, who serves no evident function and presumes too much on our common ethnicity, sidling up to me one night to engage in a little nativism directed at the Haitian immigrants: "I feel like I'm the foreigner here. They're taking over the country." Still later that evening, the drug in question escalates to crack. Lionel, the busboy, entertains us for the rest of the shift by standing just behind Stu's back and sucking deliriously on an imaginary joint or maybe a pipe.

The other problem, in addition to the less-than-nurturing management style, is that this job shows no sign of being financially viable. You might imagine, from a comfortable distance, that people who live, year in and year out, on $6 to $10 an hour have discovered some survival stratagems unknown to the middle class. But no. It's not hard to get my coworkers talking about their living situations, because housing, in almost every case, is the principal source of disruption in their lives, the first thing they fill you in on when they arrive for their shifts. After a week, I have compiled the following survey:

> Gail is sharing a room in a well-known downtown flophouse for $250 a week. Her roommate, a male friend, has begun hitting on her, driving her nuts, but the rent would be impossible alone.

> Claude, the Haitian cook, is desperate to get out of the two-room apartment he shares with his girlfriend and two other, unrelated people. As far as I can determine, the other Haitian men live in similarly crowded situations.

> Annette, a twenty-year-old server who is six months pregnant and abandoned by her boyfriend, lives with her mother, a postal clerk.

> Marianne, who is a breakfast server, and her boyfriend are paying $170 a week for a one-person trailer.

> Billy, who at $10 an hour is the wealthiest of us, lives in the trailer he owns, paying only the $400-a-month lot fee.

> The other white cook, Andy, lives on his dry-docked boat, which, as far as I can tell from his loving descriptions, can't be more than twenty feet long. He offers to take me out on it once it's repaired, but the offer comes with inquiries as to my marital status, so I do not follow up on it.

> Tina, another server, and her husband are paying $60 a night for a room in the Days Inn. This is because they have no car and the Days Inn is in walking distance of the Hearthside. When Marianne is tossed out of her trailer for subletting (which is against trailer

park rules), she leaves her boyfriend and moves in with Tina and her husband.

Joan, who had fooled me with her numerous and tasteful outfits (hostesses wear their own clothes), lives in a van parked behind a shopping center at night and showers in Tina's motel room. The clothes are from thrift shops.[3]

It strikes me, in my middle-class solipsism, that there is gross improvidence in some of these arrangements. When Gail and I are wrapping silverware in napkins—the only task for which we are permitted to sit—she tells me she is thinking of escaping from her roommate by moving into the Days Inn herself. I am astounded: how she can even think of paying $40 to $60 a day? But if I was afraid of sounding like a social worker, I have come out just sounding like a fool. She squints at me in disbelief: "And where am I supposed to get a month's rent and a month's deposit for an apartment?" I'd been feeling pretty smug about my $500 efficiency, but of course it was made possible only by the $1,300 I had allotted myself for start-up costs when I began my low-wage life: $1,000 for the first month's rent and deposit, $100 for initial groceries and cash in my pocket, $200 stuffed away for emergencies. In poverty, as in certain propositions in physics, starting conditions are everything.

There are no secret economies that nourish the poor; on the contrary, there are a host of special costs. If you can't put up the two months' rent you need to secure an apartment, you end up paying through the nose for a room by the week. If you have only a room, with a hot plate at best, you can't save by cooking up huge lentil stews that can be frozen for the week ahead. You eat fast food or the hot dogs and Styrofoam cups of soup that can be microwaved in a convenience store. If you have no money for health insurance—and the Hearthside's niggardly plan kicks in only after three months—you go without routine care or prescription drugs and end up paying the price. Gail, for example, was doing fine, healthwise anyway, until she ran out of money for estrogen pills. She is supposed to be on the company health plan by now, but they claim to have lost her application form and to be beginning

---

3. I could find no statistics on the number of employed people living in cars or vans, but according to a 1997 report of the National Coalition for the Homeless, "Myths and Facts about Homelessness," nearly one-fifth of all homeless people (in twenty-nine cities across the nation) are employed in full- or part-time jobs.

the paperwork all over again. So she spends $9 a pop for pills to control the migraines she wouldn't have, she insists, if her estrogen supplements were covered. Similarly, Marianne's boyfriend lost his job as a roofer because he missed so much time after getting a cut on his foot for which he couldn't afford the prescribed antibiotic.

My own situation, when I sit down to assess it after two weeks of work, would not be much better if this were my actual life. The seductive thing about waitressing is that you don't have to wait for payday to feel a few bills in your pocket, and my tips usually cover meals and gas, plus something left over to stuff into the kitchen drawer I use as a bank. But as the tourist business slows in the summer heat, I sometimes leave work with only $20 in tips (the gross is higher, but servers share about 15 percent of their tips with the busboys and bartenders). With wages included, this amounts to about the minimum wage of $5.15 an hour. The sum in the drawer is piling up but at the present rate of accumulation will be more than $100 short of my rent when the end of the month comes around. Nor can I see any expenses to cut. True, I haven't gone the lentil stew route yet, but that's because I don't have a large cooking pot, potholders, or a ladle to stir with (which would cost a total of about $30 at Kmart, somewhat less at a thrift store), not to mention onions, carrots, and the indispensable bay leaf. I do make my lunch almost every day—usually some slow-burning, high-protein combo like frozen chicken patties with melted cheese on top and canned pinto beans on the side. Dinner is at the Hearthside, which offers its employees a choice of BLT, fish sandwich, or hamburger for only $2. The burger lasts longest, especially if it's heaped with gut-puckering jalapeños, but by midnight my stomach is growling again.

So unless I want to start using my car as a residence, I have to find a second or an alternative job. I call all the hotels I'd filled out housekeeping applications at weeks ago—the Hyatt, Holiday Inn, Econo Lodge, HoJo's, Best Western, plus a half dozen locally run guest houses. Nothing. Then I start making the rounds again, wasting whole mornings waiting for some assistant manager to show up, even dipping into places so creepy that the frontdesk clerk greets you from behind bullet-proof glass and sells pints of liquor over the counter. But either someone has exposed my real-life housekeeping habits—which are, shall we say, mellow—or I am at the wrong end of some infallible ethnic equation: most, but by no means all, of the working housekeepers I see on my job searches are African Americans, Spanish-speaking, or refugees from the Central European post-Communist world, while serv-

25

ers are almost invariably white and monolingually English-speaking. When I finally get a positive response, I have been identified once again as server material. Jerry's—again, not the real name—which is part of a well-known national chain and physically attached here to another budget hotel, is ready to use me at once. The prospect is both exciting and terrifying because, with about the same number of tables and counter seats, Jerry's attracts three or four times the volume of customers as the gloomy old Hearthside.

Thinking about the Text

1. Barbara Ehrenreich passes back and forth in her narrative between the voice of the waitress describing her own reality and the voice of the writer who has assumed a role for investigative purposes—and of course both voices are hers. How well do those voices combine to present a cohesive narrative? Explain your answer, presenting examples from the text.

2. How typical do you suppose Ehrenreich's experience is of people who wait tables at "family restaurants" (8)? Consider evidence from your own experience and that of people you know, either as employees or as customers at such restaurants.

3. On radio and TV, in movies, and in other public forums, people like Ehrenreich's coworkers and customers, with low incomes and low social status, are often belittled and ridiculed, on the one hand, or romanticized and idealized, on the other, whether subtly or openly. One of the strengths of Ehrenreich's book is the respect with which she describes people just the way they are. Identify three **EXAMPLES** of respectful description.

4. What is the main point that Ehrenreich is making in her narrative? Where is this point most clearly stated? Do you think she made it convincingly? Why or why not?

5. Write a **NARRATIVE** describing the people and places of your daily life. If you have (or have had) a job, you may want to center your narrative there. Include plentiful **DESCRIPTIVE** details; try to present the people as vividly (and respectfully!) as you can. Make your main point something that you have learned as a result of your contact with the people you describe.

The Inner Corset

LAURA FRASER

ONCE UPON A TIME, a man with a thick gold watch swaying from a big, round paunch was the very picture of American prosperity and vigor. Accordingly, a hundred years ago, a beautiful woman had plump cheeks and arms, and she wore a corset and even a bustle to emphasize her full, substantial hips. Women were *sexy* if they were heavy. In those days, Americans knew that a layer of fat was a sign that you could afford to eat well and that you stood a better chance of fighting off infectious diseases than most people. If you were a woman, having that extra adipose blanket also meant that you were probably fertile, and warm to cuddle up next to on chilly nights.

Between the 1880s and 1920s, that pleasant image of fat thoroughly changed in the United States. Some began early on to hint that fat was a health risk. In 1894, Woods Hutchinson, a medical professor who wrote for women's magazines, defended fat against this new point of view. "Adipose," he wrote, "while often pictured as a veritable Frankenstein, born of

LAURA FRASER is a San Francisco–based writer whose work has appeared in such diverse publications as *Mother Jones, Food and Wine, Redbook, Salon,* and the *New York Times.* She focuses mainly on women's health issues, cultural aspects of food, and travel. This piece, adapted from Fraser's book *Losing It: America's Obsession with Weight and the Industry That Feeds on It* (1997), was published in 2009 in the anthology *The Fat Studies Reader.*

and breeding disease, sure to ride its possessor to death sooner or later, is really a most harmless, healthful, innocent tissue" (Hutchinson, 1894, p. 395). Hutchinson reassured his *Cosmopolitan* readers that fat was not only benign, but also attractive, and that if a poll of beautiful women were taken in any city, there would be at least three times as many plump ones as slender ones. He advised them that no amount of starving or exercise—which were just becoming popular as means of weight control—would change more than 10 percent of a person's body size anyway. "The fat man tends to remain fat, the thin woman to stay thin—and both in perfect health—in spite of everything they can do," he said in that article.

But by 1926, Hutchinson, who was by then a past president of the American Academy of Medicine, had to defend fat against fashion, too, and he was showing signs of strain. "In this present onslaught upon one of the most peaceable, useful and law-abiding of all our tissues," he told readers of the *Saturday Evening Post*, "fashion has apparently the backing of grave physicians, of food reformers and physical trainers, and even of great insurance companies, all chanting in unison the new commandment of fashion: 'Thou shalt be thin!'" (Hutchinson, 1926, p. 60).

The thin ideal that developed in the United States from the 1880s to 1920s can be traced through the evolution of three ideal types (*from left to right*): the plump Victorian woman, the athletic but curvaceous Gibson Girl, and the boyishly straight-bodied flapper.

Hutchinson mourned this trend, and was dismayed that young girls were ridding themselves of their roundness and plumpness of figure. He tried to understand the new view that people took toward fat: "It is an outward and visible sign of an inward and spiritual disgrace, of laziness, of self-indulgence," he explained in that article, but he remained unconvinced. Instead, he longed for a more cheerful period in the not-so-distant past when a little fat never hurt anyone, and he darkly warned that some physicians were deliberately underfeeding girls and young women solely for the purpose of giving them a more svelte figure. "The longed-for slender and boyish figure is becoming a menace," Hutchinson (1926, p. 60) wrote, "not only to the present, but also the future generations."

And so it would. But why did the fashion for plumpness change so dramatically during those years? What happened that caused Americans to alter their tastes, not only to admire thinner figures for a time, but for the next century, culminating in fin de siècle extremes of thinness, where women's magazines in the 1990s would print ads featuring gaunt models side-by-side with photo essays on anorexia?

Many things were happening at once, and with dizzying speed. Foremost was a changing economy: In the late 1800s, for the first time, ample amounts of food were available to more and more people who had to do less and less work to eat. The agricultural economy, based on family farms and home workshops, shifted to an industrial one. A huge influx of immigrants—many of them genetically shorter and rounder than the earlier American settlers—fueled the industrial machine. People moved to cities to do factory work and service jobs, stopped growing their own food, and relied more on store-bought goods. Large companies began to process food products, distribute them via railroads, and use refrigeration to keep perishables fresh. Food became more accessible and convenient to all but the poorest families. People who once had too little to eat now had plenty, and those who had a tendency to put on weight began to do so. When it became possible for people of modest means to become plump, being fat no longer was a sign of prestige. Well-to-do Americans of northern European extraction wanted to be able to distinguish themselves, physically and racially, from stockier immigrants. As anthropologist Margaret Mackenzie notes, the status symbols flipped: it became chic to be thin and all too ordinary to be overweight (personal communication, June 12, 1996).

In this new environment, older cultural undercurrents suspicious of fat began to surface. Europeans had long considered slenderness a sign of class distinction and finer sensibilities, and Americans began to follow suit. In Europe, during the late 18th and early 19th centuries, many artists and writers—the poets John Keats and Percy Bysshe Shelley, and authors Emily Brontë, Edgar Allan Poe, and Anton Chekhov—had tuberculosis, which made them sickly thin. Members of the upper classes believed that having tuberculosis, and being slender itself, were signs that one possessed a delicate, intellectual, and superior nature. "For snobs and parvenus and social climbers, TB was the one index of being genteel, delicate, [and] sensitive," writes essayist Susan Sontag in *Illness as Metaphor* (1977, p. 28). "It was glamorous to look sickly." So interested was the poet Lord Byron in looking as fashionably ill as the other Romantic poets that he embarked on a series of obsessive diets, consuming only biscuits and water, or vinegar and potatoes, and succeeded in becoming quite thin. Byron—who, at five feet six inches tall, with a clubfoot that prevented him from walking much, weighed over two hundred pounds in his youth—disdained fat in others. "A woman," he wrote, "should never be seen eating or drinking, unless it be *lobster salad* and *champagne,* the only truly feminine and becoming viands" (quoted in Schwartz, 1986, p. 38). Aristocratic European women, thrilled with the romantic figure that Byron cut, took his diet advice and despaired of appearing fat. Aristo-cratic Americans, trying to imitate Europeans, adopted their enthusiasm for champagne and slenderness.

Americans believed that it was not only a sign of class to be thin, but also a sign of morality. There was a long tradition in American culture that suggested that indulging the body and its appetites was immoral, and that denying the flesh was a sure way to become closer to God. Puritans such as the minister Cotton Mather frequently fasted to prove their worthiness and to cleanse themselves of their sins. Benjamin Franklin, in his *Poor Richard's Almanack,* chided his readers to eat lightly to please not only God, but also a new divinity, Reason: "Wouldst thou enjoy a long life, a healthy Body, and a Vigorous Mind, and be acquainted also with the wonderful works of God? Labour in the first place to bring thy Appetite into Subjection to Reason" (Franklin, 1970, p. 238). Franklin's attitude toward food not only reveals a puritanical distrust of appetite as overly sensual, but also pre-saged diets that would attempt to bring eating in line with rational, scien-tific calculations. "The Difficulty lies, in finding out an exact Measure;" he wrote, "but eat for Necessity, not Pleasure, for Lust knows not where Neces-sity ends" (p. 238).

At the end of the 19th century, as Hutchinson observed, science was also helping to shape the new slender ideal. Physicians came to believe that they were able to arrive at an exact measure of human beings; they could count calories, weigh people on scales, calculate "ideal" weights, and advise those who deviated from that ideal that they could change themselves. Physicians were both following and encouraging the trend for thinness. In the 1870s, after all, when plumpness was in vogue, physicians had encour-aged people to *gain* weight. Two of the most distinguished doctors of the age, George Beard and S. Weir Mitchell, believed that excessive thinness caused American women to succumb to a wide variety of nervous disorders, and that a large number of fat cells was absolutely necessary to achieve a balanced personality (Banner, 1983, p. 113). But when the plump figure fell from favor, physicians found new theories to support the new fashion. They hastily developed treatments—such as thyroid, arsenic, and strychnine—to prescribe to their increasing numbers of weight loss patients, many of whom were not exactly corpulent, but who were more than willing to part with their pennies along with their pounds.

As the 20th century got underway, other cultural changes made slen- 10
derness seem desirable. When many women ventured out of their homes

Much of the strength of this report comes from its sources. See Ch. 22 on incor-porating sources in your own writing.

and away from their strict roles as mothers, they left behind the plump and reproductive physique, which began to seem old-fashioned next to a thinner, freer, more modern body. The new consumer culture encouraged the trend toward thinness with fashion illustrations and ads featuring slim models; advertisers learned early to offer women an unattainable dream of thinness and beauty to sell more products. In short, a cultural obsession with weight became firmly established in the United States when several disparate factors that favored a desire for thinness—economic status symbols, morality, medicine, modernity, changing women's roles, and consumerism—all collided at once.

Thinness is, at its heart, a peculiarly American preoccupation. Europeans admire slenderness, but without our Puritanism they have more relaxed and moderate attitudes about food, eating, and body size (the British are most like us in both being heavy and fixating on weight loss schemes). In countries where people do not have quite enough to eat, and where women remain in traditional roles, plumpness is still widely admired. Other westernized countries have developed a slender ideal, but for the most part they have imported it from the United States. No other culture suffers from the same wild anxieties about weight, dieting, and exercise as we do because they do not share our history.

The thin ideal that developed in the United States from the 1880s to 1920s was not just a momentary shift in fashion; it was a monumental turning point in the way that women's bodies were appraised by men and experienced by women. The change can be traced through the evolution of three ideal types: the plump Victorian woman, the athletic but curvaceous Gibson Girl, and the boyishly straight-bodied flapper. By 1930, American women knew how very important it was for them to be thin. From then on, despite moments when voluptuousness was admired again (e.g., Marilyn Monroe), American women could never be too thin.

Note

This chapter is adapted from the book *Losing It: America's Obsession with Weight and the Industry That Feeds on It* (New York: Dutton, 1997). © Laura Fraser. Hillel Schwartz's *Never Satisfied* provided a good deal of background material for this chapter, and is an excellent resource on the history of dieting. Lois Banner's meticulously researched *American Beauty* traces American beauty ideals, and was also very helpful in preparing this chapter.

References

Banner, L. (1983). *American Beauty.* Chicago: University of Chicago Press.

Franklin, B. (1970). *The Complete Poor Richard Almanacks,* Vol. 1: *1733–1747.* Barre, MA: Imprint Society.

Hutchinson, W. (1894, June). "Fat and Its Follies." *Cosmopolitan.* 395.

Hutchinson, W. (1926, August 21). "Fat and Fashion." *The Saturday Evening Post,* 60.

Schwartz, H. (1986). *Never Satisfied: A Cultural History of Diets, Fantasies, and Fat.* New York: The Free Press.

Sontag, S. (1977). *Illness as Metaphor.* New York: Farrar, Straus and Giroux.

Thinking about the Text

1. A **REPORT** should have a confident **TONE** that informs rather than argues. How well does Laura Fraser satisfy that requirement? What examples from the article support your answer?

2. The dangers of obesity and efforts to combat it are prominent in the daily diet, so to speak, of virtually every general-interest American newspaper and magazine today. Fraser is certainly not arguing in favor of obesity; still, a historical point of view such as the one she presents is rarely provided in these journalistic contexts. How do you account for the omission? Is it simply an oversight? Is there some marketing strategy involved? Are Americans simply uninterested in past perspectives, at least on this issue? Would more knowledge about this history affect our perceptions of body shape? Speculate on the **CAUSES** of this situation. Why is the history of fat in the United States so little known?

3. The report cites six sources that provide relevant information. Find five citations of source material in the article, and look at how Fraser integrates the material into her text. What techniques does she use? How smooth is the integration? Make sure that your examples include both direct **QUOTATIONS** and **PARAPHRASES**.

4. Fraser explains the reemergence among Americans of an older European association of thinness with intelligence and "finer sensibilities" (7). How did that association come about? To what extent is it still active today? Provide contemporary **EVIDENCE** to support your response.

5. Benjamin Franklin is one of our nation's best-loved and most often quoted philosophers and moral leaders. His practical advice, such as "A stitch in time saves nine" or "A penny saved is a penny earned," is familiar to most Americans two centuries after his lifetime, whether they follow it or not. Fraser quotes Franklin advising that one should eat for necessity and not for pleasure. What would happen in the United States if this suggestion were taken more seriously? What would the economic consequences be? The social consequences? Write an essay in which you speculate on the changes that might occur if Americans suddenly stopped eating for pleasure.

Why *Glee* Ain't What It Used to Be

MATTHEW GILBERT

WHAT'S THE STORY, *GLEE*? Or, more accurately, *where* is the story? Fox's Tuesday night musical hit has all but chucked out story line this year, in favor of weekly lessons in tolerance, love, God, and big-time pop-artist promotion. The creators have turned their show from a sweet, twisted teen melodrama honoring the power of music into a slick soapbox-jukebox with one eye on TV ratings and the other on record sales.

Yup, I'm terribly disappointed in *Glee*, since it has become such a shrieky sensation. I certainly don't mind finding a message buried in a TV series; I suppose that every show is bent around some point of view. The *Seinfeld* writers were committed to "no learning," but their satirical thinking about urban narcissism shone through nonetheless. And I like much of what *Glee* stands for; it was saying "It Gets Better" before that became a catchphrase in response to teen-bullying suicides. The show, tonight at 8, has a good heart when it comes to issues of acceptance and diversity.

But *Glee* has given up on any semblance of subtlety and storytelling art. At this point, the show is a collection of Big Learning Scenes, writ-

MATTHEW GILBERT has written hundreds of reviews since 1998, when he became TV critic for the *Boston Globe* newspaper. His favorite programs range from the *Sopranos* to the *Office*, and he brings a light and quirky point of view to his work. This review appeared in the *Globe* on October 26, 2010, at the beginning of the second season of *Glee*.

ten to give the songs some vague narrative sense. I laugh at many of the comic lines—dumb Brittany, for instance, telling wheelchair-bound Artie she'd never made eye contact with him because "for a while I thought you were a robot." But the scripts rarely move anything significant forward. The dialogue doesn't develop character so much as hammer it home. Almost every line that comes out of Rachel's mouth is, essentially, "I am a diva—oh, and I am also a diva. I guess I shouldn't be such a diva." The writing is an afterthought on *Glee,* once the big theme and the songs have been chosen.

Indeed, song choice has become king on *Glee* as soundtrack sales have begun to break records. A few weeks ago, *Glee* became bigger than the Beatles on the Billboard charts, with 75 charting singles beating out the Beatles' 71. The promotion for the show is now all about which artist's oeuvre is going to be celebrated—Madonna, Lady Gaga, Britney Spears (whose music inspired one of the series' most nonsensical episodes so far). Rumors of a post–Super Bowl Springsteen episode have faded, but a Taylor Swift hour may be in the works. In this way, *Glee* comes off like a scripted *American Idol,* which also has single-artist episodes and has made a mega-industry out of cover tunes.

Single-theme and single-artist episodes, which are largely self-con- 5
tained, also help *Glee* in the ratings. Serialized storytelling is a risk on TV, because new viewers are reticent to jump into an ongoing plot once it has started. Serialized shows don't grow in the ratings as easily as shows with self-standing episodes. Also, hourlong shows with self-standing episodes score higher ratings when they repeat. More people will watch a repeat of *Law & Order* than of, say, *ER.* Jettisoning the story lines can only help the ratings of *Glee,* which already does remarkably well among young viewers. Now, you've got "the Britney Spears episode," and "the religion episode," instead of just another episode of the ongoing *Glee* story.

And, of course, good storytelling isn't easy. In a recent interview with E!, *Raising Hope* creator Greg Garcia talked about the pressure of coming up with plots: "I get knots in my stomach thinking about stories," he said, "because they are the hardest thing to come up with. You've just got to pull them out of thin air." But the answer isn't to just throw out the plot and jump headlong into garish chaos. Initially, *Glee* had as much intimate character development as it had broad musical theater. Now, the broadness has taken over. The song performances are all big numbers, and they are rendered especially artificial with their plastic production

Good storytelling may not be easy, but Ch. 8 provides some help.

A scene from the mash-up competition in season one's "Vitamin D" episode.

values. There's none of the imperfection you might expect from a real glee club.

Glee is now a phenomenon more than a TV high school story, and I'm sorry for that. It has become a powerful, promotional machine, long on hype and short on the human feeling—the glee—that once made it so addictive.

Thinking about the Text

1. Matthew Gilbert mentions several **CRITERIA** with which he evaluates a TV program such as *Glee*. One of these, for example, is that a program should have a good plot. Name two more of Gilbert's review criteria.

2. We all know that the high school in *Glee* is not at all typical or even terribly realistic, yet it must have enough realistic touches to be recognizable. Would you have liked to go that school? Why or why not?

3. Although Gilbert is very clear that he doesn't like the changes he sees in the new season of *Glee*, he explains in some detail the producers' probable reasoning for the changes. Why might he have done that in his review?

4. The program's name, *Glee*, is a single word with multiple meanings in everyday English. How does Gilbert echo the name of the program in order to establish his main **ARGUMENT**?

5. Are there any TV programs that you liked more in previous seasons than you do this year? Choose a program that you feel has changed for the worse and write a **REVIEW**. You will want to compare the past and present seasons according to clear **CRITERIA** that you establish.

Hidden Intellectualism

GERALD GRAFF

EVERYONE KNOWS SOME YOUNG PERSON who is impressively "street smart" but does poorly in school. What a waste, we think, that one who is so intelligent about so many things in life seems unable to apply that intelligence to academic work. What doesn't occur to us, though, is that schools and colleges might be at fault for missing the opportunity to tap into such street smarts and channel them into good academic work.

Nor do we consider one of the major reasons why schools and colleges overlook the intellectual potential of street smarts: the fact that we associate those street smarts with anti-intellectual concerns. We associate the educated life, the life of the mind, too narrowly and exclusively with subjects and texts that we consider inherently weighty and academic. We assume that it's possible to wax intellectual about Plato, Shakespeare, the French Revolution, and nuclear fission, but not about cars, dating, fashion, sports, TV, or video games.

The trouble with this assumption is that no necessary connection has ever been established between any text or subject and the educational depth

GERALD GRAFF, a professor of English and education at the University of Illinois at Chicago, is best known for his books *Professing Literature: An Institutional History*, *Beyond the Culture Wars: How Teaching the Conflicts Can Revitalize American Education*, *Clueless in Academe: How Schooling Obscures the Life of the Mind*, and (with Cathy Birkenstein) *"They Say / I Say": The Moves That Matter in Academic Writing*. This essay was written for *Clueless* in 2003.

and weight of the discussion it can generate. Real intellectuals turn any subject, however lightweight it may seem, into grist for their mill through the thoughtful questions they bring to it, whereas a dullard will find a way to drain the interest out of the richest subject. That's why a George Orwell writing on the cultural meanings of penny postcards is infinitely more substantial than the cogitations of many professors on Shakespeare or globalization.

Students do need to read models of intellectually challenging writing—and Orwell is a great one—if they are to become intellectuals themselves. But they would be more prone to take on intellectual identities if we encouraged them to do so at first on subjects that interest them rather than ones that interest us.

I offer my own adolescent experience as a case in point. Until I entered ⁵ college, I hated books and cared only for sports. The only reading I cared to do or could do was sports magazines, on which I became hooked, becoming a regular reader of *Sport* magazine in the late forties, *Sports Illustrated* when it began publishing in 1954, and the annual magazine guides to professional baseball, football, and basketball. I also loved the sports novels for boys of John R. Tunis and Clair Bee and autobiographies of sports stars like Joe DiMaggio's *Lucky to Be a Yankee* and Bob Feller's *Strikeout Story*. In short, I was your typical teenage anti-intellectual—or so I believed for a long time. I have recently come to think, however, that my preference for sports over schoolwork was not anti-intellectualism so much as intellectualism by other means.

In the Chicago neighborhood I grew up in, which had become a melting pot after World War II, our block was solidly middle class, but just a block away—doubtless concentrated there by the real estate companies—were African Americans, Native Americans, and "hillbilly" whites who had recently fled postwar joblessness in the South and Appalachia. Negotiating this class boundary was a tricky matter. On the one hand, it was necessary to maintain the boundary between "clean-cut" boys like me and working-class "hoods," as we called them, which meant that it was good to be openly smart in a bookish sort of way. On the other hand, I was desperate for the approval of the hoods, whom I encountered daily on the playing field and in the neighborhood, and for this purpose it was not at all good to be book-smart. The hoods would turn on you if they sensed you were putting on airs over them: "Who you lookin' at, smart ass?" as a leather-jacketed youth once said to me as he relieved me of my pocket change along with my self-respect.

I grew up torn, then, between the need to prove I was smart and the fear

Graff frames his position as a response to attitudes he has observed. See pp. 67–70 on responding to what others say.

of a beating if I proved it too well;
between the need not to jeopar-
dize my respectable future and
the need to impress the hoods. As
I lived it, the conflict came down
to a choice between being physically tough and being verbal. For
a boy in my neighborhood and
elementary school, only being
"tough" earned you complete
legitimacy. I still recall endless,
complicated debates in this period with my closest pals over
who was "the toughest guy in

The symbolic triumph of geek over jock: Marilyn Monroe marries Arthur Miller in 1956.

the school." If you were less than negligible as a fighter, as I was, you settled
for the next best thing, which was to be inarticulate, carefully hiding telltale
marks of literacy like correct grammar and pronunciation.

In one way, then, it would be hard to imagine an adolescence more
thoroughly anti-intellectual than mine. Yet in retrospect, I see that it's more
complicated, that I and the 1950s themselves were not simply hostile toward
intellectualism, but divided and ambivalent. When Marilyn Monroe married
the playwright Arthur Miller in 1956 after divorcing the retired baseball star
Joe DiMaggio, the symbolic triumph of geek over jock suggested the way the
wind was blowing. Even Elvis, according to his biographer Peter Guralnick,
turns out to have supported Adlai over Ike in the presidential election of 1956.
"I don't dig the intellectual bit," he told reporters. "But I'm telling you, man, he
knows the most."

Though I too thought I did not "dig the intellectual bit," I see now that I
was unwittingly in training for it. The germs had actually been planted in the
seemingly philistine debates about which boys were the toughest. I see now
that in the interminable analysis of sports teams, movies, and toughness that
my friends and I engaged in—a type of analysis, needless to say, that the real
toughs would never have stooped to—I was already betraying an allegiance
to the egghead world. I was practicing being an intellectual before I knew
that was what I wanted to be.

It was in these discussions with friends about toughness and sports,   10
I think, and in my reading of sports books and magazines, that I began to
learn the rudiments of the intellectual life: how to make an argument, weigh

different kinds of evidence, move between particulars and generalizations, summarize the views of others, and enter a conversation about ideas. It was in reading and arguing about sports and toughness that I experienced what it felt like to propose a generalization, restate and respond to a counterargument, and perform other intellectualizing operations, including composing the kind of sentences I am writing now.

Only much later did it dawn on me that the sports world was more compelling than school because it was *more intellectual than school,* not less. Sports after all was full of challenging arguments, debates, problems for analysis, and intricate statistics that you could care about, as school conspicuously was not. I believe that street smarts beat out book smarts in our culture not because street smarts are nonintellectual, as we generally suppose, but because they satisfy an intellectual thirst more thoroughly than school culture, which seems pale and unreal.

They also satisfy the thirst for community. When you entered sports debates, you became part of a community that was not limited to your family and friends, but was national and public. Whereas schoolwork isolated you from others, the pennant race or Ted Williams's .400 batting average was something you could talk about with people you had never met. Sports introduced you not only to a culture steeped in argument, but to a public argument culture that transcended the personal. I can't blame my schools for failing to make intellectual culture resemble the Super Bowl, but I do fault them for failing to learn anything from the sports and entertainment worlds about how to organize and represent intellectual culture, how to exploit its gamelike element and turn it into arresting public spectacle that might have competed more successfully for my youthful attention.

For here is another thing that never dawned on me and is still kept hidden from students, with tragic results: that the real intellectual world, the one that existed in the big world beyond school, is organized very much like the world of team sports, with rival texts, rival interpretations and evaluations of texts, rival theories of why they should be read and taught, and elaborate team competitions in which "fans" of writers, intellectual systems, methodologies, and -isms contend against each other.

To be sure, school contained plenty of competition, which became more invidious as one moved up the ladder (and has become even more so today with the advent of high-stakes testing). In this competition, points were scored not by making arguments, but by a show of information or vast reading, by grade-grubbing, or other forms of oneupmanship. School competition, in short, reproduced the less attractive features of sports culture without those that create close bonds and community.

And in distancing themselves from anything as enjoyable and absorbing as sports, my schools missed the opportunity to capitalize on an element of drama and conflict that the intellectual world shares with sports. Consequently, I failed to see the parallels between the sports and academic worlds that could have helped me cross more readily from one argument culture to the other.

Sports is only one of the domains whose potential for literacy training (and not only for males) is seriously underestimated by educators, who see sports as competing with academic development rather than a route to it. But if this argument suggests why it is a good idea to assign readings and topics that are close to students' existing interests, it also suggests the limits of this tactic. For students who get excited about the chance to write about their passion for cars will often write as poorly and unreflectively on that topic as on Shakespeare or Plato. Here is the flip side of what I pointed out before: that there's no necessary relation between the degree of interest a student shows in a text or subject and the quality of thought or expression such a student manifests in writing or talking about it. The challenge, as college professor Ned Laff has put it, "is not simply to exploit students' nonacademic interests, but to get them to see those interests through academic eyes."

To say that students need to see their interests "through academic eyes" is to say that street smarts are not enough. Making students' nonacademic interests an object of academic study is useful, then, for getting students' attention and overcoming their boredom and alienation, but this tactic won't in itself necessarily move them closer to an academically rigorous treatment of those interests. On the other hand, inviting students to write about cars, sports, or clothing fashions does not have to be a pedagogical cop-out as long as students are required to see these interests "through academic eyes," that is, to think and write about cars, sports, and fashions in a reflective, analytical way, one that sees them as microcosms of what is going on in the wider culture.

If I am right, then schools and colleges are missing an opportunity when they do not encourage students to take their nonacademic interests as objects of academic study. It is self-defeating to decline to introduce any text or subject that figures to engage students who will otherwise tune out academic work entirely. If a student cannot get interested in Mill's *On Liberty* but will read *Sports Illustrated* or *Vogue* or the hip-hop magazine *Source* with absorption, this is a strong argument for assigning the magazines over the classic. It's a good bet that if students get hooked on reading and writing by doing term papers on *Source,* they will eventually get to *On Liberty.* But even if they don't, the magazine reading will make them more literate and reflective than they would be otherwise. So it makes pedagogical sense to develop classroom units on sports, cars, fashions, rap music, and other such topics. Give me the student anytime who writes a sharply argued, sociologically acute analysis of an issue of *Source* over the student who writes a lifeless explication of *Hamlet* or Socrates' *Apology.*

Thinking about the Text

1. Gerald Graff's principal **EVIDENCE** in this essay is his own personal experience. How and how well does he present other supporting evidence? How and how well does he present the views that he is arguing against?

2. Graff notes that Laff suggests that students be encouraged to view what interests them "through academic eyes" (16). What do you and your friends discuss frequently? Sports stats? Relative merits of various cosmetics brands or video games? Who is the best dancer? rapper? Have you ever thought and written about those interests "in a reflective, analytical way" (16)? Is doing so an appealing possibility? What tools or assistance might you need in order to be able to do so effectively?

3. In introducing his argument, Graff makes frequent use of the first-person plural—"we think," "we associate," and so on (1, 2). Who is this "we"—whom does he see as his **AUDIENCE**: professors? parents? absolutely everybody? Explain the reasoning behind your answer, and provide evidence from the text. Why might Graff have chosen to use "we" this way? How does it affect your response to his argument? How do you think it would affect the response of his audience in general?

4. Graff argues that a student who learns to take an academic approach to *Sports Illustrated, Vogue, Source,* or other popular periodicals will eventually be likely to want to read traditionally academic material. Do you agree with that argument?

5. Graff recollects growing up "torn . . . between the need to prove I was smart and the fear of a beating if I proved it too well" (7). Did you have any similar experiences growing up, possibly involving fear of social rather than physical harm? Write an essay in which you **DESCRIBE** the prevailing (and perhaps conflicting) attitudes toward academic success among your friends, family members, and neighbors. Once you establish the context, write about your strategies and experiences in navigating the attitudes of those around you.

The Agnostic Cartographer
JOHN GRAVOIS

ONE FATEFUL DAY IN EARLY AUGUST, Google Maps turned Arunachal Pradesh Chinese. It happened without warning. One minute, the mountainous border state adjacent to Tibet was labeled with its usual complement of Indian place-names; the next it was sprinkled with Mandarin characters, like a virtual annex of the People's Republic.

The error could hardly have been more awkward. Governed by India but claimed by China, Arunachal Pradesh has been a source of rankling dispute between the two nations for decades. Google's sudden relabeling of the province gave the appearance of a special tip of the hat toward Beijing. Its timing, moreover, was freakishly bad: the press noticed that Google's servers had started splaying Mandarin place-names all over the state only a few hours before Indian and Chinese negotiating teams sat down for talks in New Delhi to work toward resolving the delicate border issue.

Google rushed to admit its mistake, but not before a round of angry Indian blog posts and news articles had flourished online. Some commentators posited outright conspiracy between Beijing and the search engine. "Google Maps has always been more biased towards China over

JOHN GRAVOIS is a journalist who has worked for English-language newspapers in Cambodia and Abu Dhabi and for the *Chronicle of Higher Education* in the United States. He is now an editor at *Washington Monthly*, where this article first appeared in 2010.

the Arunachal Pradesh border dispute," surmised an Indian blogger. Even more ominously, one former member of Parliament told the *Times of India*, "The Chinese know how to time their statements ahead of a bilateral meeting."

Google responded in a manner that radiated chilly omnipresence—by posting a statement in the comments section of what appeared to be every single Web site that had discussed the mix-up. "The change was a result of a mistake in our processing of new map data," Google announced. "We are in the process of reverting the data to its previous state, and expect the change to be visible in the product shortly."

One mystery remained, however: how did such an error happen in "the product" in the first place? Why did Google have that perfect set of Chinese names lying around, ready to swap in for the Indian ones?   5

Google remained silent on this point, but a Belgian blogger named Stefan Geens pieced together a compelling answer. Within China, Geens pointed out, the law commands that all maps represent "South Tibet" (aka Arunachal Pradesh) as fully Chinese. And Google Maps maintains servers in China that fall under Chinese law. In fact, Google runs an entirely separate maps site, ditu.google.cn, for Chinese users, which operates within the great Chinese firewall. This isn't just a one-off concession to the party leaders in Beijing: Google maintains thirty-two different region-specific versions of its maps tool for different countries around the world that each abide by the respective local laws. Thus on India's version of Google Maps, for example, all of Kashmir appears as an integral and undisputed part of the country—because Indian law sees it that way. Similarly, "Arunachal Pradesh" is nowhere to be found on ditu.google.cn. What you find instead are all the same Chinese place-names that caused the uproar of Google Maps in August.

"Somehow," Geens surmised, "data intended for the China map must have ended up in the global map." Was it all simply the result of an ill-fated drag-and-drop? Whatever exactly may have occurred, the whole episode illustrated the perils of geopolitics in the age of neogeography.

Just five years since the release of Google Maps and Google Earth, the corporation may well be the world's most important mapmaker. More than 600 million people around the world have downloaded Google Earth. As a testament to ambition, that number alone would be remarkable. But Google is also intent on upending our very notion of what a map is. Rather than produce one definitive map of the world, Google offers multiple interpretations of the earth's geography. Sometimes, this takes the form of customized maps that cater to the beliefs of one nation or another. More often, though, Google is simply an agnostic cartographer—a peddler of "place browsers" that contain a multitude of views instead of univocal, authoritative, traditional maps. "We work to provide as much discoverable information as possible so that users can make their own judgments about geopolitical disputes," writes Robert Boorstin, the director of Google's public policy team.

Ironically, it is that very approach to mapping, one that is indecisive rather than domineering, that has embroiled Google in some of the globe's hottest geopolitical conflicts. Thanks to the logic of its software and business interests, Google has inadvertently waded into disputes from Israel to Cambodia to Iran. It is said that every map is a political statement. But Google, by trying to subvert that truth, may just be intensifying the politics even more.

The late modern era—the age that brought us industrialization, high colonialism, and mechanized warfare—was a good time for mapmakers. Colonial authorities like the British Royal Engineers sent survey teams to the far reaches of the globe to sustain the European powers' outward march. Exuding an industrial-age clear-sightedness (and the vanity of the gainfully employed), cartographers consecrated their profession to the ideals of scientific objectivity and rational standardization—even as their work advanced the narrow mercantile and strategic aims of their state employers. 10

That progressive scientific ethic in mapmaking found its loftiest expression in 1891, when a German geographer by the name of Albrecht Penck proposed to the world's cartographers that they create a single "International Map of the World," composed of 2,500 highly standardized individual maps, each representing four degrees of latitude and six degrees of longitude, at a scale of 1 to 1 million. With great international fanfare, the project sailed off the ground in 1913, sputtered through World War I, and then suffered a blow from which it never really recovered when the program's central office, in Britain, was wrecked in a bombing raid during World War II. The very powers that had conceived of the grand project were now engaged in another enterprise: destroying each other.

The end of the colonial period, hastened by World War II, ushered in a broad crisis in geographical data collection. "The modern era collapsed under its own weight," says Michael Frank Goodchild, a British American geographer at the University of California, Santa Barbara. "By the 1970s it was apparent that it was no longer going to be sustainable to have a world in which national governments sustained geographic information."

In some ways, that postcolonial crisis of information is still with us. "The standard U.S. topographical map is now on average thirty-five years out of date," says Goodchild, who is widely regarded as a founding father of geographic information science. "Modernist government data collection efforts like the census are in decline all over the world." In certain parts of Africa, old British colonial maps are still the best thing going.

But where government surveyors have ceased to tread, satellites have zoomed in. These have helped to fill the cartographic vacuum, but not everything can be seen from an unblinking eye in space. Satellites, for example, don't know the names of local landmarks. That's where another of Google's capabilities comes in. Over just the past couple of years, Google has been able to build maps of heretofore barely charted cities in Africa, South Asia, and the Pacific Rim—maps that would have brought tears to the eyes of those who struggled for decades to assemble the International Map of the World—by tapping into the same extraordinary resource that has driven so much of the Internet's expansion: ordinary people. Using a fairly straightforward editing tool called Google Map Maker, volunteers all over the world have been shaping, revising, and detailing maps of their surroundings. "Essentially," Goodchild says, "they're replacing the traditional production systems that governments are no longer willing to fund."

That new user-generated system of production, married to the technol- 15
ogy of searchable "virtual globes" like Google Earth, has given rise to what people have begun calling "neogeography." In the colonial era, the mapmaker's imperative was to tame the foreign wilderness with names and boundaries—to discipline a profusion of facts and claims into a narrow and authoritative set of data. Now the profusion of facts and claims is a feature, not a bug. With the ability to zoom in on visual fields of higher and higher resolution, a digital map can contain more and more information—various local names for the same landmark, personal annotations, a picture of someone's dog in a field. "The modern era was an era of the expectation that every feature should have a single name, and a top-down authority would determine that," says Goodchild. "I think we're moving past that with digital technology." With policies that often favor ambiguity, Google maintains centralized control over the most official features on its maps—national borders, bodies of water, and the like—while in the "community

layer" of map information, users have an open canvas. Geography has been democratized.

This isn't to say that Google is a democracy. In its own way, Google may be just as imperious in its approach to knowledge as the nineteenth-century European powers were in their approach to territory. The corporation simply wants to have searchable dominion over as much information as possible— the more plural and local, the better. (More unique search terms mean more revenue streams.) Meanwhile, by filling the information vacuum left behind by the old state powers, Google has also made it inevitable that it will sometimes be confused for them.

At this point, Google's reach has become so vast that, whenever the corporation becomes involved in a geographical spat, it's effectively an international incident. Border disputes have become a common vexation. Earlier this year, the government of Cambodia wrote a formal letter of complaint to the corporation—and shared it with the press—because of Google's depiction of a disputed border with Thailand near an eleventh-century Khmer temple complex in Preah Vihear Province. In the letter, a senior Cambodian official very publicly declared Google's representation of the border "devoid of truth and reality, and professionally irresponsible, if not pretentious," not to mention "very wrong and not internationally recognized." Suddenly the corporation from Mountain View—which introduced its mapping platform in 2005 with the words "We think maps can be useful and fun"—was making headlines as a major party in a remote jungle conflict that has claimed at least seven lives in recent border skirmishes. Google said it would review the matter, but pointed to Tele Atlas, a third-party firm that supplied the data in question, and suggested that Cambodia should direct its complaints there.

Other disputes stem directly from Google's participatory model of mapmaking. In 2008, the small Israeli city of Kiryat Yam sued the corporation for libel after a Palestinian civilian named Thameen Darby went on Google Earth and tagged the town as the site of an Arab village destroyed by Israelis in 1948. Darby had annotated hundreds of other sites throughout the country, noting the purported locations of former Palestinian settlements that were wiped away during Israel's formative years. But the officials of Kiryat Yam took issue with Darby's geography; they claimed the city was built by Holocaust survivors on a barren stretch of dunes, not over the ruins of evicted Palestinians. Darby, they said, had sullied the city's reputation. Rather than sue Darby, though, they sued Google. The lawsuit, in other words, was an attempt to hold the corporation liable for something an ordinary user had posted to a community layer of Google Earth.

Another major genre of Google-era geopolitical dispute doesn't involve borders, but simply names. One of the most active online petitions in the world today is an Iranian campaign hosted on the Web site PetitionOnline. com. In light of recent political events, you might guess the campaign would involve some grievance against the Islamic Republic. In fact, the petition's target is Google, and its goal is to secure the "immediate and unconditional deletion of 'Arabian Gulf' from Google Earth." First posted on February 19, 2008, the online petition against that decision has gathered 1,235,743 signatures—and counting.

Since the 1960s, the disagreement over what to call the body of water   20 that separates Iran from the Arabian Peninsula has been one of geography's perennial feuds. "Persian Gulf" is the name recognized by the United Nations, while "Arabian Gulf" is a comparatively new moniker whose use came into fashion during the heyday of Arab nationalism. In the eyes of Iranians, the name "Arabian Gulf" signals a frontal assault on their national history. Defending the name "Persian Gulf" has become one of the few truly unifying pastimes in Iranian politics. Factions that bitterly oppose each other will line up together in the name's defense—or else attack each other for insufficient loyalty to it.

Unfortunately for Iran, sometime in early 2008 Google Earth decided to display the names "Persian Gulf" and "Arabian Gulf" side by side. The ensuing Iranian online petition, harking back to the values of the old nineteenth-century mapmakers, faults Google for being "unscientific" and ignorant of "international standards." The petition invokes the authority of the United Nations, whose official endorsement of the name "Persian Gulf" is grounded in a small library's worth of archival maps, literary references, and other historical source material.

Google responded to the debate with a rather novel set of cartographic norms, throwing all historical criteria out the window. Two months after the "Immediate and Unconditional Deletion" petition went live, the corporation posted a statement explaining its protocol for naming bodies of water. The statement, which made no direct mention of the Gulf or the Iranian petition, explained that Google decides what to call various geographical features purely by determining what names are in use today. Google Earth "displays the primary, common, local name(s) given to a body of water by the sovereign nations that border it," wrote Andrew McLaughlin, Google's then director of public policy (and now President Obama's deputy chief technology officer). "If different countries dispute the proper name for a body of water, our policy is to display both names."

The statement then transitioned into upbeat talk of the democratization of information. "One of the great features of Google Earth is that it enables us to provide significantly greater amounts of information than flat paper maps," McLaughlin wrote. "It is our fervent hope that different communities will use Google Earth as an open platform to create content that accurately reflects their views."

Of course, while an open platform for discussion is exactly what Iranians want in a Web site like PetitionOnline, it's not what they want in an international map. No party to a dispute likes an undecided referee. (And in fact, few parties to these disputes trust Google's claims of neutrality: much as Indians suspected foul play when the corporation dropped Chinese placenames into Arunachal Pradesh, the sponsors of the Iranian petition simply suspect a conspiracy between Google and the oil-rich Arab states on the other side of the Gulf.)

Unpopular as it may be, such uncertainty has become a central dynamic of life on the Internet. The erosion of traditional authority is followed quickly by anxiety over its absence, from Google to Wikipedia to the lesser-known precincts of PetitionOnline—where millions of people direct their impassioned grievances not to any official arbiter but straight into the ether. What results is an irony. The digital culture that encourages the inclusion of multiple names for a single feature on a map is the same digital culture that has encouraged hundreds of thousands of Iranians to voice their discontent. The very medium incites nationalism, yet also frustrates it. 25

It all points back to a simple question: What is Google? Is it a repository for all of our mutually exclusive claims, or is it a higher power to which we appeal? It cannot be both, and yet we seem to treat it as both. This tension may only heighten going forward. "In a world where mapmaking is cheap and anyone can do it," Goodchild says, "you would eventually expect things to become more and more local." In such a future, either we will reconcile ourselves to the lack of a central arbiter, or the conflicts will be all over the map.

This report has a tone that inspires trust. For tips on writing with authority, see pp. 243–45.

Thinking about the Text

1. John Gravois' report on the new problems that are emerging with new map-making technologies and practices presents a lot of information and ideas that you very likely have never had to consider. How trustworthy do you find the information, and why? In your response, consider what credentials the people and other sources Gravois mentions have, how verifiable their information is, and how clear his explanations are.

2. You may have learned in elementary school that the river that defines much of the boundary of the United States with Mexico is the Rio Grande. Are you aware that in Mexico, the same river is known as the Rio Bravo? Is the difference in name a problem? Do you think something should be done about it? If so, who should do it? Why? What might Gravois say about the situation? Think about *Google*'s policy for disputed names of bodies of water (22). Do you agree with the policy? Why or why not?

3. Gravois' article was published in *Washington Monthly*, whose print circulation is concentrated in the Washington metropolitan area. How might this magazine's **AUDIENCE** differ from that of a magazine in another area or one with national distribution? Considering Gravois' likely intended audience, who is the "we" that he addresses in the final paragraph? Are you included in it? Why or why not?

4. Before reading this report, had you ever encountered the term "neogeography"? Gravois calls attention to the term without actually providing a **DEFINITION** of it. What do you think that it means? On what information do you base your understanding of it? Does Gravois provide sufficient information for you to understand it? Explain why or why not.

5. How much do you know about the history of place names in the area where you live? Do some research on the names of streets and natural features, either in your college community or another area where you've lived, and write a **REPORT** about what you find. Are some of the names in common use just customary popular ones with no official status? Do any streets or natural features have multiple names? Did you encounter any obstacles, problems, or controversies in your investigation? Did you learn anything that made you want to mount a name-change campaign? If your answer to any of these questions is yes, discuss the issue in your report.

The Year without Toilet Paper

PENELOPE GREEN

DINNER WAS THE USUAL AFFAIR on Thursday night in Apartment 9F in an elegant prewar on Lower Fifth Avenue. There was shredded cabbage with fruit-scrap vinegar; mashed parsnips and yellow carrots with local butter and fresh thyme; a terrific frittata; then homemade yogurt with honey and thyme tea, eaten under the greenish flickering light cast by two beeswax candles and a fluorescent bulb.

A sour odor hovered oh-so-slightly in the air, the faint tang, not wholly unpleasant, that is the mark of the home composter. Isabella Beavan, age 2, staggered around the neo-Modern furniture—the Eames chairs, the brown velvet couch, the Lucite lamps and the steel cafe table upon which dinner was set—her silhouette greatly amplified by her organic cotton diapers in their enormous boiled-wool, snap-front cover.

A visitor avoided the bathroom because she knew she would find no toilet paper there.

PENELOPE GREEN is editor of the Home and Garden section for the *New York Times*. She has written for *Vogue, House Beautiful,* and *House and Garden,* among other periodicals, and her articles deal with issues ranging from window placement to a defense of messiness to an evaluation of the relative merits of different types of lightbulbs. This article appeared in the Home and Garden section of the *Times* in 2007.

Dim Lights, Big City. The Conlin-Beavan family experiment requires that lights be low in their Fifth Avenue apartment.

Meanwhile, Joseph, the liveried elevator man who works nights in the building, drove his wood-paneled, 1920s-era vehicle up and down its chute, unconcerned that the couple in 9F had not used his services in four months. "I've noticed," Joseph said later with a shrug and no further comment. (He declined to give his last name. "I've got enough problems," he said.)

Welcome to Walden Pond, Fifth Avenue style. Isabella's parents, Colin   5
Beavan, 43, a writer of historical nonfiction, and Michelle Conlin, 39, a senior writer at *Business Week,* are four months into a yearlong lifestyle experiment they call No Impact. Its rules are evolving, as Mr. Beavan will tell you, but to date include eating only food (organically) grown within a 250-mile radius of Manhattan; (mostly) no shopping for anything except said food; producing no trash (except compost, see above); using no paper; and, most intriguingly, using no carbon-fueled transportation.

Mr. Beavan, who has written one book about the origins of forensic detective work and another about D-Day, said he was ready for a new subject, hoping to tread more lightly on the planet and maybe be an inspiration to others in the process.

Also, he needed a new book project and the No Impact year was the only one of four possibilities his agent thought would sell. This being 2007, Mr. Beavan is showcasing No Impact in a blog (noimpactman.com) laced with links and testimonials from New Environmentalist authorities like treehugger.com. His agent did indeed secure him a book deal, with Farrar, Straus & Giroux, and he and his family are being tailed by Laura Gabbert, a documentary filmmaker and Ms. Conlin's best friend.

Why there may be a public appetite for the Conlin-Beavan family doings has a lot to do with the very personal, very urban face of environmentalism these days. Thoreau left home for the woods to make his point (and secure his own book deal); Mr. Beavan and Ms. Conlin and others like them aren't budging from their bricks-and-mortar, haut-bourgeois nests.

Mr. Beavan looks to groups like the Compacters (sfcompact.blogspot.com), a collection of nonshoppers that began in San Francisco, and the 100 Mile Diet folks (100milediet.org and thetyee.ca), a Vancouver couple who spent a year eating from within 100 miles of their apartment, for tips and inspiration. But there are hundreds of other light-footed, young abstainers with a diarist urge: it is not news that this shopping-averse, carbon-footprint-reducing, city-dwelling generation likes to blog (the paperless, public diary form). They have seen *An Inconvenient Truth*; they would like to tell you how it makes them feel. If Al Gore is their Rachel Carson, blogalogs like Treehugger, grist.org and worldchanging.com are their Whole Earth catalogs.

Andrew Kirk, an environmental history professor at the University of   10 Nevada, Las Vegas, whose new book, *Counterculture Green: The Whole Earth Catalog and American Environmentalism*, will be published by University Press of Kansas in September, is reminded of environmentalism's last big bubble, in the 1970s, long before Ronald Reagan pulled federal funding for alternative fuel technologies (and his speechwriters made fun of the spotted owl and its liberal protectors, a deft feat of propaganda that set the movement back decades). Those were the days when Stewart Brand and his Whole Earth writers, Mr. Kirk said, "focused on a brand of environmentalism that kept *people* in the picture."

"That's the thing about this current wave of environmentalism," he continued. "It's not about, how do we protect some abstract pristine space? It's what can real people do in their home or office or whatever. It's also very urban. It's a critical twist in the old wilderness adage: Leave only footprints, take only photographs. But how do you translate that into Manhattan?"

With equals parts grace and calamity, it appears. Washed down with a big draught of engaging palaver.

Before No Impact—this is a phrase that comes up a lot—Ms. Conlin and Mr. Beavan were living a near parody of urban professional life. Ms. Conlin, who bought this apartment in 1999 when she was still single, used the stove so infrequently (as in, never, she said) that Con Edison called to find out if it was broken. (Mr. Beavan, now the family cook, questioned whether she had yet to turn it on. Ms. Conlin ignored him.)

In this household, food was something you dialed for.

"We would wake up and call 'the man,'" Ms. Conlin said, "and he would 15 bring us two newspapers and coffee in Styrofoam cups. Sometimes we'd call two men, and get bagels from Bagel Bob's. For lunch I'd find myself at Wendy's, with a Dunkin' Donuts chaser. Isabella would point to guys on bikes and cry: 'The man! The man!'"

Since November, Mr. Beavan and Isabella have been hewing closely, most particularly in a dietary way, to a 19th-century life. Mr. Beavan has a single-edge razor he has learned to use (it was a gift from his father). He has also learned to cook quite tastily from a limited regional menu—right now that means lots of apples and root vegetables, stored in the unplugged freezer—hashing out compromises. Spices are out but salt is exempt, Mr. Beavan said, because homemade bread "is awful without salt; salt stops the yeast action." Mr. Beavan is baking his own, with wheat grown locally and a sour dough "mother" fermenting stinkily in his cupboard. He is also finding good sources at the nearby Union Square Greenmarket (like Ronnybrook Farm Dairy, which sells milk in reusable glass bottles). The 250-mile rule, by the way, reflects the longest distance a farmer can drive in and out of the city in one day, Mr. Beavan said.

Olive oil and vinegar are out; they used the last dregs of their bottle of balsamic vinegar last week, Mr. Beavan said, producing a moment of stunned silence while a visitor thought about life without those staples. Still, Mr. Beavan's homemade fruit-scrap vinegar has a satisfying bite.

The television, a flat-screen, high-definition 46-incher, is long gone. Saturday night charades are in. Mr. Beavan likes to talk about social glue—community building—as a natural byproduct of No Impact. The (fluorescent) lights are still on, and so is the stove. Mr. Beavan, who has a Ph.D. in applied physics, has not yet figured out a carbon-fuel-free power alternative that will run up here on the ninth floor, though he does subscribe to Con Ed's Green Power program, for which he pays a premium, and which adds a measure of wind and hydro power to the old coal and nuclear grid.

The dishwasher is off, along with the microwave, the coffee machine and the food processor. Planes, trains, automobiles and that elevator are out, but the family is still doing laundry in the washing machines in the base-

Colin Beavan is a regular visitor to the Union Square Greenmarket; he brings string bags and reusable cups.

ment of the building. (Consider the ramifications of no-elevator living in a vertical city: one day recently, when Frankie the dog had digestive problems, Mr. Beavan, who takes Isabella to day care—six flights of stairs in a building six blocks away—and writes at the Writers Room on Astor Place—12 flights of stairs, also six blocks away—estimated that by nightfall he had climbed 115 flights of stairs.) And they have not had the heart to take away the vacuum from their cleaning lady, who comes weekly (this week they took away her paper towels).

Until three weeks ago, however, Ms. Conlin was following her "high-fructose corn syrup ways," meaning double espressos and pastries administered daily. "Giving up the coffee was like crashing down from a crystal meth addiction," she said. "I had to leave work and go to bed for 24 hours." 20

Toothpaste is baking soda (a box makes trash, to be sure, but of a better quality than a metal tube), but Ms. Conlin is still wearing the lipstick she gets from a friend who works at Lancôme, as well as moisturizers from Fresh and Kiehl's. When the bottles, tubes and jars are empty, Mr. Beavan has promised her homemade, rules-appropriate substitutes. (Nothing is a substitute for toilet paper, by the way; think of bowls of water and lots of air drying.)

Yet since the beginning of No Impact, and to the amusement of her colleagues at *Business Week*, Ms. Conlin has been scootering to her office on 49th Street each day, bringing a Mason jar filled with greenhouse greens, cheese and her husband's bread for lunch, along with her own napkin and cutlery. She has taken a bit of ribbing: "All progress is carbon fueled," jeered one office mate.

Ms. Conlin, acknowledging that she sees her husband as No Impact Man and herself as simply *inside* his experiment, said she saw *An Inconvenient Truth* in an air-conditioned movie theater last summer. "It was like, 'J'accuse!' " she said. "I just felt like everything I did in my life was contributing to a system that was really problematic." Borrowing a phrase from her husband, she continued, "If I was a student, I would march against myself."

While Ms. Conlin is clearly more than just a good sport—giving up toilet paper seems a fairly profound gesture of commitment—she did describe, in loving detail, a serious shopping binge that predated No Impact and made the whole thing doable, she said. "It was my last hurrah," she explained.

It included two pairs of calf-high Chloe boots (one of which was paid   25
for, she said, with her mother's bingo winnings) and added up to two weeks' salary, after taxes and her 401(k) contribution.

The bingo windfall points to a loophole in No Impact: the Conlin-Beavan household does accept presents. When Mr. Beavan's father saw Ms. Conlin scootering without gloves he sent her a pair. And allowances can be made for the occasional thrift shop purchase. For Isabella's birthday on Feb. 25, her family wandered the East Village and ended up at Jane's Exchange, where she chose a pair of ballet slippers as her gift.

"They cost a dollar," Ms. Conlin said.

It was freezing cold that day, Mr. Beavan said, picking up the story. "We went into a restaurant to warm her up. We agonized about taking a cab, which we ended up not doing. I still felt like we really screwed up, though, because we ate at the restaurant."

He said he called the 100 Mile Diet couple to confess his sin. They admitted they had cheated too, with a restaurant date, then told him, Yoda-like, "Only in strictness comes the conversion."

Restaurants, which are mostly out in No Impact, present all sorts of   30
challenges beyond the 250-mile food rule. "They always want to give Isabella the paper cup with the straw, and we have to send it back," Mr. Beavan

Quoting the Conlin-Beavans' exact words lets readers know them directly; see Ch. 22 for help using direct quotes.

Michelle Conlin rides her scooter, even in the snow. "Rain is worse," she said.

said. "We always say, 'We're trying not to make any trash.' And some people get really into that and others clearly think we're big losers."

Living abstemiously on Lower Fifth Avenue, in what used to be Edith Wharton country, with early-21st-century accouterments like creamy, calf-high Chloe boots, may seem at best like a scene from an old-fashioned situation comedy and, at worst, an ethically murky exercise in self-promotion. On the other hand, consider this response to Mr. Beavan's Internet post the day he and his family gave up toilet paper.

"What's with the public display of nonimpactness?" a reader named Bruce wrote on March 7. "Getting people to read a blog on their 50-watt L.C.D. monitors and buy a bound volume of postconsumer paper and show the filmed doc in a heated/air-conditioned movie theater, etc., sounds like nonimpact man is leading to a lot of impact. And how are you going to measure your nonimpact, except in rather self-centered ways like weight loss and better sex? (Wait, maybe I should stop there.)"

Indeed. Concrete benefits are already accruing to Ms. Conlin and Mr. Beavan that may tempt others. The sea may be rising, but Ms. Conlin has lost 4 pounds and Mr. Beavan 20. It took Ms. Conlin over an hour to get home from work during the snowstorm on Friday, riding her scooter, then walking in her knee-high Wellingtons with her scooter on her back, but she claimed to be mostly exhilarated by the experience. "Rain is worse," she said.

Perhaps the real guinea pig in this experiment is the Conlin-Beavan marriage.

"Like all writers, I'm a megalomaniac," Mr. Beavan said cheerfully the other day. "I'm just trying to put that energy to good use." 35

Thinking about the Text

1. To research this **PROFILE**, Penelope Green spent time with the No Impact family in their apartment; in the article, she performs a delicate dance to indicate her own presence and reactions while at the same time keeping a distance from them. What examples of this balance can you identify in the article? How successful do you find it?

2. How far would you go to reduce your carbon footprint? Would you go as far as the Conlin-Beavan family? Which of their life changes, if any, might you be willing to make? Why? Explain your comfort limit.

3. Green's **DESCRIPTION** of the Conlin-Beavan apartment includes many sensory details. Select three such details, each one appealing to a different sense, and assess how well each contributes to the descriptiveness of the article.

4. The Conlin-Beavan family certainly made drastic changes in their lives and sacrificed many comforts in their No Impact experiment. Still, their economic circumstances and urban location offered them many privileges and other advantageous conditions that most people wouldn't have for such a project. What are some of the ways that their home life is different from yours? What elements of it may have made their experiment easier than it would be for you or your family? Are there also elements that may have made it harder? If so, explain.

5. Green suggests the possibility that the Conlin-Beavan No Impact experiment may just be "an ethically murky exercise in self-promotion" (31). Do you agree? Why or why not? Write an essay in which you **ARGUE** for or against Green's suggestion, presenting evidence from the article and any other (correctly cited) sources you feel appropriate.

Touching the Earth

BELL HOOKS

I wish to live because life has within it that which is good, that which is beautiful, and that which is love. Therefore, since I have known all these things, I have found them to be reason enough and—I wish to live. Moreover, because this is so, I wish others to live for generations and generations and generations and generations.

—LORRAINE HANSBERRY, *To Be Young, Gifted, and Black*

WHEN WE LOVE THE EARTH, we are able to love ourselves more fully. I believe this. The ancestors taught me it was so. As a child I loved playing in dirt, in that rich Kentucky soil, that was a source of life. Before I understood anything about the pain and exploitation of the southern system of sharecropping, I understood that grown-up black folks loved the land. I could stand with my grandfather Daddy Jerry and look out at fields

---

BELL HOOKS is Distinguished Professor of Literature at the City University of New York. Her works include many books for both academic and general audiences and focus on the interconnectedness and inseparability of race, economic class, and gender and the powerful role that these three factors play in maintaining the social structure of the United States. *Utne Reader* named her one of "100 Visionaries Who Could Change Your Life." This selection was originally published in the 1993 anthology *Sisters of the Yam: Black Women and Self-Recovery.*

of growing vegetables, tomatoes, corn, collards, and know that this was his handiwork. I could see the look of pride on his face as I expressed wonder and awe at the magic of growing things. I knew that my grandmother Baba's backyard garden would yield beans, sweet potatoes, cabbage, and yellow squash, that she too would walk with pride among the rows and rows of growing vegetables showing us what the earth will give when tended lovingly.

From the moment of their first meeting, Native American and African people shared with one another a respect for the life-giving forces of nature, of the earth. African settlers in Florida taught the Creek Nation runaways, the "Seminoles," methods for rice cultivation. Native peoples taught recently arrived black folks all about the many uses of corn. (The hotwater cornbread we grew up eating came to our black southern diet from the world of the Indian.) Sharing the reverence for the earth, black and red people helped one another remember that, despite the white man's ways, the land belonged to everyone. Listen to these words attributed to Chief Seattle in 1854:

> How can you buy or sell the sky, the warmth of the land? The idea is strange to us. If we do not own the freshness of the air and the sparkle of the water, how can you buy them? Every part of this earth is sacred to my people. Every shining pine needle, every sandy shore, every mist in the dark woods, every clearing and humming insect is holy in the memory and experience of my people.... We are part of the earth and it is part of us. The perfumed flowers are our sisters; the deer, the horse, the great eagle, these are our brothers. The rocky crests, the juices in the meadows, the body heat of the pony, and man—all belong to the same family.

The sense of union and harmony with nature expressed here is echoed in testimony by black people who found that even though life in the new world was "harsh, harsh," in relationship to the earth one could be at peace. In the oral autobiography of granny midwife Onnie Lee Logan, who lived all her life in Alabama, she talks about the richness of farm life—growing vegetables, raising chickens, and smoking meat. She reports:

> We lived a happy, comfortable life to be right outa slavery times. I didn't know nothin else but the farm so it was happy and we was

Kentucky morning.

happy.... We couldn't do anything else but be happy. We accept the days as they come and as they were. Day by day until you couldn't say there was any great hard time. We overlooked it. We didn't think nothin about it. We just went along. We had what it takes to make a good livin and go about it.

Living in modern society, without a sense of history, it has been easy for folks to forget that black people were first and foremost a people of the land, farmers. It is easy for folks to forget that at the first part of the 20th century, the vast majority of black folks in the United States lived in the agrarian south.

Living close to nature, black folks were able to cultivate a spirit of won- 5
der and reverence for life. Growing food to sustain life and flowers to please the soul, they were able to make a connection with the earth that was ongoing and life-affirming. They were witnesses to beauty. In Wendell Berry's important discussion of the relationship between agriculture and human spiritual well-being, *The Unsettling of America*, he reminds us that working the land provides a location where folks can experience a sense of personal power and well-being:

> We are working well when we use ourselves as the fellow creature of the plants, animals, material, and other people we are working with. Such work is unifying, healing. It brings us home from pride and despair, and places us responsibly within the human estate. It defines us as we are: not too good to work without our bodies, but too good to work poorly or joylessly or selfishly or alone.

There has been little or no work done on the psychological impact of the "great migration" of black people from the agrarian south to the industrialized north. Toni Morrison's novel *The Bluest Eye* attempts to fictively document the way moving from the agrarian south to the industrialized north wounded the psyches of black folk. Estranged from a natural world, where there was time for silence and contemplation, one of the "displaced" black folks in Morrison's novel, Miss Pauline, loses her capacity to experience the sensual world around her when she leaves southern soil to live in a northern city. The south is associated in her mind with a world of sensual beauty most deeply expressed in the world of nature. Indeed, when she falls in love for the first time she can name that experience only by

Good evidence can be more than facts and figures, as hooks shows. See pp. 289–95.

evoking images from nature, from an agrarian world and near wilderness of natural splendor:

> When I first seed Cholly, I want you to know it was like all the bits of color from that time down home when all us chil'ren went berry picking after a funeral and I put some in the pocket of my Sunday dress, and they mashed up and stained my hips. My whole dress was messed with purple, and it never did wash out. Not the dress nor me. I could feel that purple deep inside me. And that lemonade Mama used to make when Pap came in out of the fields. It be cool and yellowish, with seeds floating near the bottom. And that streak of green them june bugs made on the tress that night we left from down home. All of them colors was in me. Just sitting there.

Certainly, it must have been a profound blow to the collective psyche of black people to find themselves struggling to make a living in the industrial north away from the land. Industrial capitalism was not simply changing the nature of black work life, it altered the communal practices that were so central to survival in the agrarian south. And it fundamentally altered black people's relationship to the body. It is the loss of any capacity to appreciate her body, despite its flaws, Miss Pauline suffers when she moves north.

The motivation for black folks to leave the south and move north was both material and psychological. Black folks wanted to be free of the overt racial harassment that was a constant in southern life and they wanted access to material goods—to a level of material well-being that was not available in the agrarian south where white folks limited access to the spheres of economic power. Of course, they found that life in the north had its own perverse hardships, that racism was just as virulent there, that it was much harder for black people to become landowners. Without the space to grow food, to commune with nature, or to mediate the starkness of poverty with the splendor of nature, black people experienced profound depression. Working in conditions where the body was regarded solely as a tool (as in slavery), a profound estrangement occurred between mind and body. The way the body was represented became more important than the body itself. It did not matter if the body was well, only that it appeared well.

Estrangement from nature and engagement in mind/body splits made it all the more possible for black people to internalize white-supremacist assumptions about black identity. Learning contempt for blackness, southerners transplanted in the north suffered both culture shock and soul loss. Contrasting the harshness of city life with an agrarian world, the poet Waring Cuney wrote this popular poem in the 1920s, testifying to lost connection:

> She does not know her beauty
> She thinks her brown body
> has no glory.
> If she could dance naked,
> Under palm trees
> And see her image in the river
> She would know.
> But there are no palm trees on the street,
> And dishwater gives back no images.

For many years, and even now, generations of black folks who migrated north to escape life in the south, returned down home in search of a spiritual nourishment, a healing, that was fundamentally connected to reaffirming one's connection to nature, to a contemplative life where one could take time, sit on the porch, walk, fish, and catch lightning bugs. If we think of urban life as a location where black folks learned to accept a mind/body split that made it possible to abuse the body, we can better understand the growth of nihilism and despair in the black psyche. And we can know that when we talk about healing that psyche we must also speak about restoring our connection to the natural world.

Wherever black folks live we can restore our relationship to the natural 10 world by taking the time to commune with nature, to appreciate the other creatures who share this planet with humans. Even in my small New York City apartment I can pause to listen to birds sing, find a tree and watch it. We can grow plants—herbs, flowers, vegetables. Those novels by African-American writers (women and men) that talk about black migration from the agrarian south to the industrialized north describe in detail the way folks created space to grow flowers and vegetables. Although I come from country people with serious green thumbs, I have always felt that I could not garden. In the past few years, I have found that I can do it—that many gardens will grow, that I feel connected to my ancestors when I can put a meal on the table of food I grew. I especially love to plant collard greens. They are hardy, and easy to grow.

In modern society, there is also a tendency to see no correlation between the struggle for collective black self-recovery and ecological movements that seek to restore balance to the planet by changing our relationship to nature and to natural resources. Unmindful of our history of living harmoniously on the land, many contemporary black folks see no value in supporting ecological movements, or see ecology and the struggle to end racism as competing concerns. Recalling the legacy of our ancestors who knew that the way we regard land and nature will determine the level of our self-regard, black people must reclaim a spiritual legacy where we connect our well-being to the well-being of the earth. This is a necessary dimension of healing. As Berry reminds us:

> Only by restoring the broken connections can we be healed. Connection is health. And what our society does its best to disguise from us is how ordinary, how commonly attainable, health is. We lose our health—and create profitable diseases and dependencies— by failing to see the direct connections between living and eating, eating and working, working and loving. In gardening, for instance, one works with the body to feed the body. The work, if it is knowledgeable, makes for excellent food. And it makes one hungry. The work thus makes eating both nourishing and joyful, not consumptive, and keeps the eater from getting fat and weak. This health, wholeness, is a source of delight.

Collective black self-recovery takes place when we begin to renew our relationship to the earth, when we remember the way of our ancestors. When the earth is sacred to us, our bodies can also be sacred to us.

Thinking about the Text

1. This essay takes an explicit **POSITION**, but it is expressed in very abstract terms. What, exactly, is the author exhorting her readers to do? What concrete steps might they take to accomplish what she is recommending? Present examples from the text to support your responses.

2. What kind of environment would you say you live in—urban, rural, or something in between? How would you describe your relationship to the natural

world? What do you do in order to "touch the earth"? Would you like to be able to do more? Why or why not?

3. Hooks cites Wendell Berry, who mentions the "profitable diseases and dependencies" that people create when we fail to see "the direct connections between living and eating, eating and working, working and loving" (11). What does Berry mean by "profitable diseases and dependencies"? Profitable for whom? Why? Dependencies on what or on whom? How does Berry's assertion fit into this essay's argument?

4. Because of black Americans' particular history with slavery and racism in the United States, hooks is suggesting a particular path toward healing. Might this same path be a healing one for other groups of people? Why or why not? Might it be a healing path for you, personally, or other members of a social or ethnic group to which you belong? Why or why not?

5. Very few of us, of any racial or ethnic identity, could be said to live in harmony with nature; the demands of contemporary economic and social life, in fact, seem to take us increasingly farther afield from such a state. Take a critical look around you, at your individual, family, and community contexts. What barriers are blocking what bell hooks would call reconnection with the earth on each of those three levels? What could be done on each level to lower such barriers? Write an essay in which you take stock of your environment and **PROPOSE** concrete, doable steps in a path toward a more harmonious relationship with nature at one of these levels—individual, family, or community—or explain why this is not a desirable goal. Be sure to make clear which level your proposal is addressing.

On Getting By

ALEX HORTON

IN **MY PREVIOUS POST,**[1] I outlined some basic principles needed to successfully navigate the murky waters of education under the GI Bill. The challenges in dealing with the VA for education benefits are considerable, yet veterans new to college face an unfamiliar, unpredictable and strange environment on campus. If taken all at once, these hurdles can quickly overwhelm a student veteran and distract from the overall goal: to finish a degree on time with benefits to spare. Next week I will be in class for my fifth semester of higher education, and in my time I have tinkered with a system of how to bring up my veteran status, discussing Iraq and Afghanistan in the classroom and dealing with the myriad reactions fellow students have had. The system cannot be expected to work for everyone, but as veterans file into classrooms for the first time this spring, these tips could help in the development of a coping system better tailored for you. These should simply help to get you started.

1. "Here to There: Tips and Tricks for the Student Veteran," Dec. 29, 2009.

ALEX HORTON's blog, *Army of Dude*, has been operating since 2006 and was a finalist for Weblog Awards for Best Military Blog in 2007 and 2008. Horton, an Iraq War veteran, lives in the Washington, D.C., area and works for the Veterans Administration. This piece was posted on *Army of Dude* in 2010; links to other posts, both within and outside Horton's blog, appear as footnotes.

Modesty Is the Best Policy

Why did Horton write this piece as a process analysis, not an argument? See Ch. 12 for help choosing genres.

There are only two kinds of veterans in school: those who prattle on about their time in the military and overseas, and those who do not. The former will find any opportunity to bring up their time in Afghanistan or Iraq, even if it is not relevant to class discussion. They forget one of the tenets of military experience—the role of the consummate professional. Joining the military and serving in a time of war are sacred acts and carry a certain degree of respect and modesty. We owe it to our injured buddies and fallen friends not to brag about our exploits overseas. We have done our fair share of things that set us apart from others in the classroom, and that is exactly why it is best to retain an understated presence among others.

This is a difficult situation as it applies to reintegration, as the chasm between veterans and civilians has never been wider. From World War II to Vietnam, it would have been a difficult task to know someone that neither served overseas nor had a family member or friend who did. Now there are whole classrooms filled with those people. As Matthew McConaughey spoke prophetically in *Dazed and Confused*, "I get older, they stay the same age." An 18 year old in college this year would have been nine years old during the invasion of Afghanistan and eleven years old during the invasion of Iraq. They have grown up with war to the point of it becoming a mind numbingly prosaic concept. It would be a frustrating battle to try and close the rift with those who don't see a rift at all. The best thing to do is use your judgment when bringing up your veteran status in the classroom. I've done it just a few times and felt uncomfortable enough to think twice about the next time. Now I tend to mention it in private conversation, not when I have the floor in public, and even then it is a casual touch on the subject. When you are ready to talk . . .

. . . Prepare for a Question Salvo

No matter how much you try to keep it stashed away from students and coworkers, your military experience will come out sooner or later. There are things you simply cannot hide forever, like going to prison or reading *Twilight*. Once you begin to move past casual conversation, it's only a matter of time before that period of your life is visited. It usually begins with a discussion of age. When I tell people I'm 24, the followup questions are almost always, "What have you done since high school?" or, "Why did you wait so long to go to school?" People tend to catch on if you mention extended vacations in the Middle East or recite monologues, so at that point it is best to come clean. However, be prepared for the questions they are more than willing to hurl your way. They might not know anyone who has deployed, but our hyperviolent culture has removed any restraint left in the world and enables them to ask any question that comes to mind. Here is what you can expect, in order of the most frequently asked:

1. What's it like?
2. Was it really hot?
3. Did you kill anyone?
4. Seriously, how hot was it?
5. Do you regret it?
6. Did you see any camel spiders?
7. Were you in Iran?

It's hard to get upset at some of those questions, as I find it difficult to think of what I'd ask if the roles were switched. #3 can be blamed on ignorance and apathy, but #5 is the most troubling I've heard. It suggests that there is something shameful about service, duty and sacrifice. Both questions trivialize an important part of our lives. The best answer to #3 I've heard comes from the The Kitchen Dispatch comment section: "I will forgive you for asking that question if you forgive me for not answering it."[2] Something that personal should never be asked, only told.

The flip side to some of those cavalier probes are questions that handle 5 the topic with kid gloves. Once a coworker found out I was in the Army, she asked, "Did you go to . . . one of those places they send people?" It was uncomfortable for her just to utter those dirty "I" and "A" words, like we were speaking about some subversive topic. The kind of questions you will get will be all over the map, spanning from a place of genuine interest to the depths of sheer morbidity. Be prepared to answer anything, or politely let them know the subject isn't appropriate for casual banter.

2. 1776 on Kananai Fong, "Seven Things Never to Say to a Veteran," *The Kitchen Dispatch*, Jan. 3, 2010.

Let the Right Ones In

Popular culture is replete with images of the maladjusted veteran, from Rambo to Travis Bickle to Red Forman. These characters are ingrained in our national conscious and typically become placeholders in the event someone doesn't personally know a veteran. When these sources are taken at face value, war veterans are invariably crazy, depressive, easily startled, quick to anger and alcoholics. We come from broken homes, trying to escape jailtime and were too dumb or poor to go to college after high school. The best way to combat these silly notions is to let people get to know you, the person, before you, the veteran. Those stereotypes aren't going anywhere soon, so the best idea is to take the concept of guarding your veteran status in the classroom and carry it over to blossoming relationships. That way your service and overseas experience complement your personality and don't define it. Revealing too much at one time can damage a friendship before it takes off. Just like in the classroom, take it slow. If they are worth keeping around, they'll understand why. We have met our lifelong friends already; we can afford to be picky.

Try to Keep a Straight Face

There's a huge disparity between what you have been asked to do in the service and what you will be asked to do in school. At the very basic level you were asked to maintain a clean weapon and uniform. Many of you were tasked with watching the back of your fellow soldiers while in imminent danger or operate complex machinery and vehicles. At school, you'll be held responsible for showing up and turning in work before deadlines. That's it. Like I mentioned in the earlier post, college seems like an insurmountable gauntlet of crushed dreams when you're in the military. Once you transition to civilian life and take a few classes, you'll be astounded at the lack of discipline and drive in some of your classmates. It's a big joke, but try to maintain composure. I'm not saying it's easy the whole way through, but I guarantee you've done something harder than a five page essay. As they say, the rest is downhill.

Find Another Brother

If you were in active duty, the friends you met along the way are now scattered across the country. Perhaps I've always been an introvert, but I don't make friends as easy as some people. I've met just two people in fourteen classes that I consider friends, and one of them is an Afghanistan veteran. It's easy to understand why we get along. Do your best to find other veterans in your class and say hello. Talking to them will come easier than the 18 year old hipster next to you about his passion for ironic hats. Find out if there is a veterans' organization on campus, but be wary of their motives. While some will join to find support and befriend fellow veterans, others will use it for recognition....

Enjoy the Ride

Besides getting a degree or learning new skills, people go to college to meet new people and to experience a different life. If you've served since Sept. 12, 2001, you've already had a bit of each. But don't let that stop you from enjoying everything school has to offer. It's the last time very little will be expected of you, unless you get another government job. Then you're golden.

. . .

If you are recently out of the military and on your way to college, these 10 tenets, coupled with the GI Bill pointers, should help you get started in academia. Like most things, your experience may vary, and I would hope you don't safeguard your veteran status like it's a dark secret or the true location of Jimmy Hoffa's body. It's something to be proud of, but not flaunted. It's something to share with your friends who genuinely want to know about the world you lived in, but not with the people who have twisted notions of what you have done overseas. The last thing you want people to know you as is the guy who went to Iraq. You want them to say "Hey, that's Alex, he's good people," and not "I wonder how many ear necklaces he has. I'm betting two." Hopefully these tips will help even just a tiny bit in that regard.

Thinking about the Text

1. Alex Horton is clearly writing about a subject that he knows deeply and personally. Still, his article is not a personal narrative. What techniques does he use to maintain an **ANALYTIC** focus on his topic? Present examples from the text to support your conclusions.

2. Speaking about nonveteran students, Horton says that "you'll be astounded at the lack of discipline and drive in some of your classmates" (7). Is this a fair and reasonable assessment? Why or why not? If you're not a veteran—or even if you are one—do you think you could be seen as lacking "discipline and drive"? Why or why not?

3. Horton is writing serious advice about a serious matter, and he relieves some of the gravity with humorous touches. Find three instances of humor and explain what makes them funny. Does Horton's humor make his article more interesting? more authoritative? Why or why not?

4. Horton states with utter certainty that "we have met our lifelong friends already" (6). What does he mean by that statement? What makes him so certain? What does the brevity of that statement contribute to the article as a whole?

5. Regardless of your veteran status, you likely had a lot to learn about "getting by" in college. Think about your first weeks or months there, and write an essay that provides **DESCRIPTION** and advice for an audience of people very similar to you, in whatever ways you feel appropriate, who are about to enter your school for the first time.

My Brief Wondrous Career as a Soccer Dad

DAVID L. HOYT

SPOT CLEARLY DIDN'T WANT TO BE IN SOCCER CLASS. How could I tell? There he was, in the middle of the basketball court, crouched in turtle position with his face pressed against the floorboards as the phalanx of toddlers drove their soccer balls from one end of the gym to the other. This was a stunning, daring act of civil disobedience against the unwanted enforcement of our weekly athletics programming.

Yet it was hardly the first time Spot had protested in soccer class. It was only the most spectacular such collapse. I was confident that, as in previous crises, with a little cajoling he'd be back on his feet and off among the cones and floppy orange discs littering the floor. But this time Spot was raising the stakes. Coach Jaime swung in from the sidelines and stood protectively over my turtle boy as soccer balls careened around him. It was time for dad to intervene.

I approached Spot's successful participation in soccer class as a natural scientist might approach the outcome of a laboratory experiment. If I could control key variables in advance, I could guarantee the desired result in such a way that it could be replicated every Saturday morning at 10:30 AM. It was

DAVID L. HOYT is a stay-at-home dad living with his wife and two children in Chicago. A former professor of history, he began blogging about fatherhood with the birth of his son in 2007. This essay comes from *Daddy Dialectic*, a blog for twenty-first-century parents.

simply a matter of setting the proper controls before plugging in the box. Did I administer the mid-morning fuel booster? Check. Had I drained the bladder? Check. Did I deliver an adequate pre-class pep talk? Check. Were the sneakers on both feet with shoelaces not too tight? Check.

So, if all went well, I would soon be jumping up and down on the sidelines as Spot managed to keep his focus and dribble the ball across the court and into the goal, much as I might were I warming up the giant magnets of an underground particle accelerator and high-fiving my lab assistants as we successfully smashed tiny bits of matter into their component quarks, bosons, and perhaps even a hadron or two.

But that wasn't happening, and Spot was deploying every possible sub-   5
terfuge to sabotage the enterprise. Collapse #1 was a bogus potty alarm. Back from our unproductive run to the washroom and on the sidelines again, Collapse #2 followed with a demand for "banana." Banana peeled and in hand, Spot wandered back onto the court kicking randomly with one leg at balls that may or may not have been there, turning in ever larger, ever more meaningless circles.

Despite following every protocol and controlling for every variable, despite jerry-rigging the apparatus with a banana, this experiment was a failure. There were no quarks or Higgs bosons at the end of this accelerator. I failed to see the hand of God in the soapy tracks of my bubble chamber. No quarks or bosons, just randomly colliding soccer balls, just noise and a single rogue toddler with his banana gyrating through statistically improbable cycles of leg twitching glory.

It was at this moment that my Inner Hockey Dad awoke from its evolutionary slumber deep in the most primitive parts of my brain. This cold-blooded amphibian, this vestigial holdover from an earlier stage of male evolutionary development, lifted itself onto all four legs, swung its armor-plated tail against the more evolved portions of my consciousness, and bellowed:

"Kick the fucking ball you fucking loser! Fucking *A*! Get your ass off the floor and K.I.C.K. the B.A.L.L.!"

Now, although this crude commentary never made it out of my mouth, it nonetheless highlighted how invested I had become in Spot's performance. This was a surprise. It all began so simply: I saw a sign at the neighborhood club last spring, I signed him up, and all seemed to go well. He loved being surrounded by balls, endless piles of balls rolling everywhere, and running back and forth from one net to the other with other yelping toddlers. What joy!

Caught up in the enthusiasm, I joined an adult pick-up league, play-   10 ing real soccer with real rules for the first time in my life, and loving it as much as my son. I endured one crippling injury after another, as well as the frustration—as raw for a 40 year old man as for a teenager—of not getting enough ball time. I took the ball to the park in the twilight of September evenings and dribbled endless figure eights while Spot picked berries from nearby bushes and my dog panted blankly.

And why? How had my own expectations advanced so far ahead of my son's desires? Because, in the back of my head, I wanted to be ready to do all this with my son. I wanted to be ready to coach him when the time came. I wanted to jump into a sport that I always wished I had been able to play when I was a boy. And, more than all of that, I wanted to be able to kick the ball around with Spot.

But what if he didn't want to kick the ball, and in fact was now much more interested in picking the red berries from that bush and the black berries from this bush? So be it. He has tasted soccer, he has devoted roughly one-fifth of his brief life-span to it, perhaps it is time to sample other things. He can always come back to it, being the nimble, flexible creature that he is. It's his father, accustomed as he has become to projects requiring years of labor, who is not quite so nimble anymore.

Still feeling the effects of my Inner Hockey Dad's amphibian intrusion, I brusquely picked Spot up off the floor and carried him football-style out of the gymnasium and down the window-lined corridor. Away from the sound of bouncing balls and toddler voices, I set him down on his feet and let him run a few steps ahead. His protest was concluded. He had won. A smile returned to his overheated face. It was a sunny day and the rest of the afternoon lay before us.

He looked back at me and motioned me forward. "Not that way, this way," he said, coming back to get me. "I'll hold your hand."

Three years ago, there had been nothing in the space above that empty ₁₅ stretch of linoleum but swirls of dust floating in a ray of sunshine. Now a person stood there, and his small voice ahead of me called me forward. Only a fool would fail to listen.

> What kind of rhetorical thinking did this soccer dad do? See Ch.1 for advice about any such thinking you ever need to do.

Thinking about the Text

1. David L. Hoyt writes confidently from a first-person **POINT OF VIEW**; still, his description of Spot's experience at soccer practice is very vivid. Do you

feel yourself identifying more with Hoyt or with Spot? with both? with neither? Why?

2. In addition to the article's title, Hoyt employs other language and metaphors of work and scientific research to discuss the practice of parenting. Identify two such examples. How might each of those ideas be expressed differently, without locating them in a work or research context? Does the essential message of the narrative change? Why or why not?

3. Hoyt is writing for an **AUDIENCE** composed principally of fathers of young children. What might he have done differently if he had written this narrative for his local Sunday newspaper? for a large-circulation women's magazine? Explain your ideas.

4. What is the point of Hoyt's narrative? Where and how is it stated? How does his description of his own reactions to Spot support his point?

5. Parents have abundant daily opportunities to learn important life lessons from their children, but each of us, at one time or another, has learned something from someone much younger, be it a sibling, a neighbor, or just another kid on the playground. Write a **NARRATIVE** about an experience in which a child's challenge to an idea or belief (either yours or someone else's) taught you an important lesson. Your experience may be recent or from long ago. If you truly can't remember anything appropriate, interview an older relative or acquaintance about one of their experiences, and write your narrative in the third person.

Betraying Salinger

ROGER LATHBURY

THE FIRST LETTER I GOT FROM J.D. SALINGER was very short. It was 1988, and I had written to him with a proposal: I wanted my tiny publishing house, Orchises Press, to publish his novella *Hapworth 16, 1924*. And Salinger himself had improbably replied, saying that he would consider it.

Hapworth is Salinger's great mystical not-quite-lost work. It takes the form of a digressive 26,000-word letter sent home from summer camp by the breathtakingly precocious 7-year-old Seymour Glass. The novella took up more than 50 pages of *The New Yorker* in the issue of June 19, 1965; I was 18 then, and I still have my copy. It's the last writing that Salinger released to the world, apart from court documents blocking assaults on his privacy, and it never appeared again.

I had the idea that Salinger might find my company attractive for its smallness. (Orchises is based in Alexandria, Virginia, and at the time had about 50 titles in print, mostly poetry and reprints of classics.) I had addressed my pitch to "J.D. Salinger, Cornish, NH," figuring that the post office would know what to do. They did. Two weeks later, a short note arrived,

ROGER LATHBURY is a professor of English at George Mason University, and his publishing company, Orchises Press, has published over 100 books of poetry and other literature. He has written several books of his own and boasts of being able to yodel in six non-European languages. This article was published in *New York* magazine in 2010, shortly after the death of J. D. Salinger.

J. D. Salinger in a rare publicity photo, 1952.

signed "J D S," and saying that he'd consider my proposal. I was ecstatic, even if I doubted that he'd proceed. And then, silence.

Eight years went by. In 1996, Harold Ober Associates, which represented Salinger, asked for a catalogue and some sample books. It had been so long, I didn't make any connection, but I now see that I was being vetted. That May, I came home from vacation to find a letter from Phyllis Westberg, Harold Ober's president. She began, "It might be wiser to sit down before reading the rest of this . . ."

She summarized my communication with Mr. Salinger and said that   5 he would soon write to me. I phoned her, in shock, just to be sure. Westberg warned me that the book would have to be made to exacting standards. (I remember thinking, *That means F cloth*—the highest grade of buckram bookbinding fabric.)

Why had he said yes? I think he chose me because I didn't chase him. I had left him alone for eight years after receiving his letter; I wasn't pushy in the commercial way he found offensive.

Two weeks later, a large envelope arrived. It had been addressed on a

Royal manual typewriter, the same as the 1988 note. Inside was a full-page letter, and it took my breath away. Chatty, personal, with that rare sweet and endearing tone that characterizes the story I wanted to publish, it expressed Salinger's high pleasure in finding a way to put out *Hapworth*. He proposed a meeting. Just by chance (could this be true?), he would soon be close to Washington, D.C. Might we have lunch?

Later that week, I was in my office and the phone rang. "Mr. Lathbury, please." "That's me." "This is Salinger." I swallowed. "I, um, am glad you called. Thank you for your letter."

Then J. D. Salinger pitched me his story, like an unknown, saying that he thought it was a high point of his writing. "I don't know how I managed to finish it." Some instinct told me not to offer praise, which would have been superfluous. (Hadn't I wanted to publish the story?) He proposed a lunch at the National Gallery of Art. Shaking with astonishment, I set up a time the following Wednesday.

That week, I typed out the text of "Hapworth 16, 1924" from my old 10 *New Yorker*, and designed a dummy that I thought would meet Salinger's demands. I gave the story plenty of leading (the space between lines of type) so that, as Salinger had put it, "Seymour could breathe." That bulked up the book, solving another problem. Salinger had told me that he strongly preferred type on a book's spine to read horizontally rather than vertically, and the volume had been too slim for that.

As I worked out the specifications, I tried deliberately not to make the book "elegant." He had been quick to object to my use of the word, which to him connoted narcissism and preciousness. The buckram he asked me to use is the functional, unpretty material that libraries use to rebind worn-out books. *Hapworth*, the book, was to start out this way: straightforward and pure.

When I arrived at the National Gallery, Salinger—tall, in good shape at 77, with silver hair and a blue kerchief around his neck—was waiting. We shook hands, proceeded through the cafeteria lines, and found a table in the middle of the room. Just two guys discussing papers pulled from an old briefcase. He was losing his hearing and was slightly embarrassed about it, but if I leaned in and spoke a little louder than normal, he could manage. Salinger disconcertingly asked me to call him "Jerry." I was nervous, though small talk came easily enough. Surprisingly, he touched on matters about which I would never have dared inquire, such as his resentment over the lawyers' fees in his suit against biographer Ian Hamilton. He also made the disparaging remark that he found Little, Brown, his publisher since 1951, completely unsympathetic. I resolved that he wouldn't find Orchises so. Still, when I said, "Shall we get down to business?" he too relaxed perceptibly.

I had prepared two typographical treatments for the text, and he chose the one I thought he would. We went over small details of bookmaking. (Running heads at the top of the page? No. The fabric headband at the ends of the spine? Plain navy blue. "Can't go wrong with that!" Salinger said, with an explosive laugh.) The cover would carry just the title and, below it, his name. There would be no dust jacket. I showed him a mock-up of the spine, and when he saw the horizontal type, he said, warmly, "Oh good."

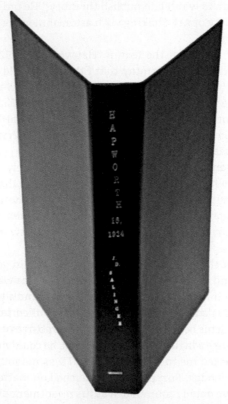

The sample cover, with type laid out to Salinger's eccentric specifications.

I confessed that my distribution wasn't great. He told me, "Nothing would make me happier than *not* to see my book in the Dartmouth Bookstore." Distributed but not distributed! Of all the writers I have published, only one has ever asked that his book be kept out of stores.

I had spotted a few inconsistencies within the text, and I brought them up, fearing the wrath of the lion. Yet he said, mildly enough, "No, no. I want it left as it is." He reminisced about reading *The New Yorker* page proofs in the car of his editor, William Shawn, while Shawn attended an event at his son's prep school.

What would be the publication date? This I had ready: "January 1, 1997." Six months off.

"That's my birthday."

"I think I knew that." In fact, I had chosen it for that reason.

We wrapped up a few details, and bussed our trays. I stopped to stare at the waterfall outside the cafeteria, which flows over a set of stone steps right up against a glass wall. Suddenly, Salinger wheeled around. "What are you looking at? *Answer quick, without thinking!*"

Taken aback, I stammered, "I like that waterfall." He seemed mollified. In a moment I understood: Had I paused so he could be secretly photographed? A friend later told me that such pictures can be sold for large sums.

Money, though, was not on my mind, nor on his. There was never talk of an advance, and although he did not want the book aggressively priced, he had told his agent, generously, to let me make some money on it. I worked out that I could sell the book for $15.95.

After refusing my offer of a ride, J.D. Salinger walked energetically across the Mall. I was both relieved and sad to see him go, and wondered if this would be the only time we would meet.

A series of letters followed. They were remarkably open, even garrulous, with notes on family life, social observations, gripes about train travel, little jokes about himself. He mentioned working on Glass-family stories, but told me nothing about what he'd written after *Hapworth*. I certainly didn't ask.

Around this time, I unwittingly made the first move that would unravel the whole deal. I applied for Library of Congress Cataloging in Publication data.

It sounds innocent. It is certainly boring. CIP data are the information printed on the copyright page. The filings are public information, but I didn't imagine that anyone would notice one among thousands. It would

Unlike Salinger, you may want your work to be published. Ch. 35 suggests how to go about it.

be like reading a list of register codes at the grocery: apples 30, bananas 45, oranges 61.

As we worked on the book, the publication date slipped from January to February. An agreement was drawn up, saying that *Hapworth* had to appear by June 1, or the deal would expire. There was also an unusual provision: All copies were to be sold at the retail price, whether to individuals or distributors or bookstores. Salinger would get his wish of limited distribution. What store would sell a book on which it could make nothing?

One thing Salinger did tell me was that he'd grown unhappy about seeing his name on the front cover, and we removed it. This was going to be a most austere book. We also learned that the type on the spine was too small to be stamped cleanly into the fabric. Salinger offered a new design, with the letters strung out diagonally. It was awful: ugly, difficult to read, ostentatiously weird. When I said so to Phyllis Westberg, she was succinct: "Bite the bullet, Roger!"

I bit. I ordered two sample cases—the covers of the book, its shell. In November, I sent one to Cornish, and kept the other. We would have *Hapworth* in stores in just a few weeks.

Then I made another, bigger mistake.

What I know now, but did not then, was that CIP listings are not only public but also appear on Amazon.com, even for books not yet published. Someone spotted *Hapworth* there, and his sister was a reporter for a local paper in Arlington, the *Washington Business Journal*. One day, after I arrived home from my job teaching at George Mason University, she telephoned.

It seems clear now how everything happened. Hindsight is always clear. I remember that the reporter told me this would be an article about Orchises Press as well as Salinger. She asked me basic questions, about how I'd got Salinger to say yes, about the size of the press run. Foolishly—if reasonably—I answered most of them. I compared our press run to those of Salinger's earlier books, mentioning them by name. I thought I could control myself, but my ego came into play. Anyway, what harm could it do? This was a tiny paper.

Then someone at the Washington *Post* saw it. A writer, David Streitfeld, called. I refused to speak at first, then answered a few questions, nervously, about what I liked about *Hapworth* and when it would appear. He asked if I'd met Salinger, and that, at least, I kept to myself.

The story appeared in the *Post* in January 1997. My phone nearly exploded. Newspapers, magazines, television stations, book distributors, strangers, foreign publishers, movie people. South Africa, Catalonia, Australia. The fax machine ran through reams of paper. People wanting review copies. (There were to be none.) People wanting interviews. I held as closely as I could to "no comment," but when asked for a publication date, I gave one—at first March 1997, then later. I held to the $15.95 price for everybody: bookstore, distributor, chain store, fruit stand, anyone who wanted *Hapworth*.

The only one who didn't call me was Salinger. I asked his agent, and repeatedly got the same answer: No news. I couldn't proceed without him, because we still had too many details unsettled.

Meanwhile, bookstore chains—frustrated by the no-discount rule—had ³⁵ decided to simply mark the book up to $22.95. I inferred (from Westberg's questions) that Salinger thought I had jacked up the price, to capitalize on the publicity and gouge everyone. I hadn't, but I'll never know for sure what he believed.

By February 1997, I had heard nothing for three months, but I had not yet given up hope. On February 20, Michiko Kakutani, working from the original text in *The New Yorker,* published a punishing review of *Hapworth* in the New York *Times*. I have no way of knowing, but this may have been the last straw. It was as rough as anything that Mary McCarthy or any other critic had ever said about Salinger's work.

I yearned to write to Salinger, but I knew that it would do no good. He must have been furious with me, for betraying him by leaking news to the press, or even confirming it. I could no longer be trusted. I had proven myself part of the crass, opportunistic world that Salinger's heroes disdain.

We were at a standoff, and soon enough, the contract's time limit passed. I lost the book on June 1. Westberg's office told me then that any subsequent moves would be up to Salinger, and that was that.

Some people, when they hear this story, blame Salinger for backing down after going this far, but I find this unfair. Such people want J.D. Salinger to be someone other than J.D. Salinger. Nor is the problem the Washington *Post*. I know where the blame lies. After thinking I could do right by a man I admired, I let him down.

In the end, I'm left with a box. It contains the buckram sample case and ⁴⁰ the die used to stamp the cockeyed spine printing. It also contains a stack of wonderful, kind letters from a man who has meant as much to readers as any writer ever can. I have not looked at those letters in years; to reread them would be too painful. Nor will I sell them. That, at least, I can do.

40

Thinking about the Text

1. Roger Lathbury presents a narrative of his experience with the famously reclusive J. D. Salinger. What point is he making in telling this story? How does the timing of its publication contribute to Lathbury's narrative? Could he have told the story in the same way while Salinger was still alive?

2. Not many people would publish stories about errors or failures they have been responsible for in the course of their work. What is Lathbury's **PURPOSE** in doing so? Why might he have needed to tell this story? What factors and circumstances contributed to his being able to do so publicly?

3. A narrative about how a book did not get published doesn't sound very exciting, yet Lathbury constructs a very compelling tale. How does he provide the tension and drama necessary to keep his readers interested?

4. Lathbury says that some people to whom he tells the story blame Salinger for backing out of the deal, but he places the responsibility for the failed publication plan squarely on himself. Do you agree? In your estimation, who bears the blame? Salinger? Lathbury? Both? Neither? Explain your reasoning.

5. The deal began to unravel after Lathbury registered the book with the Library of Congress. This routine procedure that all publishers follow set in motion the chain of events that ultimately ended in Salinger's withdrawal. Have you ever experienced or witnessed a disastrous outcome of some innocent and ordinary act, either your own or someone else's? Write a **NARRATIVE** in which you trace a sequence of events from a routine beginning to a calamitous end. Use plenty of details and try to build tension to keep your audience interested.

We, Robots

JONAH LEHRER

In 1995, Sherry Turkle, a professor of the "social studies of science" at M.I.T., published a book about identity in the digital age called *Life on the Screen*. It was a mostly optimistic account, as Turkle celebrated the freedom of online identity. Instead of being constrained by the responsibilities of real life, Turkle argued, people were using the Web to experiment, trying on personalities like pieces of clothing. As one online user told her, "You are who you pretend to be."

In Turkle's latest book, *Alone Together*, this optimism is long gone. If the Internet of 1995 was a postmodern playhouse, allowing individuals to engage in unbridled expression, Turkle describes it today as a corporate trap, a ball and chain that keeps us tethered to the tiny screens of our cellphones, tapping out trite messages to stay in touch. She summarizes her new view

---

JONAH LEHRER is a contributing editor at *Wired* magazine, and his blog, *Frontal Cortex*, appears on the *Wired* website. He is a columnist for the *Wall Street Journal* and has also written for the *New York Times*, *Boston Globe*, *New Yorker*, *Nature*, and other periodicals. He has published two books, *Proust Was a Neuroscientist* in 2007 and *How We Decide* in 2009 (see Steven Johnson's review of *How We Decide* on p. 246). In this selection, Lehrer reviews Sherry Turkle's book *Alone Together: Why We Expect More from Technology and Less from Each Other*; the review appeared in the *New York Times* in January 2011.

A child interacts with Kibo, a social robot developed by the Korea Institute of Science and Technology, at the Innorobo 2012 European summit. Kibo is designed to display more than ten different kinds of emotion and can perform complex actions with humans such as bringing them an object or hugging them.

of things with typical eloquence: "We expect more from technology and less from each other."

Alone Together is really two separate books. The first half is about social robots, those sci-fi androids that promise (one day) to sweep the kitchen floor, take care of our aging parents and provide us with reliable companionship. As always, though, she's less interested in the machines than in our relationships with them. Turkle begins with the troubling observation that we often seek out robots as a solution to our own imperfections, as an easy substitute for the difficulty of dealing with others.

Just look at Roxxxy, a $3,000 talking sex robot that comes preloaded with six different girlfriend personalities, from Frigid Farrah to Young Yoko. On the one hand, it's hard to argue with the kind of desperate loneliness that would lead someone to buy a life-size plastic gadget with three "inputs." And yet, as Turkle argues, Roxxxy is emblematic of a larger danger, in which the prevalence of robots makes us unwilling to put in the work required by real human relationships. "Dependence on a robot presents itself as risk free," Turkle writes. "But when one becomes accustomed to 'companionship' without demands, life with people may seem overwhelming." A blind date can be a fraught proposition when there's a robot at home that knows exactly what we need. And all she needs is a power outlet.

The reason robots are such a slippery slope, according to Turkle, is that they take advantage of a deeply human instinct. When it comes to the perception of other minds, we are extremely gullible, bestowing agency on even the most inanimate of objects. After children spend a few minutes playing with a Tamagotchi—a wildly popular "digital pet"—they begin to empathize with the "needs" and "feelings" of the plastic device. And it's not just little kids: Turkle describes the behavior of Edna, an 82-year-old who is given a robotic doll called My Real Baby during a visit with her 2-year-old great-granddaughter. When Edna is asked if the doll is alive, she scoffs at the absurdity of the question. But then the doll starts to cry. Edna cradles the robot in her arms and gently caresses its face. "Oh, why are you crying?" she asks the robot. "Do you want to sit up?" When her great-granddaughter starts whining, Turkle reports, Edna ignores her.

Tamagotchi come in a wide variety of colors and styles, including jungle camouflage, tropical green flowers, and translucent yellow.

After exploring the often disturbing world of social robots—we treat these objects like people—Turkle abruptly pivots to the online world, in which we have "invented ways of being with people that turn them into something close to objects." She rejects the thesis she embraced 15 years earlier, as she notes that the online world is no longer a space of freedom and reinvention. Instead, we have been trapped by Facebook profiles and Google cache, in which verbs like "delete" and "erase" are mostly metaphorical. Turkle quotes one high school senior who laments the fact that everything he's written online will always be around, preserved by some omniscient Silicon Valley server. "You can never escape what you did," he says.

But Turkle isn't just concerned with the problem of online identity. She seems most upset by the banalities of electronic interaction, as our range of expression is constrained by our gadgets and platforms. We aren't "happy" anymore: we're simply a semicolon followed by a parenthesis. Instead of talking on the phone, we send a text; instead of writing wistful letters, we edit our Tumblr blog. (Turkle cites one 23-year-old law student who objects when friends apologize online: "Saying you are sorry as your status . . . that is not an apology. That is saying 'I'm sorry' to Facebook.") And yet, as Turkle notes, these trends show no sign of abating, as people increasingly gravitate toward technologies that allow us to interact while inattentive or absent. Our excuse is always the same—we'd love to talk, but there just isn't time. Send us an e-mail. We'll get back to you.

There is no easy reply to these critiques. The Internet is full of absurdities, from the booming economy of virtual worlds—a user recently paid $335,000 for land on a fictitious asteroid in Entropia Universe—to the mass retweeting of Justin Bieber. It's always fun to mock the stilted language of teenagers and lament the decline of letter writing. But these obvious objections shouldn't obscure the real mystery: If the Internet is such an alienating force, then why can't we escape it? If Facebook is so insufferable, then why do hundreds of millions of people check their page every day? Why did I just text my wife instead of calling her?

I certainly don't expect Turkle to have all the answers, but her ethnographic portraits would have benefited from a more probing investigation of such questions. The teenagers she quotes complain about everything—phones, texting, e-mail, Skype. And yet, virtually none of them seem willing to turn off the digital spigot.

Perhaps this is because, despite our misgivings about the Internet, its [10] effects on real-life relationships seem mostly positive, if minor. A 2007 study at Michigan State University involving 800 undergraduates, for instance, found that Facebook users had more social capital than abstainers, and that the site increased measures of "psychological well-being," especially in those suffering from low self-esteem. Other studies have found that frequent blogging leads to increased levels of social support and integration and may serve as "the core of building intimate relationships." One recurring theme to emerge from much of this research is that most people, at least so far, are primarily using the online world to enhance their offline relationships, not supplant them.

　　Needless to say, the portrait painted by these studies is very different from the one in Turkle's fascinating, readable and one-sided book. We are so eager to take sides on technology, to describe the Web in utopian or dystopian terms, but maybe that's the problem. In the end, it's just another tool, an accessory that allows us to do what we've always done: interact with one other. The form of these interactions is always changing. But the conversation remains.

Lehrer criticizes Turkle for writing a "one-sided" book. See pp. 76–77 & 297–300 for tips on considering multiple viewpoints.

Thinking about the Text

1. Jonah Lehrer has written on the same themes that Sherry Turkle examines in her book, and from his **REVIEW** it could be easy to think that the two somehow disagree with one another or that they take competing positions. Would you say that Lehrer's assessment of Turkle's book is fair? Has he presented well-supported reasons? Provide examples from the text to support your conclusions.

2. According to Lehrer, Turkle is "upset by the banalities of electronic interaction," such as texting instead of calling (7). Lehrer himself admits to texting his wife when he could just as well have called. Still, conversation avoidance is only one of many possible reasons to choose texting. Do you tend to text instead of call? Look at the texts you've sent in the last couple of days, and make a list of your reasons for opting to text instead of call. What might you have gained by choosing to text? What might you have lost?

3. Lehrer begins his review of Turkle's 2011 book by mentioning a 1995 work of hers. How does his summary of the earlier work contribute to his discussion of Turkle's recent book? Explain your reasoning.

4. Lehrer says favorable things about Turkle's book, and he also makes some criticisms. On balance, would you say that Lehrer gave the book a "good"

review? Did he like it? Could you tell? Cite evidence from the text to support your conclusions.

5. Lehrer addresses the topic of social robots—androids to "sweep the kitchen floor, take care of our aging parents and provide us with reliable companionship" (3). What might you imagine having a robot for? What kinds of functions would it serve? What kind of relationship would you have with it? Write an essay in which you answer these questions by projecting yourself into a not-distant future and describing the robot you imagine having.

Home Game

MICHAEL LEWIS

WE'RE AT A FANCY HOTEL IN BERMUDA. Like fancy hotels everywhere, the place is paying new attention to the whims of small children. The baby pool is vast—nearly as big as the pool for the grown-ups, to which it is connected by a slender canal. In the middle of the baby pool is a hot tub, just for little kids. My two daughters, now ages six and three, leap from the hot tub into the baby pool and back again. The pleasure they take in this could not be more innocent or pure.

Then, out of nowhere, come four older boys. Ten, maybe eleven years old. As anyone who has only girls knows, boys add nothing to any social situation but trouble. These four are set on proving the point. Seeing my little girls, they grab the pool noodles—intended to keep three-year-olds afloat—and wield them as weapons. They descend upon Quinn, my six-year-old, whacking the water on either side of her, until she is almost in tears. I'm hovering in the canal between baby pool and grown-up pool, wondering if

---

MICHAEL LEWIS, a former Wall Street worker with a degree in art history, is the author of eight best-selling books, including *Moneyball* (2003), *The Blind Side* (2006), *The Big Short* (2010), and *Boomerang* (2011). His financial journalism has appeared in the *New York Times*, *Slate*, *Vanity Fair*, and *Bloomberg*, among other periodicals. This selection is an excerpt from Lewis' book *Home Game: An Accidental Guide to Fatherhood*, published in 2009.

I should intervene. Dixie beats me to it. She jumps out in front of her older sister and thrusts out her three-year-old chest.

"Teasing boys!" she hollers, so loudly that grown-ups around the pool peer over their Danielle Steel novels. Even the boys are taken aback. Dixie, now on stage, raises her voice a notch:

"You just shut up you stupid motherfucking asshole!"

To the extent that all hell can break loose around a baby pool in a Bermuda resort, it does. A John Grisham novel is lowered; several of Danielle Steel's vanish into beach bags. I remain hovering in the shallows of the grown-up pool where it enters the baby pool, with my entire head above water. My first thought: *Oh . . . my . . . God!* My second thought: *No one knows I'm her father.* I sink lower, like a crocodile, so that just my eyes and forehead are above the waterline; but in my heart a new feeling rises: pride. Behind me a lady on a beach chair shouts, "Kevin! Kevin! Get over here!"

Kevin appears to be one of the noodle-wielding eleven-year-old boys. "But Moooooooommm!" he says.

"Kevin! *Now!*"

The little monster skulks over to his mother's side while his fellow Orcs await the higher judgment. I'm close enough to hear her ream him out. It's delicious. "Kevin, did you teach that little girl those words?" she asks.

"Mooomm! Nooooooo!"

"Then where did she learn them?"

As it happens, I know the answer to that one: carpool. Months ago! I was driving them home from school, my two girls, plus two other kids—a seven-year-old boy and a ten-year-old girl. They were crammed in the back seat of the Volkswagen Passat, jabbering away; I was alone in the front seat, not especially listening. But then the ten-year-old said, "Deena said a bad word today."

"Which one?" asked Quinn.

"The S-word," said the ten-year-old.

"Ooooooooo," they all said.

"What's the S-word?" I asked.

"We can't say it without getting in trouble," said the ten-year-old knowingly.

"You're safe here," I said.

She thought it over for a second, then said, "Stupid."

"Ah," I said, smiling.

"Wally said the D-word!" said Quinn.

"What's the D-word?" I asked.

5

10

15

20

"Dumb!" she shouted, and they all giggled at the sheer illicit pleasure of it. Then the seven-year-old boy chimed in. "I know a bad word, too! I know a bad word, too!" he said.

"What's the bad word?" I asked brightly. I didn't see why he should be left out.

"Shutupyoustupidmotherfuckingasshole!"

I swerved off the road, stopped the car, and hit the emergency lights. I began to deliver a lecture on the difference between bad words and seriously bad words, but the audience was fully consumed with laughter. Dixie, especially, wanted to know the secret of making Daddy stop the car.

"Shutupmotherstupid fuck," she said.

"Dixie!" I said.

"Daddy," said Quinn thoughtfully, "how come you say a bad word when we spill something and when you spill something you just say, 'Oops'?"

"Stupidfuck!" screamed Dixie, and they all laughed.

"DIXIE!"

She stopped. They all did. For the rest of the drive they whispered.

So here we are, months later, in this Bermuda pool, Dixie with her chest thrust out in defiance, me floating like a crocodile and feeling very much different than I should. I should be embarrassed and concerned. I should be sweeping her out of the pool and washing her mouth out with soap. I don't feel that way. Actually, I'm impressed. More than impressed: awed. It's just incredibly heroic, taking out after this rat pack of boys. Plus she's sticking up for her big sister, which isn't something you see every day. I don't want to get in her way. I just want to see what happens next.

Behind me Kevin has just finished being torn what appears to be a new asshole by his mother, and is relaunching himself into the baby pool with a real malice. He's as indignant as a serial killer who got put away on a speeding ticket: He's guilty of many things but not of teaching a three-year-old girl the art of cursing. Now he intends to get even. Gathering his fellow Orcs in the hot tub, he and his companions once again threaten Quinn. Dixie, once again, leaps into the fray.

"Teasing boys!" she shouts. Now she has the attention of an entire Bermuda resort.

"You watch out teasing boys! Because I peed in this pool two times! Once in the hot pool and once in the cold pool!"

The teasing boys flee, grossed out and defeated. Various grown-ups say various things to each other, but no one seeks to remove Dixie from the baby

25

30

35

Lewis relies heavily on quotations to advance his narrative. Ch. 22 can help you quote effectively, as he does.

pool. Dixie returns to playing with her sister—who appears far less grateful than she should be. And the crocodile drops below the waterline, swivels, and vanishes into the depths of the grown-up pool. But he makes a mental note to buy that little girl an ice-cream cone. Even if her mother disapproves.

Thinking about the Text

1. Michael Lewis' narrative of the showdown in the baby pool uses descriptive detail to "show" readers the story. For example, when his daughter first yells at one of the bullies, Lewis recounts the reactions of adults around the pool, saying that "a John Grisham novel is lowered, and several of Danielle Steel's vanish into beach bags" (5). What other **DESCRIPTIVE** details provide vivid visual images? Give three examples.

2. Lewis is part of a new wave of fathers documenting their parenting experiences. Could the same essay have been written by a mom rather than a dad? If the account had been written without any references to the gender of the parent, would you have been able to tell that a dad wrote it? Why or why not? What clues would you be looking for?

3. Lewis jumps almost right away into the action of the narrative. The only background he gives is a brief description of the pools and a reference to his girls' ages. How effective is this strategy for the telling of the story? Did you feel that the events needed more context? Why or why not? Explain your reasoning.

4. You may not be a parent, but surely you can identify with Lewis' ambivalence. His daughter has single-handedly defeated a group of bullies much bigger than herself, but did so by using inappropriate language. Not only that, but she unabashedly reported that she "peed" twice in the pool (35). As a parent, how would you have responded? Try to project yourself into the hypothetical moment of the events and give what would have been your immediate reaction, rather than using the leisure of reflection. Explain your response.

5. The power of naughty words is a lesson that each of us learns in childhood (usually more than once!). Perhaps you remember one of your childhood experiences with naughty words, or perhaps you were involved in an incident as a parent or other responsible adult. Write a first-person **NARRATIVE** about an experience you remember with a naughty word or phrase; if you were the child, decide whether to write as a child-narrator or in hindsight, as an adult remembering and reflecting on the incident.

The Egg and the Sperm

EMILY MARTIN

The theory of the human body is always a part of a world-picture.
. . . The theory of the human body is always a part of a *fantasy*.
—JAMES HILLMAN, *The Myth of Analysis*[1]

AS AN ANTHROPOLOGIST, I am intrigued by the possibility that culture shapes how biological scientists describe what they discover about the natural world. If this were so, we would be learning about more than the natural world in high school biology class; we would be learning about cultural beliefs and practices as if they were part of nature. In the course of my research I realized that the picture of egg and sperm drawn in popular as well as scientific accounts of reproductive biology relies on stereotypes

1. James Hillman, *The Myth of Analysis* (Evanston, Ill.: Northwestern University Press, 1972), 220.

EMILY MARTIN, a professor of anthropology at New York University, is founding editor of the magazine *Anthropology Now* and has written extensively about intersections of culture and science. Her 2007 book *Bipolar Expeditions* won a prize for feminist anthropological research. This article first appeared in *Signs: Journal of Women in Culture and Society* in 1991 with the subtitle "How Science Has Constructed a Romance Based on Stereotypical Male-Female Roles." It has become a classic reading in medical anthropology.

central to our cultural definitions of male and female. The stereotypes imply not only that female biological processes are less worthy than their male counterparts but also that women are less worthy than men. Part of my goal in writing this article is to shine a bright light on the gender stereotypes hidden within the scientific language of biology. Exposed in such a light, I hope they will lose much of their power to harm us.

Egg and Sperm: A Scientific Fairy Tale

At a fundamental level, all major scientific textbooks depict male and female reproductive organs as systems for the production of valuable substances, such as eggs and sperm.[2] In the case of women, the monthly cycle is described as being designed to produce eggs and prepare a suitable place for them to be fertilized and grown—all to the end of making babies. But the enthusiasm ends there. By extolling the female cycle as a productive enterprise, menstruation must necessarily be viewed as a failure. Medical texts describe menstruation as the "debris" of the uterine lining, the result of necrosis, or death of tissue. The descriptions imply that a system has gone awry, making products of no use, not to specification, unsalable, wasted, scrap. An illustration in a widely used medical text shows menstruation as a chaotic disintegration of form, complementing the many texts that describe it as "ceasing," "dying," "losing," "denuding," "expelling."[3]

Male reproductive physiology is evaluated quite differently. One of the texts that sees menstruation as failed production employs a sort of breathless prose when it describes the maturation of sperm: "The mechanisms which guide the remarkable cellular transformation from spermatid to mature sperm remain uncertain.... Perhaps the most amazing characteristic of spermatogenesis is its sheer magnitude: the normal human male may manufacture several hundred million sperm per day."[4] In the classic text *Medical Physiology*, edited by Vernon Mountcastle, the male/female, productive/

2. The textbooks I consulted are the main ones used in classes for undergraduate premedical students or medical students (or those held on reserve in the library for these classes) during the past few years at Johns Hopkins University. These texts are widely used at other universities in the country as well.

3. Arthur C. Guyton, *Physiology of the Human Body*, 6th ed. (Philadelphia: Saunders College Publishing, 1984), 624.

4. Arthur J. Vander, James H. Sherman, and Dorothy S. Luciano, *Human Physiology: The Mechanisms of Body Function*, 3d ed. (New York: McGraw Hill, 1980), 483–84.

destructive comparison is more explicit: "Whereas the female *sheds* only a single gamete each month, the seminiferous tubules *produce* hundreds of millions of sperm each day" (emphasis mine).[5] The female author of another text marvels at the length of the microscopic seminiferous tubules, which, if uncoiled and placed end to end, "would span almost one-third of a mile!" She writes, "In an adult male these structures produce millions of sperm cells each day." Later she asks, "How is this feat accomplished?"[6] None of these texts expresses such intense enthusiasm for any female processes. It is surely no accident that the "remarkable" process of making sperm involves precisely what, in the medical view, menstruation does not: production of something deemed valuable.[7]

One could argue that menstruation and spermatogenesis are not analogous processes and, therefore, should not be expected to elicit the same kind of response. The proper female analogy to spermatogenesis, biologically, is ovulation. Yet ovulation does not merit enthusiasm in these texts either. Textbook descriptions stress that all of the ovarian follicles containing ova are already present at birth. Far from being *produced,* as sperm are, they merely sit on the shelf, slowly degenerating and aging like overstocked inventory: "At birth, normal human ovaries contain an estimated one million follicles [each], and no new ones appear after birth. Thus, in marked contrast to the male, the newborn female already has all the germ cells she will ever have. Only a few, perhaps 400, are destined to reach full maturity during her active productive life. All the others degenerate at some point in their development so that few, if any, remain by the time she reaches menopause at approximately 50 years of age."[8] Note the "marked contrast" that this description sets up between male and female: the male, who continuously produces fresh germ cells, and the female, who has stockpiled germ cells by birth and is faced with their degeneration.

Nor are the female organs spared such vivid descriptions. One scientist 5 writes in a newspaper article that a woman's ovaries become old and worn out from ripening eggs every month, even though the woman herself is still relatively young: "When you look through a laparoscope . . . at an ovary that

5. Vernon B. Mountcastle, *Medical Physiology,* 14th ed. (London: Mosby, 1980), 2:1624.
6. Eldra Pearl Solomon, *Human Anatomy and Physiology* (New York: CBS College Publishing, 1983), 678.
7. For elaboration, see Emily Martin, *The Woman in the Body: A Cultural Analysis of Reproduction* (Boston: Beacon, 1987), 27–53.
8. Vander, Sherman, and Luciano, 568.

has been through hundreds of cycles, even in a superbly healthy American female, you see a scarred, battered organ."[9]

To avoid the negative connotations that some people associate with the female reproductive system, scientists could begin to describe male and female processes as homologous. They might credit females with "producing" mature ova one at a time, as they're needed each month, and describe males as having to face problems of degenerating germ cells. This degeneration would occur throughout life among spermatogonia, the undifferentiated germ cells in the testes that are the long-lived, dormant precursors of sperm.

But the texts have an almost dogged insistence on casting female processes in a negative light. The texts celebrate sperm production because it is continuous from puberty to senescence, while they portray egg production as inferior because it is finished at birth. This makes the female seem unproductive, but some texts will also insist that it is she who is wasteful.[10] In a section heading for *Molecular Biology of the Cell*, a best-selling text, we are told that "Oogenesis is wasteful." The text goes on to emphasize that of the seven million oogonia, or egg germ cells, in the female embryo, most degenerate in the ovary. Of those that do go on to become oocytes, or eggs, many also degenerate, so that at birth only two million eggs remain in the ovaries. Degeneration continues throughout a woman's life: by puberty 300,000 eggs remain, and only a few are present by menopause. "During the 40 or so years of a woman's reproductive life, only 400 to 500 eggs will have been released," the authors write. "All the rest will have degenerated. It is still a mystery why so many eggs are formed only to die in the ovaries."[11]

The real mystery is why the male's vast production of sperm is not seen as wasteful.[12] Assuming that a man "produces" 100 million (10^8) sperm per

9. Melvin Konner, "Childbearing and Age," *New York Times Magazine* (December 27, 1987), 22–23, esp. 22.
10. I have found but one exception to the opinion that the female is wasteful: "Smallpox being the nasty disease it is, one might expect nature to have designed antibody molecules with combining sites that specifically recognize the epitopes on smallpox virus. Nature differs from technology, however: it thinks nothing of wastefulness. (For example, rather than improving the chance that a spermatozoon will meet an egg cell, nature finds it easier to produce millions of spermatozoa.)" (Niels Kaj Jerne, "The Immune System," *Scientific American* 229, no. 1 [July 1973]: 53). Thanks to a *Signs* reviewer for bringing this reference to my attention.
11. Bruce Alberts et al., *Molecular Biology of the Cell* (New York: Garland, 1983), 795.
12. In her essay "Have Only Men Evolved?" (in *Discovering Reality: Feminist Perspectives on Epistemology, Metaphysics, Methodology, and Philosophy of Science*, ed. Sandra Harding and Merrill B. Hintikka [Dordrecht: Reidel, 1983], 45–69, esp. 60–61), Ruth Hubbard points out that sociobiologists have said the female invests more energy than the male in the production

day (a conservative estimate) during an average reproductive life of sixty years, he would produce well over two trillion sperm in his lifetime. Assuming that a woman "ripens" one egg per lunar month, or thirteen per year, over the course of her forty-year reproductive life, she would total five hundred eggs in her lifetime. But the word "waste" implies an excess, too much produced. Assuming two or three offspring, for every baby a woman produces, she wastes only around two hundred eggs. For every baby a man produces, he wastes more than one trillion (10^{12}) sperm.

How is it that positive images are denied to the bodies of women? A look at language—in this case, scientific language—provides the first clue. Take the egg and the sperm.[13] It is remarkable how "femininely" the egg behaves and how "masculinely" the sperm.[14] The egg is seen as large and passive.[15] It does not *move* or *journey*, but passively "is transported," "is swept,"[16] or even "drifts"[17] along the fallopian tube. In utter contrast, sperm are small, "streamlined,"[18] and invariably active. They "deliver" their genes to the egg, "activate the developmental program of the egg,"[19] and have a "velocity" that is often remarked upon.[20] Their tails are "strong" and efficiently

---

of her large gametes, claiming that this explains why the female provides parental care. Hubbard questions whether it "really takes more 'energy' to generate the one or relatively few eggs than the large excess of sperms required to achieve fertilization." For further critique of how the greater size of eggs is interpreted in sociobiology, see Donna Haraway, "Investment Strategies for the Evolving Portfolio of Primate Females," in *Body/Politics*, ed. Mary Jacobus, Evelyn Fox Keller, and Sally Shuttleworth (New York: Routledge, 1990), 155–56.

13. The sources I used for this article provide compelling information on interactions among sperm. Lack of space prevents me from taking up this theme here, but the elements include competition, hierarchy, and sacrifice. For a newspaper report, see Malcolm W. Browne, "Some Thoughts on Self Sacrifice," *New York Times* (July 5, 1988), C6. For a literary rendition, see John Barth, "Night-Sea Journey," in his *Lost in the Funhouse* (Garden City, N.Y.: Doubleday, 1968), 3–13.

14. See Carol Delaney, "The Meaning of Paternity and the Virgin Birth Debate," *Man* 21, no. 3 (September 1986): 494–513. She discusses the difference between this scientific view that women contribute genetic material to the fetus and the claim of long-standing Western folk theories that the origin and identity of the fetus comes from the male, as in the metaphor of planting a seed in soil.

15. For a suggested direct link between human behavior and purportedly passive eggs and active sperm, see Erik H. Erikson, "Inner and Outer Space: Reflections on Womanhood," *Daedalus* 93, no. 2 (Spring 1964): 582–606, esp. 591.

16. Guyton (n. 3 above), 619; and Mountcastle (n. 5 above), 1609.

17. Jonathan Miller and David Pelham, *The Facts of Life* (New York: Viking Penguin, 1984), 5.

18. Alberts et al., 796.

19. Ibid., 796.

20. See, e.g., William F. Ganong, *Review of Medical Physiology*, 7th ed. (Los Altos, Calif.: Lange Medical Publications, 1975), 322.

powered.[21] Together with the forces of ejaculation, they can "propel the se-men into the deepest recesses of the vagina."[22] For this they need "energy," "fuel,"[23] so that with a "whiplashlike motion and strong lurches"[24] they can "burrow through the egg coat"[25] and "penetrate" it.[26]

At its extreme, the age-old relationship of the egg and the sperm takes   10 on a royal or religious patina. The egg coat, its protective barrier, is some-times called its "vestments," a term usually reserved for sacred, religious dress. The egg is said to have a "corona,"[27] a crown, and to be accompanied by "attendant cells."[28] It is holy, set apart and above, the queen to the sperm's king. The egg is also passive, which means it must depend on sperm for res-cue. Gerald Schatten and Helen Schatten liken the egg's role to that of Sleep-ing Beauty: "a dormant bride awaiting her mate's magic kiss, which instills the spirit that brings her to life."[29] Sperm, by contrast, have a "mission,"[30] which is to "move through the female genital tract in quest of the ovum."[31] One popular account has it that the sperm carry out a "perilous journey" into the "warm darkness," where some fall away "exhausted." "Survivors" "assault" the egg, the successful candidates "surrounding the prize."[32] Part of the urgency of this journey, in more scientific terms, is that "once released from the supportive environment of the ovary, an egg will die within hours unless rescued by a sperm."[33] The wording stresses the fragility and depen-dency of the egg, even though the same text acknowledges elsewhere that sperm also live for only a few hours.[34]

In 1948, in a book remarkable for its early insights into these matters, Ruth Herschberger argued that female reproductive organs are seen as bio-

21. Alberts et al. (n. 11 above), 796.
22. Guyton, 615.
23. Solomon (n. 6 above), 683.
24. Vander, Sherman, and Luciano (n. 4 above), 4th ed. (1985), 580.
25. Alberts et al., 796.
26. All biology texts quoted above use the word "penetrate."
27. Solomon, 700.
28. A. Beldecos et al., "The Importance of Feminist Critique for Contemporary Cell Biology," *Hypatia* 3, no. 1 (Spring 1988): 61–76.
29. Gerald Schatten and Helen Schatten, "The Energetic Egg," *Medical World News* 23 (January 23, 1984): 51–53, esp. 51.
30. Alberts et al., 796.
31. Guyton (n. 3 above), 613.
32. Miller and Pelham (n. 17 above), 7.
33. Alberts et al. (n. 11 above), 804.
34. Ibid., 801.

logically interdependent, while male organs are viewed as autonomous, operating independently and in isolation:

> At present the functional is stressed only in connection with women: it is in them that ovaries, tubes, uterus, and vagina have endless interdependence. In the male, reproduction would seem to involve "organs" only.
>
> Yet the sperm, just as much as the egg, is dependent on a great many related processes. There are secretions which mitigate the urine in the urethra before ejaculation, to protect the sperm. There is the reflex shutting off of the bladder connection, the provision of prostatic secretions, and various types of muscular propulsion. The sperm is no more independent of its milieu than the egg, and yet from a wish that it were, biologists have lent their support to the notion that the human female, beginning with the egg, is congenitally more dependent than the male.[35]

Bringing out another aspect of the sperm's autonomy, an article in the journal *Cell* has the sperm making an "existential decision" to penetrate the egg: "Sperm are cells with a limited behavioral repertoire, one that is directed toward fertilizing eggs. To execute the decision to abandon the haploid state, sperm swim to an egg and there acquire the ability to effect membrane fusion."[36] Is this a corporate manager's version of the sperm's activities—"executing decisions" while fraught with dismay over difficult options that bring with them very high risk?

There is another way that sperm, despite their small size, can be made to loom in importance over the egg. In a collection of scientific papers, an electron micrograph of an enormous egg and tiny sperm is titled "A Portrait of the Sperm."[37] This is a little like showing a photo of a dog and calling it a picture of the fleas. Granted, microscopic sperm are harder to photograph than eggs, which are just large enough to see with the naked eye. But sure-

35. Ruth Herschberger, *Adam's Rib* (New York: Pelligrini & Cudaby, 1948), esp. 84. I am indebted to Ruth Hubbard for telling me about Herschberger's work, although at a point when this paper was already in draft form.
36. Bennett M. Shapiro. "The Existential Decision of a Sperm," *Cell* 49, no. 3 (May 1987): 293–94, esp. 293.
37. Lennart Nilsson, "A Portrait of the Sperm," in *The Functional Anatomy of the Spermatozoan*, ed. Bjorn A. Afzelius (New York: Pergamon, 1975), 79–82.

ly the use of the term "portrait," a word associated with the powerful and wealthy, is significant. Eggs have only micrographs or pictures, not portraits.

One depiction of sperm as weak and timid, instead of strong and powerful—the only such representation in western civilization, so far as I know—occurs in Woody Allen's movie *Everything You Always Wanted to Know About Sex* *But Were Afraid to Ask*. Allen, playing the part of an apprehensive sperm inside a man's testicles, is scared of the man's approaching orgasm. He is reluctant to launch himself into the darkness, afraid of contraceptive devices, afraid of winding up on the ceiling if the man masturbates.

The more common picture—egg as damsel in distress, shielded only   15 by her sacred garments; sperm as heroic warrior to the rescue—cannot be proved to be dictated by the biology of these events. While the "facts" of biology may not *always* be constructed in cultural terms, I would argue that in this case they are. The degree of metaphorical content in these descriptions, the extent to which differences between egg and sperm are emphasized, and the parallels between cultural stereotypes of male and female behavior and the character of egg and sperm all point to this conclusion.

New Research, Old Imagery

As new understandings of egg and sperm emerge, textbook gender imagery is being revised. But the new research, far from escaping the stereotypical representations of egg and sperm, simply replicates elements of textbook gender imagery in a different form. The persistence of this imagery calls to mind what Ludwik Fleck termed "the self-contained" nature of scientific thought. As he described it, "the interaction between what is already known, what remains to be learned, and those who are to apprehend it, go to ensure harmony within the system. But at the same time they also preserve the harmony of illusions, which is quite secure within the confines of a given thought style."[38] We need to understand the way in which the cultural content in scientific descriptions changes as biological discoveries unfold, and whether that cultural content is solidly entrenched or easily changed.

In all of the texts quoted above, sperm are described as penetrating the egg, and specific substances on a sperm's head are described as binding to

38. Ludwik Fleck, *Genesis and Development of a Scientific Fact*, ed. Thaddeus J. Trenn and Robert K. Merton (Chicago: University of Chicago Press, 1979), 38.

the egg. Recently, this description of events was rewritten in a biophysics lab at Johns Hopkins University—transforming the egg from the passive to the active party.[39]

Prior to this research, it was thought that the zona, the inner vestments of the egg, formed an impenetrable barrier. Sperm overcame the barrier by mechanically burrowing through, thrashing their tails and slowly working their way along. Later research showed that the sperm released digestive enzymes that chemically broke down the zona; thus, scientists presumed that the sperm used mechanical *and* chemical means to get through to the egg.

In this recent investigation, the researchers began to ask questions about the mechanical force of the sperm's tail. (The lab's goal was to develop a contraceptive that worked topically on sperm.) They discovered, to their great surprise, that the forward thrust of sperm is extremely weak, which contradicts the assumption that sperm are forceful penetrators.[40] Rather than thrusting forward, the sperm's head was now seen to move mostly back and forth. The sideways motion of the sperm's tail makes the head move sideways with a force that is ten times stronger than its forward movement. So even if the overall force of the sperm were strong enough to mechanically break the zona, most of its force would be directed sideways rather than forward. In fact, its strongest tendency, by tenfold, is to escape by attempting to pry itself off the egg. Sperm, then, must be exceptionally efficient at *escaping* from any cell surface they contact. And the surface of the egg must be designed to trap the sperm and prevent their escape. Otherwise, few if any sperm would reach the egg.

The researchers at Johns Hopkins concluded that the sperm and egg stick 20 together because of adhesive molecules on the surfaces of each. The egg traps the sperm and adheres to it so tightly that the sperm's head is forced to lie flat against the surface of the zona, a little bit, they told me, "like Br'er Rabbit getting more and more stuck to tar baby the more he wriggles." The trapped sperm continues to wiggle ineffectually side to side. The mechanical force of

39. Jay M. Baltz carried out the research I describe when he was a graduate student in the Thomas C. Jenkins Department of Biophysics at Johns Hopkins University.

40. Far less is known about the physiology of sperm than comparable female substances, which some feminists claim is no accident. Greater scientific scrutiny of female reproduction has long enabled the burden of birth control to be placed on women. In this case, the researchers' discovery did not depend on development of any new technology. The experiments made use of glass pipettes, a manometer, and a simple microscope, all of which have been available for more than one hundred years.

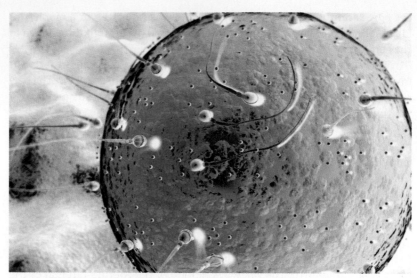

The traditional, stereotypical view of sperm as forward-thrusting aggressor, overcoming the egg's barrier.

its tail is so weak that a sperm cannot break even one chemical bond. This is where the digestive enzymes released by the sperm come in. If they start to soften the zona just at the tip of the sperm and the sides remain stuck, then the weak, flailing sperm can get oriented in the right direction and make it through the zona—provided that its bonds to the zona dissolve as it moves in.

Although this new version of the saga of the egg and the sperm broke through cultural expectations, the researchers who made the discovery continued to write papers and abstracts as if the sperm were the active party who attacks, binds, penetrates, and enters the egg. The only difference was that sperm were now seen as performing these actions weakly.[41] Not until August 1987, more than three years after the findings described above, did these researchers reconceptualize the process to give the egg a more active role. They began to describe the zona as an aggressive sperm catcher, cov-

41. Jay Baltz and Richard A. Cone, "What Force Is Needed to Tether a Sperm?" (abstract for Society for the Study of Reproduction, 1985), and "Flagellar Torque on the Head Determines the Force Needed to Tether a Sperm" (abstract for Biophysical Society, 1986).

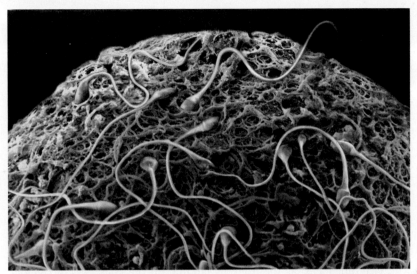

Modern research shows that adhesive molecules on the egg's surface are designed to trap sperm, forcing them to lie flat and wiggle side to side.

ered with adhesive molecules that can capture a sperm with a single bond and clasp it to the zona's surface.[42] In the words of their published account: "The innermost vestment, the *zona pellucida*, is a glycoprotein shell, which captures and tethers the sperm before they penetrate it.... The sperm is captured at the initial contact between the sperm tip and the *zona*.... Since the thrust [of the sperm] is much smaller than the force needed to break a single affinity bond, the first bond made upon the tip-first meeting of the sperm and *zona* can result in the capture of the sperm."[43]

42. Jay M. Baltz, David F. Katz, and Richard A. Cone, "The Mechanics of the Sperm-Egg Interaction at the Zona Pellucida," *Biophysical Journal* 54, no. 4 (October 1988): 643–54. Lab members were somewhat familiar with work on metaphors in the biology of female reproduction. Richard Cone, who runs the lab, is my husband, and he talked with them about my earlier research on the subject from time to time. Even though my current research focuses on biological imagery and I heard about the lab's work from my husband every day, I myself did not recognize the role of imagery in the sperm research until many weeks after the period of research and writing I describe. Therefore, I assume that any awareness the lab members may have had about how underlying metaphor might be guiding this particular research was fairly inchoate.
43. Ibid., 643, 650.

Experiments in another lab reveal similar patterns of data interpretation. Gerald Schatten and Helen Schatten set out to show that, contrary to conventional wisdom, the "egg is not merely a large, yolk-filled sphere into which the sperm burrows to endow new life. Rather, recent research suggests the almost heretical view that sperm and egg are mutually active partners."[44] This sounds like a departure from the stereotypical textbook view, but further reading reveals Schatten and Schatten's conformity to the aggressive-sperm metaphor. They describe how "the sperm and egg first touch when, from the tip of the sperm's triangular head, a long, thin filament shoots out and harpoons the egg." Then we learn that "remarkably, the harpoon is not so much fired as assembled at great speed, molecule by molecule, from a pool of protein stored in a specialized region called the acrosome. The filament may grow as much as twenty times longer than the sperm head itself before its tip reaches the egg and sticks."[45] Why not call this "making a bridge" or "throwing out a line" rather than firing a harpoon? Harpoons pierce prey and injure or kill them, while this filament only sticks. And why not focus, as the Hopkins lab did, on the stickiness of the egg, rather than the stickiness of the sperm?[46] Later in the article, the Schattens replicate the common view of the sperm's perilous journey into the warm darkness of the vagina, this time for the purpose of explaining its journey into the egg itself: "[The sperm] still has an arduous journey ahead. It must penetrate farther into the egg's huge sphere of cytoplasm and somehow locate the nucleus, so that the two cells' chromosomes can fuse. The sperm dives down into the cytoplasm, its tail beating. But it is soon interrupted by the sudden and swift migration of the egg nucleus, which rushes toward the sperm with a velocity triple that of the movement of chromosomes during cell division, crossing the entire egg in about a minute."[47]

Like Schatten and Schatten and the biophysicists at Johns Hopkins, another researcher has recently made discoveries that seem to point to a more interactive view of the relationship of egg and sperm. This work, which Paul Wassarman conducted on the sperm and eggs of mice, focuses on identifying the specific molecules in the egg coat (the zona pellucida) that are involved in egg-sperm interaction. At first glance, his descriptions seem to fit

44. Schatten and Schatten (n. 29 above), 51.
45. Ibid., 52.
46. Surprisingly, in an article intended for a general audience, the authors do not point out that these are sea urchin sperm and note that human sperm do not shoot out filaments at all.
47. Schatten and Schatten, 53.

the model of an egalitarian relationship. Male and female gametes "recognize one another," and "interactions . . . take place between sperm and egg."[48] But the article in *Scientific American* in which those descriptions appear begins with a vignette that presages the dominant motif of their presentation: "It has been more than a century since Hermann Fol, a Swiss zoologist, peered into his microscope and became the first person to see a sperm penetrate an egg, fertilize it and form the first cell of a new embryo."[49] This portrayal of the sperm as the active party—the one that *penetrates* and *fertilizes* the egg and *produces* the embryo—is not cited as an example of an earlier, now outmoded view. In fact, the author reiterates the point later in the article: "Many sperm can bind to and penetrate the zona pellucida, or outer coat, of an unfertilized mouse egg, but only one sperm will eventually fuse with the thin plasma membrane surrounding the egg proper (*inner sphere*), fertilizing the egg and giving rise to a new embryo."[50]

The imagery of sperm as aggressor is particularly startling in this case: the main discovery being reported is isolation of a particular molecule *on the egg coat* that plays an important role in fertilization! Wassarman's choice of language sustains the picture. He calls the molecule that has been isolated, ZP3, a "sperm receptor." By allocating the passive, waiting role to the egg, Wassarman can continue to describe the sperm as the actor, the one that makes it all happen: "The basic process begins when many sperm first attach loosely and then bind tenaciously to receptors on the surface of the egg's thick outer coat, the zona pellucida. Each sperm, which has a large number of egg-binding proteins on its surface, binds to many sperm receptors on the egg. More specifically, a site on each of the egg-binding proteins fits a complementary site on a sperm receptor, much as a key fits a lock."[51] With the sperm designated as the "key" and the egg the "lock," it is obvious which one acts and which one is acted upon. Could this imagery not be reversed, letting the sperm (the lock) wait until the egg produces the key? Or could we speak of two halves of a locket matching, and regard the matching itself as the action that initiates the fertilization?

It is as if Wassarman were determined to make the egg the receiving partner. Usually in biological research, the *protein* member of the pair of

48. Paul M. Wassarman, "Fertilization in Mammals," *Scientific American* 259, no. 6 (December 1988): 78–84, esp. 78, 84.
49. Ibid., 78.
50. Ibid., 79.
51. Ibid., 78.

binding molecules is called the receptor, and physically it has a pocket in it rather like a lock. As the diagrams that illustrate Wassarman's article show, the molecules on the sperm are proteins and have "pockets." The small, mobile molecules that fit into these pockets are called ligands. As shown in the diagrams, ZP3 on the egg is a polymer of "keys"; many small knobs stick out. Typically, molecules on the sperm would be called receptors and molecules on the egg would be called ligands. But Wassarman chose to name ZP3 on the egg the receptor and to create a new term, "the egg-binding protein," for the molecule on the sperm that otherwise would have been called the receptor.[52]

Wassarman does credit the egg coat with having more functions than those of a sperm receptor. While he notes that "the zona pellucida has at times been viewed by investigators as a nuisance, a barrier to sperm and hence an impediment to fertilization," his new research reveals that the egg coat "serves as a sophisticated biological security system that screens incoming sperm, selects only those compatible with fertilization and development, prepares sperm for fusion with the egg and later protects the resulting embryo from polyspermy [a lethal condition caused by fusion of more than one sperm with a single egg]."[53] Although this description gives the egg an active role, that role is drawn in stereotypically feminine terms. The egg *selects* an appropriate mate, *prepares* him for fusion, and then *protects* the resulting offspring from harm. This is courtship and mating behavior as seen through the eyes of a sociobiologist: woman as the hard-to-get prize, who, following union with the chosen one, becomes woman as servant and mother.

And Wassarman does not quit there. In a review article for *Science,* he outlines the "chronology of fertilization."[54] Near the end of the article are two subject headings. One is "Sperm Penetration," in which Wassarman describes how the chemical dissolving of the zona pellucida combines with the "substantial propulsive force generated by sperm." The next heading is "Sperm-Egg Fusion." This section details what happens inside the zona af-

52. Since receptor molecules are relatively *immotile* and the ligands that bind to them relatively *motile*, one might imagine the egg being called the receptor and the sperm the ligand. But the molecules in question on egg and sperm are immotile molecules. It is the sperm as a *cell* that has motility, and the egg as a cell that has relative immotility.
53. Wassarman, 78–79.
54. Paul M. Wassarman, "The Biology and Chemistry of Fertilization," *Science* 235, no. 4788 (January 30, 1987): 553–60, esp. 554.

ter a sperm "penetrates" it. Sperm "can make contact with, adhere to, and fuse with (that is, fertilize) an egg."[55] Wassarman's word choice, again, is astonishingly skewed in favor of the sperm's activity, for in the next breath he says that sperm *lose* all motility upon fusion with the egg's surface. In mouse and sea urchin eggs, the sperm enters at the *egg's* volition, according to Wassarman's description: "Once fused with egg plasma membrane [the surface of the egg], how does a sperm enter the egg? The surface of both mouse and sea urchin eggs is covered with thousands of plasma membrane-bound projections, called microvilli [tiny "hairs"]. Evidence in sea urchins suggests that, after membrane fusion, a group of elongated microvilli cluster tightly around and interdigitate over the sperm head. As these microvilli are resorbed, the sperm is drawn into the egg. Therefore, sperm motility, which ceases at the time of fusion in both sea urchins and mice, is not required for sperm entry."[56] The section called "Sperm Penetration" more logically would be followed by a section called "The Egg Envelops," rather than "Sperm-Egg Fusion." This would give a parallel—and more accurate—sense that both the egg and the sperm initiate action.

Another way that Wassarman makes less of the egg's activity is by describing components of the egg but referring to the sperm as a whole entity. Deborah Gordon has described such an approach as "atomism" ("the part is independent of and primordial to the whole") and identified it as one of the "tenacious assumptions" of Western science and medicine.[57] Wassarman employs atomism to his advantage. When he refers to processes going on within sperm, he consistently returns to descriptions that remind us from whence these activities came: they are part of sperm that penetrate an egg or generate propulsive force. When he refers to processes going on within eggs, he stops there. As a result, any active role he grants them appears to be assigned to the parts of the egg, and not to the egg itself. In the quote above, it is the microvilli that actively cluster around the sperm. In another example, "the driving force for engulfment of a fused sperm comes from a region of cytoplasm just beneath an egg's plasma membrane."[58]

55. Ibid., 557.
56. Ibid., 557–58. This finding throws into question Schatten and Schatten's description (n. 29 above) of the sperm, its tail beating, diving down into the egg.
57. Deborah R. Gordon, "Tenacious Assumptions in Western Medicine," in *Biomedicine Examined,* ed. Margaret Lock and Deborah Gordon (Dordrecht: Kluwer, 1988), 19–56, esp. 26.
58. Wassarman, "The Biology and Chemistry of Fertilization," 558.

Social Implications: Thinking Beyond

All three of these revisionist accounts of egg and sperm cannot seem to escape the hierarchical imagery of older accounts. Even though each new account gives the egg a larger and more active role, taken together they bring
into play another cultural stereotype: woman as a dangerous and aggressive threat. In the Johns Hopkins lab's revised model, the egg ends up as
the female aggressor who "captures and tethers" the sperm with her sticky
zona, rather like a spider lying in wait in her web.[59] The Schatten lab has the
egg's nucleus "interrupt" the sperm's dive with a "sudden and swift" rush
by which she "clasps the sperm and guides its nucleus to the center."[60] Wassarman's description of the surface of the egg "covered with thousands of
plasma membrane-bound projections, called microvilli" that reach out and
clasp the sperm adds to the spiderlike imagery.[61]

These images grant the egg an active role but at the cost of appearing 30
disturbingly aggressive. Images of woman as dangerous and aggressive, the
femme fatale who victimizes men, are widespread in Western literature
and culture.[62] More specific is the connection of spider imagery with the
idea of an engulfing, devouring mother.[63] New data did not lead scientists
to eliminate gender stereotypes in their descriptions of egg and sperm. Instead, scientists simply began to describe egg and sperm in different, but no
less damaging, terms.

Can we envision a less stereotypical view? Biology itself provides another model that could be applied to the egg and the sperm. The cybernetic
model—with its feedback loops, flexible adaptation to change, coordination
of the parts within a whole, evolution over time, and changing response to
the environment—is common in genetics, endocrinology, and ecology and
has a growing influence in medicine in general.[64] This model has the potential to shift our imagery from the negative, in which the female repro-

59. Baltz, Katz, and Cone (n. 42 above), 643, 650.
60. Schatten and Schatten, 53.
61. Wassarman, "The Biology and Chemistry of Fertilization," 557.
62. Mary Ellman, *Thinking about Women* (New York: Harcourt Brace Jovanovich, 1968), 140;
Nina Auerbach, *Woman and the Demon* (Cambridge, Mass.: Harvard University Press, 1982),
esp. 186.
63. Kenneth Alan Adams, "Arachnophobia: Love American Style," *Journal of Psychoanalytic
Anthropology* 4, no. 2 (1981): 157–97.
64. William Ray Arney and Bernard Bergen, *Medicine and the Management of Living* (Chicago:
University of Chicago Press, 1984).

ductive system is castigated both for not producing eggs after birth and for producing (and thus wasting) too many eggs overall, to something more positive. The female reproductive system could be seen as responding to the environment (pregnancy or menopause), adjusting to monthly changes (menstruation), and flexibly changing from reproductivity after puberty to nonreproductivity later in life. The sperm and egg's interaction could also be described in cybernetic terms. J. F. Hartman's research in reproductive biology demonstrated fifteen years ago that if an egg is killed by being pricked with a needle, live sperm cannot get through the zona.[65] Clearly, this evidence shows that the egg and sperm *do* interact on more mutual terms, making biology's refusal to portray them that way all the more disturbing.

We would do well to be aware, however, that cybernetic imagery is hardly neutral. In the past, cybernetic models have played an important part in the imposition of social control. These models inherently provide a way of thinking about a "field" of interacting components. Once the field can be seen, it can become the object of new forms of knowledge, which in turn can allow new forms of social control to be exerted over the components of the field. During the 1950s, for example, medicine began to recognize the psychosocial *environment* of the patient: the patient's family and its psychodynamics. Professions such as social work began to focus on this new environment, and the resulting knowledge became one way to further control the patient. Patients began to be seen not as isolated, individual bodies, but as psychosocial entities located in an "ecological" system: management of "the patient's psychology was a new entrée to patient control."[66]

The models that biologists use to describe their data can have important social effects. During the nineteenth century, the social and natural sciences strongly influenced each other: the social ideas of Malthus about how to avoid the natural increase of the poor inspired Darwin's *Origin of Species*.[67] Once the *Origin* stood as a description of the natural world, complete with competition and market struggles, it could be reimported into social science as social Darwinism, in order to justify the social order of the time. What we are seeing now is similar: the importation of cultural ideas about passive females and heroic males into the "personalities" of gametes.

---

65. J. F. Hartman, R. B. Gwatkin, and C. F. Hutchison, "Early Contact Interactions between Mammalian Gametes *In Vitro*," *Proceedings of the National Academy of Sciences (U.S.)* 69, no. 10 (1972): 2767–69.
66. Arney and Bergen, 68.
67. Ruth Hubbard, "Have Only Men Evolved?" (n. 12 above), 51–52.

This amounts to the "implanting of social imagery on representations of nature so as to lay a firm basis for reimporting exactly that same imagery as natural explanations of social phenomena."[68]

Further research would show us exactly what social effects are being wrought from the biological imagery of egg and sperm. At the very least, the imagery keeps alive some of the hoariest old stereotypes about weak damsels in distress and their strong male rescuers. That these stereotypes are now being written in at the level of the *cell* constitutes a powerful move to make them seem so natural as to be beyond alteration.

The stereotypical imagery might also encourage people to imagine that 35 what results from the interaction of egg and sperm—a fertilized egg—is the result of deliberate "human" action at the cellular level. Whatever the intentions of the human couple, in this microscopic "culture" a cellular "bride" (or femme fatale) and a cellular "groom" (her victim) make a cellular baby. Rosalind Petchesky points out that through visual representations such as sonograms, we are given "*images* of younger and younger, and tinier and tinier, fetuses being 'saved.'" This leads to "the point of visibility being 'pushed back' *indefinitely.*"[69] Endowing egg and sperm with intentional action, a key aspect of personhood in our culture, lays the foundation for the point of viability being pushed back to the moment of fertilization. This will likely lead to greater acceptance of technological developments and new forms of scrutiny and manipulation, for the benefit of these inner "persons": court-ordered restrictions on a pregnant woman's activities in order to protect her fetus, fetal surgery, amniocentesis, and rescinding of abortion rights, to name but a few examples.[70]

Even if we succeed in substituting more egalitarian, interactive metaphors to describe the activities of egg and sperm, and manage to avoid the pitfalls of cybernetic models, we would still be guilty of endowing cellular entities with personhood. More crucial, then, than what *kinds* of personalities we bestow on cells is the very fact that we are doing it at all. This process could ultimately have the most disturbing social consequences.

68. David Harvey, personal communication, November 1989.
69. Rosalind Petchesky, "Fetal Images: The Power of Visual Culture in the Politics of Reproduction," *Feminist Studies* 13, no. 2 (Summer 1987): 263–92, esp. 272.
70. Rita Arditti, Renate Klein, and Shelley Minden, *Test-Tube Women* (London: Pandora, 1984); Ellen Goodman, "Whose Right to Life?" *Baltimore Sun* (November 17, 1987); Tamar Lewin, "Courts Acting to Force Care of the Unborn," *New York Times* (November 23, 1987), A1 and B10; Susan Irwin and Brigitte Jordan, "Knowledge, Practice, and Power: Court Ordered Cesarean Sections," *Medical Anthropology Quarterly* 1, no. 3 (September 1987): 319–34.

One clear feminist challenge is to wake up sleeping metaphors in science, particularly those involved in descriptions of the egg and the sperm. Although the literary convention is to call such metaphors "dead," they are not so much dead as sleeping, hidden within the scientific content of texts—and all the more powerful for it.[71] Waking up such metaphors, by becoming aware of when we are projecting cultural imagery onto what we study, will improve our ability to investigate and understand nature. Waking up such metaphors, by becoming aware of their implications, will rob them of their power to naturalize our social conventions about gender.

71 foot-notes! Done systematically, it's not so hard. See Chs. 24 and 25 for help documenting sources.

Note

Portions of this article were presented as the 1987 Becker Lecture, Cornell University. I am grateful for the many suggestions and ideas I received on this occasion. For especially pertinent help with my arguments and data I thank Richard Cone, Kevin Whaley, Sharon Stephens, Barbara Duden, Susanne Kuechler, Lorna Rhodes, and Scott Gilbert. The article was strengthened and clarified by the comments of the anonymous *Signs* reviewers as well as the superb editorial skills of Amy Gage.

71. Thanks to Elizabeth Fee and David Spain, who in February 1989 and April 1989, respectively, made points related to this.

Thinking about the Text

1. Emily Martin has made a careful **ANALYSIS** of the ways that the sciences describe the encounter of egg and sperm in mammalian reproduction. From what kinds of sources has she drawn her **EVIDENCE**? What was the general purpose for which these sources were originally published? Did you find that the cited evidence sufficiently demonstrates Martin's point? Why or why not?

2. Surely in your school experience, you have encountered the material that Martin discusses—the egg and the sperm. Perhaps it was in high school biology, a college human development class, or both. How well does Martin's summary of traditional teaching on this topic match what you remember learning? Had you ever questioned the explanation of the fertilization process? Now that you've read Martin's article, do you think it should be questioned? Why or why not?

3. Judging from the article itself and the place where it was published, for whom was Martin writing? Who was her imagined **AUDIENCE**? What would she have had to do to make the article more suited for a general adult audience? for a high school or college-age audience?

4. **SUMMARIZE** Martin's argument about the traditional descriptions of egg and sperm. What changes does she suggest for the way the fertilization process is described in textbooks?

5. **PARAPHRASE** Martin's argument about how the models of the social sciences and the natural sciences influence one another. What does this argument have to do with descriptions of the interactions between egg and sperm?

6. Choose one of your biology or anatomy textbooks (or borrow one from someone else) and look for the kind of language that Martin found—words or phrases that characterize natural processes in terms of human actions or emotions, such as "harpoons," "an arduous journey," and "mission" (22, 10). Martin published her article in 1991; have the metaphors changed substantially in more recent texts? If so, how? Once you have five or six examples, write an essay in which you **ANALYZE** the imagery and discuss its possible social implications.

American Pie

HANNA MILLER

ALMOST EVERY AMERICAN FOOD—from egg foo yung to empanadas—is covered in the phone book under the generic heading "Restaurants." Only pizza stands alone. Pizza, a Johnny-come-lately compared with such long-standing national favorites as the hamburger and hot dog, has secured a special place on the American table. Everybody likes pizza. Even those who claim to be immune to its charms must deign to have the occasional slice; a staggering 93 percent of Americans eat pizza at least once a month. According to one study, each man, woman, and child consumes an average of 23 pounds of pie every year.

But pizza wasn't always so popular. Food writers in the 1940s who were worldly enough to take note of the traditional Italian treat struggled to explain the dish to their readers, who persisted in imagining oversized apple-pie crusts stuffed with tomatoes and coated with cheese. "The pizza could be as popular a snack as the hamburger if Americans only knew about it," *The New York Times* lamented in 1947, illustrating its plaint with a photograph of a pie subdivided into dozens of canapé-sized slices.

HANNA MILLER is a food historian based in Asheville, North Carolina, who has written on various aspects of food and ethnicity in the United States. This selection was published in *American Heritage* magazine in 2006. Unfortunately, we've been unable to locate a photograph of the author; an image of a pizza chef appears in her place.

That writer's wistful tone was supplanted in a very few years by a weary one, as culinary chroniclers became jaded by the nation's voracious appetite for pizza and the pie's never-ending parade of variations. "The highly seasoned pizza with its tough crust and tomato topping is such a gastronomical craze that the open pie threatens the pre-eminence of the hot dog and hamburger," the *Times* reported in a 1953 story about "what is perhaps inevitable—a packaged pizza mix."

Pizza had wedged its way into the nation's hearts and stomachs almost overnight, a phenomenon befitting a food that became synonymous with quick and easy. Americans seeking fun in the years after World War II found a good measure of it in pizza, a food that when eaten correctly (a matter of some debate among 1950s advice columnists) forced the diner's lips into a broad smile. Pizza, like teenagedom and rock 'n' roll, is a lasting relic of America's mid-century embrace of good times.

Modern pizza originated in Italy, although the style favored by Americans is more a friend than a relative of the traditional Neapolitan pie. Residents of Naples took the idea of using bread as a blank slate for relishes from the Greeks, whose bakers had been dressing their wares with oils, herbs, and cheese since the time of Plato. The Romans refined the recipe, developing a delicacy known as *placenta*, a sheet of fine flour topped with cheese and honey and flavored with bay leaves. Neapolitans earned the right to claim pizza as their own by inserting a tomato into the equation. Europeans had long shied away from the New World fruit, fearing it was plump with poison. But the intrepid citizens of Naples discovered the tomato was not only harmless but delicious, particularly when paired with pizza.

Cheese, the crowning ingredient, was not added until 1889, when the Royal Palace commissioned the Neapolitan *pizzaiolo* Raffaele Esposito to create a pizza in honor of the visiting Queen Margherita. Of the three contenders he created, the Queen strongly preferred a pie swathed in the colors of the Italian flag: red (tomato), green (basil), and white (mozzarella).

Thus ends the story of pizza, according to most histories of the pie. It's not a bad story, but it's only the beginning; Esposito's adventures in patriotic baking have little to do with why American pizza makers are taxed to exhaustion every Super Bowl Sunday.

Pizza crossed the Atlantic with the four million Italians who by the 1920s had sought a better life on American shores. Most Italians weren't familiar with the many regional variations their fragmented homeland had produced, but a longing for pan-Italian unity inspired a widespread embrace

Pizza pioneer: The great progenitor in its natal year.

of a simplified pizza as their "national" dish. Fraternal "pizza and sausage" clubs, formed to foster Italian pride, sprouted in cities across the Northeast. Women got in on it too, participating in communal pizza exchanges in which entrants competed with unique pies, some molded into unusual shapes, some with the family name baked into the dough.

Although non-Italians could partake of pizza as early as 1905, when the venerable Lombardi's—the nation's first licensed pizzeria—opened its doors in Lower Manhattan, most middle-class Americans stuck to boiled fish and toast. The pungent combination of garlic and oregano signaled pizza as "foreign food," sure to upset native digestions. If pizza hoped to gain an American following beyond New York City and New Haven, it would have to become less like pizza. By the 1940s a few entrepreneurs had initiated the transformation, starting a craze that forever changed the American culinary landscape.

The modern pizza industry was born in the Midwest, not coincidental- 10
ly a place of sparse Italian settlement. Although pizza had pushed into the suburbs as second-generation Italians relocated, most of the heartland was

pizza-free. Its inhabitants had neither allegiance nor aversion to the traditional pie. The region also boasted an enviable supply of cheese.

Despite such advantages, Ike Sewell still wasn't thinking pies when he partnered with Ric Riccardo to open a Chicago restaurant. Sewell, a native of Texas, planned on offering a menu of Mexican specialties. Riccardo willingly agreed, having never tried Mexican food. His first meal changed his mind so completely that, he liked to say later, he fled to Italy to recover from it. While there, he sampled classic Neapolitan pizza and found it much better than Sewell's Mexican offerings. Sewell eventually agreed to forgo enchiladas for pizza, but not until he'd inflated the thin-crusted Neapolitan recipe to make it more palatable to Americans. "Ike tasted it and said nobody would eat it, it's not enough," Evelyne Slomon, author of *The Pizza Book*, said. "So he put gobs and gobs of stuff on it."

Sewell's lightly seasoned deep-dish pie, introduced in 1943, the signature item at Pizzeria Uno, was the first true American pizza. The pie was a uniquely Chicago institution, like a perennially losing major-league baseball team, that other cities showed no interest in adopting. Until Uno's opened its first location outside Chicago in 1979, people had to go to East Ohio Street to sample anything like Sewell's idea of a pie. But its success liberated pizzeria owners nationwide to tinker with their product, ultimately paving the way for the megafranchises.

Sewell was followed in the next two decades by scores of independent operators who deleted the traditional herbs and went easy on the garlic in hopes of gaining a bigger clientele. Pizza was no longer the province of first- and second-generation Italians. Americans of every ancestry wanted a slice of this pie. "I make any kinda pizza you want," the New York pizzeria owner Patsy D'Amore told *The Saturday Evening Post* in 1957. "One day a man order a lox pizza with cream cheese. It turn my stomach, but I make it for him." Professional pizza chefs like the unnamed Japanese-American woman who stumped the panel of the TV show *What's My Line?* in 1956, and the Mexican-Americans who helped make pizza the second-best seller at the 1952 Texas State Fair (edged out only by the irresistible corn dog), and fledgling franchises like Pizza Hut, gradually shed all Italian imagery from their advertising campaigns.

But despite the best entrepreneurial efforts, most Americans remained unfamiliar with pizza well into the 1940s. "We had to give it away at first," Eugenia DiCarlo told a McNeese State University interviewer of her husband's attempt to establish a pizzeria in Lake Charles, Louisiana, in

1947. "They had never, never heard of it down here. And, boy, every time they'd take a piece of it, they liked it. And more and more liked it, told other people, and then got to the place where that was the biggest part of our business."

The urge to tell other people about pizza was apparently a universal 15 impulse that seized knowing literati like Ora Dodd—who in 1949 penned a two-page paean for the *Atlantic Monthly*: "It is piping hot; the brown crust holds a bubbling cheese-and-tomato filling. There is a wonderful savor of fresh bread, melted cheese and herbs. This is a *pizza*"—and World War II servicemen returning from Italy. Veterans ranging from the lowliest private to Dwight D. Eisenhower talked up pizza.

Led by the servicemen's newfound cravings, Americans timidly sampled their first pies. Most weren't crisp, bathed in olive oil, or sprinkled with mozzarella; if cooks followed the advice offered by *Good Housekeeping* in 1951, their pizzas were biscuit rounds or English muffins topped with processed Cheddar cheese, chili sauce, salt, pepper, and salad oil. Cooks could also opt to add deviled ham, stuffed olives, or canned tuna to the "cheese treatment."

Americans who ate at any one of the country's rapidly proliferating pizzerias (the number of parlors in the United States skyrocketed from 500 in 1934 to 20,000 in 1956) enjoyed a pie that cut a neat compromise between the traditional Italian pizza and *Good Housekeeping*'s "Yankee" variety. Pizzas at the Pennsylvania parlor where Andy Zangrilli got his first job were massive rectangles speckled with slithery pepperoni disks. "It was a hit," said Zangrilli, who today owns a chain of pizzerias. "If you didn't like the pepperoni, you'd take it off. It was the Model T of food."

Unlike other ethnically derived foods that enjoyed faddish popularity in modern America, pizza never masqueraded as exotic. Its consumers didn't aspire to be cosmopolitan or courageous. They were simply drawn in by the bewitching interplay of tomatoes, bread, and cheese—drawn in so strongly that by 1958 the novelty singer Lou Monte could issue an album called *Songs for Pizza Lovers*.

But it wasn't just the taste that Americans liked. The social aspect of the pie appealed to a nation riding the postwar boom economy. It seemed uniquely suited to the fun that defined the 1950s, easy for "the gang" to share and informal enough to figure in slumber parties and sock hops. While the early New York pizzerias had been forced to sell by the slice to draw lunchtime business, most pies outside the five boroughs were sold whole, making

Who knew the history of pizza could be so interesting? Ch. 10 tells how to report "facts" in a way that gets an audience interested.

it nearly impossible to eat pizza alone (although Jackie Gleason attributed his girth to having accomplished the feat many times, sometimes within the span of a single meal).

"I call it happy food," Slomon said. "It's a communal thing. You can have 20
two people enjoying a pizza or you can have a group." Sophia Loren in 1959 told the Los Angeles *Times* that having been raised in Italy to consider pizza the food of poverty, she pitied Americans when she saw how many pizza joints they had. "So I think America not so rich after all. Then I find eating pizza here is like eating hot dog—for fun."

Eliminating cutlery made pizza eating seem raffish to more staid diners. Although Dear Abby urged her readers to respect the pizza as a pie and reach for a fork, the etiquette authority Amy Vanderbilt condoned eating slices "out of hand," adding that "pizza tastes best as a finger food." *Look* magazine in 1954 published an illustrated step-by-step guide, instructing readers to hold pizza from "the arc edge," rather than the measly tip, and "roll it in a log." Bob Hope still had reservations when his buddy Jerry Colonna prepared a pie. "It's a tough baby to cut," Hope complained. "I never cut it," Colonna responded. "It's hand food. Chew it down and have fun."

Pizzeria owners accelerated the fun by hiring dough-tossing showmen to divert patrons by spinning pies skyward, sometimes sending the dough 12 feet into the air (and creating an overly dry pizza in the process). Tossers such as Aldo Formica, who demonstrated his talent on Tennessee Ernie Ford's television show, became second-rung celebrities. "Then it started coming out that maybe the guy with the hairy arms in the dough wasn't turning people on, and maybe he was turning people off," the pizza consultant John Correll said of the tosser's ultimate disappearance from the scene. "But pizza has stayed locked in to the image of fun and frolic."

The image was polished in 1953 when Dean Martin swung his way through "That's Amore!," an Italian-flavored love song that famously compared the moon to "a big pizza pie" (a phrase that irritated exacting food writers, who insisted it was redundant).

By the mid-1950s pizza was everywhere. Although it would be another decade before baseball stadiums and zoos offered the snack, political parties, fundraising groups, and synagogue sisterhoods were plying their members with pizza. Fun and flavor aside, the price was right: Zangrilli sold two slices at his Pennsylvania State College parlor for a quarter. "Pizza fit students' needs perfectly," Zangrilli said. Sometimes too perfectly, as a 1950s Atlanta restaurateur discovered when he added pizza to his menu and im-

JANET MICK, MISS RHEINGOLD 1961

Friendly, fresh'ning, happily <u>dry</u>
–that's fine cold Rheingold

Dry beer is cleaner-tasting, smoother, more thirst-quenching than beers that aren't dry.
This very real difference brings out the refreshing beer flavor that is Rheingold's alone.

COPR. 1961, LIEBMANN BREWERIES, INC. NEW YORK, N. Y., ORANGE, N. J • BREWERS FOR 124 YEARS. ESTABLISHED 1837 • PHOTOGRAPH BY PAUL HESSE   TEAL TRAINA costume selected by HARPER'S BAZAAR

Miss Rheingold enjoys a match made in heaven in the early 1960s.

mediately attracted hordes of Georgia Tech students who would congregate around a single pie and linger for hours. He dropped the pies.

An anonymous pizza baker in 1957 blamed James Dean for inducting 25 teens into the pizza fraternity. "Jimmy loved pizza," he complained to *The Saturday Evening Post.* "His fans knew that, so they loved it too." Pizza was pitched as the ideal snack for hard-to-please high schoolers by companies such as General Mills, whose Betty Crocker character appeared in a 1960 comic strip to solve the "Problem of the Puzzled Parent," who is perplexed by what to serve her daughters' friends after a roller-skating outing. What do "most teenagers" like? she wonders. Refrigerated pizza dough, Betty Crocker assures her. Betty is proved right, as always. "Gee, Mrs. Steward, you sure know what's good," one handsome teen raves (although he disconcertingly appears to be eyeing her twin daughters rather than her pie). By 1963 pizza was a staple of the school lunch menu. The American School Foodservice Association that year announced it was bested only by hamburgers and hot dogs in the cafeteria popularity contest.

Adults weren't ready to cede pizza to children, though. People of every age and income bracket went for it, as Lucille Ball, who met her second husband, Gary Morton, on a blind date in a pizza parlor, could attest. George Liberace was so enamored with pizza that in 1959 he contemplated abandoning the brothers Liberace to open a parlor, reconsidering only when brother Lee, the pianist of the duo, teased him ruthlessly.

Pizza's mid-century journey from unknown to unparalleled was captured in a raucous 1956 skit aired on *Caesar's Hour,* the show's second gag that year grounded in pizza adoration. Pizza was to Sid Caesar's writing team what domestic tranquility was to the creative staff over at *The Adventures of Ozzie and Harriet:* a source of endless inspiration. In "The Commuters," three couples are absorbed in a competitive Scrabble game. The word *pizza* is played, but nobody's too sure how to spell the name of their new favorite food (the word routinely shows up on first-grade spelling lists today). So the couples consult a dictionary, taking care not to drool on the definition. The men, now rapturous at the thought of a pie, flee for the nearest pizzeria, promising to return with pizza for everyone. This being comedy, they hit a snag on the way home: Their car breaks down, and the pizzas are in danger of getting wet. One of the men decides to shield the pizzas beneath the hood, a bit of chivalry that manages to jump-start the engine. Powered by pizza, the men arrive home to find their wives asleep, to be awoken only by having fragrant slices of pizza dragged beneath their noses. Pizza was a dream come true.

The premise of Caesar's skit quickly became dated as Tom Monaghan institutionalized the innovation that transformed America's infatuation with pizza into a lasting relationship: home delivery. In 1960 Monaghan and his brother James bought an Ypsilanti, Michigan, pizza joint called Dominick's (James traded his share to Tom one year later in exchange for a Volkswagen Beetle). According to Correll, Monaghan was forced to rechristen the store as Domino's when Dominick complained he was "besmirching his name" with a lousy product. But Monaghan wasn't fixated on quality: He decided to best the competition by offering free delivery, a service that every major chain later added to its repertoire. Pizza purveyors tested lots of new concepts in the 1970s and '80s: There were restaurants that explicitly wedded pizza to entertainment, such as Chuck E. Cheese's, where a life-sized rat boogied through the arcade, and restaurants that emphasized fresh and novel ingredients, such as California Pizza Kitchen, home to the caramelized pear and gorgonzola pie. Nothing, however, has yet supplanted the large pepperoni pie delivered hot within the hour as the quintessential American pizza experience.

Pizza's firm hold on the American appetite is unlikely to slip anytime soon. With very little nudging from pizza marketers, Americans have made pizza the traditional food of the emerging national holiday Super Bowl Sunday; almost 70 percent of viewers eat pizza while watching the game. Both spontaneous and economical, ordering pizza remains a signifier of carefree camaraderie; pizza seems to automatically make any event a little more fun. "We will have pizza(!)," the Carleton College history department announced last year in a memo meant to lure students to a meeting. It's hard to imagine fried chicken or tofu having the same drawing power. "Pizza is more popular than ever," Slomon said. Not bad for a food that most Americans had to have explained to them just 50 years ago.

Thinking about the Text

1. Hanna Miller provides a wealth of historical information in her **REPORT**. Given that there are no footnotes or other formal source citations in the article, how trustworthy do you find the information? What does she do to establish her **AUTHORITY** to write about this topic? Should she have done anything differently? If so, what? Why?

2. Miller states several times that pizza is widely considered a "fun" food, and its presence signals an enjoyable gathering. Do you associate pizza with a good time? Do you have pizza at your parties? Do you ever order a pizza to put some life into a dull evening or relieve anticipated stress at a meeting? What is your emotional relationship with pizza? **FREEWRITE** on the topic to stimulate your reflections.

3. Miller's article was published in *American Heritage*, a magazine of U.S. history. What might she have done differently if she had been writing for *Bon Appetit* or *Saveur*, where the emphasis is more on the food itself than its history? What kinds of information might she have added for this different **AUDIENCE**? What might she have omitted?

4. It may seem strange that the modern pizza industry was born in the Midwest, where few Italian immigrants had settled, but Miller claims that it was no coincidence. What reasons does she give? **PARAPHRASE** her explanation.

5. Few U.S. communities are without a pizza source; even in the few places that don't have pizzerias as such, there are likely restaurants that include pizza on their menus as well as frozen pizzas in grocery stores. Conduct a survey of your town or neighborhood, listing all of the pizza sources you can identify. Using your list as a basis, conduct some on-site observations and perhaps interviews of restaurant or store personnel, and use the results to write a **REPORT** about pizza consumption in your community. What are the demographic characteristics of the clientele of the respective places? Are there patterns based on age? ethnicity? social class or status? What events or occasions are associated with pizza? How much of it is delivered or taken out rather than consumed on the premises?

Why Does Monsanto Sue Farmers Who Save Seeds?

MONSANTO

MONSANTO PATENTS MANY of the seed varieties we develop. Patents are necessary to ensure that we are paid for our products and for all the investments we put into developing these products. This is one of the basic reasons for patents. A more important reason is to help foster innovation. Without the protection of patents there would be little incentive for privately-owned companies to pursue and re-invest in innovation. Monsanto invests more than $2.6 million per day in research and development that ultimately benefits farmers and consumers. Without the protection of patents, this would not be possible.

When farmers purchase a patented seed variety, they sign an agreement that they will not save and replant seeds produced from the seed they buy from us. More than 275,000 farmers a year buy seed under these

---

MONSANTO, founded in 1901, was one of the first agribusiness corporations; its first product was saccharin, an artificial sweetener sold to Coca-Cola. Today, it is one of the largest and most profitable firms in its field, best known for its herbicides and genetically modified seeds. Monsanto has been heavily involved in litigation as both plaintiff and defendant in a wide variety of cases. The corporation is currently under investigation by the Securities and Exchange Commission for issues involving customer incentives and by the Department of Justice for alleged antitrust activities. This selection was posted on Monsanto's website in the "News and Views" tab, where the corporation responds to critics and presents its own arguments.

Corn is ready for pollination. Crops of the future—including new varieties of corn and soybeans with healthier oils—blossom in sweltering greenhouses atop Monsanto's research headquarters in St. Louis, Missouri.

agreements in the United States. Other seed companies sell their seed under similar provisions. They understand the basic simplicity of the agreement, which is that a business must be paid for its product. The vast majority of farmers understand and appreciate our research and are willing to pay for our inventions and the value they provide. They don't think it's fair that some farmers don't pay.

A very small percentage of farmers do not honor this agreement. Monsanto does become aware, through our own actions or through third-parties, of individuals who are suspected of violating our patents and agreements. Where we do find violations, we are able to settle most of these cases without ever going to trial. In many cases, these farmers remain our customers. Sometimes however, we are forced to resort to lawsuits. This is a relatively rare circumstance, with 144 lawsuits filed since 1997 in the United States, as of April 2010. This averages about 11 per year for the past 13 years. To date, only 9 cases have gone through full trial. In every one of these instances, the jury or court decided in our favor.

Whether the farmer settles right away, or the case settles during or through trial, the proceeds are donated to youth leadership initiatives including scholarship programs.

We pursue these matters for three main reasons. First, no business can 5 survive without being paid for its product. Second, the loss of this revenue would hinder our ability to invest in research and development to create new products to help farmers. We currently invest over $2.6 million per day to develop and bring new products to market. Third, it would be unfair to the farmers that honor their agreements to let others get away with getting it for free. Farming, like any other business, is competitive and farmers need a level playing field.

In placing this argument on its website, Monsanto had to consider multiple audiences, as anyone writing on the web must do. Ch. 2 offers some help.

Saved Seed and Farmer Lawsuits

Enforcing patent law is not much different from the enforcement of other laws. Most people respect the law. Often, honest citizens will report those who break the law. The same is true for patent infringement involving saved seed. The vast majority of farmers respect patent laws and honor their agreements to abide by that law. When one farmer sees another farmer saving patented seed, they will often report them. Many of the tips Monsanto gets about farmers saving patented seeds come from other farmers in the same community.

Usually, cases come to us when someone reports they believe seed is being saved illegally. Monsanto's attorneys look into these allegations and may have a licensed private investigator look into the facts. If infringement is a possibility, a Monsanto manager will meet with the individuals involved. There have been farmers who were contacted and provided information that resulted in Monsanto closing the case. The vast majority of farmers who are presented with facts showing infringement admit the violation and pay a settlement.

Since 1997, we have only filed suit against farmers 145 times in the United States. This may sound like a lot, but when you consider that we sell seed to more than 250,000 American farmers a year, it's really a small number. Of these, we've proceeded through trial with only eleven farmers. All eleven cases were found in Monsanto's favor.

A very small number of farmers involved in patent infringement cases with Monsanto have sought publicity around their cases, and have characterized the company's actions in a negative light. In some other situations, outside parties have portrayed particular cases negatively. We take exception to any misleading allegation of wrong-doing. Our employees and contractors respect our customers and their property.

Gary Rinehart

Gary Rinehart has been quoted in several articles as saying that Monsanto 10 investigators approached him in his store in Missouri for no cause and threatened him. Articles have characterized Rinehart as "incredulous" that Monsanto would approach him as he is neither a farm owner nor a seed dealer.

Gary Rinehart was indeed approached by Monsanto investigators in response to a report of patent infringement. The investigators had seen unmarked, brown-bagged seed (generally indicative of saved seed) delivered to a couple of fields. When asked whom they should talk to about the farm, Gary Rinehart's son, Jeremy, directed them to see his father at the store he operates. When investigators approached him at the store, Gary Rinehart acknowledged that he sharecropped with his brother. He was otherwise uncooperative. He became angry, attracting the attention of others in the store, prompting Monsanto's representatives to leave. They were there for less than two minutes.

With the knowledge that there was saved seed on the property, and his statement that he sharecropped that property, Monsanto filed suit against Gary Rinehart. We had attempted to discuss the matter with him in the store, but he was uncooperative. Lawsuits are a legal, and often the only, option available when one party in a dispute is uncooperative.

As part of the lawsuit, Monsanto attorneys filed an affidavit stating that investigators had observed Gary Rinehart driving a pickup truck used to transport the saved seed. Gary Rinehart refuted this allegation. We conceded this point and determined that his nephew, Tim, was the person who planted the saved seed on Gary Rinehart's land. We dismissed the case against Gary Rinehart.

Monsanto eventually reached an agreement to settle the case with Tim Rinehart, his brother's son. The settlement involved Tim Rinehart agreeing to settle on the seed that he had planted. Interestingly, Tim Rinehart never followed through with the agreed settlement. The matter with Tim Rinehart remains unfulfilled to this day. Monsanto has not collected one cent and this farming operation remains unlicensed to use this technology.

Thinking about the Text

1. Monsanto presents its **ARGUMENT** in very clear and straightforward language. Is this posting intended to contribute to an ongoing conversation—to express one point of view on a complex issue—or is the intent more to shut down and defuse other points of view? How fully and accurately does Monsanto give attention to views other than its own? Explain your conclusions.

2. Most people in the United States today buy most, if not all, of our food in stores; by the time we take possession of it, it has been washed and trimmed, at the very least, and often fully prepared. We are generally very removed from the sources of our food, and we know very little about its production. Do you think we should make an effort to know more? Why or why not?

3. Why does Monsanto emphasize that much of its information about farmers who save seed comes from other farmers? Why is the source of the information so important?

4. Monsanto refers to the case against Gary Rinehart. Donald L. Barlett and James B. Steele's article (see p. 683) also deals with Rinehart's case. Which of the two accounts, in your estimation, is more comprehensive? Which is more credible—and why?

5. Write a response to Monsanto's argument. In what ways do you agree with it? In what ways do you disagree? Provide clear **REASONS** and **EVIDENCE** for your position, and be sure to cite any sources that you consult for additional background on the issue.

Nation Shudders at Large Block of Uninterrupted Text

THE ONION

WASHINGTON—Unable to rest their eyes on a colorful photograph or boldface heading that could be easily skimmed and forgotten about, Americans collectively recoiled Monday when confronted with a solid block of uninterrupted text.

Dumbfounded citizens from Maine to California gazed helplessly at the frightening chunk of print, unsure of what to do next. Without an illustration, chart, or embedded YouTube video to ease them in, millions were frozen in place, terrified by the sight of one long, unbroken string of English words.

"Why won't it just tell me what it's about?" said Boston resident Charlyne Thomson, who was bombarded with the overwhelming mass of black text late Monday afternoon. "There are no bullet points, no highlighted parts. I've looked everywhere—there's nothing here but words."

"Ow," Thomson added after reading the first and last lines in an attempt to get the gist of whatever the article, review, or possibly recipe was about.

At 3:16 p.m., a deafening sigh was heard across the country as the nation grappled with the daunting cascade of syllables, whose unfamiliar 5

Some of the humor rests on crisp, tight sentences. Ch. 29 offers techniques for producing sharp, memorable sentences like these.

THE ONION calls itself "America's Finest News Source," a claim so preposterous and silly that it has never been seriously challenged. In fact, silliness is the guiding principle of the *Onion*, which has published satire of the news for nearly twenty-five years. A core element of its humor is articles written in sensationalist style about ordinary people engaged in perfectly routine or trivial activities. This article appeared in 2010.

The giant mass of prose lacked even a large pull quote for readers to glance at before moving on.

letter-upon-letter structure stretched on for an endless 500 words. Children wailed for the attention of their bewildered parents, businesses were shuttered, and local governments ground to a halt as Americans scanned the text in vain for a web link to click on.

Sources also reported a 450 percent rise in temple rubbing and under-the-breath cursing around this time.

"It demands so much of my time and concentration," said Chicago resident Dale Huza, who was confronted by the confusing mound of words early Monday afternoon. "This large block of text, it expects me to figure everything out on my own, and I hate it."

"I've never seen anything like it," said Mark Shelton, a high school teacher from St. Paul, MN, who stared blankly at the page in front of him for several minutes before finally holding it up to his ear. "What does it want from us?"

As the public grows more desperate, scholars are working to randomly italicize different sections of the text, hoping the italics will land on the important parts and allow everyone to go on with their day. For now, though, millions of panicked and exhausted Americans continue to repetitively search the single column of print from top to bottom and right to left, looking for even the slightest semblance of meaning or perhaps a blurb.

Some have speculated that the never-ending flood of sentences may be 10 a news article, medical study, urgent product recall notice, letter, user agreement, or even a binding contract of some kind. But until the news does a segment in which they take sections of the text and read them aloud in a slow, calm voice while highlighting those same words on the screen, no one can say for sure.

There are some, however, who remain unfazed by the virtual hailstorm of alternating consonants and vowels, and are determined to ignore it.

"I'm sure if it's important enough, they'll let us know some other way," Detroit local Janet Landsman said. "After all, it can't be that serious. If there were anything worthwhile buried deep in that block of impenetrable English, it would at least have an accompanying photo of a celebrity or a large humorous title containing a pop culture reference."

Added Landsman, "Whatever it is, I'm pretty sure it doesn't even have a point."

Thinking about the Text

1. The *Onion*'s **REPORT** is, of course, a work of fiction. Still, for the humor to be effective there must be an element of truth in the underlying idea. A good report, as Chapter 10 explains, presents trustworthy information. How do you react to the "information" in the *Onion*'s report? Does it meet journalistic standards? Does it seem reliable? Why or why not?

2. The *Onion* article capitalizes on the fact that new technologies have altered our expectations and standards for writing as well as our attention spans with regard to reading. Although it is a work of satire, how strongly does the *Onion*'s report resonate with you? Do you avoid reading large blocks of text? Has your reading attention span changed over time? **FREEWRITE** or make an idea map to stimulate your reflections.

3. What does the *Onion* do to make its writing read like a newspaper? What are the journalistic features that you can identify in this article? Provide examples to support your answers.

4. In the concluding paragraphs of the report, someone is cited as saying that what is written in the impenetrable block of text can't possibly be important, because if it were, there would be a celebrity photo or an attention-grabbing popular culture reference. What broader **ARGUMENT** about the media would you say the *Onion* is making here? Based on the media that you read, watch, or listen to, is there any truth to this argument? Provide **EVIDENCE** to support your **REASONING**.

5. Observe the people around you in their everyday activities. Select one incident, and write a startling news report about it, as the *Onion* might. You might choose, for example, "Man Pulls Out of Parking Space without Thanking Car That Stopped for Him," or "Boy Scouts Find Nonsticky Spot on Movie Theater Floor," or even "Birthday Sweater Sent by Grandparents Actually Fits!"

Who Moves? Who Stays Put? Where's Home?
PEW RESEARCH CENTER

The Many Definitions of Home

HOME IS A PLACE IN THE HEART as well as a place on the map—and for more than one-in-five Americans, these are different places.

Some 23% of all adults born in the United States say the place they consider home isn't the community where they're living now. Among those who have lived in more than one place at some point in their lives, fully 38% say their "heart home" isn't where they're living now. And a third (32%) of adults who have moved say there's someplace other than where they live now that they identify with almost as much as their current home.

THE PEW RESEARCH CENTER is a privately funded and well-respected research organization based in Washington, D.C., that conducts a wide range of investigative projects both in the United States and internationally and publishes the results openly at no charge. The group's projects include the Pew Forum on Religion & Public Life, Pew Internet & American Life Project, Pew Hispanic Center, and Pew Research Center for the People & the Press. This selection is an excerpt from a 2008 report on a study by the Social & Demographic Trends project.

Go to wwnorton .com/write/ everyonelinks to read the full report.

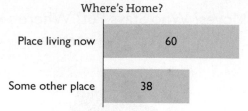

Where's Home?

Place living now   60

Some other place   38

Note: Based on U.S.-born adults who have moved to a different community at least once in their lives.

What makes these mobile Americans think of a place as their "heart home"? There's a wide range of reasons. About a quarter say it's the place they were born or raised, while about one-in-five say it's where they live now and another one-in-five say it's where they have lived the longest. Also, some 15% say it's where their family is from. Just 4% say it's where they went to high school.

Meantime, nearly four-in-ten U.S.-born adults have no reason to be conflicted about where home is: They never left the communities where they were born.

The survey finds that notions of home are also complicated for immi-   5
grants, who make up about 13% of the total U.S. population. Among these new Americans, the tug and pull of current and former lives act differently on different people. Slightly more than half (54%) say they consider the United States to be their home, while 38% say their native country remains closest to their heart. The longer an immigrant has lived in this country, the more likely the U.S. is considered to be home.

Among many U.S.-born Americans, neither the passage of time nor the accumulation of multiple moves undoes the ties that bind them to the place they consider home. More than half of all Americans who moved to their current community at least 20 years ago still identify some other place as their "heart home" (21%) or say somewhere else is nearly as special to them as their current home (37%).

The good news for U.S.-born movers who strongly identify with some other community is that you *can* go home again, especially to visit. Fully 45% say they visit their "heart home" at least several times a year, while just 7% say they never go back. In addition, more than half say they call family or friends in their other hometown at least once a week and send email or text messages to them nearly as often.

But would they want to return there to live? Here, opinion is divided. About four-in-ten whose heart is somewhere else say they'd like to go back "home" to live, while about half say they're glad to be living elsewhere.

What Makes a Place Feel Like Home

"Home" means different things to different people. For about one-in-four movers, home is where they were born or raised. Nearly as many say home is where they currently live, while slightly fewer than one-in-five say it's where they've lived the longest. Somewhat fewer identify the place where their family comes from as home, and just 4% cite where they went to high school.

Different demographic and social groups give different definitions of home. Among movers, blacks are significantly more likely than whites to say they consider home to be where they were born or raised (35% vs. 25%). Whites, on the other hand, are about as likely to define their homes as where they currently live (23%) as they are to say it's where they were born or grew up. And about a quarter of all Hispanics consider home to be where their family comes from, roughly double the proportion of whites or blacks who described home in the same way.

Not surprisingly, movers under the age of 30 are the most likely of any age group to say the place they were born or raised is their hometown. Fully a third (33%) of all young adults say home is where they were born or raised compared with only 19% of adults 65 or older. Correspondingly, these older Americans are twice as likely as young people to say the place they currently live is their home (30% vs. 15%).

What may be surprising is the degree to which older people who retire to another community embrace their new surroundings as their home. Among older adults who said a major reason they moved was to retire, fully 28% say their home is where they live now, while 25% identify their home as where they were born or raised and 17% say it is where they lived the longest.

The length of time someone has lived in a community and the type of community a person lives in also are associated with different definitions of home. Among movers who have lived in their present community 10 years

Imagine reading this statistical data in a paragraph. See pp. 149–52 and Ch. 30 for tips on designing tables and other visuals.

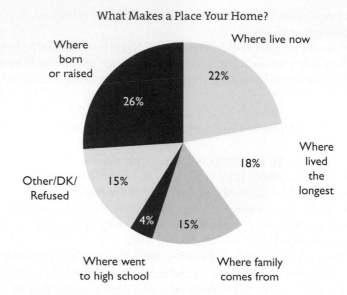

What Makes a Place Your Home?

Where born or raised — 26%

Where live now — 22%

Where lived the longest — 18%

Other/DK/Refused — 15%

Where went to high school — 4%

Where family comes from — 15%

Note: Based on U.S.-born adults who have moved to a different community at least once in their lives.

or more, fully a quarter (25%) say home is where they live now—a view shared by just 16% of those who have lived in their current communities for less than 10 years. Suburbanites are more likely to identify their home as the place they were born or raised (31%), compared with people who live in small towns (23%) or rural areas (22%).

Social networks, attitudes toward one's community and one's overall outlook on life also have an impact on definitions of home. Fully 26% of those who rate their current community as "excellent" or "very good" say home is where they now live, compared with 10% of those who rate their towns as "only fair" or "poor" places to live. Similarly, those who say they have a lot of friends in their current community are nearly twice as likely to call it home than are those who say the number of friends they have is fewer than average (24% vs. 14%). And being a happy person is associated with warm feelings toward one's current community: Fully 25% of movers who describe themselves as "very happy" say their home is where they live now, compared with 17% who describe themselves as "not too happy."

Where Mobile Americans Feel at Home

The "where's home?" question is easy for the 37% of Americans who never 15
left the community where they were born. But for the 63% majority who
have lived in two or more communities, the answer is less obvious. Among
these mobile Americans, a 38% plurality say somewhere else feels like
home to them. A third (32%) call two places home—their current community, and another place where they once lived. Only 29% of all movers say
the community where they now live is the only place that feels like home
to them.

The sharpest demographic differences are between movers who say
their current community is home and those who identify some other place
as their "real" home. Among the most striking difference between these
two groups: Fully 54% of blacks but 35% of whites say they consider home
to be somewhere other than their current community. Hispanics fall in the
middle, with 40% saying someplace else was their home.

Other demographic differences are less striking. Young movers are
the most likely to say their home is somewhere other than the community
where they now live (55% vs. 22%). That's because people tend to move the
most when they are younger, and because it takes time to become completely comfortable in a new community.

That pattern is reversed among older Americans who have made at
least one move in their lives. About a third of all adults 65 and older say
home is where they currently live, compared with 28% of those under the
age of 65. A somewhat smaller proportion (29%) say somewhere else is home,
compared with 40% of Americans younger than 65.

Those who say their current community is their home differ modestly
in terms of income and education from those who identify some other place
as their real home. Fewer than one-in-four Americans (23%) with family incomes of $75,000 or more say their current community is home, compared
with about three-in-ten other movers. And fully a third (34%) of adults with
a high school education or less say where they live now is home, compared
with about a quarter of adults who have more than a high school diploma.

Americans who have made multiple long-distance moves or lived in 20
more than two states also are more likely to say somewhere else is home.
Among movers who have lived in two states, three-in-ten (30%) say somewhere else is home, compared with 43% of those who have lived in four or
more states.

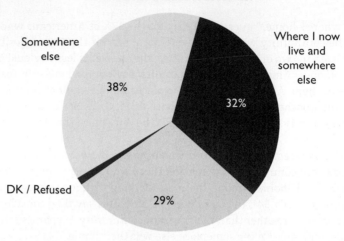

What Makes a Place Your Home?

Somewhere else 38%

Where I now live and somewhere else 32%

DK / Refused

Where I now live 29%

Note: Based on U.S.-born adults who have moved to a different community at least once in their lives.

Regionally, more than four-in-ten residents of the South (44%) say their home is someplace other than where they are currently living. That compares with 33% of those living in the East and Midwest. Part of the reason is that the South claims the largest share of residents who moved there from somewhere else.

"Dual Loyalty" Movers

The 32% of adult movers who say there is a place they identify with almost as much as their current community are different from other Americans in one striking way: They're wealthier.

Fully four-in-ten adults with family incomes of $75,000 or more identify their current community as their home but say there is another place they identify with nearly as much. For these "dual-loyalty" movers, the needlepoint on the mantel might read, "Home Sweet Homes."

In addition, Hispanic movers are more likely than are blacks to consider two places to be home (37% vs. 22%). The differences on this question be-

WHERE'S HOME? MOVERS ARE TORN

	Where Live Now %	Another Place %	Here, Other Place %
Total	29	38	32
Gender			
Men	30	35	33
Women	27	40	31
Race/Ethnicity			
Whites	31	35	32
Blacks	24	54	22
Hispanics	20	40	37
Age			
18–29	22	55	23
30–49	31	34	34
50–64	27	37	33
65+	33	29	34
Education			
College grad+	24	42	34
Some college	26	37	34
High school grad or less	34	36	28
Family Income			
$75,000+	23	35	40
$50–$75k	31	41	28
$30–$50k	33	38	29
< $30k	28	42	28
Region			
East	33	33	32
Midwest	30	33	35
South	28	44	27
West	25	36	36

Note: Based on U.S.-born adults who have moved to a different community at least once in their lives. "Don't know/Refused" responses are not shown.

tween Hispanics and blacks, as well as between blacks and whites, is not statistically significant, in part because the relatively small numbers of Hispanics and blacks interviewed for this survey.

Thinking about the Text

1. The Pew Research Center set out to explore people's reasons for staying in their communities of origin as well as their reasons for moving elsewhere; it issued a **REPORT** that analyzed the findings along a number of dimensions and provided a wealth of statistical data. As Chapter 10 explains, a good report has a confident **TONE** that informs rather than argues. How well does the Pew report satisfy this requirement? Provide examples to support your conclusions.

2. Do you still live in the community where you were born? Where do you consider "home"? How would you place yourself in Pew's data groups? Are you typical of the demographic groups to which you belong? Why or why not?

3. A person's "heart home" is a central concept in the report. Is the concept clear to you? How does Pew define it? Do you find the **DEFINITION** adequate? Why or why not?

4. In the table on p. 893, the highest percentage among all those given—55 percent—is that of young people (ages 18–29) who consider "home" to be someplace other than where they currently live. How does Pew explain this high figure? Can you come up with other possible reasons for it? (If you fall into that age bracket, think about your own experience, and talk with a few peers.)

5. Conduct your own mini–research project with questions similar to the ones that Pew asked. Choose ten people to interview across as broad an age range as possible. Compile your data and write a **REPORT** that **COMPARES** them with those of the Pew Research Group. Are they roughly comparable? Speculate on possible **REASONS** to account for any large differences you encounter.

Mind over Mass Media

STEVEN PINKER

NEW FORMS OF MEDIA have always caused moral panics: the printing press, newspapers, paperbacks and television were all once denounced as threats to their consumers' brainpower and moral fiber.

So too with electronic technologies. PowerPoint, we're told, is reducing discourse to bullet points. Search engines lower our intelligence, encouraging us to skim on the surface of knowledge rather than dive to its depths. Twitter is shrinking our attention spans.

But such panics often fail basic reality checks. When comic books were accused of turning juveniles into delinquents in the 1950s, crime was falling to record lows, just as the denunciations of video games in the 1990s coincided with the great American crime decline. The decades of television, transistor radios and rock videos were also decades in which I.Q. scores rose continuously.

For a reality check today, take the state of science, which demands high levels of brainwork and is measured by clear benchmarks of discovery. These days scientists are never far from their e-mail, rarely touch paper and

STEVEN PINKER is a professor of psychology at Harvard University and is known for his scholarly research on language and cognition as well as his best-selling books written for a general audience. He writes regularly for the *New Republic* and the *New York Times* and has twice been nominated for a Pulitzer Prize. This essay was published in 2010 in the *New York Times*.

cannot lecture without PowerPoint. If electronic media were hazardous to intelligence, the quality of science would be plummeting. Yet discoveries are multiplying like fruit flies, and progress is dizzying. Other activities in the life of the mind, like philosophy, history and cultural criticism, are likewise flourishing, as anyone who has lost a morning of work to the Web site Arts & Letters Daily can attest.

Critics of new media sometimes use science itself to press their case, 5 citing research that shows how "experience can change the brain." But cognitive neuroscientists roll their eyes at such talk. Yes, every time we learn a fact or skill the wiring of the brain changes; it's not as if the information is stored in the pancreas. But the existence of neural plasticity does not mean the brain is a blob of clay pounded into shape by experience.

Experience does not revamp the basic information-processing capacities of the brain. Speed-reading programs have long claimed to do just that, but the verdict was rendered by Woody Allen after he read "War and Peace" in one sitting: "It was about Russia." Genuine multitasking, too, has been exposed as a myth, not just by laboratory studies but by the familiar

Genuine multitasking has been exposed as a myth, as anyone who's witnessed a distracted driver crossing lanes can attest.

sight of an S.U.V. undulating between lanes as the driver cuts deals on his cellphone.

Moreover, as the psychologists Christopher Chabris and Daniel Simons show in their new book *The Invisible Gorilla: And Other Ways Our Intuitions Deceive Us,* the effects of experience are highly specific to the experiences themselves. If you train people to do one thing (recognize shapes, solve math puzzles, find hidden words), they get better at doing that thing, but almost nothing else. Music doesn't make you better at math, conjugating Latin doesn't make you more logical, brain-training games don't make you smarter. Accomplished people don't bulk up their brains with intellectual calisthenics; they immerse themselves in their fields. Novelists read lots of novels, scientists read lots of science.

The effects of consuming electronic media are also likely to be far more limited than the panic implies. Media critics write as if the brain takes on the qualities of whatever it consumes, the informational equivalent of "you are what you eat." As with primitive peoples who believe that eating fierce animals will make them fierce, they assume that watching quick cuts in rock videos turns your mental life into quick cuts or that reading bullet points and Twitter postings turns your thoughts into bullet points and Twitter postings.

Yes, the constant arrival of information packets can be distracting or addictive, especially to people with attention deficit disorder. But distraction is not a new phenomenon. The solution is not to bemoan technology but to develop strategies of self-control, as we do with every other temptation in life. Turn off e-mail or Twitter when you work, put away your BlackBerry at dinner time, ask your spouse to call you to bed at a designated hour.

And to encourage intellectual depth, don't rail at PowerPoint or Google. 10
It's not as if habits of deep reflection, thorough research and rigorous reasoning ever came naturally to people. They must be acquired in special institutions, which we call universities, and maintained with constant upkeep, which we call analysis, criticism and debate. They are not granted by propping a heavy encyclopedia on your lap, nor are they taken away by efficient access to information on the Internet.

The new media have caught on for a reason. Knowledge is increasing exponentially; human brainpower and waking hours are not. Fortunately, the Internet and information technologies are helping us manage, search and retrieve our collective intellectual output at different scales, from Twitter and previews to e-books and online encyclopedias. Far from making us stupid, these technologies are the only things that will keep us smart.

See pp. 297–300 for tips on acknowledging and responding to other perspectives, as Pinker does here.

Thinking about the Text

1. Steven Pinker presents points of view other than his own mainly in order to rebut them. How fairly does he represent these positions? Provide evidence from the text to support your response.

2. Pinker asserts that in addition to science, "other activities in the life of the mind" are flourishing (4), and he cites as evidence the website *Arts & Letters Daily*, a portal page that leads to recent articles in dozens of academic and popular periodicals. Is the essential point the proliferation of articles and the "collective intellectual output" (11) they represent, as Pinker argues, or is it our easier access to them? If access is the only thing that has changed, does that weaken Pinker's **ARGUMENT** about the vitality of contemporary intellectual activity? Why or why not?

3. This piece was originally published as an op-ed column in the *New York Times*. Judging from its **TONE**, do you think Pinker was writing for an **AUDIENCE** that was already inclined to agree with him? How can you tell?

4. What does the title of the essay mean? To what phrase is it an allusion? (Use a *Google* search on parts of the title if you're not already familiar with the phrase.) Why might Pinker (or his editors at the *Times*) have chosen that particular title? How does it contribute to his argument?

5. Pinker comments that "the constant arrival of information packets can be distracting or addictive" (9). What has been your own experience in this area? Reflect on the question, and then write a response that supports or refutes Pinker's claim.

What's Eating America

MICHAEL POLLAN

DESCENDANTS OF THE MAYA living in Mexico still sometimes refer to themselves as "the corn people." The phrase is not intended as metaphor. Rather, it's meant to acknowledge their abiding dependence on this miraculous grass, the staple of their diet for almost 9,000 years.

For an American like me, growing up linked to a very different food chain, yet one that is also rooted in corn, not to think of himself as a corn person suggests either a failure of imagination or a triumph of capitalism.

Or perhaps a little of both. For the great edifice of variety and choice that is an American supermarket rests on a remarkably narrow biological foundation: corn. It's not merely the feed that the steers and the chickens and the pigs and the turkeys ate; it's not just the source of the flour and the oil and the leavenings, the glycerides and coloring in the processed foods; it's not just sweetening the soft drinks or lending a shine to the magazine cover

MICHAEL POLLAN, a professor of journalism at the University of California at Berkeley, has won numerous awards and honors for his books and articles about food, agriculture, ecology, health, and other related topics. One of his best sellers, *The Omnivore's Dilemma*, was named one of the ten best books of 2006 by both the *New York Times* and the *Washington Post*. In 2010, Pollan was included in *Time* magazine's list of the 100 most influential people in the world. This selection first appeared in 2006 in *Smithsonian* magazine.

over by the checkout. The supermarket itself—the wallboard and joint compound, the linoleum and fiberglass and adhesives out of which the building itself has been built—is in no small measure a manifestation of corn.

There are some 45,000 items in the average American supermarket, and more than a quarter of them contain corn. At the same time, the food industry has done a good job of persuading us that the 45,000 different items or SKUs (stock keeping units) represent genuine variety rather than the clever rearrangements of molecules extracted from the same plant.

How this peculiar grass, native to Central America and unknown to the   5
Old World before 1492, came to colonize so much of our land and bodies is one of the plant world's greatest success stories. I say the plant world's success story because it is no longer clear that corn's triumph is such a boon to the rest of the world.

At its most basic, the story of life on earth is the competition among species to capture and store as much energy as possible—either directly from the sun, in the case of plants, or, in the case of animals, by eating plants and plant eaters. The energy is stored in the form of carbon molecules and measured in calories: the calories we eat, whether in an ear of corn or a steak, represent packets of energy once captured by a plant. Few plants can manufacture quite as much organic matter (and calories) from the same quantities of sunlight and water and basic elements as corn.

The great turning point in the modern history of corn, which in turn marks a key turning point in the industrialization of our food, can be dated with some precision to the day in 1947 when the huge munitions plant at Muscle Shoals, Alabama, switched over from making explosives to making chemical fertilizer. After World War II, the government had found itself with a tremendous surplus of ammonium nitrate, the principal ingredient in the making of explosives. Ammonium nitrate also happens to be an excellent source of nitrogen for plants. Serious thought was given to spraying America's forests with the surplus chemical, to help the timber industry. But agronomists in the Department of Agriculture had a better idea: spread the ammonium nitrate on farmland as fertilizer. The chemical fertilizer industry (along with that of pesticides, which are based on the poison gases developed for war) is the product of the government's effort to convert its war machine to peacetime purposes. As the Indian farmer activist Vandana Shiva says in her speeches, "We're still eating the leftovers of World War II."

F1 hybrid corn is the greediest of plants, consuming more fertilizer than any other crop. Though F1 hybrids were introduced in the 1930s, it wasn't

Crop duster spreading fertilizer over a cornfield.

until they made the acquaintance of chemical fertilizers in the 1950s that corn yields exploded. The discovery of synthetic nitrogen changed everything—not just for the corn plant and the farm, not just for the food system, but also for the way life on earth is conducted.

All life depends on nitrogen; it is the building block from which nature assembles amino acids, proteins and nucleic acid; the genetic information that orders and perpetuates life is written in nitrogen ink. But the supply of usable nitrogen on earth is limited. Although earth's atmosphere is about 80 percent nitrogen, all those atoms are tightly paired, nonreactive and therefore useless; the 19th-century chemist Justus von Liebig spoke of atmospheric nitrogen's "indifference to all other substances." To be of any value to plants and animals, these self-involved nitrogen atoms must be split and then joined to atoms of hydrogen.

Chemists call this process of taking atoms from the atmosphere and 10 combining them into molecules useful to living things "fixing" that element. Until a German Jewish chemist named Fritz Haber figured out how to turn this trick in 1909, all the usable nitrogen on earth had at one time been fixed by soil bacteria living on the roots of leguminous plants (such as peas or alfalfa or locust trees) or, less commonly, by the shock of electrical lightning, which can break nitrogen bonds in the air, releasing a light rain of fertility.

See how smoothly Pollan weaves the ideas of others in with his own. Find out how to do that in your writing in Ch. 21.

In his book *Enriching the Earth: Fritz Haber, Carl Bosch and the Transformation of World Food Production*, Vaclav Smil pointed out that "there is no way to grow crops and human bodies without nitrogen." Before Haber's invention, the sheer amount of life earth could support—the size of crops and therefore the number of human bodies—was limited by the amount of nitrogen that bacteria and lightning could fix. By 1900, European scientists had recognized that unless a way was found to augment this naturally occurring nitrogen, the growth of the human population would soon grind to a very painful halt. The same recognition by Chinese scientists a few decades later is probably what compelled China's opening to the West: after Nixon's 1972 trip, the first major order the Chinese government placed was for 13 massive fertilizer factories. Without them, China would have starved.

This is why it may not be hyperbole to claim, as Smil does, that the Haber-Bosch process for fixing nitrogen (Bosch gets the credit for commercializing Haber's idea) is the most important invention of the 20th century. He estimates that two of every five humans on earth today would not be alive if not for Fritz Haber's invention. We can easily imagine a world without computers or electricity, Smil points out, but without synthetic fertilizer billions of people would never have been born. Though, as these numbers suggest, humans may have struck a Faustian bargain with nature when Fritz Haber gave us the power to fix nitrogen.

Fritz Haber? No, I'd never heard of him either, even though he was awarded the Nobel Prize in 1918 for "improving the standards of agriculture and the well-being of mankind." But the reason for his obscurity has less to do with the importance of his work than an ugly twist of his biography, which recalls the dubious links between modern warfare and industrial agriculture: during World War I, Haber threw himself into the German war effort, and his chemistry kept alive Germany's hopes for victory, by allowing it to make bombs from synthetic nitrate. Later, Haber put his genius for chemistry to work developing poison gases—ammonia, then chlorine. (He subsequently developed Zyklon B, the gas used in Hitler's concentration camps.) His wife, a chemist sickened by her husband's contribution to the war effort, used his army pistol to kill herself; Haber died, broken and in flight from Nazi Germany, in a Basel hotel room in 1934.

His story has been all but written out of the 20th century. But it embodies the paradoxes of science, the double edge to our manipulations of nature, the good and evil that can flow not only from the same man but from the same knowledge. Even Haber's agricultural benefaction has proved to be a decidedly mixed blessing.

When humankind acquired the power to fix nitrogen, the basis of soil 15 fertility shifted from a total reliance on the energy of the sun to a new reliance on fossil fuel. That's because the Haber-Bosch process works by combining nitrogen and hydrogen gases under immense heat and pressure in the presence of a catalyst. The heat and pressure are supplied by prodigious amounts of electricity, and the hydrogen is supplied by oil, coal or, most commonly today, natural gas. True, these fossil fuels were created by the sun, billions of years ago, but they are not renewable in the same way that the fertility created by a legume nourished by sunlight is. (That nitrogen is fixed by a bacterium living on the roots of the legume, which trades a tiny drip of sugar for the nitrogen the plant needs.)

Liberated from the old biological constraints, the farm could now be managed on industrial principles, as a factory transforming inputs of raw material—chemical fertilizer—into outputs of corn. And corn adapted brilliantly to the new industrial regime, consuming prodigious quantities of fossil fuel energy and turning out ever more prodigious quantities of food energy. Growing corn, which from a biological perspective had always been a process of capturing sunlight to turn it into food, has in no small measure become a process of converting fossil fuels into food. More than half of all the synthetic nitrogen made today is applied to corn.

From the standpoint of industrial efficiency, it's too bad we can't simply drink petroleum directly, because there's a lot less energy in a bushel of corn (measured in calories) than there is in the half-gallon of oil required to produce it. Ecologically, this is a fabulously expensive way to produce food—but "ecologically" is no longer the operative standard. In the factory, time is money, and yield is everything.

One problem with factories, as opposed to biological systems, is that they tend to pollute. Hungry for fossil fuel as hybrid corn is, farmers still feed it far more than it can possibly eat, wasting most of the fertilizer they buy. And what happens to that synthetic nitrogen the plants don't take up? Some of it evaporates into the air, where it acidifies the rain and contributes to global warming. Some seeps down to the water table, whence it may come out of the tap. The nitrates in water bind to hemoglobin, compromis-

Pollution from nitrate fertilizers has boosted the growth of algae. In this image, masses of seaweed are cleared from the French coastline in August 2011.

ing the blood's ability to carry oxygen to the brain. (I guess I was wrong to suggest we don't sip fossil fuels directly; sometimes we do.)

It has been less than a century since Fritz Haber's invention, yet already it has changed earth's ecology. More than half of the world's supply of usable nitrogen is now man-made. (Unless you grew up on organic food, most of the kilo or so of nitrogen in your body was fixed by the Haber-Bosch process.) "We have perturbed the global nitrogen cycle," Smil wrote, "more than any other, even carbon." The effects may be harder to predict than the effects of the global warming caused by our disturbance of the carbon cycle, but they are no less momentous.

The flood of synthetic nitrogen has fertilized not just the farm fields 20 but the forests and oceans, too, to the benefit of some species (corn and algae being two of the biggest beneficiaries) and to the detriment of countless others. The ultimate fate of the nitrates spread in Iowa or Indiana is to flow down the Mississippi into the Gulf of Mexico, where their deadly fertility poisons the marine ecosystem. The nitrogen tide stimulates the wild growth of algae, and the algae smother the fish, creating a "hypoxic," or dead, zone as big as New Jersey—and still growing. By fertilizing the world, we alter the planet's composition of species and shrink its biodiversity.

And yet, as organic farmers (who don't use synthetic fertilizer) prove every day, the sun still shines, plants and their bacterial associates still fix nitrogen, and farm animals still produce vast quantities of nitrogen in their "waste," so-called. It may take more work, but it's entirely possible to nourish the soil, and ourselves, without dumping so much nitrogen into the environment. The key to reducing our dependence on synthetic nitrogen is to build a more diversified agriculture—rotating crops and using animals to recycle nutrients on farms—and give up our vast, nitrogen-guzzling monocultures of corn. Especially as the price of fossil fuels climbs, even the world's most industrialized farmers will need to take a second look at how nature, and those who imitate her, go about creating fertility without diminishing our world.

Thinking about the Text

1. Michael Pollan's **ARGUMENT** presents a very succinct treatment of a complex topic. Did you find the background information it provides appropriate and adequate? Why or why not? Provide examples to support your evaluation.

2. Were you already aware of the immense role played by corn in the American diet? According to Pollan, "more than a quarter" (4) of the 45,000 food items sold in supermarkets list corn or its derivatives among their ingredients; in addition, the major dairy and meat animals—chickens, pigs, cows—eat a corn-rich diet themselves. Keep a corn content journal for two days, carefully monitoring the ingredients of the foods you eat and cook with on those days, and maintaining a list of the corn products used in them. Be as thorough as possible; in addition to reading labels at home, question the staff of restaurants or campus dining facilities if necessary. On the third day, reflect on the list. Are there more corn products than you expected? fewer? **DESCRIBE** your thoughts and impressions.

3. Pollan's article was published in *Smithsonian*; from its **TONE** and content, what can you tell about this magazine's **AUDIENCE**? Think about demographic factors such as age, gender, education, income, occupation, and geographical location. Jot down your responses to the question; then go to wwnorton .com/write/everyonelinks to connect to the reader demographics section of the magazine's website and see how close you got.

4. What is Pollan's **THESIS** in this argument? Write a concise one-paragraph **SUMMARY** of the article, emphasizing the thesis.

5. Despite all that we know about the disruption or damage our shopping and eating habits cause to the environment, making substantial changes in them is difficult—often impractical, and sometimes even undesirable for economic, social, or other reasons. What, if anything, would you be willing to do personally (or have you done already) to reduce the environmental impact of what you buy and eat? What wouldn't you be willing to do? Write a carefully considered essay **ARGUING A POSITION** on these questions, justifying your responses in the context of your social and economic circumstances. Just explain *your own* attitudes and practices on this issue and the reasons for them (not what you think society in general should or shouldn't do), and you need not be defensive or aggressive in doing so.

Blue-Collar Brilliance

MIKE ROSE

MY MOTHER, ROSE MERAGLIO ROSE (Rosie), shaped her adult identity as a waitress in coffee shops and family restaurants. When I was growing up in Los Angeles during the 1950s, my father and I would occasionally hang out at the restaurant until her shift ended, and then we'd ride the bus home with her. Sometimes she worked the register and the counter, and we sat there; when she waited booths and tables, we found a booth in the back where the waitresses took their breaks.

There wasn't much for a child to do at the restaurants, and so as the hours stretched out, I watched the cooks and waitresses and listened to what they said. At mealtimes, the pace of the kitchen staff and the din from customers picked up. Weaving in and out around the room, waitresses warned

MIKE ROSE, a professor of education and information studies at UCLA, is interested in the various aspects of thinking and learning, including the ways that people teach and practice critical thinking and problem solving. His work has focused on developing better teaching methods, on understanding people's engagement with the written word, and on bridging gaps between academic disciplines and between the academic and nonacademic worlds, among many other issues. Rose has published ten books, including the semiautobiographical *Lives on the Boundary* (1989) and *Why School? Reclaiming Education for All of Us* (2009). He also maintains a blog at mikerosebooks.com. This article was originally published in 2009 in the *American Scholar*, a magazine sponsored by the Phi Beta Kappa Society.

behind you in impassive but urgent voices. Standing at the service window facing the kitchen, they called out abbreviated orders. *Fry four on two*, my mother would say as she clipped a check onto the metal wheel. Her tables were *deuces, four-tops,* or *six-tops* according to their size; seating areas also were nicknamed. The *racetrack*, for instance, was the fast-turnover front section. Lingo conferred authority and signaled know-how.

Rosie took customers' orders, pencil poised over pad, while fielding questions about the food. She walked full tilt through the room with plates stretching up her left arm and two cups of coffee somehow cradled in her right hand. She stood at a table or booth and removed a plate for this person, another for that person, then another, remembering who had the hamburger, who had the fried shrimp, almost always getting it right. She would haggle with the cook about a returned order and rush by us, saying, *He gave me lip, but I got him.* She'd take a minute to flop down in the booth next to my father. *I'm all in*, she'd say, and whisper something about a customer. Gripping the outer edge of the table with one hand, she'd watch the room and note, in the flow of our conversation, who needed a refill, whose order was taking longer to prepare than it should, who was finishing up.

I couldn't have put it in words when I was growing up, but what I observed in my mother's restaurant defined the world of adults, a place where competence was synonymous with physical work. I've since studied the working habits of blue-collar workers and have come to understand how much my mother's kind of work demands of both body and brain. A waitress acquires knowledge and intuition about the ways and the rhythms of the restaurant business. Waiting on seven to nine tables, each with two to six customers, Rosie devised memory strategies so that she could remember who ordered what. And because she knew the average time it took to prepare different dishes, she could monitor an order that was taking too long at the service station.

Like anyone who is effective at physical work, my mother learned *to* 5 *work smart*, as she put it, *to make every move count.* She'd sequence and group tasks: What could she do first, then second, then third as she circled through her station? What tasks could be clustered? She did everything on the fly, and when problems arose—technical or human—she solved them within the flow of work, while taking into account the emotional state of her co-workers. Was the manager in a good mood? Did the cook wake up on the wrong side of the bed? If so, how could she make an extra request or effectively return an order?

Rosie solved technical and human problems on the fly.

And then, of course, there were the customers who entered the restaurant with all sorts of needs, from physiological ones, including the emotions that accompany hunger, to a sometimes complicated desire for human contact. Her tip depended on how well she responded to these needs, and so she became adept at reading social cues and managing feelings, both the customers' and her own. No wonder, then, that Rosie was intrigued by psychology. The restaurant became the place where she studied human behavior, puzzling over the problems of her regular customers and refining her ability to deal with people in a difficult world. She took pride in *being among the public*, she'd say. *There isn't a day that goes by in the restaurant that you don't learn something.*

My mother quit school in the seventh grade to help raise her brothers and sisters. Some of those siblings made it through high school, and some dropped out to find work in railroad yards, factories, or restaurants. My father finished a grade or two in primary school in Italy and never darkened the schoolhouse door again. I didn't do well in school either. By high school I had accumulated a spotty academic record and many hours of hazy disaffection. I spent a few years on the vocational track, but in my senior year I was inspired by my English teacher and managed to squeak into a small college on probation.

My freshman year was academically bumpy, but gradually I began to see formal education as a means of fulfillment and as a road toward making a living. I studied the humanities and later the social and psychological sciences and taught for 10 years in a range of situations—elementary school, adult education courses, tutoring centers, a program for Vietnam veterans who wanted to go to college. Those students had socioeconomic and educational backgrounds similar to mine. Then I went back to graduate school to study education and cognitive psychology and eventually became a faculty member in a school of education.

Intelligence is closely associated with formal education—the type of schooling a person has, how much and how long—and most people seem to move comfortably from that notion to a belief that work requiring less schooling requires less intelligence. These assumptions run through our cultural history, from the post–Revolutionary War period, when mechanics were characterized by political rivals as illiterate and therefore incapable of participating in government, until today. More than once I've heard a manager label his workers as "a bunch of dummies." Generalizations about intelligence, work, and social class deeply affect our assumptions about ourselves and each other, guiding the ways we use our minds to learn, build knowledge, solve problems, and make our way through the world.

Although writers and scholars have often looked at the working class, 10 they have generally focused on the values such workers exhibit rather than on the thought their work requires—a subtle but pervasive omission. Our cultural iconography promotes the muscled arm, sleeve rolled tight against biceps, but no brightness behind the eye, no image that links hand and brain.

One of my mother's brothers, Joe Meraglio, left school in the ninth grade to work for the Pennsylvania Railroad. From there he joined the Navy, re-

With an eighth-grade education, Joe (hands together) advanced to supervisor of a G.M. paint-and-body department.

turned to the railroad, which was already in decline, and eventually joined
his older brother at General Motors where, over a 33-year career, he moved
from working on the assembly line to supervising the paint-and-body department. When I was a young man, Joe took me on a tour of the factory. The
floor was loud—in some places deafening—and when I turned a corner or
opened a door, the smell of chemicals knocked my head back. The work was
repetitive and taxing, and the pace was inhumane.

Still, for Joe the shop floor provided what school did not; it was *like
schooling*, he said, a place where *you're constantly learning*. Joe learned the
most efficient way to use his body by acquiring a set of routines that were
quick and preserved energy. Otherwise he would never have survived on
the line.

As a foreman, Joe constantly faced new problems and became a consummate multi-tasker, evaluating a flurry of demands quickly, parceling
out physical and mental resources, keeping a number of ongoing events in
his mind, returning to whatever task had been interrupted, and maintaining a cool head under the pressure of grueling production schedules. In the
midst of all this, Joe learned more and more about the auto industry, the

Rose started by observing —and by listening. Listening is a key part of thinking rhetorically; read more about it in Ch. 1.

technological and social dynamics of the shop floor, the machinery and production processes, and the basics of paint chemistry and of plating and baking. With further promotions, he not only solved problems but also began to find problems to solve: Joe initiated the redesign of the nozzle on a paint sprayer, thereby eliminating costly and unhealthy overspray. And he found a way to reduce energy costs on the baking ovens without affecting the quality of the paint. He lacked formal knowledge of how the machines under his supervision worked, but he had direct experience with them, hands-on knowledge, and was savvy about their quirks and operational capabilities. He could experiment with them.

In addition, Joe learned about budgets and management. Coming off the line as he did, he had a perspective of workers' needs and management's demands, and this led him to think of ways to improve efficiency on the line while relieving some of the stress on the assemblers. He had each worker in a unit learn his or her co-workers' jobs so they could rotate across stations to relieve some of the monotony. He believed that rotation would allow assemblers to get longer and more frequent breaks. It was an easy sell to the people on the line. The union, however, had to approve any modification in job duties, and the managers were wary of the change. Joe had to argue his case on a number of fronts, providing him a kind of rhetorical education.

Eight years ago I began a study of the thought processes involved in work 15 like that of my mother and uncle. I catalogued the cognitive demands of a range of blue-collar and service jobs, from waitressing and hair styling to plumbing and welding. To gain a sense of how knowledge and skill develop, I observed experts as well as novices. From the details of this close examination, I tried to fashion what I called "cognitive biographies" of blue-collar workers. Biographical accounts of the lives of scientists, lawyers, entrepreneurs, and other professionals are rich with detail about the intellectual dimension of their work. But the life stories of working-class people are few and are typically accounts of hardship and courage or the achievements wrought by hard work.

Our culture—in Cartesian fashion—separates the body from the mind, so that, for example, we assume that the use of a tool does not involve abstraction. We reinforce this notion by defining intelligence solely on grades in school and numbers on IQ tests. And we employ social biases pertaining to a person's place on the occupational ladder. The distinctions among blue, pink, and white collars carry with them attributions of character, motivation, and intelligence. Although we rightly acknowledge and amply compensate the play of mind in white-collar and professional work, we diminish or erase it in considerations about other endeavors—physical and service work particularly. We also often ignore the experience of everyday work in administrative deliberations and policymaking.

But here's what we find when we get in close. The plumber seeking leverage in order to work in tight quarters and the hair stylist adroitly handling scissors and comb manage their bodies strategically. Though work-related actions become routine with experience, they were learned at some point through observation, trial and error, and, often, physical or verbal assistance from a co-worker or trainer. I've frequently observed novices talking to themselves as they take on a task, or shaking their head or hand as if to erase an attempt before trying again. In fact, our traditional notions of routine performance could keep us from appreciating the many instances within routine where quick decisions and adjustments are made. I'm struck by the thinking-in-motion that some work requires, by all the mental activity that can be involved in simply getting from one place to another: the waitress rushing back through her station to the kitchen or the foreman walking the line.

The use of tools requires the studied refinement of stance, grip, balance, and fine-motor skills. But manipulating tools is intimately tied to knowledge of what a particular instrument can do in a particular situation and do better than other similar tools. A worker must also know the characteristics of the material one is engaging—how it reacts to various cutting or compressing devices, to degrees of heat, or to lines of force. Some of these things demand judgment, the weighing of options, the consideration of multiple variables, and, occasionally, the creative use of a tool in an unexpected way.

In manipulating material, the worker becomes attuned to aspects of the environment, a training or disciplining of perception that both enhances knowledge and informs perception. Carpenters have an eye for length, line, and angle; mechanics troubleshoot by listening; hair stylists are attuned to shape, texture, and motion. Sensory data merge with concept, as when an auto mechanic relies on sound, vibration, and even smell to understand what cannot be observed.

Planning and problem solving have been studied since the earliest days 20 of modern cognitive psychology and are considered core elements in Western definitions of intelligence. To work is to solve problems. The big difference between the psychologist's laboratory and the workplace is that in the former the problems are isolated and in the latter they are embedded in the real-time flow of work with all its messiness and social complexity.

Much of physical work is social and interactive. Movers determining how to get an electric range down a flight of stairs require coordination, negotiation, planning, and the establishing of incremental goals. Words, gestures, and sometimes a quick pencil sketch are involved, if only to get the rhythm right. How important it is, then, to consider the social and communicative dimension of physical work, for it provides the medium for so much of work's intelligence.

Given the ridicule heaped on blue-collar speech, it might seem odd to value its cognitive content. Yet, the flow of talk at work provides the channel for organizing and distributing tasks, for troubleshooting and problem solving, for learning new information and revising old. A significant amount of teaching, often informal and indirect, takes place at work. Joe Meraglio saw that much of his job as a supervisor involved instruction. In some service occupations, language and communication are central: observing and interpreting behavior and expression, inferring mood and motive, taking on the perspective of others, responding appropriately to social cues, and knowing when you're understood. A good hair stylist, for instance, has the ability to convert vague requests (*I want something light and summery*) into an appropriate cut through questions, pictures, and hand gestures.

Verbal and mathematical skills drive measures of intelligence in the Western Hemisphere, and many of the kinds of work I studied are thought to require relatively little proficiency in either. Compared to certain kinds of white-collar occupations, that's true. But written symbols flow through physical work.

Numbers are rife in most workplaces: on tools and gauges, as measurements, as indicators of pressure or concentration or temperature, as guides to sequence, on ingredient labels, on lists and spreadsheets, as markers of quantity and price. Certain jobs require workers to make, check, and verify calculations, and to collect and interpret data. Basic math can be involved, and some workers develop a good sense of numbers and patterns. Consider, as well, what might be called material mathematics: mathematical functions embodied in materials and actions, as when a carpenter builds a cabinet or a flight of stairs. A simple mathematical act can extend quickly beyond itself. Measuring, for example, can involve more than recording the dimensions of an object. As I watched a cabinetmaker measure a long strip of wood, he read a number off the tape out loud, looked back over his shoulder to the kitchen wall, turned back to his task, took another measurement, and paused for a moment in thought. He was solving a problem involving the molding, and the measurement was important to his deliberation about structure and appearance.

In the blue-collar workplace, directions, plans, and reference books 25 rely on illustrations, some representational and others, like blueprints, that require training to interpret. Esoteric symbols—visual jargon—depict switches and receptacles, pipe fittings, or types of welds. Workers themselves often make sketches on the job. I frequently observed them grab a pencil to sketch something on a scrap of paper or on a piece of the material they were installing.

Though many kinds of physical work don't require a high literacy level, more reading occurs in the blue-collar workplace than is generally thought, from manuals and catalogues to work orders and invoices, to lists, labels, and forms. With routine tasks, for example, reading is integral to understanding production quotas, learning how to use an instrument, or applying a product. Written notes can initiate action, as in restaurant orders or reports of machine malfunction, or they can serve as memory aids.

True, many uses of writing are abbreviated, routine, and repetitive, and they infrequently require interpretation or analysis. But analytic moments can be part of routine activities, and seemingly basic reading and writing can be cognitively rich. Because workplace language is used in the flow of other activities, we can overlook the remarkable coordination of words, numbers, and drawings required to initiate and direct action.

If we believe everyday work to be mindless, then that will affect the work we create in the future. When we devalue the full range of everyday cognition, we offer limited educational opportunities and fail to make fresh and meaningful instructional connections among disparate kinds of skill and knowledge. If we think that whole categories of people—identified by class or occupation—are not that bright, then we reinforce social separations and cripple our ability to talk across cultural divides.

Affirmation of diverse intelligence is not a retreat to a softhearted definition of the mind. To acknowledge a broader range of intellectual capacity is to take seriously the concept of cognitive variability, to appreciate in all the Rosies and Joes the thought that drives their accomplishments and defines who they are. This is a model of the mind that is worthy of a democratic society.

Thinking about the Text

1. Mike Rose begins his analysis with a pair of extended examples along with a brief personal narrative, and readers may not figure out until later what, exactly, he is analyzing. What is Rose's subject, and what is the question that directs his inquiry?

2. Because of the academically oriented prejudices that Rose mentions, you may never before have read anything that focuses on the cognitive tasks involved in blue-collar work. Were you surprised by anything that Rose said—or not? Reflect on your own attitudes about blue-collar work; in what ways did Rose confirm or challenge them? Describe your reactions and reflections.

3. Why might Rose have chosen to begin his analysis with the extended information about his mother and uncle, himself, and other members of his family? Do you find these **EXAMPLES** and **NARRATIVES** effective rhetorical strategies for introducing an analysis of this topic? Why or why not?

4. Rose is suggesting that blue-collar workers merit more recognition for the cognitive skills that they bring to their work, but that is not all he is arguing. What is the overarching **ARGUMENT** that Rose is making in his article? What **EVIDENCE** in the text supports your answer?

5. Conduct a brief interview with someone who works a blue-collar job—for example, a mechanic, a sewing-machine operator, a hairstylist, a restaurant server, a janitor or housekeeper, or a truck driver. Find out what factors someone needs to take into consideration to perform the job successfully; in other words, what does the person have to be aware of while working? To keep the interview focused, start with one of the following questions: What effect does the weather have on what you do? (Heat, humidity, cold, and other weather elements often affect even indoor work.) What are the most common mistakes a beginner in your job might make? Using the information from your interviewee, write an **ANALYSIS** of the cognitive tasks involved in his or her ordinary workday. Use clear and precise language, and be sure to include the insights that you gained in the analysis.

What Would Happen If You
Threw a Revolution and Everyone Showed Up?

GEORGE RUSSELL

COINCIDING WITH THE RISE OF THE INTERNET as a fact of everyday life there is a certain sub-genre of current affairs writing that has become popular over the past decade. Books like *The Tipping Point, Freakonomics, The Long Tail,* and *Here Comes Everybody* are examples of pop-academia. In other words, laymen interpreting complex subjects that typically take years of study to comprehend.

Besides cute attempts at coining catch phrases, these books suffer from a common malady: massive errors in logic and basic research which result in sweeping generalizations that sound great when you're being interviewed on *The Daily Show* or *Real Time with Bill Maher,* but don't stand up when scrutinized. Their appeal comes from brash positivity—the arguments brought forth seem to imply a hidden world of technological bliss that the authors can see but we can't. It's as if they're living in a Utopia of perception which gives them the convenient ability to dismiss any argument against their premises as "negativity."

GEORGE RUSSELL is a Los Angeles–based writer and features editor for *PopMatters,* an online international magazine of cultural criticism. Russell writes reviews and criticisms on diverse aspects of popular culture, including books, music, film, and the industries that produce them. This review of Clay Shirky's 2010 book, *Cognitive Surplus,* appeared in *PopMatters* in July 2010.

Clay Shirky is one of those authors, becoming a part of the crowd in 2008 with his book, *Here Comes Everybody*. You could call him a techno-idealist. Despite trying to sound even-handed the downside never seems to make its presence felt. We get the feeling that he really, really, likes the Internet. Yet, underneath the writing the desperate need to come up with a "Big Idea" is ever-present. Despite what can only be assumed are his best efforts, the idea never materializes.

With his attempt at a turn of phrase, Shirky calls "cognitive surplus" a new phenomenon because of the decade long explosion of a new way to use our collective free time—the Internet. Instead of the usual time-waster Television, he argues that we are now being productive because we're able to "create and share" (like a kindergarten teacher the book sickeningly uses that phrase ad nauseam) with one another via blogs and websites like You-Tube. Shirky also points out that because of the Internet's inherent mass-organizing ability, by using it we are able to contribute to society. He gives several examples of websites that have helped organize everything from rideshare programs to women's rights in India.

Shirky writes as if he just discovered the Internet. He's like the nouveau 5 hipster who dresses out of the Urban Outfitters catalog and shows up at the party wearing last year's tight neon pants. Sorry man, the novelty's over with. He states sweeping generalizations as if they were fact, "When the general public began using digital networks, the idea that everyone would contribute something to the public sphere was assumed to be contradictory to nature." That sentence reveals more about Clay Shirky than it does about people in general. First, who did all this assuming? He never tells us. Second, has he never heard of church organizations, non-profits, volunteer groups, the Boy and Girl Scouts, neighborhood watch programs, rideshare programs, Little League, food banks, the Lions Club . . . ? The list is virtually endless. Shirky doesn't contribute things to the public sphere, that doesn't mean that most people don't.

Countless times in the book Shirky strikes a note of revolution, as if anything has changed significantly because of the once-fabled Internet. The last time I checked we still have to go to work every day and despite some momentary upheavals, the Internet has become one more way for savvy large corporations (and many parasitic start-ups) to make money. At one point he writes, "We are all living through the disorientation that comes from including two billion new participants in a media landscape previously operated by a small group of professionals." This repeated statement

The lighter side of our cognitive-connectivity: an Internet-generated flash mob. British voters take part in a flash mob sword fight with rolled up newspapers in London's Parliament Square to campaign for a Hung Parliament in 2010.

by Shirky, that because you can upload and watch videos on YouTube (or if you're cool, Vimeo), or write a review on Amazon.com, or organize your BFF's birthday party via Facebook means that a societal revolution has occurred is a profound error at the core of *Cognitive Surplus*'s logic. The Internet is a small step forward for humanity, but it's a giant step forward for business.

Now that the novelty has worn off, it's plain that the Internet is nothing new for people—that's why it has fit so seamlessly into our daily lives and will continue to do so as the smartphone industry expands. The Internet is like the classified ads on steroids, it's like's the late edition of the newspaper but updated every second, it's the Yellow Pages but with reviews, but Shirky writes as if this is a technological Valhalla. He misses that most signs are pointing to a coming consolidation of Internet information and Television entertainment into a single entity (Shirky even inadvertently points this out in an anecdote at the end of the book about a friend's young daughter asking for "the mouse" while watching TV).

This coming single entity, cable Television and the Internet combined, will be powered by international media conglomerates and companies like Google that trade at $500.00 a share. The Internet is a battlefield, not an altruistic orgy of "creating and sharing," as Shirky puts it. The war is over eyeballs and eventually wallets.

To write his review, Russell had to think carefully about his own ideas. Get suggestions for questioning yourself on pp. 9–10.

From Malcolm Gladwell to Clay Shirky there is currently an odd streak in technology related cultural writing that proclaims the revolutionary aspect of access to information while not actually bothering to learn from any of the information while writing their books. Shirky has a habit of describing everything from Vladimir Lenin to the Protestant Reformation in the language of intellectual laziness. In describing social vs. individual values he writes, "Neither perfect individual freedom nor perfect social control is optimal. Ayn Rand and Vladimir Lenin both overshot the mark." As if to say that Lenin's problem was simply too much enthusiasm for his task of enabling the death of five million of his own countrymen and destroying an entire population's ability to feed itself after the Russian Revolution.

Shirky's logic is agonizingly error ridden at so many points that you begin to wonder if this is some sort of Comcast funded plot to erode faith in the written word. How is the reader supposed to take anything else Shirky says seriously when in reference to the invention of the printing press he produces a sentence like, "When a scholar could read both Aristotle and Galen side by side and see that the two sources clashed, it corroded reflexive faith in the ancients. If you couldn't trust Aristotle, who could you trust?" 10

Were our 15th century counterparts that easily confused? The real question is: why didn't someone make a t-shirt with "If you can't trust Aristotle who can you trust?" on it and make a few bucks?

There is actually something worthwhile in *Cognitive Surplus*. Arriving at the middle section of the book, the two chapters called "Opportunity" and "Culture" are like hitting an oasis in an unforgiving wasteland. Taken together, they provide interesting and useful information, serving to function as a directory of lesser-known websites that can truly be called a step forward (though hardly revolutionary) in human society. What changed from the rest of the book is that Shirky toned his rhetoric down and started talking about something he knows intimately—exceptional web design and its provable effects.

These two chapters, had they been expanded to form the basis of the book, could easily have become a much needed compendium of positive, grass-roots aspects of the Internet. Then the book would contain mostly first-person accounts, real-world scenarios, provable effects; the stuff of good non-fiction. Unfortunately, they are sandwiched between 100 pages of conjecture laden pop-academia.

Don't worry about Shirky. He'll get the result that this book was intended for (as of this writing the book was #1 in three different categories on Amazon.com). The big secret of Pop-Academia, or Pop-Economics, or Pop-Whatever writing is that the writing is less about the subject and more about the author. The books in this new genre are intended as marketing tools for the authors themselves, while masquerading as serious thought.

The authors get to appear on talk shows, have their books quoted and reviewed in newspapers and magazines (the irony is that non-Internet sources are still the legitimizers) and as a result they will get to take another step forward in their careers, be it at NYU or *The New Yorker*. Sadly, in a world that seems to be moving faster than most people have the cognitive framework to comprehend, readers will continue to consume these types of intellectual bags of Hot Cheetos because they don't know any better.

Thinking about the Text

I. George Russell has written a very critical **REVIEW** of Clay Shirky's book, which was otherwise generally quite well received. Do you think his assessment was fair? Why or why not? Present evidence to support your evaluation.

2. You may never have lived in an internet-less world in order to be able to do a before-and-after comparison; still, you can evaluate both Shirky's and Russell's claims. Think about your online activities. Are they predominantly "grassroots" activities, such as reading and writing personal blogs or vlogs, communicating and keeping up with friends, organizing meet-ups or parties? Or are your on-line activities mainly the consumption of commercially produced material, such as streaming videos, shopping sites, directories, periodicals and commercial-site blogs? Assess your everyday online activities, and discuss whether your experience supports Shirky, Russell, both, or neither.

3. Russell's review was written for an online magazine that claims one million unique monthly readers and prestigious status with readers in the 18-to-34 age range. What might Russell have done differently if he had been writing for a print **MEDIUM**? Select a specific newspaper or magazine and imagine what Russell would have had to do in order to appeal to the different audience. In your response, consider not only how he might have altered his argument and his tone, but also how he would have had to change the background information.

4. Russell claims that Shirky and other pop writers are talking less about their respective subjects and more about the authors themselves. Could this claim be applied to Russell as well?

5. Russell concludes his review with a claim that might feel insulting to those who count themselves among the "most people" that Russell says "don't know any better." Do you feel insulted? Why or why not? Write a direct response to Russell either agreeing or disagreeing with his **POSITION**. Use your own experience as a basis for your response.

Why McDonald's Fries Taste So Good

ERIC SCHLOSSER

THE FRENCH FRY [was] ... almost sacrosanct for me," Ray Kroc wrote in his memoir, "its preparation a ritual to be followed religiously." The success of Richard and Mac McDonald's hamburger stand had been based as much on the quality of their fries as on the taste of their burgers. The McDonald brothers had devised an elaborate system for making crisp french fries, one that was later improved by the restaurant chain. McDonald's cooked thinly sliced Russet Burbanks in special fryers to keep the oil temperature above 325 degrees. As the chain expanded, it became more difficult—and yet all the more important—to maintain the consistency and quality of the fries. J. R. Simplot met with Ray Kroc in 1965. The idea of switching to frozen french fries appealed to Kroc, as a means of ensuring uniformity and cutting labor costs. McDonald's obtained its fresh potatoes from about 175 different local suppliers, and crew members spent a great deal of time peeling and slicing potatoes. Simplot offered to build a new factory solely for the manufacture of McDonald's french fries. Kroc agreed to try Simplot's fries, but made no long-term commitment. The deal was sealed with a handshake.

ERIC SCHLOSSER, a California-based investigative journalist, is author of *Reefer Madness: Sex, Drugs, and Cheap Labor in the American Black Market* (2003), and his articles appear regularly in *Rolling Stone, New Yorker, Vanity Fair*, and the *Atlantic*, among other publications. This selection is from his best seller, *Fast Food Nation* (2001), which he subsequently helped make into a feature-length documentary.

McDonald's began to sell J. R. Simplot's frozen french fries the follow-ing year. Customers didn't notice any difference in taste. And the reduced cost of using a frozen product made french fries one of the most profitable items on the menu—far more profitable than hamburgers. Simplot quickly became the main supplier of french fries to McDonald's. At the time, Mc-Donald's had about 725 restaurants in the United States. Within a decade, it had more than 3,000. Simplot sold his frozen fries to other restaurant chains, accelerating the growth of the fast food industry and changing the nation's eating habits. Americans have long consumed more potatoes than any other food except dairy products and wheat flour. In 1960, the typical American ate eighty-one pounds of fresh potatoes and about four pounds of frozen french fries. Today the typical American eats about forty-nine pounds of fresh potatoes every year—and more than thirty pounds of frozen french fries. Ninety percent of those fries are purchased at fast food restaurants. Indeed, french fries have become the most widely sold foodservice item in the United States.

Schlosser's analysis gets very techni-cal, but he begins by describing something totally fa-miliar. Read about that technique on pp. 143–44.

·   ·   ·

Food Product Design

The taste of McDonald's french fries has long been praised by customers, competitors, and even food critics. James Beard loved McDonald's fries. Their distinctive taste does not stem from the type of potatoes that McDonald's buys, the technology that processes them, or the restaurant equipment that fries them. Other chains buy their french fries from the same large process-ing companies, use Russet Burbanks, and have similar fryers in their res-taurant kitchens. The taste of a fast food fry is largely determined by the cooking oil. For decades, McDonald's cooked its french fries in a mixture of about 7 percent cottonseed oil and 93 percent beef tallow. The mix gave the fries their unique flavor—and more saturated beef fat per ounce than a Mc-Donald's hamburger.

Amid a barrage of criticism over the amount of cholesterol in their fries, McDonald's switched to pure vegetable oil in 1990. The switch presented the company with an enormous challenge: how to make fries that subtly taste like beef without cooking them in tallow. A look at the ingredients now used in the preparation of McDonald's french fries suggests how the problem was solved. Toward the end of the list is a seemingly innocuous, yet oddly mysterious phrase: "natural flavor." That ingredient helps to explain not only why the fries taste so good, but also why most fast food—indeed, most of the food Americans eat today—tastes the way it does.

Open your refrigerator, your freezer, your kitchen cupboards, and look ₅ at the labels on your food. You'll find "natural flavor" or "artificial flavor" in just about every list of ingredients. The similarities between these two broad categories of flavor are far more significant than their differences. Both are man-made additives that give most processed food most of its taste. The initial purchase of a food item may be driven by its packaging or appearance, but subsequent purchases are determined mainly by its taste. About 90 percent of the money that Americans spend on food is used to buy processed food. But the canning, freezing, and dehydrating techniques used to process food destroy most of its flavor. Since the end of World War II, a vast industry has arisen in the United States to make processed food palatable. Without this flavor industry, today's fast food industry could not exist. The names of the leading American fast food chains and their best-selling menu items have become famous worldwide, embedded in our popular culture. Few people, however, can name the companies that manufacture fast food's taste.

For decades, beef tallow gave McDonalds' french fries their unique—and immensely popular—flavor. But after changing over to pure vegetable oil in 1990, the company had to develop a "natural flavor" to mimic the original taste.

The flavor industry is highly secretive. Its leading companies will not divulge the precise formulas of flavor compounds or the identities of clients. The secrecy is deemed essential for protecting the reputation of beloved brands. The fast food chains, understandably, would like the public to believe that the flavors of their food somehow originate in their restaurant kitchens, not in distant factories run by other firms.

The New Jersey Turnpike runs through the heart of the flavor industry, an industrial corridor dotted with refineries and chemical plants. International Flavors & Fragrances (IFF), the world's largest flavor company, has a manufacturing facility off Exit 8A in Dayton, New Jersey; Givaudan, the world's second-largest flavor company, has a plant in East Hanover. Haarmann & Reimer, the largest German flavor company, has a plant in Teterboro, as does Takasago, the largest Japanese flavor company. Flavor Dynamics has a plant in South Plainfield; Frutarom is in North Bergen; Elan Chemical is in Newark. Dozens of companies manufacture flavors in the corridor between Teaneck and South Brunswick. Indeed, the area produces about two-thirds of the flavor additives sold in the United States.

The IFF plant in Dayton is a huge pale blue building with a modern office complex attached to the front. It sits in an industrial park, not far from a BASF plastics factory, a Jolly French Toast factory, and a plant that manufactures Liz Claiborne cosmetics. Dozens of tractor-trailers were parked at the IFF loading dock the afternoon I visited, and a thin cloud of steam floated from the chimney. Before entering the plant, I signed a nondisclosure form, promising not to reveal the brand names of products that contain IFF flavors. The place reminded me of Willy Wonka's chocolate factory. Wonderful smells drifted through the hallways, men and women in neat white lab coats cheerfully went about their work, and hundreds of little glass bottles sat on laboratory tables and shelves. The bottles contained powerful but fragile flavor chemicals, shielded from light by the brown glass and the round plastic caps shut tight. The long chemical names on the little white labels were as mystifying to me as medieval Latin. They were the odd-sounding names of things that would be mixed and poured and turned into new substances, like magic potions.

I was not invited to see the manufacturing areas of the IFF plant, where it was thought I might discover trade secrets. Instead, I toured various laboratories and pilot kitchens, where the flavors of well-established brands are tested or adjusted, and where whole new flavors are created. IFF's snack and savory lab is responsible for the flavor of potato chips, corn chips, breads,

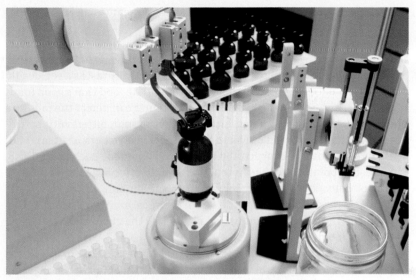

A robotic arm prepares flavor samples at a flavor company factory.

crackers, breakfast cereals, and pet food. The confectionery lab devises the flavor for ice cream, cookies, candies, toothpastes, mouthwashes, and antacids. Everywhere I looked, I saw famous, widely advertised products sitting on laboratory desks and tables. The beverage lab is full of brightly colored liquids in clear bottles. It comes up with the flavor for popular soft drinks, sport drinks, bottled teas, and wine coolers, for all-natural juice drinks, organic soy drinks, beers, and malt liquors. In one pilot kitchen I saw a dapper food technologist, a middle-aged man with an elegant tie beneath his lab coat, carefully preparing a batch of cookies with white frosting and pink-and-white sprinkles. In another pilot kitchen I saw a pizza oven, a grill, a milk-shake machine, and a french fryer identical to those I'd seen behind the counter at countless fast food restaurants.

In addition to being the world's largest flavor company, IFF manufac- 10 tures the smell of six of the ten best-selling fine perfumes in the United States, including Estée Lauder's Beautiful, Clinique's Happy, Lancôme's Trésor, and Calvin Klein's Eternity. It also makes the smell of household products such as deodorant, dishwashing detergent, bath soap, shampoo, furniture polish, and floor wax. All of these aromas are made through the same basic process: the manipulation of volatile chemicals to create a particular smell.

The basic science behind the scent of your shaving cream is the same as that governing the flavor of your TV dinner.

The aroma of a food can be responsible for as much as 90 percent of its flavor. Scientists now believe that human beings acquired the sense of taste as a way to avoid being poisoned. Edible plants generally taste sweet; deadly ones, bitter. Taste is supposed to help us differentiate food that's good for us from food that's not. The taste buds on our tongues can detect the presence of half a dozen or so basic tastes, including: sweet, sour, bitter, salty, astringent, and umami (a taste discovered by Japanese researchers, a rich and full sense of deliciousness triggered by amino acids in foods such as shellfish, mushrooms, potatoes, and seaweed). Taste buds offer a relatively limited means of detection, however, compared to the human olfactory system, which can perceive thousands of different chemical aromas. Indeed "flavor" is primarily the smell of gases being released by the chemicals you've just put in your mouth.

The act of drinking, sucking, or chewing a substance releases its volatile gases. They flow out of the mouth and up the nostrils, or up the passageway in the back of the mouth, to a thin layer of nerve cells called the olfactory epithelium, located at the base of the nose, right between the eyes. The brain combines the complex smell signals from the epithelium with the simple taste signals from the tongue, assigns a flavor to what's in your mouth, and decides if it's something you want to eat.

Babies like sweet tastes and reject bitter ones; we know this because scientists have rubbed various flavors inside the mouths of infants and then recorded their facial reactions. A person's food preferences, like his or her personality, are formed during the first few years of life, through a process of socialization. Toddlers can learn to enjoy hot and spicy food, bland health food, or fast food, depending upon what the people around them eat. The human sense of smell is still not fully understood and can be greatly affected by psychological factors and expectations. The color of a food can determine the perception of its taste. The mind filters out the overwhelming majority of chemical aromas that surround us, focusing intently on some, ignoring others. People can grow accustomed to bad smells or good smells; they stop noticing what once seemed overpowering. Aroma and memory are somehow inextricably linked. A smell can suddenly evoke a long-forgotten moment. The flavors of childhood foods seem to leave an indelible mark, and adults often return to them, without always knowing why. These "comfort foods" become a source of pleasure and reassurance, a fact that fast food chains work hard to promote. Childhood memories of Happy Meals can translate into frequent adult visits to McDonald's, like those of the chain's "heavy users," the customers who eat there four or five times a week.

The human craving for flavor has been a largely unacknowledged and unexamined force in history. Royal empires have been built, unexplored lands have been traversed, great religions and philosophies have been forever changed by the spice trade. In 1492 Christopher Columbus set sail to find seasoning. Today the influence of flavor in the world marketplace is no less decisive. The rise and fall of corporate empires—of soft drink companies, snack food companies, and fast food chains—is frequently determined by how their products taste.

The flavor industry emerged in the mid-nineteenth century, as processed foods began to be manufactured on a large scale. Recognizing the need for flavor additives, the early food processors turned to perfume companies that had years of experience working with essential oils and volatile aromas. The great perfume houses of England, France, and the Netherlands produced many of the first flavor compounds. In the early part of the twentieth century, Germany's powerful chemical industry assumed the technological lead in flavor production. Legend has it that a German scientist discovered methyl anthranilate, one of the first artificial flavors, by accident while mixing chemicals in his laboratory. Suddenly the lab was filled with the sweet smell of grapes. Methyl anthranilate later became the chief flavoring compound of grape Kool-Aid. After World War II, much of the perfume industry shifted from Europe to the United States, settling in New York City near the garment district and the fashion houses. The flavor industry came with it, subsequently moving to New Jersey to gain more plant capacity. Man-made flavor additives were used mainly in baked goods, candies, and sodas until the 1950s, when sales of processed food began to soar. The invention of gas chromatographs and mass spectrometers—machines capable of detecting volatile gases at low levels—vastly increased the number of flavors that could be synthesized. By the mid-1960s the American flavor industry was churning out compounds to supply the taste of Pop Tarts, Bac-Os, Tab, Tang, Filet-O-Fish sandwiches, and literally thousands of other new foods.

The American flavor industry now has annual revenues of about $1.4 billion. Approximately ten thousand new processed food products are introduced every year in the United States. Almost all of them require flavor additives. And about nine out of every ten of these new food products fail. The latest flavor innovations and corporate realignments are heralded in publications such as *Food Chemical News, Food Engineering, Chemical Market Reporter,* and *Food Product Design*. The growth of IFF has mirrored that of the flavor industry as a whole. IFF was formed in 1958, through the merger of two small companies. Its annual revenues have grown almost fifteenfold since the early 1970s, and it now has manufacturing facilities in twenty countries.

The quality that people seek most of all in a food, its flavor, is usually present in a quantity too infinitesimal to be measured by any traditional culinary terms such as ounces or teaspoons. Today's sophisticated spectrometers, gas chromatographs, and headspace vapor analyzers provide a detailed map of a food's flavor components, detecting chemical aromas in amounts as low as one part per billion. The human nose, however, is still more sensitive than any machine yet invented. A nose can detect aromas present in quantities of a few parts per trillion—an amount equivalent to 0.000000000003 percent. Complex aromas, like those of coffee or roasted meat, may be composed of volatile gases from nearly a thousand different chemicals. The smell of a strawberry arises from the interaction of at least 350 different chemicals that are present in minute amounts. The chemical that provides the dominant flavor of bell pepper can be tasted in amounts as low as .02 parts per billion; one drop is sufficient to add flavor to five average size swimming pools. The flavor additive usually comes last, or second to last, in a processed food's list of ingredients. As a result, the flavor of a processed food often costs less than its packaging. Soft drinks contain a larger proportion of flavor additives than most products. The flavor in a twelve-ounce can of Coke costs about half a cent.

The color additives in processed foods are usually present in even smaller amounts than the flavor compounds. Many of New Jersey's flavor companies also manufacture these color additives, which are used to make processed foods look appealing. Food coloring serves many of the same purposes as lipstick, eye shadow, mascara—and is often made from the same pigments. Titanium dioxide, for example, has proved to be an especially versatile mineral. It gives many processed candies, frosting, and icing their bright white color; it is a common ingredient in women's cosmetics; and it is the pigment used in many white oil paints and house paints. At Burger King, Wendy's, and McDonald's, coloring agents have been added to many of the soft drinks, salad dressings, cookies, condiments, chicken dishes, and sandwich buns.

Studies have found that the color of a food can greatly affect how its taste is perceived. Brightly colored foods frequently seem to taste better than bland-looking foods, even when the flavor compounds are identical. Foods that somehow look off-color often seem to have off tastes. For thousands of years, human beings have relied on visual cues to help determine what is edible. The color of fruit suggests whether it is ripe, the color of meat whether it is rancid. Flavor researchers sometimes use colored lights to modify the influence of visual cues during taste tests. During one experiment in the early 1970s, people were served an oddly tinted meal of steak and French fries that appeared normal beneath colored lights. Everyone thought the meal tasted fine until the lighting was changed. Once it became apparent that the steak was actually blue and the fries were green, some people became ill.

The Food and Drug Administration does not require flavor companies 20 to disclose the ingredients of their additives, so long as all the chemicals are considered by the agency to be GRAS (Generally Regarded As Safe). This lack of public disclosure enables the companies to maintain the secrecy of their formulas. It also hides the fact that flavor compounds sometimes contain more ingredients than the foods being given their taste. The ubiquitous phrase "artificial strawberry flavor" gives little hint of the chemical wizardry and manufacturing skill that can make a highly processed food taste like a strawberry.

A typical artificial strawberry flavor, like the kind found in a Burger King strawberry milk shake, contains the following ingredients: amyl acetate, amyl butyrate, amyl valerate, anethol, anisyl formate, benzyl acetate, benzyl isobutyrate, butyric acid, cinnamyl isobutyrate, cinnamyl valerate, cognac essential oil, diacetyl, dipropyl ketone, ethyl acetate, ethyl amylketone, ethyl butyrate, ethyl cinnamate, ethyl heptanoate, ethyl heptylate, ethyl lactate, ethyl methylphenylglycidate, ethyl nitrate, ethyl propionate, ethyl valerate, heliotropin, hydroxyphenyl-2-butanone (10 percent solution in alcohol), α-ionone, isobutyl anthranilate, isobutyl butyrate, lemon essential oil, maltol, 4-methylacetophenone, methyl anthranilate, methyl benzoate, methyl cinnamate, methyl heptine carbonate, methyl naphthyl ketone, methyl salicylate, mint essential oil, neroli essential oil, nerolin, neryl isobutyrate, orris butter, phenethyl alcohol, rose, rum ether, γ-undecalactone, vanillin, and solvent.

Although flavors usually arise from a mixture of many different volatile chemicals, a single compound often supplies the dominant aroma. Smelled alone, that chemical provides an unmistakable sense of the food. Ethyl-2-methyl butyrate, for example, smells just like an apple. Today's highly processed foods offer a blank palette: whatever chemicals you add to them will give them specific tastes. Adding methyl-2-peridylketone makes something taste like popcorn. Adding ethyl-3-hydroxybutanoate makes it taste like marshmallow. The possibilities are now almost limitless. Without affecting the appearance or nutritional value, processed foods could even be made with aroma chemicals such as hexanal (the smell of freshly cut grass) or 3-methyl butanoic acid (the smell of body odor).

The 1960s were the heyday of artificial flavors. The synthetic versions of flavor compounds were not subtle, but they did not need to be, given the nature of most processed food. For the past twenty years food processors have tried hard to use only "natural flavors" in their products. According to the FDA, these must be derived entirely from natural sources—from herbs, spices, fruits, vegetables, beef, chicken, yeast, bark, roots, etc. Consumers prefer to see natural flavors on a label, out of a belief that they are healthier. The distinction between artificial and natural flavors can be somewhat arbitrary and absurd, based more on how the flavor has been made than on what it actually contains. "A natural flavor," says Terry Acree, a professor of food science at Cornell University, "is a flavor that's been derived with an out-of-date technology." Natural flavors and artificial flavors sometimes contain exactly the same chemicals, produced through different methods. Amyl acetate, for example, provides the dominant note of banana flavor. When you distill it from bananas with a solvent, amyl acetate is a natural flavor. When you produce it by mixing vinegar with amyl alcohol, adding sulfuric acid as a catalyst, amyl acetate is an artificial flavor. Either way it smells and tastes the same. The phrase "natural flavor" is now listed among the ingredients of everything from Stonyfield Farm Organic Strawberry Yogurt to Taco Bell Hot Taco Sauce.

A natural flavor is not necessarily healthier or purer than an artificial one. When almond flavor (benzaldehyde) is derived from natural sources, such as peach and apricot pits, it contains traces of hydrogen cyanide, a deadly poison. Benzaldehyde derived through a different process—by mixing oil of clove and the banana flavor, amyl acetate—does not contain any cyanide. Nevertheless, it is legally considered an artificial flavor and sells at a much lower price. Natural and artificial flavors are now manufactured at the same chemical plants, places that few people would associate with Mother Nature. Calling any of these flavors "natural" requires a flexible attitude toward the English language and a fair amount of irony.

The small and elite group of scientists who create most of the flavor in 25 most of the food now consumed in the United States are called "flavorists."

They draw upon a number of disciplines in their work: biology, psychology, physiology, and organic chemistry. A flavorist is a chemist with a trained nose and a poetic sensibility. Flavors are created by blending scores of different chemicals in tiny amounts, a process governed by scientific principles but demanding a fair amount of art. In an age when delicate aromas, subtle flavors, and microwave ovens do not easily coexist, the job of the flavorist is to conjure illusions about processed food and, in the words of one flavor company's literature, to ensure "consumer likeability." The flavorists with whom I spoke were charming, cosmopolitan, and ironic. They were also discreet, in keeping with the dictates of their trade. They were the sort of scientist who not only enjoyed fine wine, but could also tell you the chemicals that gave each vintage its unique aroma. One flavorist compared his work to composing music. A well-made flavor compound will have a "top note," followed by a "dry-down," and a "leveling-off," with different chemicals responsible for each stage. The taste of a food can be radically altered by minute changes in the flavoring mix. "A little odor goes a long way," one flavorist said.

In order to give a processed food the proper taste, a flavorist must always consider the food's "mouthfeel"—the unique combination of textures

Domenico Milano, research and development manager of Torani, samples some new flavors of vanilla-flavored syrup inside the company development lab. Milano, one of Torani's two "flavor masters," takes extracts from plants grown around the world and experiments until he arrives at the perfect essence of vanilla, raspberry or coconut.

and chemical interactions that affects how the flavor is perceived. The mouthfeel can be adjusted through the use of various fats, gums, starches, emulsifiers, and stabilizers. The aroma chemicals of a food can be precisely analyzed, but mouthfeel is much harder to measure. How does one quantify a french fry's crispness? Food technologists are now conducting basic research in rheology, a branch of physics that examines the flow and deformation of materials. A number of companies sell sophisticated devices that attempt to measure mouthfeel. The TA.XT2i Texture Analyzer, produced by the Texture Technologies Corporation, performs calculations based on data derived from as many as 250 separate probes. It is essentially a mechanical mouth. It gauges the most important rheological properties of a food—the bounce, creep, breaking point, density, crunchiness, chewiness, gumminess, lumpiness, rubberiness, springiness, slipperiness, smoothness, softness, wetness, juiciness, spreadability, springback, and tackiness.

Some of the most important advances in flavor manufacturing are now occurring in the field of biotechnology. Complex flavors are being made through fermentation, enzyme reactions, fungal cultures, and tissue cultures. All of the flavors being created through these methods—including the ones being synthesized by funguses—are considered natural flavors by the FDA. The new enzyme-based processes are responsible for extremely lifelike dairy flavors. One company now offers not just butter flavor, but also fresh creamy butter, cheesy butter, milky butter, savory melted butter, and super-concentrated butter flavor, in liquid or powder form. The development of new fermentation techniques, as well as new techniques for heating mixtures of sugar and amino acids, has led to the creation of much more realistic meat flavors. The McDonald's Corporation will not reveal the exact origin of the natural flavor added to its french fries. In response to inquiries from *Vegetarian Journal,* however, McDonald's did acknowledge that its fries derive some of their characteristic flavor from "animal products."

Other popular fast foods derive their flavor from unexpected sources. Wendy's Grilled Chicken Sandwich, for example, contains beef extracts. Burger King's BK Broiler Chicken Breast Patty contains "natural smoke flavor." A firm called Red Arrow Products Company specializes in smoke flavor, which is added to barbecue sauces and processed meats. Red Arrow manufactures natural smoke flavor by charring sawdust and capturing the aroma chemicals released into the air. The smoke is captured in water and then bottled, so that other companies can sell food which seems to have been cooked over a fire.

The Vegetarian Legal Action Network recently petitioned the FDA to issue new food labeling requirements for foods that contain natural flavors. The group wants food processors to list the basic origins of their flavors on their labels. At the moment, vegetarians often have no way of knowing whether a flavor additive contains beef, pork, poultry, or shellfish. One of the most widely used color additives—whose presence is often hidden by the phrase "color added"—violates a number of religious dietary restrictions, may cause allergic reactions in susceptible people, and comes from an unusual source. Cochineal extract (also known as carmine or carminic acid) is made from the desiccated bodies of female Dactylopius coccus Costa, a small insect harvested mainly in Peru and the Canary Islands. The bug feeds on red cactus berries and color from the berries accumulates in the females and their unhatched larvae. The insects are collected, dried, and ground into pigment. It takes about 70,000 of them to produce one pound of carmine, which is used to make processed foods look pink, red, or purple. Dannon strawberry yogurt gets its color from carmine, as do many frozen fruit bars, candies, fruit fillings, and Ocean Spray pink-grapefruit juice drink.

In a meeting room at IFF, Brian Grainger let me sample some of the company's flavors. It was an unusual taste test; there wasn't any food to taste. Grainger is a senior flavorist at IFF, a soft-spoken chemist with graying hair, an English accent, and a fondness for understatement. He could easily be mistaken for a British diplomat or the owner of a West End brasserie with two Michelin stars. Like many in the flavor industry, he has an Old World, old-fashioned sensibility which seems out of step with our brand-conscious, egocentric age. When I suggested that IFF should put its own logo on the products that contain its flavors—instead of allowing other brands to enjoy the consumer loyalty and affection inspired by those flavors—Grainger politely disagreed, assuring me such a thing would never be done. In the absence of public credit or acclaim, the small and secretive fraternity of flavor chemists praises one another's work. Grainger can often tell, by analyzing the flavor formula of a product, which of his counterparts at a rival firm devised it. And he enjoys walking down supermarket aisles, looking at the many products that contain his flavors, even if no one else knows it.

Grainger had brought a dozen small glass bottles from the lab. After he opened each bottle, I dipped a fragrance testing filter into it. The filters were long white strips of paper designed to absorb aroma chemicals without producing off-notes. Before placing the strips of paper before my nose, I closed my eyes. Then I inhaled deeply, and one food after another was conjured from the glass bottles. I smelled fresh cherries, black olives, sautéed onions, and shrimp. Grainger's most remarkable creation took me by surprise. After closing my eyes, I suddenly smelled a grilled hamburger. The aroma was uncanny, almost miraculous. It smelled like someone in the room was flipping burgers on a hot grill. But when I opened my eyes, there was just a narrow strip of white paper and a smiling flavorist.

Thinking about the Text

1. Eric Schlosser's **ANALYSIS** of McDonald's fries may appear to veer off in several non-fries directions. Does all of the **EVIDENCE** that Schlosser presents turn out to be relevant to the subject at hand? Does he tie it all together? Is the analysis cohesive? Why or why not?

2. That our foods contain long lists of difficult-to-pronounce chemicals is not exactly news; still, Schlosser's analysis probably told you much more than you had ever imagined about what goes into them. Has what you read affected your appetite for processed foods? For fast-food restaurants like McDonald's and Burger King? Why or why not? Explain your reflections and reactions.

3. Schlosser is dealing with a subject that is quite emotionally charged and controversial—chemicals that go into food. How would you describe the **TONE** and the language of his analysis? Given that the subject matter has great potential for sensationalism, do you think that Schlosser has exploited that potential? resisted it? neglected it by writing in too understated a way? Explain your conclusions, providing examples from the text.

4. What is Schlosser trying to do in his analysis? Does he want to persuade his readers to stop eating fries or fast food in general? Does he hope to inspire them to lobby for changes in packaging? in processing? Or does he want to just make them think about what's in their food? **SUMMARIZE** this text, making Schlosser's **PURPOSE** the central feature of your summary.

5. Choose a processed food product that you buy regularly—such as cookies, ice cream, frozen pizza, and so on—and make a note of each ingredient listed on the packaging, paying particular attention to the ones with chemical names. For each one, find out where it comes from, how it is made, and what its function is in the food. Write a **REPORT** on what you find, and include your reaction to the results. Will you continue to eat that item? Why or why not?

Why Colleges Shower Their Students with A's

BRENT STAPLES

THE ECONOMIST **M**ILTON **F**RIEDMAN taught that superior products flourished and shabby ones died out when consumers voted emphatically with their dollars. But the truth of the marketplace is that shabby products can do just fine if they sustain the veneer of quality while slipping downhill, as has much of higher education. Faced with demanding consumers and stiff competition, colleges have simply issued more and more A's, stoking grade inflation and devaluing degrees.

Grade inflation is in full gallop at every level, from struggling community institutions to the elites of the Ivy League. In some cases, campuswide averages have crept up from a C just 10 years ago to B-plus today.

Some departments shower students with A's to fill poorly attended courses that might otherwise be canceled. Individual professors inflate grades after consumer-conscious administrators hound them into it. Professors at every level inflate to escape negative evaluations by students, whose opinions now figure in tenure and promotion decisions.

The most vulnerable teachers are the part-timers who have no job security and who now teach more than half of all college courses. Writing in

BRENT STAPLES, who has a PhD in psychology, is a member of the *New York Times* editorial board and is a frequent contributor to the newspaper. He writes about politics and cultural issues, with particular focus on controversies about race and about education. This selection appeared in the *Times* in 1998.

the last issue of the journal *Academe,* two part-timers suggest that students routinely corner adjuncts, threatening to complain if they do not turn C's into A's. An Ivy League professor said recently that if tenure disappeared, universities would be "free to sell diplomas outright."

The consumer appetite for less rigorous education is nowhere more evident than in the University of Phoenix, a profit-making school that shuns traditional scholarship and offers a curriculum so superficial that critics compare it to a drive-through restaurant. Two hundred colleges have closed since a businessman dreamed up Phoenix 20 years ago. Meanwhile, the university has expanded to 60 sites spread around the country, and more than 40,000 students, making it the country's largest private university. 5

Robert Wancha in the library of the University of Phoenix in Southfield, Michigan, in December 2006. Wancha, who is pursuing a bachelor's degree, has criticized its standards. The University of Phoenix became the nation's largest private university by delivering high profits to investors and a solid, albeit low-overhead, education to midcareer workers seeking college degrees. But its reputation is fraying as prominent educators, students and some of its own former administrators say the relentless pressure for higher profits, at a university that gets more federal student financial aid than any other, has eroded academic quality.

Phoenix competes directly with the big state universities and lesser-known small colleges, all of which fear a student drain. But the elite schools fear each other and their customers, the students, who are becoming increasingly restive about the cost of a first-tier diploma, which now exceeds $120,000. Faced with the prospect of crushing debt, students are treating grades as a matter of life and death—occasionally even suing to have grades revised upward.

Twenty years ago students grumbled, then lived with the grades they were given. Today, colleges of every stature permit them to appeal low grades through deans or permanent boards of inquiry. In *The Chronicle of Higher Education,* Prof. Paul Korshin of the University of Pennsylvania recently described his grievance panel as the "rhinoplasty committee," because it does "cosmetic surgery" on up to 500 transcripts a year.

The argument that grades are rising because students are better prepared is simply not convincing. The evidence suggests that students and parents are demanding—and getting—what they think of as their money's worth.

One way to stanch inflation is to change the way the grade point average is calculated. Under most formulas, all courses are given equal weight, so math, science and less-challenging courses have equal impact on the averages. This arrangement rewards students who gravitate to courses where high marks are generously given and punishes those who seek out math and science courses, where far fewer students get the top grade.

Valen Johnson, a Duke University statistics professor, came under 10 heavy fire from both students and faculty when he proposed recalculating the grade point average to give rigorously graded courses greater weight. The student government beat back the plan with the help of teachers in the humanities, who worried that students might abandon them for other courses that they currently avoided. Other universities have expressed interest in adopting the Johnson plan, but want their names kept secret to avoid a backlash.

Addicted to counterfeit excellence, colleges, parents and students are unlikely to give it up. As a consequence, diplomas will become weaker and more ornamental as the years go by.

Staples presents a lot of information but makes it readable. How did he do it? More importantly, how can you do it? See Ch. 10.

Thinking about the Text

1. Brent Staples presents a great deal of information in a very brief opinion piece. Does the piece live up to the promise of its title—that of explaining the cause of A abundance? Why or why not?

2. Staples argues that the proliferation of A grades devalues a degree by demonstrating the lack of academic rigor of any college that grants so many A's. How do you feel about the degree that you are working toward? If you had the choice of two colleges equally accessible to you in terms of distance and cost, and one had a reputation for academic rigor and maintained high standards for grades, while the other had a mediocre academic reputation but bestowed abundant high grades, which would you choose? Why?

3. Staples' essay was published as an opinion piece in the *New York Times*, which has a readership of millions. Staples was surely aware of the breadth of the **AUDIENCE**, but was he really addressing all of those millions, or was his true intended audience a particular subset of the *Times*' readership? Explain the reasoning behind your answer.

4. Staples mentions the proposal of Valen Johnson as a way of dealing with "counterfeit excellence" (11). Is he advocating Johnson's proposal? opposing it? not taking a position one way or the other? How do you know?

5. Imagine that the administration of your school is undertaking a major evaluation of the grading system, with the ultimate goal of enhancing the academic rigor of the institution. They have asked members of the academic community at all levels, including students, to present opinions and suggestions. Write an essay in which you **ARGUE A POSITION** on grading policies, particularly with respect to grade inflation. Give a carefully reasoned argument backed up by **EVIDENCE** from your own experience.

The Joy of Texting

LYNNE TRUSS

AS SOMEONE WHO SENDS TEXTS MESSAGES more or less non-stop, I enjoy one particular aspect of texting more than anything else: that it is possible to sit in a crowded railway carriage laboriously spelling out quite long words in full, and using an enormous amount of punctuation, without anyone being aware of how outrageously subversive I am being. My texts are of epic length. "SMS 4" I am notified on-screen, but I merely smile inwardly at this warning against extravagance, and see if I can finish (for once) without getting to "SMS 5." No one around me can tell, as I thumb the keys, that my secret delight is to shorten no words, use no smiley faces, eschew predictive text, and employ no handy abbreviations except for "LOL"— which I always use, wilfully incorrectly, to signify "lots of love."

We pedants are supposed to hate texting, but we don't. We are in love with effective communication, and there's nothing more effective than sending a message direct from your phone to someone else's, sometimes from the hairdresser's (which I mention for a reason). "I CANT BELIEVE U

LYNNE TRUSS, an English writer and journalist, may be best known for her 2004 book *Eats, Shoots and Leaves: The Zero Tolerance Approach to Punctuation.* She has also written several novels and comic radio dramas and is a regular columnist and radio commentator. This piece was originally published in 2008 in the British newspaper the *Guardian*, where it accompanied David Crystal's essay "2b or Not 2b" (p. 745).

Truss was able to make a mundane topic interesting by thinking hard about her own habits and opinions. Learn more about how to do that on pp. 13–14.

PUT APOSTROPHE IN HAIRDRESSERS," a friend texted me recently (he obviously had a bit of time on his hands, too). "Oh, I felt the apostrophe was required," I texted back, happily—in both upper and lower case, with regular spacing, and a comma after "Oh."

I am aware that I am breaking unwritten rules all the time with texting. The etiquette is a bit baffling, so I err on the side of overdoing it. For example, I reply on immediate receipt of texts, and I suspect that such overt eagerness is probably desperately uncool. I have one friend who is, I think, trying to train me in the proper (cool) art of texting, which involves waiting a day or two before dispatching a response. But even if I get a text at 1:30 in the morning, I still write back within two minutes, because I'm just too excited not to (and anyway, I've woken up and put the light on). I also conscientiously supply answers to questions, which I find is not the norm, either. As with email, the recipient of a texted question seems to have the option to ignore it, while nevertheless saying hello, lovely day, and so on.

There are deeper etiquette issues, of course. A friend of mine once received a text with the news that another friend had committed suicide. This is not the right sort of information to convey by text; just as it wouldn't be the right sort of news to leave on an answering machine. Texting is a supremely secretive medium of communication—it's like passing a note— and this means we should be very careful what we use it for. I have been thinking about the great plots in our literature that would be improved (or destroyed) by the use of texting. The convenient plot device of the wrong-letter-in-envelope in Ian McEwan's *Atonement,* for example, would be far more plausible as a text sent in error (Robbie had meant to save it in "Drafts"!). But Tess's confession about her baby would be much too big to put in a text to Angel Clare in *Tess of the d'Urbervilles.* Even in a world of texting, Tess still has to put that letter under that fateful door.

Whether one should read texts in company is the trickiest issue. In   5
America, now, where nearly everyone seems to own a BlackBerry, there is a new facial expression I have observed which involves a fixed smile and panicky swivelled eyes, which means, "I am still listening to you, but I can see I have a message, but I am honestly still listening to you, I will read the message later, so tell me again, what did you say, I wish I could read my effing message." Asking permission from fellow diners to read messages seems fairly acceptable ("Ooh, can I just see who this is from?"), but nodding and sniggering at the content, without sharing it, is not. Composing a quick reply while in company is likewise quite rude. I often excuse myself and then text

The question of whether to read texts in company is a tricky issue: asking permission to read messages seems fairly acceptable, but reacting to the content, without sharing it, is not.

feverishly from the lavatories, which seems less socially offensive, even if I'm gone for at least 20 minutes (what with all the spelling out of long words, punctuating and so on).

Texting is a fundamentally sneaky form of communication, which we should despise, but it is such a boon we don't care. We are all sneaks now. It's as if we have an endless supply of telegram boys who, in a matter of seconds, can not only locate anyone on the planet on our behalf, but also tap him on the shoulder and hand over a sealed envelope marked "For Your Eyes Only." My favourite text—which I lovingly preserve—was sent to me by a friend in Greece, when I was staying the other side of the harbour from his house. "AM WAVING" it said, and I looked across with my binoculars, and so he was. The oldest form of communication was thus served by the latest. It seemed daft, but also right.

Thinking about the Text

1. Lynne Truss takes an analytic look at her own habits and standards of texting, while acknowledging that they are different from those of most people that she knows. Although your texting practices may be very different from hers, do you agree that she has identified the etiquette dilemmas that the medium raises? Why or why not?

2. While acknowledging that the medium is more conducive to messages that are very short, Truss describes the great pleasure she gets from creating very long texts and relates an astonished response from one of her correspondents. Do you enjoy getting long texts? Why or why not?

3. Truss takes a flippant and casual **TONE** with a relatively serious topic. Does her tone enhance her **AUTHORITY** on this topic? undermine it? neither? How would you describe the ethos that Truss constructs for herself in this article?

4. In a very short essay, Truss manages to both criticize and applaud SMS messages and the social practices of sending and receiving them. Are her arguments consistent with one another? How would you **SUMMARIZE** her main point?

5. How do you use texting in your life? What social activities and interactions does it facilitate? Are there any ways that it makes your life more complicated? Write an essay in which you **ANALYZE** your own texting and **DESCRIBE** both how it facilitates and complicates your life. (Before you write, it may be helpful to keep a log of all your texts for forty-eight hours—sent and received—so that you have evidence to draw from.)

The Sims Medieval

KEVIN VanORD

PLAYING **THE SIMS MEDIEVAL** is like looking at your neighbor's vacation slides: You're hearing about someone else's grand adventure rather than having one of your own.

The Good
- Has all that Sims charm, from animations to voice-overs
- You can approach quests in a number of different ways
- Some of the hero-specific skills are really neat

The Bad
- Quests become a repetitious chore
- Too little freedom to live as you wish
- Dollhouse elements are greatly restricted

The Sims Medieval brings some irony to this popular series of life simulations. Whereas the proper Sims games make the mundane aspects

KEVIN VanORD is a California-based staffer on *GameSpot*, which calls itself "the go-to source for all things video games"; he writes game reviews and hosts a blog about game-related themes. *The Sims*, a game franchise that began in 2000 and has become one of the best-selling video games ever, has branched off into numerous updates and spinoffs. This review was published in April 2011.

How does
a reviewer
determine
how much
background
information
to include?
Find some
help on pp.
234–37.

of everyday life interesting, this Renaissance faire spin-off takes interesting concepts and makes them mundane. It's initially entertaining, fueled by the peculiar charms that have always made these games so delightful. But eventually, the pleasures of calling the local bard a lack-witted cur are undercut by the sensation that you're just treading water and never really getting anywhere. Of course, you could say this about those previous Sims games, but their joy came from your ability to make a life as worthy as you liked. Just as your little digital people built relationships with each other, so you built relationships with them, and the stories you played out in the game were born of your own imagination. In The Sims Medieval, you don't play out your own stories—you play out someone else's. And you do so over and over again in a weird computer-game version of *Groundhog Day*. The first 10 hours or so are pleasant ones, and some worthwhile ideas work out rather well. But in the end, The Sims Medieval lacks imagination—and it lacks the tools to let you flex your own.

The game begins by letting you create a sim called a hero; in this case, your hero is a monarch in charge of a kingdom. Your king (or queen) doesn't have an enormous selection of outfits to choose from, but this is more like Ye Olde Sims, so you wouldn't expect a plethora of sunglasses and tank tops. Luckily, the create-a-style feature from The Sims 3 returns, which lets you customize those garments using various patterns and colors. So, at least initially, you get a taste of that dollhouse appeal you expect coming into the game. You gussy up your monarch, give him or her a couple of traits (fun loving, vain, and so forth) and a fatal flaw (perhaps gluttony or hubris). Then you head to your castle, where you might expect to find raucous adventures or, at least, a chance to exercise your decorating skills.

As it turns out, you find both, but not in ways you might have expected. Your first tasks are to collect flowers, write laws, and defeat a giant bear—an eclectic array of activities for the kingdom's ruler, to be sure, though this introduction is expanded upon in due time. After the multi-hour tutorial (during which, incidentally, you cannot save your game), you are whisked to a kingdom view, where you get the chance to add a new structure to your land and possibly a new hero to create along with it. Some structures, such as the lighthouse, don't come with a new sim. But if you build a wizard's tower, you get to create a wizard to live within it. If you go for the barracks, you get to design a knight to enjoy it. Each of these heroes can interact with various objects, and each other, in typical Sims fashion. Sidle up to locals and get to know them. (Or spit in their faces, if you fancy your sim one of

those aforementioned curs.) Head to the fireplace and whip up some vegetable stew or bear meat soup. Head to the docks or to a local stream and see
if you can catch a few fish. You can also use a chamber pot, take a bath, or
enjoy the tunes from a music box, but you don't need to give the usual basic
needs too much concern: The only such needs you're required to meet are
hunger and energy.

Different heroes get entirely different sets of skills outside of these ba-   5
sics, however. Take the Peteran priest. She can convert locals to the Peteran
faith, deliver sermons, pray, and evangelize out in front of the church. Your
doctor collects leeches from streams, gathers herbs and flowers, and treats
citizens in a creepy-looking contraption. Some of these new elements are
fun to play with and exude the usual Sims silliness and tongue-in-cheek
melodrama. The bard, for example, writes poems and recites them to others.
To make him do so, you have him talk to other sims for inspiration, visit the
docks and ponder the night sky, or just hang around the forest. Once he has a
variety of subjects to write about, you send him to his desk and choose what
subjects to write about, and he puts pen to paper. Or perhaps you'd rather he
write a play. In this case, you follow a similar procedure, but once the play
is complete, you recruit an actor, and the bard and his protégé act out this
comedy or tragedy on the stage at the local tavern. It's a joy to watch this
little play come to life, with the sims hamming it up like community theater
thespians taking on *Macbeth*.

These are neat twists on the Sims formula, and at first, they're differ-

Religious conversions in The Sims Medieval are a quick and easy process,
just as they are in real life.

ent enough and entertaining enough to inspire the benefit of your doubt. Each campaign (called an ambition) is divided into a series of quests, which you choose from a list after you complete the latest one. Quests have you controlling one or two sims, using these skills to find out, for example, what disease might be affecting the populace or where you might find a proper suitor for the queen. When taking on a quest, you might be given multiple ways to approach it. An evil witch has returned. Do you marry her, rob her of her power, or kill her off for good? Only certain sims (or pairs of sims) can carry out certain paths, so the king takes the marriage path, whereas the wizard (or the physician, or the priest) takes the power-robbing path. From here, you control one or two heroes and perform individual tasks that lead to quest completion. This means having the blacksmith forge weapons, the merchant trade in faraway lands you never get to see, and the bard write a play so magnificent that the local critic declares it a perfect work of art. As they write, study, and pray, your heroes level up, opening up new possibilities. (Make armor faster! Fight more effectively!)

There are moments within each quest in which you get to choose how to proceed, and these are legitimately interesting. Do you ask the queen's advisor for guidance, or do you search for clues on your own? Do you choose a gender for your monarch's child, or do you leave it to chance? The quest might play out differently, depending on what you decide, though some decisions are less significant. For instance, when your king holds court, a citizen may ask for permission to have a child. You could offer your blessing or treat the citizen with disdain, which is a neat touch—the first time. But when you hold court a few times, and these folks eventually ask you the same questions ad nauseam, you can only decide whether to tax goat milk so many times before you tire of it. When the same beggar approaches you as you leave the market time and again, and the same dream interrupts your sleep, it stops being a cute diversion and becomes an annoyance.

It's unfortunate, given the series' pedigree, that the moment-to-moment gameplay gives you so little room to be creative. Rather, it pushes you from one very specific task to another, and it punishes you when you exercise some freedom. Should you spend too much time doing something other than assigned activities, you receive fewer renown points (used to purchase new structures) when completing your quest. In addition, you need to keep your heroes focused. The more focus they have, the greater the chance of completing a successful task. And the easiest way to earn focus is to complete two *additional* specific activities each day, like healing a patient (if you're a doctor) or mining for gems (if you're a blacksmith). And, so, instead of creating a family and living a dream, your sims are chained to specific deeds like slaves. (Shirking these responsibilities can even get a sim sent to the stocks.) And you as the player are no longer the puppeteer but rather the puppet yourself, and you're rewarded only for doing what the game wants you to do. How odd that the opening cinematic informs you that you are playing The Maker—that is, God—when, in fact, you are now more of a middle manager, telling your sims to do what the game demands of you, not what you want them to do.

The game's large-scale structure merely accentuates this monotony. Each time you begin a new ambition, you start with a blank slate in the exact same kingdom. Everything is in the same place—the plants you pick, the ore you mine, the graveyard your dead father haunts. And you perform many of the same quests as well. Granted, the opportunity to complete them differently freshens things up a bit, but it's never enough to make all of this content feel like more than a 15-hour game stretched to what seems like infinity. Eventually, you use the time-manipulation feature to speed through almost every individual task just so you can see how things play out. And once you're done, you realize that you didn't have an adventure—you were only told of one. In previous Sims games, your journey might only have been a vacation to the beach or a picnic at the park, but it was still one you experienced and molded. In The Sims Medieval, you don't see the epic battle between your knight and a dragon; you learn of the details in a quest update. The only battles you experience are presented like any other social or object interaction—they just involve the slicing of swords rather than the flapping of gums.

If you like Sims games for their creation aspects, you will be disappoint- 10 ed to learn that you don't get to build your castle from the ground up. You can decorate interiors with wall hangings, toss in some barrels, change wall and floor textures, and buy a fancy claw-footed bathtub from your hoity-toity merchant. There's a good selection of decorative and useful items alike to purchase, so the cathedral and monastery can look as holy—or as intimidating— as you like. What you *can't* do is add walls or tear them down. There is no true building element to The Sims Medieval. This dollhouse only allows you to play as interior decorator, but not as castle architect. Even the camera is limited here, forcing you into a cutaway view rather than allowing you to rotate around your handsome interior. The camera is an issue in other ways as well. It swoops about cinematically when you want to move quickly to the village square or local forest, but it gets stubborn as you pan across the terrain.

The Sims Medieval is an interesting, and initially enjoyable, mixture of life simulation and role-playing game. But this is an uneasy partnership. The RPG facet has you doing all the busywork to prepare for epic quests you never experience for yourself. The Sim aspect, meanwhile, limits too many of the features that give this series its unique identity. Creating spells with your maniacal wizard, bleeding sick patients with leeches, and sermonizing at the cathedral's pulpit are all smart new activities that lend a bit of freshness to the Sims formula. But these additions are overshadowed by the forced grind that comes from leading these heroes through lives of indentured servitude.

Thinking about the Text

1. Kevin VanOrd's review was written for a very specific **AUDIENCE** of gamers. A good review, as noted in Chapter 11, is sensitive to the needs, interests, and expectations of its readers. Does VanOrd satisfy this requirement? Why or why not? Provide examples to support your conclusions.

2. It could be argued that *The Sims Medieval* provides a learning experience about life in the Middle Ages. Do you think that a video game designed in collaboration with historians and other academics could be used in place of a textbook for history classes? Do you think such a game could improve academic accomplishment? Why or why not?

3. VanOrd's evaluation of *The Sims Medieval* is generally negative, although he does note a number of good features. Do you find his **TONE** authoritative and credible? Why or why not? What does he do to establish his **CREDIBILITY**?

4. What does VanOrd mean by the phrase "indentured servitude" (11)? What historical era does it refer to? (Do some research if necessary to find out.) Why might he have chosen to use such a phrase to conclude his review?

5. Write a **REVIEW** of your favorite video or computer game (or of one that you know well but don't like). If you are not a game player, ask a friend or classmate to share one with you or recommend one that you can try out online. In your review, make sure that readers can tell what **CRITERIA** you're using for the evaluation. Whether you are giving a favorable or unfavorable review to the game, acknowledge other points of view about it if necessary, and support your **REASONS** with **EVIDENCE**.

The Social Network

ALISSA WILKINSON

IT'S **AUGUST 2004.** I'm sitting in an ugly chair in the student union with my laptop balanced on my knees, checking my senior year course schedule. I had spent the summer working as a student orientation advisor for incoming freshmen. My coworkers and I had had a fantastic time working and living together, and we're sad that we can't keep up with one another as well as we'd like, now that classes are starting and the campus is filling back up.

I open my email and there's an invitation to join a site called thefacebook.com. I think it might be spam, and I'm about to delete it when two girls walk by and I hear them say something about a "face book." *Well, okay,* I think. And I click on the link.

A week later, campus productivity has all but disappeared. We routinely tell people to "just facebook me." Many of us now know things about that guy we sat next to in physics last year that we used to not know about some of our friends: political and religious beliefs, favorite bands, relationship status. To my excitement, this website means my friends and I can now keep

ALISSA WILKINSON, a former Wall Street analyst and technical writer, teaches writing at King's College in New York. Her research interests include such diverse topics as the politics of food, the relationship between theology and political philosophy, and contemporary American literature. This review of the 2010 film *The Social Network* appeared in *Christianity Today*, a monthly magazine, in October 2010.

in touch more easily, even though we've all gone back to our daily world of classes, homework, and clubs.

Six years later, I (and five hundred million other people) can hardly remember that world, in which if you failed to get someone's phone number, you might never see them again; where you couldn't see pictures from last night's party online the next day; where leaving a note on your friend's "wall" was an act of vandalism, or would at least leave a few thumbtack holes.

In spring 2003, not long before his website changed our world, a mis- 5 anthropic but vaguely hapless sophomore at Harvard named Mark Zuckerberg (played by the excellent Jesse Eisenberg) could bring down an entire network in a couple of hours by just throwing together a website between late-night beers. *The Social Network* is his story—kind of. It's also the story of his friends and acquaintances, of those suing him and those wondering why it all matters. It's the curious tale of a social outsider who became the gateway for social interaction. And most importantly, it's a story that embodies the generation that was willing to redefine privacy to digitize their world.

Writer Aaron Sorkin (*The West Wing, A Few Good Men, Charlie Wilson's War*) tackles the tricky task of untangling the Facebook founding myth. The facts have never been very clear, and everyone's account differs. So Sorkin simply gives us the various versions of the truth and lets us wonder. (You might ask: Who cares who actually came up with the idea for Facebook? Well, for starters, the site is now worth around $25 billion, and Zuckerberg owns half of it.)

Zuckerberg's success with Facemash—the site he put together in the middle of the night—attracted the attention of Harvard officials, who put him on academic probation for violating privacy restrictions and bypassing security regulations, and some fellow students—twins Cameron and Tyler Winkelvoss (Armie Hammer and Josh Pence) and their business partner, Divya Narenda (Max Minghella), who were developing a website called the Harvard Connection. Like MySpace, the site would let users create a profile and add others as friends; unlike MySpace, the site would be exclusive, available only to those with a harvard.edu email address.

What exactly happened next is unclear. The film skillfully skips between the narrative (much of which is imaginative reconstruction of what could have happened) and testimonies in various lawsuits brought against Zuckerberg. What we do know is that Zuckerberg never ended up writing code for the Harvard Connection, but did end up writing a website he called

Jesse Eisenberg as Mark Zuckerberg in *The Social Network*.

TheFacebook.com that became a social institution overnight, funded by his friend Eduardo Saverin (brilliantly portrayed by Andrew Garfield), who became CFO of the company. They did become campus celebrities, and soon much more. The site did expand beyond the Harvard campus and dropped the "the" to become Facebook. Zuckerberg and Saverin did meet Napster founder Sean Parker (Justin Timberlake, ideal in this role), who introduced them to the venture capitalists who made them very rich young men. There were two lawsuits brought against Zuckerberg—one by the Winkelvoss twins and Narenda, and one by Saverin.

Facebook grew so rapidly that today, if it were a country, it would have one and a half times the population of the United States. And Zuckerberg, at 26, is the youngest billionaire in the world.

The Social Network is a story, not a history or a biopic, and unfortunate-   10
ly it's hard to know how much of this movie is just made up. But that's also somehow fitting, because it also marks director David Fincher's return to one of his favorite themes: anarchy. To be someone like Zuckerberg or Parker (who boasts of bringing down the recording industry, even though he's now bankrupt) is to not simply subvert, but completely ignore the usual channels through which power flows: wealth, authority, age, experience. . . . All of his protagonists are antiheroes on the outside, always looking in, always more clear-eyed than the folks who are content to live a conventional life.

So it's no surprise that while *The Social Network* is a glossy, sexy film, it's mostly not about glossy, sexy people. Zuckerberg has a talent for alienating people and is utterly incapable of reading social cues or making nice for his own gain; he and his few friends, even the coolest among them, don't represent the pride and joy of Harvard the way the strong-jawed, well-spoken Winkelvoss twins do. Plenty of popular kids hang around this movie, but this isn't their story. Every bit of it buzzes with a kind of underground frenetic energy—from the signature Sorkin rapid-fire dialogue (can you keep up?) to the soundtrack (co-written by Nine Inch Nails's Trent Reznor) to the dynamic cast, who had the unenviable task of trying to portray their contemporaries (Eisenberg is a mere six months older than Zuckerberg).

Most everything about *The Social Network* is successful, but its real achievement stretches beyond the Facebook story. Decades from now, when we've all forgotten what Facebook even was, *The Social Network* will still tell us what it was to be part of the generation sociologists are calling the Millennials. I'm part of this generation, and I teach students who are, too, and what

How do you provide enough information in a movie review without giving away too much of the story? See Ch. 11.

I see is this: Like Zuckerberg, who argues against advertising that would take away Facebook's "cool" factor, Millennials care more about constructing their image and gaining influence than having a lot of money. Privilege and wealth are useful tools toward constructing an attractive identity, but knowing the right people, listening to the right music, and being in the right place at the right time is much more important.

Millenials are defined by their craving to belong; Zuckerberg desperately wants to be part of one of the private social clubs at Harvard because "they're exclusive, and fun, and lead to a better life." They're willing to radically redefine the idea of privacy—to post their political views and favorite bands and pictures from summer vacation on a website for their "friends" to see—in order to gain that sense of belonging. Millennials won't listen to you unless they first like you: because Parker fascinates and pursues Zuckerberg, because Parker seems to care first about power and image and then about money, Zuckerberg trusts Parker—maybe too much.

So in some ways, Zuckerberg is the archetypal Millennial. But is Zuckerberg the villain of this story? No. In fact, we can't help but agree when he tells someone that he's not a bad guy. Confused, yes; angry, yes; young and impulsive and occasionally stupid, yes. It's just that his youthful indiscretions and missteps, though they lost him friends, also made him into a billionaire and a kind of anti-celebrity.

But thanks to Zuckerberg's creation, which effectively puts real life online—where, as one character points out, history is written in ink, not pencil—a whole generation can follow in his footsteps. Whatever might be true in *The Social Network,* one fact is undeniable: what Zuckerberg did was change the world.   15

Thinking about the Text

1. Alissa Wilkinson establishes that she has been in on *Facebook* since its first days, and her review of the film relies heavily on her personal experience as a Millennial and an early *Facebook* citizen. Does her degree of involvement enhance her **AUTHORITY**, or does it cloud her judgment? Explain your reasoning.

2. Wilkinson speculates about a time "decades from now, when we've all forgotten what *Facebook* even was" (12). Imagine, for example, the world of 2040. Will *Facebook* have disappeared altogether? Why or why not? Use your imagi-

nation and consider the technological trends and developments that you've experienced in recent years.

3. Wilkinson weaves back and forth between history as she is living it and the narration of history that the film presents. What signposts does she offer in her writing to help readers know which she is talking about? Give examples. Were you ever not completely sure? Why or why not?

4. Wilkinson identifies herself and her students, along with Zuckerberg and the other people portrayed in the film, as Millennials, and she defines the characteristics of this group. Do you belong to the generation of Millennials? If you do, how well does Wilkinson's characterization apply to you? Why? Whether or not you are a Millennial, many of your classmates surely are. How well does the characterization apply to the Millennials that you know? Provide **EXAMPLES** to support your conclusions.

5. Think of a movie that depicts lives substantially similar to your own, however you choose to identify with them. (The movie need not depict contemporary American life; perhaps you identify strongly with distant times or places.) Write a **REVIEW** of the film that takes an approach like Wilkinson's—that relies heavily on your own experience and its relevance to the themes presented. Be sure, though, that your assessment presents **REASONS** and **EVIDENCE** based on other appropriate **CRITERIA** in addition to your individual ones.

Credits

ILLUSTRATIONS

p. 350. Copyright © 2003, Southern Political Science Association. Reprinted with the permission of Cambridge University Press. 427 Courtesy The Bark. 431 Courtesy of Forum on Religion and Ecology, Yale University and J. Baird Callicott. 434 Reprinted with permission of EBSCO Publishing, 2010; 451 United Artists/The Kobal Collection; 459 Paramount/Rafran/The Kobal Collection

Chapter 25: 474 From *Endless Forms Most Beautiful: The New Science of Evo Devo and the Making of the Animal Kingdom* by Sean B. Carroll. Copyright © 2005 by Sean B. Carroll. Used by permission of W. W. Norton & Company. This selection may not be reproduced, stored in a retrieval system, or transmitted in any form or by any means without the prior written permission of the publisher. 471 Lisa Takeuchi Cullen, "Freshen Up Your Drink": Copyright TIME INC. Reprinted by permission. TIME is a registered trademark of Time Inc. All rights reserved; (Stern): Amanda Friedman/Icon International; (Timberlake): Tobias Schwartz/Reuters; 480 Reprinted from the Federal Reserve Bank of San Francisco Economic Letter 2001-29. The opinions expressed in this article do not necessarily reflect the views of the management of the Federal Reserve Bank of San Francisco, or of the Board of Governors of the Federal Reserve System. Glenn D. Rudebusch; 483 Ethics & Behavior 18(1), 59-92 (c) Taylor & Francis Group LLC; 485 Reprinted with permission of EBSCO Publishing, 2008

Chapter 26: 515 left Spelling/The Kobal Collection; 515 right ABC/Paramount/The Kobal Collection; 517 Paramount Television/The Kobal Collection; 518 © Kevin Epling; 521 Courtesy of Marilyn Hagerty; 522 left Reuters/Newscom; 522 right PRNewsFoto/Twin Peaks, Gregg Ellman/AP Photo; 524 Rebecca Homiski

Chapter 27: 527 Danny Shanahan/The New Yorker Collection/www.cartoonbank.com; 528 Courtesy

of Stephanie Parker; 531 Yelp.com; 532 Courtesy of Kathryn Jagelavicius; 535 Spaghettimeatballs.com

Chapter 28: 543 top left Bart Nijs fotografie/Hollandse Hoogte/Redux; top right Lorenzo Moscia/Archivolatino/Redux; center left Roberto Caccuri/Contrasto/Redux; center right Pierre BESSARD/REA/Redux; bottom left CAMERA PRESS/Cedric Arnold/Redux; bottom right AP Photo/The Northern Star, Jerry Burnes

Chapter 29: 568 Ray Garbo/WENN.com/Newscom

Chapter 30: 571 left Wikimedia Commons; 571 right http://www.youtube.com/watch?feature=endscreen&NR=1&v=xiMf5cCDy1I; 577 iStockphoto; 578 http://www.youtube.com/watch?v=yl2xhfVUu0Y; 579 left js AFP/Newscom; 579 right MCT/Newscom; 580 imagebroker/Simone Brandt/Newscom; 581 Reuters/Landov; 582 Yingling/MCT/Newscom; 585 http://www.ted.com/; 587 http://www.nationalgeographic.com/; 588 Saurabh Vaish; 589 http://prezi.com/uh_7jvp0ykpf/great-jazz-bassists-and-their-influence-through-the-ages/; 590 http://www.pecha-kucha.org/presentations/349

Chapter 32: 647 Courtesy of Carole Clark Papper.; 651 https://stonybrook.digication.com/egimenez/Welcome/published

Chapter 35: 665 W,W, Norton & Co.; 666 W,W, Norton & Co.; 667 Wikimedia Commons; 668 http://www.scribd.com/collections/2837873/For-the-Love-of-Food; 669 http://austenauthors.net/category/pp200/page/4; 670 http://www.pen-international.org/the-pen-logo/; 671 Courtesy of Carrie Barker

Readings: 679 Courtesy of Kevin Arnovitz; 680 Gary Bogdon/KRT/Newscom; 683 Photo by Nick Kelsh; 684, 699 © Kurt Markus; 705 Courtesy of Dennis Baron; 706 iStockphoto; 707 (top left) Wikimedia Commons; 707 (top right) Marie-Lan Nguyen/Wikimedia Commons; 707 (middle) Wikimedia Commons; 708 (top) Wikimedia Commons; 708

TEXT

Credits

About the Authors

ANDREA LUNSFORD is Professor of English and Rhetoric at Stanford University and is on the faculty at the Bread Loaf School of English. Her scholarly interests include contemporary rhetorical theory, women and the history of rhetoric, collaboration, style, and technologies of writing. Among her favorite courses to teach are "The Language Wars" and "The Rhetoric of Graphic Narratives." She's received the Braddock and Shaughnessy Awards (with Lisa Ede), and in 1994 she received the CCCC Exemplar Award. One of her most recent books is *The Sage Handbook of Rhetorical Studies*, and she's currently at work on *The Norton Anthology of Rhetoric and Writing*.

MICHAL BRODY is a linguist, independent scholar, and lecturer. She was a founding faculty member of Universidad de Oriente in Yucatan, Mexico, and teaches now in California, most recently at Sonoma State University and San Francisco State University. Her scholarly work centers on language pedagogy and politics in the United States and Mexico. Her favorite courses to teach include "Theories of Writing Systems" and "Linguistics of Cartoons and Comics." She's the author (with Keith Walters) of *What's Language Got to Do with It?* and the editor of *They Say / I Blog*.

LISA EDE is Professor of English at Oregon State University, where she's directed the Center for Writing and Learning and teaches courses in language and technology, composition, rhetoric, and literacy studies. One of her favorite classes is "Language, Culture, and Technology." Together with Andrea Lunsford, she's been the recipient of the Braddock and the Shaughnessy Awards for their research on audience and collaboration. Her recent books include *Situating Composition: Composition Studies and the Politics of Location* and (with Andrea) *Writing Together: Essays on Collaboration in Theory and Practice*.

BEVERLY MOSS is Associate Professor of English at The Ohio State University, where she teaches in the Rhetoric, Composition, and Literacy program, and is on the faculty at the Bread Loaf School of English. Her research and teaching interests focus on community literacy, composition theory and pedagogy, and writing center theories and practices. Some of her favorite courses to teach are "Memory in African American Literary and Public Discourse" and "Issues and Methods in Tutoring Writing." Her books include *Literacy across Communities* and *A Community Text Arises: A Literate Text and a Literacy Tradition in African American Churches.*

CAROLE CLARK PAPPER is Associate Professor in the Department of Writing Studies and Composition at Hofstra University, where she also directs the University Writing Center. Prior to that, she served as the Director of the Ball State University Writing Program (winner of the CCCC Certificate of Excellence). Her scholarly interests include visual literacy, composition theory and pedagogy, and writing center theories and practices. Her favorite courses to teach include the practicum in writing center pedagogy, "From Pictograph to Pixel: The Impact of Writing Technologies on Literacies," and "Navigating the Information Ocean: Research, Writing, and the Web."

KEITH WALTERS is Professor and Chair of Applied Linguistics at Portland State University, where he teaches sociolinguistics, discourse analysis, and research design and methods. Among his favorite courses are "Language and Nationalism in the Middle East" and a writing workshop for TESOL students. Much of his research has focused on issues of language and identity in Tunisia, where he served as a Peace Corps volunteer, and the Arab world more broadly. He's the author of two other textbooks, *Everything's an Argument with Readings* and *What's Language Got to Do with It?*

About the Alphabet

THE ALPHABET song may be one of the first things you learned to sing: *a - b -c-d-e-f-g/h-i-j-k-l-m-n-o-p/q and r and s and t/u-v-w-x-y-z / Now I know my abc's / Next time won't you sing with me?* And maybe you had a set of alphabet blocks, 26 little letters you could use to make words of your own. Combined, those letters yield everything from the word *Google* to the complete works of Shakespeare. So alphabets are versatile, and perhaps that's part of their fascination. In our grandmothers' day, young women often made alphabet samplers, using fancy stitches to create the letters. Earlier, in medieval times, scribes labored to create highly ornate letters to adorn manuscripts whose words were "illuminated" by the intricate letters, often done in silver and gold.

We had these illuminated letters in mind when we asked Carin Berger to create a modern-day illuminated alphabet for this book. You'll see the results in every chapter, each of which begins with one of the letters Berger created. To us, they represent our old alphabet blocks, our grandmothers' samplers, and the illuminated letters that still dazzle us after thousands of years. But look again and you'll see that these letters are also vivid, striking images. And instead of being decorated with precious silver and gold leaf, our letters are decorated with bits of everyday text—maps, comics, stationery, receipts, school papers, checks, and so on. In our alphabet, old and new, low tech and high tech, word and image come together to create evocative, timely letters for our book.

And just as modern-day type fonts have names, so too does our alphabet. We call it Author.

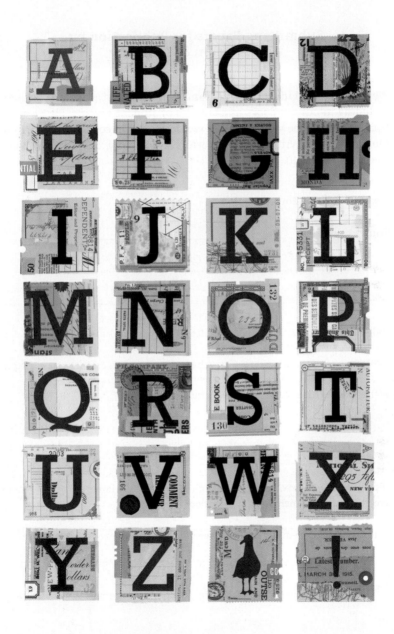

Submitting Papers for Publication by
W. W. Norton & Company

We are interested in receiving writing from college students to consider including in our textbooks as examples of student writing. Please send this form with the work that you would like us to consider to Marilyn Moller, Student Writing, W. W. Norton & Company, 500 Fifth Avenue, New York NY 10110.

Text Submission Form

Student's name _____

School _____

Address _____

Department _____

Course _____

Writing assignment the text responds to _____

_____

_____

_____

_____

_____

Instructor's name _____

Please write a few sentences about what your primary purposes were for writing this text. Also, if you wish, tell us what you think you learned about writing from the experience writing it.

_____

_____

_____

_____

_____

_____

_____

_____

_____

_____

Contact Information
Please provide the information below so that we can contact you if your work is selected for publication.

Name _____

Permanent address _____

Email _____

Phone _____

Author / Title Index

Note: Page numbers in *italics* indicate figures.

Glossary / Index

Note: This glossary / index defines key terms and concepts and directs you to pages in the book where you can find specific information on these and other topics. Please note the words set in SMALL CAPITAL LETTERS are themselves defined in the glossary / index. Page numbers in *italics* indicate figures.

AGREEMENT The correspondence between a SUBJECT
and VERB in person and number (*the dog chases the
children down the street*) or between a PRONOUN and
its ANTECEDENT in gender and number (*the cat nursed
her babies; the children flee because they are afraid*).
  pronoun-antecedent, 612–13
  subject-verb, 624–31

ANALOGY, 305–6 A strategy for COMPARISON by explaining something unfamiliar in terms of something
that is more familiar. *See also* faulty analogy

ANALYSIS, 137–81 A writing GENRE and strategy that
breaks something down into its component parts so
that those parts can be thought about methodically in
order to understand the whole. Features: a question
that prompts a closer look • DESCRIPTION of the subject
being analyzed • evidence drawn from close examination of the subject • insight gained from the analysis •
clear, precise language *See also* CAUSAL ANALYSIS; DATA
ANALYSIS; INFORMATIONAL ANALYSIS; INSTRUCTIONAL
ANALYSIS; PROCESS ANALYSIS; RHETORICAL ANALYSIS
  across academic fields, 138

ANECDOTE Brief NARRATIVE used to illustrate a point.

ANNOTATED BIBLIOGRAPHY, 377–80 A writing GENRE that gives an overview of published research and scholarship on a topic. Each entry includes complete publication information for a source and a SUMMARY or an ABSTRACT. A *descriptive annotation* summarizes the content of a source without commenting on its value; an *evaluative annotation* gives an opinion about the source along with a description of it. Features: complete bibliographic information • a brief SUMMARY or DESCRIPTION of the work • some indication of how the SOURCE will inform your RESEARCH • consistency

ANTECEDENT, 612–15 The NOUN or PRONOUN to which a pronoun refers: *Maya lost her wallet.*

APA STYLE, 463–510 A system of DOCUMENTATION used in the social sciences. APA stands for the American Psychological Association.

ARTICLE, 592–93 The word *a*, *an*, or *the*, used to indicate that a NOUN is indefinite (*a writer, an author*) or definite (*the author*).

AUDIENCE, 21 Those to whom a text is directed—the people who read, listen to, or view the text. Audience is a key part of any RHETORICAL SITUATION.

AUTHORITY, 369, 370 A person or text that is cited as support for a writer's ARGUMENT. A structural engineer may be quoted as an authority on bridge construction, for example. *Authority* also refers to a quality conveyed by a writer who is knowledgeable about his or her subject.

B

equal weight to each one (*bacon _and_ eggs; pay up _or_ get out*).

correctness, 516

COUNTERARGUMENT, 86, 253 In ARGUMENT, an alternative position or objection to the writer's position. The writer of an argument should not only acknowledge counterarguments but also, if at all possible, accept, accommodate, or refute each counterargument.

COUNT NOUN, 592–93 A word that names something that can be counted (*one book, two books*). *See also* NONCOUNT NOUN

CQ Researcher, 353

CREDIBILITY, 88, 193–95, 211 The sense of trustworthiness that a writer conveys through his or her text.

credit, giving, 12, 15, 390, 401–6
Crick, Francis, 14–16

CRITERIA, 252–53, 255 In a REVIEW, the standards against which something is judged.

critiquing, 663
culture
    analysis and, 140–41
    arguments and, 64–65
    reports and, 187
    reviews and, 233

CUMULATIVE SENTENCE, 558–59 A sentence that begins with a main idea expressed in a MAIN CLAUSE and then adds details in PHRASES and DEPENDENT CLAUSES that follow the main clause. *See also* PERIODIC SENTENCE

D

Dame Rhetorica, *512*

DATA ANALYSIS, 149–52, 165–66 A kind of ANALYSIS that looks for patterns in numbers or other data, sometimes in order to answer a stated or implied question.

databases, 351–53
    author, title, and subject searches and, 342–43
    documentation of, 366, 433, *434*
    keyword searches and, 341–42
    open-access, 345
    subject-specific, 353
Davidson, Owen, 533
DavisWiki, 668

definite article. *See* ARTICLE

DEFINITION, 311–13 A strategy that says what something is. *Formal definitions* identify the category that something belongs to and tell what distinguishes it from other things in that category: a worm is an invertebrate (a category) with a long, rounded body and no appendages (distinguishing features); *extended definitions* go into more detail: a paragraph or even an essay explaining why a character in a story is tragic; *stipulative definitions* give a writer's own use of a term, one not found in a dictionary. Definition can serve as the organizing principle for a paragraph or whole text.

Demosthenes, *37*
Descartes, René, 12

DESCRIPTION, 313–15 A strategy that tells how something looks, sounds, smells, feels, or tastes. Effective description creates a clear DOMINANT IMPRESSION built from specific details. Description can be *objective, subjective,* or both. Description can serve as the organizing principle for a paragraph or whole text.
    analysis and, 143–44
    argument and, 313–15
    dominant impression and, 313
    narrative and, 111–12, 313
    photographs and, 577
    profile and, 313
    review and, 241, 253, 254
    visuals and, 314, *314,* 577
    of your work, 647, 648

DESIGN, 570–92 The way a text is arranged and presented visually. Elements of design include fonts, colors, illustrations, layout, and white space. *See also* MEDIUM

LITERACY NARRATIVE A GENRE of writing that tells about a writer's experience learning to read or write. Features: a well-told story • vivid detail • some indication of the narrative's significance

LOGICAL APPEAL, 289–95 Ways an author uses REASONS and EVIDENCE to persuade an AUDIENCE to accept a CLAIM. *See also* EMOTIONAL APPEAL; ETHICAL APPEAL

LOOPING, 26 A process for GENERATING IDEAS AND TEXT in which a writer writes about a subject quickly for several minutes and summarizes the most important or interesting idea in a sentence, which becomes the beginning of another round of writing and summarizing, and so on, until finding an angle for a paper.

M

MAIN CLAUSE, 553, 557 A CLAUSE, containing a SUBJECT and a VERB, that can stand alone as a sentence: *She sang. The world-famous soprano sang several arias.*

MEDIUM, 19, 23, *59*. A means for communicating—for example, in print, with speech, or online. *See also* DESIGN

N

NONCOUNT NOUN, 592–93 A word that names something that cannot be counted or made plural with certain modifiers or units: *information, rice.*

NONESSENTIAL ELEMENT, 596–97 A word, PHRASE, or CLAUSE that gives additional information but that is not necessary for understanding the basic meaning of a sentence: *I learned French, which is a Romance language, online.* Nonessential elements should be set off by commas.

NOUN A word that refers to a person, place, animal, thing, or idea (*director, Stephen King, forest, Amazon River, tree frog, notebook, democracy*).

R

RESEARCH METHODS, 337–61 The ways a writer conducts research for writing—for example, in a library (either in person or remotely), through the internet, or with interviews, polls, or observations in the field.

RESEARCH QUESTION, 339–40 A question that guides research. A good research question should be simple, focused, and require more than a simple "yes" or "no" answer.

restrictive element. *See* ESSENTIAL ELEMENT

RÉSUMÉ, 49–50 A GENRE that summarizes someone's academic and employment history, generally written to submit to potential employers. DESIGN and word choice depend on whether a résumé is submitted as a print document or in an electronic or scannable form. Features: an organization that suits goals and experience • succinctness • a design that highlights key information (for print) or that uses only one typeface (for scannable)

REVIEW, 229–62 A writing GENRE that makes a judgment about something—a film, book, product, restaurant, whatever—based on certain CRITERIA. Features: relevant information about the subject • criteria for the evaluation • a well-supported evaluation • attention to the AUDIENCE's needs and expectations • an authoritative TONE • awareness of the ethics of reviewing

REVISION, 27–28 The process of making substantive changes, including additions and cuts, to a draft so that it contains all the necessary information in an appropriate organization. During revision, a writer generally moves from whole-text issues to details with the goals of sharpening the focus and strengthening the argument.

RHETORIC, 1–56 One of the three original disciplines in the ancient world (along with grammar and logic), rhetoric has been defined in many ways down through the centuries. In this book, we define rhetoric as the art, practice, and theory of ethical communication.

RHETORICAL ANALYSIS, 163–64 A kind of ANALYSIS that takes a close look at how a text communicates a message to an AUDIENCE. *See also* ANALYSIS

RHETORICAL SITUATION, 18–23 The circumstances that affect writing or other communication, including PURPOSE, AUDIENCE, GENRE, STANCE, MEDIA, DESIGN, and CONTEXT.

STANCE, 65 A writer's or speaker's attitude toward his or her subject—for example, reasonable, neutral, angry, curious. Stance is conveyed through TONE and word choice.

STANDARD EDITED ENGLISH, 517–18, 543–44 The conventions of spelling, grammar, and punctuation expected in academic discourse, which tends to be more formal than conversational English. The *standard* is set by well-educated people, but standard English varies from country to country and changes over time. *Edited* refers to the care writers take in reviewing their formal written work.

STASIS THEORY, 279–80 A simple system for identifying the crux of an argument—what's at stake in it—by asking four questions: (1) What are the facts? (2) How can the issue be defined? (3) How much does it matter, and why? (4) What actions should be taken as a result?

SUBJECT, 616–19, 624–31 A word or word group, usually including at least one NOUN or PRONOUN plus its MODIFIERS, that tells who or what a sentence or CLAUSE is about. In the sentence *A frustrated group of commut-* *ers waited for the late bus*, the subject is *A frustrated group of commuters*.

SUBJUNCTIVE MOOD, 640–41 The MOOD of a VERB used to express wishes or requests or to indicate unlikely conditions: *Most people wish that global warming were not so evident.*

SUBORDINATE CLAUSE, 556, 557, 604–5, 616–19 A CLAUSE that begins with a SUBORDINATING WORD and therefore cannot stand alone as a sentence: *She feels good when she exercises. My roommate, who was a physics major, tutors students in science.*

SUBORDINATING CONJUNCTION, 556 A word such as *because, in order that*, and *while* that introduces a SUBORDINATE CLAUSE: *The ice sculpture melted because the room for the wedding reception was too warm.*

SUMMARY, 388, 398 The use of one's own words and sentence structure to condense someone else's text into a briefer but still faithful version in lieu of QUOTING. As with paraphrasing and quoting, summarizing requires DOCUMENTATION.

TOPIC SENTENCE, 544 A sentence, often at the beginning of a paragraph, that states the paragraph's main
point. The details in the rest of the paragraph should
support the topic sentence.

TRANSITIONS, 545, 555–57 A word or PHRASE that
helps to connect sentences and paragraphs and to
guide readers through a text. Transitions can help
show comparisons (*also, similarly*); contrasts (*but,
instead*); examples (*for instance, in fact*); sequence
(*finally, next*); time (*at first, meanwhile*); and more.

U

V

VANTAGE POINT The physical position from which a
writer DESCRIBES something. *See* perspectives; POINT
OF VIEW

VERB, 632–41 A word that expresses an action
(*dance, talk*) or a state of being (*be, seem*). A verb is an
essential element of a sentence or CLAUSE. Verbs have
four forms: base form (*smile*), past tense (*smiled*), past
participle (*smiled*), and present participle (*smiling*). *See
also* HELPING VERB; IRREGULAR VERB; TENSE

W

MLA DOCUMENTATION DIRECTORY

APA DOCUMENTATION DIRECTORY

APA In-Text Documentation

APA Reference List

Books   *471*

Documentation Map   *474*

Periodicals   *476*

Documentation Map   *479*

Online Sources   *480*

Documentation Maps   *482, 483, 485*

Other Kinds of Sources   *487*

Menu of Readings ∽

Readings by Genre ∽

Argument

Narrative

*Student writing